Gunfire!

British Artillery in the Second World War

Stig H. Moberg

FRONTLINE BOOKS

Dedicated to the Royal Regiment of Artillery
in honour of its 300 years of distinguished service

Gunfire: British Artillery in the Second World War

This edition published in 2017 by Frontline Books,
an imprint of Pen & Sword Books Ltd,
47 Church Street, Barnsley, S. Yorkshire, S70 2AS

Copyright © Stig H. Moberg, 2017

The right of Stig H. Moberg to be identified as the author of this work has been asserted by him in accordance with the Copyright, Designs and Patents Act 1988.

ISBN: 978-1-47389-560-7

All rights reserved. No part of this publication may be reproduced, stored in or introduced into a retrieval system, or transmitted, in any form, or by any means (electronic, mechanical, photocopying, recording or otherwise) without the prior written permission of the publisher. Any person who does any unauthorized act in relation to this publication may be liable to criminal prosecution and civil claims for damages.

CIP data records for this title are available from the British Library

For more information on our books, please visit
www.frontline-books.com, email info@frontline-books.com
or write to us at the above address.

Printed and bound by CPI Group (UK) Ltd, Croydon, CR0 4YY

Typeset in 10.25/12 point Plantin Light

Contents

Foreword by Brigadier (retd) Ken Timbers RA   12
Preface   14
Acknowledgements   18

Part 1
Historical Background – War and Rearmament

1. The Period Before the First World War   25
    Two pictures   25
    The Black Prince takes to the guns   26
    A permanent artillery organisation   27
    The establishment of the Royal Regiment of Artillery   27
    Twenty-two years of war against Napoleon   29
    A paradigm shift   30
    Ubique – Quo Fas Et Gloria Ducunt   32

2. The Period up to the Second World War   33
    The great wars and the next paradigm shift   33
    The Territorial Army – using society's best resources in times of national crisis   34
    Artillery develops into a mighty force during the Great War   35
    'It can be presumed…'   37
    Development against the odds   37
    Goodbye to the horse   38
    Organisational adaptation   38
    Traditions and names   39

3. Twilight – War and Mobilisation   40
    The Territorial Army (TA) doubles   40
    To war with obsolete guns   42
    Artillery mobilisation   45

4. A Decisive Rearmament   48
    Construction takes five years   48
    A new light standard gun for divisional artillery   50

Contents

Mobilisation of industry	52
The 25-pounder is well received by artillery units	54
The old mountain howitzer	54
Army and corps artillery modernised with new medium guns	55
Heavy artillery neglected	57
The 'Bishop', the 'Priest' and the 'Sexton' on stage	58
The Congreve legacy – rocket renaissance	60
Modernisation of anti-tank artillery	61
Anti-aircraft guns in ground role	62

5. **Artillery Grouping, Organisation and Equipment** — 64
   - 'Indirect fire system' — 64
   - Artillery grouping and command structure — 66
   - 'System management' and command — 67
   - Organisation of the Field Regiment — 68
   - Manoeuvre organisation of batteries — 70
   - The vehicles — 72
   - Self-propelled guns required a modernised stock of vehicles — 73
   - Organisation of Medium and Heavy Regiments — 73
   - Manpower and equipment specifications for the different types of regiment — 74
   - The communication function and equipment of a Field Regiment — 74

6. **Looking Far into the Battlefield** — 81
   - Army Cooperation Squadrons, RAF — 81
   - Air Observation Posts — 83
   - The Sound Rangers – the 'ears' of the artillery — 86
   - Radar – a new intelligence resource — 89
   - 'Flash spotting' – artillery observation bases — 89
   - Supporting intelligence resources were Corps units — 92

7. **Airborne Artillery** — 93
   - Construction takes time — 93
   - Air-transported artillery another option — 97

Part 2
Gunnery Methods, Procedures, Tactics, Staff Work

8. **How to Hit the Target – Technical Gun Characteristics** — 100
   - Internal ballistics — 100
   - External ballistics — 100

	Declining muzzle velocity a scourge	101
	Range Tables provide information on trajectory physics	102
	Fire dispersion unavoidable	103
	Tactical advantages of different charges and fuzes	104
9.	How to Hit the Target – Geodetic Requirements	108
	Good maps a must	108
	Which 'North' to use?	108
	Traditional survey again honoured	109
	Target acquisition – the most difficult task	112
	How to deal with geodetic relations at the gun positions?	112
10.	How to Hit the Target – Gun Laying	114
11.	Preparations for Opening of Gunfire	117
	Deployment and gun orientation	117
	Fire observation and control	123
	Other preparations before opening fire	125
12.	Artillery Battle Techniques and Tactics	126
	When everything that could be calculated had been done – ranging complements	126
	After ranging – fire for effect	130
	Battle techniques – general factors and dilemmas	131
	The doctrine was there, but battle techniques were to be gradually developed	133
	Violent, persistent – battle techniques for attack	135
	Unplanned heavy blows might be lashed after the barrage	141
	Be prepared to hit back hard! Battle techniques for the defence	142
	Some battle techniques used in both an offensive and in defence	143
	Counter-bombardment always a priority	145
	The human factor	149
13.	Train, Train, Exercise, Exercise…!	150
	Fast-track training	150
	War-oriented officers training	152
	Exercises at all levels an ongoing process	154
14.	Success Requires Efficient Staff Work	155
	Three disciplines	155
	The artillery – one of the best providers of tactical information	157

Coordinated planning and order production – keys to success	158
The Order is given, control and support follow	161

Part 3
How British Artillery Resources Were Used – Descents into Battle History

15. Introduction	164
16. Artillery to the Field – Across the Channel	165
The 'Phoney War'	165
End of the respite – April 1940	170
'David 6 – David 6 – David 6'	171
'Impress on the troops that this is the real thing and not a Divisional Exercise'	174
The BEF outflanked but avoids encirclement	177
What role did the British Artillery play?	180
Withdrawal under artillery protection	182
Fatigue takes its toll	185
Lysanders – not suitable for air observation	185
The artillery is once again concentrated	186
The counter-attack at Arras – no role for the artillery	187
BEF under extreme pressure but holds the right flank thanks to its artillery	188
Fragmentation – the 'indirect fire system' put out of order	190
The unremitting work of the surveyors	190
The last shots – the gunners fire to the end	193
The battle is over – but not south of Somme!	196
Summary of the role of British Artillery in France 1940	197
17. Failed Intervention in Norway	199
Norway a country of strategic interest	199
Planning of the attack	200
To forestall or be forestalled – the battle begins	201
The allies give priority to northern Norway	202
But where was the artillery?	204
The only artillery unit	205
Positions are taken in the Narvik area	206
An experienced mountain warrior takes over	208
Auchinleck's assessment	208
The southern front a great concern	209
How to employ 203 Battery RA?	210
Narvik recaptured	211

The large evacuation – a failed campaign is over	212
Summary of the (limited) role of artillery in Norway	213

18. From Imminent Invasion Threat to Offensive Training — 214
Restoration	214
A new regimental organisation is born	217
First phase of invasion defence – the threat and need for improvisation	218
Second phase of invasion defence – continued rearmament, training, development of new methods	221
The third phase – preparations for an offensive overseas	226

19. 'It will be a killing match' – El Alamein — 229
Varying initiatives	229
Qattara Depression – its historical importance	230
How had the artillery resources been employed before El Alamein?	231
Montgomery in command	232
Recovery and then – a new battle	234
Montgomery's plan for his own great offensive	236
The situation before the great offensive	238
Intelligence status good	240
No ammunition shortage	242
The coordinated fire plan	242
Where are we? Finding the way ahead	243
Intensive covering fire – but no barrages	244
21.40 hours on 23 October 1942	245
The initial attack – success and setbacks	246
Continuous artillery fire for twelve days	250
What about 'simplicity'?	254
One million shells	255
Summary of the role of artillery at the last battle of El Alamein	256

20. A New Front is Opened – Normandy — 258
Preceding bombardment – the task of the navies and air forces	258
Large amounts of artillery landed	260
Covering fire after the initial bombardment	262
Continuous landing of artillery resources	264
Consolidation and enlargement of the bridgehead	265
Operation Goodwood – an attempt to break out?	267
French observers	269

'The scourge' — 270
Finally – material superiority counts — 270
Summary of the role of artillery in the British sector — 272

21. 'BERLIN Tonight' – Arnhem — 275
    'A bridge too far' — 276
    The artillery plan – Operation Market — 278
    The artillery plan – Operation Garden — 281
    From plans to action — 284
    The artillery starts the battle in the south – XXX Corps breakout — 286
    The fighting north of the Rhine intensifies — 288
    The Guards Division head north — 291
    The air-transported reinforcement division — 294
    The artillery dispersed but finally concentrated again — 295
    The medium and heavy guns rush forward — 298
    How had the artillery intelligence resources been employed? — 303
    The role of airpower — 304
    Disappointed Scottish gunners — 305
    The end of the battle and evacuation — 306
    How had the gunners contributed to making the evacuation possible? — 307
    Operation Market Garden – still controversial — 310
    Summary of the role of artillery in Operation Market Garden — 312

22. The Final Onslaught – The Rhine Crossing — 315
    Artillery planning initially concentrated at Corps headquarters — 322
    Hard, exhausting staff work — 324
    Ten hours of counter-bombardment — 326
    Strong support of the Commando Brigade – Operation Widgeon — 326
    And then: concentrated firepower in support of the main attack
        – Operation Torchlight — 328
    Massive XXX corps artillery support – Operation Turnscrew — 329
    The mistakes at Arnhem should not be repeated – Operation Varsity — 330
    A short but intensive artillery fire preparation before the air-landings — 334
    A good start – the plans for Operation Plunder take effect — 335
    Operation Varsity – another catastrophe? — 336
    Breakout towards the Baltic coast — 340
    Summary of the artillery role in Operation Plunder – the Rhine Crossing — 341

23. From Defeat to Success – Burma — 343

Ubique! 343
   The new enemy 343
   First Phase – Malaya and Singapore 344
   Next Phase – Burma 346
   The many artillery problems in Burma 349
   The last artillery battle of the war 352

24. Gunners We Have Met 353
   They forged the sword 353
   Distinguished Territorial officers 356
   They used the sword – the subalterns 357

Epilogue Interview with Major General (retd)
   Jonathan B.A. Bailey CB, MBE, PhD 360

Selection of Symbols, Terms and Acronyms 365
Maps 369
Appendices 401
Notes 414
Sources and Literature 429
Index 442

Foreword

'O, wad some Power the giftie gie us
To see oursels as others see us!'
ROBERT BURNS

Having spent my working life either serving in the Royal Regiment of Artillery or as the Curator of its famous historical collections, I was inevitably hooked by the idea of a book on the Regiment's role in World War II. It was without doubt a period when British artillery reached a peak of power and performance, prompting encomiums from wartime military leaders of the calibre of FM Montgomery and General Horrocks, both of whom attributed much of the British Army's success to its artillery. Finding that the book was written by a Swedish artillery officer added to my interest.

In addition to a successful career in his field of expertise, with managerial roles in electrical engineering and power supply companies, Stig H. Moberg's experience as a reservist artillery officer in Sweden is extensive. He served from 1957 to the late 1980s, keeping up to date by attending courses and field exercises at many levels. His interest in history and the principles of indirect fire led him to explore the subject, settling on British artillery in the Second World War as the 'state of the art'. His choice was influenced by finding that the archives in England were full of valuable sources, making it much easier to study the subject.

The author has done an immense amount of research in producing this book, which covers a wide range of topics, including a historical background that explains how artillery firepower developed, particularly with the dramatic switch from direct to indirect fire shortly before the First World War. He discusses the many consequent changes in technology, including improvements in range, weight of fire, accuracy, communications, transport and logistics, showing a system at its peak when that war ended. However, the system lay dormant in the period between the wars, and enormous efforts were needed to get the Royal Artillery's performance back to a level where it could begin to help turn the tide against the Axis powers in the Second World War. In this context he highlights the decisive contribution by Brigadiers (later Generals) Sidney Kirkman and Jack Parham. Their initiative led to new tactical and gunnery principles which enabled swift and unmatched massing of artillery.

This book takes the reader through that period of development, showing not only the technical improvements and advances, but also illustrating them with accounts of events and actions during the early days of the War. It goes on to discuss organisations and equipment, both of which are helped by clear illustrations and photographs. A masterly account of the progress of the War shows how artillery made its contribution. A glance at the bibliography and the detailed footnotes show how much work has gone into producing a comprehensive account of his subject. The book is a translation from the original publication in Sweden, but it has been closely reviewed by the author in the process, resulting in a thoroughly readable exploration of the subject. It is of particular interest because it is a study by an officer of a foreign army, who provides an extraordinarily detailed analysis of the role of artillery in the Second World War.

Brigadier Ken Timbers (late RA), September 2016

Preface

This book was first published in Sweden in 2013, written for those interested in military history, in particular artillery history. The English version is a slightly revised edition in order to take into account valuable comments and suggestions received from readers and experts in Sweden and U.K. Many photographs have been replaced by substitutes made available from various sources during the process of preparation.

The conceptual idea was to provide insights as to how artillery resources were established, developed technically and tactically and used during the Second World War, with the British Royal Artillery as an example. This is often very sparsely dealt with in the voluminous literature on Second World War battles.

The book is not a scientific treatise, neither regarding theory nor methodology. It is based on observations of particular interest to me, hoping, however, that this will give readers a better understanding of the role of artillery in the Second World War.

The reason for selecting the British artillery as a subject for this book is partly a consequence of different coincidences, but it is also due to contacts with some British war veterans during the early 2000s. I have also been inspired by a statement about the British artillery that Lieutenant General Brian Horrocks often gave in his forewords to various publications, but also expressed in many public contexts. He was, as is familiar to many readers, one of Field Marshal Bernard L. Montgomery's most valued and engaged Corps Commanders during the war. One of his statements reads as follows: 'Although I am an infantryman, and proud of it, I have many times said that the Royal Regiment of Artillery, in my opinion, did more to win the last war, more than any other Arm of the Service.'

After having seen similar statements several times, my interest arose to investigate what really laid behind these positive words about the British artillery effort. In my studies, I first examined the artillery resources built up by the British, what equipment they had, how the resources were organised, what technical, tactical, and combat methods etc. that were applied, all against an historical background. The latter is important to have some knowledge of, thus giving a better understanding of the position of the British Artillery just before and during the Second World War. Great Britain had, as is well known, hundreds of years back in time a vast empire, with India as the largest and richest possession. The Army's main task had historically been geared primarily to defend this empire. For the artillery this meant 'policing' with smaller units, a few guns organised into troops and batteries. It was due to this 'historical burden', but also because of serious negligence in the interwar period, that Britain was ill prepared in the late 1930s for a modern continental war. It became a rude awakening, and we can see that the necessary renovation, modernisation and adaptation of a new organisational structure and modernised methods and tactics, which started in late 1938, was a process that was to take about five years to complete. This despite the fact that the country and its industry were put on a war footing in 1939 for fastest possible rearmament.

The build-up of new resources and associated technical requirements and capabilities as well as modernised tactics is discussed in the book's first two parts, Part 1 and Part 2. It should be stressed here that artillery fire was not just about guns and shells. The context is a complete system with many components; it is usually called the 'indirect fire system'. It was the system efficiency that was crucial and a prerequisite for success in battle. A distinction to mention here is that I have only written about what usually is called field artillery. Anti-aircraft, anti-tank, coastal artillery and artillery for the protection of merchant navy ships are largely left aside. As the two former artillery services beyond their primary functions sometimes were used also in ground combat in addition to field artillery, they are, however, sometimes discussed briefly in this book. It should also be noted that artillery commanders in higher units, corps and divisions, were in command of all the artillery participating in battle, i.e. the field artillery as well as anti-aircraft and anti-tank units.

The *Royal Regiment of Artillery*, colloquially *Royal Artillery* or only *RA*, from the early 1700s is the formal home of all artillery units employed for combat since. It was, and is, itself not a combat unit but a sort of umbrella organisation. Hence, the existing resources in 1939 and those gradually established later during the war had their home, so to speak, within this organisation. The resources were organised in regiments, which in their turn consisted of 3–4 batteries. I have chosen to retain the term 'regiment' in order not to obscure the connection to the source material and the parlance accepted in UK, *Field Regiment*, *Medium Regiment* etc. The reader should, however, be aware that a British artillery regiment was roughly the same as 'artillery battalion' in other countries' armies.

The book's third section, Part 3, describes how the British artillery resources actually were used during the war. Obviously, it has been impossible to analyse and describe this for all kinds of battles that took place. The selection of battles made has intended first to describe the use of, or lack of use, of artillery during the early war years, with the resources then available and methodological conditions prevailing – in the campaigns in France and Norway in particular. Then I have devoted much attention to the most important battle in the middle of the war, namely El Alamein that took place on 23 October to 4 November 1942. This battle meant a new trend in terms of mass employment of artillery and close air support. During the last two years of the war the British artillery was at the height of power and versatile capabilities. This is covered in some chapters on some of the major operations in Northwest Europe in 1944–1945, the grand finale being the Allied crossing of river Rhine in March 1945. The British artillery can be said then to represent the *state-of-the-art*. The same or similar technologies, organisation, tactics etc. came to survive relatively unchanged in most countries for another 40–50 years, i.e. basically the Cold War period. With computers, GPS, gyro compasses and precision ammunition the next trend came, or if you like, the next paradigm shift, say around 1990.

One of the concluding chapters briefly deals with the fighting against the Japanese in Southeast Asia in 1941–1945. The gunners were there to face a different, extremely brutal and ruthless opponent characterised by a different culture and a different view on human value than they had met in Europe, an opponent who also was extremely dedicated and talented in everything he undertook. They also had to face him there under appalling terrain and climatic conditions. The use of artillery resources was influenced by all of this, and was thus quite different to the role of artillery in North Africa and Western Europe. The brief presentation included here may be seen as an introduction for further discussion in another context.

I have had the ambition to base my studies and my writing on original sources as much as possible, especially when it comes to specific artillery issues and the use of artillery resources. The sources used are reported in the Notes and the subsequent reference lists (Sources and Literature). These include war diaries, reports of various kinds as well as personal accounts written by artillery officers at various levels, but also by other gunners. Official documents such as regulations, training manuals and handbooks, technical manuals, etc. have also been extensively used. It has not been war diary sheets as such that have been of primary interest. These are of much varying quality and credibility. The diary annexes, however, have been of much greater value to study. These normally consist of written plans, planning instructions, operation orders for higher and lower units, situation and intelligence reports as well as battle logs and detailed fire plans for major battles etc. Of great value have also been all the experience reports from various battle theatres, which were collected and distributed by means of the *Royal Artillery Notes* from 1943 onwards. I have also to some extent used existing English literature on artillery practices and history and would particularly like to refer to books by Major General J.B.A. Bailey and Brigadier A.L. Pemberton and the latest editions of *The History of the Royal Regiment of Artillery* authored by General Sir Martin Farndale. A source of great value has also been *The Journal of Royal Artillery*. However, as regards the course of the Second World War in general in the various theaters of war, I have often made use of the voluminous literature published up to the present day, mainly English and Swedish works. In this context I also want to mention all the valuable information that various veterans have kindly given to me in connection with visits and through extensive correspondence (letters and e-mails).

Although the book's presentations often go down to details, the book still has a rather superficial treatment of the subject. Much more can and should be studied, such as the effect of the British artillery fire on its opponents. A more systematic analysis as to how the German/Italian and Japanese opponents were affected in terms of material and human losses would be of interest, and how this affected their ability to retain, or lose, initiative and freedom of action. These issues are only briefly reviewed. Some general statements from prisoners of war have, however, been included. In particular some comparisons with the Soviet artillery on the Eastern Front are of interest.

Overall, the book gives interested readers, who do not have experience of artillery practice and knowledge about the design and operation of the 'system indirect fire', some insights into how it technically worked and how it was used during the Second World War.

A marginal note finally is, not least when seen in a British historical perspective, that the artillery as a resource almost always is underestimated during long periods of peace and sometimes mishandled. As history shows, it takes many years, and the cost in human lives is high, to correct mismanagement. Many have testified that the decisive role of artillery in war cannot be overstated.

The book deals with the Second World War artillery and its historical background. To give a better perspective on the conditions prevailing during the war and thereafter that influenced the British Army's development I have included in an Epilogue a discussion that I had in September 2011 with Major General (ret.)

Jonathan B.A. Bailey, CB, MBE, PhD. General Bailey has authored many books on artillery history and its future development. He is also an authority on security policies and strategies in general.

Kungsängen, 2017
Stig H. Moberg

Acknowledgements

This book could not have been written without the help and encouragement from many people. I am indebted to them all. My thanks first and foremost go to all the veterans whom I have met or had contact with otherwise. In this context I want to thank especially David Baines, Douglas Goddard, Sir Gilbert Heathcote, Tony Richardson, Johnny Walker and Peter Wilkinson, who generously shared source material with me as well as offered time for correspondence and lengthy discussions about their own war experiences. They were all young artillery officers during the war and made impressive careers after this, the four former mentioned military and the latter two civilian. Douglas Goddard too, after having left the Army in 1957, made an impressive civilian career eventually on several high civil positions in the industry and community.

My thanks also go to two veterans who served as infantry platoon commanders during the last years of the war. They are John Coghlan, who served with the Black Watch (Royal Highland) Regiment, and L van Aardt who fought with the King's African Rifles. Their accounts have provided interesting perspectives on the fighting in Italy and Burma.

Many veterans, who had already passed away when my work began, have, however, through their documents given me valuable insights into their war experiences. I would like to mention in particular Sidney Beck, whose extraordinary war diary, notes and photographs have been most valuable, and I am indebted to his son Benjamin Beck, who has kindly assisted me with this material. I also thank Jim Whetton, who has helped me with unpublished material from his uncle John T. Whetton, the distinguished commander of 4 Survey Regiment RA, who became Professor of Geology and Mining Sciences after the war. He was one of many talented Territorial Army officers in the Royal Artillery.

Another two deceased veterans I want to mention and thank here. One of them is G.W. Robertson, who served in one of the many field regiments during the war. After the war he wrote a comprehensive regimental history, *The Rose & The Arrow*. His regiment took part in the fighting in Burma for several years. I have benefited greatly from this work and extracted some quotations from the book and I am much grateful for these. The second one I am indebted to is the late Robert Woollacott who, like the aforementioned Johnny Walker and Peter Wilkinson, served in 1 Airlanding Light Regiment RA. He has written the regiment's history in the book *Winged Gunners,* from which I have taken some quotations after consultation with Bob Gerritsen, holder of Woolacott's background material. I extend my thanks to him.

Related to the same regiment's history is Peter Wilkinson's excellent book *The Gunners at Arnhem,* another important source for my writing. In this context I would like to extend my special and deeply felt thanks to Peter Wilkinson for his kindness to review and comment on the chapters on airborne artillery and Operation Market Garden. Sadly, he passed away a couple of months after I received his last comments.

Brigadier (ret.) David Baines has been so kind as to give me a copy of his personal war diary and given me permission to refer to it. For this and interesting communication with him I am very grateful.

I would also like to thank Philip Crawley, Permanent Secretary of the Burma Star Association, who conveyed valuable contacts with Burma Veterans and has assisted me also in tracing holders of copyrights.

It is natural that a work of this kind also leads to contacts with contemporary historians with different specialties. First I must express my gratitude to the too early deceased secretary of the Royal Artillery Historical Association Lieutenant Colonel William Townend, who was a frequent and prominent battlefield guide. His special interest was the battle of Normandy, which we had many discussions about. Much appreciated by me was the extensive correspondence that we exchanged. We also came to discuss issues regarding the future of the Territorial Army on which he had written an academic treatise. Amongst other people interested in military history, whom I want to thank for valuable exchanges of ideas about war historical events and conditions, are the late Ian Daglish, Major (ret.) Stephen King and Bill Hardy. Stephen King has reviewed five of the technical chapters of the book and given me a large number of most valuable comments for which I would like to extend a special thank you. I am indebted to Bill Hardy for an exciting excursion to and around the airfield where II Army Cooperation Squadron RAF was based during the war. I owe much to Nigel Evans, whose website about all aspects of the British artillery during World War II has been of great help to me (see http://nigelef.tripod.com).

As mentioned, I had frequent contacts with Major (ret) Douglas Goddard over many years. He so generously put his large private archive at my disposal and he was always ready to answer many questions on gunnery problems and various war subjects. Douglas Goddard sadly passed away in 2011 and I am grateful for the permission given by his children Tina Hutton and Nigel Goddard for me to quote from his rich material.

I would like to extend my thanks to Major General, PhD, Jonathan BA Bailey, who made himself available for the interview I have recorded in the Epilogue. He is an authority on British artillery history, and has in his extensive writings also analysed superpower strategies in both Europe and the Far East. He has taken an interest in the problems of nation building in countries becoming independent, but also countries where military intervention has thrown dictators out of the saddle, for instance Iraq and Sierra Leone. In our dealings, I have had the opportunity to discuss many of the observations and conclusions, which I have presented in summaries at the end of several of the chapters of the book. For this and the interview I am General Bailey much indebted.

I then turn to three Dutch friends who have also been instrumental. Robert Voskuil is an eminent authority on the Battle of Arnhem, Operation Market Garden. Over the years he has been most helpful through discussions and provision of documents and photographs that I thank him very much for. I also owe him my sincere thanks for reviewing and commenting on the chapter about this controversial battle. Hans Onderwater, who although he is a Dutch is the Official Historian for the RAF's Second Army Cooperation Squadron, has given me much information and material on this RAF Squadron, which I appreciate. One of the main tasks during the war was interaction with artillery, both in terms of intelligence survey and fire control in depth of the battlefield. He has given me access to interesting aerial photographs related to such tasks. For that I thank him very much. The third Dutch expert to thank is Louis Meulstee, who is an expert on British communication equipment used in the war and has published several books on this. I thank him especially for the large number of photographs that he has put at my disposal, some of which are included in this book.

My book is based on extensive archival studies in the UK for many years. I want to thank the staff at the Imperial War Museum's records department and photo archive for valuable help throughout the years. Sincere thanks also to the British National Archives at Kew, London, which is a real 'gold mine' for anyone looking for original sources. The staff are very service-oriented, always offering kind and efficient assistance when it comes to finding and producing interesting documents for review. I am very grateful for all the assistance I have received and having been given permission to use my own digital camera when visiting the institution.

My principal thanks as regards help from various archives go to the Librarian at the James Clavell Library, Paul Evans. The library, now closed, was the official repository and archive of the Royal Artillery Museum at Woolwich Arsenal in southeast London. No one has helped me as much, and with such an interest, as Paul Evans. For more than a decade, he has during all my visits with the utmost readiness and skill sought and found numerous original documents for my review. He has well understood what kind of photographs that I have been interested in and has presented a large number, of which many now are reproduced in the book. I also want to thank Paul Evans' research assistant during the first two years of my research, Matthew Buck. He introduced me to the archive collections and gave valuable assistance by providing long lists of documents of potential interest to me and, after my review, readily got them out in the light for my detailed examination. I owe Matthew Buck too, my sincere thanks.

My thanks also go to the former Curator of the now closed Royal Artillery Museum, Woolwich, Mark Smith, and his staff for their help on many occasions to find objects in the museum's collections that have been of particular interest to me. For many interesting photographs that the museum's staff have provided, I am much indebted.

In this context, I would like to extend my sincere thanks to the formal owner of the museum's collections and archives, the Royal Artillery History Trust. Thanks to the Trust's generosity, I have been able to copy and use numerous original documents and – not the least – photographs.

My thanks go to the Association of Friends of the museum and its former chairman the late Major General Mike Steele for many valuable contacts. From the Association's Secretary Philip Jobson I have been much supported as regard terms and acronyms. His magnificent 'Royal Artillery Glossary of Terms and Abbreviations. Historical and Modern', has been of great value in my work.

The Royal Artillery Publications have given me permission to include in my book several quotes from the two journals 'Royal Artillery Journal' and 'The Gunner'. For this, I convey my sincere thanks to the Regimental Secretary, HQS RA, Colonel R. Robson.

Another institution that I would like to thank for valuable help, not least in connection with copyright issues, is the Royal Artillery Association.

The large number of photographs that can be found in this book originate partly from some private collections, but to a large extent from the artillery museum's archive, i.e. James Clavell Library representing the Royal Artillery History Trust, and from the Imperial War Museum. I especially thank the staff of these two institutions for all their help with the finding of suitable photographs and providing copies from the original negatives. Several photographs have been provided also from other public sources such as Australian War Memorial. I extend my sincere thanks to these institutions.

I am much indebted to Major Jon McCleery, who, when commanding the 'O' Headquarters Battery (The Rocket Troop) 1st Regiment Royal Horse Artillery, kindly helped me with photographs of the paintings in the officers' mess showing the British rocket artillery in action at Leipzig in 1813. The Rocket Troop then fought under Swedish command against Napoleon. My thanks go to McCleery's successor as commander of the battery Major J.E. Allen for reconfirming the permission to include one of them in this book.

My special and heartfelt thanks go to my late brother, Åke Moberg, who helped me by producing twenty of the book's thirty-six maps. This help has been invaluable. Unfortunately, he suddenly and unexpectedly passed away, when he was just about to take on the remaining maps. For preparation of these, I later received excellent help from Oskar Karlin. I am grateful for his willingness to help me. My thanks go also to Mrs. Amis Halldin who quickly and skillfully drew printable copies of all sketches and numerous diagrams; and to my brother Jan Moberg for valuable general support and improvement of some illustrations and maps.

I want to convey special thanks to two prominent Swedish gunners who reviewed my first, Swedish, manuscript. They are Colonel 1.Cl. Gustaf Ankarcrona and Colonel Leif Mårtensson, the latter now head of the National Artillery Museum in Kristianstad, Sweden. Both have spent a lot of time on critical review of my draft material and have provided many valuable suggestions for improvements and additions.

When expressing my gratitude to many persons for help given to review and comment on my manuscript, I must stress that the responsibility for the book's subjects and facts, however, rests entirely on myself.

I have endeavored to find all relevant copyright-holders, but despite extensive inquiries failed in some cases. I hope this can be excused and that those concerned still can feel satisfaction that their documents and pictures will be well observed by others, as they deserve. To all those who have generously given me permission to use copyright material, including illustrations, I extend my sincere thanks.

It was a great privilege to me when the Publisher Martin Mace offered to publish an English version of my book. It has been a great pleasure to cooperate with Martin and his staff at Frontline. Thank you all!

My sincere thanks go also to the Commissioning Editor Mark Khan who has been so kind to undertake the onerous task of bringing my translation from Swedish to become more like English as it should be written by people having English as their mother tongue. Mark has with great patience and good humour been an excellent teacher. For this I am very grateful.

During the preparatory phase, Brigadier (ret.) Ken Timbers offered to submit the Foreword now included in the English version. For this I extend my sincere thanks.

Last but not least I extend a warm thank to my dear wife Gunilla who during the long time that I have worked on this project often saw me disappear into work and thoughts in the 'writer's study', to which came my absence for all trips to British archives and other places. My subject matter has not been particularly attractive to her, but has rather been a source of reminders of war atrocities and human suffering. Despite this, I have got a very valuable help with the reading of the script and wise comments on what I tried to express. Her good sense of languages has led to many proposals for text enhancement for which I express my great gratitude.

'The war was to show that where
artillery was used correctly,
battles were won,
where it was not they were lost'

General Sir Martin Farndale, KCB

Part 1
Historical Background – War and Rearmament

Fig. 1-1 2nd Rocket Troop Royal Horse Artillery under Swedish Command in action in the battle against Napoleon outside Leipzig, October 1813 (McCleery, O/HQ Battery [Rocket Troop] Royal Horse Artillery)

1. The Period Before the First World War

Two pictures

It is a battle, an intensive battle. A village can be partly seen in the background, some of its houses seem to be in flames, and in front of them we can visualise one of the combatants' soldiers fighting their opponents in the foreground. Gunpowder smoke is dense. Between them a couple of fallen soldiers, the horse of one of them already dead, the other one in death-throes. The head and neck are stretched forwards in panic, the left leg seems to be kicking intensively, and soon life will be gone. A mounted troop in colourful uniforms is in the right corner of the picture, led by their commander with drawn sabre. Order is given: Attack!

As far as this, it could be any painting of a battle from older days. But there is an unusual element. Behind the mounted troop, there are two horizontal arcs of fire and smoke heading straight into the formation of soldiers at the opposite side. Rockets! And closer to the observer: soldiers in the same uniforms as the mounted troop is carrying can be seen. They are preparing rockets attached to wooden rods ready to fire, in a great haste, as it seems. See **Fig. 1-1**.

The other picture is a photograph. And it is one from the Second World War, published more often than most photographs from this war. It can be seen in hundreds, not to say thousands of books and magazine articles. On the western shore of the River Rhine the top war leaders from Britain can be seen. Churchill, Alan Brooke and Montgomery are having lunch. It is 26 March 1945. Two days earlier, the Allies had crossed River Rhine in a grand concentration of their military resources, not least artillery. Churchill and Brooke had come over from London in order to witness the crossing in company with their host Field Marshal Bernard L. Montgomery. The crossing operation commenced the night between 23 and 24 March 1945. Although numerous artillery rounds were fired after the crossing, this was the great finale on the part of the British artillery, and I will come back to this later in this book.

When looking closer at the photograph **Fig. 1-2**, we can see that Churchill is comfortably seated and has put his walking stick into the ground behind him; his back against the photographer. He is holding a glass in his hand. To the right of him is the host Field Marshal Montgomery, Commander of the British 21st Army Group. Opposite Churchill is the Commander Imperial General Staff, Field Marshal Alan Brooke (later Viscount Alanbrooke). Slightly bent forward, he keeps his eyes on Churchill, and we might assume that the latter is speaking just when the photograph was taken. Maybe their discussion not only dealt with the events of the last few days, but also with a question raised by Montgomery to his guests during the morning 24 March, when they witnessed the large air-landing operation taking place east of the River Rhine: 'Now British soldiers are again fighting on German soil, when did it last take place?' Churchill, knowing his history, told the others that it was on 18 October 1813. The British Rocket Brigade, attached to the Swedish Army,

Fig. 1-2 'Picnic' on the western shore of the River Rhine for the three British war leaders Churchill, Brooke and Montgomery, just after Operation Plunder, the Rhine Crossing 23–24 March 1945. Churchill could tell the others of the role played by the British 2nd Rocket Troop when attached to the Swedish Army in the battle at Leipzig in October 1813 (©Imperial War Museum BU 2636)

took part in the battle against Napoleon; The Swedish Army was member of the Northern Alliance of four armies under command of the Swedish Crown Prince Karl Johan (former French Marshal Bernadotte)[1]

From other sources we know that the unit was 2 Rocket Troop Royal Horse Artillery and not a complete brigade. The Troop was the only British unit taking part in the Battle of Leipzig. The fact that it actually was there may seem a bit strange, as the British Army under the Duke of Wellington fought against the French on the Iberian Peninsula. The explanation is said to be that the Duke did not like rockets:[2] 'I do not want to bring cities into flames. I cannot see any other use of rockets'. Also later in 1815 at Waterloo he demonstrated his sceptical view on the use of rocket artillery.

Rockets had been used before 1800, e.g. in India, but the one who developed the technology and organised field units in England around the period of the Napoleon wars was Sir William Congreve. He developed a set of rockets with different weights for firing at ranges of 2–3km, i.e. much longer than the range of the guns of that time. Congreve organised the rocket artillery into brigades, which in their turn comprised a number of Troops, all eager to get involved in the war against Napoleon. Upon the Duke's dismissal, 2 Rocket Troop was sent to Northern Germany and became attached to the Swedish Army. The unit went into action after necessary adaptations and training, foremost at the Battle at Leipzig. It is said that the painting reproduced in **Fig. 1-1** illustrates the Troop in action there. During the battle the Troop Commander Captain Bogue was killed and his grave is at Paunsdorf just outside Leipzig. The memory of his and the Troop's magnificent participation in the battle is held in highest esteem in Britain.

A fact less observed is that the British rocket artillery accompanied the Swedish Army after the battle of Leipzig and took part also in the Swedish siege of the Danes at Glücksberg in December 1813 before returning to Britain in January 1814. The Crown Prince appreciated the contribution of the British gunners in the battles and awarded Lieutenant Strangways, who was nominated commander after Captain Bougue had been killed, a golden medal for gallantry in the field and also silver medals to a few other British gunners. After Strangways, Lieutenant Wright took command of the Rocket Troop and he too was awarded a gold medal before the Swedish-British cooperation ceased.[3]

After having heard the answer given by Churchill, Montgomery turned to his artillery chief and asked him to check as to whether any artillery formation in 21st Army Group was holding an honour title in commemoration of the battle of Leipzig and the role of the Rocket Troop in it. It was later found that the bearer of the tradition in this case was 'O' Battery (The Rocket Troop) Royal Horse Artillery. However, this battery was not in the vicinity at the time. It was part of a Field Regiment fighting in Italy. The discussion is a good illustration of the importance of traditions in the British Army, not least in the Royal Artillery.

The memory of the rocket gunners today is the responsibility of 'O'/Headquarters Battery (The Rocket Troop) 1st Regiment Royal Horse Artillery. A photograph of the painting here reproduced, as **Fig. 1-1** was kindly put at my disposal in 2005 by the then Battery Commander Major Jon W. McCleery. The painting is placed at the Officers' Mess, where a dinner is organised every year in October in commemoration of the Rocket Troop and its participation in the battle at Leipzig in October 1813.[4]

In order to get a broader perspective on the history of British Artillery and its development as regards organisation, equipment, tactics, etc., we will take a historical journey, through the centuries up to 1939; and we start long before the nineteenth century.

The Black Prince takes to the guns
Different types of weapon had been used in battles through the centuries, among them bows and arrows and heavier equipment based on mechanical energy to throw stones and other types of projectile. These could include incendiary projectiles. Amongst battles much written about where such equipment was used is the Battle at Hastings in 1066 when William the Conqueror defeated the Anglo-Saxons under Harold Godwinson. The famous Bayeux tapestry shows how this was done.

It would take a long time until chemical energy had replaced mechanical energy as the driving force for throwing projectiles against the enemy. Exactly when gunpowder came to use is uncertain, and it is still in debate. It is, however, confirmed through literature and paintings that a kind of gun was used during the first decades of the fourteenth century. The Navy's battle against the French Navy in 1340 is mentioned in British military literature as one of the earliest battles where guns were used. There are also paintings of guns in England dated as early as 1326.[5]

As to field artillery, there is a place and a year that most often references are made to in the literature and this is Crécy 1346. One can state that it was here that the British artillery emerged as a lasting force of power to determine the outcome of battles. The son of Edward III, the Black Prince, won a decisive victory over a superior French force. He managed to accomplish this thanks to a skilful use of archers and artillery. Maybe it can be stated that the paradigm shift from mechanical to chemical propellant, then gunpowder, was completed in Europe.

A permanent artillery organisation
Although guns were taken into operation during the fourteenth century, it would take a long time before artillery received a more permanent organisation in Britain. This happened first in 1486, when Henry VII created a special authority, Master of the Ordnance, appointed artillery commander and employed twelve paid gunners. They were located at the Tower of London. Later the organisation was extended with a number of Master Gunners positioned at various castles and citadels. They were to take care of the equipment when no war was taking place. Furthermore, they were also made responsible for the training of gunners and recurrent exercises. The gunners were civilians who against payment were called in to serve the guns. This artillery was organised in *Traynes*, an organisational form that would last for another 150 years.[6] A minor exception from this structure was the establishment by Henry VIII in 1537 of the Guild of St. George, which oversaw what later became Honourable Artillery Company (HAC), the duty of which was 'to be overseers of the science of artillery […] for the better increase of the defence of our realm'.[7] At its establishment, it was given the magnificent name Fraternity of Guild of Artillery of Longbows, Crossbows and Handguns; hence it did not have much in common with 'artillery' of later years.[8] Artillery pieces were not provided until the late eighteenth century. The HAC has always had a close relation to the city of London and from time to time reinforced the local police.

When the Territorial Army was established (see below) the HAC was attached to the artillery as well as infantry units. Four Field Regiments were mobilised by HAC in the Second World War. Amongst ceremonial duties it fires salutes from the Tower of London, a responsibility given in 1924. The HAC is considered to be amongst the oldest regiments of the British Army.

We are returning now to the sixteenth century and the establishment of the British Empire, which had commenced with Queen Elizabeth I as one of the key persons behind it. The interest on the part of the Queen was aimed primarily to establish trade links and to take advantage of colonisation.[9] Of particular interest was India, which brought about the establishment in 1600 of the East India Company, a company that later gradually established a strong Indian artillery force.

The building and defence of the Empire caused a number of wars with other colonial powers, in particular France, the Netherlands and Spain. The British participation in the North American War of Independence was also an important struggle. Defending the Empire would cause numerous engagements of British artillery through various local wars up to the present time. The need for 'policing' was always there. Here is one of the most important legacies that have influenced the development of organisation, equipment, and tactics etc., from long ago and into the twentieth century.

Artillery was not very mobile up to the seventeenth century; it was therefore foremost used at sieges and defence in static situations. Improved mobility, and with this adaptation of tactics, was to characterise the seventeenth and eighteenth centuries. The reforms during the former century by the Swedish King Gustav II Adolf [Gustavus Adolphus] also had some influences on the British artillery.

The establishment of the Royal Regiment of Artillery
With the frequent wars within the country and on the world arena, it finally became impossible to base the engagement of British artillery on the system with Master Gunners and civilian soldiers and civilian resources for transportation. When artillery support could be delivered, it was often too late. The battle was already over; and this usually had negative consequences for the British Army. Such experience led to a historical

decision by the Duke of Marlborough in 1716. Two regular artillery companies were set up at Woolwich, Southeast London. These constituted 'The Royal Ordnance'. Each company had 5 officers and 99 NCOs and ORs. The Commanding Officer was a Captain. A few years later, in 1722, two independent companies were attached, one of them at Gibraltar. The formations were now given the name the Royal Regiment of Artillery; today and at earlier times just known as the Royal Artillery or by the acronym RA.

The first Colonel of the regiment was an old very experienced officer born in Denmark, Albert Borgard. **Fig. 1-3** illustrates his bust, which was inaugurated in the Danish city Holbœk in 1947. His original Danish name spelt with 'aa' is there used, but I will here use the name as it is spelt in Britain, i.e. with one 'a'.

To some extent Borgard was familiar to the Swedes of his time. He commenced his military career by participating in the fierce Danish-Swedish battles in 1676 in the southern province of Sweden, Skåne [Scaniae], including the siege of the fortress at Kristianstad on 25 August and the decisive battle at Lund on 3 December. Borgard has written about his long gunner career and tells us how he became a gunner in Sweden:

> In the Month of September several young Men that were all recommended were taken out of the Foot Regiments to be made Gunners of the Artillery of which I was one of the number & served as such in the great Battle fought at Lund (in the month of December) between the Swedes and the Danes, which continued from Sun rising to Sun setting. This was counted a drawn Battle because both Armies' Artillery remained in the Field that night.[10]

Borgard later entered Foreign Service on the Continent, disappointed for not being promoted at home, and in 1692 came to serve under the English banner:

> [. . .] I marched with the Army to the Camp at Genep (Genappe) where in the month of July I entered as Firemaster into the English Artillery [. . .].[11]

When he much later was appointed the first Colonel of the Regiment, he had served for more than 40 years as a gunner and had numerous successful battles behind him. He was correctly known as one of the foremost gunners of his time.

The new regiment quickly developed under Borgard's leadership, and a special spirit of corps was established. Borgard demanded from his gunners that they should always fight till the end, regardless of an enemy's superiority. They were to continue firing their guns till the last round or were killed on post! This spirit was well observed and maintained over the years and was one important component of the legacy when the Second World War commenced.

Woolwich was developed into a huge artillery centre during the eighteenth century.[12] The number of companies increased, and in 1757 there were 24 grouped into two battalions. Recruitment of civilian horses and drivers still took place, when reinforcement was needed. Basic training was organised as was officer training. The latter took place at Royal Military Academy Woolwich founded in 1741. Here, all artillery and sapper officers were given qualified

Fig. 1-3 The veteran artillery officer Alfred Borgard, a Dane by birth, was the first Commander of Royal Regiment of Artillery. He assumed command at the age of 63 years in 1722 (RAHT)

training. Manufacture of ammunition had begun at Woolwich in late seventeenth century and was gradually expanded. Also manufacture of guns was initiated at Woolwich, and the place remained as a large defence centre until the end of the twentieth century.

In parallel with this progress, the country was involved in many military actions and campaigns around the world where much experience was gained. It was, for instance observed that Frederick the Great established a more solid organisational artillery structure, in which the Battery was the prime unit.[13] Mobility of artillery was also to increase, and again Frederick the Great played an important future role, when he created the mounted artillery for the first time and established a special organisation for it. His idea was to make it possible for the artillery to follow the cavalry in swift attacks, in particular at the flanks. For this fairly light guns were needed; it was also necessary to have all the serving gunners mounted on horses.

In England, or now more correctly to say the United Kingdom, as the union between England, Scotland, Wales and Ireland now had been created, Fredrick's ideas were found interesting and well worth copying. In this regard Britain had its own experience from India. This led to the establishment of the Royal Horse Artillery (RHA) in 1793. Two mounted Troops were organised. RHA is, as is well known, still in existence and is often regarded as a *corps d'élite* in the RA.

On the equipment side, no revolutionary developments took place during the eighteenth century even if new guns were supplied from time to time, but these were all still designed for direct fire against the enemy. Guns with flat trajectories, as well as howitzers with high, curved trajectories, were available. The ammunition was round solid shells, in most cases. However, a more advanced type of ammunition was developed towards the end of the century. It had a high explosive core. Simple case-shot with numerous small iron balls spread in front of the guns had for long been used, but only on a very limited scale. In 1783, Lieutenant Henry Shrapnel invented a more sophisticated version of this type of ammunition. It contained numerous small rifle bullets, which were spread by means of explosive powder.[14] This type of ammunition was still being widely used at the beginning of the nineteenth century.[15]

Military music is part of old traditions of the artillery. The Royal Artillery Band was established in 1762 and still exists today; it is considered to be Britain's oldest military band.

Before leaving the eighteenth century we will observe another important change, which was to become very important during the world wars of the twentieth century. The first artillery formations for volunteers, Volunteer Gunners, were established in 1797. This took place when the country was under pressure from Napoleon and his France, with which the country was at war since 1793.[16] These formations of volunteers were predecessors to the Territorial Army of the twentieth century and the artillery regiments of this army, and to which I will come back later.

Twenty-two years of war against Napoleon
The war against France, which broke out in 1793 and lasted until Napoleon was defeated finally at Waterloo in 1815, was a war effort of extreme scale. This war was fought at many places outside Europe under participation of The Royal Artillery before its culmination with the battle between Wellington's British Army and French armies on the Iberian Peninsula 1808–1814. The Royal Artillery had grown to impressive strength already before this war. In 1806 twelve mounted Troops were mobilised from the Royal Horse Artillery and no less than 102 companies of field artillery organised into nine artillery battalions.[17]

Napoleon himself was a commander who ascribed a very important role to the artillery in battle; in static positions as well as in swift manoeuvres. He is said to have stated: '[Artillery] Fire is everything, the rest does not matter' and 'Great Battles are won by artillery.'[18] He strived for physical concentration of the artillery and had special artillery commanders nominated at army and corps levels in order to make concentration possible. The British did not have as much artillery as Napoleon and had to prioritise support for divisions. In order to facilitate this Wellington organised his artillery in brigades. The mounted artillery was used as a complement to the slower field artillery and the Troops of Royal Horse Artillery became a decisive mobile artillery reserve for Wellington in many battles.[19] An experience of lasting importance was the need for a new command structure. An established example implied that artillery commanders should be assigned to all tactical levels.[20] We will later see how this was applied many times during the twentieth century. Again, an important part of the historical legacy!

Much did not happen on the technical side. However, development of ammunition continued, and ammunition with high explosive capability and time fuzes came into use more and more as were shrapnel and case-shot.

We have at the beginning of the chapter touched upon William Congreve's development of rockets. He, and others interested in new devices, saw the rocket as a means to overcome disadvantages of traditional artillery, in particular the short range of fire and low mobility. Rockets could be fired up to 3km, and it was easy to bring fire over the walls of fortresses at sieges. From naval ships fire on land targets could easily be brought down in heavy concentrations, which the Danes had experienced at Copenhagen in 1807 when the Royal Navy attacked the city. Rockets set large parts of the city on fire.

An advantage of the rockets, much appreciated, was its psychological effect and ability to 'frighten the horses of the enemy'. Their poor precision was however a decisive disadvantage.[21]

An important lesson from the Napoleon wars was that the best effect was accomplished when artillery-infantry-cavalry arms were well coordinated both in defence and in offensive campaigns. This required officers with the right understanding of the characteristics of each 'component' of the all-arms system and how to coordinate them. Another important lesson – not the least – was that they must understand the need for joint exercises. It is amazing that the British forgot most of these lessons soon after the defeating of Napoleon. Tactics and battle methods were not developed further during the subsequent forty-year period; and no all-arms training was arranged, for which a high price had to be paid in the next major battle, the Crimean War.[22]

The problem returned through the decades, and to learn from history seems to be an 'eternal' difficulty! All-arms exercises are not particularly popular in time of peace; there seldom seems to be time for them. First when put at test in war, the fatality of such negligence is recognised – and the price is high in terms of human lives. We will return to this when coming to the Second World War campaigns in this book.

When it comes to the role played by British artillery during the nineteenth century, this was also determined by technological conditions and status. It was possible to act in support of infantry with direct fire and – by means of the mounted artillery – the cavalry. The second important task was to attack the enemy's artillery.[23] Hence, it was always important to find a balance between different prime tasks, a duty that really had not lost its interest when the Second World War approached.

A paradigm shift
The Crimean War was a great war for Britain, but hardly for its artillery. Too much had been neglected during the forty years that had passed since Waterloo. These actions, although often heroic, were achieved by single guns or smaller formations. At these levels much was accomplished, but it had no strategic importance. Such actions led, however, to the awarding of the new Victoria Cross to nine gunners; Britain's highest ranked award for gallantry in battle.

Another important sequence of events during this century was the Indian Mutiny, in some countries called the 'Sepoy Uprising'. In India it has been regarded as a Battle for Freedom. It commenced in 1857 when Indian soldiers mutinied against their European masters in some British-Indian Army units. Even some artillery companies of East India Company took part in the mutiny, although many others remained loyal to the British. The mutineers committed dreadful excesses against the European population, including massacres of women and children, e.g. in Delhi. Several cities, where Europeans had sought shelter under protection of British armed forces, were under siege for a long time. The British response was a massive military intervention using forces in place, but also by formations sent from Europe. The siege and capture of Lucknow was one of the decisive trials of strength between the opposing forces.[24] The mutiny was finally crushed in 1858.

A young Swedish Officer serving in the Royal Navy, Axel Lind of Hageby, took part in the fighting when the guns of his ship were taken ashore and organised in a artillery 'sea-brigade', which was sent to Delhi to reinforce the British forces there. His account [in Swedish] is an interesting report of what happened there.[25]

This violent confrontation led to

disbandment of East India Company when the rule of India was taken over by the British Government. All military units of the Company were either disbanded or taken over by the British Army. This included a large number of artillery companies that were transferred to the Royal Artillery.

In this context it should be remembered that despite the severe conflict Indians were to serve the British with great loyalty and skill after 1858 and during the coming decades. During the Second World War units of the Indian Army with both British and Indian personnel played an exceptionally impressive role on several major theatres.

Captain Sing a retired Indian officer represents many distinguished Indian officers and soldiers (**Fig. 1-4**).

In 1859, the British artillery was reorganised and 'Brigade' was introduced instead of the 'Battalion', and 'Company' became 'Battery', an order that was to last until 1938. An important technical step of development was taken, also in 1859, when Armstrong's rifled breech-loading gun with cylindrical high explosive shells was introduced. This was followed by the introduction of 12-pounders for the Field Regiments and 9-pounders for the mounted regiments of the Royal Horse Artillery.[26] This meant longer ranges and higher fire intensity at the same time as the need for mobile artillery reserves was reduced.

The development of guns went on, and buffer and recuperator devices for control of recoil and return of the barrel to the firing position after firing were eventually invented. This reduced the need for re-laying of the gun after every round. Hence, fire intensity could be further increased. A further modernisation of the guns was the application of shields for protection of the detachment from enemy infantry fire.

All artillery had become more mobile, but it was still necessary to fire direct, i.e. the target must be seen from the gun. Neither sights nor communication equipment were as yet available for indirect firing with the fire observer placed far from the guns. This meant a tactical disadvantage that still prevailed.

New artillery practice camps were established during the second half of the nineteenth century. Besides Woolwich Shoe-buryness came in 1859, Okehampton in 1875 and finally, the one that was later to become Britain's primary artillery centre during the twentieth century, Larkhill on the Salisbury Plain, in Wiltshire.

The practical war experience was limited to such that emerged from all small wars at the outskirts of the Empire, which were going on almost continuously. Britain was at the end of the century ill prepared for large wars against well-equipped and well-trained opponents. The Royal Artillery remained very skilled in employing in action small formations up to the strengths of battery, or just a section of guns, sometimes single guns.

An organisational change came in 1899 when the Royal Artillery was split up into a 'mobile' part and a 'static', or at least a less mobile part. The former part comprised the Royal Field Artillery (RFA) with the Royal Horse Artillery (RHA). The latter was named the Royal Garrison Artillery (RGA). Coast artillery and heavier guns for primarily static deployment and Mountain Artillery formations were all included in RGA. This order lasted until 1924 when all formations again became the Royal Artillery, in which RHA retained its special rank.

Fig. 1-4 The retired Indian Officer Captain Sing may represent all distinguished Indian Officers and soldiers serving the British Empire in the World Wars (RAHT)

Before leaving the nineteenth century, we will notice a special formal legacy which survived the Second World War and still is in use and much respected.

Ubique – Quo Fas Et Gloria Ducunt

The British Army had, as was the case in most armies, honoured important battle victories on banners and standards. The problem arose when formations like the RA were continually fighting wars, albeit these were small-scale wars. Many of these gave reasons for proud remembrance. How to pay tribute to all these victories and proof of extraordinary gallantry? After all, there was not much room on flags and standards for this. This Gordian knot was resolved by royal initiative in 1833, when William IV decided to grant the Royal Artillery the right to bear the motto *Ubique*, which means 'Everywhere' in Latin, as replacement for all previous Battle honours. A second motto, *Quo Fas Et Gloria Ducunt,* which means 'Whither right and honour lead' was granted too by the king. The two combined over and below a gun constitutes the regiment's Coat of Arms, which is much used, e.g. as a cap badge. The present design is from 1902 (the gun is a 9-pounder from 1871). **Fig. 1-5** illustrates the badge with its proud mottos. It should be observed that the royal crown is as shown in the illustration when the monarch is a king; when a queen the design is as it is today. It may be added also that the Royal Horse Artillery within the Royal Artillery has its own cap badge. Furthermore, the fact that the guns always are the Regiment's Colour should be observed.

Certainly the Regiment has been standing up to its first motto during the past three hundred or more years, and the Second World War was definitely no exception.

Fig. 1-5 The Coat of Arms of Royal Regiment of Artillery was granted by HM King William IV in 1833. It was intended to replace victory names on standards and flags. It is used in many contexts including as a cap badge. Its motto 'Ubique – Quo Fas Et Gloria Ducunt' means 'Everywhere – Whither Right and Glory Lead'. The guns are the Colours of the regiment (RAHT)

2. The Period up to the Second World War

The great wars and the next paradigm shift
The introduction of gunpowder as propellant can be regarded as a paradigm shift. The first years of the twentieth century would see changes emerge.

For Britain the Boer War 1899–1902 became the first 'modern' large-scale war. Here the British had to face a strong, well-equipped and mobile enemy, who had access to more long-range firing artillery than they possessed themselves. The Boers had acquired such modern guns, which also had higher fire intensity, based on German technology. The British came to the battlefield with guns, although rifled and breech-loaded, that could not match those of their opponent in terms of range and fire intensity. The traditional doctrine calling for deployment of the guns close behind the infantry, and sometimes in front of those to be supported, did not work. Direct fire at the enemy's artillery and infantry implied an unacceptable exposure, which caused great losses. To this can be added that the Boers had more modern infantry weapons, which they could use from hidden positions, at longer ranges.

The situation forced the British to withdraw their guns to positions where they were sheltered, and from which a kind of simplified indirect fire was applied. As the technical means for indirect fire had not been introduced, they had to improvise. A fire observer could, for instance, be placed not far from the guns at the crest of a ridge or a hill, where he could see the target. He directed the fire by shouting changes regarding the gun laying to the gun detachments. A provisional use of aiming markers was used to refer to the direction of the target.

Indirect fire had been discussed among gun manufacturers and military users for quite some time. Germany had already come far on this when the new century came and had in use new sights for indirect fire already in 1892. In Britain, however, it was difficult to get acceptance for the new technology. Captain C.D. Guinness analysed in an article 1897 the advantages and disadvantages of indirect fire and concluded that the British artillery should continue with direct fire. He accepted, however, that one should try to avoid too exposed deployments. He concluded: '[. . .] Indirect fire was contrary to the spirit of the Royal Artillery's sense of sportsmanship.'[27]

The Boer War initiated, however, a quick development of new guns to meet the new challenges. The need for this had also become obvious during the war between Russia and Japan 1904–1905. Just in time for the First World War a new modern 13-pounder gun had been introduced for Royal Horse Artillery, and an 18-pounder for Royal Field Artillery. A new 4.5-inch howitzer was also developed, as was a new medium gun, the 60-pounder. Incidentally, we may here notice that the British used different systems for denomination of their artillery pieces. Sometimes the denomination was based on the weight of the projectile to be fired by the gun, sometimes on the calibre in inches, the latter for howitzers predominantly.

The first gun sight for indirect fire came in 1913, i.e. more than 20 years later than the first German sight had emerged.

The Mountain Artillery formations that existed, in particular in India, had towards the end of the nineteenth century been equipped with the famous 2.5-inch (63.5-mm) gun, the screw gun, well known from a famous poem by Rudyard Kipling. This was later replaced at the beginning of the twentieth century by modernised 2.75-inch (70-mm) mountain guns and eventually with the 3.7-inch howitzer (94-mm).

With the change to 'indirect fire' as the primary task of the artillery, opportunities emerged for an earlier unknown concentration of firepower across large areas and at long distances. Almost all 'corners' of the battlefield could now be reached, not only the nearest enemy infantry lines and the artillery deployed just behind. This meant a real paradigm shift. Bailey (2004) writes:[28]

> Indirect fire had been used in siege warfare for centuries, but its use on the battlefield was the most important conceptual and technical innovation in over five hundred years of artillery practice.

The new technology required a change of organisation and more advanced methods in order to improve the precision of artillery fire. The need for communication with fire observers at long distances became another prerequisite for concentration of firepower from many units dispersed over a large area. A 'loud' and 'distinct' commanding voice with or without megaphone was not any longer enough! The one who developed new artillery tactics based on the advantage of 'indirect fire' was a winner.

This, however, did not take place in Britain; conservatism was too strong. And it seems that those concerned had been too much influenced by all the small colonial wars against weaker and technology-wise inferior opponents and thus being less willing to take on the new possibilities. Hence, Britain went to war in 1914 with modern guns but with obsolete tactics, and for 'indirect fire' less developed methods. Britain lacked qualified staff and command resources for concentration of firepower. A large war on the European Continent with British participation had for long not been regarded as a likely threat. Bailey (2004) again: '[. . .] At the turn of century British artillery remained essentially but a collection of batteries.'[29]

The wake-up was to be dramatic! Before proceeding and summarising artillery development during World War I, we will first note an organisational change of utmost importance to the British artillery during the twentieth century; i.e. the taking advantage of the defence interest by Volunteers.

The Territorial Army – using society's best resources in times of national crisis

We have seen that artillery units of volunteers were already organised in 1797. Other types of formation also existed such as the Yeomanries, a kind of local militia in the counties for protection against external enemies and internal troublemakers. At the beginning of the twentieth century, it was found appropriate to reorganise units of volunteers and establish a more powerful resource, which could be used as reinforcement of the regular army. The Secretary of State for War in the new Liberal Government, which took office in 1906, was a man of strong will, Richard Burton Haldane. He clearly saw a need for reform. The growing and more united Germany was seen as a coming threat to Britain and he felt that Britain must be prepared to send a strong Expeditionary Force to Continental Europe in case Germany attacked for instance Belgium or France. It should have a strength of at least 120,000 men and should be ready to deploy across the Channel within fifteen days.

In support of this force, which must be a professional regular army, another army must be available at home for the protection of the national territory. It had been seen during the Boer War that the demands from Southern Africa had drained the homeland of military resources and made the country indefensible. In the future this must be avoided and the solution was the creation of a Territorial Force, also called the Home Force, later renamed the Territorial Army. After a lot of political struggles and squabbles the Parliament approved a new law, the Territorial Reserve Forces Bill, which basically became an approval of Haldane's reform proposal. According to this at least fourteen fully equipped divisions with supply and artillery would be established (Haldane had originally suggested the double this amount). Fourteen cavalry brigades and a number of divisional formations were to be set up in addition to the mentioned divisions. The former Militia was integrated with the regular army and became an important Special Reserve. The law became effective on 1 April 1908 and two years later, a Territorial Army of 286,618 men had been created on voluntary basis.[30]

After this reform, other reforms followed regarding staff work, training and exercises etc. for the entire Armed Forces.

The system with a Territorial Army meant that Britain had got the ability to quickly reinforce the regular army with qualified formations, albeit not immediately after mobilisation. A six months respite for additional training was called for. A great advantage was, and so it prevailed, that valuable civilian competence from many areas of society would be provided. Not the least for the artillery, this was of great importance. Another advantage was that defence interest in the society could be taken care of. As we will see later, this was to become of immense, not to say decisive, importance for the rearmament of artillery before and during the Second World War.

Those who had joined the Territorial Army had to serve in evenings, normally two days a week, up to 20 hours annually as well as attending a two-week summer practice camp.

Artillery develops into a mighty force during the Great War

Britain went to war in the summer 1914 when the First World War broke out, the war that was to be called the Great War. The army did so burdened with traditions, obsolete doctrines and incomplete methods. The opportunities provided by the paradigm shift to indirect fire, and its consequences in a broader sense, were not fully observed and implemented. It was thought that the war would be characterised by swift manoeuvres with mobile units supported by relatively independent batteries with the new light guns. It would be a war for the Royal Horse Artillery and Royal Field Artillery and not for the heavier guns of the Royal Garrison Artillery. In total 72 Field Regiments were mobilised but only six Heavy Batteries.[31]

Ammunition expenditure was estimated based on experience from the Boer War. It was planned for a maximum consumption of 1,000 rounds for each 18-pounder gun of which only 176 would be available forward at the front. At home another 300 rounds per gun were to be stocked and another 500 were planned for manufacture within six months. If lessons from Russian–Japanese War had been taken into account, quite larger volumes would have been secured. However, it did not take much time until it had been made clear that a modern war raised other demands. In 1918, for instance, it was considered necessary to prepare supply of at least 600 shells per day for an 18-pounder, when a major attack was planned. In total some 100 million shells were fired during the war with this type of gun.[32]

As most people know the war soon changed to a static war with the opponents dug in into vast systems of trenches. However, both sides made many large and small attempts with attacks to break the deadlock. Not until the final phase of the war, large mobile operations took place. As to the artillery, focus was soon geared towards 'destruction' and 'annihilation' rather than 'neutralisation'. Hence, the need for heavy guns increased dramatically, and these should be howitzers due to their curved trajectories with a steep descent towards the ground. By this type of fire, enemy soldiers in the trenches were easier to hit. As far as the British army was concerned, such guns were provided from Royal Garrison Artillery, but numerous new ones were manufactured too. Some of them were equipped with wheel carriages; others were mounted on railway carriages. The calibres were many:[33]

- 60-pounder
- 6-inch 26cwt howitzer
- 8-inch howitzer
- 9.2-inch siege howitzer
- 9.2-inch railway gun
- 12-inch siege howitzer
- 14-inch railway gun

It is interesting to notice that the introduction of all these heavy guns gradually lead to provision of motor transport to replace the horses. It was out of the question to use horses to draw the heaviest guns. Instead steam-driven tractors were supplied (which in fact had been tested on a small scale during the Boer War), but also petrol-fuelled combustion tractors were used. More than 1,000 American Holt tractors moving on tracks were purchased.[34] Moving the guns was still a slow undertaking: more than 3–5 miles an hour could seldom be achieved. Furthermore, the largest guns had to be dismantled into several parts easier to transport.

Britain went to war with only six heavy batteries, as mentioned above. It must be regarded as an outstanding industrial achievement that quite soon some 440 heavy and super-heavy batteries could be set up complete with guns and ammunition.[35] With these new guns Army and Corps artillery were established organisationally for the first time as a complement to the divisional artillery, i.e. the light Field Regiments.

However, long-range guns with fairly flat trajectories were also needed in large quantity. This need was fulfilled by the light guns mentioned above, although the quantity of these was too low initially. The number of batteries increased gradually and amounted to 568 at the end of the war as compared with 72 when the war commenced. The stock of guns comprised 3,000 18-pounders with eight million shells and around a thousand 4.5-inch howitzers with two million shells.[36]

The ammunition was developed also. When the war commenced 1914 only shrapnel shells were available for the 18-pounders, but these were gradually complemented with high explosive shells, smoke shells and shells for chemical warfare (tear gas and mustard gas).[37]

With this enormous artillery rearmament a need for a new artillery command structure arose. Artillery commanders were introduced at all high levels; and staff resources for efficient coordination of the plans for the artillery battle with those of the infantry, i.e. all-arms coordination and planning, were organised. This was also a prerequisite for concentration of firepower from as many fire units as possible irrespective of 'ownership'. The need for systematic counter-battery fire against the enemy's artillery and other types of fire in depth also required a more advanced command structure. Fire planning including extensive fire plans for barrages, unknown in 1914, became normal practice.

Fire observation and control was enhanced by the use of aircraft, albeit initially at a small scale, and balloons. Artillery intelligence was also improved by use of air resources and the possibilities to provide air photographs of the enemy's artillery positions. Another way of improving intelligence was the invention and introduction of sound ranging systems as well as resources for coordinated observation against enemy artillery, flash spotting. We will see more of these methods later in this book.

A major problem was communication across the battlefield. Radio was not yet available, so one had to rely on telephone communication with field lines. Dispatch riders were retained as well for transmitting orders, fire plans etc. Huge amounts of telephone wires were laid but often destroyed by enemy artillery fire, horses, and vehicles etc. Hence, large resources were required for repairing lines cut off. This problem was to repeat itself in the Second World War.

With the change to 'indirect fire' a new problem faced the gunners: How to hit the target with accuracy, when it could not be observed from the guns? And to do this with all units to be engaged irrespective of where they were deployed? A small error in fire direction or gun elevation would result in a large impact deviation relative the target, this when the firing ranges had increased considerably with new guns. The impact of weather conditions on shell trajectory became a critical factor, as were changes of muzzle velocity. The voluminous firing during the war meant significant wearing of barrels with a reduction of the latter as a consequence that must be observed and corrected. Furthermore, indirect fire required better data as regards the location coordinates of gun deployments and targets. This could be achieved by introduction of efficient resources for survey and better maps. Methods and resources to match all these new requirements were gradually provided during the war. It is interesting to notice that the British Expeditionary Force had only one single officer specialised in survey when the war commenced; and he had only one assistant! Four years later, when the war ended, there were almost 10,000 surveyors, out of which 4,000 were officers.[38]

Methods for daily regular acquisition of weather data (several times a day) were introduced. The aim was to determine strength and direction of wind at different heights above ground where the shell trajectory was to pass. Even air pressure at different heights had to be measured. With such weather data the trajectory could be corrected in advance in order to improve accuracy, thus making it more likely that the target would be hit. Procedures for 'calibration' of the guns to correct deviation of muzzle velocity were also by necessity developed. I will later in the book discuss more in detail the problems related to hitting the target.

When the First World War commenced 'mobility' was the word of honour, then it soon changed to 'firepower'. However, towards the end of 1917 and early 1918 the former doctrine again began coming into focus, but still at the battle at Vimy 1917, the operation commenced with a huge fire plan, which went on for seven days! Of course no elements of surprise preceded that attack, this to the advantage of the defenders.

Another part of the new doctrine that was developed gradually during the war was that artillery should in the first place be used against targets in depth, and not only against the nearest enemy lines on the battlefield as before. Bailey (2004) is summarising the doctrine during the last year of the war as follows:[39]

> A typical fire-plan attacked enemy headquarters communication systems, artillery logistics, bridges, and depots simultaneously. It blinded enemy observers and destroyed strong points and field defences. It attacked enemy positions in depth, especially the enemy reserve before it could join the contact battle, sealing off the battlefield. At the same time it provided close support to the manoeuvre force as it advanced on its objectives. All this was accompanied by ruses and deceptions, including a complete dummy fire-plan if necessary. The planning for operations was conducted at high level under centralised command, but measures were taken to make the plan responsive to the unexpected events that inevitably occurred.

Basically this doctrine came to last over the

Second World War and long after that war, but as Bailey noted, in 1914 it would have been regarded as 'bizarre'!

The First World War ended on 11 November 1918 with the British artillery comprising 540,000 men and 2,000 batteries of various types.[40] Only a minor part comprised regular formations, the majority had been established by means of soldiers conscripted from civilian resources.

Barnett (2000) is summarising in his book *Britain and her Army* that the army of civilians had become battle-experienced. The British soldier was stubborn and resolute but not very 'dashing'. The British Army was good at organising and controlling the attack in detail. Barnett meant that there was a rigidity and concentration to hierarchy and firm control from the top that would hamper individual initiatives and actions to take advantage of rapidly changing situations (see interview with General Bailey in the Epilogue).[41]

At the end of the Great War, an organisational, technical and tactical foundation had been laid for the future British artillery.

'It can be presumed…that the British Empire will not get engaged in a major war during the next ten years'
This was the directive of the British Government in 1919 as the basis for all military planning after the devastating Great War. The 'Ten Years Rule' would be seen applied until 1932 when politicians had to reluctantly admit that the trend not only in Europe, but also in the Far East, required a new policy to be implemented.

The dreadful number of victims of the Great War (three-quarters of a million killed and more than one and a half million wounded from the United Kingdom alone) caused widespread pacifist sentiments in Britain.

In this context, the above directive was not to be seen as unreasonable. After demobilisation of the conscripted men that dominated the armed forces during the Great War, the Army had to revert to its traditional role as a sort of 'imperial police force'; so also the role of the artillery.

The Great War brought about, however, some actions also closer than those that occurred in the colonies. In the allied occupation of what was called the Rhine-Land, which lasted ten years until 1929, several batteries from Royal Field Artillery and Royal Garrison Artillery were engaged. The allied protection of the border between Poland and Germany also required participation of batteries from the Royal Artillery. Britain also became involved in the Russian Civil War after the Bolshevik revolution in 1917. This included engagement of several thousand men in many places in Northern Russia; many British and Canadian batteries came into action as well.

The British landed in 1918 on the coast of the Kola Peninsula and at Archangelsk. The North Russia Expeditionary Force became involved in heavy fighting with the Bolsheviks along the two railways running in north–southerly direction, Murmansk–Petrograd and Archangelsk–Vologda/Moscow, until finally withdrawing and being evacuated in 1919. This engagement had required great skill in adaptation to the severe climatic conditions and movement in a land almost without roads. The art of fighting (down to the northern shores of Onega) also required adaptation of organisation and methods for the use of the guns available (some 18-pounders and howitzer were placed on railway trucks and river steam boats). This is a good example of the outstanding ability on the part of the Royal Artillery to get engaged 'Everywhere' as expressed in its Motto, *Ubique!*

Development against the odds
Much of lessons learned and experience from the large-scale of the First World War took time to implement during the years between the two World Wars. There were, of course, people looking ahead. Some gave much thought to the development and role of armoured formations in future conflicts. A test concept was devised, the Experimental Mechanized Force (EMF).[42] It was however disbanded towards the end of the 1920s, and much was again to remain as before. The different arms slipped away from each other, and the interest for all-arms training faded away, each arm proceeded on its own.

However, it is worthwhile to observe, that the Royal Artillery tested self-propelled (SP) guns in the 1920s. Some attempts in this regard had been made already during the war, but it was too early. When the EMF concept went to the grave, the interest for development of such guns was dropped. Again, Britain should lose ground to other more progressive countries. Towards the end of the 1920s, and at the beginning of the 1930s, another debate emerged: would aircraft replace heavy guns? Those arguing for aircraft as a substitute for heavy guns, amongst them the later well-known 'entrepreneur', Major General Hobart, were of the opinion that in a modern mobile war would heavy guns never stand a chance to follow the infantry and armour, only heavy bombers could! As a consequence of this debate Britain lacked modern heavy guns when the Second World War broke out.

As far as light artillery is concerned, the lessons learned were taken into account, not least the enormous logistic challenges encountered in a modern war such as the First World War. These had been particularly severe due to the fact that many different types of gun had been employed. It was wisely decided soon after the war that one new standard light gun should be developed as a substitute for the RHA 13-pounders, the 18-pounders and the 4.5-inch howitzers of RFA. In order to achieve this the new gun must combine the characteristics of these guns by given the possibility to fire with flat trajectories at long ranges like a true gun, but also with steeper, curved trajectories as an howitzer. Maximum range should be 15,000 yards (13,650m).

This opened the stage for heavy debate and squabbles regarding different issues such as calibre, types of shell, weight of shell, type of carriage and many more details. It would therefore last twenty years before everything was settled and a new gun could be introduced in the organisation, which eventually took place in 1940.

The first issue that had to be settled was the weight of the shell; it was decided that it must be 25 pounds. This in combination with the range requirement determined the calibre, approximately 88-mm, which was slightly larger than that of the 18-pounder. The range was an issue for much discussion too, and it was not settled until long into the 1930's. It had to be reduced to 13,000 yards (11,880m), this due to another requirement. The maximum weight of the gun should not be more than 30cwt (approximately 1,500kg).

Regarding the type of carriage, the struggle was as to whether the traditional British box-type should be selected or an open V (split trail) type with two legs. This took time to agree on. Before this could take place towards the end of the decade, a modernised 18-pounder was designed and manufactured, with a new barrel, and a 25-pound shell could be used. The gun also had pneumatic rubber tyres. It was designated Ordnance QF 25-pounder Mark I, but daily just the 18/25-pounder, or for short the 25-pounder. When the 'real' new 25-pounder, Mark II, eventually arrived, the former was often inadvertently taken as the latter. I will come back to it in Chapter 4.

One of the most important development steps between the World Wars was the introduction of radio. Trials with short-wave devices were made as early as 1928. The following year, 1929, Colonel, later Field Marshal, Alan Brooke wrote that a successful introduction of radio communication would imply that no need for artillery below the divisional organisational level would exist in the future. What he had in mind was that an observer by utilising radio equipment could concentrate all available artillery in the division not only for divisional attacks, but also in support of attacks by battalions or even companies. Exchange of intelligence data, orders and other type of information between units would also be much facilitated. The trend gained momentum and when the Second World War commenced all Observation Officers and their parties were equipped with wireless sets.[43]

Goodbye to the horse
A radical change took place on the transportation side. With inspiration from the experience of the First World War, the development of motor vehicles for the artillery was going on for many years between the wars, and this not only for the heavy artillery but also for the lighter guns. While this was going on, the light artillery was still horse-drawn and the mounted gunners could continue galloping in good old style.

But then came the important decision to retire the horse for good. This was not an easy decision to make in the Army with its traditions and conservatism. However, the process commenced in 1937 and by 1939 the artillery was fully motorised. An exception was the few Mountain Regiments, which retained their horses and mules by necessity. The Royal Artillery had now become the first major artillery force in the world to be almost completely motorised. The change brought about another important change, viz., re-equipment of the guns with pneumatic rubber tyres. These changes together implied that British artillery went to the new war with much improved mobility.

Organisational adaptation
Finally, a few changes of the artillery organisation

during the years between the two World Wars will be observed. The split enacted in 1899 of the Royal Artillery into a mounted part, Royal Horse Artillery and Royal Field Artillery, and a dismounted part, the Royal Garrison Artillery, i.e. basically the light artillery, the heavy artillery and coast artillery, was abolished in 1924 and once again it was only the Royal Regiment of Artillery, or Royal Artillery for short.

The 'brigade' became 'regiment' in 1938. Field Regiments normally had four six-guns batteries. This was now changed, a regiment was to consist of two twelve-gun batteries and these were divided into three four-gun troops. It was to be shown later that this was not an optimal organisational structure, and a revision was to take place in 1940–1941.

An important reinforcement of the Territorial artillery took place beginning in 1920. It was the transformation of a number of Yeomanries to artillery formations. This process went on until it was basically completed in 1940.[44] Many old volunteer cavalrymen found it an awful change to become gunners, others found it quite exciting and an inspiration; after all they still had to use horses. Many of the converted formations were to become a *corps d'élite* in the Territorial Army.

Traditions and names

Artillery formations have had, as seen, various names and denominations through the centuries. The senior title has, however, since 1722 been the Royal Regiment of Artillery. This as such has not been a fighting formation of its own, but has served as an 'umbrella' for numerous formations organised for war and which have had their own titles. When we now are coming to the end of this brief historical review, it might be of interest to have a look at some examples of formation names from the years preceding the Second World War. The Royal Artillery had, as mentioned earlier, their guns as their Colours and since 1833 'Ubique' as the regimental motto A system of Honour Titles granted to batteries in commemoration of victories and gallantries was later introduced.

The field (light) artillery was organised in 'Field Regiments' with traditions from horse-drawn as well as mounted artillery formations. A few examples:

- *1st Regiment RHA*
- *115th Army Field Regiment RA*
- *24th Field Regiment RA*
- *112th (Wessex) Field Regiment RA, TA*
- *11th (Honourable Artillery Company) Field Regiment RHA*
- *150th (South Notts Hussars) Field Regiment RA (converted Yeomanry)*

Medium, Heavy and Super Heavy Regiments mostly used a numbering system:

- *64th Medium Regiment RA*
- *3rd Heavy Regiment RA*
- *1st Super Heavy Regiment RA*

But there were also a few heavy regiments which were converted Yeomanries, an example:

- *52nd (Bedfordshire Yeomanry) Heavy Regiment RA*

Regiments consisted of 2–4 batteries. It was the batteries who were to be the bearers of traditions and honour titles, not regiments. The title was attached to the organisational number and name of the battery and could be the name of a place where a notable action had taken place, or it could be the name of an old formation or a distinguished commander. As is known, this system is still in use. A few contemporary examples are the names of the batteries of *12th Field Regiment RA*:[45]

- *12 (Minden) Battery RA*
- *9 (Plassey) Battery RA*
- *58 (Eyre's) Battery RA*
- *'T' Headquarters Battery (Shah Sujab's Troop) RA*

And as we saw in Chapter 1 the memory of the British rocket gunners taking part in the battle at Leipzig in October 1813 is commemorated through the honour title granted to a Battery of 1st Field Regiment RHA:

- *'O' Headquarters Battery (The Rocket Troop) RHA*

As seen above 'RA' stands for the 'Royal Regiment of Artillery' and 'RHA' for the 'Royal Horse Artillery'. On maps contained within this book I have, in order to save space, written FR for Field Regiments; MR for Medium Regiments and HR for Heavy Regiments.

3. Twilight – War and Mobilisation

The war leader-to-be Winston Churchill remained loyal to the 'ten-years rule' for many years, but asserted that he abandoned it in 1929, and that he was right! This was because it took ten years, until 1939, before any major war broke out. However, it would take a few years into the 1930s before the political establishment reluctantly was forced to realise that international security steadily deteriorated as a result of Germany's, under Hitler, aggressive politics. Another worry on the part of Britain was Japan's aggressive foreign policy; this was seen as a threat to the 'crown jewel' in the British Empire, India, and the colonies east of this sub-continent, not least Singapore. Japan's invasion of China in 1937 caused chock waves in London. Worrying from the British perspective was increasing demands for independence in India, with the Congress Movement under Gandhi as a driving force.

World recession at the beginning of the 1930s was a true burden and prevented a substantial rearmament, with politicians preferring to concentrate as long as possible on other issues than 'bullets and guns'. Not much was done to prepare Britain for a large European war, nor for a war in the Far East. This was certainly the case as far as the Army, and thus the artillery, was concerned. The Royal Navy and the Royal Air Force were better off and could invest for an approaching large conflict. The different arms were oriented inwards. Focus on coordinated operations was of no interest, except for a few foresighted individuals. All-arms training did not take place during these years.

The last years of the 1930s were a period of appeasement. 'Herr Hitler' was a man with whom to discuss and enter into agreements with and not to confront militarily. The same applied for 'Signore Mussolini' who more and more became a threat against British interests in the Mediterranean area and in East Africa. All this culminated in September 1938 with the negotiations in Munich between Hitler, Mussolini, Daladier of France and Britain's Prime Minster Chamberlain on the future of the so-called Sudetenland, i.e. the 'Czech issue'. Was Europe to be thrown into a new devastating war or not? But a settlement came: 'Peace is saved!' as it was stated to the international journalists at a dramatic press conference in the middle of the night.[46]

According to this, Hitler could without risking intervention occupy the German-speaking Sudetenland in Czechoslovakia.

Hitler and Chamberlain then entered into a written agreement regarding the future relations between the two nations. 'Consultations' was the method to be applied, not war. Well-known is the situation when Chamberlain returned and at the airport triumphantly waved with the agreement in hand towards the journalists and photographers and expressed: 'Peace in our time!' Unknown to him at the time, this was to become a future symbol of the appeasement policy.

The two dictators (Hitler and Mussolini) had, as we know, their own agenda. In 1935 Italy had invaded Abyssinia, and Hitler had re-militarised the Rhine-Land in 1936 and annexed Austria in 1938, the latter based on the Munich Agreement. The Sudetenland was occupied in October this year. The final sign of the complete breakdown of the hitherto followed 'Appeasement policy' was the German invasion of Czechoslovakia in March 1939. But now 'heels were set in the ground': No more concessions! If Germany intended to occupy also Poland and Romania, it meant war with Great Britain and France. Although in reality, military resources were lacking for guaranteeing these countries' independence such guarantees were given. This was urged by the unexpected German–Soviet Non-Aggression Pact signed on 23 August 1939. When the German attack on Poland came on 1 September, the new Great War was unavoidable.

The Territorial Army (TA) doubles
Even though the politicians hoped that the appeasement policy would secure peace, the British public became more and more worried with what they saw, and the will to defend the country rose.

Many became convinced that a war could not be avoided and a rush to join the Territorial Army took place; the will to do something voluntarily became strong in all classes. Germany's invasion of Czechoslovakia led to a very important decision in the Parliament in March 1939. The Territorial Army was to be doubled immediately from its present size amounting to 150,000 men on mobilisation to around 300,000. No plan how to accomplish this existed, however, neither how all new units would be equipped and trained. But the British are used to rapidly adapt to a new situation and accept the situation as it is.

The Royal Artillery responded immediately setting up new regiments by splitting the existing 'parent regiments' into halves and then gradually expanding these up to nominal size and required level of training. As an example, 112 (Wessex) Field Regiment RA came to existence from the splitting of 55 (Wessex) Field Regiment. The latter had until 1938 comprised of four six-gun batteries, which were to merge into two twelve-guns batteries. Before this was completed, two of the original batteries were transferred to the new regiment, 112 (Wessex) Field Regiment, which by this arrangement got a first core of trained personnel when established in 1939.[47]

Another example was the establishment of the later much appraised 64 Medium Regiment RA. Here, the process was a bit slower, however. Denis Falvey, who was recruited to the regiment from the beginning and remained in service for seven years until its demobilisation after the war has told the story:[48] At Offord Road, Islington in the northern part of London there was a Training Hall for the Territorial Army, which also was the headquarters of 55 Medium Regiment RA, another territorial formation from the Great War 1914–1918. When the Territorial Army was doubled Falvey's regiment, 64 Medium Regiment RA was created. A squad of officers and NCOs were sent to this regiment to take care of training of recruits, which in peace-time took place one evening every week and at a two-week long training camp in the summer, as was normal for territorial units. Falvey tells us that a normal evening training sequence was often followed by a round or two at a nearby pub.

The newly recruited and registered soldiers represented a cross-section of the society: technicians, drivers, office clerks, grocers and many others. They had reported on 1 April 1939, filled in a form and answered a few questions from the Sergeant in charge. 64 Medium Regiment used the Drill Hall on another evening than the 'parent' regiment. The soldiers came in their ordinary civilian clothes, as no uniforms were as yet available.

The officers (many of them bankers, brokers or workers from the City) were given the prudent task to place the 600 recruits in positions in accordance with some kind of coherent principles. School education was the first criterion. Most of the recruits had left elementary school at the age of 14–15 years, but there were some forty with higher education and these were divided between the two batteries. One was a middle age Architect and Falvey himself was also amongst the graduates. This group of new more skilled people were nominated as 'specialists' and were to become real 'professionals' in the art of gunnery.

Those with appropriate physical strength were to handle the heavy guns and ammunition; lorry drivers became drivers of military vehicles, and those with good brains became signallers or gun layers. All these initial assignments were of course provisional and had to be modified later based on performance.

Falvey also tells us that when training commenced the regiment had no equipment of its own, and no guns of its own. 53 Medium Regiment was equipped with old 6-inch howitzers. These were on loan to 64 Medium Regiment for basic training in deployment, gun laying, and ammunition handling etc.

As with all territorial units before them, 64 Medium Regiment was sent to a summer camp in 1939, and here they were issued with uniforms for the first time. Still they had to use vehicles on loan as was the case also for other types of equipment needed. This was to be the first and only summer camp as far as this regiment was concerned. It mobilised on 1 September. After a couple of months the regiment got some civilian vehicles for the first time, all requisitioned for use by the Army. Dennis Falvey's group was given a small truck with 'Jones, the Fishmonger' displayed on it. More vehicles came later and around New Year 1939/1940 the first guns of their own were provided. The regiment received six old 6-inch howitzers. Some personal weapons were also provided. During the spring 1940 the guns were exchanged for 60-pounders, but not until the autumn could the first rounds be fired for practice, i.e. a whole year after mobilisation.[49]

The Territorial Army grew from 54 Field Regiments in May 1938 to more than 100 in September 1939, a unique rearmament process, albeit it would take much time until all units were ready for war. There were also nine Medium Regiments and fourteen Heavy Regiments.[50] Here, it should be observed that the Territorial Army also mobilised a large number of Anti-Aircraft Regiments as well as some Anti-Tank Regiments, all of which belonged to the Royal Artillery.[51]

To war with obsolete guns
The organisational structure of the Royal Artillery at that time was a legacy from the Great War:

- Army artillery
- Corps artillery
- Division artillery

There were a number of Mountain units as well, particularly in India. No artillery units were permanently attached to formations below the level of division. At the lower levels only mortars were permanently included.

The first two levels included mostly all Medium and Heavy Regiments, the use of which was for counter-battery fire and fire against other types of target in depth, but also for reinforcement of divisional artillery. At these highest levels, regiments called Army Field Regiments (AFR) could also exist to some extent. Divisional artillery had as their main task to support its own division, but could also be used for concentrations of fire across the boundaries of their division. The grouping of batteries and troops will be discussed later. First, let us have a look at the guns available when the Second World War commenced in 1939.

It may be recalled that the development of new field guns went on during the period between the wars, but they were not ready when the war commenced. The formations had to use the vintage guns from the Great War, albeit modernised. With the motorisation in 1938–1939, the old wooden, iron-clad wheels had been replaced by pneumatic tyres that had increased mobility. Some guns of the stock of modernised old guns are seen in **Fig. 3-1**.

The much-awaited standardisation of field guns for the divisional artillery was not yet in place. Older guns and howitzers were to be

Fig. 3-1 The gun legacy – The British artillery went to war with a set of obsolete guns. Here are the most commonly used light guns. Many 18-pounder Mark IVP guns were modernised before the war with a new barrel to be called 18/25-pounders or 25-pdr Mark I.

QF 18-pdr Gun Mark IIP (RAHT)

QF 18-pdr Gun Mark IVP (RAHT)

3.7-inch Howitzer (RAHT)

QF 4.5-inch Howitzer (RAHT)

replaced by the new 25-pounder gun, but these were not yet in production. Only prototypes had been manufactured. A large number of a modernised 18-pounder in versions Mark IV and Mark V had been manufactured before the war. This gun had also been modernised with a new barrel lined for 25-pound ammunition besides pneumatic tyres. The piece was, as mentioned, called 'QF 25-pounder Mark I' or for short the '18/25-pounder'.

Territorial regiments had still to stick to the 18-pounder. In these regiments the old 4.5-inch howitzers were also still in use, cf. **Fig. 3-1**.

Mountain Regiments were equipped with the old 3.7-inch pack howitzer, which could be dismantled for transport by means of mules in mountainous terrain without roads. Modernised version with pneumatic rubber tyres were later supplied; with or without a gun shield for protection.

It should be observed that guns and howitzers were manufactured in many versions. Guns with different barrels were called Mark I, Mark II, etc. The same for different carriages, e.g. Mark I, Mark II. As an example it can be mentioned that the 18-pounders still in use when the war commenced had different modernised carriages given the designations Mark II, Mark III, Mark IV and Mark V. When reequipped with pneumatic wheels a 'P' was added, i.e. Mark IVP. This reflects the new requirements as regards mobility, but also regarding firing range and thus elevation.

The plethora of gun versions makes it difficult to summarise technical data for a particular type of gun. The weight differs between versions, as does firing range. Performance data are valid only under nominal weather conditions, for a specified ammunition type, etc. In the tables that follow, data can be interpreted as a correct in order of magnitude, but not necessarily being exact.[52] First we have in **Table 3-1** data for light field guns.

Before leaving the light guns we will forestall the coming presentation of the Battle of France in 1940 (Chapter 16). When the British Expeditionary Force was evacuated from Dunkirk late in May 1940 and during the first days in June 60–70 per cent of the entire stock of guns of the Royal Artillery was lost. Facing the threat of an imminent German invasion of the British Isles, Britain made the extraordinary decision to lease from United States some 900 guns of the famous

Table 3-1. Gun data – light guns

Gun	Calibre cm	Weight kg	Shell weight kg	Max. range m
18-pounder gun	8.4	1,400	3.4	9,000
18/25-pounder gun (QF 25-pdr Mark I)	8.8	1,560	11.3	10,800
4.5-inch howitzer	11.4	1,500	15.7	6,000
3.7-inch pack howitzer	9.4	800	9.1	4,000–6,500

French design, the 'soixante-quinze'.[53] This 75-mm gun was designed already in 1896 and was considered to be one of the best in the Great War. Thanks to this, the Americans had bought a large number at the end of the war. There was no use of them after the war, so they were placed in warehouses and well greased for protection against rust. Although they were absolutely obsolete, they filled well a need in Britain in 1940 for a temporary substitute for the lost guns, when the defence against invasion was to be organised after Dunkirk. They were good for basic training of all the new gunners. But the reception of the guns differed. Johnny Walker tells us of his experiences:

> I was at first placed at a provisional mortuary where we had to take care of the victims from Dunkirk. It was the first time I came in touch with killed soldiers [. . .] it was to become many more occasions later on in the war. But it was here that I for the first time came across the light French gun. After extensive cleaning we were to make a test firing out into the Channel. Excitement was great to all, but it did not result in a real bang. But more like a weak crack. The projectile landed in the middle of Dover! A bit embarrassing, but such things can happen in war. It was decided that we should fire another round. The same result! After that 'cease fire' and we never were to fire the gun again.[54]

Other gunners however found the gun much more useful. 136 Field Regiment RA received the gun in August 1940:

> A gunner without a gun is like a dog without a tail; with eleven months of the war already

completed the Regiment had still not received its full complement of twenty-four guns. [. . .] But in the third week in August the news was received with no little surprise that more guns were on the way. Nobody can now recall at what stage we learnt that these were to be the famous 'soixante.quinze' – the French-built 75-mm gun. We were most certainly astonished and not a little shocked. The gunners were even more surprised when they went to Yoxford station to collect the new weapons. They were quite small with four-foot diameter wooden spoked wheels and were covered in grease. They did not look very robust [. . .] Each Battery set to clean the guns and this took several days [. . .] The barrels were packed tight with grease from muzzle to breech and proved very difficult to clean. The local residents – the few still left – were asked to produce all the old clothing and bed linen they could spare to assist in the task [. . .] Before the guns could be taken to their firing positions [. . .] it was essential to test each one. The guns were taken four at a time to a field about two miles from the coast and placed on accurately surveyed positions. On the cliff edge in front of the guns the Regimental Survey Party had placed their equipment through which the fall of the shells into the sea would be observed. This would enable the accuracy and consistency of each gun to be determined. [. . .] Everybody held their breath when the order 'Fire' was given, but they need not have worried. The gun behaved perfectly and the round exploded on hitting the sea at the desired spot. [. . .] During the day the other guns fired their trial five rounds and to everybody's astonishment and delight they all performed exactly as [the first one]. From that day the gun detachments accepted their new equipment with complete confidence and held them in the highest regard.[55]

It may be added that some of these guns later were equipped with pneumatic tyres and could then be towed after a truck on roads. The gun could fire up to 7km and fired a fixed round (the projectile and cartridge case fixed together as a single item). The weight of the projectile was a modest 16 pounds. From the deployment point of view, the maximum elevation of 17° was a problem; this meant a very flat trajectory.

The Medium Regiments also had to stick to vintage pieces, albeit somewhat modernised. The two old pieces that were retained for the time being were the BL 60-pounder gun and the BL 6-inch 26-cwt howitzer, **(Fig. 3-2)**. During the initial battles in North Africa the former was often used with its old iron clad wooden wheels, whereas the pneumatic rubber tyres were used at home. Some of these guns were modernised with a new 4.5-inch barrel. As seen in **Fig. 3-2**, a few other old pieces were also parts of the arsenal. Approximate gun data are given in **Table 3-2**.

Table 3-2. Gun data – medium guns

Gun	Calibre cm	Weight kg	Shell weight kg	Max. range m
6-inch 26 cwt howitzer Mark I	15.2	4,000	39/45.4	10,000
60-pounder Mark II	12.7	5,500	27.2	11,250–14,900

No development of a modern heavy piece took place before the Second World War, despite the fact that the need for heavy guns had been distinctly recognised during the Great War 1914–1918. Only a limited number of formations with obsolete guns were retained. As mentioned, it was stated in the 1930s by the RAF, and by some army officers, that bomber aircraft could take over the role of heavy artillery in the future, so there was no need to develop new guns of this type, it was argued! Hence, 'a dead hand' was laid over the development programme. Those units, which were retained despite this attitude, were in most cases equipped with the 6-inch Mark XIX gun and the 8-inch howitzer. The Heavy Regiments typically had one battery equipped with the former and two or three with the latter. The even heavier 9.2-inch and 12-inch howitzers still existed in a limited number when the war broke out as were some railway guns. See **Fig. 3-2**. Approximate gun data for the heavy pieces are seen in **Table 3-3**.

The Royal Artillery went to war also with a large number of anti-aircraft and anti-tank guns, and in addition to these coast artillery guns as well. These will, however, not be further discussed here.

When it comes to other types of equipment for artillery such as motor vehicles, survey instruments, communication equipment, personal weapons, etc., we will come back to the rearmament aspects later. It should be observed however that there was a severe shortage of everything during the first year

Fig. 3-2 The gun legacy – As well as the light field guns, obsolete medium and heavy guns were at hand when the war broke out.

BL 60-pdr Gun (RAHT)

BL 6-inch 26-cwt Howitzer (RAHT)

6-inch Gun (RAHT)

BL 12-inch Howitzer (RAHT)

Table 3-3. Gun data – heavy guns

Gun	Calibre cm	Weight kg	Shell weight kg	Max. range m
6-inch gun Mark XIX	15.2	9,400	45.4	17,000
8-inch howitzer Mark VI	20.3	9,000	90.7	11,000
9.2-inch howitzer Mark II	23.4	16,500	131.5	12,750

of the war, in particular as regards the needs of the Territorial Army units. Interesting to note is that the Royal Artillery was far better off in terms of radio equipment than the infantry when the war broke out. At least in theory, all Observation Officers could communicate with the guns by means of radio and telephone equipment. It has been stated that a British infantry division had only 75 radio sets, out of which, 55 were held by its artillery regiments. Many older infantry commanders found it sufficient with a loud voice and dispatch riders. The war changed this attitude. In 1944 a division had around a thousand radio sets. The artillery had doubled its stock.[56]

Artillery mobilisation

Brian Hulse has told BBC how he experienced the mobilisation in September 1939.[57] He had, when sixteen years old, reported for enlistment as a volunteer for the artillery regiment Bedfordshire Yeomanry. He was to serve through the entire war, and for him it became, as for others survivors, seven years in uniform before returning to civilian life. In May 1941 he was commissioned as artillery officer.

In August 1939, Hulse tells, all knew that war was unavoidable; it was only a matter of when. For all who had reported for enlistment as volunteers, for men this in the Royal Navy Voluntary Reserve (RNVR), Territorial Army (TA) or Royal Air Force Voluntary Reserve (RAFVR) and for women in Women's Royal Naval Service (WRNS or 'Wrens'), the Auxiliary Territorial Army (ATS) or Women's Auxiliary Air Force (WAAF), it was of no surprise when on 1 September 1939 it was announced in radio broadcasts that all men and women in the Armed Forces should immediately report to their respective unit. So, this was exactly what was done, pencils, saws, spades and other tools were laid down, professions were left and a marching-out took place from the job sites. Many found it exciting. While the mobilisation went on, the last dramatic contacts at the diplomatic levels took place between Britain and France on the one side and Germany on the other. After he had entered into the Non-Aggression Pact with Stalin on 23rd August, Hitler had decided to 'resolve' the 'Danzig Issue' by implementing military means, and the issue regarding a corridor to East Prussia in the same way. Negotiations with Poland were out of question. Hitler had also rejected the proposal by the French Premier Daladier about further negotiations. Britain had on 25 August reaffirmed its intention to protect the independence of Poland. On 28 August the British Ambassador to Germany, Sir Neville Henderson, returned to Berlin with the message from the British Government that it would stick to this and that any form of aggression was unacceptable. Then followed the fatal day, Sunday 3 September 1939. At 11.15 a.m. Chamberlain opened his speech to the nation in a BBC broadcast. His voice was grave and he spoke slowly:

> This morning, the British Ambassador in Berlin handed the German Government the final note stating that unless we had heard from them before eleven o'clock where they declare that they at once will withdraw their troops from Poland, a state of war will exist between us. I have to tell you now that no such undertaking has been received, and consequently this country is at war with Germany. You can imagine what a bitter blow this means to me after my long struggle for peace [. . .]. [58]

When the war broke out Britain was militarily a weak nation and lacked the resources for meeting its obligations. It is a good example of a failed, not to say non-existent, coordination of foreign policy and national strategy. Appeasement turned out to be a failure, and when this at the beginning of September 1939 was realised by the politicians, it was too late. Certainly they had decided to double the Territorial Army, and also to introduce conscription, but it was not realised that any rearmament, worth its name, would take several years. The transfer of industry from peacetime production to a wartime footing with a capacity to provide all the old and new military formations with modern equipment was an immense challenge, which certainly could not be met overnight.

Furthermore, training of all officers and men that was required for getting all formations ready for war was indeed another significant challenge taking a long time to meet.

The situation in September was such that Britain could mobilise less than a million men to compare with the five million in France. In the spring of 1939 the British Government had decided to plan for an army comprising 55 fighting divisions (15,000 to 20,000 men per division), these were to be established by all Commonwealth countries in cooperation. Britain's own share was to be 32 divisions. The build-up should be completed by September 1941, i.e. after about two and half years. The number was reduced in February 1940 to a total of 36 divisions.[59]

The Commander of the British Expeditionary Force (BEF) sent to France, Lord Gort, estimated that 19 divisions would be needed. The day after the war had commenced he was ordered to start the preparations for a build-up in France. At his disposal that day only 3–4 divisions were available. In the Middle East and North Africa 6-7 divisions could be mobilised and in India 1–2 divisions. In South East Asia (Malaya) there were two brigades.

Luckily enough, there was only one enemy at the beginning, Germany, and, furthermore, the country thanks to the period known as the 'Phoney War' did not have to commence fighting for another eight months. Launching any offensive was out of the question. It would be almost a year before British & Commonwealth forces were in action against Italian forces. Where Britain was weakest, in South East Asia, the respite was slightly more than two years. As far as artillery is concerned, the regular organisation comprised 37 Field Regiments, 7 Medium Regiments and one Heavy regiment.[60] In addition to these formations there were in 1938 54 Field Regiments in the Territorial Army, 9 Medium Regiments and 14 Heavy Regiments. As mentioned, all these regiments were to be doubled. To the Territorial Army also a few converted Yeomanries came. As seen not all new regiments were in place when the war broke out, and many of the TA formations were not ready for war. When we summarise all formations (regular and territorial) we find that the Royal Artillery went to war with roughly the following numbers of regiments:

- Field artillery   116 Regiments
- Medium artillery   25 Regiments
- Heavy artillery   5 Regiments

The number of heavy regiments is uncertain. Most of the heavy regiments of TA in 1938 do not seem to have been mobilised. On the other hand a few new regiments were established during the autumn 1939. The number here given is to be seen as the order of magnitude.

Besides those in the list, a number of independent batteries of various type existed. It might be of interest also to take note of the fact that some infantry battalions had been converted to ant-aircraft units during the 1930s.

On 31 December 1939 the total strength in manpower was 122,017.[61] In this number some Anti-Tank Regiments and depot units are included as well.

4. A Decisive Rearmament

Construction takes five years

The prime task of the British army was to equip and train the British Expeditionary Force (BEF) when the war broke out and to get it deployed in France. Available regular regiments were the core as far as artillery was concerned, but they had to be supplemented with a large number of Territorial regiments. In addition to this, it was important to set up artillery formations for all the 32 divisions that were planned in 1939, but also to establish more of army and corps artillery, local defence units, defence regiments, training regiments and various reserve units etc.

Initially the situation was not good, but Britain decisively met the challenge to rebuild what had been destroyed between the wars, and this systematically. It was realised that the nation did not have the capacity to meet Hitler alone, and neither was this needed. The fight against Hitler was to be made by a coalition with France. The huge resources and, as it was deemed, good quality of these gave hope. As far as the Far East was concerned, there were hopes to get USA as a coalition partner, if and when Britain had to go to war against Japan.

Which were then the personnel resources available to secure the size of the armed forces? First and foremost, there were the regular forces with men who had signed up for 12 years. Before the war, the formations were often undermanned, but the mobilisation quickly brought them up to nominal strength. This was possible due to existing practice. Normally soldiers were not obliged to serve the whole 12-year period. After 5–7 years they normally left for a civilian life and became reservists. An obligation remained, however, for the reservists to return immediately to service in case of war, as now was the case. So, in September 1939 numerous experienced veterans were called back to the regular formations, but often also as reinforcement to Territorial regiments. This was a good support to all young and inexperienced recruits during this first critical phase of rearmament. The other most important addition of resources was all the civilians that had volunteered for service in the Territorial Army.

Conscription had been instituted by the Parliament early 1939 through the Militia Act. This applied initially only for men in the ages 18–20 years, who were to be called in for six months training in peace-time. Later during the war conscription was extended to apply for all men between 21 and 41 years of age. This greatly increased the manpower resources needed for rearmament. A special clause of the Act said that those who voluntarily went to Territorial Army could not be forced by the authorities to be enlisted into a formation as ordered by them. Many men realising what would come, and who wanted to enlist in a formation of their own preference, availed themselves of this clause. A well-known formation near the home was often preferred to an unknown post somewhere else in the country. This created a massive inflow of recruits to old and new Territorial Regiments. On one hand, this was positive, on the other hand however it caused large problems due to their lack of training and the shortage of equipment.

Even if personnel resources initially were available in sufficient quantity, more was needed later in order to bring up all formations to nominal strength as required by the War Establishment. Large human resources were also needed for all new formations gradually being set up, the so-called War Formations. How this gradual increase in manpower went on can be followed in national statistics. From this, we can see that the artillery rearmament took around four years until it reached its maximum. This was despite the fact that the nation in September 1939 was set on a 'war footing'. Training and provision of equipment and material set the limits.

As far as the Royal Artillery was concerned, the number of men engaged was in the statistics divided into two major groups. One was Field Artillery and the other Coast Defence/Anti-Aircraft. The first group comprised all Field, Medium and Heavy Regiments, which this book is about, but also Anti-Tank Regiments, Headquarters and a few others. Those of the second group were mainly mobilised initially for the defence of the homeland, but to some extent also to meet the needs of the field army as regards light and heavy anti-aircraft resources.

On 31 December of each respective year the group Field Artillery, as so defined, had the following manpower strength:[62]

- 1939 122,017 men
- 1940 186,149
- 1941 196,078
- 1942 213,993
- 1943 227,231
- 1944 237,491

When the war in Europe had ended, the number had reached 254,103 men (30 June 1945).

We can also see that in July 1943 the two groups together comprised almost 700,000 men, which was 26% of the total army strength, which was around 2,700,000 men.[63] The total strength of the infantry and armoured forces was less than that of the Royal Artillery!

The total strength of the Field Artillery group as compared with the total number of men in the Royal Artillery is illustrated in **Fig. 4-1**.

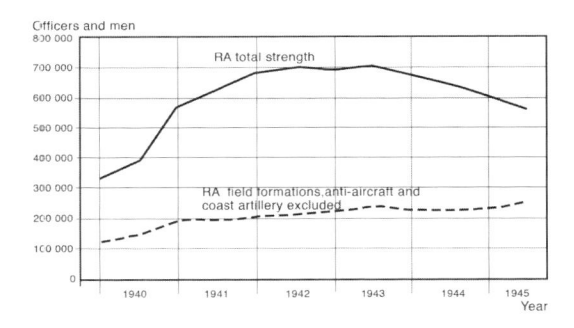

Fig. 4-1 The strength of the British artillery 1939–1945 (Author)

From this it can be understood that there initially was an extremely rapid growth of anti-aircraft and coast artillery resources during the first half of the war, which reflects the severe threats of a German invasion and attacks by *Luftwaffe* bomber armadas in 1940 and 1941 operating against British territory. Anti-aircraft and coast artillery resources were roughly twice the size of the field artillery.

In this context it is interesting to note the remarkable war effort made by women. In total not less than 70,000 women were enlisted into anti-aircraft regiments. Mixed units, with men and women, served in most cases at home with a few exceptions.

Both a large number of light and heavy anti-aircraft regiments existed, as were quite a number of rocket-launching batteries and searchlight units. When the threats from the air and against the coast gradually declined, the share of anti-aircraft and coast artillery in the manpower strength of the Royal Artillery also gradually declined, and at the end of the war it was about the same as for field artillery.

The manpower needs for anti-tank units was around 30,000 men. The increase of the number of regiments of different types during the war is illustrated in **Fig. 4-2**. The various sources consulted are not always coherent, sometimes certain regiments are missing, and sometimes regiments had been counted twice.[64] However, although the graph may not give exact numbers, it is considered to be correct as far as orders of magnitude are concerned and fairly well illustrates trends during the war. In 1942 and 1943 many new 'war formations' were possible to establish thanks to the increased production capacity of the industry. Deliveries of guns, vehicles, optical instruments and other sorts of equipment along with improved availability of trained people made this successful final phase of the rearmament possible.

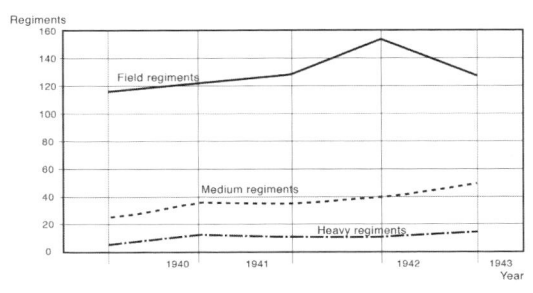

Fig. 4-2 Increase of artillery resources 1939–1945 in terms of regimental types (Author)

During the war no new regular formations were organised and the number of mobilised regiments, around 40, was roughly constant during the war. The number of territorial regiments, inclusive of those, which had come to existence through doubling of existing regiments, did not increase much either during the war and stayed at around 100–110. The increase thus came about by all the new formations established, i.e. the 'war formations', a process that culminated by the first half of 1943. By then, some 50 'war formations' had been organised. Some of these did not survive for long due to war losses. Others were converted or disbanded for various reasons. Hence the number of active regiments was to change over the years of war.

After the peak in 1943, the number of field regiments was affected by decisions to convert light (field) regiments to medium or heavy regiments during the last few years of the war. As regards these categories the number of regiments increased in 1944 and 1945. Increased deliveries of guns from the domestic and Commonwealth industries, and from USA, as well as battle experience, were driving forces in this process.

A new light standard gun for divisional artillery

As seen, the Royal Artillery went to war with – albeit modernised – obsolete guns, and these were furthermore available in insufficient quantity. To fully equip the around 120 field regiments mobilised at the end of 1939 2,880 pieces were needed (24 per regiment). In addition to these many more were needed for training, replacement of damaged or lost in battle etc. An estimated increase to a total number of around 3,500 pieces would be required. Roughly half this number was available.[65]

The fighting in Belgium and France in May–June 1940, which ended with the evacuation at Dunkirk, had a disastrous consequence as regards the stock of artillery equipment. This was particularly the case as regards the most 'modern' guns, the 18/25-pounder guns. Only some 1,100 of this type had been delivered to the Army and most of them had been sent with BEF to France. One source (uncertain) says that only 334 of these were saved and brought back to England. Most likely these were saved from Cherbourg and a few other southerly ports in France and not from Dunkirk.[66]

When this catastrophe came, and indeed it was a catastrophe, the manufacture of the new 'real' 25-pounder, i.e. Mark II, had begun, but only a very limited number, if any, had been delivered to active units. In any case, none had been delivered to BEF. The first version of the new gun was designated QF 25-pounder Gun Mark II. The weight of the gun was 1,750kg. Three versions are illustrated in **Fig. 4-3**. The piece was a gun-howitzer with the calibre 87.6mm. It may be called 'gun-howitzer' as it was able to fire at long ranges with a flat trajectory but also with higher trajectories with steep descent like a howitzer. In order to facilitate this, the shell was not fixed to the cartridge case but the shell was first inserted into the barrel and then a separate cartridge case. The latter was filled with bags of propellant, the number of which was dependent on which charge that was to be used: Charge 1 for short ranges (blue bag), Charge 2 (blue + white bags), Charge 3 (blue + white + red bags) and for the longest ranges – Super Charge. Some additional propellant bags were supplied later during the war as Charge Increments. These charges gave more alternatives for affecting the trajectory; e.g. Charge 2 + incr. These options were in particular used in Italy and Burma, when firing at targets behind mountains and ridges was required, i.e. with elevation higher than 45°: this is called the 'Upper Register'.

The fourth charge, Super Charge, was one entity and could not be combined with the others. With this the gun could be fired at maximum range, around 12,250m (13,500 yards), i.e. further than the 18/25-pounder could. This charge was also used when direct firing with anti-tank rounds at short distances was needed, this thanks to the greater muzzle velocity it provided. However, it should be observed that this highest charge was normally available only for around 25% of the stock of ammunition supplied to the guns. This had to be taken into account tactically when employment of the guns was ordered. It was important to avoid plans requiring extreme ranges, as there could be a shortage of ammunition due to this restriction. The 18/25-pounder could not use Super Charge.

As mentioned, it would have been better if the new gun could have fired one or two kilometres further, as initially was specified. But this wish had to be abandoned as it was in conflict with the requirement to have the weight of the gun under approximately 30cwt (approx. 1,500kg).

After many years of discussions, not to say squabbles, it was agreed that the gun carriage should be of the box-trail type and not a split-trail carriage. This meant that traverse within the carriage was limited to 5° in both directions. That

Fig. 4-3 The new generation of field guns. The 25-pdr became standard field gun but several versions were manufactured during the war. From 1943 it was equipped with a muzzle brake

QF 25-pdr Gun Mark II (RAHT)

QF 25-pdr Mark III with muzzle brake (©Imperial War Museum B 9985)

25-pdr with the so-called Jury axle adapted for conditions prevailing in Burma (Author's collection)

disadvantage was eliminated with a creative design solution: a firing platform on which the gun was placed and locked. The platform was designed to absorb the recoil, which thus could be avoided as far as the box-trail was concerned. No spade was needed. Hence it was very easy to traverse the barrel 360° around.

Elevation was limited to 40–45° and depression to 5°; however, higher elevation was found necessary. A special sight was introduced to make this possible, but one still had to improvise the deployment of the gun. This could, e.g., be done by placing the wheels of the guns higher than usual or digging a pit into which the end of the box-trail could be lowered. By such arrangements elevation up to around 70° could be applied (**Fig. 10-7**).

An ammunition limber was hooked to the gun during transport. This contained a ready for use stock of ammunition comprising 32 complete rounds. When firing ceased, and redeployment was ordered, the gun was hooked to the limber and this to the tractor. This was the same arrangement as for the 18/25-pounder. It can be seen as a kind of legacy from the earlier period when guns were horse-drawn.

When the new gun went into service, three types of shell were supplied, a high explosive shell (HE), a solid armour-piercing projectile and a smoke shell. Later also a chemical shell was manufactured, but it was fortunately never to be used.

The HE shells could be used with different types of fuze. By means of these, bursts above ground, on (Instant Impact, IA) or below it (Delayed Impact) could be arranged. A variant of delayed burst was the 'ricochet burst' which required fairly flat trajectory and flat ground.

Time fuzes of different types were available, both one based on a burning train of gunpowder (combustion) and one based on a mechanical (clock) device. The mechanical time fuzes were not introduced until 1941.

The armour-piercing projectile had a tracer element attached to it to facilitate observation when fired.

The first smoke projectile produced white smoke, but other smoke colours were also available later in the war. Projectiles for artificial light were available too, but this type does not seem to have been used very much.

A special projectile was the propaganda projectile. It could be filled with numerous printed propaganda sheets, which when fired were spread a few hundred metres above the enemy positions.

We will discuss the use of different types of projectile and fuze in Chapter 8.

Several versions of the 25-pounder were introduced during the war. The latest was Mark III, which had a slightly modified box-trail and firing platform. It was also equipped for the first time with a muzzle brake. A lighter version was developed for use in hilly terrain in Burma - the Jury axle 25-pounder. The distance between the wheels, which were smaller, had been reduced and thus also the firing platform. The shield could also be removed for lower gun weight during transport. One example of this version could be seen at the Royal Artillery Museum, Woolwich Arsenal (**Fig. 4-3**).

The gun detachment normally comprised six gunners led by a Sergeant. During long battles it was possible to manage firing by using three to four men only. Hence, working in shifts was possible to arrange. A pre-requisite was that sufficient volumes of ammunition had been stocked up at the gun site before the battle. In some battles as much as 500–600 projectiles were stockpiled.

Mobilisation of industry

The manufacturing of the 25-pounder started in 1939 by Royal Ordnance Factory (ROF) Woolwich and by the private company Vickers Armstrong. In the middle of 1930s there still were three government-owned factories in operation and another three 'moth-balled'. The industrial production could therefore gear up as **Table 4-1** illustrates.[67]

Of the various industries, five were designated as manufacturers of 25-pounders, or more specifically, the most demanding parts of the gun, the barrel and the breech. They also were responsible for final assembly of the guns after carriages and other parts had been delivered to

Table 4-1. Royal Ordnance Factories

	Factories	Employees
March 1938	10	28,479
March 1939	16	32,794
December 1939	29	54,249
1942	40	>300,000

Source: Hughes (1992), pp. 200–202

them from other industries. The number of barrels manufactured by the different industries is presented in **Table 4-2**.

Table 4-2. Deliveries of 25-pounder barrels - ROF

	Barrels delivered
ROF Cardiff	786
ROF Dalmuir	350
ROF Hayes	1,822
ROF Leeds	1,358
ROF Woolwich	163

Source: The Production History of the 25-pdr Field Equipment. Ministry of Supply. Feb. 1947. The Directorate of Weapons Production

Besides Vickers Armstrong another five private industries were engaged late 1940 and early 1941 for manufacture of barrels as presented in **Table 4-3**.

Table 4-3. Deliveries of 25-pounder barrels – private industries

	Barrels etc delivered
Wm. Beardmore (Parkhead)	900
Wm. Beardmore (Dalmuir)	95
Metro-Vickers	450
A. & W. Smith	3,348
Watson Leidlaw & Co.	1,101
Vickers Armstrong	1,827

Source: The Production History of the 25-pdr Field Equipment. Ministry of Supply. Feb. 1947. The Directorate of Weapons Production

Manufacture of carriages with buffer/recuperator, wheels, platform and trail was a suitable task for private industries. Five industrial groups had to be established in order to meet the requirements. Many sub-contractors had to be engaged as well. The leaders of the groups were companies manufacturing barrels and breeches. All the groups cooperated closely and with the Royal Ordnance factories in order to meet delivery time obligations, not the least this cooperation was necessary as regards supply of raw materials and components. The five groups were normally responsible for final assembly of complete guns.

For manufacture of carriages five groups were also established including sub-contractors. The leading private companies were to deliver the number of carriages etc. given by **Table 4-4**.

Table 4-4. Deliveries of 25-pounder carriages etc – private industries

	Carriages etc. delivered
G. & J. Weir	3,625
Crossley Bros.	1,752
Baker Perkins	1,965
W. & T. Avery	680
L.M.S. Derby	500
Vickers Armstrong	1,700

Source: The Production History of the 25-pdr Field Equipment. Ministry of Supply. Feb. 1947. The Directorate of Weapons Production.

The G. & J. Weir Company was contracted already in May 1939 and, as seen in Table 4-4, they were to manufacture and assemble the largest number of guns. **Fig. 4-4** is a good illustration from their workshops. Note that women dominate the workforce. In total 12,500 barrels were manufactured by British industry and 10,222 carriages. The first number is often in the literature presented as the number of 25-pounders manufactured, but as we see from the second number, the lower number is a more correct number of complete guns manufactured. To this number, however, a number of self-propelled guns (Sextons) manufactured in Canada can be added.

The overall planning had the target of 350 guns per month manufactured. This was accomplished, but not until mid-1941, i.e. two years after the redirection of the industry had taken place. The accumulated number of delivered barrels and carriages over time is presented in **Fig. 4-5**. At the end of 1939, 189 barrels with breeches had been delivered, but deliveries of carriages did not take place until March 1940, when the first eight could be delivered from Vickers Armstrong. In April they could deliver another sixteen carriages, and G. & J. Weir could deliver the first five of their manufacture. Manufacture then increased rapidly, but at the end of 1940 only 1,356 carriages had been delivered, so the Army requirement could not yet be filled. It was to take another two years before that target was met. When this had taken place around the end of 1942, the industry could be directed

Fig. 4-4 The industry was reorganised for mass-production of 25-pdrs. Here is an interior from the firm G & J Weir Ltd. (RAHT MD)

towards manufacture of other types of gun.[68] A special program for manufacture of muzzle brakes had, however, to be organised from the end of 1943.

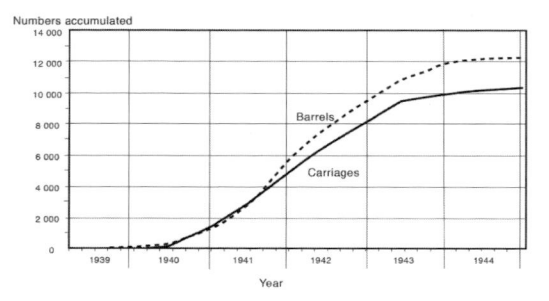

Fig. 4-5 Deliveries of the main parts of 25-pdr Guns (Author)

The 25-pounder is well received by artillery units

The new gun immediately became popular amongst gunners for its robustness and reliability as many war diaries and other accounts tell us. An example below illustrates this.

Of course some 'teething problems' could not be avoided. A real and thorough test came in North Africa during the battle of El Alamein in October 1942 where the huge barrages required the guns to fire 600 rounds each during the first 24 hours. It was noticed here that the upper part of the carriage with its cradle was a weak point. Quite a large number of guns had to be removed and taken to repair shops.

136 (1st West Lancashire) Field Regiment RA did not receive their new 25-pounders until August 1942 when it had been decided that the regiment was to embark for Burma. There was still a shortage of guns so the regiment had to take over guns from 174 Field Regiment RA in exchange of their 18/25-pounders. A bad exchange for the latter! The arrival of the new guns at 136 Field Regiment RA has been described as follows:[69]

> For a year we had been the proud 'owners' of twenty-four 18/25-pdrs, which the gunners had learnt to handle and appreciate. Naturally we had hankered after a set of the new 25-pdrs [...] we had only occasionally spotted an example in our travels [...] The arrival of the new guns at each Battery caused great excitement and they were at once surrounded by all ranks. It is the gun, which is the centre of all activities and purpose in an Artillery Regiment in much the same way that the aircraft is in an RAF Squadron. For the next few days the gunners were busy learning all about their new charges and were very pleased with every aspect of the design and construction. They were worth waiting nearly three-and-a-half years for.

Before leaving the 25-pounder we will summarise some data in **Table 4-5**.[70]

The old mountain howitzer

The old much appreciated 3.7-inch (94-mm) mountain howitzer remained in the Royal Artillery through the whole war, in several slightly revised versions. In addition to this, another gun was provided for certain light regiments. It was the American 75-mm pack howitzer, which came into service 1943 and was

Table 4-5. Gun data – 25-pounder Mark II

Calibre cm	Weight kg	Type of shell	Shell weight kg	Charge	Muzzle velocity m/s	Max. range m
8.76	approx. 1,750	High Explosive (HE)	11.3	1	198	3,565
				2	305	7,130
				3	453	10,810
				Super	532	12,250
		Armour piercing	9.1	3	472	1,830
				Super	564	2,750
				Super + inc.	656	2,750
		Smoke		10.0	—	—

Sources: 1) Nigel F. Evans website: British Artillery in WW 2, Chapter The Guns 25-pdr 2) Range Tables QF 25-pounder Mark II

supplied to the airborne divisions. When it came, it was still equipped with wooden, ironclad wheels. Len Gittings has the story:[71]

> When we saw the 75-mm howitzers with the cart wheels we had a good laugh. Then they told us we could go off on two weeks leave and, when we returned, the gun had been modified with rubber tyres.

More about these guns can be found in Chapter 7, where we are to look at the artillery of airborne forces.

Army and corps artillery modernised with new medium guns

The Medium Regiments had initially to be satisfied with the vintage 6-inch howitzer and the 60-pounder gun. A few of the latter had been upgraded with 4.5-inch lined barrels, but this did not help much; the medium artillery was not up to standard as regards firing range and mobility. Development of new guns had during the 1930s had to stand back for priority development of the 25-pounder and the new heavy anti-aircraft gun (3.7-inch) for high altitude fire.

When the war broke out, no complete designs for new medium guns had been approved. In January 1939 a specification had, however, been agreed on. This said that the new gun was to have the calibre 5.5-inch (140-mm) and a firing range of maximum 16,000 yards (14,600m) when firing a shell with the weight of 100lb (45.6kg). It should be a gun-howitzer, and thus be able to fire flat trajectories as well as higher ones with steeper descent. In this book we will call it 'Gun' for short. The carriage could be a modernised 60-pounder carriage. Gun weight should not exceed 5.5 tons.[72] Later during this year this was found to be a bad idea as far as the carriage was concerned. A completely new carriage design was required, therefore, to be provided.

Furthermore, it had been decided, in haste, that a second medium gun with smaller calibre must be produced as well; it should be a 4.5-inch gun (114mm). The weight of projectile should be 55lb (25kg). By reducing the propellant and shell size, it would be possible to increase firing range up to maximum 20,500 yards (18,700m). It was also decided that this gun, a true gun, was to have the same carriage as the 5.5-inch gun. The latter is shown in **Fig. 4-6**.

Manufacture of prototypes of the two new medium guns took place during the first year of the war followed by final tests. Now, it really was urgent! Production was speeded up before all 'teething troubles' had been found and been remedied. Towards the end of 1941 the first Medium Regiments could be reequipped with new guns. For instance, 64 Medium Regiment RA, which took part in the battle of El Alamein,

Fig. 4-6 The new generation medium guns began to arrive in 1941. The two types of gun with the calibres 4.5-inch and 5.5-inch had the same carriage (split trail). Here is the latter. Concentration of manufacture to the 5.5-inch Gun followed quite soon (RAHT).

Table 4-6. Gun data – medium guns

Calibre cm	Weight kg	Type of shell	Shell weight kg	Charge	Muzzle velocity m/s	Max. range m
11.4 (4.5-inch)	Approx. 5,800	High Explosive (HE)	24.9 (55lb)	1	381	10,150
				2	533	13,710
				3	686	18,740
14.0 (5.5-inch)	Approx. 6,200	High Explosive (HE)	45.4 (100lb)	1	233	6,220
				2	350	9,780
				3	419	11,790
				4	510	14,800
		High Explosive (HE)	36.3 (80lb)	1	290	6,950
				2	381	10,150
				3	465	12,610
				4	556	15,360
				Super	594	16,540

Sources: Nigel F. Evans website: British Artillery in WW2, Chapter The Guns, Data Sheet Medium Guns

was re-equipped in May/June 1942. One of its batteries received 4.5-inch guns and the other 5.5-inch gun-howitzers.

Denis Falvey serving in this regiment has in his account described how positive it was to receive the new guns as substitute for the obsolete ones. All gunners were 'entranced, intoxicated' by the new guns. Never had such 'beautiful' guns been seen. The effect on morale was, he said, dramatic.[73]

Experience from the battlefield soon showed that a lighter shell for the 5.5-inch gun was needed instead of the 100lb shell. The new shell was deemed to have the weight of 80lb (36.3kg). This would reduce the load on the mechanism and barrel and by that reduce the risk of fire interruptions. At the same time a gain in range of up to 18,000 yards (16,500m) would be accomplished, indeed an important improvement tactically. However, it was not until 1944 the new shell became available in larger quantities. This new development virtually made the 4.5-inch gun superfluous with its lower impact effect and about the same maximum range. Hence, production was reduced and focus was entirely turned to the 5.5-inch gun. Thanks to this change, all new Medium Regiments could be equipped with the latter in both batteries. After the initial 'teething troubles' had been resolved, the gun became very popular, also in many other countries, and was still used in the 1980s. The 4.5-inch gun, however, went to the 'grave' right after the war.

It is interesting to note that the new generation of guns had a split-trail, which was a deviation from the British earlier preference for the box-type trail. The detachment for handling the new medium guns comprised ten men. A few technical data in **Table 4-6** illustrate the performance qualities of the two pieces.[74]

Manufacture was urgent, and the first pieces were delivered in August 1940 and before the end of the year 57 barrels with breeches had been delivered. All came from the only manufacturer of medium guns, ROF Nottingham. Later, in March 1942, also ROF Dalmuir joined. Vickers Armstrong delivered the first privately produced medium guns in January 1941. No other private companies were engaged in manufacturing the guns. However, as regards carriages six private manufacturers were engaged in the programme besides Vickers Armstrong. ROF Nottingham supplied carriages from January 1941 and had six months later supplied 75 of them. The other manufacturers followed suit, and at the end of the year the total delivery capacity had reached 40 pieces per month. A total of 227 guns had been manufactured at the end of 1941. However, the target was set high, 100 guns per month, but that could never be reached. A maximum was 92 guns in February 1942. One reason was that the gun went into production before the design was fully tested and ready for mass production. Changes thus had to be introduced in parallel with the production; one such change was introduction of welding methods as a substitute for riveting.

At the beginning as many 4.5-inch guns as 5.5-inch guns were manufactured, but as previously mentioned a shift towards the latter gradually took place. At the end of the war 754 barrels of the smaller calibre had been manufactured as compared with 2,250 with the larger calibre. In total 2,453 carriages were manufactured.[75] Manufacturing was forced heavily until the end of 1943 when a drastic reduction of the monthly output came, and it continued thereafter at a low level. Also when looking at this part of the artillery rearmament, we can note that it took about five years to complete, despite the massive mobilisation and redirection of industry.

None of the medium guns were up to the reliability standard of the 25-pounder. Problems arose already at the beginning with the carriages, later also as regards buffer/recuperators and breeches. These 'teething troubles' emerged at first in connection with the large and extended fire programmes at El Alamein in October 1942. There also occurred some prematures with devastating consequences for the gun detachments. In Burma in particular, such problems were quite frequent, which reduced the gunners' confidence in this type of gun.

Initially the life of the barrels was estimated to be equivalent to 3,000 rounds fired, but after El Alamein this was reduced to 2,000 rounds. An advantage was, however, that it was easy to replace a worn-out barrel, even in the field.

Whilst the introduction of the lighter 80lb shell was in order to accomplish the longer range, the other likely reason was, as mentioned, to reduce the mechanical strain on the barrel and thus to reduce the damage risk.

Heavy artillery neglected

Even if the design and manufacture of new medium guns had had to stand back because of the development of the 25-pounder and the 3.7-inch heavy anti-aircraft gun, the situation was much worse as regards the necessary development of new heavy guns, the Heavies. We may recall the ongoing discussions during the 1930s as to whether bomber aircraft could take over the role that the heavy guns had had in the Great War. These discussions did not end before the new war broke out, but also national economy and shortage of industrial resources led to a negative impact on the development of heavy guns. And the result was, as we have seen, that no modern heavy guns were available when the war broke out in 1939. This was not only the case as regards guns in the calibre range of 6-8 inches (15–20 cm), but also guns with even larger calibre, the Super Heavies. New guns were not available.

In order to improve the situation somewhat, and reduce the number of calibres and related logistic problems, it was decided in the autumn 1940 to concentrate on one calibre, the 7.2-inch (183-mm). This should be accomplished by providing a new barrel on carriages of the vintage 6-inch gun and – in particular – the

Fig. 4-7 No new heavy guns were designed and manufactured during the war. An old howitzer was however modernized with a 7.2-inch barrel. Modern heavy guns were bought from USA.

A new 7.2-inch barrel was applied to the carriage of the old 8.2-inch Howitzer (RAHT)

155-mm Gun, 'Long Tom', American manufacture (RAHT)

vintage 8-inch howitzer. Some new carriages of this design were manufactured too, by which 160 pieces were made available. These guns were of course applied with pneumatic tyres and modern dial sights. A detachment of thirteen men was required for serving the gun. We can see the howitzer in **Fig. 4-7**. The weight of the piece was around 10.3 tons and it fired a 200lb (91.6kg) projectile up to 17,000 yards (15,450 m) when using Charge 4.

A great disadvantage was that it lacked a buffer to absorb the entire recoil energy when firing. This was instead taking care of by placing ramps behind the wheels. When the howitzer was fired the piece moved up the ramps settling back to its original firing position again afterwards. This implied that no one could stand close to the piece when firing. This arrangement also made it necessary to re-lay (re-sight) the piece after each round. Hence the fire intensity was by necessity low, normally less than one round per minute.

Even if cooperation between artillery and the air force became very efficient from 1942, there was still a need for heavy artillery with capacity for long range firing. This was accomplished during the last years of the war, when 155-mm guns were bought from USA. The gun was the famous 'Long Tom', as it was called. It had a carriage with eight wheels and a fire platform-facilitating traverse. It could launch a 95lb (43kg) projectile 25,000 yards (23,000m), which made it one of the most versatile guns during the war. It has been stated, although it has not been able to confirm, that Britain bought 111 pieces for delivery in 1943 and 1944.[76] We can see the gun in **Fig. 4-7**.

New American guns were supplied towards the end of the war for the Super Heavy Regiments, although on a limited scale, a few tens of them only. They had the calibres 203mm (8-inch) and 240mm (9.4-inch). The former is seen in **Fig. 4-8**.

The 'Bishop', the 'Priest' and the 'Sexton' on stage

So far we have looked at towed guns and howitzers, and these dominated the stock. But self-propelled pieces were gradually added, in particular to meet the requirements of the

Fig. 4-8 A few super heavy guns were purchased from USA and used during the final years of the war. Here an 8-inch gun (RAHT)

armoured divisions for better mobility. As mentioned above, some experiments with such guns had already been made during the 1920s as part of the work on the Experimental Mechanised Force (EMF). One was the Birch Gun, which was an 18-pounder combined with a remarkably modern tracked carriage. Some experiments with application of armoured protection for the gun detachment were also made. However, the project was dropped when the EMF was disbanded and no further development took place.

During the first years of war in North Africa it was realised that one had been on the right track twenty years earlier. In haste was the 'Bishop' developed. It was an 18/25-pounder applied to the light tank carriage Valentine. It came into service just before the battles at El Alamein in 1942 and can be seen on **Fig. 4-9**. It cannot be claimed to have been a success. The gun was slow and the large armoured upper structure on its top made it difficult to conceal, and at the same time the elevation was restricted to 15°. This made the maximum range less than approximately 6,000 yards. The weight was however a modest 8 tons. In any case it was to serve well during the North African Campaign and was also used on Sicily.

Again, the Americans could help. They had developed a light self-propelled howitzer of 105-mm calibre on an M3 tank carriage. The weight was 22 tons. The British could acquire a number of these self-propelled (SP) guns just in time for the battle of El Alamein. The protecting armour plate around the carriage for an anti-aircraft machine gun gave it a special look, which inspired the British gunners to call it the 'Priest' as the carriage had a slight resemblance to a church pulpit. The piece is also illustrated on **Fig. 4-9**. It proved to be a good and useful piece of equipment and it was supplied to many regiments by the British and was used for two years in North Africa, Italy and Northwest Europe. In Burma it was used until the end of the war in August 1945, albeit on a limited scale.

There was for logistic reasons a strong need for standardisation. To facilitate training this was also wanted. Hence a new self-propelled carriage with the 25-pounder applied to it was urgently needed. The task was given to the Canadians and they developed the Sexton using a RAM tank carriage (**Fig. 4-9**). Just before the D-Day landings in Normandy, re-equipment of British

Fig. 4-9 Self-propelled guns became an important addition to the artillery of armoured divisions from 1942

Bishop Entered service in 1942 just before the battle of El Alamein, a 25-pdr on a Valentine tank-carriage (RAHT)

Priest American design and equipped with a 105-mm howitzer. The first guns arrived basically at the same time as the 'Bishops' (RAHT)

Sexton A 25-pounder applied on a RAM tank-carriage. Change to this piece in British regiments commenced in the middle of 1944 (RAHT)

regiments commenced; the 'Priests' left and in came the 'Sextons'. In total 1,450 pieces were provided for British and Canadian regiments.[77] The design proved to be very good and the British retained it for active service into the 1960s. The weight was around 25 tons and due to its design the maximum range of a 25-pounder could be used, which was much more than that of the 'Priest'.

A detail in this context is that when the 'Priests' were taken out of service in 1944 the guns were removed and the carriages adapted for transport of infantry. In this shape it was called Kangaroo and was to be the first armoured fighting vehicle (AFV) after the Bren Carrier.

The Congreve legacy – rocket renaissance
The rockets designed by William Congreve played an important role in the Royal Artillery even a few decades after Waterloo 1815. But the interest for them gradually declined in parallel with the decline of their comparative advantage relative ordinary artillery, the longer range. Furthermore, artillery had the advantage of much better accuracy. But some rocket competence was, however, always retained although no further technical development took place. When the Second World War broke out in 1939, no rocket artillery for ground targets existed in the artillery arsenal.[78]

It had, however, been observed that something was under way in Germany in the 1930s and in some other countries too, amongst them the Soviet Union. A high-level committee was therefore established under General Sir Hugh Elles, Master Gunner of Ordnance, to give it a closer look. The committee concluded already in 1936 that development of new rockets should be commenced in accordance with the priority:

1. Anti-aircraft rockets
2. Long-range rockets against ground targets
3. Rockets for fighter-bomber application
4. Rockets for take-off assistance for heavy aircraft

A concentrated development effort was initiated on the first priority rockets and some test launchings had materialised when the war broke out. Rockets with diameters of two to three inches (50 to 75mm) were manufactured for these tests. Various types of launching arrangement were also tested. Much remained however to be done; which included development of suitable fuzes to be adopted for ignition of the high explosive loads of the rockets. An interesting idea was the attempts to develop a fuze based on photo-electrical principles, which was to react on the shadow of an enemy aircraft when approaching it. This was a foregoer to the VT-fuze to be developed for field artillery towards the end of the war, and which was to use a radar signal to determine the distance to the target with great accuracy.

It was decided that each rocket was to have its own launching ramp, which later was to be modified implying a ramp built for two rockets or, to some extent eight rockets. In March 1941 the Royal Artillery was ready to establish its first rocket anti-aircraft regiment and already in the following month an enemy aircraft was shot down for the first time. Rearmament went on, and in December 1942 there were no less than 91 anti-aircraft batteries in active service, each of them equipped with 64 launching ramps for two rockets. This was the situation, when the threats from the air over the British Isles had declined significantly.

The development of rockets as of Priority 2 was slow. The interest on the part of the Royal Artillery was limited. The technology was not considered promising enough. Development to meet Priority 3 took over, as was development of anti-submarine rockets. With inspiration from the failed assault landing at Dieppe in 1942, development of rockets that could be massively launched from amphibious landing ships took place. The anti-aircraft rockets could easily be adapted for this purpose. Although accuracy still was bad, it was considered that there was a great psychological effect, negative for the defenders and positive for the attackers. Such rockets were used on a large-scale basis, at first at the landings in Italy in 1943 and later in connection with the Normandy landings on 6th June 1944. At the latter occasion rockets for fighter-bombers were extensively used for the first time (Typhoon aircraft in particular).

When it comes to the Priority 2, task suspiciousness was still widespread as to whether it was a good idea to use rockets against ground targets, which can be considered a bit strange as the British were well aware of the extensive use of such rockets by the Red Army on the Eastern Front. Industry made an attempt in 1943 to raise the interest by suggesting to the infantry and the artillery that a new five-inch rocket with improved flying characteristics should be developed. But, no! Not until March 1944, it was accepted that such a rocket should be developed. The range to target was to be increased up to around 9,000 yards (8,000m) with better accuracy than earlier rockets had shown. By this the rocket (salvo) became an attractive weapon for causing impacts over a fairly large area.

A prototype was available for demonstration in June 1944 to the concerned authorities. It was not the 'thumb down', but enthusiasm was still pending. This changed when the Canadians in July 1944 saw the new rocket in action. They immediately asked for as many as could be delivered without delay. They deemed the rockets to be an excellent complement to traditional artillery in large barrages designed to support large-scale attacks. Twelve mobile units each with 30 launchers were soon supplied to the Canadian Army. A technical feature was introduced in order to make it possible to vary the firing range. This was done by means of a kind of 'spoilers', which affected the air resistance in the trajectory. However, another problem remained; the accuracy could not be improved as much as was wanted. A battery salvo covered for instance an area of around 700x700 yards.

But despite this disadvantage, the Canadians used rockets several times with success during the battles in Northwest Europe during the autumn 1944 and later, not least the massive allied crossing of the River Rhine in March 1945 (**Fig. 4-10**). Concentrated rocket salvoes definitely proved to have a decisive psychological effect against the opponents. Now some rocket units in the Royal Artillery had been organised, so – at last – rockets became part of the Royal Artillery arsenal, although not as much as on the Eastern Front. Positive experience achieved made rockets again a permanent complement to traditional artillery and have remained so even today.

Modernisation of anti-tank artillery

As mentioned at the beginning of this book I am not attempting to cover the story of the Royal Artillery Anti-Tank formations. They will, however, not be completely overlooked; one reason being the fact that anti-tank guns often were included in large plans for attack covering fire during the last years of the war.

Britain went to war with anti-tank guns with about the same calibres and capability as those of her opponents. The main gun was the 2-pounder which had a calibre of 1.6 inch (40mm) and which was manufactured in large numbers till the end of 1940. It was towed by a truck but could also be taken loaded on a truck or lorry, Portee. The latter arrangement made it possible to make surprise attacks at short distances, which partly compensated for the poor penetration capability in armour.

The gun was the standard equipment of the Anti-Tank Regiments that were gradually established during the 1930's in the Royal Artillery, and which were to be attached at a divisional level. A regiment had 48 guns distributed amongst four batteries. Some of these regiments were part of Army and Corps artillery.[79]

Beside the 2-pounder there were also a number of Bofors 37-mm anti-tank guns. The British had just before the war placed an order with Bofors for delivery of 250 guns, but only 80 could be supplied before the war broke out.[80] These were given to formations sent to Egypt during the first years of the war. Apart from the Anti-Tank Regiments of the Royal Artillery, there were a few independent batteries as well. It is interesting to note that, for instance, 3 Field Regiment RHA had a 'Bofors Battery' attached.[81]

The war would soon demonstrate that the calibre was insufficient when meeting modern German tanks, which forced the British to use the 25-pounder with its armour-piercing shell as an anti-tank weapon; this as an interim solution in 1941 and early 1942 while waiting for a new stronger gun. However, a problem was that maximum range for penetration of the armour of the enemy tanks was around 700–800 yards with the 25-pounder, whereas the most modern

Fig. 4-10 Rockets were first introduced as a complement to anti-aircraft guns, later also as 'ground artillery' for ground targets. The Canadians were here the driving force. The picture is taken at a Canadian rocket battery towards the end of the war (©Imperial War Museum BU 1755)

German tank could fire with accuracy up to around 2,000 yards.

A better gun, the 6-pounder, was on the drawing table just before the war, but a strategic decision was made to prioritise manufacture of the 2-pounder, a decision that proved to be a mistake. Not until November 1941 was manufacture of this new gun commenced; the first would enter service just before the battle of El Alamein in September and October 1942. The 6-pounder had a calibre of 2.2 inch (57mm) and could penetrate armour twice as thick as the 2-pounder, around 74mm at a range of 1,000 yards. This was increased to 146mm in 1944 when sub-calibre, high velocity ammunition, using a Sabot projectile, was introduced for the first time.[82] The gun soon became the standard piece, and from 1943 the 25-pounders were not used any more for direct anti-tank fire, except occasionally, when attacked.

An even more powerful anti-tank gun, the 17-pounder, was designed in haste in 1940 and was ready for supply to anti-tank regiments in 1942. This took place just in time for the great allied invasion in North Africa in November 1942. A 'teething trouble' was that it lacked its carriage, which had been delayed. This problem was provisionally resolved on initiative by the Managing Director of G. & J. Weir Ltd, who was much involved in manufacture of 25-pounders, as we have seen. He suggested that the new gun initially should use the standard 25-pounder carriage. This was accepted, and the temporary solution was called the 17-pounder Hybrid Anti-Tank gun. On pictures from the campaign in North Africa this gun can be seen there. See also **Fig. 4-11**.

The 17-pounder had the calibre 3.0-inch (76.2-mm) and was capable to penetrate 231-mm armour with high velocity ammunition (Sabot) at a distance of 1,000 yards.[83]

This gun was also used for the Archer Self-propelled anti-tank vehicle and a version of it in Sherman Firefly tanks.

Anti-aircraft guns in ground role

Anti-aircraft guns were really important during the first years of the war as protection for artillery units and their guns, together with RAF fighter squadrons. The gunners had their own light anti-aircraft guns and machine guns, but for fire at higher altitudes they were dependent on support from the Royal Artillery Anti-Aircraft Regiments. Divisions normally had one Anti-Aircraft Regiment equipped with the famous Bofors 40mm automatic gun. This gun was introduced by the Swedish industry just in time before the war, when most countries had started to re-arm their armies with modern anti-aircraft capacity. It became an amazing export success for the Swedish manufacturer.

Britain decided in 1937 to acquire this gun and ordered 100 pieces with ammunition, spare parts, etc. Another 1,000 guns, along with one million shells, were contracted to be supplied the following year.[84] Even more guns were needed,

Fig. 4-11 The 17-pounder anti-tank gun was introduced in the middle of the war and it was the most powerful anti-tank weapon in the British Army. The gun was installed also in Sherman tanks and in a SP-carriage, the Archer (RAHT)

so Britain entered into a license agreement with Bofors giving British industry the right to manufacture the gun. As in several other countries, the gun became standard for British Light Anti-Aircraft (LAA) Regiments one of which was attached to a division. Such a regiment had, as the anti-tank regiments, 48 guns divided into four batteries. The main task was of course fire against enemy aircraft as is illustrated in the drawing, **Fig. 4-12**. It was however soon found that due to its versatility it could also be used for other tasks, for instance as an anti-tank gun. Another application taken advantage of already at El Alamein in 1942 was to fire bursts of tracer rounds to mark boundaries between attacking formations or to show the direction of attacks.

For fire against enemy aircraft flying at very high altitudes, which bombers often did, the new 3.7-inch (94-mm) heavy anti-aircraft gun was provided. For protection of Army units in the field the guns were organised in Heavy Anti-Aircraft Regiments (HAA), which each one comprised of 3–4 batteries. Each battery had two troops that comprised four guns. In total, each regiment thus comprised of 24–32 guns. As the air threat gradually declined, many of the regiments were converted to other formations, but those left got more and more involved in fire against ground targets. This was due to two important characteristics of the gun. First, its long firing range, up to more than 20,000 yards (18,000m) at ground targets.[85] Second, its time fuze, which was perfect when firing at such targets. For instance, when taking part in counter-battery firing it was easy to arrange airbursts with good accuracy at a suitable height over the target. A third important characteristic was its natural ability to fire at elevations above 45°, which for instance in Burma was an asset, but also when firing against enemy mortar positions, which normally were dug in into mortar pits. **Fig. 4-13** illustrates the gun in a ground role in Burma.

We will later in the book see how light and heavy anti-aircraft guns complemented the field artillery.

Fig. 4-13 The 3.7-inch anti-aircraft gun was standard in heavy anti-aircraft regiments for fire against aircraft at high altitudes. Its long range and suitable fuzes made it also very useful for counter-battery fire and fire against other distant ground targets. Such a gun is here seen firing in a ground role in Burma (RAHT Collection MD/2791)

Fig. 4-12 The main task for anti-aircraft units was to fire against enemy aircraft. However, when the threat from the air declined, anti-aircraft guns were more and more used in a 'ground role'. This was also the case as regards the Bofors 40-mm guns, which could be supporting the field artillery in fire preparations before large infantry attacks. They could also be used for marking attack directions and boundaries between formations by firing tracer bursts (drawing by J.T. Kenney/RAHT)

5. Artillery Grouping, Organisation and Equipment

'Indirect fire system'
Yes, indeed, the guns are the main equipment of artillery and the projectiles delivered can thus be regarded as the principal weapon. Furthermore, they can be delivered by means of both direct and indirect fire.

In the former case, guns acted independently as the target can be seen by the detachment, and aiming can be done even if the target is moving. In the latter case, indirect fire, the target cannot be seen from the guns. Hence these must be complemented with other devices and functions into a complete system. Without this working as it should, no fire can be brought onto the target. The indirect fire method meant a paradigm shift for the artillery in early twentieth century.

Before proceeding and discussing the organisation and equipment of British artillery in the Second World War, a few words about the 'indirect fire system' and its components. In its simplest form the following main components can be identified, all of which were found in every regiment and battery:

- **Intelligence function** – for target acquisition and sometimes fire control
- **Fire observation and control function** – for target acquisition and fire control
- **Communication function** – *for* transmission of information and orders
- **Calculation function** – for calculation of gun aiming data and various corrections of shell trajectory
- **Fire unit** – one or numerous guns for execution of fire orders
- **Administrative, supply function** – for supply of ammunition, fuel, food etc.

In order to improve and strengthen the effectiveness of the 'system' resources could be provided from outside the regiments, in particular the following:

- Survey resources
- Special intelligence resources such as sound ranging troops, flash spotters, radar (in the latter years of the war) for location of enemy artillery and mortars
- Air Observation Squadrons for target acquisition and fire control
- Army Cooperation Squadrons RAF for target acquisition in depth and sometimes fire control

As is the case for all systems, the 'indirect fire system' also had a command and control function, which included tactical coordination with commanders of infantry and armoured units to be supported and overall control of fire.

We will now have a closer look into the various functions and will start with the Intelligence function.

Intelligence function
Indirect fire with artillery guns requires detailed identification, classification and location of potential targets. The character of these can vary substantially. It can be attacking infantry or armoured units lacking protection from fortifications or terrain features. Or, on the contrary, it could be just that! Artillery might be required to fire against an enemy well dug in and who maybe has had the time for construction of fortifications and shelters as protection for machine guns, anti-tank guns etc. Enemy units might have deployed behind mountainous slopes, or in close woods, or in more or less impenetrable jungle. In such situations it might be a matter of concealed mortars or infantry reserves. The target can also be the enemy's artillery, headquarters or supply bases i.e. targets in depth far from the front lines. It might also be a matter of disrupting his transport and supply or troop concentrations with artillery fire.

The intelligence resources available were in the first place the batteries' own observation parties that accompanied forward infantry companies in defence or offence, but they could be assisted by such units that could 'look' far beyond the front line, i.e. by support resources as those mentioned above.

Fire control function
This function with its observation parties was the primary function for intelligence and fire control at the front line with the infantry and armoured units that were to be supported. Troop Commanders and, less frequently, Battery Commanders served as Fire Observation Officers; this as the first alternative. When losses struck the units, subalterns could be called forward from gun positions as replacements.

Besides acquisition of targets and determining their characters and location, the primary task was to order and control the artillery fire. All officers were trained for this, and they could therefore replace each other. Another important task was to send tactical reports about the general battle situation, a very important source of information for commanders and headquarters at higher levels.

Each battery had two observation parties and as a regiment normally comprised three batteries there were six observation parties per regiment.

No other rank suffered as high losses as the observation officers. They were always at the front line, not far back as most of the other gunners were.

The observer had to be supported by assistants for various duties at the observation post in the front line; one could be to measure distances to targets or terrain features important as reference objects. The signallers, one or two per observation party, were another very important group of assistants. And this will carry us on to next function in the system for indirect fire.

Communication function
Information and orders from observation officers should be transmitted to the guns, and often also to various headquarters. This was accomplished by means of telephone lines or radio communication. In mobile battles the latter was the only option.

Signallers were detached to take care of this at the observation posts and the firing units, the guns, under overall command of signal officers. Ways of oral communication was strictly regulated and signal discipline was always enforced in the Royal Artillery. Resources must be available not only for radio communication but also for laying telephone lines and for repairing them when required, which could be quite frequent during the course of a battle.

Telephone lines were often cut by enemy artillery fire, tracked vehicles, etc. Of course, resources must also be available for retrieval of the cables in connection with redeployment. More about communication later in the book.

The terminal function at the firing unit was also to be seen as part of the 'indirect fire system'. All received information should be taken care of by those who were to undertake calculations of gun data. This leads us to the Calculation function.

Calculation function
The information regarding target classification and location, purpose of fire etc was to be transformed into aiming data for the guns, and for making ammunition of the right type ready for fire including setting of fuzes when so required. Time schedules for firing should also be given to the guns in an appropriate way depending on the tactical situation. Hence, a calculation function was a must, and normally one was available at each troop, Troop Command Post, but also another for the whole battery, Battery Command Post, which acted as coordinator and controller of the calculations made by the former.

Fire unit
The fire unit, which was ordered to deliver fire of some kind and intensity, could be a single gun (rarely), a section of guns (two), a troop (four guns normally) or more often a battery (eight guns, four if a heavy battery). But a whole regiment (24 field guns, 16 if a medium or heavy regiment) or numerous regiments could also constitute a 'fire unit', which required an extensive radio or telephone communication system.

Administrative, supply function
Without ammunition, no artillery fire! Obviously, but how was ammunition supplied to the guns? A first-hand stock was brought by the guns themselves, or more specifically by gun trailers and tractors. The Battery Ammunition Detachment could provide more and also fetch more at ammunition depots organised by the Royal Army Service Corps (RASC). Companies of the latter were a joint resource at the division level and they could fetch ammunition at railway stations or harbours. When larger operations were planned, these companies could transport large amounts of ammunition and stockpile it just where the guns were deployed, up to 600 shells per field gun was not an unusual requirement.

Although resources for supply of fuel, water, food, medicine, spare parts etc, were not needed directly for the artillery fire, they were necessary for securing sustainability of the formations. This includes numerous vehicles to meet capacity requirements.

The 'indirect fire system' needs of course human resources as well. These must be well trained and motivated if to secure a well-functioning system. And an appropriate organisation of all resources must be established; and this must be under competent command and control. Before going into details regarding organisation and structures, we will have a brief look at the overall artillery grouping and command structure.

Artillery grouping and command structure

As already mentioned artillery formations mostly comprised of regiments. The following types were the normal arrangement:

Formations with light guns **(<114-mm, 4.5")**
- Field Regiments with towed guns
- Field Regiments with self-propelled guns
- Airlanding Light Regiments
- Mountain Regiments
- Assault Regiments
- Jungle Field Regiments

The two last mentioned types were organised only in Burma as complement to regiments of the normal type, i.e. the two first mentioned.

Formations with medium guns **(114-mm–140-mm, 4.5"–5.5")**, *heavy guns* **(150–200-mm, 6"–8")**, *super heavy guns* **(>200-mm, 8")**
- Medium Regiment
- Heavy Regiment
- Super Heavy Regiment

The main task for all artillery formations was to support infantry and armoured units and to combat and destroy enemy artillery. They could be permanently attached to the unit to be supported, thus being an organisational part of the latter. They could also be attached for a specific operation, for marching and other temporary purposes. Often a combined grouping was chosen, as we will see several examples of later in Part 3 of the book.

Only Field Regiments were permanently attached to the infantry and armoured units, most of them at the divisional level. An infantry division normally had three regiments and an armoured division two regiments, one with towed guns and one with self-propelled guns. The regiments constituted the 'divisional artillery', a denomination I will refer to many times. In this context we must not forget the artillery regiments attached to airborne divisions, nor the few mountain regiments supporting various types of formation.

This grouping of field artillery was due to the fact that an infantry division normally comprised of three infantry brigades and the armoured division of one infantry brigade and one armoured brigade.[86] The towed guns were to support the infantry brigade and the SP guns the armoured brigade (compared with mounted artillery supporting the cavalry in earlier years). When a division was to take part in a large operation it was normal practice to organise support also from external regiments, as we will see later in the book.

Brigades normally lacked their own field regiments, i.e. 'under command'. Regiments could be attached and given the role to be 'in support' depending on the operational and tactical situation. The divisional level was thus the lowest level as regards permanent allocation of artillery resources.

A British Army or Corps did not have a permanent, fixed organisation. They were organised on a temporary basis with a structure chosen to meet the requirements of a specific operation. This was also the case as regards medium and heavy regiments. Their role was to reinforce divisional artillery or to execute special tasks, for instance bombardment of enemy artillery. Hence, they could normally be regarded as 'army artillery' or 'corps artillery'. At these higher levels a few field regiments were also found, called 'Army Field Regiments'. Their role was to reinforce other artillery units.

Soon after the Battle of El Alamein in October/November 1942 a new permanent organisation was introduced for reinforcement of artillery at these higher levels. 'Army Groups Royal Artillery', or just 'AGRAs' for short, were established. The composition of such groups varied, but normally they comprised:

- 1–2 Field Regiments
- 3–4 Medium Regiments
- 1–2 Heavy Regiments

Even if the denomination 'AGRA' suggests that the 'Group' operated at the highest level, the Army level, an 'AGRA' normally was attached to a Corps, hence they can be regarded as Corps formations. From 1943 and onwards ten such formations were established.

Besides all its divisions the British Army included also a number of independent infantry and armoured brigades. Not even these had a permanent stock of artillery, but a Field Regiment could be attached for shorter or longer periods as support to a brigade.

The general methods of allocating artillery to infantry and armoured formations was, as mentioned, to either order an artillery unit to come 'under command' or be 'in support' of the subject formation. The first expression meant that the infantry/armour commander had the artillery formation at his full disposal, and that he was authorised to give tactical orders in all aspects. It meant, on the other hand, that he was made responsible also for the artillery unit as regards march, protection, supply etc.

The expression 'in support' meant that the artillery formation was at the infantry/armour commander's disposal just as a tactical fire unit. No other responsibility was laid on the commander's shoulders. This of course did not exclude that assistance and supply could be given when needed. Forward Observation Parties, dispatch riders, liaison officers and others vital for the fire support to function well must of course always be taken good care of as if they had been part of the commander's own organisation.

The method of ordering 'under command' could be applied on parts of a regiment, for instance one of its batteries or just a troop, which could be allocated to an infantry battalion. One artillery unit could also be placed 'under command' of another artillery unit, for instance when a long march was to take place. The latter type of arrangement was more common during the first years of the war than later.

'System management' and command

The 'indirect fire system' must, as all systems, be managed efficiently. Often it was not a matter of one system only, but several linked together. Support of a battalion attack required one type of system, a divisional attack a different, much larger and more complex one. In common they comprised functions such as 'intelligence', 'fire observation and control', fire unit(s) etc. as described above. It was important that the system was flexible enough to meet suddenly changing battle circumstances.

As an example we can imagine a situation where a Troop Commander as Forward Observation Officer is supporting an infantry company by means of the four guns of his own troop. Suddenly the tactical situation changes, and support from all the 72 guns of his division or even many more is required. This required well-established procedures and efficient 'system management' in order to face this situation and adapt artillery support efficiently.

'The indirect fire system' was based on organisational units with competent and well-trained men with adequate equipment. It was a matter of regiments, batteries and troops etc. Tactical and technical 'system management' was imperative, but not sufficient alone. Ordinary command and administrative procedures as such were also required at all organisational levels.

In the British Army two types of management were established. On one hand, commanders of the various units were to command their units as usual. On the other hand, nominated 'artillery commanders' were acting at higher levels as advisors to the infantry or armoured units to be supported. This implied normally certain authorities to decide how to use artillery units even when not 'under command'. The task and responsibility of an officer acting as 'artillery commander' was to ensure efficient overall tactical and technical management of the artillery resources, i.e. 'system management'. This was one lesson learnt during the Great War; 'artillery commanders' were required at all operational and tactical levels.

Certain artillery commanders with headquarters were permanently detached to higher formations such as divisions, corps or armies. At lower levels, brigade, battalion, company, artillery commanders were allocated on a case-by-case basis depending on the role and task of these. As a normal arrangement, a regimental commander was acting as brigade artillery commander and under him battery commanders were assigned the role to act as battalion artillery commanders. Troop commanders, sometimes young subalterns, were normally acting as detached company artillery commanders.

An overall view of the artillery command structure is given in **Table 5-1** as it was from

Table 5-1. Artillery Command Structure

Formation	Artillery Commander	Rank	Acronym	Number of regiments (number of guns)
Theatre/Regional Command	Commander Royal Artillery	Major General	MGRA	
Army Group/Army (>500,000 men)	Commander Royal Artillery	Brigadier	BRA	Great variation (1,000–2,000)
Artillery Group Royal Artillery (AGRA)	Commander AGRA	Brigadier	CAGRA	Example: 2 Army Field Regiments, 4 Medium Regiments, 1 Heavy Regiment (128)
Corps (50,000–100,000 men)	Corps Commander Royal Artillery	Brigadier	CCRA	Great variation (300–600)
Infantry Division (15,000–20,000 men)	Commander Royal Artillery	Brigadier	CRA	3 Field Regiments (72)
Armoured Division (14,000–15,000 men)	Commander Royal Artillery	Brigadier	CRA	1 Field Regiment, towed guns, 1 Field Regiment, self-propelled guns (48)
Airborne Division (10,000–13,000 men)	Commander Royal Artillery	Lt. Colonel / Brigadier (from 1944)	CRA	1 Light Airlanding Regiment (24)
Brigade (3,000–5,000 men)	Brigade Artillery Commander (assigned for a specific operation)	Lt. Colonel (a Regimental Commander)	—	Temporary allotment, normally one of the divisional Field Regiments (24)
Battalion (700–1,000 men)	Battalion Artillery Commander (assigned for a specific operation)	Major (a Battery Commander)	—	Temporary allotment, normally a Battery (8)
Company (100 – 150 men)	Company Artillery Commander (assigned for a specific operation)	Captain (a Troop Commander)	—	Temporary allotment, normally a Troop (4)

1943 to the end of the war. A few comments might be worthwhile.

The artillery commanders at the highest levels, i.e. theatre of war, army group or army, were not normally engaged as commanders of operations. They can be seen as responsible for provision of adequate resources and general support. They had ranks such as Major General Royal Artillery Middle East, Major General Royal Artillery 21st Army Group etc.

An army artillery commander could have a similar role, but often also had an operative role as we will see examples of later in the book, Part 3.

It should also be noted that there were two commanders at the Corps level during the first years of the war. The one with the principal role was the Commander Corps Royal Artillery (CCRA). He had the rank of Brigadier. But a second Brigadier was the Commander Corps Medium Artillery. The role of the latter was to act as counter-battery commander, but the medium guns were also to reinforce divisional artillery and thus the risk for 'twin-command' was obvious. Hence, after a couple of years this position was changed when the AGRA was instituted (see above). The commander of such an army artillery group was automatically subordinated the CCRA as an AGRA normally was attached in support of a Corps.

Finally, it is again stressed that the British doctrine was that artillery fire was to be concentrated from as many guns as possible irrespective of normal organisational affiliation, temporary grouping or boundaries between formations. Hence, when looking at **Table 5-1**, an artillery commander in the lower part of the Table could often take advantage of all artillery as of the upper part of the Table. We will now have a closer look at the details of regiments' organisation and equipment.

Organisation of the Field Regiment

As mentioned above, the 'Regiment' was re-introduced as a substitute for [Artillery] 'Brigade' in 1938, which had been used historically. At the same time the 'Regiment' took over most of the tactical and administrative role that the 'Battery' traditionally had had for long. The 'Battery' had been introduced in the middle of the nineteenth century as a substitute for 'Company' and had since then had a very important role in the British Army in respect of the frequent need for 'policing' around the outskirts of the Empire. The enormous expansion of the artillery during the Great War can be seen as a special exception from the traditional role of British artillery.

I have in this book consequently stuck to the denomination 'Regiment' and not used 'Battalion' or 'Artillery Battalion' which are normally used in most armies. Their tactical role was about the same, but the British formation had more guns than its international counterparts, still grouped in a number of Batteries as the latter.

Until 1938 the Field Regiments (former Brigades), i.e. the divisional artillery, had four six-gun Batteries. Now this was changed to two twelve-gun Batteries, which in their turn comprised three four-gun Troops. The change took time to implement and was not completed when the war broke out in September 1939. However, most of the regiments sent to battle in France with the British Expeditionary Force (BEF) had this organisational structure. The artillery sent to Norway in April 1940 also had been re-organised the same way. Later, as we will see, this regimental organisation did not meet the requirements of a modern, large-scale war.

The infantry divisions normally had three brigades. The usual allocation of artillery 'in support' was one field regiment for each one. For cooperation at the battalion level with three infantry battalions in the brigade, and only two batteries available in an artillery regiment, one infantry battalion therefore lacked an artillery support unit; this was the consequence of the 1938 organisation. It was also to be clearly seen in France that a twelve-gun battery was too complicated to manage and supply, in particular when the battle was very mobile. It was therefore decided in the autumn 1940, after Dunkirk, that the 24 guns of the Field Regiment should be divided into three Batteries instead, each one of these comprising two four-gun Troops. This change could not be implemented quickly however. Shortage of equipment and trained staff delayed the process. Towards the end of 1942, the new organisation was fully implemented, and it proved to be adequate throughout the war. Only minor adaptations were sometimes needed. Under the very specific conditions prevailing in the Burma theatre of war, a few variants of the normal structure had to be introduced, however, not in large numbers.

When now turning to the details of the organisation of a Field Regiment and its three Batteries, we will refer to the one prevailing from 1943 and onwards. The starting point is the official specifications of organisation and equipment given by the [Unit] War Establishment (WE) and the Unit Equipment Table. These documents illustrate the resources available, but as we will see, the organisation applied in the field was different from the official organisation specified in the WE. The former was called Organisation for Manoeuvre.

It must also be observed that the Field Regiment had a fixed allocation of resources from other arms and corps. To regimental headquarters and headquarters at higher levels, signallers with commanding officers from Royal Corps of Signals were provided. Signallers in batteries were, however, Royal Artillery staff. Technical staff for maintenance and repair of equipment came from Royal Army Ordnance Corps. In 1942 a new Corps was formed – the Corps of Royal Electrical and Mechanical Engineers, to fulfil this role. Cooks came from the Army Catering Corps when this entity was established in 1941. The Regimental Medical Officer was allocated from Royal Army Medical Corps.

The main parts of the regimental organisation are summarised in **Fig. 5-1**.

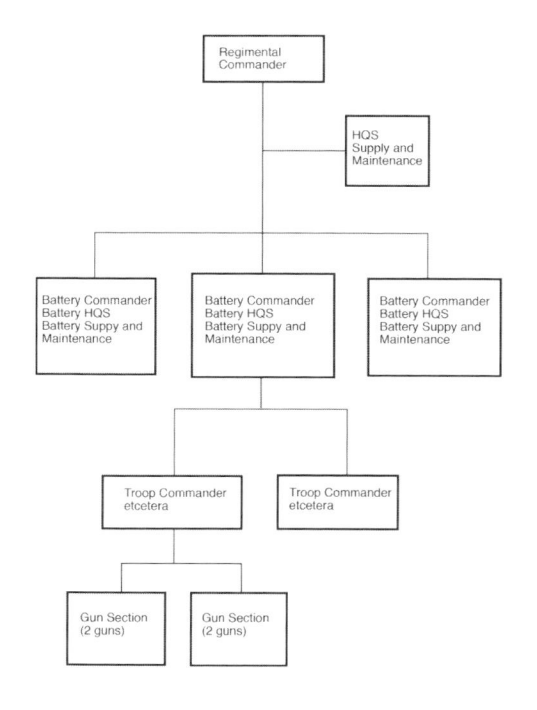

Fig. 5-1 The principal organisation of a Field Regiment (Author)

The Batteries comprised around 200 men each, (approximately 600 men for all three gun batteries). The balance of 122 men was needed for the Regimental Headquarters and Administrative functions. The total number 722 men, (plus around 50 replacement staff to cover up for illness and battle losses), comprised a regiment.

The Regiment's Commanding Officer was an officer with the rank of Lieutenant Colonel. His deputy, Second in Command, was a Major. The latter was responsible for deployment reconnaissance. He often commanded the Regiment on marching and deployment and was the commanding officer at the headquarters when the Commanding Officer was absent, which he normally was as he acted as Brigade Artillery Commander with the support of a small headquarters detachment.

Looking now at the different 'boxes' of **Fig. 5-1** and how they were organised more in detail during march and deployment, i.e. the Manoeuvre Organisation, the following detachments can be identified.[87] First, Commanding Officer's Group and Regimental Headquarters:

a) Commanding Officer's Party:
   -Commanding Officer and Second in Command
   -Signals Officer (Subaltern)
   -Survey Officer (Captain/Subaltern)
   -Staff Officer (Subaltern)
   -Other ranks (Signallers, surveyors, dispatch riders etc.)

b) Adjutant's Party:
   -Regimental Adjutant (Captain)
   -Other ranks (Staff assistants, signallers, dispatch riders, mechanics, local defence)

c) Survey Party:
   -Survey Officer and Surveyors with equipment

d) Regimental HQ Group
   -Medical Officer
   -Regiment Sergeant Major
   -Other ranks (medical orderlies, signallers, staff assistants, technicians, dispatch riders
   (This group was larger than the others and needed several vehicles for transport)

e) 'B' Echelon and Light Aid Detachment REME:
   -Regimental Quarter Master
   -Ordnance technicians
   -Other ranks (cooks, store keepers, technicians etc.)
   (Besides several vehicles for supply transport, two vehicles with 20mm anti-aircraft guns on travelling platform. One PIAT anti-tank weapon and six light machine-guns for local defence were also transported).

We will now look at the detachments and groups in which the Batteries were grouped on transport and deployment.

Manoeuvre organisation of batteries
As **Fig. 5-1** illustrates, each Battery comprises two four-gun Troops. A pair of guns was called a Section.

The leader was the Battery Commander with the rank of Major. His deputy was the Battery Captain. Normal practice was for the former to act as Battalion Artillery Commander and thus as advisor to the commander of the battalion. In this role he could also directly observe and control artillery fire when the situation so required. The Battery Headquarters remained at the gun deployment area, where also resources for supply were deployed.

The deputy had nothing to do with fire control once the battery had been deployed. His post normally was at the Wagon Line where the battery's all vehicles were kept. His main task here was to manage the supply of the battery with ammunition, fuel, food etc.

The person in charge of final deployment of the guns and then control and direction of the firing was the Battery Command Post Officer (CPO). He was also responsible for organising the local defence of the gun positions. It was customary that he was the most senior of the subalterns. When leading the preparations for fire and directing it, he was assisted by Specialists, some whom were NCOs, and some signallers.

The two Troops were commanded by the Troop Commanders with the rank of Captain. We have seen that they normally were posted as Observation Post Officers (OPO). Their role was to act as Forward Observation Officers (FOO) when the infantry or armour attacked. Hence they seldom were close to their guns during battle. With support of Specialist(s) and signallers they were detached to the commander of the infantry or armoured unit to be supported by artillery fire, normally a company. By means of telephone or, more often, radio they could communicate with the former, but also with their Battery Commanders and the gun positions. More about this later.

The four guns of a troop were deployed quite close to each other. The distance between the two troops normally was 300–500 yards. The deployment could be much tighter when terrain and battle conditions so required. The deployment of a troop was the responsibility of a deputy, the Troop Leader, who often was a young subaltern. The technical gunnery services, i.e. preparation for and direction of fire, were the responsibility of the Gun Position Officer (GPO) assisted by Specialists and signallers. They established the Troop Command Post for this purpose. As we will see later, a telephone line to the Battery Command Post was established as soon as possible and also forwards to the Troop Commander if there was time to do so. Most often the substitute was radio communication.

Towards this background, we will now look closer at the Organisation for Manoeuvre and its division into groups and parties when the battery was on the march for deployment:

a) Battery Commander's Party:
   -Battery Commander
   -Command Post Officer
   -Other ranks (Specialists, signallers, dispatch riders etc.)
   (The Battery Commander used a jeep, a tank or a half-track vehicle for transport).

b) Observation Party (2 of them):
   -Troop Commander
   -Other ranks (Specialists, signallers, carrier drivers etc.)
   (Normally an 'O' Party was equipped with a light armoured carrier, the Universal Carrier, or more often called the Bren Carrier. If the party was to support an armoured unit, it was in most cases given a tank instead).

c) Headquarters Party:
   -Battery Captain
   -Assistant Gun Position Officer(s)
   -Other ranks (Specialists, staff assistants, signallers, local defence and drivers).

d) Gun Position Party (one or two):
   -Gun Position Officers (A Tp GPO and B Tp GPO)
   -Battery Sergeant Majors (A Tp BSM and B Tp BSM)
   -Other ranks (Specialists, assistants, technicians and drivers etc.)

e) Gun Group (one or two):
   -Troop Leader (A Tp Leader and B Tp Leader)
   -Four gun detachments with driver and technician
   -Other ranks (Specialists, drivers, local defence etc.)
   (A Gun Section had three tractors, Tractor 4x4, field artillery. Two of these towed the guns and their ammunition trailers, the third carried ammunition in two trailers for both guns. The tractor was the famous Quad, a four-wheel drive tractor that carried the gun crew with their personal equipment and belongings and in addition to that 32 complete rounds of ammunition, of which eight were armour-piercing).

f) Ammunition Group:
   -Ammunition crew, medical orderlies, assistants, local defence)
   (The Group was transported in three 3-ton lorries, 4x4, G.S. In total 480 complete rounds of ammunition were transported on these vehicles. They also brought camouflage nets, PIAT anti-tank guns and machine guns for local defence. Two 20mm anti-aircraft guns on separate vehicles were also attached to the Group).

g) 'B' Echelon:
   -Battery Quarter Master Sergeant
   -Supply crew, staff assistant, cooks, electrician, vehicle mechanic, water attendant, drivers

The total number of vehicles in the Field Regiment was 110–130 plus a few motorcycles. When on march this meant a column about 5–6km long.

We may also note that when the war broke out only a few gunners had personal weapons. Most of them were unarmed, probably a reminiscence from the Great War when the gun positions, well protected behind static fronts, very rarely risked an enemy infantry attack.

The vehicles
When the war broke out the British Army had not standardised its stock of vehicles and thus many different types of various manufacture existed. This situation prevailed during the course of the war and was further complicated during the last few years of the war by addition of many American and Canadian vehicles to those manufactured in Britain. In particular foreign-built vehicles were used for heavy transport.

All vehicles used by the Royal Artillery can thus not be illustrated in one, not even in a couple of photographs, but a selection of them are presented in **Fig. 5-2**.

Vehicles with two-wheel and four-wheel drive were used. Many special vehicles were also used, for instance for water transport or as ambulances. Many were used as vehicles for radio communication or staff work.

One special vehicle was the mentioned Quad, the tractor for the 25-pounder and its related ammunition trailers. It existed in many versions designed and manufactured by several manufacturers in Britain and overseas. In total some 22,000 are said to have been manufactured.[88] The Quad was very robust and reliable, but a disadvantage was its weak engine, which caused problems in difficult terrain and when steep hills had to be climbed.

During the final years of the war, plans were made to replace the Quad with a half-track tractor, after inspiration from Germany, to be implemented as a standard vehicle for field regiments but also for anti-tank and anti-aircraft guns. Nothing, however, materialised during the war. For medium guns a suitable tractor, the Matador, existed which also was used for heavy anti-aircraft guns. For the vintage heavy guns the Scammel tractor was much used.

Supply transport were normally undertaken by means of 3-ton lorries, some of them with four-wheel drive. Another much used vehicle was the light truck, the 15 cwt truck 4x4, which also was used for many other tasks. The Jeep did not exist during the first years of the war, but when it arrived in 1942, it became immensely popular for all sorts of purposes; e.g. towing of supply trailers, mountain guns and pack howitzers. It replaced many older small British-made vehicles.

As mentioned, the standard vehicle for observation parties with the infantry divisions was the Universal Carrier, which was retained through the war. An example of this use of the carrier is illustrated in **Fig. 5-3**.

Fig. 5-2 A sample of vehicles used by artillery formations for different purposes

The Quad was through the war the standard gun tractor for regiments equipped with the 25-pdr gun. It was made by many different manufacturers in Britain and Canada (RAHT)

The Matador was used as gun tractor for medium and heavy anti-aircraft guns (RAHT)

The 15-cwt light lorry was used as a radio car, for transportation of observation parties and other purposes (RAHT)

Fig. 5-3 A sample of vehicles used by artillery commanders and observation parties

The light Universal Carrier was the standard vehicle for the observation parties in the field regiments of infantry divisions. The main radio was the No. 22 wireless set which was fixed in the vehicle. A remote control unit made traffic possible at distances up to some 700 yards from the carrier. Note the telephone cable at the front (RAHT)

During the final years of the war halftracks were often used by the artillery in armoured divisions. This one is from a post-war museum (Shutterstock.com No. 74245039)

Observation parties of the armoured divisions had to use tanks or halftracks in order to be able to follow armoured units to be supported. One alternative was the Churchill tank seen here, Sherman tanks were also used frequently. To provide necessary space for signallers and wireless sets the gun of the tank was often removed and the barrel replaced by a wooden dummy (Author's collection)

Self-propelled guns required a modernised stock of vehicles

Field Regiments equipped with self-propelled guns required more of skilled maintenance and supply personnel than the ordinary regiments such us gun technicians, and mechanics etc. Around 25 more men were needed in these regiments, the size of it thus increasing to around 750 men for the Sexton-equipped regiments organised from 1944 onwards.

As regards transport vehicles, one major difference was that the Commanding Officer, all Observation Post Officers (OPOs) and the Gun Position Officers (GPOs) were given tanks, the total number normally being thirteen. Furthermore, the medium trucks (15cwt 4x4) that were equipped with radio equipment were replaced by half-track vehicles. In total 46 such vehicles were available in the regiment. These changes of vehicles implied much better protection and improved mobility.

During the last years of the war it was quite common to dismantle the guns of Sherman and Churchill tanks used by the gunners and install a wooden dummy in order to give more room for signallers and their radio equipment. **Fig. 5-3** illustrates some vehicle alternatives.

Organisation of Medium and Heavy Regiments

As mentioned the Medium Regiments nominally had two Batteries, each with eight guns. Although the gun detachments were larger than those of the 25-pounders, ten instead of six men, the total size of the regiment was smaller, around 590 men. Apart from the gun tractors these types of regiment had the same types of vehicle as the Field Regiments. The gun tractors were bigger and stronger than the Quads, the Medium Regiment had as mentioned the Tractor, 4x4 medium or just Matador, which is shown in **Fig. 5-2**. This was a powerful and reliable tractor. The gun tractor for the vintage 7.2-inch howitzer of the Heavy Regiment normally was the old-timer, but efficient, Scammel, but the Matador was also used. The Observation Post Officers and their parties were transported by means of the Universal Carrier as was the case in the Field Regiments. But two tanks were also provided, one for each Battery Commander.

A limited number of Medium Regiments were equipped with the two types of medium gun, the 4.5-inch and the 5.5-inch gun. The former in one battery and the latter in the other.

During the last few years of the war, when quite a large number of Medium Regiments were set up, focus was shifted entirely to the 5.5-inch gun. Most regiments were equipped with this gun only, which of course implied many advantages, not least logistically.

Heavy Regiments had during the second half of the war four batteries. Two of them were equipped with the modernised vintage 7.2-inch howitzer, the other two had the modern American 155-mm gun ('Long Tom'). The Heavy Regiment had around 780 men, and thus was the largest type of regiment as far as the manpower size was concerned. The heavy guns all required strong six-wheel tractors/trucks, often of US manufacture.

Manpower and equipment specifications for the different types of regiment

Data on the principal types of regiment discussed are presented in the specifications in **Table 5-2**. It must again be stressed that organisational structures as well as equipment were changed many times during the war, and local adaptations had sometimes to be made to meet specific requirements. However, the illustration is deemed to fairly well represent the order of magnitude of the Royal Artillery resources. Manpower provided by other British Army Corps are included in numbers given.[89]

From this data we can see that the divisional artillery of an infantry division comprised around 2,000 men and 400 vehicles. This was approximately 10% of the division's strength, also as regards the number of vehicles.

In the presentation above communication equipment has not been included. Neither has it been shown how the communication function of the 'indirect fire system' was arranged. These aspects will now be presented in the following section with a Field Regiment as the basis for the discussion.

The communication function and equipment of a Field Regiment

When the regiment had been deployed after a completed march and was ready for firing, it was important to establish one or several communication systems as soon as possible. The indirect fire required communication between Forward Observation Parties (FOPs) and the gun positions in the first place. Troop Command Posts must thus be connected by means of telephone lines or radio to the Troop Commanders acting as FOOs in support of an infantry or armoured company near the front. The latter must also be connected with their Battery Commanders as to make it possible to arrange fire with more guns than those of their own Troops, in the first place all the eight guns of their own Battery.

The Battery Commander acting as Battalion Artillery Commander was to be connected to his Battery Command Post; and preferably also to the Regimental Headquarters and the Regimental Commander, who normally was acting as Brigade Artillery Commander in close contact with the Brigade Commander. At the next level upwards, communication with the Divisional Artillery Commander, 'CRA', and his Headquarters must be arranged. The CRA in his turn must be able to communicate with the Corps Artillery Commander, 'CCRA', and so on upwards.

Once this hierarchal communication function was ready, the foundation was established for concentration of fire on a specific target from a few guns up to not only the 72 of the regiment, but also from most guns of the Corps or even an Army, which meant several hundreds and even more. Douglas Goddard wrote about the importance of this communication system/function in 1944:

> There is no doubt that the tremendous firepower available to the FOO's was entirely due to the efficiency of the wireless communications at all levels.[90]

Which were then the resources available for making this happen? Basically the types of resource were four:

- Telephone lines and exchanges
- Radio networks
- Flags, signs, signal lamps, heliographs etc.
- Dispatch riders and liaison officers

The third method was in principle obsolete, but was sometimes successfully used as a complement to the others, for instance in East Africa, Malaya and Singapore. Some signals officers and signallers were always eager to establish some kind of back-up communication. But to become efficient, those using them must

Table 5-2. Manpower strength and equipment of regiments 1943–1945

Resource	Field Regiment (towed guns)	Field Regiment	Medium Regiment	Heavy Regiment (self-propelled guns)
Manpower, men	720	750	590	780
Number of batteries	3	3	2	4
25-pounder guns	24	24 'Sexton'	—	—
4.5-inch guns	—	—	8(0)	—
5.5-inch guns	—	—	8 (16)	—
7.2-inch howitzer	—	—	—	8
155-mm gun ('Long Tom')	—	—	—	8
Jeeps	21	21	16	13
Automobiles	3	1	3	3
Light truck (15 cwt)	43	13	37	47
Lorry 3 tons	29	30	30	36
Heavy lorry	1	1	1	1
Gun tractor, Quad	36	—	—	—
Gun tractor, Medium	—	—	18	—
Gun tractor, Heavy	—	—	—	36
Tank Observation Post	3	13	2	—
Universal Carrier	6	3	4	4
Armoured Car	—	—	—	4
Half-Tracks	—	46	—	—
Motor Cycles	31	38	24	30
Light Machine Guns	26	27	18	26
Anti-tank Gun (PIAT)	14	14	10	18
Anti-Aircraft Gun, 20-mm	8	—	6	6
Artillery ammunition (with the guns)	2 592 (108/gun)	3 216 (134/gun)	640 (40/gun)	240 (7.2.inch how), (30/how) 480 (155-mm gun), (60/gun)
Artillery ammunition (with ammunition group)	1 440 (60/gun)	912 (38/gun)	960 (60/gun)	208 (7.2-inch how), (26/how) 160 (155-mm gun), (20/gun)

Note. Data for the Medium Regiment is when equipped with 5.5-inch guns only. Source: War Establishment

have knowledge of the Morse Code.

The fourth option was often the only feasible when the technical options had broken down or if they lacked the necessary communication range. Weak communication during nights and under severe atmospheric disturbances could result in leaving the fourth option as the only feasible one. Large orders and fire plans could seldom be transmitted by any other method than application of the fourth option.

The two first mentioned options were to be used for normal firing communication. Telephone communication required normally own cables to be laid and kept in working order day and night. Permanent telephone lines and systems were normally not available in the field. The laying of cables was done by signallers on foot or from adequate vehicles. It was a dangerous job, in particular once the battle was under way. Equally dangerous was repair of lines damaged by enemy fire, tracked vehicles etc. Enemy patrols were another hazard. But also other, unexpected events could cause interruptions of communication lines. Peter Wilkinson MC has an example:

When Tudor [Troop Commander] first set up his O.P., he decided to lay a telephone line for better communication to the guns. He and his party with the Battery commander set out, laying line as they went. When they reached the O.P. however the line was dead, so Dennis [Battery Commander] left Tudor there and went back down the line with a signaller to find out what was wrong. When they reached the village, they discovered that a two hundred yard length of the line had been removed. Walking into the village, they noticed some washing hanging on a clothes-line of wire. Dennis saw red at this and stormed into the cottage, making it quite clear to the occupants that if they did not produce the rest of the wire they would be in serious trouble. The signaller fortunately spotted the missing length coiled beneath a pile of logs. So, after further threats of what might happen, they repaired the telephone line and all was well. A case of sabotage, probably unwitting.[91]

If the telephone lines worked, they were the best and most reliable communication alternative. Bur this was not always the case. The cables were normally laid direct on the ground, only occasionally hung up in trees and bushes or dug down. Hence they were regularly damaged by enemy artillery fire or own vehicles, to the regret no doubt of many tank commanders.

Those tasked with repairing the lines were also at high risk of being attacked. G.W. Robertson relates an example of this:

> For the first fortnight these [repair] parties were being sent out several times a day [. . .]. It was hoped that the breaks were caused by animals, but there was no proof. Consequently the line maintenance men would have to follow the line with caution – one eye on the cable and the other watching out for a Jap ambush. It was a very nerve-wracking business and although none of our parties were trapped at this time, those from other units in the area did suffer casualties from either Jap ambush or their fighting patrols. It was certainly the signallers who had the toughest time during the first weeks in action and they rose to the occasion and did a magnificent job.[92]

It was normal practice to double the lines if enough cable was available. Arranging a kind of meshed network was another alternative for establishing back-up communication. A Field Regiment normally brought some 25km of cable, to which came a large stock also from attached units from Royal Corps of Signals.[93] Hence, there was room for improvisation!

At command posts and headquarters the lines were connected to manual exchanges, the smallest for 20 lines and the largest for several hundreds.

An example of a regimental telephone network is illustrated in **Fig. 5-4**.

Radio was the principal artillery communication alternative when battle was imminent. This technology meant a revolution when compared with earlier wars. Thanks to this means fire concentrations could quickly be executed over a large area, even in mobile battles. The Royal Artillery took on the opportunities offered by the wireless technology early and was fairly well equipped when the war broke out. This was not the case as regards other arms.

Battle methods and procedures required the radio system to make communication all over the artillery hierarchy possible, but communication directly with units to be supported must also be established, as a FOO or an Artillery

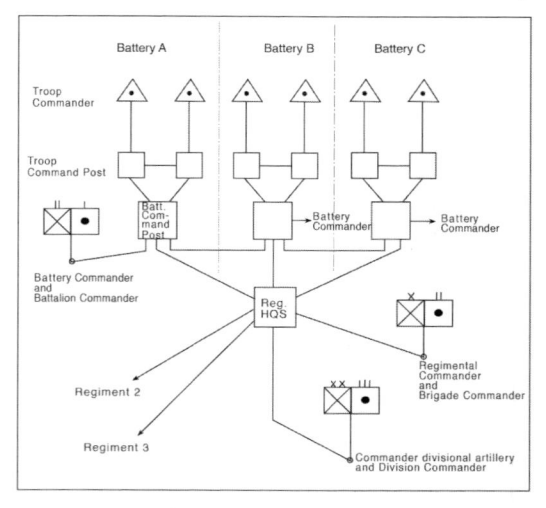

Fig. 5-4 It was always an ambition to establish a telephone network for the regiment. It was to be used for orders as well as for other purposes such as fire control. Seen here is a network for a field regiment, which is supporting an infantry brigade. The Commander of the regiment is Commander Royal Artillery in support of the Commander of the brigade. The three battery commanders are acting as artillery commanders for the brigade's battalions (Author)

commander could not always be on speaking distance to the commander of the supported unit. The gunner officer was keen to establish himself where the best opportunities for observation of potential targets were offered. If he supported an armoured unit he and his counterpart were moving in different fighting vehicles/tanks he also required to be in radio communication with the supporting unit.

The communication systems required wireless sets with different capacity and other characteristics. Radio technology was fairly new and many practical constraints were typical of the time (long before introduction of transistors and modern circuit technologies). The High Frequency (HF) band was almost totally dominant until the last year of the war when also Ultra High Frequency (UHF) sets were introduced on a small scale based primarily on American and German technologies. But there were exceptions to the general HF picture. As far as the artillery was concerned, one exception was communication with Army Cooperation Squadrons of RAF, which used the UHF frequency band for artillery reconnaissance and air support.

Observation Post Officers needed small and light devices, which could be easily carried when they were accompanying the infantry or armour. But this was at the expense of communication range. Longer ranges required heavier wireless sets with accompanying larger battery loads. This made installation in vehicles necessary; if not left at headquarters and gun positions. If the sets were needed where motor vehicles were not available for transport, it was necessary either to use mules or by manhandling of the device dismantled into several loads.

The general system of classification of wireless sets in the British Army had ten principal classes depending on where the sets were used. When two digits were applied, the first digit represented wireless type and the second the class. The digit 1 showed that the use primarily was within a brigade, digit 2 use at the divisional level or higher when the range was fairly short. For longer ranges the digit 3 was used. Lighter sets to be carried by one man was the class 8. Sets to be installed primarily in tanks and other fighting armoured vehicles were in class 9.

The Royal Artillery had two sets, WS No. 8 and WS No. 11, when the war broke out. The first one was planned to be a set to be man-carried also by infantry. The latter was too heavy for that and was intended for vehicle installation or a more stationary emplacement. Both were soon replaced by new types of equipment, although the No. 11 was retained by some artillery formations through the war. After 1942, the WS No. 18 became the standard set for Observation Officers' communication with commanders of units to be supported. For the communication within the artillery regiment and with higher formations the WS No. 22 became the standard set thanks to its longer range. It was however heavy and therefore it was installed in carriers or in static positions. When necessary, it could however be transported dismantled in several loads by three to four men. The No. 18 set could of course also be used by the regiment when its smaller range was sufficient.

For use in AFVs [Armoured Fighting Vehicles] the WS No. 19 was introduced during the war. It had capacity for longer ranges than the No. 22 and was therefore also used by some high level headquarters.

The No. 18 set was further developed during the war, for instance in Canada, Australia and United States with the objective to reduce weight or increase the communication range. British artillery was therefore to use also the No. 38, No. 48 and No. 68 sets. The latter was, for instance, used by the air-landing regiments.

Table 5-3. Key technical data for some wireless sets used by the artillery

Type No.	Transmission	Frequency Mc/s	Power W	Range km	Aerial Type
11*	R/T C/W	4,2–7.5	6	15–30	Rod 3m
18	R/T C/W	6–9	0.25	4–8	Rod 2m
19**	R/T C/W	2–8	12	15–30	Rod 2.4m
22	R/T C/W	2–8	1–1.5	15–30	Rod 4m
38	R/T	7.3–8.8	0.2	1	Rod 1.3m
48	R/T	6–9	0.25	4–6	Rod 2m
68	R/T	3–5.2	0.25	8–15	Rod 3.3m

*) Data for the strongest versions are presented here. Earlier versions had about half the power and half the range.

**) A more powerful version had 30 W of power and a range of 40–80km.

Fig. 5-5 The most common wireless sets used by the artillery, all operating in the frequency band 2 – 8 MHz. Range depended on type of aerial used.

WS No. 38 – Observation officers supporting armoured units and moving in a tank, normally used WS No. 38. Here is one version of this set shown (Louis Meulstee)

WS No. 18 – Standard radio for communication between fire observation officers and the commanders of infantry units to be supported. Observe the morse key. Another alternative was WS No. 68, which was used by airborne units in particular. With telegraphy the range was up to 10 – 15 km, with radiotelephone communication about half this range (Louis Meulstee)

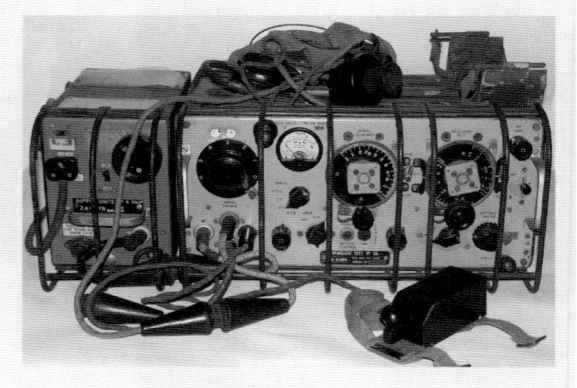

WS No. 22 – This set was standard within artillery regiments due to its fairly favourable range, 15–20 km with radiotelephone communication and 30–35 km with telegraphy. It was generally fixed into vehicles, but an observation party could act from a post 500–700 yards from the vehicle by means of a remote control devise. WS No. 19 set was a version that was the first hand alternative for AFVs (Armoured Fighting Vehicles). It was used by artillery formations equipped with self-propelled guns. It was also used for other purposes when its long range was needed, e.g. by airborne units (Louis Meulstee)

Some technical data for the sets used by the Royal Artillery are presented in **Table 5-3**.[94] 'R/T' means radio-telephony communication and 'W/T' wireless telegraphy. Range data are approximate as they depended much on terrain and atmospheric conditions. It was also dependent on whether communication took place during the day or during the night. Night communication was almost impossible in tropical areas particularly; this is due to lack of sky wave reflection. Another factor with great impact on communication range was the type and length of the antenna/aerial that was used, which was different for ground wave and reflected sky wave communication.

The portable smaller sets had a weight slightly under 20kg, the larger much more. As mentioned, the No. 22 set required 3–4 men to carry it dismantled. Extra batteries and sometimes a battery charger were needed when an Observation Post Party was to be away from the gun position for a couple of days. In such cases 8–10 men would be needed; besides the set and the batteries they also had to carry their personal weapons and belongings and in addition to that also food and water. Under difficult terrain and weather conditions such as those prevailing in Burma and Italy, the signallers indeed had a really tough job. If mules were at hand, the situation became much easier.

Fig. 5-5 illustrates some of the wireless sets most frequently used by the Royal Artillery.

Normal practice in an artillery regiment was to establish two types of radio communication net. One was the Battery net, which gave communication between the OPOs and the Troop Command Posts and the Battery Command Post. The Wagon Line could also be connected to this net. The No. 22 set was used; the No. 19 set if the regiment was equipped with self-propelled guns.

The Troop Commanders in the regiments of an infantry division were transported as mentioned in Universal Carriers in which the No. 22 set was permanently installed. As this vehicle often could not be taken close to the observation post, a remote control unit could be used. By means of this device, radio communication could take place 500–600 yards from the carrier.

The FOO used a No.18 set or a No.38 set for the communication with the infantry commander to be supported. Although the equipment was there, it was still often difficult to establish good communication from the observation post due to enemy fire and other means of interference.

From an observation post established by 2 Field Regiment RA during the battle in the Anzio bridgehead in Italy in January 1944, the following story is related:

> On January 30th, one of the infantry battalions which the regiment were supporting, came under extremely heavy artillery fire. The remote control cable from the artillery observation post to the wireless set was repeatedly cut. Bombardier Charles Ranks carried fire orders from the O.P. to the wireless truck. Several times as he crawled backwards and forwards shells landed within a few feet of him; several times he had narrow escapes from machinegun bullets. Twice he lay out in the open, mending the cable as shells and mortar bombs made the air hideous with noise and flying, whirling fragments. When, at length, the cable could no longer be mended he continued his message carrying.[95]

Besides the Battery Nets a Regimental Net for orders and firing was established (**Fig. 5-6**). As we can see, the three Battery Command Posts on this net were linked to the Regimental Headquarters. Sometimes a separate net for Administration and Supply could be established, this when equipment and frequencies were available. This was a good arrangement in larger mobile battles to secure supply of ammunition, fuel and other stores.

Skilled signallers often got the communication lines to work well despite technical constraints. One method was to use a number of extra sets as relay stations to bridge gaps in communication ranges. This could be accomplished automatically by connecting two No. 22 sets to each other, but oral transfer from one signaller to one or several others serving other sets was another method often used. Sometimes this required several steps. Lieutenant J-W. Widdicombe has the story of such an event:

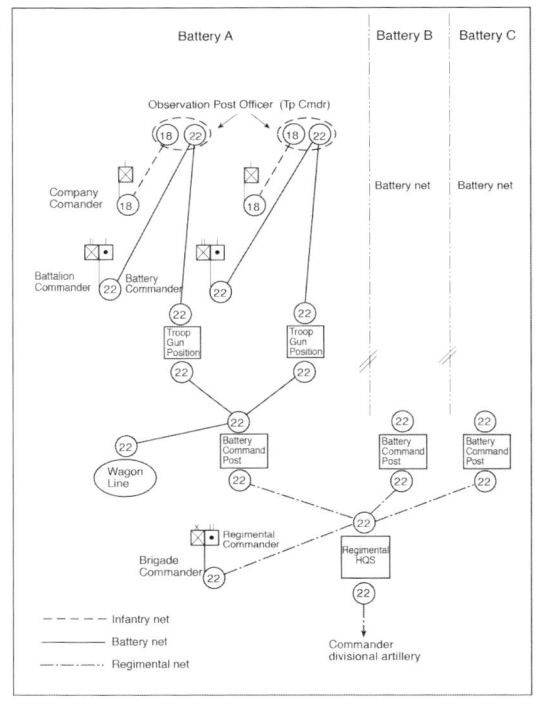

Fig. 5-6 Example of a regimental radio network. Normally, there was a unique battery network for each one of the three batteries and a regimental network for battery headquarters and the regimental headquarters, which could include a connection to the artillery commander of the division as well. Other artillery formations could also connect to this regimental network (Author)

Our Battery motto was 'Bash On' and soon we were beyond the town and in positions about three miles on. We had one interesting shoot from Teddy Thompson doing F.O.O. He sent down the map reference of a target out of our range but we were able to shoot a troop of medium guns who were well behind us. Sam Wilkinson and I were shouting orders from one wireless set to the other since we had shifted the sets out of the Command Post and into jeeps on the road ready to move forward. The orders were passed back to the guns through five wireless nets! (A number of sets operating on the same wavelength). The report of "shot one" from the 5.5-guns was reaching the F.O.O. long before the shell fell and that after being relayed through ten sets![96]

It is obvious that this type of improvisation would not materialise unless the signallers were skilled and well trained.

Shortage of nets and frequencies raised the demand for rigid voice discipline, and much training to maintain this. Standardised acronyms and codes etc. were gradually introduced to make telecommunication more efficient. In particular communication of fire orders and control of fire required a special nomenclature to speed up this type of communication and for avoidance of mistakes. Expressions and words used must be exactly understood and known by all. It is said that the Americans were not so strict on this and when, using one example, an American FOO said: '*Frank, you may fire when I tell you*', a British FOO in the same situation would give the command: '*Fire by order!*' when ranging had been completed. The order 'Fire for effect' would then follow. All concerned in the British unit knew exactly what the expression meant.

Identification abbreviations were for security reasons used for calls between sets, and these could be changed one or more times every 24 hours. In most cases they comprised three or four letters.

Frequencies were changed fairly often also for security reasons, although there was a general shortage of frequencies, which made changes difficult or even impossible during large operations with numerous formations involved.

A special standardisation in this context were the denominations of certain officers:

'*Sunray*' meant the officer in charge
'*Acorn*' was used when communication with the Intelligence Officer was requested
'*Seagull*' meant a high-ranked Staff/Planning Officer
'*Molar*' was called when communication with the Officer in charge of Administration was wanted
'*Sheldrake*' was the artillery commander or his representative at an infantry headquarters

At higher levels various types of cipher machine were used for strictly confidential messages about operational plans. At lower levels temporary coded words, names and orders were used to protect sensible information for shorter periods at least. In 1943 the Slidex system was introduced for improvement of security. It was a simple manual encoding system. The principle was to conceal expressions, names and numbers of units, names of places and commanders etcetera with a four-letter code. Cards were prepared for different types of military formation and activity such as artillery, plans and signals, engineers and so on. There were 12 x17 rectangles (204) on each card. The cards fitted into a frame with horizontal and vertical flanking cursors that were movable. By changing the cursor letters/keys and their positions a coded message could be devised. Keys were changed on army basis and normally at midnight, but it could be done more frequently.[97]

6. Looking Far into the Battlefield

The artillery regiments we have studied above all had good resources for delivering efficient support for the infantry and armoured formations. But the artillery also had the important task to prevent, or at least reduce, the enemy's artillery and mortar fire. This fire by the enemy made the own fighting more difficult and it could cause significant losses. This was not only a scourge for the infantry, but also for gunners. Colonel E.R.D. Palmer, who took part as a young command post officer in the evacuation of 27 Field Regiment RA at Dunkirk in early June 1940 (the battle of France is discussed in Part 3 of the book), has illustrated this in his account *Last Days at Dunkirk*, the Royal Artillery Journal, Vol. CXVII, No. 2, p. 19:

> At intervals during the next 40 minutes D Troop continues to be heavily shelled but it was in short bursts and very fortunately none fell sufficiently close to the guns while they were actually being fired to cause any further casualties. However it was an unpleasant time for the troop as they had only rudimentary gunpits due to the high water table and, from my command post 300 yards away, I quite frequently could see no sign of the guns as they were hidden by the smoke and dust from the bursting shells.

Well, this time it did not end too badly. The enemy probably could not direct too much of his resources against this target. Generally, counter-battery fire was very important for both sides. This type of artillery engagement was a prioritised task at the beginning of major operations. As much as possible of available resources were then concentrated. But in order to succeed finding the exact location of enemy batteries was a prerequisite, the same as regards his mortar deployments. Another prerequisite was well-deployed guns with adequate range. On the British side Medium and Heavy Regiments were the primary resource for counter-battery fire, but also regiments with light/field guns had always to be prepared to participate when possible.

The first resource for target acquisition and fire control was the Observation Post Officers (OPO) in the front line, this in cooperation with commanders of units to be supported. A problem, however, was that they normally lacked opportunities to look very far beyond the front line, to the terrain where enemy batteries were deployed. This became instead the role of the specific intelligence units established and equipped for survey deep into the battlefield. These supporting resources were as mentioned earlier in the book (Chapter 5) the following:

- Survey Regiments RA
- Army Cooperation Squadrons, RAF
- Air Observation Posts, RA/RAF

In the Survey Regiments three types of resource were at hand:

- Surveyors for geodetic work
- Sound Rangers
- Flash Spotters

The Surveyors had an important role when concentration of artillery fire was required over large areas and at long distances. Their methods are a matter of technology and procedures and this will later be discussed more in detail, when gunnery and tactics will be in focus. So, for now, we are leaving them and should just remember them as an intelligence resource. The two other resources of the Survey Regiment will be presented in this Chapter, but first let us look at the air resources available for target acquisition far beyond the front line.

Army Cooperation Squadrons, RAF
The Royal Air Force had a number of Army Cooperation Squadrons when the war broke out. Their role was primarily survey and air-photography. Later they were also to assume fighter-bomber tasks and were equipped for such a role. In 1940, there were five squadrons equipped with Westland Lysanders. This was a single-engine high-wing aircraft, which made its first flight in 1936 and entered active service in

1938. Besides the pilot, it could take one passenger/observer. It was manufactured in many versions; one is seen in **Fig. 6-1**. In total 1,786 aircraft were delivered to several air forces.

This aircraft was used for cooperation with the artillery, in the first place for intelligence tasks as the basis for planning of counter-battery fire. A special procedure for communication between the aircraft and the ground staff was introduced called Arty/R, 'R' for reconnaissance.

This procedure included ways to communicate during fire observation and – later – fire direction. It was, however, found to be difficult to do this, as it required close and adequate communication between the pilot and observer. Many have witnessed the difficulties and the thorough training that was needed for making it work efficiently. Some squadrons specialised in this, but generally speaking the fire observation and control tasks to be undertaken by the observer were not successful.

During the battle in France 1940, it was found that the Lysander was not up to the standard required. It was too vulnerable unless the RAF had gained air superiority, which was not the case in France. The aircraft was too slow and not swift enough to manoeuvre away from attacking enemy fighters.

Rearmament was necessary, and the Army Cooperation Squadron's Hurricanes were provided as replacement already in 1940. A bit

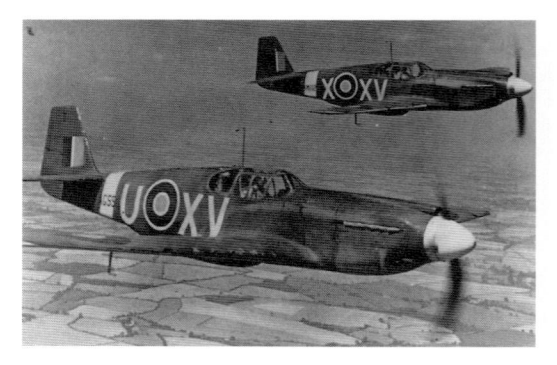

Fig. 6-2 After the Lysander several types of aircraft were tested, but it was not until 1941 a really good replacement was found. It was the first version of the American Mustang fighter. The 'XV' on the plane shows that this aircraft belonged to II Army Cooperation Squadron RAF (II Army Cooperation Squadron RAF via Hans Onderwater)

Fig. 6-3 Targets for artillery were surveyed by means of air photography. Contrary to the Lysander, the Mustang had a fixed oblique camera fixed to it just behind the pilot (II Army Cooperation Squadron RAF via Hans Onderwater)

later some squadrons got Spitfires and the first version of the American-built Mustangs. The new aircraft were single seat; hence the pilot must be trained to undertake the observation tasks himself. The Mustang is seen in **Fig. 6-2**, and in **Fig. 6-3** is seen its camera equipment for oblique photography.

The RAF Army Cooperating Squadrons played an important role during the war. Not least the fourth battle at Cassino in Italy in May 1944 was a good demonstration of the state-of-the-art, but they were still only a complement to the artillery's own resources. Other types of air observation resources were needed and this led to the creation of own resources within the Royal Artillery.

Fig. 6-1 RAF Squadrons for cooperation with the artillery were equipped with the two-seater Lysander aircraft when the war started. It was manufactured in several versions. When the fighting had commenced in May 1940 in Belgium/France, it was found that the aircraft was too vulnerable and unsuitable for this task (II Army Cooperation Squadron RAF via Hans Onderwater)

Air Observation Posts

The Counter-Battery Officer of the 17th Indian Infantry Division reported a mission flown by an Air Observation Officer on 23 March 1945:

> Evening sortie again with success. Flashes of two guns were seen at map ref 287363 and 288363 which compared favourably with HB 2836 JY originally fixed by Obs Sec at 28912 36200. A Div concentration was put down at 1900 hrs same evening, 88 guns fired scale 3.[98]

This is an example from the final phase of the war, when significant air observation resources were available, and the experience in their use also was significant. But the road to this status had been hard and lined with bureaucratic difficulties and lack of genuine interest at concerned decision-making levels.

A few artillery officers had commenced arguing already at the beginning of the 1930s for the Royal Artillery to acquire air resources of its own; resources that could communicate direct with artillery units and that could be deployed close to the guns. One of these officers was Jack Parham, one of the real innovators in the Royal Artillery, to whom we will come back to many times later in the book. He suggested as an alternative that autogyros should be used as air observation posts.[99] A test was made in 1935, which showed the alternative to be uneconomic and less effective.

The artillery officers interested in flying aircraft established the *Royal Artillery Flying Club*, where off-duty they could exploit their interest in flying. Here was the embryo of an own air observation organisation. When the war broke out, 100 officers with flying certificates were members. The Club Chairman was Brigadier H.R.S. Massy and Secretary Captain Charles Bazely. These two gentlemen and Parham argued intensively before the war for the establishment of 'Air Observation Posts' with pilot and observer being the same person; and – of course – he should be a Gunner! A small aircraft that could be based close to a battery was what was required. The plan implied that observation some 5–6km into enemy-held territory should be made. Observation further deep was to be the role of the RAF Army Co-operation Squadrons.

A formal decision was made in 1938 to undertake practical trials with an artillery air unit. The Air Ministry was strongly against the whole idea, which it regarded as impinging on its territory, and also warned of risks in splitting air resources between the arms. But in December 1938, the Ministry reluctantly accepted that trials were to be undertaken. The Air Officer Commanding the Army Cooperation Command remarked sourly: 'There is nothing new in this. An old horse resuscitated at War Office request. As long as they [RA] provide the bodies to be shot down, I do not mind . . .'[100]

The trials were successful and resulted in the proposal that 'Air Observation Posts' would be established permanently and co-deployed with RAF Artillery/Reconnaissance Squadrons. The 'Lysander' was unsuitable and a new light aircraft was to be provided. In the autumn of 1939 the organisational set-up was clarified. The RAF was to organise a number of AOP Squadrons with Gunner Officers as pilots.

The Cabinet had in November 1939, after the Chief of Imperial General Staff had strongly argued in writing that air resources under control of the Army should be established, found that '…it serves no meaningful purpose now to take up the issue as to whether the Army should have control over an air force of its own.'

This message calmed down those worried at the Air Ministry and RAF (it would last until 1957 before the Army got its own Army Air Corps). Trials could now be initiated with light aircraft of the Taylorcraft, Cagnet, Comper and Stinson manufacture. The trials were to be undertaken in England, but also at the Saar Front in France. A special unit (D Flight) was set up for the trials. The task was to find a suitable aircraft and a suitable organisation for Air Observation Posts. Amazingly enough some of the trials in France were to coincide with the German invasion in May 1940. The Flight narrowly managed to escape back to England on 20 May.[101] Two of the types of aircraft were found to be the best alternatives, the American-built Taylorcraft and Stinson. Both were high-winged, which made observation easier. A British firm, Taylorcraft Aeroplanes (England) Limited, had a licence to manufacture the former; and this was the aircraft selected.

After the retreat from France, RAF had other things to attend to. The invasion threat became imminent and one lost interest in the trials. Towards the end of 1940, the RAF wanted them totally disbanded. By intervention from

General Sir Alan Brooke (background as a Gunner Officer) this was however prevented. So, in August 1941 the very first AOP Squadron 651 RAF Air Observation Squadron was formed.[102] This and two other squadrons were planned to be equipped with Stinson aircraft, but this did not take place. During 1941 a new version of the Taylorcraft aircraft had been developed specifically for these first squadrons. This aircraft was the Taylorcraft Auster simply known as the 'Auster'. It was to be manufactured in several successively improved versions; in total 1,604 aircraft were delivered to British and Commonwealth Air Forces (**Fig. 6-4**).

It was to take more than a year before the new organisation was tested in battle for the first time. This took place in Operation Torch, the allied invasion in Northern Africa in November 1942. The person who made it happen was a very able man. It was Jack Parham, i.e. one of the pioneers, now Brigadier and Commander Royal Artillery of the 1st British Army. He took a personal interest in this test.

Several AOP Squadrons were under establishment and training in Britain at the beginning of 1943. A second squadron was ready for active service in March, the 654 AOP Squadron RAF, which was transferred to the front in Tunisia. The denomination 'AOP' had now been established as an acronym for 'Air Observation Post'. This type of squadron was now well established as an intelligence and fire control resource for the Royal Artillery. In parallel with provision of more squadrons during the war, tactics and methods were gradually further developed and improved. The flying gunner officers became more and more skilled to use their 'instrument'; they understood well when a single target like a gun or a tank was best engaged by one heavy gun or when the target was best engaged by a concentration of 600 guns, e.g. when a large enemy counter-attack was to be stopped. They also determined when the best fire alternative was engagement by ships of the Royal Navy. An extra-ordinary example of this flexibility took place on 17 September 1944, when the fire from the coast artillery at Dover together with the fire from huge railway guns destroyed several German coast artillery guns across the Channel, which was arranged in connection with a Canadian assault.[103]

When the organisation based on experience in battle had stabilised, a typical AOP Squadron could have the composition as is here illustrated with 656 AOP Squadron as an example; this squadron became operative on 31 December 1942:

- RA Officers (all pilots)   23
- RAF Officers (not pilots)   3
- RA Other Ranks   90
- RAF Other Ranks   80

i.e. in total   196 men

The emblem of this squadron is shown in **Fig. 6-5**.

The manpower was distributed in Squadron Headquarters and three Flights (A, B and C Flight). The latter were in their turn divided in Flight Headquarters and four Sections. A Section was commanded by a RA Captain/Pilot as was the Flight. The Section had one aircraft, which was maintained by technicians from the RAF. A signaller from RA was responsible for radio communication with the aircraft equipped with a No. 22 wireless set. For communication with the artillery regiment to be assisted a second set of the same type was used. The headquarters of the RAF Squadrons and Flights had the same type of radio communication equipment. In the Section there was also a gunner serving as Batman/Driver.

The AOP Squadron thus normally had twelve aircraft, but in some of them a fourth Flight was attached, i.e. the number of aircraft was increased to sixteen.[104]

Fig. 6-4 Fire control from the air became a more common method closer to the front than deeper into the theatre where the RAF Army Cooperation Squadrons operated. Air squadrons with gunners as pilots and at the same time fire observation officers used the Auster type of aircraft and were commissioned in 1942 (RAHT)

Fig. 6-5 The emblem of 656 AOP Squadron RAF illustrates the cooperation between the gunners and RAF (RAHT)

One could perhaps perceive a 'hybrid' formation of this kind, with manpower from both RA and RAF, to experience some 'frictions' between the two groups. This seems, however, not have been the case, on the contrary, many statements of the opposite can be found. Fighting spirit was normally remarkably good.[105]

The twelve – by and by – AOP Squadrons were together with the RAF Army Cooperation Squadrons the main resources available to the artillery as regards intelligence acquisition and fire control from the air. But situations appeared when the resources were not sufficient and some kind of improvisation was required. This was in particular the case in Burma, where the jungle often made direct observation on the ground impossible or at least very difficult. Airborne resources were therefore very welcome as a complement. London could not allocate more than one squadron to this theatre, 656 AOP Squadron mentioned above. Its twelve aircraft certainly could not meet the demand when the fighting was dispersed over a very large area. But in the 14th Army an innovative spirit was always at hand when difficulties arose. The commanders and their units were used to improvisation and keen to find local solutions to emerging problems.

A very valuable resource in this context was the US Army Air Force, which had a large number of Stinson L-5 light aircraft organised in Liaison squadrons. One of these was attached to each British Corps in Burma. The primary tasks were liaison flights and evacuation of wounded. Besides the pilot and a passenger the aircraft could transport one stretcher with a wounded soldier. The versatility of the aircraft gave it the nickname '*The flying Jeep*'.

A few British artillery units, amongst them 136 Field Regiment RA, which was one of the regiments of the 7th Indian Division, persuaded the American pilots and their chiefs to let them use the aircraft also for fire observation and control. Neither the pilots nor the gunner officers had any training whatsoever for this, so training and exercises were organised, and this with great enthusiasm on both sides! The pilots found this more advanced type of flying much more exciting than the daily duties as 'taxi and ambulance drivers'. And the Observation Post Officers indeed appreciated the much improved observation opportunities. The Artillery Commander RA of the 19th Indian Division also recognised the advantages and took similar steps. So, in parallel with the professional 656 AOP Squadron resources were created for fire observation and control from the air by means of, as they were called, *Amateur Air Ops*.[106]

Air observation units were Corps units and were concentrated in the European theatres of war. Normal practice was to attach one squadron to each British Corps and having its three Flights delegated with one to each division of the Corps. If an Army Group Royal Artillery (AGRA) was allotted to a Corps, this was normally also given an AOP Flight with four aircraft. But before all resources had been provided, it was necessary to make the best of the situation and allocate scarce resources to formations where they were most needed. Four AOP Squadrons were eventually allotted to the Italian theatre and seven to the Northwest European theatre. As mentioned, only one was provided in Burma; with normal practice four would have been given.

The light aircraft only required around 100 yards to take off, so a take off/landing strip of 250-300 yards was sufficient to find. Hence, it was often easy to deploy the aircraft close to artillery headquarters and deployed guns.[107]

It was often stressed that the pilots/observers must be skilled in their profession. Here is an example:

> On one urgent occasion a pilot carried out 5 registrations, all to verified short brackets, in one sortie. Subsequent shooting proved that all targets had been correctly registered. The value of a pilot who can shoot like this is out of all proportion to his flying ability.[108]

The Sound Rangers – the 'ears' of the artillery

When the Commanding Officer of 5 Survey Regiment RA in June 1945 summarised the activities of his regiment during the war, and in particular in Northern Italy, he wrote about his sound rangers:

> Conditions of weather and country on the Po plain were excellent; there were many guns against us and these two factors contributed chiefly to the large number of locations of a high order of accuracy the S rgs [sound rangers] have obtained. Whereas after the African campaign surveyors and gunners had doubts of the value of S rg, S rg has now proved itself to be of excellent value.[109]

Each Corps had one Survey Regiment RA which, when the war broke out, comprised three batteries besides its headquarters: A Survey Battery, a Flash Spotting Battery and a Sound Ranging Battery. During exercises at home in England and – in particular – under fighting conditions in North Africa it was found that this grouping often was not feasible. Each division needed resources of all the three types, and fighting over large areas made it difficult to have resources centralised into batteries of the aforementioned types. It was therefore decided, at first informally, and later during the war (1943) formally, to establish batteries comprising all three disciplines. These were known as Composite Batteries. Such a battery was then attached to a division. We will not here look into the process of change as such, but instead look into the technical means and procedures of the three disciplines.

It was not a new challenge to fix the location of the enemy's artillery. The methods and technology had been invented already during the Great War, but had of course since then been improved in the inter-war period. When the war broke out, the British had sound ranging equipment named S.R. Mark I and II. This comprised, as is illustrated in **Fig. 6-6**, 5-6 of microphones which were placed behind the front lines in locations over a width 6–8km, sometimes up to 10km, i.e. the distance between the microphones being around 1,500 m or more. The microphones were dug into the ground and were connected by telephone cables to the evaluation/plotting centre. One or often two observers were posted at Advance Posts (AP) about a kilometre in front of the microphone base. Their role was to activate the equipment at the evaluation centre when measuring was to take place. This was done by pressing a button at their end of a telephone line. The registration equipment could not stay switched on all the time but had to be activated, when required. Another important role on the part of these posts was to submit general tactical information about the activities of the enemy, not least the deployment of artillery and mortar units.

Serving in an 'Advance Post' (AP) was a risky undertaking. Certainly the idea was to get the post deployed well behind the infantry, but the front was not always clear and easy to identify. One could suddenly be surrounded by enemy patrols or attacking units. Jock Stubbs serving with 7 Survey Regiment RA tells his story of what could happen:

> The next morning the party set off. The halftrack was taken part of the way, and from there we began the climb to the farmhouse where the AP [Advance Post] was situated […] The farmer, his wife and family (four or five daughters from about 16 to a babe in arms) were in residence. There was no need for digging for we were able to use a spacious "hide-hole" which had been used during the occupation when the Germans came looking for labour for the land or for the factory. The cover over it had now been removed of course, and a little ladder led down to a vault lined with straw.
>
> As a novice AP man I was given training in the skills needed before my first stint. Any information about movement of transport, armour etcetera that might be useful had to be passed back. There were some enemy mortar and patrol activity. Each day the mortars went round their HF [Harassing Tasks] tasks, and our time came about 1040 hrs most days. Fortunately the farm house was not hit. It was some days before the

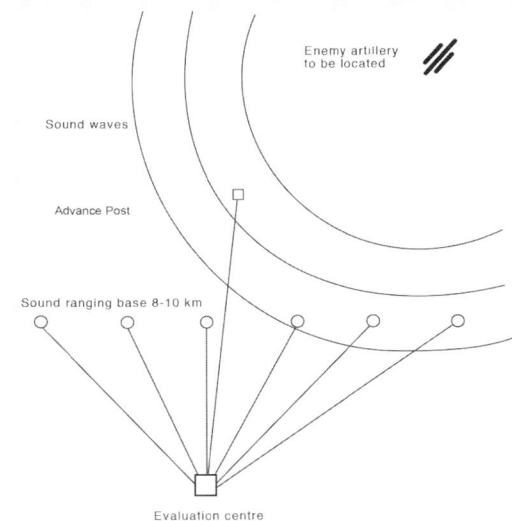

Fig. 6-6 8–10 hours were normally needed to establish a sound ranging base due to the extensive work required for building the necessary telephone lines. The microphones were connected to the registrator. The time difference between the arrival of the sound wave to the microphones gave the direction to the object to be located (Author)
Top picture: Advance post and base set-up

Below left: Six microphones (©Imperial War Museum NA 13030)

Below right: Evaluation of data and fixing coordinates of firing enemy guns (©Imperial War Museum NA 5246, NA 5249)

surveyors (at HQ) got clear enough readings to locate their positions and pass it to the gunners who signalled when fire was to be expected. As we squinted out of a side window it was just possible to observe the fall of shot. Satisfying!

A German patrol did pass within 20 yards of the post when Mr. Duncan (a visitor for the night) was taking an early watch, but I, asleep below, knew nothing of it, until he wakened me before alerting others. No more was seen of it, but some shots from the rear indicated contact with an infantry post. Thus passed our days at the Maas AP, till we tramped back down the way we had come after taking fond leave of the family.[110]

When the AP activated the registration equipment at the evaluation/spotting centre, the information was recorded on film. When the sound wave reaches the microphones a distinct 'click' and oscillation is recorded on the film, one for each microphone. Depending on the direction to the gun to be located from the microphones the sound wave will arrive to a pair of microphones with a time difference that is recorded as the time difference on the film between the 'clicks'. On a plotting board the directions from all the pairs of microphones are evaluated by means of a graphical method, normally called the hyperbola asymptote method.[111] The intersection between the plotted directions gives the location of the firing gun the AP observer had noticed.

The evaluation and plotting took some time

as the photographic film must be developed and fixed before becoming available for plotting. The sound wave was affected by weather conditions (temperature, wind, air pressure) and also the terrain characteristics. This made it necessary to correct the time difference recorded in order to determine the direction to the firing gun with acceptable accuracy.

The evaluation/plotting centre was normally located several kilometres behind the microphones, Connecting the APs and the microphones with the centre thus required extensive cable laying before any measuring could commence. Another time consuming preparatory activity was survey of the microphone locations to get these accurately fixed in the co-ordinate grid system used by own guns to be employed in the counter-battery fire. Taking all activities together the establishment of a working sound ranging base normally took 10–12 hours. If good topographical maps (Scale 1:25 000) were available one could start measuring a bit earlier subject to completion of line laying. But the accuracy was not always up to required standard in such cases. Final survey was essential in order to get accurate coordinates for all microphones.

An ever-lasting problem was to keep all the telephone cables in order. They were frequently damaged by enemy fire and tracked vehicles. Signallers must always, day and night irrespective of weather conditions, be prepared to go out and find line breaks and get them repaired as soon as possible. The risks for meeting enemy patrols was very trying and imminent. Jack Jobbit writes:

> Here my most uncomfortable experience was looking for a break in the line in no-man's-land during the night (the party comprised Capt Small, Sam Kemp and myself). We got to the forward infantry and told them of our intentions. Then we went ahead of them between the exchange of spasmodic bursts of small arms fire – very quietly toe-tipping along the grass verge of the road between ominous looking thick woods on each side. We found the line and fixed the telephone on. Now came the awkward moment. I'd got to give a buzz on that telephone when even breathing seemed to create too much noise. I waited for a burst of machine gun fire…it came – and I buzzed. Another wait for a burst of fire before I could speak. No answer! I breathed a sigh of relief, for that meant the break in the line must be further back nearer home.[112]

When a gun fired, three different types of sound could be registered. The first one was the signature when the shell left the gun, which was a fairly low-frequency dull noise. This was what the sound rangers wanted to record. The second type was the sound from the flying shell, which if it travelled in supersonic speed, produced a sharp, high-frequency sound, – the bow-wave sound. The third type was the sound of the bursting shell. Guns of different type and calibres produced different marks/'clicks' on the recorder's film. An experienced person at the plotting board could distinguish these differences from each other and thus determine what type of enemy gun that had been recorded; a valuable piece of information for the counter-battery office besides the location of the gun.

The Germans had not as much artillery as the Allies, but they had many mortars. The ordinary sound ranging equipment was not very effective in locating enemy mortars, although it was not impossible altogether. In the summer 1944 a new lighter type of sound ranging equipment was provided which was much more adapted to the task of locating mortars. It was the 4-pen recorder. Recording was made on a strip of paper and not on a photographic film. An electrical signal initiated by a mortar firing burned an oscillating strip on the moving paper. Without the need for developing and fixing a photographic film the paper strip could immediately be taken care of by the plotter. Evaluation thus could be speeded up. As mortars produced a sound with different frequency as compared with artillery, the microphones were equipped with filters adapted to this frequency, which prevented other battle noises to disturb the recording.

A microphone base for the '4-pen recorder' was shorter, around 1,500m and comprised only 3–4 microphones, which were located fairly close to the evaluation/plotting centre. This meant that a sound ranging base of this type could be ready for measuring within a couple of hours. The Army was provided with this lighter equipment during the autumn 1944 and into early 1945. Experience was very favourable, and it became a very good tactical complement to the traditional 'heavier' equipment. Further on in this book, I will call a base with the '4-pen recorder' a 'light' sound ranging base when not using the term '4-pen recorder'.

The accuracy in sound ranging was, as mentioned, affected by many factors. Correct survey for determination of microphone coordinates was one factor; another was the influence from terrain and its dispersing effects on sound waves. The weather conditions were of utmost importance also to have a firm grip on, as these affected the speed of sound waves and dispersion of waves. The sound rangers needed weather data to correct for deviations from nominal conditions. Data was delivered by a RAF metrological section attached to the headquarters of the Survey Regiment.

The enemy gun to be located must not be too far away from the microphone base. As a rule of thumb the British used to state that the maximum distance for location should preferably not be more than 0.6–0.8 times the length of the microphone base, i.e. 6–8km (the 'heavy equipment'). When all conditions were favourable this could, however, be extended.

A difficulty for all sound ranging programs was that the fire from own artillery could make measurement impossible. To avoid such problems, a pause was sometimes included in the fire plan for a short period. This could be an option, for instance, when the firing of an extensive barrage took place.

In order to give those concerned with counter-battery fire planning a better idea of the accuracy of the locations submitted, a classification system was applied by which the expected maximum deviations from correct location was given. The likely maximum deviation was:

- J 10 yards
- W 25 yards
- Z 50 yards
- A 100 yards
- B 200 yards
- C 300 yards
- D 400 yards

It seems that 'Z' was regarded as a kind of acceptable quality standard when using the traditional ('heavy') equipment.[113]

Radar – a new intelligence resource

An almost unfailing method for mortar location is radar by which the trajectory of the mortar shell from the firing place to ground impact is measured. The trajectory is near to a parabola curve and fixing it by recording one point in the upward part of it and one point in the descending part gives the mortar location with good accuracy.

This technology was to become available for the artillery intelligence in the last year of the war. Some trials had been undertaken already in 1943 with the anti-aircraft radar GLIII but without success. Towards the end of 1944 a new version had been provided by which the mortar location could be determined with an accuracy of 25–50 meters. The type classification was AA No. 3 Mk 2 (F), which is shown in **Fig. 6-7**.

Towards the summer 1945 it was finally concluded that radar was the technology of the future for mortar location. Work was thus continued on developing equipment specially designed for this role. Besides being a device for the field artillery, a version specially adapted for air-landing was contemplated to meet requirements of airborne formations. Experience from Normandy landings gave inspiration also for implementing radar on landing crafts. Radar could there, it was thought, be used for mortar location in the beach defence positions. However, none of these ideas materialised during the war.

'Flash spotting' – artillery observation bases

Firing guns and other heavy weapons had in all times been at risks of being revealed due to muzzle flash and smoke. In open terrain, as in the deserts in North Africa, this was a particularly serious problem. It was reduced to some extent when flashless propellant was

Fig. 6-7 During the final months of the war radar equipment was provided for location of enemy mortars. This is a GLIII radar originally developed for anti-aircraft purposes (RAHT)

Fig. 6-8 Cooperating observation posts established by Flash Spotting Troops and being connected in short- and long-bases were carefully surveyed and had to be concealed towards the enemy side. Besides observation theodolites telescopes were used as well (©Imperial War Museum NA 11823)

introduced, at first by the Germans. But it was not possible to avoid flash completely. Both sides therefore went on using bases for visual observation towards firing guns. This was done from observation posts well located and well surveyed in. It was an ambition to locate the latter at high places with good sight into the battlefield to facilitate observation. In Europe church towers or house attics were good for such location of observers. If this was not possible observers had to dig in and camouflage the post as best as they could for instance on a hill, ridge and the like. An example is given in **Fig. 6-8**.

Measurements were made simultaneously from a number of observation posts, normally four, sometimes five to six, which all had to be accurately fixed in the grid system. The base had a width of several kilometres, quite similar to a sound range base. The observers could have various instruments for recording the bearing to the flash of an enemy gun. Typically, *a Instrument Flash Spotting* was used, but also Telescopes. The former was a kind of theodolite (**Fig. 6-9**).

Sometimes 'directors' with their less accuracy could also be used; or even hand compasses. Measured directions to the enemy gun from the observation posts were reported on telephone lines or radio to an evaluation/plotting

Fig. 6-9 'Flash Spotting' was facilitated by means of accurate observation theodolites (RAHT)

centre. Here a plotting board with a coordinate grid was used. The intersection of the reported bearings gave the coordinates of the enemy gun/battery. An observation base of the described type was called *Long Base*.

If time was scarce, a simplified base with only 2–3 observation posts could be used as a start. Coordinates could be taken direct from a map, if it had adequate scale and quality. As soon as possible, this base could then be extended up to normal shape and standard with observation posts fixed by means of theodolite or 'director' survey. If so, enemy guns/batteries could be located up to around 20km from the observation base with an accuracy of 25–50m or less.

It was important to establish observation posts as high as possible, but high buildings and the like were not always easy to find. An alternative practiced by the British was high (10m or more) mobile towers made in sections or sometimes of telescopic design. These were transported on lorries and raised by means of, for instance, winches when deployed. In particular in North Africa and Italy, such towers were much used. An early example is seen in **Fig. 6-10**.

A graphic illustration of a 'Long Base' in seen in **Fig. 6-11**. Typically, the width of the observation base was fairly large relative to the measuring distance to the target. Another option applied was the *Short Base*. This used only a limited number of observation posts, normally two only, deployed quite near to each other. Hence, the observation base was short relative to the measuring distance. In order to still accomplish high accuracy the coordinates of the posts must be fixed with best possible accuracy, which required survey with theodolites; and bearings to targets must be measured with (binocular) theodolites and not directors. If so established and equipped a 'Short Base' could provide data on enemy gun locations with almost the same accuracy as the 'Long Base'.

A Flash Spotting Troop was included in the 'Composite Batteries' of a Survey Regiment RA. The troop was used for observations as described above. Again, it must be stressed that the 'Flash Spotters' were an excellent resource

Fig. 6-10 'Flash Spotting' was facilitated by means of high observation posts. Observation opportunities must always be balanced against the risk for enemy fire against the observation post (RAHT)

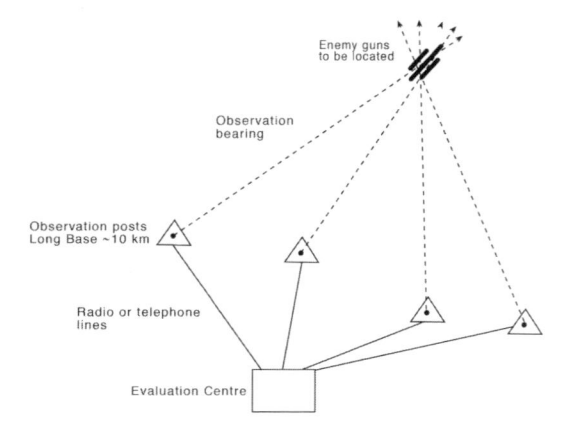

Fig. 6-11 Observation bases of the long-base type were normally established by the Flash Spotting Troops of the Survey Regiments. The bearing to the object to be located was determined by means of directors or observation theodolites. In order to make an accurate evaluation the participating observation posts must be carefully surveyed and their location determined with precision (coordinates) (Author)

also for acquisition and distribution of tactical information from the front such as movements and deployment of enemy infantry units, tanks, artillery, supply vehicles etc. The observation bases were also used for fire control in depth, when measurement towards high bursts (40–50m) could be made during ranging at distant targets. The same method was also used sometimes when fighting was very mobile and various artillery formations were to be fixed into the same grid and time for normal survey was not at hand. Another example of the versatility of observation bases is their use as a tool for calibration of guns, by which determination of deviations of muzzle velocities from nominal conditions could be accomplished (more about this later in the book).

Supporting intelligence resources were Corps units
We have now seen that the artillery could muster a number of different intelligence resources besides their own fire observation posts. Well-organised support from the Royal Air Force Army Cooperation Squadrons was also an option. So, it is not wrong to talk about a system of co-operating intelligence resources made available by the gunners. Correctly used, they provided necessary data for counter-battery fire against enemy artillery and mortars, anti-aircraft and anti-tank batteries but also data on other types of target in the depth of the battlefield. They also delivered tactical information to supported commanders, who often lacked possibilities to collect data easily with own resources.

Organisationally, the intelligence resources of the artillery were Corps units under the command of the Corps Commander Royal Artillery (CCRA). This was not only the case as regards the AOP Squadrons but all resources of the Survey Regiments. When the war broke out there were only four such regiments, 1–4 Survey Regiment RA, two of which were regular formations and two Territorial Regiments. When the Royal Artillery set up more and more field, medium and heavy regiments, the need for more survey regiments also came. The maximum number, eleven Survey Regiments, was achieved in early 1943.[114]

When the batteries that originally were parts of a survey regiment had been reorganised to become Composite Batteries, it became normal practice to attach one to each division, where they operated independently. By this arrangement a division had access to all the three types of discipline needed, i.e. 'survey', 'sound rangers' and 'flash spotters'. In the headquarters of the Survey Regiment RA a survey section was retained. Such sections were later up-graded to complete 'Survey Troops' by which 'Short Bases' could be established also centrally.

Before leaving Part 1, and its review of the artillery resources with which Britain went to war and created during the rearmament years, we will in the following Chapter 7 have a brief look at air-landing artillery of the British Army.

7. Airborne Artillery

Construction takes time
Peter Wilkinson, one of the pioneer airborne gunners, wrote to me:

> Towards the end of the course [OCTU], each of us was asked if we wished to opt to go into any particular branch of the artillery – coastal, heavy, medium, field, anti-aircraft, anti-tank etc [. . .] Keith had a brother who had been through Woolwich just before the war and was currently serving in a battery of Light Artillery which were, in effect, descendants of the old mountain artillery with their screw guns that had served on the north-west frontier of India. We felt that this was an interesting and exciting branch to go to and duly applied for Light Artillery. [. . .] In March 1942, having completed the course, we received our commissions. Carmel and I were posted to 458 Independent Light Battery RA and, after some leave, we joined the battery at their base near Newbury in Berkshire. We had heard rumours that the Battery had been selected to form part of the newly forming Airborne Division. When we arrived we found that this was the case. [. . .] A month or so after I joined the Battery, we moved to a new base at Bulford on Salisbury Plain where the rest of the embryo Airborne Division was located. Here our training to become an airborne force started in earnest. Apart from improving our skills as gunners we had to experiment in ways of being transported by air. We knew that we were to travel in gliders although the Horsa was not yet available. There were smaller gliders [most likely the Hotspur, author's note] and there seemed to be good supply of 'Dakota' aircraft for towing and loading experiments. Most of the officers and a number of signallers were sent on parachute courses as some would be expected to drop with the parachute infantry that they would be supporting.[115]

Yes, this is how it all started. Italy, the Soviet Union and Germany had already during the later part of the 1920s (Italy) and the 1930s begun establishment of airborne troops, and also to provide artillery for them. In Britain nothing happened in this field, however, and the country was 'caught napping' in 1940 when the Germans successfully used such formations, at first in Denmark and Norway and then in the 'Blitzkrieg War' in Belgium and the Netherlands. These units had, however, no artillery.

The German examples immediately triggered demands in Britain for establishment of something similar. Churchill requested his generals to create and train an airborne formation of 5,000 men as soon as possible. Later, in September 1941, a formal decision was made to establish a complete airborne division, the 1st Airborne Division as it was to be called. The very first field artillery of the division was Peter Wilkinson's 458 Light Battery RA, which in June 1942 was re-named to become the 1 Airlanding Light Battery RA.

In September 1942 a Commander Royal Artillery (CRA) was appointed and in February 1943 the 1 Airlanding Light Battery RA was extended up to the full size of a regiment. The 1 Airlanding Light Regiment RA was born.[116] The same method as the one applied when the Territorial Army was doubled was applied also here to raise the strength of the new Regiment. The only existing Battery was split into three Cadre-Batteries, which later when new officers and recruits had been provided became complete Batteries. Many of the recruits had only six weeks of basic training behind them.

The CRA with his tiny headquarters did not have the same status as the CRA of an ordinary infantry division. Although having command also over two anti-tank batteries besides the Light Regiment no major managerial or co-ordinating problems were anticipated. So, the CRA had the rank of Lieutenant Colonel and not Brigadier as in infantry divisions. This was changed in late 1944 based on experiences from Normandy and Arnhem, which I will discuss more later on.

Initially the vintage 3.7-inch mountain howitzers of the 458 Light Battery were used when waiting for something better to come. The

Fig. 7-1 The 75-mm mountain howitzer made in the USA was the standard howitzer used by the light air-landing regiments of the British airborne divisions. It is here seen when used by a mountain regiment in Italy. Re-supply of ammunition with the help of mules is going on (RAHT)

towing by jeep. There were a few more minor shortcomings to rectify when the Regiment, in haste, was ordered to move to North Africa in May 1943. By using spare guns the difficulties were overcome.

This howitzer was to prove its value in the coming battles, not least due to its longer range, about 9km. The vintage mountain howitzer had only a range of 4–5km, so this was a significant improvement. Another advantage was better ammunition with stronger impact effect. In the normal case the gun detachment comprised the howitzer with a towing vehicle, a Jeep, and an ammunition trailer. In addition to this a second Jeep with two trailers for ammunition and supplies were part of the gun detachment.

As Peter Wilkinson told us the plans were to have the Light Regiment transported in Horsa Gliders except for Observation Parties and some signallers, who were to be dropped with parachutes. Before the Horsas became available, training had to be performed with the smaller Hotspur gliders and other types of aircraft, but these were not capable of transporting of heavy equipment such as guns and Jeeps.

25-pounder was not an alternative as it was too heavy for transportation in gliders, and furthermore it was not available as yet in sufficient quantities. In the spring 1943 it was, however, possible to equip the entire Light Regiment with the American 75-mm pack howitzer mentioned earlier (**Fig. 7-1**).

When this gun arrived it was not yet adapted for airborne units. It still had for instance iron-clad wooden wheels. But they were immediately 'pneumatised' and were provided with means for

When the Horsa came it was big, in a double sense. This elegant glider could transport some 25 soldiers with equipment, and it could as an alternative take on-board an air-landing howitzer with its Jeep and trailer with ammunition. Net weight of the load was maximum 3,130kg. In

Fig. 7-2 The British Horsa was possibly the best glider in the war. It could a load of 25 soldiers. Alternatively a mountain howitzer with its tractor or other types of heavy equipment could be transported to the battlefield. Transportation of ammunition for the parachute units was another task for the Horsa (US National Archives)

total 137 rounds per gun were carried. If the formation was not to be transported a very long distance up to 242 rounds could be taken, but the ammunition Jeeps had to be left behind. The Horsa is seen in **Fig. 7-2**.

Transporting the whole light regiment with equipment and supplies would need 115 gliders. It was often not possible to get as many as that, so other transport alternatives also had to be devised. Once, it was requested that the regiment should use only 36 gliders, a completely unrealistic alternative. Less than 115 gliders meant that the regiment must be reduced. When the 1 Airlanding Light Regiment RA had arrived in Tunisia in May 1943, several transport alternatives were devised in detail including the adoption of load tables for every glider. By means of the latter any over-loading of a glider was prevented. Based on these tables standing regimental orders were prepared. The main alternatives are summarised in **Table 7-1**.

Table 7-1. Air transportation of 1 Airlanding Regiment RA

Alternative	Number of gliders	Units
A	87	Entire regiment with reduced equipment
B	69	Regiment with three six-gun batteries
C	62	Regiment except one battery
D	50	Regimental HQS plus two six-gun batteries
E	27	One normal 8-gun battery

Britain was to set up a second complete airborne division, the 6th Airborne Division, a process that commenced in early 1943. This division also had its own artillery, the 53 Airlanding Light Regiment RA. This was a converted anti-tank regiment, and was ready for action in November 1943. A third airborne formation was organised in India and came into action during the final phase of the Burma campaign.

Besides the Horsa a larger glider had been developed, the Hamilcar, which could carry a much heavier load, up to 8 tons. It could therefore transport the heavy 17-pounder anti-tank gun with its tractor or a light tank. Although it was not planned it could also transport a 25-pounder. This glider was available in a limited numbers, however. It lacked a nose-wheel, which often was a disadvantage when landing on rough fields. The risk for over-turning was great, and when it happened the consequences often were catastrophic, both for the pilots in the raised

Fig. 7-3 By the artist Terence Cuneo, this scene depicts an airborne assault underway during the Second World War. Note that Cuneo has included a number of General Aircraft Limited GAL. 49 Hamilcar gliders and Light Tank Mk VII Tetrarchs (The National Archives)

cockpit at the top of the glider and the passengers. A Hamilcar being unloaded after landing is seen in **Fig. 7-3**.

Both airborne divisions were to suffer from severe shortage of gliders in the operations to come. Ideally, a complete division should be transported in one lift only, or if a second was necessary, this should arrive the same day. The capacity for this was not available in the operations of 1943 and 1944, it was only so for the first time in the final major airborne operation of the war, the Rhine Crossing in March 1945.

In an operation the gliders were allotted two to three separate landing zones where the terrain was open, preferably with fields without ditches. Of course also the parachute formations were to be dropped in open terrain, if possible. To speed up unloading of the Horsas the tail section was removed after landing, if possible just before the glider had reached its final standstill. A later version of the Horsa was designed for unloading at the front after the cockpit section had been opened and turned to the side.

The light artillery regiment was expected to be ready to fire at 360°, immediately after landing and re-assembling.

The landing zones could look quite chaotic with all the gliders scattered around as can be seen in **Fig. 7-4**. This photograph was taken by an AOP pilot in Normandy, in July 1944.

Fig. 7-4 The shortage of gliders was for long a major problem. When the 6 Airborne Division was landed in Normandy on D-Day, 6 June 1944, only one of the three batteries of its light artillery regiment could be landed from the air (RAHT)

One would expect an airborne division to have three field artillery regiments as the ordinary infantry division. Certainly, this should have been the case but it was far from possible at the time. The regiments had been able to organise and train, but the necessary transport capacity was not available, far from it. Instead the airborne division had to rely on support from other artillery resources on the ground and – sometimes – the guns of ships of the Royal Navy.

Tactically, the airborne division was to land and capture territory, bridges etc, of strategic importance and hold it for a few days only with its own resources until other attacking formations could reach the area and relieve, or at least support, the air-landed troops. It was furthermore anticipated that the artillery of the relieving formations would be deployed within range of the bridgehead to provide supporting fire as early as possible. But in order to facilitate such support more FOOs were needed.

The solution adopted was the creation of special observation units called Forward Observation Units (FOU). Two of them were established in 1944, the 1 and 2 Forward Observation Unit RA for employment in North West Europe and a third one, the 3 Forward Observation Unit RA, was organised later and deployed in Italy. All three were strong and comprised a commanding officer with headquarters and three sections, each one with six FOOs. A section was to support a brigade attaching one FOO team to each one of the three battalions of the brigade, one to be kept as a reserve. The remaining two were to be used as liaison detachments at the brigade headquarters with the task to operate radio communication with the artillery of the approaching formations.[117] 60 men of the FOU were dropped by parachute or landed with gliders together with formations of the airborne division.

This method for reinforcing the brigades of the airborne divisions worked well in Normandy, but as we will see later it was not a complete success at Arnhem, for several reasons.

We have now briefly reviewed the field artillery resources of the airborne divisions, but before leaving this subject it must be stressed that the airborne divisions, besides the Air-landing Light Regiments RA, also were supported by a large number of anti-tank guns and mortars in the parachute and air-landing infantry battalions, a most valuable direct support as many books about the battle at Arnhem illustrate.

Air-transported artillery another option

During the war, methods for 'air transportation' of ordinary ground forces were also developed. This was not the same as 'air-landing' for which only 'air-borne troops' could be used. The transport as such was not part of the battle technique and tactics, but a means for deploying ground forces from one geographic area to another, where they were to operate as usual. For this purpose ordinary types of transport aircraft were to be used, and not gliders. However, much training was needed to make air transport a versatile option and this applied to the artillery in particular.

An infantry division preparing for battle after air transport was the 52nd (Lowland) Infantry Division. In this Scottish division the three Field Regiments 79, 80 and 186 Field Regiment RA constituted the divisional artillery. The two first mentioned were TA-regiments and the latter a new regiment established during the war (ready for operation in December 1942). A mountain regiment was attached as well, 1st Mountain Regiment RA. Major Walter J.M. Ross commanding a battery in 80 Field Regiment RA tells us how the artillery prepared itself for a role as 'air-transported' regiment.[118]

Until 1944 the regiment had acted as other field regiments equipped with 25-pounders. But:

> On Tuesday morning everyone at MONTROSE was told on a muster parade that the Division was to prepare for Air-transportation to a still undisclosed theatre of operations: The aircraft to be used were DAKOTA C 47, with a payload of 5000lb, and a man with his kit was to be taken as weighing 248lb. More would be known on the return of the G.O.C. from the War Office, and meantime, officers were to be earmarked for a short course at the Airborne Training Development Centre, AMESBURY; but nothing was to be discussed outside billets or mentioned in letters. The C.O. then left by car for HAWICK to break the news to 317, whose Bty. Comdr's lively curiosity had already been whetted by cryptic signal messages orienting him that something was in the wind.
>
> On 29 June the problem was expounded in greater detail. The role of the Division was twofold:
>
> Role A: To be landed by air in enemy occupied territory. In this operation 186 Fd. Regt. RA were to be flown in armed with 3.7 [-inch] howitzers, followed, if necessary, by 80 Fd. Regt. RA also armed with 3.7 howitzers. If 80 were not required to go by air, they were to go by sea, at assault scale, armed with 25 pdrs.
>
> Role B: To be landed by air behind our own forward troops. In this operation both 186 and 80 were to be flown in armed with 25 pdrs.

The vintage mountain howitzer was something new for the regiment (**Fig. 7-5**). They received four guns for quick training from 3 Mountain Regiment RA.

Now an intensive program for training and adaptation for the air-transportable role with 25-pounders also commenced. The regiment constructed 'mock-ups' of Dakotas with the right dimensions and placement of the loading doors. Loading ramps were made for attachment to the doors with the correct angle. The 25-pounder could not be loaded in one piece; it had to be 'stripped'. The shield was removed as was the platform and certain other pieces to make it less voluminous. This was also necessary in order to get the right weight distribution inside the aircraft.

It was heavy work indeed, to load and lash the gun and then to unload it. But practice gave muscles and the right handling. According to the regulations the whole procedure was not to take more than 25–30 minutes, i.e. to dismantle the gun, load and lash it, and then to reverse it all and restore the gun to one piece after unloading. Most of the gun crews, thanks to enthusiastic work, managed to get down to 17–20 minutes after many exercises.

The gun crews also had to acquaint themselves with Jeeps, a new type of vehicle for them. Their usual 'Quads' were too big and heavy for air transportation. These had to be taken by sea transport together with the rest of the regimental heavy equipment. In replacement of the Quads the regiment was given 100 Jeeps to be used as gun tractors after landing and transport of a first-hand stock of artillery ammunition, com-

Fig. 7-5 One of the armament alternatives for formations preparing for air transportation to a battle theatre was an adapted version of the old British 3.7-inch mountain howitzer (RAHT)

munication equipment, weapons for local defence, personal kit etc. So, now the gunners had to practice driving and loading of the Jeeps, and, not the least, to get them loaded into a Dakota. This too, required much training, which was not out of problems for the gun crew and the aircraft.

Detailed loading tables had to be prepared to ensure that all necessary items of equipment were taken and that there was no overloading or dangerous distribution of weight. These tables specified the positions where all men, irrespective of rank, would sit in the aircraft and how much personal kit they could take.

Besides basic gunnery training and later firing practice with the mountain howitzers new procedures and standing orders for reconnaissance and deployment had to be worked out. The first regimental firing exercise with live ammunition took place a couple of weeks after the training had commenced, and the result was good. The air-transported gunners-to-be felt ready to go into battle, but they still had to wait for it. Hence, the training programme continued up to August 1944, as were various improvements to get the regiment even more fit for fight. As the regiment must be ready also for a seaborne assault, this had to be prepared as well. But this alternative the regiment felt well acquainted with. It had been practiced numerous times in Scotland long before the air-transportation alternative emerged.

Now, how were the 52nd (Lowland) Division and its artillery to be engaged in real battle? Well, I will come back to that later in the book.

Part 2
Gunnery Methods, Procedures, Tactics, Staff Work

8. How to Hit the Target – Technical Gun Characteristics

To hit the target, gunners must master:

- The internal ballistics of the gun
- The external ballistics of the shell
- The geodetic relation between the gun and the target

First, we will now have a look at the two first-mentioned aspects.

Internal ballistics
When discussing the movement of the shell through the barrel and the velocity of it when leaving the muzzle we are talking about the *internal ballistics*, often also called the *interior ballistics*. The most important factors affecting this ballistics are:

- Weight of projectile and fuze
- The rotation of the projectile imposed by the rifling in the barrel
- Length of barrel
- Wearing of barrel
- Size and composition of cartridges (propellant) and thus the chemical energy released
- The temperature of the propellant, which also affects the energy
- Vibrations of the barrel
- Loading force when the shell is inserted into the barrel

As seen, some of the factors are unique for each gun, whereas others are the same for several guns, for instance of a battery to which certain batches (consignments) of shells and propellant had been supplied. It would then be natural to assume the same weight of shells from such a batch for all guns of the battery and, similarly, the same temperature for charges taken from the same batch.

Upon ignition of the propellant a rapidly increasing gas pressure is built up which pushes the projectile through the barrel accelerating it up to its maximum speed. Once the projectile leaves the muzzle the driving gas pressure instantaneously drops to zero. Part of the gas pressure is sometimes used to dampen the recoil by means of a 'muzzle brake'.

External ballistics
The trajectory of the projectile would be close to the parabola if no air was present and the elevation of the barrel would then determine the range. Maximum range would be reached at 45° elevation. Reality is, however, more complicated. A number of factors have an impact on the trajectory, such as:

- Shape and weight of the projectile including the fuze
- Rotation of the projectile
- The earth's rotation
- Air pressure
- Air temperature
- Wind direction and strength along the trajectory

Range Tables were available for all types of gun and the different types of ammunition to be used by those guns. Basic data such as muzzle velocity, elevation, trajectory peak, range, impact angle, flying time and much more of nominal data could be retrieved from the tables. But the gunners also needed to know the magnitude of influences on the trajectory due to deviations from nominal data, for instance various weather data, in order to calculate necessary corrections of aiming data needed for hitting the target. When it comes to wind speed the nominal value was 0ft/s, but if the wind was 30ft/s obliquely from left or right against the projectile, it would be necessary to know exactly how to make corrections for that. This could be done by means of information from the 'Range Tables'. The projectile is affected by meteorological deviations at all heights throughout its trajectory and the problem is to determine the significant deviation and its level. Ideally this should be determined just when the projectile was to fly towards its target.

Weather data could be collected at various heights by means of a small balloon, the route of which was monitored by means of a theodolite, (**Fig. 8-1**). This function was performed during the war for the Royal Artillery by Mobile Met Units of the Royal Air Force. This was developed and improved initially by attaching such a unit to HQRA at Corps and one each to the Survey Regiments and AGRAs. Later improvements saw units attached down at divisional levels.[119]

The weather data was collected for the various heights every four hours using a theodolite to record the bearing and angular height to a met balloon after a set time. From 1943 and onwards also radar could be used for tracking the balloon. Recorded data were presented in a met telegram, which was distributed to all artillery regiments and headquarters in the relevant battle area. When a particularly important ranging was to take place a special 'met telegram' could be provided as near as possible to this in order to get up-to-date and accurate weather data. When the battle at El Alamein was prepared 'met telegrams' were provided every 30 minutes. Yet, sudden and local changes of weather conditions often remained unrecorded.

Weather data were also collected by aircraft, which often was a very valuable complement to ground data.

Declining muzzle velocity a scourge

The projectile's range was affected by muzzle velocity, which in turn is very dependent on the degree of the wear to the bore of the barrel. A decline of the velocity was inevitable when the numerous rounds had caused barrel wear. If this reduction was, for instance, 5% this implied a significant reduction of the range that must be compensated. A problem to be encountered was the lack of instruments for measuring the decline in the muzzle velocity. The wear as such could be measured, but what it meant in reduced muzzle velocity was not obvious. The method adopted was to undertake calibration shoots. These were made against a target well defined geodetically, i.e. well-known coordinates were at hand. Other factors influencing the trajectory were also to be recorded as accurately as possible, leaving the muzzle velocity as the remaining unknown variable. Such calibration shoots could be done for one gun only or for many, for instance all of a regiment. In order to make it easier special 'calibration troops' were organised by the Royal Artillery. They had guns with well-defined muzzle velocity for comparisons. The guns to be 'calibrated' fired at the well-defined target as did the gun(s) of a 'calibration troop' and impact differences were measured and used for velocity corrections, which were done on the range marker of the gun. Hence, the calibrated velocity could be used as a known, fixed quantity, in the target data calculations leaving fewer factors to be corrected for the calculation of the gun laying data. See **Fig. 10-1** and **10-3**.

In peacetime calibration was seldom necessary due to the limited number of rounds fired in exercises. No significant barrel wearing took place. In war the situation was completely different, which if not dealt with correctly, could imply serious deviations from the planned point of impact. The 25-pounders were the guns suffering least from the problem, more critical it was for medium and heavy guns. One of the Gun Position Officers of 112 (Wessex) Field

Fig. 8-1 Acquisition of best possible weather data along the trajectory of the shells was always important. Recording the route and speed of a balloon by means of a thedolite was the principal method to get wind data needed. The method applied during the war remained also after the war as this image illustrates (RAHT)

Regiment RA, Douglas Goddard, related that his 25-pounders fired around 15,000 rounds per gun from landing in Normandy 1944 to the end of the war in May 1945 and yet calibration was undertaken only once in this period. It took place just after the breakout from the Normandy bridgehead and the advance northwards was halted at river Seine at the end of August 1944.[120] Other batteries it must be said were calibrated more often.

As the deviation of muzzle velocity from the nominal values of the 'Range Table' was one of the most critical factors affecting the trajectory of a gun it was always a matter of constant observation. Calibration was never neglected in battle pauses or when units were withdrawn for recovery, if needed. We get an example in the War Diary of 69 Medium Regiment RA for 29 October 1942 at 17.45 hrs when the battle at El Alamein still was raging:

> From 1400 hours when not firing at targets Regt fired calibrations shoot from pivot gun of each troop in conjunction with 4th Survey Regt. Data from this shoot proved that the average loss of M.V. since the offensive started was 55 f/s. The necessary adjustment to the sights was made.[121]

From this example we can see that the barrel wearing of a medium gun could be considerable after one week of continuous fighting only. It has been stated that calibration shoots were to take place every three days for these guns.[122]

The problem occupied central authorities throughout the war and various policies were implemented. The voluminous shooting during the war resulted in empirical data on the relation between measured barrel wearing and the decline of muzzle velocity, which were added to the 'Range Tables' as valuable pieces of information in the field. By means of this data it was possible to make adjustments to the gun sights also between formal calibration shoots.

As a policy it was later decided that every regiment was to have at least one gun, called the standard gun, which should be well calibrated all the time. The other guns of the regiment could use this one for comparative shootings. It was furthermore made clear that the commanding officer of the regiment was responsible for this arrangement, and he was also to make sure that his battery commanders really undertook calibration shootings regularly.

Several factors of influence could be determined at the gun position, but not all of them. The difference between chemical energy of different batches of propellant was unknown at the gun positions. It was also difficult to get a grip of the impact of extreme air humidity, which for instance was a big problem during the monsoon periods in Burma. To 'keep the gunpowder dry', this good old rule was not always easy.

Range Tables provide information on trajectory physics

As mentioned the 'Range Tables' are rich sources of data on the physics of the trajectory of guns firing various types of ammunition. With the 25-pounder as an example we will have a look at the magnitude of the impact caused by variations in nominal data. First, a list of the latter given for Charge 3:

- Muzzle velocity: 1,450ft/s (442m/s)
- Air pressure: 30 inch Hg (762mm)
- Air temperature: 60°F (15.6°C)
- Wind velocity: 0 ft/s (all directions relative fire)
- Propellant (Cordite) temperature: 60°F (15.6°C)

Now, if other values were applied what did it mean to the change of the point of ground impact, or in other words: what will the range be as compared with the one achieved under nominal conditions? **Fig. 8-2** illustrates the deviation as a function of nominal range for the following variations of nominal values:[123]

- Muzzle velocity: -100 ft/s (-30.5m/s)
- Air pressure: -3.0 inch Hg (-76.20mm Hg)
- Air temperature: -20°F (-11.1°C, i.e. 4.4 °C absolute)
- Wind straight against the shell: +30 ft/s (+9.1m/s, i.e. 9.1m/s absolute)

The graph clearly indicates the importance of checking the degrading of the muzzle velocity. Weather data should also be recorded as up-to-date as possible; otherwise the shells might descend far away from the target, in particular when the range is long. The wind was often hitting the shell from an acute direction, or across it. Such wind directions required correction not only of the range but also the firing bearing.

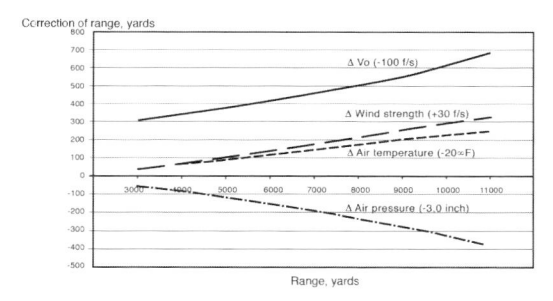

Fig. 8-2 An illustration of various factors influencing the shell trajectory of a 25-pdr firing high explosive shells with Charge 3. As an example, if the range to target is 10 000 yards the gun must be aimed for the range 10 600 yard if the muzzle velocity has declined by 100 ft/s through wearing (Author, data from Range Tables Part 1 for QF 25-pdr Guns, Mark I and II, 1944)

In the first place corrections to meet adverse conditions were calculated. The combined result of all corrections was called Correction of the Moment (CoM) and could as seen in **Fig. 8-2** have a high impact, in particular along the firing bearing. Even if the calculations have used the best possible data there was often a remaining uncertainty. This could be determined only by means of shooting and correcting the ground impact of the shells towards the target; this was called ranging, which we will come back to later in the book.

It is understandable that the staff working in Troop and Battery Command Posts had to cope with a hectic situation when they had to make lots of calculations of corrections, in particular when the situation changed dramatically or when huge fire plans for numerous targets had to be prepared. In order to make it a bit easier calculation procedures had been standardised and appropriate data forms provided.

Fire dispersion unavoidable

Even if extensive calculations had been made it did not imply hole-in-hole ground impact of the rounds fired. If one single gun fired a large number of projectiles without change of the gun's elevation and fire direction a dispersion pattern would be observed. Normal probability rules gave the shape of the area within which the projectiles hit the ground. The distribution within this area followed standard statistical models. To make it easier the Royal Artillery gave the dispersion length for 50%, 82%, 96% and 100% of the projectiles, **Fig. 8-3**[124] and **Fig. 8-4**. Similar

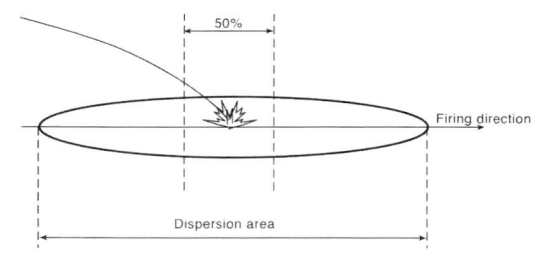

Fig. 8-3 If a number of shells are fired against the same aiming point they will on hitting ground be dispersed over an area as illustrated. Range Tables provide information on the size of the area within which the shells will fall with 50% probability. This is given along the firing direction as well as the size straight across this. As indicated, the latter is normally much smaller (Author, data from Range Tables Part 1 for QF 25-pdr Guns, Mark I and II, 1944)

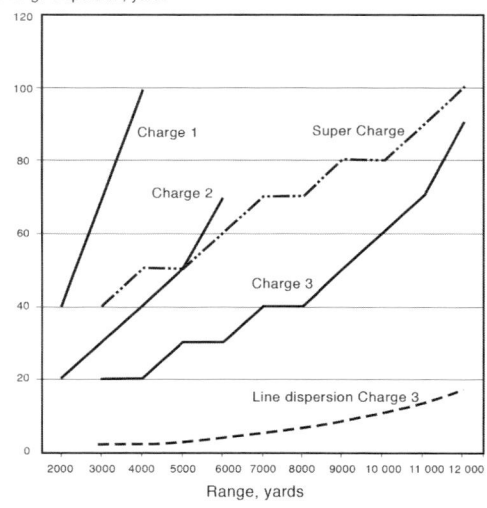

Fig. 8-4 The size of dispersion at various ranges for a 25-pdr Gun for different Charges. For Charge 3 the dispersion across the firing direction is indicated. Observe that Super Charge implies bigger dispersion than Charge 3 due to its less elevated trajectory (Author, data from Range Tables Part 1 for QF 25-pdr Guns, Mark I and II, 1944)

errors also occurred in the line of fire and the two patterns were called Probable Error Range and Probable Error Line respectively. If doubled these measures gave the whole dispersion area and they are given in the Range Tables. The graphs of **Fig. 8-4** have been prepared by using data for different charges.[125]

When observing the nature of gunfire dispersion it is realised that fire from a large number of guns towards the same geographic point would be dispersed over a fairly large area, the shape of which was affected by the deployment of the guns and the difference between them in terms of range and line. Artillery of the time was not a precision weapon but a wide-area hitting weapon. This was both an advantage and a disadvantage depending on the tactical situation and thus had to be taken into account when the best battle technique had to be applied.

The following data illustrate in approximate numbers the size of the area within which planners had to expect the fire to be effective:[126]

- · Troop 100x100 yards
- Battery 150x150 yards
- Regiment 250x250 yards
- Divisional artillery 350x350 yards
- Divisional artillery + an AGRA 400x400 yards

As we will see later it was not always a matter of having all the guns aiming at the same spot. Battle techniques and the tactical situation could make it more appropriate to take advantage of the system characteristics and spread the fire, from for instance a number of batteries or regiments, over a larger area or along a line target by having the guns to aim at different points/coordinates in a controlled manner. Instead of the normal practice to have the guns of troops or batteries to fire with parallel barrels the fire from them could be more concentrated or spread out by means of individual aiming data. There were indeed many options! Skilled and innovative gunners did not want to get into a rut.

Tactical advantages of different charges and fuzes

As if it was not enough with options for variation of the location and area of the fire impact, opportunities for changing the trajectory profile were also included in the tactical 'tool box'. This could be done by firing with different charges.

Most guns with a calibre less than 105mm were in Britain called Quick Firing Guns (QF), a term introduced already in the last years of the nineteenth century. It implied that the gunpowder (propellant) was contained in a brass cartridge case. Before firing a number of propellant filled bags were placed inside the cartridge case. Each 'Charge' had its number of bags. In order to reduce the risk for mistakes the bags had different colour. The projectile was first rammed into the barrel and then the cartridge case was inserted before the breech was closed. For certain guns such as the modern anti-tank guns the projectile and the cartridge case was loaded as one entity.

When rammed into the barrel the driving band of the projectile fitted into the rifling of the barrel by which it would rotate upon ignition of the propellant. Another purpose was to prevent any gas leakage between the barrel and the projectile. Besides being a container for the propellant bags, the primary role of the cartridge case was to prevent gas leakage backwards through the breech, which for the QF 25-pounder was of the sliding block type. For ignition the case was fitted with a base primer.

The first versions of the QF 25-pounder had as we have seen three different charges and a fourth came later, the Super Charge. The latter became available for the first versions once these guns had been equipped with a muzzle brake and was used for extension of the range, but could also be used when the gun was in an anti-tank role firing directly towards enemy tanks with armour-piercing projectiles. The need for firing in elevations above 45° (upper register) in mountainous terrain as in Burma and Italy, made it necessary to introduce not only a revised carriage but also additional charges, intermediate charges, often called just incremental bags, which were added to the base charge. With these the 25-pounder could use seven different charges, i.e. it was a real 'gun-howitzer'. This was typical for howitzers and gun-howitzers. The old QF 3.7-inch mountain howitzer could use up to six charges. Several versions with different types of breech existed during the war.

The medium and heavy guns were classified as Breech Loading Guns (BL) the propellant cloth bags were not contained in a brass case but were inserted directly into the barrel once the projectile first had been rammed into position and obturation forwards had been secured. To prevent leakage backwards the breech was of the screw type with interrupted threads. A special primer was used for ignition of the propellant. The BL 5.5-inch gun-howitzer used four charges.

During the war many different types of propellant were devised. Various types were tested in

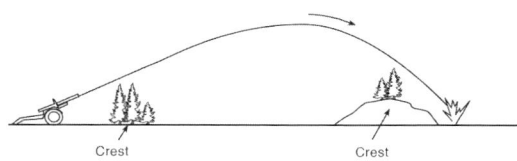

Fig. 8-5 When planning firing one has to select an adequate charge so that the shell does not hit any hindrance in the upward part of the trajectory, neither in the downward part of it. Such a hindrance could be buildings or some trees behind which a concealed deployment has been made (Author)

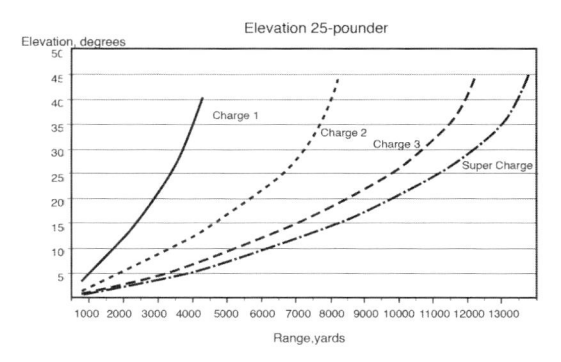

Fig. 8-6 Elevation for different charges of a 25-pdr Gun as a function of the range to the target (Author, data from Range Tables Part 1 for QF 25-pdr Guns, Mark I and II, 1944)

order to find optimum relations between the chemical composition and released chemical energy per weight unit, rate of burn, etc. Different additions to the propellant for reduced barrel wearing and muzzle flame were tested as well.

The reasons for using different charges in the field were twofold. First, it made it easier to conceal the guns after deployment behind trees, hills, and buildings etc., thus preventing direct observation from the enemy side. It was then necessary to select a charge that made the trajectory pass over the obstacles taking into account the distance between the guns and the obstacles. Similarly a steeper trajectory with higher descent angle could make it easier to avoid obstacles near the target (**Fig. 8-5**). A steeper trajectory required higher elevation, which in its turn required a lower charge. This meant a shorter range, which could be a trouble tactically.

The other reason for using different charges was related to the impact of the projectile. A trajectory with higher descent angle could be an advantage if the enemy was dug down in trenches or the like. Again, this called for a low charge number. In other situations a flat trajectory was preferred, even if the range was reduced, for instance when the gun was used in an anti-tank role or when fire against bunkers or other types of fortification was required. The former situation was quite common in North Africa before replacement of obsolete anti-tank guns had taken place. The latter situation was not an unusual task for the gunners in Burma.

Fig. 8-6 illustrates the elevation of a 25-pounder as a function of the range. As can be seen various charges can be selected if the range to the target is, say, less than 7,000 yards, but above 10,000 yards only Charge 3 and 'Super Charge' could be used, the latter giving the maximum possible range. It should be noted that normally only some 20–25% of the projectiles supplied in the field could be fired with the highest charge, 'the Super Charge'. This was a factor not to be overlooked when planning for an operation and deciding where to deploy the guns, particularly not in mobile battles. Artillery out of range due to lack of appropriate stock of charges when needed is useless!

Now turning to types of bursts and how these were accomplished by means of various fuzes. See **Fig. 8-7**.

When the war broke out there were not many different types of fuze to consider. Shrapnel shells with their type of fuzes had been removed from service in the middle of the 1930s. They were replaced by 'High-Explosive' shells that, upon bursting, gave a large number

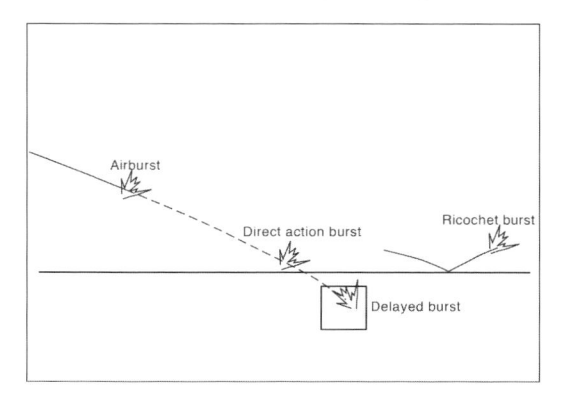

Fig. 8-7 By means of different fuzes and the setting of these the shells can be brought to burst as is best in respect of the tactical situation. Percussion fuze, which implies direct impact burst when the shell hits the ground, were most commonly used (Author)

of very sharp splinters over a wide area. The detonation took place when the projectile hit the ground. This was accomplished by using a fuze called 'Direct Action Percussion Fuze'. As illustrated it happened that best effect was reached when the ignition was delayed a little, for instance when the enemy took shelter in bunkers or other types of fortification with a roof preventing the enemy from being hit by splinters if the burst took place at ground impact. The fuze for this was called 'Graze Percussion Fuze'. This could also be used to get airbursts if the descent angle was small enough to make the projectile ricochet upwards after hitting ground. It required a fairly flat and hard ground surface.

It was soon realised after having fought many battles during the first years of the war that the effect of bursting projectiles would be much better if the burst took place above ground, say 8–10 m up for a 25-pounder. This required another type of fuze, which caused the fuze to ignite the shell after a pre-planned flying time. This was accomplished with the 'Time Fuze'. Three types were provided, one with a burning igniferous train that ignited when the shell left the gun. The burning time was set before firing and took into account the range to target and the required height of the burst. Another type used a mechanical clock, which was set to provide ignition after the set time. A third type was developed during the war, but was not available until the last few months of the war. It was the 'VT' fuze, or 'Proximity Fuze', which had a small 'radar' device, which ignited the shell when the fuze registered the proximity of the ground. 'VT' stands for 'Variable Time'. This was the most accurate type of fuze for airbursts, but again, it arrived too late to have any significant impact on the few remaining battles.

When an OPO/FOO wanted to fire airbursts he had to take into account the unavoidable dispersion along the trajectory, this when the 'Time Fuzes' were applied. During the first years of the war it was considered to be too complicated a task on the part of young OPO/FOOs with less training to control and direct the fire in three dimensions which delayed the supply of such fuzes to the field units. But at last, in November 1941, deliveries started.[127] Gradually the interest for these increased. Not least the Canadians who were eager to avail themselves of the opportunities provided. The difficulties on controlling and directing air burst fire were dramatically reduced when the 'VT' fuze came during the last few months of the war.

As mentioned the dominating shell was the 'HE' shell which besides its charge for fragmenting it into sharp splinters also carried some phosphorous material to create a small white cloud of smoke, which could facilitate observation of the fire. In addition to the 'HE' shell there were others, the armour-piercing projectile already mentioned. Another one, which was used frequently, in particular during the battles of the second part of the war, was the smoke projectile. Less frequently used were projectiles creating artificial light or dispersion of propaganda material over the positions of the enemy. For these special types of fuze were needed. A gas projectile had also been introduced, but it was never used during the war.

Development of ammunition during the war was an ever-ongoing process and it was a large number of different propellants and fuzes that were devised.[128] A few of the fuzes most commonly used were the following:

- No. 117. Direct action percussion fuze, which were the standard for 25-pounders when delivered from factories
- No. 119. Percussion fuze with graze options
- No. 210. Time fuze
- No. 231. Similar to the previous but specially designed for 'bouncing' (ricochet) bursts
- No. 213. A combined percussion and time fuze. Time function was based on a mechanical clock mechanism
- No. 221. Fuze designed for special projectiles and which had a time function based on a burning gunpowder string
- T 97. Proximity fuze ('VT') designed for the 25-pounder and the 3.7-inch mountain howitzer
- T 100. Proximity fuze ('VT') designed for the 5.5.-inch gun and the 7.2-inch howitzer

Time fuzes with mechanical time function were preferred as they implied less dispersion along the trajectory when firing 'HE' projectiles. But they were more expensive than those using a burning string. But the latter were good enough for smoke and other special projectiles, as these were not dependent on the same accuracy as the

Fig. 8-8 The selected fuze and its setting (fuze length) determined whether the burst should take place above, on ground impact or below ground level. Fuze keys were used to attach the fuze to the shell and to set the time to burst (fuze length). Such a key was on display at Royal Artillery Museum (No. 9) (Author's collection)

former. Even more costly were the 'VT' fuzes with their superior accuracy. Evans tells that 2/3 of the bursts were at the correct height after ranging when using the fuzes with mechanical time function and up to 90% when firing with 'VTs'.[129]

The possibilities to fire high air bursts against points with known coordinates became a popular method to bring different fire units into the same grid when the battle was very mobile and good maps were missing. This was the case when Eighth Army rushed westwards in pursuit of Rommel after the battle at El Alamein in October/November 1942.

One gets, however, the impression that use of percussion fuzes for direct ground impact was by far the dominating method throughout the war. Hence, the potential of firing airbursts with their superior effect on the enemy seems to have been much neglected.

For gun crews the use of different fuzes always required strict observance, and needed special handling when the standard fuze was not to be used. For instance when a time fuze was ordered the correct flying time to the burst above ground must first be determined by means of a Fuze Indicator. Correct flying time was then to be fixed on the fuze using a Fuze Key. Such a key can be seen on **Fig. 8-8**. The method was improved during the war and later a special Fuze Setter was introduced. This was so designed that exactly the same flying time could be fixed for all projectiles to be fired.

After this short review of technical aspects of gun firing and the ammunition applied it would perhaps be most logical to look at gun laying and how this was done to secure target hits. We will however first look at another prerequisite for target hitting, the geodetics required for determining and fixing the geographic relation between guns and targets, which must be accomplished and this in three dimensions.

9. How to Hit the Target – Geodetic Requirements

Good maps a must

A first question is related to maps, grid systems and bearings etc., i.e. what for hundreds of years has been the profession of surveyors. In the British Army the responsibility for this rested with the Corps of Engineers [RE]. Their primary task was to provide good maps for the fighting units wherever in the world they had to fight. Either own maps were produced, as was the case in the British Empire, or maps were acquired from authorities in other countries and adapted to meet British requirements. The latter was applicable for Italy and France who had modern national maps of their own.

Britain standardised map scales for the Army around 1936 as follows:

- 1:250,000 for planning and high-level command of operations and transports
- 1:100,000 for tactical planning and command of mobile operations, in particular for armoured units
- 1:50,000 for ordinary planning and command of operations
- 1:25,000 for artillery fire planning and control

The classic British map scales, ¼ inch to the mile and one inch to the mile were much used as well, in particular within the British Isles.

The Gunners had chosen the 1:25,000 scale as standard as it was sufficient for giving gun deployments and target locations with sufficient accuracy for firing without ranging. The requirement for this was a maximum radial deviation of 15 yards.

The maps should preferably be in four-colour print with elevation curves inserted. As it was to be shown this was quite often a problem. Another problem that sometimes occurred was that heights could be given either in feet or in metres, which could be confusing if not properly observed. Aerial mapping could give reliable data but was a scarce resource during the first years of the war.

Maps as such were not enough. All military activities, not least those of the artillery, required fixing of locations by means of grid coordinates. No universal grid (reference) systems existed at the time. A grid system covering a large operational area, a theatre grid, was always preferred. The RE's ambition was to introduce such grids on all maps, but it was not always possible. In particular during the first years of the war it was often necessary to use local grids, sometimes without any. In Egypt, for instance, before the final battle at El Alamein in 1942 two different grid systems existed, and far to the west none existed. Fortunately the boundary between the two systems was east of El Alamein, but some mistakes occurred from time to time when two different systems had to be used for location data.

If no grid system existed, or was not available for any reason, when the Gunners were to fire their guns, it was necessary to establish a grid as soon as possible for the establishment of correct geodetic relations between gun deployments and targets. This was built from the lowest levels, for troops or batteries, and was then gradually extended to become a regimental grid. And from this level it was always important to extend this to be used by all artillery units within the divisional area, a divisional grid. Sometimes, even a corps grid could be devised.

The Gunners had methods and procedures to change from one preliminary grid system to a permanent one, once this had been made available. Locations for the guns and targets could be corrected using these coordinates. Sometimes this also included a slight correction of the 'North' direction.

Which 'North' to use?

A correct grip on geodetic relations also required that bearings could be correctly determined. This in turn required that the difference between various 'North' were known and correctly observed. These normally were the following:

- Meridian North, i.e. the circle through the terrestrial poles, *True North*

- Magnetic North, i.e. the magnetic northern pole
- Grid North, i.e. the northern direction of the grid system

As is well known the 'Magnetic North' is changing all the times. The deviation (m) from the 'Meridian North' is normally given in maps and is not only changing by time but is also different depending on where on the earth you are located. During the war 'm' was quite big on the British Isles, around 10°, whereas in Burma it was not more than around 1.5°. In the fire plan for the large allied Rhine Crossing in March 1945 the 'm' was given as 5°.

When devising new grids for operative use it was an endeavour to make the difference between 'Meridian North' and 'Grid North' as small as possible, normally 0°–1.5°.

Deviation from 'Meridian North', 'True North', was given as 'western' or 'eastern'. In calculations it was important to know whether the deviation was positive or negative. But was it important to observe the deviation? Certainly it was!

If the Gunners at the Rhine Crossing had not observed the deviation the fire would have hit ground some 400 yards from the intended impact point (target) when the firing range was as moderate as 5km. The fire of the medium and heavy guns with their range of 10–20km would show an even more destructive dislocation. This illustrates the need for good procedures, including control functions, when it comes to the technical gunnery requirements.

If you had the 'correct' north somewhere, how to get others to get it too? Well, there were several methods. Most important was the traditional survey methods.

Traditional survey again honoured

The most important methods for establishing correct geodetic relations between two locations were:

- Triangulation
- Traverse
- Astronomic bearing fixing
- Simultaneous measuring towards a celestial object

Astronomic determination of a bearing was normally done by means of a theodolite or a sextant, which could be done in daytime towards the sun or during night towards a star such as the North (Pole) Star. Calculations were quite demanding but were a routine for experienced surveyors.

Simultaneous measuring towards a celestial object could be done by Gunners, as well as by surveyors. Where directors (an instrument like a theodolite) were available, as was the case at the gun deployment areas and often at observation posts, this was a practicable method. When applied, for instance the course of North Star across the sky was followed by those taking part in the process. The director that had the correct bearing, which was to be transferred to the others, was leading. Once all, who were in connection with each other by means of telephone or radio, followed the star they were at a certain exact moment ordered to stop following the movement of the star. The leader then informed the others in which bearing their director now was fixed. To be sure the measurement could be repeated a couple of times.

Good maps with grid systems inserted gave a good picture of geodetic relations between guns and targets by using coordinates, but it was not always possible to determine the coordinates with sufficient accuracy. Fixing the grid relations between different gun deployment areas from the maps only was not always possible either. Other methods were necessary.

Fixing more exact coordinates for the gun deployment required survey. The first question was where to commence the survey, the starting point. It was normally the responsibility of RE to provide exact coordinates and a sample of bearings at a number of trig points, sometimes called just trigs, from which the artillery surveyors could start transferring data to the gun deployments by means of the survey methods mentioned above. 'Trig points' were often presented as a network of many such points which had been fixed by Ordnance Survey or RE through the classic survey method, triangulation.

The principle of 'triangulation' is based on the fact that if one side and two angles of a triangle are known, the two other sides of the triangle can be calculated by means of elementary trigonometry. When this has been done a new 'trig point' has been fixed, and the process can continue with an adjacent triangle for fixing of another 'trig point' etc.

The surveyors preferred locations at heights, ridges etc., which were visible over large areas. The 'trig points' were marked with a piece of an iron pipe or a concrete pole in the ground. In the field trig points could be marked also with a special beacon tissue to increase its visibility from long distances. An example is shown in **Fig. 9-1**, although it is post-war photograph.

If good maps were available and objects that easily could be identified such as road junctions, bridges, churches etc., 'trigs' could be fixed without triangulations. An example when this was possible was the Normandy invasion. In preparation of this a cluster of trig points was printed on maps for the whole area (see Kirkman papers, RAHT).

These 'trigs' supplied by the RE surveyors formed the starting point for the artillery surveyors for their own schemes. As mentioned above, one Survey Regiment RA was attached to each Corps. These regiments also had qualified survey personnel and the necessary instruments, including theodolites. The latter can be seen in use in **Fig- 9-1**.

The task of the surveyors was the establishment of a common grid for the artillery units to be engaged. They were to provide correct bearings when such were not available otherwise, called Orientation, and, which was the most common task, to survey the Battery/Troop positions as accurately as available time and enemy actions made possible. Determination of coordinates was called Fixation.

The resources were not sufficient enough to survey every single troop or battery, not to say the single gun. What they could do was to fix a single point near the guns, a Bearing Picket, where the artillery regiment's own survey groups could themselves proceed by traverse and fix coordinates for a Bearing Picket near their guns and also bring forward to this a true bearing to be used in gunnery calculations. The surveyors would leave a card at the Bearing Picket giving the true bearing to one or several easily identifiable points, such as buildings, church towers, a single tree, a power line pole etc. The correct co-

Fig. 9-1 When artillery units were surveyed into the same coordinate grid the surveyors from a Survey Regiment started from a so-called trig-point with well-defined and accurate coordinates. Bearings to reference objects, which were well identifiable, could here also be provided. The data were brought to regiments and batteries, observation posts etc. by means of different survey techniques. A beacon was placed at the final control point called Bearing Picket (BP). A BP Card gave the coordinates and reference bearings. From this accurate data were brought to the unit through survey by the unit's own staff. This post-war image illustrates the procedure, which was used also during the war (RAHT)

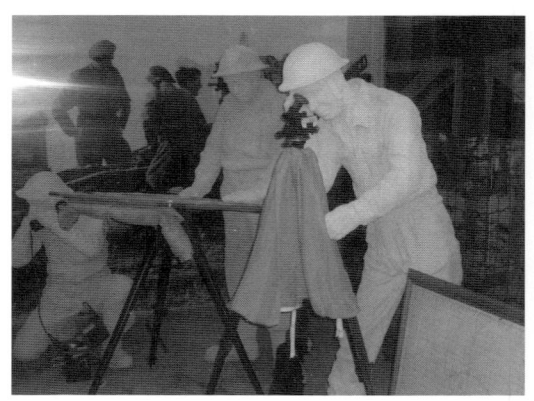

Fig. 9-2 Battery staff used a 'director' for surveying the location of troop deployments. This instrument was also used when the guns were to be aimed into the zero line with parallel barrels. The procedure was illustrated in Royal Artillery Museum (Author's collection)

How to Hit the Target – Geodetic Requirements

Fig. 9-3 The distance of the legs of traverse were preferably measured by means of a measuring string or wire (AWM No. 0944306)

ordinates were also given on the card.

In the regimental headquarters and in the battery headquarters too, survey groups were attached who could undertake the final survey as indicated. These groups were normally using directors and not theodolites. The former was a less complex survey instrument with lesser accuracy than the latter, but it was sufficient for survey close to the guns. A version of this instrument, a Director No. 7, used by a Gunner was shown at the Royal Artillery Museum, (**Fig. 9-2**). The method to carry a bearing from one place to another within a regimental or battery deployment area was traverse by means of 'directors'.

Traverse in this context means that angles are recorded at various positions in the terrain and bearings calculated starting with the bearing at the first point of the traverse polygon. The distance between measuring points is measured also, using either a measuring tape or line or by pacing, i.e. counting walking steps. **Fig. 9-3** gives an example.

When applying an open traverse, bearings are recorded for each leg of a polygon. An alternative is a closed traverse measuring also the way back to the starting point, which is undertaken as a control of the traverse. These principles are illustrated in **Fig. 9-4**.

In view of the importance of correct orientation the data from the survey scheme to the BP needed to be self-checking. This could be accomplished using a second team working on a line close to the first team, this was known as Parallel Traverse. It could also be done by combining the polygons of two close, but independent, schemes to produce the BP data by having the two polygons to cross each other a couple of times. The number of small closed polygons thus accomplished gave further check points. This method was known as Diamond Traverse. In both cases the location and orientation data for the BP card had to agree within fine tolerances, if so the scheme was then 'closed'.[130]

Sometimes coordinates could be fixed also by means of Resection or Intersection. The former method implied measuring the bearings to three or four objects with known coordinates from the position with unknown coordinates. The crossing of the measured lines on a map or an evaluation board gave the unknown coordinates. This method was often used in the deployment area of own units.

The latter method, 'intersection', implied measuring the bearings from a few of positions with known coordinates to the position to be fixed. Again, the intersection of the bearings gave the unknown coordinates. This was the natural method to be used when positions outside own deployment areas were to be fixed, for instance targets.

Finally analysis of air-photographs was another method to determine exact location of

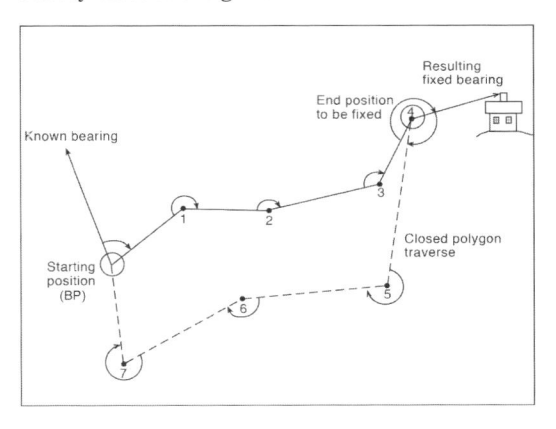

Fig. 9-4 Known coordinates and bearings presented at the control point (BP) by the Survey Regiment were carried forward by means of a traverse using a Theodolite or Director. The instrument was used for measurements of angles by the regimental or battery survey resources to batteries, observation posts etc. where accurate survey data were needed. In order to get the results of measurements checked and mistakes avoided, the traverse was often closed as the picture also illustrates. The distance between the points where the instruments were placed had also to be measured as accurately as possible (Author)

targets beyond the front line such as enemy gun positions.

Target acquisition – the most difficult task

Each infantry or armoured commander would be accompanied by an officer and an observation party from the supporting artillery unit. On contact with the enemy, the Gunner officer's task was to identify and locate the enemy position in order to bring down immediate protective fire. Maybe the enemy fire was coming from several positions, or from a cluster of farm buildings, or from a section of the woods, or anything else. The Gunner officer must quickly relate the enemy's ground location to his map and pass that data to his guns in preparation for providing the supporting fire for the ensuing attack, but how? The coordinates must be fixed and communicated to the gun position. It was not a good idea to ask the infantry commander. He rarely could tell. If anybody could, it was the Gunner. He had followed the advance on the map and had a brief knowledge where the advance had been stopped, but a more detailed 'map reading' was necessary to find the exact coordinates. In most cases he only had his compass and binoculars as help, but he could also be assisted. Occasionally his observation party had an optical instrument for measurement of distances, a rangefinder, which could be used as a complement.

Map reading was one of the fundamental skills that the Gunner officer had to learn and master. This involved determining the correct coordinates of targets quickly and frequently when exposed to enemy fire and foul weather conditions. Johnny Walker told me that, during his first service as 2nd Lieutenant, he was drilled in this art by his battery commander. At any time during an exercise he could get the question from the commander: 'Can you see the big oak over there? What are the coordinates? If one could not provide the correct answer an extra exercise in map reading after the normal work on Saturdays was imposed.'[131]

Map reading in North Africa was particularly difficult because of the lack of distinguishable terrain formations and similarly in Burma's close jungles. It is easy to understand that the impact of artillery fire could be completely wrong under such conditions.

Under more stationary conditions map reading could be complemented by other means for fixing targets or potential targets. First of all it was a matter of getting a good overview of the coming fighting area. Besides the personal binoculars and hand compass instruments like a director, observation binoculars, a rangefinder or a theodolite could be helpful. With these the Observation Officer could fix coordinates for important terrain objects and potential targets etc., and document the data on a panorama sketch. Intersection from cooperating observation posts was another method, often used. These could be manned by the Observation Officers of the batteries but could also be posts manned by the Flash Spotting Troops of Survey Regiments.

Targets were of course also to be located deep into the battlefield beyond the reach of human eyes. This required observation from RAF aircraft or by gunner officers in Air Observation Posts (e.g. Auster aircraft); but also by means of such methods as sound ranging and, during the final phase of the war, radar.

Despite all instruments and elaborated methods accurate target acquisition was not always possible to accomplish. In such cases only one additional method remained: ranging of artillery fire to fix the exact target location. We will come back to this later in the book.

How to deal with geodetic relations at the gun positions?

As discussed above, the geodetic relationship between the guns and target had to be established correctly in order to hit the target but the coordinates for these two locations had to be from the same grid system. But how to get projectiles fly between the two points determined?

At first the firing bearing from the Troop or Battery position must be determined and then the range to cover. This could be done trigonometrically when the coordinates were known. At the troop and battery command posts forms, logarithm tables etc., were available for such calculations. Slide rules were also used to facilitate calculations.

Graphic methods were more commonly used. For these the command posts had one or two artillery boards. Two sizes were available, one 21.5 x 21 inches, the other was larger, about 31 x 31 inches. The board was overlaid with a tracing paper with a grid in scale 1:25,000 or 1:50,000 and numbered such that the planned shooting zone was well covered. On the board a metallic bearing arc was attached with the zero line in the centre. Sometimes limiting boundaries in line and range for potential fire beyond which no fire was permissible could be drawn.

On the board the position of the deployed Troop was marked with a drawing pin. A metallic range arm was attached from this pin. The pin was placed exactly where the right fourth gun of the Troop is positioned, the pilot gun as it was called. The coordinates of this gun were thus representing the location of the Troop. Similarly the 'pilot gun' of the left Troop in a battery represented the location of the battery. The arm was graduated in yards up to 12,000 or 16,000 yards depending on type selected. A plotting protractor could be of help when plotting on the artillery board.

When arranged as presented, the artillery board could be used for graphic solutions of any problem involving map references, coordinates, bearings, ranges, switches from the zero line etc. Normally, it was used for determination of switches and ranges for targets with reported map coordinates. It could also be used the other way around, i.e. to deduce coordinates of targets to which switch of line and range have been recorded after firing.

An artillery board could be used for survey purposes as well, for instance by plotting a traverse from a trig point to a bearing picket near the guns. Targets from gridded oblique air photographs could also be transferred to the artillery board.

When the coordinates of a target had been communicated from the OPO/FOO to the command post, the exact location of the target was plotted on the board. By means of the range arm and the bearing arc the firing line (bearing) to it could be easily read. As the range arm had a graduated range scale the distance to the target could also quickly be fixed.

As every Troop command post had its own artillery board and the Battery command post also its own, it was easy by means of the latter to get a double check of the data the troops had found from their artillery boards.

It was also important as seen to determine the height difference between the target and the guns, as this had an impact on gun laying.

The line and range determined at the artillery board had to be corrected for factors influencing the projectile trajectory as discussed in the previous Chapter 8. Of particular importance were corrections due to deviating weather conditions. The summary of corrections calculated was the Correction of the Moment (CoM). When 'CoM' had been calculated and added to the data from the artillery board, laying data to the guns could be ordered from the command post.

An 'Artillery Board' is seen in **Fig. 9-5**. The board shown has data from the battle of El Alamein in October 1942 and was on display at the Royal Artillery Museum.

Fig. 9-5 An Artillery Board was used at Troop and Battery Command Posts for establishing the geodetic relation between guns and target. The Board is prepared with a reference coordinate grid on a paper in scale 1:25 000 or 1:50 000 on which the gun deployment is represented by the pivot marker at the coordinates of the battery or troop pilot gun. From this a steel range arm was placed towards a bearing arc. The range and bearing from the guns to the target could easily be determined when the target had been plotted on the Board by means of its coordinates. This example was seen at Royal Artillery Museum (Mark Smith RAHT)

10. How to Hit the Target – Gun Laying

Indirect fire, i.e. when the target cannot be seen from the gun, is achieved using an auxiliary aiming mark, but as this mark can be any well-defined object around the gun, a specialised sight is needed. Such sights were introduced by the Royal Artillery at the beginning of the twentieth century. One of these was Dial Sight No. 7 used for the 18-pounders in the Great War 1914–1918. This had one scale for line laying (direction to target). Later, during the 1930s, a second scale was applied in order to make it easier to apply corrections for the individual gun.

Fig 10-1 Most British guns had up to 1943 a dial sight of the type Dial Sight No.7 B. A similar improved version, 'Dial Sight No. 9', was introduced 1943–1944. This was used long after the war and is shown here. (RAHT)

This was a 'slipping scale'. The revised version was called Dial Sight No. 7A, others were Dial Sight No. 7B and Dial Sight No. 7C. These were the most commonly used sights for all types of gun during the Second World War. They were in 1944 followed by an improved version, the Dial Sight No. 9. We can see a sight with double scales for line laying in **Fig. 10-1**. One of the line scales was marked (engraved) clockwise and the other anti-clockwise. The top of the sight could be released and turned easily towards an aiming point before locked again, when it was to be moved/turned by means of graduated scale micrometers, one for each one of the line scales.

The sight top, the upper prism, could be revolved horizontally 360° and thus directed to any aiming point around the gun while the layer looked through the lower telescope part, which always was directed straight forward. When looking into the sight the layer could see two engraved cross lines, which should be laid against the aiming point(s) once the ordered direction towards the target had been applied. This was done by means of the traversing hand wheel. Upon arrival at a new position all the guns were to have their barrels in parallel in the ordered direction, the zero line. More about this in Chapter 11.

The range, i.e. the distance to the target, was a function of barrel elevation, which in its turn was dependent on the projectile muzzle velocity and applied corrections for factors like weather conditions, projectile weight etc. British guns had Calibrating Sights, which meant that the range could be set directly by the layer. The range scale was engraved, as far as the 25-pounder was concerned, on a cone being part of the sight carrier. A fixed reader arm with markers for different charges was used. These could also be adjusted to make allowance for decreasing muzzle velocity. By means of the range indicator wheel the cone was moved till the ordered range was set against the marker. Then the barrel was brought into the correct position by means of the elevation hand wheel and a Sight Clinometer water bubble, which was to come into level position (**Fig. 10-2**).

Fig. 10-2 On the 25-pdr, range was set by means of wheels affecting the unique range cone/drum seen here. The cone has engraved lines for different ranges. Markers for each Charge were on the ruler beyond the cone. Lower ruler is engraved with muzzle velocity scale (Author's collection)

Fig. 10-4 Sight Clinometer with spirit (bubble) level for adjusting the elevation with the angle of sight to be set by means of a separate scale (Author's collection)

If there was a difference in height between the gun and the target, an angle of sight corresponding to this difference must be taking into account when laying the gun (**Fig. 10-3**).

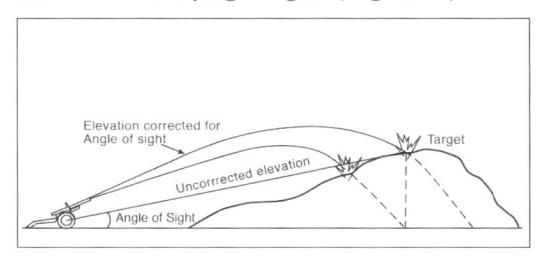

Fig. 10-3 The geodetic relation between firing units and targets must be determined in three dimensions. This implied that the gun elevation must be corrected with the angle of sight if the height difference is significant. If not, the shell will fall short of the target as illustrated here (Author)

The Sight Clinometer is shown in **Fig. 10-4**.

We can see that the trajectory must be raised a little in order to get projectile impact at the correct place. This was called a non-rigidity correction. The magnitude was found in the 'Range Tables' and the correction was set on the 'Sight Clinometer' by which the elevation, and thus the range, was adjusted to bring the projectile to touch ground at the right place.

We may in this context observe that the layer of a 25-pounder operated both the traversing hand wheel and the elevation hand wheel (**Fig. 10-5**).

For other guns such as the modern medium guns, the same types of dial sight were used but the range laying was made by means of readers set against engraved range scales on a vertical plate. The readers, one for each charge could be moved to compensate for changes in muzzle velocity. Once the reader had been set against the range scale the barrel was brought into right elevation by means of the clinometer's water bubble, which was to be level when the laying had been completed. See the arrangement for a 5.5-inch gun-howitzer in **Fig. 10-6**.

Fig. 10-5 Laying of a 25-pdr. This was done by the layer who operated both the traversing hand wheel and the range (elevating) wheel. The dial sight is set on the line bearing and the range on the cone/drum using the charge marker (AWM No. 041956)

Additional corrections in line and range could be given to the gun layers, who had to set them on the dial sight. When ranging, changes in line and range were similarly ordered to the guns.

The British guns were designed for a maximum elevation of 45°. In mountainous terrain as the Gunners met in Italy and Burma the guns sometimes had to be fired, as mentioned, with higher elevation in order to get a suitable trajectory with steep descent; this was called the Upper Register.[132]

Improvisation was then needed to raise the front part of the gun by raising the wheels from the ground. We can see in **Fig. 10-7** what it could look like. Later during the war a revised sight carrier was introduced to facilitate laying. As seen above Incremental Charges were also provided to make firing easier in this 'Upper Register'.

Fig. 10-6 Laying of a 5.5-inch gun-howitzer. Medium guns had the same dial sights as the 25-pdr. The sight objective is in this example directed forwards to an aiming point in front of the gun. Firing range was set against graphic scales on a quadrant. We can here see the ruler with its five markers for different charges. The sight clinometer with its bubble level is to the right behind the quadrant (RAHT)

Fig. 10-7 British guns were not designed for firing at elevations above 45° (Upper Register). With the 25-pdr this could be overcome by an improvised support placed under the wheels as shown here. By means of this arrangement and introduced incremental charges it was possible to fire above high mountains and hit targets behind them in e.g. deep valleys (©Imperial War Museum NA 20531)

11. Preparations for Opening of Gunfire

Deployment and gun orientation
British artillery was normally deployed with the two troop positions of a battery some 300–400 yards from each other. The four guns of a troop were positioned with a gap of 25–35 yards between them. With parallel barrels this meant that the width of fire from a troop was 75–100 yards. Fire control for the troops was the responsibility of the Troop Command Post (TCP). This was deployed fairly centrally behind the guns. Between the two troops the Battery Command Post (BCP) was deployed. The normal deployment scheme is illustrated in **Fig. 11-1**.

The geodetic position of the battery was, as mentioned above, the coordinates of the 'pilot gun' in the left troop, i.e. the fourth gun to the right.

If a concentration of the fire against one point was ordered instead of having the troops to fire with parallel barrels, deployment corrections could be given to each gun. A graphic tool was available for the calculations, the Sand Graph.

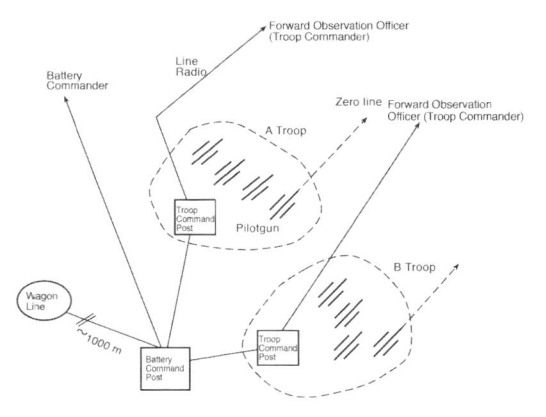

Fig. 11-1 Normal deployment of a battery, 20–30 yards between the guns, 200–300 yards between the troops. If the terrain was difficult, e.g. dense jungle, guns sometimes had to be squeezed into a very narrow area. This was often the case in Burma. An advantage, however, was that local defence of the deployment then was facilitated (Author)

Once the guns had arrived and been deployed it was important to move all vehicles away to a special parking area, the Wagon Lines, some 500–1,000 yards behind the gun positions. This was also the place for technicians and supply groups. Extra ammunition could also be stocked up here.

Reconnaissance and preparation of alternative gun positions was another important task in connection with redeployment. The Commanding Officer of 136 Field Regiment RA in Burma, Lieutenant Colonel Armstrong wrote in a newsletter about some lessons learned. One was:

> The value of pre-reconnoitred alternative gun positions [was unquestionable]. Bad ones were better than none. Three times I had to move guns at night because enemy parties were over-looking them and preventing them doing their job by day.[133]

Special gun positions sometimes had to be reconnoitred where direct fire against enemy tanks could be fired. In order to avoid revealing the gun deployment in connection with ranging, one or two guns could be moved to temporary positions away from the main battle position for such tasks.

The other batteries of the regiment were deployed in the same way as has been here described for one of the three batteries. The distance between the three should, however, not exceed say 2–3km in order to make it easier to concentrate fire from them against the same target. Another reason for not spreading out the batteries too much was to facilitate telephone and radio communication between the batteries and the regimental headquarters.

The normal deployment pattern could not always be observed. Sometimes, as in Burma, dense jungle terrain could make it impossible. Mountainous terrain without good roads as on Sicily could also make it necessary to improvise and make the best out of the situation and deploy guns much tighter than normally. During the final years of the war when the risks for enemy air attacks and counter-bombardment had been drastically reduced it could be acceptable to deploy the guns very close to each other and without any camouflage, almost wheel to wheel.

Now, how could the guns be deployed where they should? Once a deployment had been advised by a superior commander it was important to dispatch a reconnaissance team at once to that area for a detailed reconnaissance. Normal practice in a regiment was allocation of responsibility for the overall reconnaissance and coordination of that to be undertaken for the three batteries to the Second-in-Command. If a battery was to act independently it was of course the Commanding Officer of the battery who had to undertake the reconnaissance himself.

When larger operations were planned with numerous regiments involved it was important to provide clear orders to the regiments where they were expected to deploy and thus where to reconnoitre. Such initial overall planning could take place at Corps level but also at divisional level.

A battery reconnaissance was made under the command of the 'Battery Command Post Officer' (CPO). He decided where the troops were to be deployed and where the 'Battery Command Post' (BCP) should be located. He also had to organise the initial local defence. At the troop position the 'Gun Position Officer' had to decide the exact position for every gun and his own 'Troop Command Post'.

The 'Wagon Lines' was reconnoitred by the 'Battery Captain' (Battery Commander's deputy) and the 'Battery Quarter Master Sergeant'.

What factors had to be taken into account when reconnoitring a new deployment? Some of them were these:

- The tactical task assigned to the regiment/battery
- The area to be covered by artillery fire, sometimes maximum and minimum range
- Ordered zero line
- Crest
- Communication opportunities
- Prevention of enemy observation of the deployed guns
- Protection against enemy air attacks
- Ground digging conditions
- Protection against enemy infantry and tanks
- Transport roads for supply of ammunition and other necessities
- Availability of space for 'Wagon Lines' and alternative gun positions and suitable roads for their access

Under ideal conditions reconnaissance and survey took place in daytime. Sometimes there was time for other necessary activities such as digging shelters and gun pits, the laying of telephone lines etc. March to and deployment normally, however, took place when it was dark. The unit could be taken to a nearby hiding place during the day or direct to the new position during the night. The vehicles of a troop were led by one of the younger subalterns, the Troop Leader.

Naturally, the situation was often far from the ideal. The 2nd-in-command of 112 (Wessex) Field Regiment RA, Major Gilbert Heathcote (later Brigadier), tells us about the critical situation when the 1st Airborne Division should be relieved at Arnhem in September 1944:

> We went into action as far forward as possible south of the Waal but the Airborne perimeter at Oosterbeek was well out of range. 129 Brigade became involved in fierce battle at Elst on the main road to Arnhem. 130 Brigade were then ordered to advance via the lanes west of this axis to secure the village of Driel. They set out at first light on 23 September but even more urgent had been the need to get field guns within range of the Airborne perimeter. My guess is that it was in the late afternoon of 22 September that Bill Heath [divisional artillery commander] called me to the set. I was to set off at once to recce a gun position within range of Oosterbeek and Arnhem. 'But, Sir, it will be dark within an hour or so'. (In our formative years, IGs [Instructor Gunnery] had stressed: 'Never recce a gun position in the dark, always disaster next day') Bill's answer was not unexpected, it was crisis time: 'Don't argue. Get on with it'. Perhaps because of the abrupt exchange, I failed to ask who had gone before up this route. I collected elements of my Recce Party and discovered that I would be accompanied by the CRE [Commander Royal Engineers], Jim Evill. Dark was with us very quickly as the narrow lanes with dykes on either side made progress slow. To our right the battle for Elst was providing

a major and noisy fire-work display with tracer making its seemingly lazy arcs in the sky [. . .] Rain added to the darkness of the night. The site in this polder country was flat, soggy but looming, everywhere there seemed to be good concealment from high hedges and trees. 'Got to start somewhere', I thought: here was a small farm, with a cellar, do for RHQ; work outwards from there, on foot, pacing each field, sudden freeze, who was pacing with me? Into the hedge, slip a round into the breech of my airborne carbine [. . .] There was at dawn, just time to correct my most awful errors before the guns arrived. The hedges and trees were now far less protective; we could clearly see Arnhem which made it as clear that once guns were in action, we would become an attractive target. Rarely, had gunpits been dug deeper or more quickly.[134]

Once the guns had arrived at the new battery deployment area a hectic work followed to get the unit ready for firing. The guns were to be oriented with parallel barrels along the zero line and 'aiming posts', or 'aiming parallelo-scopes', were to be placed in the vicinity of the gun to get it ready. Careful control of this was made to avoid erroneous shooting. A first-hand stock of ammunition was placed close to the gun.

At the 'troop command posts' and the 'battery command post' the artillery board was prepared for firing within the ordered area. Range tables, various forms, logarithm tables, slide rules etcetera were brought out for use. Correction of the Moment was to be calculated when 'meteor data' had been provided as were other corrections to be used for the coming gun laying.

Communication between the command posts and the guns had to be prepared as well. This could be done with the establishment of a simple 'tannoy' system, which can be seen on **Fig. 4-3** (the 25-pounder with muzzle brake).

When the war commenced such systems were not available in large numbers. The alternative was to give the guns the laying data by loud voice and a megaphone. As regards more comprehensive data for the guns, such as those required for the execution of extensive fire plans, the data could be given in writing by means of a Gun Programme. This was particularly necessary when large barrages were to be fired over many hours.

Much of the preparations followed strict procedures and had been rehearsed many times. It was therefore not amazing that a troop could report ready for fire within five minutes after the arrival of the first vehicle.

As soon as the guns had reported ready for fire other activities followed. At first the local defence must be prepared to protect the guns and command posts against enemy attacks. This could include readiness to use the hand-held PIAT (**Fig. 11-2**). Of high priority was the personal protection. All the staff should have

Fig. 11-2 Local defence had to be organised around the deployment. It could include barbed wire fence, alarm systems, slit trenches, fox holes etcetera but also positions for anti-aircraft and anti-tank weapons, here the light PIAT (RAHT)

access to dug slit trenches and shelters. Such were normally each arranged for two men of the gun crew around the gun pit.

Then followed digging of gun pits and sheltered pits for command posts. The gun pits were quite shallow in order not to obstruct firing, but they still provided good protection for the gun when exposed to enemy artillery fire or air attacks. They were to be carefully camouflaged by means of nets, tree branches etc. Normally, hasty protection had to be arranged for command posts, guns and crews, but this could then be gradually improved if the unit was to remain deployed for a longer period. **Fig. 11-3** illustrates a dug in troop command post in Burma and **Fig. 11-4** a well-camouflaged gun in its dug gun-pit.

The British were strict on personal hygiene and therefore latrines also had to be dug as soon as possible and washing facilities arranged. Special 'sleeping pits' often had to be dug as well.

Sergeant Bob Cotterhill who was a gun crew No. 1 in Burma gives his story to us about deployment activities:

Fig. 11-3 Efficient teamwork was a must when firing. Here is a troop command post in Burma in action. It is dug in for protection (©Imperial War Museum SE 3360)

> On reaching the new position the gun would be got into action and Zero Lines recorded whilst the quad would be emptied of its load of gun ammunition, gun stores, camouflage nets and the crew's kit. It would be driven to the Wagon Lines, off the gun position, but close at hand. Then could come the call from the G.P.O., for various jobs to be done – a man to assist the cooks, one to dig latrines, one for digging defence posts. A detachment would usually be left with the No.1 and two men.
>
> The next job was to dig in. Slit trenches for each of the six men of the detachment would be dug to a depth of 18 inches to two feet. When these had all been completed to this depth, they would be dug to the full five feet depth, six feet long and two feet wide. When these were finished a start would be made on the gun pit. Because of our isolated position and the fear that an attack could come in from any direction, the gun pits were made full size so that they were big enough for the gun to be moved around to fire at any point of the compass.
>
> Digging would continue throughout the day with only brief breaks for mugs of tea, a bully beef and biscuit snack at midday and a hot meal about 17.00. It was extremely hot working in the blazing sun although stripped to the waist. Because we were always down in the low-lying ground there was never a breath of wind.[135]

Fig. 11-4 When deploying guns it was always an endeavour to get them protected behind a shelter in a gun pit. If deployed at the same place for a longer period gun crews had to improve the shelter as much as they could by means of logs and planks, empty ammunition boxes, sand bags etc. Camouflage nets reduced the risk for enemy intervention (AWM No.024828)

As we have seen in Chapter 5 quite a lot of resources were available for local defence. As protection against tanks the own guns were of course the primary resource, but gradually also the hand-held anti-tank weapon PIAT was provided. Anti-tank mines were also added. Own resources for anti-aircraft protection were a limited number of 20mm anti-aircraft guns. In addition to personal weapons (rifles, sub-machine guns and pistols) local defence could also be reinforced by means of light machine-guns, personnel mines and alarm devices.

Protection of the own gun position was in a modern war of extreme importance, and all were concerned. An artillery officer in Burma wrote:

> The lessons we learnt were many, but one in particular, that every cook, ammunition number, etc., must know the defence layout and what his job is if an attack comes in.
>
> There was never time to issue orders when troubles began. Each man had to do his job unsupervised, and the only motto for success on such occasions, or indeed at any time in battle is, keep your head and resolve to kill as many Japs as possible.[136]

The reason why local defence was of particular importance in Burma was the fact, that the primary Japanese method of countering artillery fire was infiltration into the gun positions in the dark.

Enemy attacks by tanks on artillery deployments were a reality that one always had to take into account, particularly in North Africa. Such an event is described in the *Royal Artillery Commemoration Book:*[137]

> 'Tank Alert!' but although we could hear the rumbling of tanks it seemed an age before anything happened. At last six black objects huddled together in groups of three appeared to the right front of the Troop. It was still very dark and difficult to judge the range, but we set our sights at 400 and opened fire.
>
> The first shot from No. 1 gun set the leading tank on fire. No.2's first round lifted the turret clean off another tank – a good start, but we had stirred up a hornet's nest. Soon there were 15 or more tanks firing at us with 75mms and machine guns. We scored hit after hit, but I fancy we put a number of shells into tanks that were already dead. During this period two officers – the only officers with the guns – and four other ranks were hit. The tanks were now working round our right towards E Troop. Just as our No.1 gun swung round to engage them, a 75mm shell landed on the trail, killing all the detachment and setting fire to a box of cartridges. At the same time a gun of E Troop received a direct hit on the shield, disabling the whole detachment.

Another threat against deployed artillery was the enemy's own artillery and mortars. The only protection against this hazard was digging and counter-bombardment, in particular forestalling enemy fire. We will not look deeper into this context here, but will return later.

The guns should be deployed in such a way that shielding obstacles such as trees or buildings did not prevent supporting artillery fire. The centre of the area to be covered was given by the zero line, i.e. the bearing in which the guns were initially oriented with parallel barrels. This must be carefully observed and the accuracy of this orientation had a decisive impact on the subsequent precision of the first rounds fired. As mentioned, the required minimum and maximum ranges would affect selection of gun positions in respect of shielding crests. Requirements as regards left and right boundaries of the area to be covered by fire must also be observed when deciding gun positions.

Upon arrival at the new positions the guns were first roughly laid by means of hand compass along the 'zero line'. As soon as possible the exact orientation with parallel barrels would be done. When this was done the dial sight was oriented towards one or several reference points, Gun Aiming Points (GAP).

The GAP could be a distant object such as a tree, a church steeple, and the corner of a visible building, etc. Another alternative was to use two aiming posts, Gun Aiming Posts, often equipped with marked crossing bars, placed near the gun, normally 50 and 100 yards away. A further alternative for arranging a nearby GAP was the paralleloscope. By means of the two latter devices deviations of required line due to traverse or movement of the gun, as a result of firing, could be compensated when laying the gun. GAPs with light to be used during nights also had to be arranged, often one for all the guns of a troop or battery.

Orientation of the guns to get barrels in parallel along the 'zero line' was a procedure starting at a Battery Aiming Point (BAP), where a director was placed. This was a 'Bearing Picket' with known coordinates and surveyed-in bearings to certain beacons or visible terrain objects. The angle between the known bearing and the ordered 'zero line' was then calculated and used when the director was oriented against the beacon. Then the director head was turned towards the dial sight of each gun and the bearing read. After correction with 180° this bearing was given to the layer, who had to set it on the dial sight by means of the line micrometer screw. After this, he turned the barrel with the traversing hand wheel to the zero line position, which was reached when he had oriented the cross lines of the dial sight exactly towards the director. The relations between the various bearings and angles in this process, and how the bearing was ordered to each gun, are illustrated in **Fig. 11-5** and **Fig. 11-6**.

Without moving the barrel the layer then had to turn the head of his dial sight towards the GAPs selected. The bearings to these were read and normally recorded by chalk on the shield. The lower micrometer screw, the Slip Scale, could then be released and be fixed in the position 0° when the barrel was directed along the zero line. Looking at various photographs of deployed guns we can see that the head of the dial sight sometimes is directed to the left, sometimes to the right or almost straightforward depending on the place of the GAPs.

When the fire direction to an identified target was ordered, this was done relative to the zero line, as an example Zero 16°, for which the slip scale was used when laying the gun. But the bearing to the target could also be given as this could be set on the fixed line scale by means of the micrometer screw for this scale.

In order to facilitate orientating the guns the director used had two scales, one a clock-wise scale and the other anti-clockwise.

Amongst necessary preparations after deployment, ammunition supply must be mentioned. Prior to large operations this could imply stockpiling of 500–600 shells at each gun,

Fig. 11-6 When bringing the gun barrels in parallel positions the bearing to be set on each gun sight was given by means of a loudspeaker system or a megaphone. Once set, the layer at each gun was to aim exactly at the Director by traversing the barrel [this seems to be a No.7 Director] (©Imperial War Museum SE 3365)

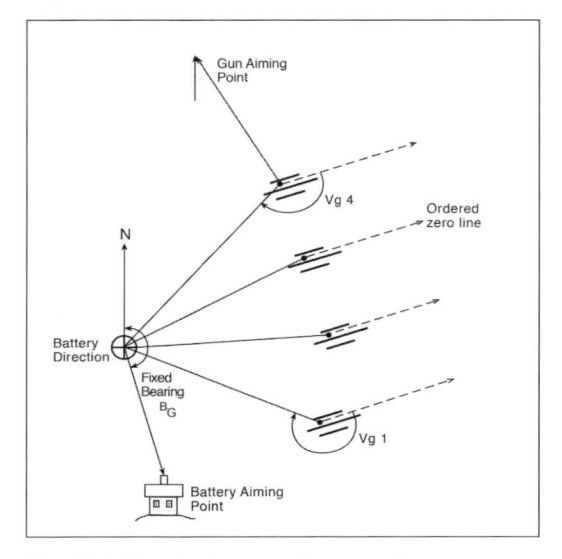

Fig. 11-5 After deployment the guns of a troop were to be aligned with the zero line with parallel barrels. This was accomplished with the help of a Director placed at the control point that had been fixed by the surveyors and where a correct reference bearing was given by a BP Card, here denominated B_G. By using this bearing and the zero line bearing an angle was calculated for each gun, which was to set at the dial sight, here denominated V_{G1} for gun No. 1, V_{G2} for gun No. 2 etc. When the angle was set on the dial sight the layer should turn the traversing hand wheel such, that he was aiming the sight exactly on the Director. With the barrel now in correct position he could release the sight head and turn it towards the gun's aiming point and then to fix it again to the sight carrier. Other methods for getting the guns parallel existed (Author)

Fig. 11-7 Once the guns had been deployed ammunition must be stockpiled to meet the requirements of coming fire plans. Ammunition supply was a logistic challenge that must be met day and night (RAHT)

often done during nights. **Fig. 11-7** is an indication of the important logistic function, which also is a component of the 'system indirect fire'.

Fire observation and control

As mentioned troop commanders normally were 'Observation Post Officers'. Once they had got their orders whom to support and preliminary orders where to establish their observations posts and which area to observe, they went forward for establishing contact with the infantry or armour commander and for detailed reconnaissance of observation possibilities. The need for good observation often made it impossible to establish the observation post exactly where the commander to be supported had his headquarters or was on the march. This could be compensated by means of radio communication. For this the FOP was equipped with the WS No. 18 set (or a similar set) and tuned in on the frequency used by the commander to be supported. Sometimes a telephone line could be used.

Besides the requirement for good observation possibilities over the area ordered, the OPO/FOO had to take into account the need for protection and opportunities for good camouflage. In this context it was also important to make sure that relieving personnel had safe access to the observation post avoiding exposure to direct enemy observation and fire. Another pre-requisite was the communication with the OPO/FOO's own battery. For this he had the WS No. 22 or its remote control. We recall that this set with its batteries was quite heavy and was not portable, but the remote control unit made it possible to use it at the observation post, while the set was kept backwards in the OPO/FOO's (Bren) carrier. As soon as possible a telephone line should be laid between the observation post and the troop position. If the situation made it possible, the OPO/FOO tried to find places with the best observation conditions, for instance up in a church steeple or a water tower, but house attics were often good as well. The latter is illustrated by the artist in **Fig. 11-8**.

At the observation post, the OPO was assisted by a Specialist, who was a NCO and trained in target acquisition and fire observation. He had the qualifications for replacement of the OPO if needed. There are many accounts where skilled assistants took over from the OPO, when the latter was killed or wounded badly, and directed artillery fire from many units. As many other accounts show it could also happen that the OPO quickly had to take over the command of the supported unit, when its ordinary commander was killed. But sometimes a skilled OPO had to combine the two jobs, indeed a real challenge.

At the observation post, the OPO also was assisted by one or more signallers who manned the radio sets and telephone devices. Staying behind at the carrier was the driver and sometimes also a few signal replacements.

Fig. 11-8 A Forward Observation Officer always tried to find a place with best possible view over the target terrain he had to fire at, here the attic of a house. As he was a valuable target for snipers he and his party had to act very carefully and not exposing themselves carelessly towards the enemy lines. It was also important for him to secure good communication by means of radio or telephone line with the infantry or armoured unit that he was to support with artillery fire (Drawing by J.T. Kenney/RAHT)

Once the observation party had established itself at the selected position, fire preparations followed. First the exact coordinates of the positions had to be determined. The OPO was to 'visualise' the firing zero line/direction of his guns and to 'fix' it against some easily visible terrain objects. Then he was expected to draw a panorama sketch over the area to be observed. Again, this had been included in his basic training and he knew that the best start was to draw the horizon and then continue with terrain formations and typical objects between his position and the horizon. He made notes of firing bearings to potential targets, the coordinates of which he also determined and inserted. In order to further enhance the panorama he could mark deviations of, say, 2°, 4° or 8° from the zero line and also try to identify them in the terrain ahead.

Although it was pretty well prescribed in training manuals how to make such a panorama, it was stated that no 'artistic excesses' should be done. There are, however, many panorama sketches done with much talent and that have a clear artistic value. Even nice water-coloured sketches can sometimes be found. Obviously the OPO had had plenty of time to make it, instead of being engaged by fire observation duties.

Anyway, it was a well-honoured tradition in the Royal Artillery to prepare informative panorama sketches and instructions were quite elaborated.[138] Major General Jack Parham was very talented in making sketches and used panorama sketches throughout his career, not only such drawn at observation posts.

As the OPO must be prepared to direct fire not only from his own guns but from numerous others as well, he had to determine the coordinates of potential targets, this in addition to the primary task, which was indicating the firing line of his own guns. This was called Silent Registration.

An example of a panorama sketch made at an observation post in Burma is seen in **Fig. 11-9**. It is drawn on the backside of a paper form.

If time was available, preparations for target engagement could be done by fire ranging various potential targets or suitable terrain objects. Such ranging was completed by recording them with a number and – at the command posts – recording data with or without the 'Correction of Moment'.

All preparations done would facilitate quick action when fire was requested by the supported unit, either this would need further ranging or fire for effect could be ordered directly. We will return to this subject later.

The OPOs and their assistants had a dangerous job and it was important to be extremely careful as to not expose oneself to enemy fire. An experienced officer shared his experience from Italy in this respect:[139]

> Do not wear a tie at the OP, or walk about with binoculars round your neck. Snipers are on lookout for such people – and they seldom miss if you are careless.

Another piece of advice was:

> Be very careful of ALL wireless aerials at the OP – whether a vehicle set or a No. 18 or No. 38 set. Aerials are picked out quite easily. On vehicles – bend them back and tie them with string.

A regimental commander in Italy found good reasons for writing down a number of 'DOs and DONTs for Op Officers', the introduction was:

> Undue exposure and carelessness do not show bravery – they show that you are a bloody fool. You may get away with it for days and then find that just when observation is vital the Boche will neutralise your OP.[140]

I have now discussed which preparations for firing that were made in more stationary situations. In mobile operations there would not be time for achieving everything. Improvisations were needed and it was important that the artillery officer, now often called Forward Observation Officer (FOO), followed the commander of the supported unit close to him in order to meet his requests for fire without undue delay. His ability in map reading was then critical as was the ability of accompanying signallers to keep radio communication open. The observation party's duties were particularly challenging when an advancing armour unit needed support from the gunners. This required transport in a tank or a half-track so as to keep up during the fast advance.

Other preparations before opening fire
We have already discussed the importance of efficient survey as a necessary basis for concentration of accurate artillery fire from many guns. This should, however, not prevent an earlier engagement based on as good data as then

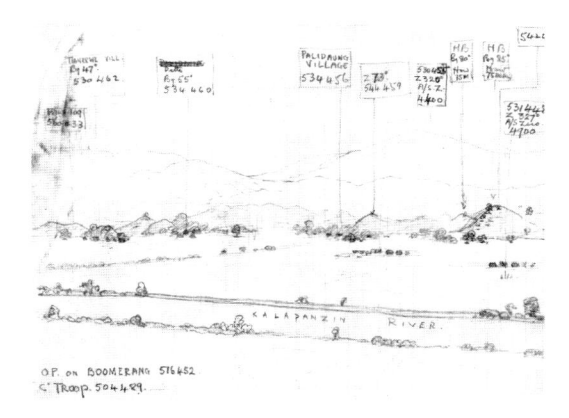

Fig. 11-9 A Forward Observation Officer always tried to find a place with best possible view over the target terrain he had to fire at, here the attic of a house. As he was a valuable target for snipers he and his party had to act very carefully and not exposing themselves carelessly towards the enemy lines. It was also important for him to secure good communication by means of radio or telephone line with the infantry or armoured unit that he was to support with artillery fire (Drawing by J.T. Kenney/RAHT)

available. An exception might be a situation where a huge concentration was to be fired with surprise without previous ranging. This should not be done without appropriate survey data.

As already discussed, establishing telephone and radio communication for the whole regimental and divisional areas was always given high priority as well.

Normally the batteries brought a sufficient first-hand stock of ammunition loaded on their own vehicles. But when large operations required intensive firing, maybe over several days, this stock had to be complemented with extra ammunition. As we will see in Part 3 of the book, it could be required to store some 500–600 shells at each gun position. The RASC might take a whole week to deliver the stockpile of ammunition because most driving would be done at night with minimal convoy lights.

We have now looked at the 'system indirect fire' and how its different sub-functions were designed and were supposed to be established before firing for effect commenced. Next, we will review the different tactical procedures and techniques that were applied, in particular during the second half of the war. Ranging is the first procedure to have a look at, this in the next Chapter.

12. Artillery Battle Technique and Tactics

When everything that could be calculated had been done – ranging complements

As seen one of the preparations to be done before firing could commence was calculation of adjustments to gun laying in order to take into account all known factors influencing the shell trajectory, the Correction of the Moment (CoM). Despite all calculations made, however, a remaining uncertainty as to the possibilities to hit the target could not be avoided. Not least quickly changing weather conditions added to this uncertainty. Hence, a control by fire had to be done. This could be aimed at checking the definite value of 'CoM'. In such a case firing could be done against a point ahead with well-fixed coordinates, a 'Datum Point', provided it was easy to observe the fire against it. When the fire had been gradually corrected, so as to get the impact right at the 'Datum Point', it was easy to calculate backwards getting the corrections to be used when all guns were to fire in the vicinity, provided they were all surveyed into the same grid. Targets to be engaged should not be too far away from the 'Datum Point', say maximum 1,000 yards. Otherwise the CoM might be different.

Another prerequisite for a direct hit upon the target was that its exact locations, i.e. its co-ordinates, had been fixed. The conditions discussed were not always at hand. Then (fire) ranging had to be applied. Once this had been completed the target had been fixed and trajectory corrections had been determined. All that was needed for hitting the target by all participating guns had been done. The resulting 'CoM' could be used for fire for effect upon other nearby targets fixed in relation to the former.

Before looking further into the ranging technique, we will notice a reflection made by Major W.P. Lunn-Rochliffe. Ranging should not be just a routine. He presented in the Royal Artillery Journal his view on this based on his experience from Tunisia and Italy:

The gunner is a 'rep' in direct support of another arm must not only interpret his commander's requirements for fire, but be capable of discussing plans and suggesting solutions whenever called upon for advice. Then, of course, the gunner must be thoroughly proficient in all technical matters: the O.P. officer who does no more than follow the rules of ranging is no better than 'a good plain cook'. A thoroughly proficient O.P. officer, with his better knowledge and wider experience, will have all kinds of tricks up his sleeve with which to solve his problems.[141]

Well, certainly a relevant comment. Ranging was the primary method for compensation of poor ballistic and geodetic data. However, it could be tactically counter-productive and in such situations other methods from the palette of different techniques had to be selected.

If surprise was the priority, it might be better to cover a larger area with fire, which was not accurate enough, rather than trying to obtain maximum precision. Of course this required good availability of ammunition. Surprising fire without ranging was called Predicted Fire.

Ranging on to the target was always the first choice for achieving a target round and had to be mastered by all OPOs, not only the skilled professionals but also the less talented. Ranging, or more normally Registration, was done in accordance with standard procedures, something like this to follow.

The OPO decided which gun or guns in his Troop that he wanted to be engaged for ranging. Normally he selected a 'Section', i.e. two guns, or only one or as a third options, all the four guns of the troop.

When the first alternative was considered to be the best, he normally selected the right section of his troop, as the rightmost gun, the 'pivot gun', was one of the guns in this section. The two guns were furthermore in the middle of the battery position if they belonged to the left troop. When the ranging commenced the OPO gave the order 'troop target, right ranging, 6800. Fire' If only one gun was to be used he gave the order 'troop target, No. 1 ranging, 6800, fire' or likewise for other guns. We may now recall that the dial sights had a line scale graduated in degrees and minutes. The elevation scales for different charges were graduated in distance to target (range) and not degrees. It was an ambition that switches, i.e. correction of line and range, should be applied directly at the sight obviating further recalculations.

Before the firing could commence the OPO had to give the line to the target from the guns. One method was map references (coordinates), another method was ordering the line relative to 'zero line', for instance 'zero, six degrees, 20 minutes, angle of sight 25 minutes elevation'.

The OPO rarely was positioned just under the line from guns to target, his observation direction formed an angle against the firing direction. See **Fig. 12-1**.

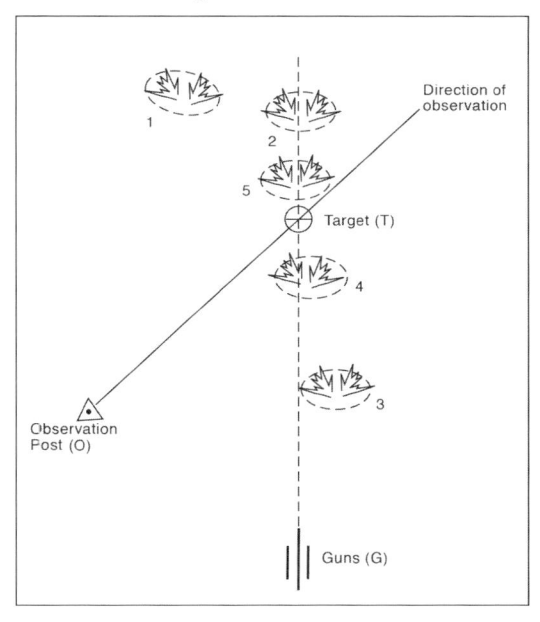

Fig. 12-1 An example of ranging with two guns (a Section). After each pair of rounds, as here are given a number, the Observation Officer had to order changes to the guns relative the guns –target bearing (GT) and not relative his observation direction (OT). This was not easy when the angle between these two bearings was large. In order to facilitate the impact location he has here changed in such a way that the impact of the second pair of rounds is close to the line GT. After this he has changed along this line with a pair of rounds on each side of the target, gradually decreasing the width of the 'fork' around the target until target impact has been accomplished (Author)

Despite this angle he had to give his correction of the fall of shot relative the latter direction, i.e. the 'GT' line. As an example: 'zero, more two degrees, add 200. The first was the change of line and the latter change of range.

A target's coordinates and height to be ranged were passed to the 'troop command post' by means of its coordinates and height. Its position was there marked at the 'Artillery Board', from which line and range were extracted. To these data the 'CoM' corrections were added and laying data were then passed to the guns. When ready the gun, or the guns ordered, fired a first round. If the target had been correctly fixed (coordinates) and 'CoM' also was correct the shell impact(s) would take place right at the target apart from a deviation due to the unavoidable dispersion. If a direct hit took place, the ranging could be suspended and fire for effect by all guns needed could be ordered. In such a case the target data could be recorded and a number given. This was called registration.

As discussed, the ideal situation was rarely at hand. Some uncertainties in laying data normally could not be avoided. This caused a deviation of the impact from the correct position. In difficult terrain such as woods or, in particular, the jungle, it could happen that nothing could be seen of the ground impact (fall of shot) of the first round(s). The method then to be applied was 'bracketing' along the 'GT' line or across of it. In order to obtain the bracket the OPO had to correct line and range one or a few times till a bracket around the target had been established, i.e. he had observed rounds on both sides of the target This was then made shorter, for instance halved. By such changes the OPO ended with having the target in the middle of a short bracket, which meant that he had fixed the target. If the angle between his observation line and the gun line was small it might be necessary to 'bracket' both along this line and across it, or making brackets along the direction of observation, i.e. 'OT' in **Fig. 12-1**. The figure illustrates ranging by means of such a 'bracketing' with a section of two guns along the 'GT' line. The number of the different rounds indicates how the impacts gradually were brought closer to the target. Rounds '4' and '5' were so close to the target that the ranging was sufficient. It was now possible to fire for effect or just to record the target for use later.

Upon completion of the ranging, the

command posts could analyse the result and try to find out whether deviations from initial laying data were due to incorrect target data than had been assumed, or deviations were due to change of ballistic influences from new weather conditions, in particular wind direction and strength. Of course it could be a combination. Whatever the reasons were, it did not matter if fire for effect was to take place immediately once the ranging had been completed. In such cases the target could be recorded uncorrected. If other targets were to be engaged the same 'CoM' could be used provided a new target could be fixed relative to the one used for the initial ranging. If this could be done the latter used to be called 'Witness Point'.

If, on the other hand, firing was to take place later, when a new weather situation had emerged, the target location could be recorded without the 'COM' used, the target was then recorded corrected.

Ranging along the 'OT' line would of course be the best method from an observation point of view. The problem was, however, that the OPO still had to give the changes relative the 'GT' line so as to save recalculations at the command post. Some graphical and numerical means of assistance to be used when ranging along the OT line were often available.[142]

In order to speed up the ranging a few alternative methods existed. One was to visualise the firing line, i.e. 'GT' line, by ordering two different ranges, one to be used by one of the guns in a section, the other by another gun: 'Right ranging 65–58. Fire'. This implied a round from the No. 1 gun at the range 6,500 and five seconds later a shot from No.2 at the shorter range, 5,800. The OPO could repeat with other ranges if necessary. Once he had found out where the 'GT' line was in the observation zone, he could either continue ranging with the two guns at the same elevation/range or he could proceed with one gun only.

Another, even more effective, method to visualise the 'GT' line was to use all four guns of the troops and order 'Ladder ranging, 15 seconds, 6000, up 300', this as an example. The method had been learnt from the Royal Navy and was suitable, in particular, when ranging at long distances with long time of flight should take place. Time could be spared, by having several projectiles in the air simultaneously. In this example No. 1 fired at the range of 6,000 [yards] and 15 seconds later the No. 2 followed at the range of 6,300, followed another 15 seconds later by a round from No.3 at 6,600, and finally the No.4 completed the 'ladder' after another 15 seconds with its elevation at 6,900. Again, this could be repeated, for instance after a switch of line. When the OPO was certain about the line in the terrain, he could proceed with an ordinary type of ranging with one or two guns.

The purpose of ranging was, as discussed, to prepare fire for effect such that the shells would fall on the right spot, the target to be engaged. If there was a risk at hand that the fire would not land there, ranging was a must. On the other hand if the OPO during ranging found that he could accomplish a direct hit he could immediately stop the ranging and go to fire for effect, or just get the target registered.

The procedures briefly described were applied when ranging of the OPO's own troop or battery was to take place. But the overruling doctrine was to concentrate fire from many more guns when the tactical situation called for this. If for instance the OPO wanted to concentrate fire from all the three batteries of his regiment, not to say all the batteries of the divisional artillery, how to undertake the ranging in such a case? Obviously he could not keep track of the 'zero lines' of all these troops/batteries and communicate switches relative to these. If fire for effect was required before all the units had been surveyed into the same grid, the situation was even more complicated.

The solution as far as ranging was concerned was the introduction in 1941 of the *cardinal point method*. Quite simply this implied that the OPO undertook ranging as usual with one section or a single gun, but now gave the switches to all participating units by giving them an order for correction of the fire such as 'all 300 northeast' (example). The cardinal points were eight directions around the compass (North, Northeast, East, Southeast, etc.). When the fire correction was received, the command posts had to mark it on their artillery boards from which they could determine the switch in line and elevation applicable for their own guns. If all units to be used in target engagement were on the same grid, ranging was, as mentioned, done by means of a section of two guns or just one. All other troops just had to follow the corrections on the artillery board and then register the target position. On the other hand, if they were not on the same grid all units had to be ranged before fire for effect.[143]

It was important for artillery commanders and observation officers alike to understand the constraints but also technical options that could make the fire support as efficient as possible, given the specific tactical situation and fighting techniques to be applied by the infantry and armoured units supported. Ranging or not, was one question to raise amongst many. What were the requirements as regards accuracy? And how far should ranging be pursued in order to obtain best accuracy?

The AT Volume III advised:

> Since the time available will almost always be limited, speed is vital. This speed in ranging will not be achieved by slavish adherence to rigid rules, but only by a proper grasp of the principles set out [...]. Except when a target is close to one which has already been engaged, any attempt to save time by opening fire for effect, without carrying ranging to the degree appropriate to the nature of target, is a gamble which is almost certain to result in waste of time as well as ammunition. Conversely, to carry ranging beyond the appropriate degree may result in loss of what may be only a fleeting opportunity of inflicting loss on the enemy.[144]

Ranging by means of high airbursts, 30–50 metres above ground, was a special type of ranging. It could be used just for determining COM data. Another purpose could be to bring many units on to the same grid when time was not available for ordinary survey. The batteries taking part fixed their positions through intersection to a couple of air bursts fired against two or more points with coordinates calculated by the leading unit/battery. This method was successfully used as the only possible during the rapid pursuit westwards in November and December 1942 of Rommel's army after the battle at El Alamein. A third optional use of high airburst was when directing fire against targets deep beyond the front line, for instance enemy batteries. Ranging then took place with the help of sound rangers.

In order to facilitate concentration of artillery fire from many units a standardised set of terms was introduced for classification of targets, and at the same time ordering fire against them with a specified number of units. They were:

- A target ordered as 'Troop Target' implied engagement by the four guns of the troop
- A 'Battery Target' was to be engaged by the eight guns of the battery
- A 'Mike Target' was to be engaged by the 24 guns of a regiment (3 batteries)
- An 'Uncle Target' was to be engaged by all the divisional artillery, normally 72 guns
- A 'Victor Target' was ordered when the artillery of a Corps was required. It could imply engagement of 300–400 guns, sometime even more

An Army Group Royal Artillery (AGRA) was engaged by the order 'Yoke Target'. Such a concentration could involve 80–140 guns of different type, mainly medium and heavy guns.

If a particular target was expected to be engaged several times, or was included in a written fire plan, it was given a number, which was preceded by a letter. A regimental target, 'Mike', was allotted the letter 'M' and a number, for instance 'M 678'. A second letter could be added if there was a need to distinguish it from other regiments' targets, for instance it could be 'ML 678' and 'MK 678'.

In fire plans it was a normal practice to group a number of targets under a common name. A large fire plan could comprise several such groups of targets given for instance names of cities, 'Aberdeen', 'Glasgow', 'Edinburgh' etcetera. Prepared targets for defensive fire (more about that below) normally were denominated 'DF 456', 'DF 457' etcetera. 'DF' was the acronym for Defensive Fire.

It should finally be observed that whenever fire was to be opened, either it was a matter of ranging or fire for effect; the OPO/FOO was expected to convey tactical information besides the more technical data. It could be what type of target he intended to engage, what he could see of enemy actions, transport etcetera. Command posts and headquarters were then in a better position to understand what kind of fire that was expected from them and whether, for instance, time was a critical factor. The more of information about enemy activities and battle progress that could be conveyed also to commanders and headquarters of units to be supported, the better it was.

After ranging – fire for effect

When ranging a target to be engaged had been completed fire for effect was ordered by the OPO/FOO. As long as this was to include only his own troop, a few standardised order alternatives were available:[145]

- Gun fire
- Section fire
- Troop fire
- Troop salvo

The first one meant that guns engaged fired independently as soon as they had been laid. As an example: 5 rounds gunfire required the gun(s) to fire the five rounds as quickly as possible. This was often used when a target had been ranged, or been registered earlier, and observed fire was to come. If the OPO/FOO wanted to start the engagement with only two guns he could order: 'Right Section, 2 rounds gun fire', which meant that Guns Nos. 1 and 2 each should fire two rounds as quickly as possible. But an interval between the rounds could alternatively be ordered.

'Section fire' was ordered when the OPO/FOO wanted each section of the troop to take part. The guns were then fired in succession from right of each section. It could be like: '4 rounds section fire, 20 seconds', by which order No. 1 and No. 3 guns opened and were then followed 20 seconds later by No. 2 and No.4, and then another 20 seconds later No. 1 and No. 3 fired again etcetera, until all guns had fired four rounds.

The order 'Troop fire, 15 seconds' implied that the four guns fired, starting from right, with a time lap of 15 seconds between them.

If surprise was required the OPO/FOO could order a 'Salvo'. Following the order all guns were loaded and reported 'ready' to the command post. They all then fired simultaneously upon a signal or order from the latter.

The OPO/FOO could if necessary stop firing or change the ordered interval between rounds.

It was often the 'quick-firing' method, i.e. 'gun fire' that was applied when concentration of fire from one or several regiments was required. In order to obtain surprise the final order for effect could be given when all were ranged and the target registered. This had been prepared by the order 'fire by order' from the OPO/FOO. A more refined order could be: 'Target Uncle seven, scale four, all engage at 1400 hours'. An even more refined version was to take into account the time of flight from respective gun position to the target and giving the time when all shells were to hit the target. The order for this alternative was 'time on target'. This alternative required more of preparations at the command posts and thus often delayed the fire for effect. It was not applied very often in connection with observed fire as speed often had highest priority.

An important factor indicated by the above orders for concentrations from several units was that in the British Army an OPO/FOO could give order to all units that he wanted to engage without first requesting permission to do so. A troop commander always was authorised to engage his own troop, a battery commander his battery and sometimes also the whole regiment etcetera upwards in the hierarchy.

Even if not authorised to engage the whole regiment, a troop commander acting as OPO/FOO could order 'Mike Target'. His order was then communicated via his own command post to the regimental headquarters, where the final decision was made as to whether the regiment was to fire. Before accepting the order the commanding officer or his representative had to ask a few additional questions about the tactical situation in order to get convinced that the order was justified. If this was the case, it might still happen that not all batteries could participate due to other tasks. This could then be compensated by an additional order to the two other batteries to make up for the missing third battery by firing additional rounds. If for instance the OPO/FOO had ordered '*scale four*', this implied that all guns were to fire four rounds if all of them in the regiment would participate, i.e. 4x24 rounds in total, i.e. 96 rounds. If, as in our example, only two batteries were available they had to each fire six rounds per gun (6x16 = 96 rounds). The command 'scale' could also imply immediate compensation for guns not available due to damage or crew rest, etc. Hence, this command gave excellent flexibility and was normally used by OPO/FOOs wanting to fire with more than his own guns as he/they rarely could know exactly the number of guns available.

A method to bring authorisation closer to the OPO/FOOs, or a subordinate artillery commander's tactical headquarters, and thus to speed up execution of larger engagements, was delegation of authorization from, say a divisional artillery commander to an officer acting as his representative, a CRA Representative. This could for instance be worthwhile when the whole divisional artillery was made available for the support of a brigade attack. The 'CRA Rep' went to the brigade commander for direct liaison. In the same way a regimental commander could authorise a battery commander to act as his representative.

When engaging enemy targets the fire in most cases was directed to a single point. The natural dispersion still made the artillery fire to cover an area, the size of which was dependent on the number of guns engaged. A troop normally covered a 100x100 yards area, a regiment maybe 250x250 yards. Sometimes a bigger area covered was required. Two methods to accomplish this were at hand. One was to have the engaged troop or battery to increase the impact area by increasing the width of the fire by ordering a switch of line by the command 'Sweep' and/or a change of range by the command 'Search'. The switch of the line was given in degrees and minutes relative the target centre line. And the change of range was given in yards. Thus the coverage area could be extended to fit the tactical requirements.

The second method was to order the various batteries apart such that, as an example, one battery was aimed at a point 200 yards northwest of the ranging point, and another over a dangerous area some 100 yards east of the ranging point. A large area to be covered with artillery fire could be covered by dispersing a number of 'Mike' targets (regimental targets) over it.

An important question to raise is: How much ammunition shall be used? The answer depends on the tactical situation and battle techniques to be employed by the artillery. I will discuss this later, but first a few general aspects regarding battle techniques.

Battle techniques – general factors and dilemmas

The battle techniques applied by the British artillery were influenced by technical factors discussed above, but were also based on the general nature of artillery fire of the time. Some of these were:

- Artillery was best suited for area targets
- It was easy to vary the size of the area to be covered with fire
- Comparatively long ranges made effect possible over a large area with redeployment of the guns
- Artillery fire could be concentrated and moved over a large area within a few minutes
- Artillery fire concentration was a means to accomplish local tactical superiority
- Artillery fire was an effective means to react on a crisis and thereby protecting own forces
- Remote engagement without own troops was possible
- 'The system indirect fire' offered a complete intelligence system with widespread coverage
- Although indirect fire was the prime task, this did not exclude direct fire over open sights, e.g. against attacking enemy tanks
- Contrary to air forces, artillery could be used day and night under all weather conditions

The technical constraint most affecting the battle techniques was lack of precision, which was the reason for the first observation in the list above. The effect over an area was reinforced by the use of high explosive shells spreading a large number of lethal splinters over the area where the impact came. Thus its characteristics as a weapon for area coverage could be turned into tactical an advantage in many situations, often a decisive one.

The battle technique to be applied must take into account the fact that it often was very difficult, not to say impossible, to fix the target exactly in relation to the guns. Furthermore one had to take into account that the exact location of the enemy positions might be unknown. Nor was it always obvious where the enemy would emerge and what his intentions were.

A classic dilemma on the part of the gunners therefore was whether the best method to engage the enemy was with predicted fire without having first ranged the potential target. This meant taking advantage of surprise. But it could be argued that ranging was to take place first in order to become certain that the fire for effect went down exactly where its effect could be maximised. Hence, what is best from a tactical point of view: Surprise or precision? The problem has existed since indirect fire was introduced at the beginning of the twentieth century. And indeed it was a matter of much controversy in Britain throughout the war with many opinions in the air.[146]

Those in favour of 'predicted fire' stressed the importance of surprise, often with arguments that the enemy should be exposed to the artillery fire when most vulnerable, which was before taking shelter in trenches and other fortified positions. One should furthermore not reveal own intentions, for instance a planned attack, by first ranging. Tactically this was of course correct, but only if the fire hit the right place at the right time. However, bad preparations might lead to missing the target and all would be wasted.

The opponents against 'predicted fire' argued that, almost every time, it was a waste of valuable artillery resources. Hence, always give priority to 'ranging' and other good preparations using a limited number of guns before the giant knockout blow was struck. Superior effect required artillery fire at the right place, was the message! And furthermore, it was not always necessary to do the ranging against the ultimate target. A nearby point could be chosen, if its geodetic relation (bearing, distance) to the real target was known, i.e. go for a Witness Point!

The reader might wonder how this delicate choice of alternative was made in daily situations. The answer is that the experienced and skilled OPO/FOOs and artillery commanders, who were well familiar with the artillery characteristics, shifted between the two strategies with the objective to suit the tactical requirements; quite often also combining the two. The less experienced and more cautious, and those less spirited, used to stick to a more routine-like action. Of course this could imply that the most forceful option was overlooked.

In this discussion we should, however, not forget that ranging required good observation opportunities, not least that the target itself could be observed, and observed fire control being possible to pursue. If this was not possible, 'predicted fire' was the only option. As we have seen, sometimes help with fire control could be given by the 'sound rangers', a sort of middle-alternative. We will touch on these problems again when counter-bombardment is discussed.

Another problem often encountered by OPO/FOOs was whether the artillery fire was intended for destruction or neutralisation. The former meant annihilation of the enemy soldiers and their equipment, fortifications, etc. The latter method implied making the enemy unable to fight during the course of the bombardment, for instance when the own infantry was attacking his positions. During the Great War the first method had been extensively used, but it was often found to be uneconomic, as enormous amounts of ammunition could be spent without resulting in destruction of an enemy well dug in and protected by strong fortifications. In this stationary war they had had plenty of time to construct and improve fortifications continuously. Besides the cost of wasted ammunition all the craters from exploding shells completely destroyed the terrain and made it much more difficult for advancing troops and vehicles. In other words, it meant a counter-productive use of artillery.

Hence, it was better to use the artillery to force the enemy soldiers to keep their heads (and weapons) down while own infantry attacked, unprotected as they were. This became the leading doctrine during the Second World War, as far as the British were concerned, but still a matter at issue all the time. It worked well in Europe, but in Burma the British met the Japanese, who were masters of digging shelters and building strong, deep fortifications. As they also were opponents who fought fanatically without respect for their own security, the British found the need for strong artillery fire that could lead to destruction, much stronger in this theatre than in Europe. This was a problem, as the projectiles of the lighter guns (25-pounders and 3.7-inch mountain howitzers) rarely could penetrate the ground sufficiently. More medium and heavy guns than allotted to this theatre were thus needed desperately. The few available could, however, often be efficiently used as 'bunker-busters' by means of direct fire against enemy fortifications.

The relation between effect and ammunition spent was a matter for many systematic analyses during the war. Investigations in the field, when the result of a known ammunition spending could be studied in terms of killed soldiers, destroyed equipment and fortifications etc., gave good answers as to the physical effects. It was much more difficult to analyse psychological effects of the fire. How many shells were needed for neutralisation of a battle-experienced group of soldiers as compared with neutralisation of un-experienced soldiers? What did fire intensity mean? And would a fewer number of large-calibre shells be better than a larger number of smaller? Such questions were many, and finding definite answers was difficult.

Anyway, an illustration of the relation between ammunition consumption and effect is given in **Table 12-1**, which is made from data presented by Nigel Evans.[147] In this table 'Neutralisation' has the meaning discussed above, i.e. the enemy soldiers cannot observe and use their weapons as long as the artillery firing is going on. 'Demoralisation' means that there is a lasting effect long after the fire has ceased. Reduced ability or will on the part of the enemy to continue fighting is noticed. Finally, 'Partial Destruction' means that about 2% of the soldiers in trenches are killed or wounded, 20% if they lack this kind of protection. In the table, the area covered by fire is assumed to be 100x100 yards.

Table 12-1. Ammunition required for effect

Effect	25-pounder	5.5-inch Gun
Neutralisation	8–32 rounds/min	3–12 rounds/min
Demoralization	40 rds/hr during 4 hours	16 rds/hr during 4 hours
	100 rds/min during 15 min	30 rds/min during 15 min
Partial destruction of unit equipments	40 rds	16 rds

Note. For more precise definition of effects see Evans 'British Artillery in World War 2, Effects and Weights of Fire'

The effect of protection on ammunition consumption is illustrated in **Table 12-2** by means of data from Evans.[148]

Table 12-2. Relative risks of becoming casualty

Protection level/position	Relative probability
Standing	1
Lying	1/3
Firing from open trench	1/15 – 1/50
Crouching in open trench	1/25 – 1/100

The figures show the relative likelihood for being hit by shell splinters. Not least the final line illustrates very clearly how important it was to dig in as soon as possible whenever this was possible. It became routine for British gunners to dig themselves in as they always were at risk for being exposed to enemy counter-bombardment when near the guns or at observation posts. 'Sweat saves blood!' was an undisputed lesson from the war.[149]

The doctrine was there, but battle techniques were to be gradually developed

Lieutenant P. Boyle of 17 Field Regiment RA acted as FOO in the attack by the 38th (Irish) Brigade at Centuripe (Sicily) in July 1943. He tells that he sent thousands of shells over the enemy positions. On one occasion he and the commander of the unit he was supporting observed large enemy formations moving at the opposite side of a ravine and the commander felt that the enemy was preparing a counter-attack. Boyle judged the character of the target to justify a few rounds with the entire regiment, so he gave the order 'Monkey [Mike] target' (code word for engagement by regiment) and the map references for it. He first fired a few ranging rounds, and when the fire was close enough he ordered '10 rounds gunfire'. Within 60 seconds 240 shells landed within an area less than a football ground.

The company commander at his side obviously was very impressed, to such a degree that he excused himself and asked for another round. As Boyle saw it, it was not necessary as the risk for an enemy attack had been eliminated, but he used to follow the principle that if his infantry commanders requested something, he gave them what they wanted. Without further discussion he therefore turned to his signaller Corbet and said, 'Repeat' and another 240 shells whistled above them and landed right upon the target.[150]

The account tells us of some aspects of British artillery doctrine during the war. These and a few others are:

- A commander (infantry/armour) to be supported should have the FOO or the artillery commander with him for close liaison
- The artillery plan should always be well integrated with the plan of the supported commander
- A FOO could always 'order' fire and did

not have, as in other armies, first to request permission to do so. At company and battalion level immediate support by a troop (4 guns) or a battery (8 guns) could thus be provided. Often the FOO, as indicated in the example above, was authorised in advance to engage his whole regiment, sometimes many regiments

- Ammunition shortage normally was not an issue. Hence, speed and concentration of fire were the priorities
- Speed and concentration of fire often was a higher priority than precision and extensive fire preparations
- Striving for surprise was always encouraged
- Artillery was to be used also for deception purposes
- Fire plans should always be as simple as possible, even when large, in favour of speed and reduced risks for errors in calculations at command posts
- The British batteries had more guns (normally 8) than was common in other armies (4–6). This facilitated concentrations of firepower

This is how the central features of the British artillery doctrine can be summarised. The doctrine was well established already when the war started. But the battle techniques necessary for implementation were less advanced. Hence, concentration of firepower was not normal practice, maybe for historical reasons. The 'Battery' was the administrative unit and central point for fire engagement rather than the 'Regiment'. Arms prestige and rivalry had not favoured the so important all-arms exercises, which were almost non-existent between the world wars. Commanders of tank formations seemed to believe that they did not need any artillery support at all, 'they had their own guns'. Perhaps a modern 'Balaklava Syndrome'?[151]

Brigadier R.G.S. Bidwell touched upon the problem in an article 1967:

> The British Army has [...] another fatal mental habit, which is to consider problems on a single arm instead of an army basis. An American, a Russian or a German commander would be astonished at the doctrine, which British gunners tamely accept, that it was (and is) part of an artillery commander's duty not only to instruct the other arms in the correct use of artillery, but to go cap in hand selling his wares.[152]

The development of radio communication technology had not been taken advantage of by the infantry. Many old-timers considered it unnecessary to use radio sets. A loud and clear voice would do! And if this was not enough one could always use dispatch riders. With this attitude it was even more difficult to establish an efficient all-arms cooperation including artillery, not least when it came to concentration of firepower in mobile battles.

The doctrine introduced later during the war that artillery resources were to be tactically led at highest possible level, Centralised Command, and the technical management at lowest level, Decentralised Control, was not even well understood and accepted in the Royal Artillery during the first years of the war. A consequence was that it was more difficult to live up to the doctrine of rapid concentration of firepower.

Although not an organisation with just fairly lame interest in modernisation, it took time until development of tactics and battle techniques in the Royal Artillery geared up; when it did so, this was in the first place attributed to devoted efforts by a few determined men. Generals Jack Parham and Sidney Kirkman, (Brigadiers in 1941–1942), must be mentioned as the foremost of these.

After the evacuation from France in May/June 1940, which will be discussed in detail in Chapter 16, it was easier to get acceptance for changes, this in the light of bitter experience from the campaign in France and Belgium. But the leadership had to come from individuals with the correct understanding of the modern war but also the opportunities offered by the technological development. In order to succeed these individuals had to be well respected for their professionalism and, not the least, be in possession of a true entrepreneurial spirit. Jack Parham was a man of this calibre. Another was the mentioned Sidney Kirkman. We will come back to these distinguished men several times later in the book.

During the critical period 1940–1942 both were as mentioned Brigadiers after Dunkirk and enjoyed strong support from General Alan Brooke, who himself had a background as gunner, and during the first critical years had the important position of Commander-in-Chief Home Forces (from 25 December 1941 Chief

Imperial General Staff). Another supporter was Brooke's artillery commander Otto Lund, Major General Royal Artillery.

Back to Brigadier Bidwell:

> [...] Fortunately some single-minded and determined men, acting largely on their own and sometimes in defiance of accepted habits of thought, forced their ideas on the Army, but this is not the way to handle great affairs. As long as wars are fought the business of artillery is the business of all.[153]

In this context we must not forget the Corps and Division Commanders who early in the war understood the importance of all-arms training, one of them the renowned commander of V Corps (later commanding XII Corps and South-Eastern Army, Home Forces during the early years) Lieutenant General Bernard L. Montgomery.

The old doctrine got its real meaning through further development of methods and techniques and – not the least – training. It is well justified to state that the most important phase of the new trend was concluded in the autumn 1941 with the historical huge army Exercise *Bumper*. I will discuss later what it meant. At this stage, I would however like to say that the battle methods and techniques presented in this book from here onwards represent state-of-the-art from 1942 to the end of the war, although some adaptations of these had to be made during the final years in the light of new experience gained and increased resources.

Now we are to look a bit more closely at battle techniques applied for attack, i.e. offensive actions.

Violent, persistent – battle techniques for attack

Even if the objectives of the artillery fire could vary quite a lot, and there was room also for flexibility in its application, a few basic techniques were to be used. They can be summarised under the term 'Covering Fire'. These were:

- Facilitating the attack by supported units by launching a barrage
- By means of immediate observed fire supporting an attack when this was pursued, once the primary objectives had been reached
- Assisting with fire in protection of seized ground/terrain
- Harassing with fire on depth enemy's transport, supplies, work at headquarters, communication centres, etc.
- Providing forceful counter-bombardment against enemy artillery and mortars before and during attacks by own forces
- Sealing off part of the battle theatre with smoke
- Providing some artificial light in support of attacks during nights
- Taking part in deception operations

It might be added that the artillery bombardment sometimes was carefully coordinated with fire from naval artillery, strategic bomber formations and fighter-bombers, the latter using guns and rockets. This kind of cooperation was in particular arranged in connection with the huge landings in Italy and Normandy, but also in connection with the smaller operations in Burma. In these cases officers from the Royal Artillery were engaged for liaison and fire control. It is not possible in this book due to lack of space to discuss the details and outcome of such cooperation. Later on I will, however, briefly touch upon some related issues.[154]

The large barrages fired during the war became a special token on the part of the British. But only after three years of war the resources were available and the competence at hand. It was then possible to fire a barrage for several hours in support not only of divisional attacks, but also one or two coordinated Corps attacks could be well supported by this kind of covering fire. This was at the upper end of the scale, in the lower end were barrages fired for single companies and battalions. Even in such situations the aim was to concentrate firepower from more units than normally attached to them for support.

Robertson (1986) gives an example from Burma in the spring of 1944:

> At 22.20 the guns opened up on Cain, Rabbit and Poland – all hell was let loose. In the Kalapanzin Valley the guns of 136th, 139th, 7th Indian and 6th Medium and from west of the Mayu 130th Field and 1st Medium fired simultaneously. Seventy-two 25-pdrs, sixteen 3.7-inch howitzers and thirty-two 5.5-inch guns poured a torrent of shells on the two features for twenty minutes. The

noise of the guns firing and the shells exploding echoed and re-echoed off the many ridges of the Mayu in a fantastic volume of sound. It was a very bright moon that night but the continuous flashes from each of the gun areas looked like bursts of summer lightning.

All the noise ceased as abruptly as it started, to be replaced by a new sound. In the Gun and Happy Valleys we were roughly five thousand yards, say three miles, from the forward infantry of the 1/11th Sikhs whose attack went in the moment the fire of guns ceased. But we could hear their shouts and war cries as they went in with the bayonet. …] and nothing could have withstood the ferocity of their attack, and they gained their objectives in grand style. The attack was followed at once by that of 4/15th Punjabis on Point 142 which had also been included as one of the targets of the artillery concentrations […].[155]

Large barrages needed extensive preparations with many fire plans and plans for ammunition supply and stocking in advance, sometimes also plans for redeployment of hundreds of guns and much more. Hence, a lot of paper work was required! The principle was to have strong artillery fire on the enemy front positions when the own troops approached the starting line for their attack. When this was commenced the artillery fire was moved in steps backwards into the area held by the enemy aiming at neutralising him when the infantry approached their positions. Sometime the objective could also be destruction of such positions and heavier weapons such as machine guns and anti-tank guns.

'Covering fire' was planned in accordance with one of two principles:

- Fire concentrations at selected well-defined targets for a certain period of time, and opening of fire at specified times. The fire was subsequently moved ahead in line with the attack to new targets until the attacking infantry/armour had reached their objectives. These were 'Timed Concentrations'
- Rolling or creeping Barrage against line targets, shifting from one line to another after a couple of minutes determined by the speed of the attackers

Robertson's account above is an example of application in accordance with the first principle. A prerequisite was that the enemy positions had been fixed exactly from previous fighting and/or intelligence sources (not least using the intelligence resources of the artillery). It was also necessary to determine when and where the enemy would be most dangerous against the attackers during various phases of the attack. The advantage with this method was that precious artillery ammunition was not wasted on non-existent positions.

Some of the described techniques were standardised and much practiced during exercises and other attacks thus to facilitate planning and distribution of orders. The aim was always to reduce the necessary paper work during preparations. The paper work at headquarters and command posts was still a real burden. It was a manual work with paper and pen with the support only from standard forms, logarithm tables, and paper traces etc. Not easy a task when one is exhausted due to lack of sleep and exposed to enemy fire! Douglas Goddard recalls how it was when the 112 (Wessex) Field Regiment RA planned for Operation Clipper, the offensive at Geilenkirchen in November 1944:

> Spent very cold morning at new gun positions. At front line and rather lively. Rained all evening and my bivouac got soaked through. Constantly working on fireplans. The night's air activity had hordes of ours going out and some of their coming in [. . .][156]

A measure taken to make the planning of 'Timed Concentrations' a bit easier was, as mentioned above, to use standardised terms for description of targets and how much artillery to engage depending on the size and importance of targets, Mike Target (regimental), Uncle Target (divisional), etc. They could help when this type of 'covering fire' was planned.

Targets to be engaged in support of infantry/armour attacks were given letters and numbers showing what kind of target they represented, 'M1234' for a 'Mike' target, 'U1234' for an 'Uncle' target and so on. In the fire plan the map references (coordinates and heights) were given for such targets, and with which units to engage them. Time when the fire was to start had to be given as well. Type of ammunition and fuzes must, as well as the fire intensity, be given in the fire plan. In case some kind of ranging was needed this should also be noted (although not often).

Provided batteries were to be laid at the same point for all guns in a regimental concentration (25-pounders) covered an area of around 250x250 yards and a divisional around 350x350 yards or a bit more. If medium guns were engaged as well, this area increased to around 400x400 yards. These dispersions of fire must be taken into account in the planning as must related safety distances for the advancing infantry/armour.

The fire plan was as discussed above carefully coordinated with the plan of the commander of the attacking units, taking into account the time needed by these to reach the 'start line' for the attack. Sometimes the fire had to remain in this position quite a long time, maybe up to an hour or so before the attack commenced. When it was underway, the fire had to be moved in steps into the enemy's area, i.e. a Creeping Barrage. Ideally the attackers should follow the fire, just close behind it, thus taking advantage of its neutralising effect. Normally the fire plan included all the shifts forward needed until the attacking units had reached their first-hand objectives.

Next, the plan was designed to give as good support as possible when the attackers were to pursue their advance towards the second objectives. This would in most cases require more neutralising fire for some time against the most dangerous enemy positions (targets). Such neutralising concentrations were often to begin with a massive punch with all participating guns shooting as quickly as possible a certain number of rounds, remember the fire order '6 rounds gunfire' or the like, this before the enemy took shelter in slit trenches or fortifications. Then firing could proceed more slowly during the time needed for neutralisation. As a basis for planning of 'covering fire' a set of standardised terms for fire intensity existed, which are shown in **Table 12-3**.

It might be added that a 25-pounder crew when ordered 'Gun fire' used to fire 6–8 rounds/minute.[157] If, however, firing at this rate for a long period was ordered this could result in over-heating of the barrel, in particular when high charges were used. When planning this was another factor to take into account, especially when large fire plans were to be implemented. Large operations often included fire plans lasting as much as 5–10 hours of continuous firing. To avoid over-heating fire intensity was kept as low as possible. Another measure was taking the guns out of action every 45 minutes for a 10-minute break. This was an appreciated break also for the crews. An even more drastic measure to deal with over-heating was to spray the barrels with water, if available.

The safety distance, i.e. how close to the moving fire the attackers could proceed without being hit by own shells, varied with calibre. As a rule of thumb the British used 150 yards for shells fired by 25-pounders and 300 yards if they attacked behind the fire of medium guns. These distances were approximate and were valid when the direction of fire and the direction of attack roughly coincided. If the angle between the two was 90° one had to increase the safety distance for 25-pounders to around 200 yards, which was due to the fact that the fragments from the bursting shells were dispersed more across the fire direction than along it.

We will now have a look at the second principle for arranging covering fire, i.e. the *Barrage* principle. This fire could be either a creeping or rolling belt of fire against linear targets. It was much used, in particular when the artillery was to support major operations. The advantage was that the fire covered the whole area over which the attackers were advancing, irrespective of whether a section of it was more dangerous than the other. The disadvantage was that it required much more ammunition and that quite a lot of this might fall where no enemy positions existed.

The whole front was initially to be covered with fire as close as possible to the attacking units, the 'opening line'. From this the fire would move from one line to another in intervals equalling the pacing speed of the attackers. For infantry a shift of 100 yards every 2–4 minutes

Table 12-3. Intensity of covering fire (Rounds per minute)

	25-pounder	Medium guns (4.5-inch/5.5-inch)	Heavy guns (7.2-inch)
Intense	5	2	1
Rapid	4	1 1/2	1/2
Normal	3	1	1/3
Slow	2	2/3	1/4
Very slow	2	1/3	1/8

was considered appropriate, and for tank formations 200 yards every second minute.

The term 'barrage' is in literature often used incorrectly as a term for heavy artillery fire in general, either in defensive or offensive operations, but the term had a well-stipulated meaning implying a stationary or moving belt of fire providing a protective screen behind which the attackers advanced.[158]

The method (principle) was not new, it had been practiced already in the Great War, but it was refined during the Second World War. In its simplest form it was designed as illustrated in **Fig. 12-2**.

This figure illustrates how a regiment fired a 'barrage'. As seen, the fire from two batteries was arranged beside each other. It was calculated that the width of the fire of a troop was 140 yards, i.e. a battery covered a front of 270 yards and the two 560 yards. The fire of the third battery was superimposed over the two other batteries. If the 'barrage' was to cover the advance of tank formations, the regimental belt could be reduced to around 400 yards. Several regiments, engaged in parallel, might support a larger formation's attack. As we will see some large operations would require a front of simultaneous fire covering several kilometres.

Referring to **Fig. 12-2** with its illustration of the basic design of a regimental 'barrage', the opening fire was on line a–a and when the attackers commenced their advance the fire was shifted to line b–b and then to c–c after 2–4 minutes etcetera, until the last line had been reached. If deemed advantageous, pause lines could be included in the fire plan, for instance when the first objectives had been captured and redeployment of the attackers was necessary before continuing the advance. In Part 3 of the book we will see several examples of 'barrages' with many regiments participating. A 'barrage' over a front of 4km and a depth of 4km or even more became quite common in large operations. In such cases pause lines were necessary and they could imply a break in the advance for an hour or more.

The advantage of the 'barrage' was that it was not necessary to know exactly where the enemy had his positions, which in particular often would be difficult towards the depth of the battle area. Another advantage it offered the attackers was the psychological support they experienced from the continuous fire close ahead of them but also further back. The disadvantages were several. One was that the fire not always fell on top of the enemy positions, which could imply less efficient neutralisation when this was most needed. Another was, as mentioned, the waste of ammunition.

The preparations for a covering fire of this type were simple. Regimental headquarters and battery command posts received the corner coordinates, for instance 'B' in **Fig. 12-2**, and the main direction of the 'barrage'. They also had to know the moving speed of the advance. With this information it was easy for command posts to prepare a 'gun programme' for every gun. This was possible, as all calculations in relative terms had been calculated beforehand. It was then easy to recalculate from the real coordinates, adding when needed also 'Corrections of the Moment' (CoM).

One problem was that the enemy's position might be non-linear, hence they would not conform to the linear barrage format. Positions were placed with regard to the terrain and tactical considerations. This meant that neutralisation was effective where the fire belt coincided

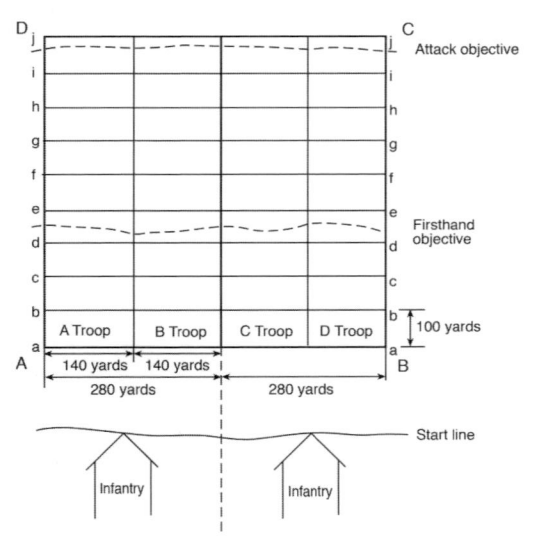

Fig. 12-2 Standard barrage to be fired by one field regiment. The fire from two of the batteries are beside each other along the first line, the third battery is imposed over the two. The fire was moved forward to subsequent lines with a speed adapted to the advancing speed of the attacking infantry or armoured units, for infantry normally 100 yards every 2–3 minutes, for armoured units a bit faster, say 200 yards every 2–3 minutes (Author)

with the enemy positions whereas the fire was a failure when not. The remedy, at least partially, was to adapt the 'barrage' layout in such a way that fire belts better overlapped positions, at least when the fire was to commence and where it was to cease. Two variants existed.

One of them was called the '*wheel method*'. Adaptations of the fire belts to the enemy positions were made such that the distance between belts were made shorter at one flank while it was retained at 100 yards on the other side. One never increased the distance above 100 yards. This design implied that the attackers had to advance with different speed when it was wanted to get them into all enemy positions simultaneously. It could work if the speed difference was not too big.

The other method was called the '*echelon method*'. As with the previous method the opening line and the last were designed to overlap enemy positions as well as it was possible. The fire belts between these were located with equal distance between them. Hence, the advancing speed was expected to be the same. The disadvantage was that attackers had to cover different distances before breaking in with their bayonets. Which method to choose had to be carefully considered in respect of the overall plan for the attack. This is an example where close cooperation between the commander of the attackers and his artillery commander was necessary in order to maximise the effect of the artillery support. In large operations the two methods had to be applied in parallel on different sectors.

The 'barrage method' worked well when the terrain was fairly unobstructed and the attacker's rate of advance easily predicted. In a very hilly terrain this was not possible, in particular when the slopes were covered with dense jungle as in Burma. The speed of an attack in deep snow could also be very difficult to estimate in advance. Under these circumstances it was better to plan the covering fire with 'timed concentrations' with appropriate pause lines. Preparations for changing of the timings and switches of fire, as well as shifts to other targets, must also be done, i.e. flexibility was required.

If medium guns were available normal practice was to have them firing on a belt or target beyond that of the 25-pounders, i.e. a bit further away from the attackers in respect of their larger safety distance. If the area to capture was deep and availability of artillery permitted it, several belts/lines behind each other could be fired at simultaneously and with the fire from medium guns superimposed over the fire from 25-pounders.

Taking as an example a 'barrage' designed as in **Fig. 12-2**. One field regiment could fire at the line a–a and another at b–b and a third one at c–c with a medium regiment also firing at c–c. If a Creeping Barrage was planned all the units moved one line ahead simultaneously, say every second minute, without changing the positions between. An alternative was the Rolling Barrage implying that the regiment firing on a–a, after say, two minutes, 'jumped' over the two nearest, which regiments continued their bombardment, to line d–d. After another say, two minutes, it was followed by a 'jump' by the second field regiment from b–b to line e–e. Two minutes later this was followed by the third field regiment and the medium regiment which both 'jumped' from c–c to f–f and so on. Hence, the barrage 'rolled' forwards further into the area to be captured by the attackers. A distinct advantage with this method was that a regiment could 'stay' firing at every line engaged longer than in the 'creeping barrage' alternative, hence the need for re-laying the guns was reduced. This method was often preferred when attack by tank units were supported. Further examples will be presented in Part 3 of the book.

The standard-pattern type of barrage was easy to implement at command posts. The disadvantage was that the line targets not always covered the terrain where enemy positions were to be engaged. In order to get a better coverage two alternative methods were used as indicated in **Fig. 12-3**.

To the left of the middle section, which is the simple standard version, the pattern called 'wheel method' is shown. As seen the line targets have been adjusted to cover the enemy positions better, but they are therefore not parallel. In the left part the attackers had to slow down while those on the right side had to cover a longer distance before they all broke in on the defenders simultaneously. The method required more of calculations at command posts.

To the right of the middle section all line targets still are parallel but the first one is placed over the enemy position, and possible the first objective, the so-called echelon method. As seen the final lines do not cover the final objective.

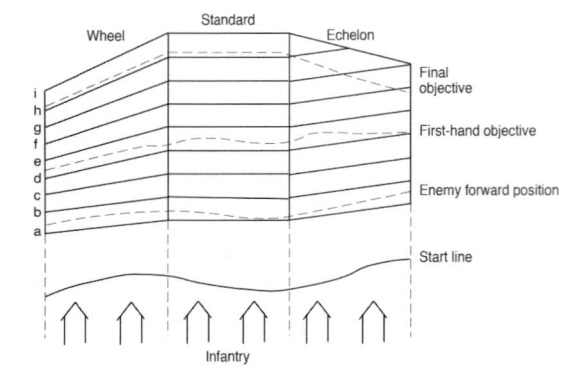

Fig. 12-3 Examples of so-called Crooked Barrages. The left section was designed in accordance with the *wheel method*, where the different line targets were placed to cover enemy positions and are not parallel, which meant that the advancing attackers had to cover different distances. They, however, reached the final enemy positions simultaneously. The middle section has the standard design as this covers the enemy positions quite well. The right section is designed in accordance with the *echelon method*. The first line target fits quite well to the initial enemy position. All other line targets are in parallel with this first one. Hence, the final fire will not cover all parts of the final enemy positions at the same time and the attackers will not engage them simultaneously (Author)

The advantage is that all attackers can advance the same distance and pace between the lines. The disadvantage is obvious. All the attackers will not reach the final objective simultaneously. Those advancing to the left will have to wait for more fire lifts before they have covered a longer distance and reached the enemy position.

A large fire plan in support of a major attack could comprise both 'timed concentrations' on individual targets and 'barrages' with several sections of the various types discussed above. The plan was in writing and could include map overlays for graphic illustration of targets, barrage lines etcetera and tables with data on participating units, schedules and more. The details were given in Task Tables. In Part 3 a few examples will illustrate some large barrages.

Fig. 12-4 is an example of a Gun Programme, which was given as the fire order to each gun based on the unit's fire order. It was the responsibility of No. 1 to order laying of his gun and preparation of ammunition in accordance with the programme and then to fire the gun in strict adherence of the time ordered for each serial.

Sometimes the paper work was as mentioned very challenging, in particular when fire plans and gun programmes for huge operations such as attacks by a division or a Corps were to be prepared. The distribution of orders and fire plans in time was also a large undertaking.

Ammunition had to be brought forward and stocked close to each gun when large fire plans were to be executed. Special transport had to be organised, as it could be a matter of stocking say 500–600 shells with cartridges, cases and fuzes of different types. Transportation normally took place at night hence the dumping programme might take a week. To re-supply the guns with new ammunition to cope with the needs for the fighting under days or weeks after the initial attack was another logistic challenge of great magnitude.

During the final phase of the war plans for large operations often included participation of anti-tank guns, tanks, heavy machine guns and also anti-aircraft guns in a ground role. Special fire plans for such participation, which was called '*Pepperpotting*', were carefully drawn up as a complement to the artillery plans.

Sometimes special plans for attacks on

Fig. 12-4 When a fire plan had been prepared, each gun got a 'Gun Programme', where it was described exactly when the gun should fire, how it should be layed and ammunition type to be used as well as fire intensity. This example refers to a barrage that was to be fired for half an hour (Douglas Goddard archive)

enemy anti-aircraft positions also had to be prepared. This kind of engagement plans for own artillery was called an *'Apple Pie'* [Programme].

The time needed for all these preparations including distribution of orders was necessarily variable, but training manuals gave as guidance the following:

- A fire plan for a regiment: 3 hours
- A fire plan when all the divisional artillery is to participate: 10–12 hours
- A fire plan for all the artillery of a Corps: 24 hours

For the simplest form of a standard 'barrage' as illustrated in **Fig. 12-2**, a written order was not necessary. The limited number of data required could easily be transferred to those concerned by radio communication. Hence, it was often called a *Quick Barrage*, which became a very popular method towards the end of the war, in particular when the number of participating units was limited. This technique was the object for much training aiming at reducing the time for fire preparations as compared to these given above. If no re-deployment of guns was needed the time could be reduced to the following values:

- A regimental 'barrage': 60–80 minutes;
- All divisional artillery to be engaged: 2 hours.

Before leaving this section of the chapter we will look at an account by a platoon commander, Lieutenant W.H. Pope, illustrating how he experienced covering fire when this worked, as it should. He tells that he reached the opening line just at H hour with his platoon in column behind him. Everything happened so quickly that it was impossible to really find out where the attack objects were. In the early morning with haze and smoke from bursting shells he recognised a hill on top of which there were a few buildings. As the barrage moved in steps of 100 yards upwards on the slope he quickly decided the buildings to be his first-hand objective.

Pope's soldiers followed the barrage as close to it as they dared, i.e. around 100 yards behind the bursting shells. He tells us that as soon as he saw bursts 100 yards nearer the enemy he dashed forward and jumped into a pit after the burst and found the walls of it still hot after the explosion 30 seconds earlier. If no enemy shells mixed up with their own nothing could stop them advancing, only short stops after each hundred-yard dash. He felt proud of his platoon attacking for the first time. No German soldier could be seen; they were all forced to keep their heads down in their slit trenches. Not without satisfaction he noticed the great advantage of following the barrage closely, the platoon reached its objective before the enemy noticed them.[159]

Unplanned heavy blows might be lashed after the barrage

The pre-planned fire plans for attack covering had their end, but the attacks normally went on. But sometimes things did not develop as planned, and an attack had to be stopped. This also called for the artillery fire plan to cease and a new plan hastily improvised by the commanders of the supported arm and the artillery. What was to follow was *'Observed Fire'* against targets suddenly emerging and not included in any previous plans, against *Opportunity Targets*. The whole palette of possible actions by the guns was then to be used, from quick-firing troops and batteries to the real big strokes with all the artillery of a division or a Corps. I have described the methods and techniques before and will not repeat them here. I will end this section with two examples illustrating how artillery could be used in such situations. First we will see what a subaltern, Fairley Mowat, had to say in his account from the battles in the mountainous terrain of Sicily.

One hour after sun set the infantry unit he was supporting was exposed to heavy enemy artillery fire. When this ceased a battalion of grenadiers attacked from the northwest. They were met, stopped and thrown back much thanks to concentrated fire from three British regiments, which was ordered via radio ['Uncle Target']. Twice the grenadiers tried to climb the slope; twice they were thrown back.[160]

We will then look at a statement from a high level officer, the commander of XXX Corps, Lieutenant General Brian Horrocks. He recalls how he used to take advantage of the artillery firepower during the battle of Normandy in 1944:

Those fine Infantry Divisions […] had been fighting in the thick Normandy Bocage for many weeks; not only were they physically exhausted but they had also suffered heavy casualties – as always, among the leaders of all ranks. When we heard over the air that our advance was held up by tough enemy resistance we would halt our infantry and tell them to be prepared to launch another assault in X minutes. I would then switch the whole of the Corps Artillery on to the point of resistance [hence a *Victor target*] – a ten-minute concentration was usually enough. The next message we received was always to the effect that our troops were advancing again.[161]

To protect attacking units, when they had taken their first objectives, defensive fire could be prepared in advance, the plan being part of the overall plan for covering fire. The battle technique was the same as that to be used in stationary situations, which we will have a look at in the next section. The creation of smoke screens by means of smoke shells as a component of the covering fire was also a technique often applied. Sometimes artificial light over the battlefield was required, and this could also be delivered by the gunners. Plans for harassing fire and counter-bombardment on enemy artillery and mortars normally were made as well. I will discuss these techniques later, but first we will look at battle techniques used in defence.

Be prepared to hit back hard! Battle techniques for the defence

The techniques applied by the artillery in stationary defence situation were the same as applied in quickly emerging situations during an offensive, for instance when the captured objectives had been taken and had to be defended. The basic difference was time for preparations. The methods were in summary:

- Concentration of fire towards an area where the enemy was deploying as preparation for a counter-attack
- Defensive fire close to own positions to stop an on-going enemy attack
- Covering fire in support of own counter-attacks
- Counter-bombardment, i.e. fire aiming at neutralisation or destruction of enemy artillery and mortars

In a defensive position it was necessary to be able to concentrate as much artillery as could be made available against an enemy concentrating forces for an attack. The aim was to launch a quick but massive response necessitating early preparations. This was called '*Counter Preparation Fire*' (CPF). The target map references could be the same for all units to participate, but fire could be prepared also against a wider and deeper target if found appropriate. Sometimes a CPF-target was designated as a '*Murder Target*' when all divisional artillery regiments were to fire at the same point on the ground.

In order to finally stop the enemy attacking if 'Counter Preparation Fire' failed, or to counter an attack where such fire had not been prepared, defensive fire was prepared along the whole front of own positions, and close to these. This was normally prepared by registering targets with extended width, i.e. line targets located beside each other. To facilitate such preparation a standardised concept was introduced, it was called '*Stonk*'. This was a line target where the fire from a regiment was spread over 525 yards, i.e. slightly wider than the regimental targets of the standard 'barrage'. The depth of the fire was not specified, it was to be determined by the dispersion of the shells. To register a 'Stonk' it was sufficient with the map reference of the middle of the target and the bearing of the target.

The method had been invented in North Africa towards the end of 1942. Width and depth were then not fixed and many versions were applied initially, but from 1943 the above specification was decided. This did not, however, prevent the New Zealanders from using their own variant, which implied a width of 1,200 m and a depth of 300 m.

Fire to stop an attacking enemy close to own positions by means of 'Stonks' or concentrations was called *Defensive Fire* (DF) or *SOS Fire*. The latter was one of the targets deemed to be in the most dangerous direction. All guns not engaged in other activities should be laid on this particular target. By this arrangement opening of fire could take place on order without any further preparations. Registered targets for defensive fire were given a number preceded by the letters 'DF', i.e. 'DF 123' as an example.

A 'chain' with 'DF-targets' were located around most of the defenders' own positions and call for fire could be made on radio or telephone

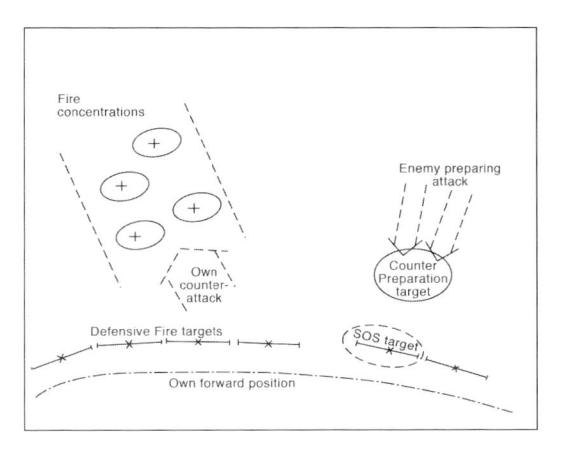

Fig. 12-5 The battle techniques in defence. Where an attack by the enemy was most likely to take place, fire by all available artillery units was organized. It was called 'Counter Preparation Fire'. To meet an attack that had not been possible to prevent beforehand, targets just in front of own positions were planned with a number of such targets beside each other. This was called 'Defensive Fire'. When no other activity was going on, all guns should be layed on the most dangerous part of this line of targets, 'SOS Fire' as it was called. Normally, own counter attacks were also prepared. These could be supported by means of either rolling or creeping barrages, but as indicated in the picture timed concentrations could be an alternative (Author)

or signal pistol (Very light). Using Very lights could be a good reserve alternative. Two or three signals from a signal pistol could mean that a particular section of the defensive fire, or the 'SOS Fire target', should be engaged by the guns immediately. These signals were of different colour, preferably say two green and one red. By such arrangements mistakes and confusion could be avoided.

In support of own counter-attacks the simplest form of covering fire, for instance a Quick Barrage, could be prepared, or improvised when needed. Such improvisations tended to replace written orders towards the end of the war. Again, speed in action was always a priority.

A summary of battle techniques applied in defence is given in **Fig. 12-5**. As mentioned earlier some of these techniques could also be applied in attack, once the attacker had reached their objectives and had to defend the ground captured.

Some battle techniques used in both an offensive and in defence
Harassing fire

An important element in the preparations for an offensive, but also in defence, was plans for fire into the depth of enemy positions, *'Harassing Fire'*. This could be fired by single guns only, but also by many more, for instance a battery or several batteries. A few rounds or a salvo was fired against locations where the enemy's supply transport were to pass, for instance an important road junction, or towards positions where enemy headquarters were expected to be located. Supply depots could be the targets too. The fire was taking place irregularly and preferably during the nights with the intention to disturb and worry, if possible also to cause damage. In order to avoid counter-bombardment from the enemy artillery the 'harassing fire' was fired from other gun positions than those to be used in covering the attack of own troops.

War diaries reveal that this type of firing normally was part of the ordinary routine, night after night for long periods preceding large offensive operations. Plans for this type of engagement could on the other hand also be part of the plans for a major attack.

This way of using the artillery had both its advocates and opponents. The former argued that it could affect the enemy's morale and fighting spirit and his endurance. The latter, on the other hand, were sceptic about the benefits and pointed at difficulties to get the fire at the right spot and at the right moment. In stationary situations 'harassing fire' could be applied more systematically and with better precision by taking advantage of the artillery intelligence resources such as the sound rangers, AOPs, etc.

Lieutenant Colonel T. P. Keene presented in an article in the Royal Artillery Journal a good example of the application of 'harassing fire' in December 1944. He was second-in-command of a field regiment, which was deployed for some time between Venlo and Roermond just west of river Maas. He was ordered to plan and implement a 'harassing' programme with his regiment, which was to be fired against selected targets very irregularly. It could take place within ten minutes or whenever during a period of ten hours, or it could be no fire at all!

For the programme Keene reconnoitred a special battery position to which his three batteries were rotated in turn. Good gun-pits and slit trenches and shelters for gun crews were dug as best protection against enemy artillery and mortars. Each battery fired 'harassing fire' for four days before relieved. In certain serials 4.2-inch mortars also were engaged. This was a typical day sequence:

> 07.30–07.50: Each troop fired one round against three selected targets. One of these was engaged a second time. The targets were enemy soldiers in farm buildings or in encampments. The time for this fire was chosen to coincide with catering or relief of units. The firing by the two troops and mortars were well synchronized even when engaging different targets.
> 15.00: Each troop fired one round against two different targets, often the same as had been engaged during the morning.
> 20.30: At this moment transport by means of motor vehicles across a tank ditch used to take place. A battery round was fired.
> 23.55: One troop fired one round against a likely headquarters position.
> 03.20: Ditto.

The following day and night the programme was quite different.[162]

The concealing smoke
Sometimes the battlefield had to be sealed off with smoke to prevent enemy observation and for concealing attack preparations. During the course of attack smoke was often an effective means for making it impossible for the enemy to use his heavy weapons such as machine guns and anti-tank guns, this in particular on the flanks. Blinding his artillery observation posts was another good objective. Sometimes smoke could also be used to protect sappers when building bridges. This was the case when the 43rd (Wessex) Infantry Division was to cross river Seine in France in August 1944. Douglas Goddard:

> On the 27th we should have crossed the river to a gun position in the bridgehead but two survey officers were captured with details of our existing and future gun positions so the Regt made a quick move to St Just, a hundred yards from the river and fired a continuous smoke screen to cover Sappers building the Class 40 bridge.[163]

A smoke screen comprised a series of impact points, the number of which was dependent on the length of the screen and the wind direction. If the two directions coincided a smaller number was needed as compared with the situation when the wind blew 90° across the screen direction. As an example; 300 yards in the first case and 75 yards in the latter. A smoke screen must be regularly maintained by firing repeatedly for hours, sometime days. An example of a smoke

Fig. 12-6 Smoke fired along a line was an efficient way of preventing enemy observation towards own positions. It could also blind enemy anti-tank guns. The 25-pounders were often successfully used for this type of fire. Observe the white trajectories of the shells coming in here from the left (©Imperial War Museum NA 12255)

screen fired by the artillery is shown in **Fig. 12-6**. The shells coming in from the left side can be clearly seen.

In connection with large operations the resources of the artillery were not always sufficient. After all there were other important tasks to pay attention to. In such cases Royal Engineers could activate stationary smoke generators along the front line. This was the case when the fourth battle at Cassino in Italy in May 1944 was to take place. Such generators were also used extensively for the 'great finale', when the Rhine Crossing operation in March 1945 was prepared (**Fig. 22-4**).

The gunners could fire coloured smoke although white smoke was more normal. This was often applied in Burma for provision of guidance to bombers and fighter-bombers, where the dense jungle often made it difficult to recognise targets from the air. For ordinary engagement of guns it was often found productive to commence ranging with one or two rounds with smoke shells, by which it was easier to get a better judgement of the fall of incoming rounds.

When firing a 'barrage' it could also be helpful to include a series with smoke shells, for instance to indicate a coming shift from one belt/line to the next one or for indicating that a pause would come. Marking attack objectives could be another use of smoke shells, in particular with coloured smoke.

Artificial light
Firing illumination rounds was never a great issue in the British artillery as regards provision of artificial light. During the first years of the war this type was in very short supply. Hence, other methods were applied. First, the date of an attack was chosen such that attackers could avail themselves of strongest possible moonlight, as was the preferred method in North Africa. Second, artificial light was provided by means of 90cm searchlights from the anti-aircraft regiments, which were lit towards the bottom of clouds and there reflected.[164] It was found that two searchlights could be sufficient when an infantry brigade was to attack in nights. Sometimes searchlights were used also for direct illumination of enemy positions, which could be quite a thrilling action.

Mortars could fire parachute illumination flares, which seems to be a method applied much more than having the artillery to fire such shells.

Artillery participating in deception and propaganda
The British were renowned for their skilful deceptive operations, small and huge. Such programmes could include participation of the gunners with fire and other means to conceal the real intentions such as preparations and deployment of forces for a large attack, the planned main directions of attacks etcetera. A deceptive plan could include the firing of an ordinary type of 'barrage', although at the wrong place, or timed concentrations for quite a long period far from the sector where the real attack was to be launched.

As seen earlier in the book, propaganda shells were available for the 25-pounders. Not least in connection with some stationary situations in Italy this type was frequently used to drain the enemy's morale.

Counter-bombardment always a priority
The Germans had less artillery units and guns than their British opponents, although they were skilled at concentrating fire from available resources. Priority had been given before the war to *Luftwaffe* and during the war there was not time enough for decisive artillery rearmament. This was much easier to accomplish as regards mortars and rocket-firing pieces, which towards the end of the war became a real scourge for the British. Not least were the salvos from the much-feared *Nebelwerfer*. This device was produced in several variants with different calibres. In **Fig. 12-7** is shown one, which seems to launch rockets of larger calibre than the 150mm most commonly used.

The stock of guns in the *Wehrmacht* and in the Italian Army was limited but yet large enough to cause problems for the allies, when to attack or in defence. Besides many batteries with 105-mm howitzers and other light guns, including captured Russian artillery pieces, the impact of quite a number of heavier long-range guns were also to be experienced. **Fig. 12-8** illustrates one version of the 105-mm howitzer, which was the standard piece of German divisional light artillery.

Fig. 12-9 is a photograph of a 170-mm gun in Egypt.

Enemy artillery could never be overlooked and systematic counter-bombardment programmes must always be part of all operations.

In South East Asia the Japanese opponent was not rich in artillery either and, although

Fig. 12-7 An ever-existing threat against the British troops were mortars and, as shown here, the 'Nebelwerfer', which fired six rockets. Several versions with different calibres were used. For Air Observation Officers they were good targets as it was very easy to detect their deployment thanks to the rocket trail (RAHT)

skilled in whatever he undertook, often lacked logistic resources for mass engagement of artillery (except when Singapore was besieged). Hence, artillery firepower was rarely applied. The Japanese infantry units had to stick to direct support from single guns or just a few. Counter-battery fire was thus rarely applied in this theatre and never caused the British too many problems.

Counter-bombardment against enemy artillery required accurate fixation of enemy gun positions, normally quite far beyond the front line, but a problem was that they rarely could be observed from own observation posts. Instead the intelligence resources, i.e. sound rangers, short and long observation bases and, not the least air observers and RAF air-co-operating squadrons, had to be used for the fixation of gun positions. A special, important task was bombardment of not only field guns but also enemy anti-aircraft positions when airborne formations were to be landed.

Towards the end of the war British heavy anti-aircraft guns were much used in counter-bombardment programmes, i.e. in a ground role, thanks to their long range and accuracy. Suitable fuzes added to their versatility.

Counter-bombardment was the responsibility of every artillery unit, but the large-scale programmes gradually became the prime task of medium and heavy batteries/regiments organised in a number of 'Army Groups Royal Artillery', 'AGRA' for short. This meant that the task more and more was centralized to Corps level, in particular during large operations. In the Corps artillery headquarters a special branch was therefore introduced for planning and implementing large counter-bombardment programmes. The head was the *Counter Battery Officer* (CBO) who was assisted by a group of officers and assistants. The acronym also meant Counter Battery Office. For efficient communication of data on enemy gun positions a special radio net normally was reserved; no 'middlemen'

Artillery Battle Techniques and Tactics

Fig. 12-8 The German 105-mm Leichte Feldhaubitze 18 was the standard gun in German divisional artillery. Most of the guns were horse-drawn, but half-track vehicles were also extensively used as gun tractors (RAHT)

should interfere! Speed was crucial, and as we will see, ten minutes from location of an enemy battery until receiving the British shells was considered an acceptable, and necessary, standard.

In stationary situations and before larger offensive operations, long lists with map references (coordinates) for those enemy batteries that had been located in advance were

Fig. 12-9 A German 170-mm gun in North Africa. This was one of several guns with long ranges (up to 30km) that the British must be prepared to destroy either by means of fighter-bomber aircraft or own long-range artillery (RAHT)

produced. This was made by artillery headquarters. The lists were continuously updated and often complemented with special reports from analyses made regarding the enemy artillery and its deployment.

Counter-bombardment was normally executed by means of a first heavy strike followed by neutralisation for some time. The doctrine required the fire to be planned for a superiority of at least 10–20, which meant that each enemy gun should be engaged by 10–20 British guns, hence a battery of four guns would attract the fire from 40–80 guns! This often made it necessary to bombard enemy batteries in turn. A programme like this was popularly called a '*Milk Round*'. The 'milk round' should be kept fairly short with minimum delay before the attack. When the attack was on, some units should be ready to repeat counter-bombardment against batteries that had survived the first blow. It also happened quite often that new, earlier undiscovered batteries opened up and required immediate counter-battery fire.

If counter-bombardment took place without preceding ranging, which was normal in large operations, i.e. predicted fire was applied; huge ammunition spending was required in order to acquire the wanted effect. Systematic investigations about the accuracy of the large counter-bombardment programmes fired in Operation Veritable 7–8 February 1945, close to river Rhine, gave the disappointing result that only 5.1% of the shells fired at enemy gun positions fell within 100 x 100 yards from

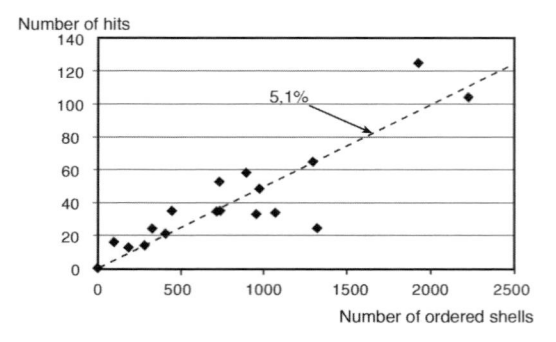

Fig. 12-10 The number of rounds hitting an area of 100x100 yards as a function of the number of rounds fired as 'Predicted Fire' in connection with the counter-battery programs of Operation Veritable in March 1945 (Source: Data have been compiled by the Author from Report No.21: Accuracy of Predicted Fire – Operation Veritable. Operational Research Sections with 21 Army Group, June 1944–July 1945. RAHT Collection MD/1479)

the centre of the target area.[165] In **Fig. 12-10** the result of the investigation is shown graphically. From this it can be seen the number of hits within 100 x 100 yards as a function of the ordered number of rounds.[166]

Efforts were made to find the reasons for the poor accuracy and several factors were discovered. This included erroneous trigonometric calculations, wrong graphic interpolations and other errors related to human behaviour, but also in-built system deficiencies and natural dispersion of shells. But the dominating factor by far was seen to be incorrect 'Corrections of the Moment' (CoM), i.e. basically weather data. Wind data for various trajectory heights that was not up to date did not help, but also, it was found, there was much stereotyped use of wind data. Resulting errors of up to 700 yards were confirmed, but most of them were in the order of 200–250 yards. The fact that acceptable effect of the fire yet was accomplished, despite the bombardment systematic errors, seems to be due to the large amount of ammunition spent.

In defence, counter-bombardment was equally important when pre-planned, but also when Opportunity Targets were to be engaged. As mentioned, the aim was to open fire on such targets within ten minutes.

War experience showed that the increasing threat from mortars and *Nebelwerfer* required better resources and methods for counter-bombardment against such pieces. On the intelligence side better resources were provided in 1944 when the 4-pen recorder came. Towards the final months of the war radar for location of mortars was also provided, albeit at a small scale. Combating mortars and *Nebelwerfers* was done with the 25-pounders and 4.2-inch mortars. Sometime heavy anti-aircraft guns could also be used with great effect on account of the steep angle of descent of their shells.

But improved coordination and control was a must. It was found that this ought to be decentralised to the brigade level. Hence the position *Counter Mortar Officer* (CMO) was introduced at brigade headquarters. The CMO was assisted by an Assistant CMO, an Intelligence Officer and a few staff assistants. An additional advantage with this reorganisation was that a closer cooperation between the artillery and the mortars of the infantry units emerged. By this the latter learned to apply artillery methods more effectively.[167] The arrangement also meant that combating mortars at the brigade level could be implemented much quicker, as compared with the previous practice when planning and control had first to be done at a higher level. This did not exclude intelligence and planning resources also at the divisional level for all kinds of counter-bombardment.

Furthermore, it was the responsibility of the artillery also to plan engagement of light bombers and fighter-bombers as parts of counter-bombardment programmes. The methods for this were refined towards the end of 1943.[168]

This review of some of the artillery battle techniques is far from complete. For much more of detailed information the reader is referred in the first place to all Artillery Training Manuals, some of which are listed in 'Sources'. It should be observed that there was a large 'palette' of techniques available for skilled gunners to use depending on the tactical and operative situation. Needless to say, this required well-trained gunners at all levels as well as numerous adequate exercises, otherwise the potential of the 'system indirect fire' would be to no avail. It must, however, be said that despite all good ambitions and good training things could go wrong, terribly wrong. Before proceeding to the next Chapter, it is worthwhile with a few words about the 'human factor' and what it could cause.

The human factor

It might be well understood that good training, adequate methods and well-conceived procedures plus the right equipment, were necessary in order to use the artillery efficiently. The gunners were expected always to perform perfectly, even when exposed to enemy fire or just were exhausted from lack of sleep. And they were also expected to take good care of their equipment, never failing to maintain it properly.

Good ambitions to do what was required were generally demonstrated, but, for instance, a signaller could fail to read correctly a written message to be transmitted, a GPO could record the coordinates of a target at the wrong place on the artillery board, a gun layer could forget to check the laying in line after having set a correction on the scales of his dial sight, the gun crew may insert Charge 2 instead of Charge 3 into the cartridge case before firing and an OPO/FOO may read the wrong bearing to a target etcetera, etcetera. It was impossible to completely avoid such mistakes; human wrong handling could take place. The 'human factor' could turn around the 'system indirect fire' and get it to fail. Of course, many control procedures existed to minimise such risks. When it still went wrong, a simple human action could result in fatal consequences.

Major Robin Powell recalls an example from Burma:

> [. . .] but at some point during the afternoon the observation post saw a number of Japanese infantry marching westwards from Buthidaung, and Colonel Mattingley, judging these to be part of a force about to form up for the counterattack we expected, asked for a salvo from the Divisional artillery on the area in which the enemy appeared to be concentrating. I consulted Dick McCaig at HQ RA at once and he sanctioned five rounds gunfire from all available guns by predicted shooting on the target indicated. This was the signal for one of those accidents of War, which are inescapable and probably more frequent than is sometimes supposed. The first round of the five from one of the 5.5-inch guns landed in the compressed area of Battalion HQ. To experience and survive one and to know that there will be four more shells to follow without having the time or chance to stop them, counts as one of least pleasant experiences of my life. When the dust had settled after the salvo ceased and the remaining four medium shells had done their worst, the toll of casualties was headed by the instant loss of Colonel Mattingley and a number of Jocks who received a direct hit in the temporary dressing station where they lay. In addition, the KOSB Signals and Intelligence officers, and many other HW staff, were wounded, [. . .]. I have always hoped that the rest of the artillery strike found its mark on the Japanese and justified poor Mattingley's last request of his Gunners.[169]

Unfortunately this was not unique a mishap. At responsible quarters all were well aware of the risks. In an evaluation report after the fighting in Italy 1943–1945 it was expressed:

> Unless CsRA [Commanders Royal Artillery] and Cos [Commanding Officers] make constant checks, the necessary standard of accuracy of all types of supporting fire will not be maintained.[170]

Without good training and frequent exercises artillery would not be the battle winning resource as it could and should be. We will now take on this subject.

13. Train, Train, Exercise, Exercise…!

Fast-track training
When the war broke out, an enormous need for training of soldiers and officers arose. It was a matter of supplying all the mobilised and new regiments with manpower. Rearmament was, as we have seen, a process going on for around four years from the day when mobilisation was ordered in September 1939. After this period, the demands lessened but never ceased entirely due to battle losses and various other reasons, a challenge becoming more and more difficult to meet.

Problems with manpower supply and training became acute already in 1938 when the sudden change of the willingness to prepare for war came as a consequence of the serious political changes in Europe. The rush to the recruitment offices of the Territorial Army (TA) was enormous. Many of the formations had for long been under nominal strength, but now people willing to enlist, often had to be referred to waiting lists. That year more than 60,000 recruits were registered.[171] The training needs became even more drastic, when the Government on 23 March 1939 decided to double TA. The decision about a month later to introduce conscription of all men at the age of 20 years, made the situation even worse.

The Royal Artillery met the 'doubling' decision by creating a new TA regiment for each of the existing ones; a kind of 'daughter' regiment was quickly formed. From the 'mother' about half of the officers and NCOs were transferred to the new formation, a consequence of which was a shortage at each of them. No equipment was initially available for the new one, neither could uniforms be provided. Training with borrowed equipment had to be improvised, at first focused on personal training. Training at unit level had to come later.

Vehicles were gradually provided, starting with the 'Fishmonger's', the 'Plumber's' and other civilian vehicles that were requisitioned by the authorities for military use. The few guns made available, besides borrowed ones, were often vintage. At the most these could be used for formal gun drills, i.e. laying, loading, deployment etc., they were labelled '*for drill purposes only*'. Rifles and other personal weapons could not be given to everyone. The few available had to be used by sentries and security squads.

True to British Army traditions, commanders emphasised personal smartness, hygiene and cleanliness. *'Spit and polish'* was the required standard! Daily parades and marches, under the command of zealous Sergeant Majors and other NCOs imposing strict discipline and correct marching order, became routine. Parades and marches to the church on Sundays were also routine, i.e. Church Parades.

It would take a year or so until the new TA regiments had been equipped and trained enough to be ready for practice firing with guns for the first time; and their staff to shoot the first few rounds with their personal weapons at a shooting-range.

Commanders at all levels were responsible for the training of their units. This was a big challenge on the part of regimental and battery commanders. Their skill in this respect was really put to the test. The room for private initiatives and creativity was always large. In particular, this was the case when personal skill of the gunners in their basic roles had been accomplished and the training began to focus on teamwork, either for a troop, a battery or the whole regiment.[172]

For practicing gun firing with field artillery several practice camps were available in 1939:[173]

- *No. 1 Practice Camp*, Larkhill/Tilshead
- No. 2 Practice Camp, Okehampton, Dartmoor
- No. 3 Practice Camp, Redesdale, Northumberland
- No. 4 Practice Camp, Trawsfynydd, Wales

Two new camps came in 1940:

- *No. 5 Practice Camp*, Otterburn, Northumberland
- No. 6 Practice Camp, Sennybridge Redesdale, Northumberland

Fig. 13-1 Direct fire against attacking tanks was much practised during the first years of the war, not least at locations along the coasts of England (©Imperial War Museum H 10910)

In 1942 the Westdown (part of Larkhill) and Okehampton ranges were handed over to the Americans, now in Britain.

As the demands on safety could be lessened a little in wartime, firing with live ammunition took place also outside the practice camps. Other training areas with live firing facilities were also set-up e.g. the South Downs in Southern England is an example. Also practice firing in areas such as Scotland took place and became routine.

Practices to improve the capability to combat enemy tanks by means of direct fire from the guns were arranged at many places along the coasts, one being Lydd in Kent. At these places firing against a moving, towed target was practiced (**Fig. 13-1**).[174]

Basic training of the mobilised units was not enough; more resources were required. Hence, a fairly large number of Training Regiments were established from autumn 1939. Twelve of these were organised to meet the training needs of field regiments as well as the needs of medium and heavy regiments. Furthermore, six such regiments were established for training of artillery signallers and two for survey units. However, a few of these training regiments could in 1940 be disbanded and most of them were closed in 1943, when the rearmament was almost completed.

Training regiments had the task to provide training in basic soldiering and gunnery skills needed by gun crewmembers, layers, fire control and command post assistants, driver's etc., before being posted for active service. During the very first years of the war, not much more than six weeks of primary training, marching and arms drilling could be done before the recruits were posted. The situation gradually improved, and when in 1943, the worst crisis had been overcome; training programmes for replacements had been extended as follows:[175]

- Primary training for all, 6 weeks, followed by further training depending on positions
- Gunners, 8 weeks
- Drivers, 12 weeks
- Specialists, 12 weeks
- Signallers, 18 weeks

Before being posted, some additional training could take place at one of the Reserve Regiments which were established to provide five weeks of unit training, primarily the functions of a troop with four guns.

For a reader today, it might seem amazing that those to become 'drivers' needed as much training as the 'specialists' (command post and fire control assistants). The reason was quite natural. At this time, not many had a driver's license from their civilian life, so training had to start from the bottom. Captain Johnny Walker recalls the problem when his battery was to take delivery of lorries from the Ford factory at Dagenham:

> It was soon discovered that of the draft of 'drivers' we received for the new trucks not one was able to drive a motorised vehicle!. They were mostly farm labourers used to working with horses! What happened consequently was commendable and one of the first examples of the resourcefulness and willingness to overcome odds that quickly became ingrained amongst the officers and men of the Regiment [1st Airlanding Regiment RA]. Remarkably, all the draft were able to go to solo after a few days intensive tuition and every one of the vehicles was safely delivered from Dagenham without a scratch.[176]

Once the basic training arrangements had got their final forms in 1943 and become a routine after much of improvisations during the first years of the war, the seven then operating training regiments for field artillery were 'producing' 120 trained gunners every two weeks. The regiment that still was active for training of replacements for medium and heavy regiments had around 200 men leaving every two weeks. The training regiments for signallers left 60 recruits every two weeks.

War-oriented officers training

Before the war, those to become regular artillery officers were trained at the Royal Military Academy at Woolwich, in southeast London, popularly called *The Shop*. Officers of the Royal Corps of Engineers and the Royal Corps of Signals were also given their officer training at this prestigious school. The courses took two years to complete.

For the Territorial Army it was different. Officers were commissioned after individual evaluation of fitness and civilian educational background and profession. The training was then performed within the own unit and the length of it varied.

Boys were often well prepared for future military service right from time at school. Most grammar schools had a special organisation for basic military training of the senior pupils, the so-called Officer Training Corps (OTC). After having passed the training, a certification was awarded to the students, Cert A, which was an indication of the student's suitability for the officer profession in the army. Similar organisations existed for preparing schoolboys for the profession in the Royal Navy and the Royal Air Force.

When the war broke out in 1939, the system for training of candidates for the officer trade was changed overnight. 'The Shop' was closed and a new system for selection of individuals was implemented, the Special Army Entry, and six special cadet schools were established, the Officer Cadet Training Units (OCTUs):

- 121 OCTU, Alton
- 122 OCTU, Larkhill
- 123 OCTU, Catterick
- 124 OCTU, Llandrindod
- 125 OCTU, Ilkley
- 133 OCTU, Shrivenham

121 and 123 OCTU were established for field artillery training, 124 and 133 OCTU for anti-aircraft artillery. In 1941, 122 and 125 OCTU were directed towards anti-tank officer training. From 1943 when the demand for new officers became smaller, the number was decreased to three, one each for field artillery, anti-aircraft artillery and anti-tank artillery.[177]

The officer training had also to be improvised initially. The length varied between three and five months, eventually to be standardised to six months for all OCTUs.[178]

Senior pupils from grammar schools were recruited to the OCTUs, but also NCOs who had in active service proved to be suitable for the officer trade. They were selected by a special War Office Selection Board (WOSB).

Douglas Goddard told me how he experienced his training as a Cadet at the 123 OCTU:

> I have still the personal diary I kept which certainly confirms that it was a very busy and demanding half year.[...] I found it a fascinating account of physical and mental exhaustion which I am rather surprised I survived – a number of original 40 cadets dropped out. To summarise the

more significant elements: the first month or so spent on introduction lectures, basic infantry drills and exercises, physical endurance tests and assault courses. From then we had leadership instruction and group tasks; constant artillery drill, exercises and firing camps; training in public speaking including lecturettes; physical toughening exercises; ceremonial parades; small arms firing; lectures and demonstrations on explosives by an explosives fanatic. Finally we went to the Lake District for a gruelling ten day- and night-battle course up and down mountains and then off to an artillery range for an advanced gunnery exercise. It was a good preparation for officer leadership in war.[179]

As was the case for all trainees, there was no time for exercises at unit level. This had to be arranged when the new Second Lieutenants came to the units to which they were posted. When *RA Notes 1943* wrote about training of gunners, officers' training was included as follows:

> Training of RA officers is carried out at three OCTUs – one each for Fd, AA and Atk. The object aimed at is to turn out a young officer who is technically sound, has a reasonable knowledge of tactics, has had a grounding in the administrative work of a unit, and is, therefore, able to assume duty as GPO or other regimental subaltern.
>
> It is important that the Regimental Commanders should appreciate that subalterns joining from OCTUs have had little opportunity of putting their theoretical knowledge into practice and that further instruction and assistance is necessary in such subjects for instance as 'man management'. In Fd Branch an attempt is made to bridge the gap between the OCTU and Regiment so far as GPOs technical work is concerned, by the institution of a Young Officers course which all ex-cadets attend before joining their Regiments.[180]

We might here add that one basic skill that was extremely important to acquire for a young gunner officer was map reading. Many commanders skilled in training used to observe the need and thus seldom missed an opportunity to train their new officers. We have in a previous chapter seen a good example of that.

This particular need inspired Colonel C.E. Ryan to an engaged article in the Royal Artillery Journal in 1941. The headline was *Map Reading Exercises* and he commenced with the words: 'DEPLORABLY LOW, INEXCUSABLY BAD. These words have been used to pillory the general standard of map reading. [...].'[181]

The good Colonel continues by saying that map reading is much more than the words tell. It is a matter of visualising the information tactically and technically, to see possible advance routes and suitable deployment positions and to work from map to ground and vice versa. 'In short, all that goes to make up and develop an eye for country and a bump of locality. Viewed thus, map reading is a fundamental military accomplishment', he adds. He says that training in map reading can be as 'dull as "ditch water" if perfunctory, but it can also be of great interest if carefully planned.' In his article he is presenting a set of fundamental exercises collected together from various sources. He does not claim them to be enough for producing good map readers, but 'they have been "tried on the dog" in the shape of some hundreds of officers, NCOs and, some of them, on men too.' But more is needed to accomplish good results from training in map reading. He urges unit commanders: 'Energy, a little imagination, and determination as always make for success.' True!

Young officers were as seen given basic training at OCTUs and other ranks at 'Training Regiments', processes which were repeated continuously during the war. To this came complementary training by the units to which the recruits were posted. If time was available, the units also tried to widen their basic skills. Gunners posted to man guns could be given training not only in serving and loading the guns but also, if talented, to be able to act as layers; signallers could be trained to serve as command post specialists, drivers to act as fire control assistants and so on. By this the unit was better prepared to meet casualties during extended battles.[182]

A number of central schools and institutions offered courses and special training programmes for widening of officers' qualifications. Officers were sent to courses in, for instance, motors, signals, intelligence, parachute jumping, headquarter staff methods and much more. The School of Artillery at Larkhill was a large and important centre for all training activities. During the war, the School was expanded to a huge institution. It had most qualified and experienced teachers and instructors covering all aspects of gunnery and the use of the 'indirect fire system'. At Larkhill, a systematic collection and evaluation of war experience also took place.

Exercises at all levels an ongoing process
Repeated drill in all basic skills needed at the guns, at command posts, at observation posts, at headquarters, by signallers, etc., was never neglected by the Royal Artillery formations. Skills needed by everyone, irrespective of position, should never fail and duties be performed even when one was exhausted or wounded. The risk for human errors must be minimised as discussed above. Drill was also seen as a good means for imposing and retaining discipline and a good spirit in the field.

But drilling in individual roles was not enough; drilling gun crews, battery and troop command post staffs and others must also accomplish teamwork. After such training, exercises at higher levels had to be run for training of troops, batteries and regiments to be able to act efficiently as coherent units in all tactical situations.

Now a few words about one of the most important challenges, all-arms-training, i.e. exercises for artillery to function efficiently in cooperation with those to be supported by artillery fire. This had been much neglected before the war, and this with sad consequences when the realities of war came. Some senior commanders with foresight drew the right conclusions and changed the attitudes and behaviour. Not least large all-arms exercises, performed before planned large operations, were arranged later during the war, and this with decisive results.

And with the real battle, the final type of training came, on-the-job-training! So in summary, the British gunners had to, all the time, Exercise, Exercise, Exercise – when done properly the battle could be won.

I will come back to these issues later in the book.

No engagement by large formations became effective unless their headquarters worked efficiently and systematically, i.e. proficient staff work of 'high calibre' was necessary for success in battle. Without it, even the best commander would fail, whoever he was. Having now reviewed artillery battle techniques and tactics, we will briefly look at the organisation of staff work.

14. Success Requires Efficient Staff Work

Three disciplines

Large battles described in literature and films with formation symbols and coloured arrows might give the impression that the General with his pen and a few words was leading his troops to victory. Everything looks so simple! But reality was far from this. A commanding General might have the right visions about what his troops should accomplish and how they would act in order to defeat the enemy, but without efficient staff work nothing would materialise.

Staff work was needed at all hierarchal levels, let alone to much varying extent. A Corps headquarters and a battalion headquarters had quite different volumes of work to do, and of course the staff resources available for it were quite different. Looking at principles, however, much work was the same. During the Second World War staff work included the following tasks in most cases:

- Monitoring and evaluating the tactical situation including preparation of various reports
- Planning of battles and other activities in the short and long term, often based on alternative scenarios
- Production of written orders or key data for oral orders to be given
- Participation in presentation of orders to subordinated commanders and units
- Distribution of orders
- Planning and leading supply of ammunition, fuel, food, spare parts etc.
- Administration of human resources including taking care of killed, wounded and prisoners of war. Distribution of information, arranging entertainment and leave schemes

In the British Army, the staff was organised in three disciplines. 'G' Staff was responsible for operations, intelligence, communication and training. 'A' Staff was responsible for manpower administration including disciplinary actions. 'Q' Staff had to take care of administration of supplies. In principle, the functions existed at all headquarters, but at lower levels some of them could be allocated to the same officer or a small group of officers.

At higher levels, officers with different ranks could be organised to take care of the different disciplines. In their turn, they were supported by assistants of lower rank, signallers and others. Looking at a divisional headquarters, as an example, the following staff members were on board:

General Staff Officer, Grade 1 (GSO 1)[183]
His task was to manage all the staff functions and, if needed, be capable of replacing the Divisional Commander. It can be said that he was responsible for the detailed operative planning and acted as Chief of Staff. He was assisted by
General Staff Officer, Grade 2 (GSO 2), who primarily was engaged in preparation of orders, planning of marches etc. In his turn he was assisted by
General Staff Officer, Grade 3 (GSO 3[O]) and General Staff Officer, Grade 3 (GSO 3 [I]). The latter was responsible for the important 'Intelligence' function. In order to secure continuity he was supported by an Intelligence Officer (IO).

When the war broke out, the staff also included an officer responsible for actions against chemical warfare and related exercises, GSO 3 (CW).

To provide effective liaison with subordinate units, there were three Motor Contact Liaison Officers (MCLO).

At the divisional level, security was extremely important to be observed in all radio and telephone communication. The officer in charge was the Cipher Officer.

The leader of the so important administrative function was the Assistant Adjutant and Quarter Master General (AA&QMG) assisted by Deputy Assistant Adjutant General (DAAG), who was responsible for disciplinary issues at the highest level and Deputy Assistant Quarter Master General (DAQMG) who was responsible for supply of ammunition and other necessities as well as equipment maintenance and repair.

The chief officers mentioned headed the various groups of staff officers, assistants and service personnel. In total the number of staff members was around 20 officers and around 120 other ranks (1942).[184] Besides the own staff also officers from other arms with their headquarters were attached to the divisional headquarters, i.e. artillery, engineers, signals officers and an RASC detachment.

As far as the artillery is concerned, we have seen that there was the Commander Corps Royal Artillery (CCRA) with his Headquarters Royal Artillery (HQRA) at Corps level and at the divisional level the Commander Royal Artillery (CRA) and his HQRA.

At higher headquarters liaison officers with the Royal Air Force and, sometimes, the Royal Navy, were important staff members. Well known is that Montgomery always kept quite a large group of young liaison officers to be sent out from his headquarters to his Corps and divisions. Their task was to convey orders and to collect detailed information about the current tactical situation, an arrangement not liked by all. Personal visits by the C-in-C would have been preferred.

The denominations of the leading staff officers were different at lower levels. At the brigade level, the 'Chief of Staff' was the Brigade Major. Responsible for intelligence was the Brigade Intelligence Officer and there could be a Staff Captain ('A'&'Q' matters) as well.[185]

At the operative and tactical levels, the above mentioned artillery headquarters Regimental Headquarters, were the most important. It should furthermore be noted that the commander of an 'AGRA' (Army Group Royal Artillery) had his own staff for leading army and Corps artillery. As mentioned earlier, a special counter-bombardment staff was organised towards the end of the war, the Counter Bombardment Office. The artillery headquarters at the Corps and divisional levels had a Brigade Major as 'Chief of Staff' and he was assisted by a Staff Captain and an Intelligence Officer, the two latter Captains in rank.

A Signals Officer was detached from Royal Corps of Signals to the divisional artillery commander's staff as were a Captain from Royal Electrical and Mechanical Engineers and a 'Met Officer' from the Royal Air Force. Two padres were normally attached to this headquarters too. So, in total there were nine staff officers at the divisional HQRA, four of which were gunners. They were supported by 47 other ranks, 28 of which were gunners.[186]

The HQRA of an armoured division was bigger as they often had to act at a forward tactical headquarters in addition to the main headquarters. Furthermore the administrative burden was larger as the staff had to take care of not only wheeled vehicles, as in an infantry division, but also numerous tracked vehicles and half-tracks. Hence, maintenance and repair was much more demanding.

The regimental headquarters was led by the Regimental Adjutant, who was assisted by the Orderly Officer; the latter acting also as 'Intelligence Officer'. For the survey function, there was a Survey Officer and for administrative tasks a Quarter Master.

Communication matters were the responsibility of the (Regimental) Signals Officer detached from Royal Corps of Signals. Maintenance and repair was the responsibility of an officer from Royal Electrical and Mechanical Engineers supported by a Warrant Officer. Finally, a Regimental Medical Officer and a Regimental Chaplain were attached at the regimental headquarters as well. In total, the regimental headquarters was manned by 6–8 officers and around 50 other ranks supporting them.

The numerical strength of the Corps artillery headquarters was smaller, around 30 all ranks. But in connection with larger operations the staff had to be reinforced, sometimes significantly. For instance, this was the case when the fourth battle of Cassino in Italy in May 1944 was planned. The artillery commander of the leading XIII Corps was supported by no less than 250 people. This is an illustration of the experience gained that the staff workload could vary significantly. At the lowest level, when battle activities were at their lowest and planning was on the agenda, it might be sufficient with a couple of individuals keeping track of what was going on. They should also keep communication lines open, should anything unexpected happen. During nights, it might even be sufficient with only one officer in charge supported by a few signallers, while the rest of the staff were asleep apart from those officers who were out visiting subordinate units. The duty assigned to the staff

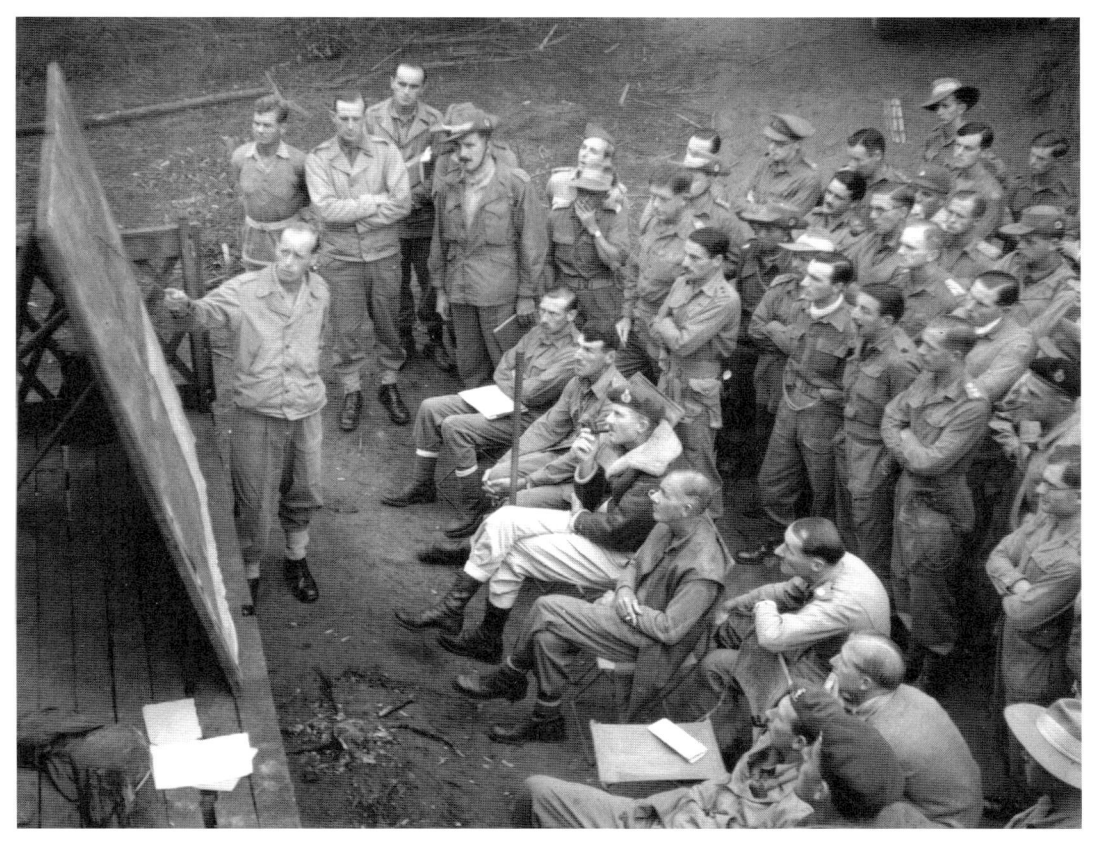

Fig. 14-1 Headquarters staff must always strive to maintain a common view of the actual battle situation. This was accomplished through regular briefings, here is pictured one held at the headquarters of 36 Infantry Division in Burma. The Commanding Officer, General F.W. 'Killer' Festing, sitting in the middle of the first row (©Imperial War Museum SE 2162)

member in charge was basically to monitor the tactical situation and immediately take action to alert the others if needed or ordered from a higher level.

The artillery – one of the best providers of tactical information

The mentioned monitoring of the tactical situation was an activity that never was allowed to fail. What the enemy was up to as well as the engagements of own troops on the battlefield must always be closely monitored. From all conceivable sources such information was all the time collected by the Intelligence people and systematically evaluated. Based on this, regular Intelligence reports, 'Sitreps', Intelligence Summaries, Engagement Reports, etc. were prepared and distributed. Amongst sources for such information were reports from reconnaissance patrols and interrogations of prisoners of war. One of the most important groups of information suppliers were the intelligence resources of the artillery. The network of observation posts, sound rangers, flash spotters and air reconnaissance resources were all important as were liaison officers and – not the least – the radio and telephone communications systems.

Irrespective of the work that was under way at the headquarters, it was important to regularly inform all staff officers about the current tactical situation. It was normally done every morning, sometimes called 'morning prayers' when all were on duty after the night's rest or other activities; and as 'evening prayers' when activities were reduced for the night. An example of such a briefing is shown in **Fig. 14-1**.

When the commanding officer and his staff had received orders for a new operation, it was also important to call staff representatives, and visiting representatives from subordinated units, to special staff briefings to clarify the latest situation and what actions that were needed. This had to be done when the battle was raging and the tactical situation changed repeatedly. Those best to inform were representatives from a skilled intelligence group that worked systematically. When deemed appropriate, the group would be supported by officers responsible for planning and production of orders.

From the information about the current situation, the intelligence officers had also to look ahead and try to understand what the enemy had in mind. It was necessary to find out what his next tactical intentions might be, and what resources he had gathered and what alternatives for their use that could be seen. Those making the best judgments were those with in-depth knowledge about the enemy's organisation, tactics and weapons, and who had the ability to see not only details, but also the broader overall perspectives. Brigadier Hallifax used to emphasise this as a good talent in general, when he talked to young officers:[187] 'To command one must have perspective. In a technical arm one cannot gain perspective without complete mastery of technical job, which must be second nature.'

Coordinated planning and order production – keys to success

An element of the British doctrine was, as seen, that the artillery commander and the commander of the unit to be supported should work close together, this at all levels. The artillery plan could then be part of the overall operation plan and the artillery resources could be used in the best way, often a prerequisite for success in battle. How the cooperation between the two commanders was to take place, and how their headquarters were to do their job, can partly only be understood from looking at the organisation. Even when this was the same, the tactical situation would significantly influence the work, as would the personalities of commanders and staff members. Hence, the 'informal' organisation was as important as the 'formal'.

It is very obvious, when looking at the highest levels, how the way in which commanders acted influenced very much the work that their staff had to execute. Eisenhower, for instance, wanted his staff to prepare a number of alternate plans and present them to him. After review of them, he selected one of them as the best one in his mind. His headquarters then had to work out all the details to a complete operational order.

Montgomery on the other hand, worked differently. He had strong opinions regarding the objectives of a coming operation and the methods needed to reach them. He used to write down this in a long list with numbered points. His staff then had to convert all these points into plans and orders. Only one person could sometimes get him to change his ideas a little. It was his Chief of Staff, Major General Francis de Guingand, who Montgomery much respected. He had himself recruited de Guingand after having taken command of Eighth Army in August 1942. But once he had made up his mind it was indeed not easy even for de Guingand to get Montgomery to abolish his conviction about the ways the battle should be launched.

A high-ranked officer working more along a line between the above two extremes was Field Marshal William Slim. He has in his much-appraised book *Defeat into Victory* given an interesting account of his way to act when a new operation was to be planned and prepared.[188] He states that all his operational plans were based on a few fundamental principles:

- The ultimate goal must be offensive
- The plan must be simple
- The goal and the idea of the operation must be very clear and everything must be subordinated to this
- The plan should include a certain amount of surprise

He writes that he used to start the process by himself considering a number of main alternatives followed by informally discussing these with the two senior staff officers closest to him. These were the Brigadier General Staff (BGS) and the Major General Administration (MGA), i.e. the two highest staff officer responsible for planning of operations and administration. The latter had the highest rank as the supply of the army in this theatre was of extreme importance and complexity. Slim also consulted the highest air force commander (who had the same formal position as he himself). Together they agreed on at least two, often three to four, alternatives. These were put into the hands of a group of specially selected staff officers (BGS nominated them), to which team also air force officers were attached.

This team made a first quick analysis of the presented alternatives to find advantages and disadvantages. They were free to come up with own ideas and suggestions for improvements. They were also allowed to 'pick raisins from the cake' and combine parts from the different alternatives, thus making a completely new one. In this respect Slim was absolutely free from own prestige (cf. Montgomery). The team presented their results in a list of 'bullets' and tables with short comments. After this, a new 'consultative round' took place to arrive at the best alternative. This involved representatives of all arms at the headquarters and the heads of supporting arms, amongst them the artillery commander.

During these consultations, all major problems were identified and what decisions that had to be made to get around them. A final agreement with the air force commander was made at this state about the participation of bombers, fighters, air reconnaissance and – not least – air supply resources. After this detailed staff work for the production of army orders took place. This was also done by the artillery commander and his staff.

Slim informs that a dozen orders for large operations were issued during the war in South East Asia in his name. He writes that one clause of every order he always wrote himself – Intention. This clause was often the shortest of all in the order, but it was the most important, Slim stated. It expresses, or should express, what the Commander wants to achieve. This is the overriding point of the order under which all others are subordinated. It must be understood and followed by every man in the army. Hence, it should be formulated by the Commander himself. And this was how Slim acted.

Based on the operational orders from the high commander, in this case the Commander of XIV Army, a similar process followed at the next lower level, the Corps level, and so it proceeded on down the hierarchy. As mentioned, it was important to have well-coordinated operational orders and artillery orders at all levels in order to make sure that artillery resources were used in the best possible way (cf. General Farndale's statement before Part 1). At the divisional level, the commanding officer and his artillery commander had to work close together. In **Fig. 14-2** we can see an example.

When the Intention and other key elements had been fixed all other parts of the order could be worked out, normally with all disciplines participating. The divisional artillery commander engaged his own staff to do the job as far as the artillery in support of the division was concerned. A standard structure/model for such an order had the following clauses:

- Information
  - Enemy
  - Own troops
- Intention (the overall role of the artillery)
- Tasks
  - Allotment of artillery
  - Reconnaissance
  - Deployment areas
  - Alternative gun positions
  - Fire observation resources and liaison
  - Allotment of AOP resources
  - Fire zones
  - Special plans for ranging and registration
  - Local defence
- Fire plans
  - Attacks
  - Defence
  - Advance/March
  - Retreat
- Survey

Fig. 14-2 In order to make best possible use of the artillery resources, the artillery plan must be well coordinated with the plan made by the commander of the formation to be supported. Here is the Commanding Officer 78 Infantry Division, Major General V. Evelegh, conferring with his Commander Royal Artillery, Brigadier J. Maxwell, before an attack in Tunisia in April 1943 (©Imperial War Museum NA 2242)

- Air-Cooperation
- Administration/Supply
- Communication
  - Headquarters
  - Liaison Officers
  - Telephone
  - Radio
  - Frequencies
  - Call signals
  - Code words
  - Communication with air bases and air units
- Time
- Order distribution

Planning and production of the regimental operation order started when the regimental headquarters received an order from the artillery commander of the division (CRA) with applicable items of this structure filled in. The regimental order needed more of technical details than the divisional order, for instance regarding gun positions, marching orders, fire zones, fire observation and control etc. Fire plans often had to be broken down to the battery levels, as were orders for registrations and fire ranging.

Sometimes were written marching orders prepared at higher levels, for instance when redeployment of numerous units in preparation for a large operation required coordination and many details to set and control regarding traffic discipline.

As regards supply, strict coordination was often needed regarding ammunition dumping and replacement. Location of dressing stations and evacuation of wounded could also require coordination at high levels, the same also for maintenance and repair services.

When larger operations were to be launched, the supply matters normally required their own order, an Administrative Order. Sometimes special orders were required due to all the details that had to be fixed, and which

Fig. 14-3 In the hierarchical structure of command that prevailed during the war orders must be prepared and submitted at all levels based on the orders from the top level. Here is a unit commander giving his order to subordinates (RAHT)

were not required by all, but only concerned specialists. Detailed instructions on communication might be such an area; another could be detailed task tables for OPO/FOOs and guns.

The Operation Order was the fundamental order, but a few others might be noted:

- Standing Order
- Warning Order
- Operation Instruction

The first mentioned contained numerous items, which were not specific for a particular operation, but would apply for all operations. Such an order could stipulate, for instance, how reconnaissance was to be undertaken and by whom, who would lead the march to new gun positions and be in command during deployment, how local defence should be organised and prepared etc. The second order type aimed at getting an early start of preparations for a coming operation or engagement before complete orders could be finalised for distribution. An example could be an order to get reconnaissance for new gun positions started as early as possible. Much could be gained by not losing time!

The third type was often used when the largest operations were to be planned and work at different levels was required. It was to be seen as an order for planning given to the first subordinate level from which later 'operation orders' were prepared. Sometimes a sequence of 'Operation Instructions' would be required before a final 'Operation Order' could be fixed and distributed. We will in Part 3 see examples of such a process.

Once an order had been prepared and signed, it would be distributed to all units concerned. At the highest levels, it was normal practice to call commanders of subordinated units or their authorised representatives to a conference at the headquarters of the commander responsible for the order. At the conference, the latter presented the order with the help of senior staff members after which a written copy was distributed. An alternative could be to distribute orders by means of liaison officers. Commanders had their preferences, but the tactical situation had also to be taken into account. General William Slim preferred to travel around to his Corps and Divisional Commanders handing over his order 'face to face'.

At regimental levels, oral orders from the commanding officer were normal, but in such cases the practice was to distribute a short written confirmation as soon as possible afterwards. An example showing a commander presenting an order to his subordinates is given in **Fig. 14-3**, although the participants are not gunners.

Among practical things to attend to at a headquarters was acquisition and distribution of maps. At Army and Corps levels, and often at the divisional level as well, this was a demanding task, in particular in mobile operations over a large area.

The Order is given, control and support follow

The headquarters of higher formations, including attached artillery headquarters, were quite big and required quite a large force for their local defence. It was discussed from time to time where the headquarters should be located in relation to the forward front line. Telecommunication, accessibility for visitors from units at the front and so on, were arguments for a forward location. Against it were the risks for artillery shelling and surprise attacks from patrols, so a compromise was needed. It might also be recalled that the heaviest burden on staff officers was imposed during the planning phase of an operation. When the orders had been given, the work was reduced to monitoring the battle progress; focus was changing towards future operations. Hence, it was not so important then to be close to the front.

The immediate, short-term control of the on going fighting was the responsibility of the commanding officer with the assistance of a small group of staff officers and assistants. It was a matter of giving additional oral orders, or to alter some items of the written order, when needed. Hence he had to, with 'perspective' (cf. above), understand how the battle developed and react quickly on critical changes. This was best done when being close to the foremost fighting units. A Tactical Headquarters (Tac HQS) was established in that area, sometimes also called Advance Headquarters, whereas the main part of the headquarters stayed behind and could be called Main or Rear Headquarters.

From this it follows that an artillery commander of a Corps or a Division should be well forward too, supported by as small a number of staff officers as possible. For the regimental headquarters the requirements were different. It should not be split up. Its resources were needed close to the front as it formed a central part of the artillery communication system and thus the control of the regimental fire. The headquarters worked as a hub, when concentration of fire from all available guns was called for, while the commanding officer was liaising elsewhere with the commanding infantry/armour officer to be supported. In such situations the 'Regimental Adjutant' was the key figure leading and coordinating the work at the regimental headquarters, indeed a busy time for him!

High commanders did not stay at their 'tactical headquarters' all the time. Often they wanted to be even closer to the front to support their soldiers and officers doing the ongoing fighting, in particular at the most important frontal sector. Working radio communication was then a must. A commander could rest assured of this to be the case when his artillery commander was with him. The gunners were very good at radio communication and thus could act also as a 'back-up' for supported unit commanders. The battle of Arnhem in September 1944 gave good and clear examples of what the gunners could do.

A commander who liked to execute his control of the ongoing fighting in this way, and always had his artillery commander in sight, was the Commander of XXX Corps Lieutenant General Brian Horrocks. We can see him in this role in **Fig. 14-4**. The photograph was taken when his Corps just had crossed river Rhine in March 1945 and fought to extend the bridgehead.

Please note the radio equipment in his Jeep. Is it maybe his artillery commander standing with the map behind his back?

Fig. 14-4 When the battle was in full swing given orders must be checked and monitored. When needed they must be altered to cope with the actual course of the battle through new verbal orders. Driving commanders wanted to be forward near the front line units and from there give new orders if and when needed. Here is the Commanding Officer XXX Corps, Lieutenant General Brian Horrocks, seen in this role in connection with the Rhine Crossing in March 1945. Observe the radio equipment in his Jeep (©Imperial War Museum BU 2410)

Part 3
How British Artillery Resources Were Used
– Descents into Battle History

15. Introduction

In Part 1 and Part 2 of the book, we have seen what artillery resources that Britain mobilised and established during the rearmament taking place in the first four years of the war, the equipment provided and how they were organised and trained. Gunnery methods, battle techniques and tactics gradually developed and applied have been discussed. Hence, the book has described the main features of the 'indirect fire system', how it was designed and worked.

In this Part 3, we will proceed and look into the actual use of the available resources, this by diving into the war history of a sample of selected theatres and specific battles. At the same time, we will see how the efficient use of artillery was gradually pursued and how the general doctrines were followed and – sometimes – more or less dismissed.

Giving a complete presentation of the role of artillery on every theatre of war is obviously not possible within the space available. A selection must be made. At first I have selected the campaign in France and Belgium 1939–1940 for my review, then the intervention in Norway 1940 followed by a discussion of what happened artillery-wise at the Home Front after Dunkirk. Then I am turning to the decisive events in North Africa in 1942, in particular the third battle at El Alamein, which became a turning point. After this, I am making a jump to 1944 and the period up to the end of the war in 1945. Three central battles during this period are analysed. The first one is the battle of Normandy beginning with the landings on 6 June 1944, then the battle of Arnhem in September 1944 and finally the great artillery finale, the Rhine Crossing in March 1945. Very briefly, I will also touch upon the problems and challenges encountering the gunners in Burma.

Within the scope of the objects selected, the use of the artillery resources and the basic conditions for this is briefly discussed, but sometimes deeper into details. As a background an overview of the respective campaign is given. This is far from complete and I refer for more information to the manifold literature about World War II.

Even with the limitations in scope made, it is not possible to discuss exactly the same aspects of the use of artillery for every campaign or battle selected. The availability of literature and original sources, and the content and quality of these, have determined what can be presented and discussed. Combined, however, the various presentations give a fairly good picture of the use and standard of the artillery as far as the British are concerned and the results achieved.

When I have studied the British artillery, some issues raised have been the following. It should, however, be observed that it has not been possible to find answers to them all for every campaign and battle reviewed:

- What artillery resources were employed?
- How was the plan for their use?
- Was the planning well coordinated with the planning by the infantry and armoured units to be supported? Did all-arms training take place?
- What battle techniques were applied?
- What fire plans were prepared?
- Was concentration of artillery fire prepared?
- Was artillery ammunition in sufficient quantity available? Any constraints regarding supply of ammunition, fuel, food and water etc.?
- How were the intelligence resources used?
- Did radio and telephone communication and dependent command functions work?
- Can any specific 'system deficiencies' be observed?

I will in my presentation in some cases touch upon cooperation with naval and air forces. Some specific issues related to provision of manpower and exercises will be discussed as well.

16. Artillery to the Field – Across the Channel

The 'Phoney War'
The final planning for the transport and deployment of British Expeditionary Force (BEF) in France was initiated on 4 September 1939 and orders were given. The BEF was to be commanded by General Lord Gort and subordinated the French High Command, more specifically the commander of the North Eastern Area of Operation, General Georges, and under him the Commander 1st Army Group, General Bilotte. The troops were to be transported from harbours in South England to French ports, primarily Cherbourg and Le Havre, but the smaller ports of Boulogne and Calais were also used for disembarkation of troops. The BEF was to be deployed on the border of neutral Belgium apart from one division, which was to be deployed in Eastern France just behind the Maginot Line.

The regular 1st and 2nd Infantry Divisions were the two divisions first in place. Their first units left England on 22 September and were almost completely deployed at the end of the month. They were part of I Corps commanded by General Sir John Dill. Soon after this the two divisions of II Corps followed, the 3rd and 4th Infantry Division. The commander of this Corps was the distinguished and much respected General Alan Brooke, as mentioned a former Gunner. His two divisions had to take on a large number of reservists and conscripts to get up to nominal strength and needed thus more time for mobilisation and training. They were deployed in France on 12 October. The total strength of BEF had now reached 158,000 men and 25,000 vehicles. But real fighting was still many months away. Both sides needed more time for mobilisation and additional training for more troops to come later. Hence, a 'Phoney War' followed.

As far as the British were concerned, preparations for war continued systematically and eventually the BEF reached its final strength around 400,000 men, when the fighting started on 10 May 1940. Ten fighting divisions in three Corps were then ready. Some of them were regular formations; others came from the Territorial Army (TA) and had arrived at the beginning of 1940. In addition to these ten divisions, there was another three without artillery deployed along the supply lines. In total a respectable expeditionary force, but still too small an army.

On the allied side, there were in total no less than 139 divisions. Besides the ten British divisions, 22 divisions from neutral Belgium, 5 from the Netherlands (also a neutral country), and 102 French were ready. Of the French divisions 27 were stationary fortress divisions. Against the allies were 137 German divisions.[189]

It should be noted that a fourth British Corps was planned to be taken over to France and BEF later in 1940, IV Corps, which had two TA divisions under training in England in the spring.

The responsibility of BEF was to cover only 50km of the front, which went from the Channel along the Belgian border, then along the Maginot Line down to the border with Switzerland, a total length of no less than 600km. To its left, the BEF had the French 7th Army and to the right the French 1st Army. The sector assigned to the BEF made it possible to deploy four British divisions beside each other, the rest had to be deployed further back (southwards). One division, the 51st (Highland) Division, was alone deployed behind the North Western part of the Maginot Line at the German border, just north of the city Metz (i.e. the Saar Front). All the allied divisions were deployed along the long front line without any strategic reserves behind them.

Many of the British artillery formations came to France along with their divisions, some were, however, sent in advance. Those regiments, which were Army and Corps formations, came as soon as they had been mobilised and equipped. With a reservation for minor errors (for some formations the time of arrival in France is uncertain) the build-up of the artillery strength is illustrated in **Fig. 16-1**.[190]

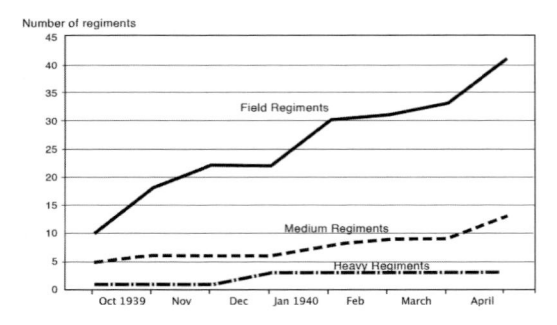

Fig. 16-1 Growth of BEF:s artillery resources was a process taking half a year. At first regular regiments were transferred to France and later Territorial Regiments. Most of the latter must first be equipped and undergo complementary training in Britain before being sent to France (Author)

As we can see, more than 40 field regiments with more than 1,000 guns were ready when the fighting began. Most of the guns were 18/25-pounders, but some TA regiments had vintage18-pounders (Mark II and Mark IV) and the old 4.5-inch howitzers. The BEF had a few hundreds of 18-pounders and around sixty of the latter.

We can also see that the number of medium and heavy regiments was limited. Around fifteen medium regiments, each with sixteen guns, had been allotted to the BEF. Their guns were basically the vintage 6-inch howitzer and the 60-pounder gun, 200 and 60 pieces respectively. Many of these old guns were still equipped with ironclad wooden wheels. The price for neglect during the inter-war period was too short ranges and poor mobility for a modern war.

The three heavy regiments sent to France had the old 6-inch gun and the obsolete 8-inch and 9-inch howitzers, a legacy from the Great War. Some of the old field, medium and heavy pieces are illustrated in Part 1, **Fig. 3-1** and **Fig. 3-2**.

The Field Regiments had the 1938 organisation, i.e. they comprised two 12-gun batteries besides the regimental headquarters. Each battery had three 4-gun troops. Regiments from the Royal Horse Artillery had smaller batteries, two 8-gun batteries.

Medium Regiments had two 8-gun batteries, each comprising two 4-gun troops. The Heavy Regiments had 2–4 batteries depending on the type of gun/howitzer.

The Royal Artillery Order of Battle early May 1940 is presented in **Appendix 1**. From this we can see the distribution of resources in **Table 16-1**, with a summary of number of regiments per formation.[191]

All the 'front divisions' had the nominal number of regiments, i.e. three, except one, which had two (42nd Infantry Division). Besides these divisions, there were as mentioned another three further back along the supply lines to the ports in the South, the 12th, 23rd and 46th Infantry Divisions, which had no artillery.

It may be noted also that no armoured divisions had been deployed in France when the fighting broke out on 10 May 1940. About one and a half weeks later, however, the first units of the 1st Armoured Division arrived in Cherbourg. The two field regiments of this division were in place already in the autumn of 1939 and were grouped as 'GHQ Troops'.

Half the artillery force came from the TA as far as field artillery was concerned. Two thirds of the medium artillery force were TA forma-

Table 16-1. British artillery resources in France on 1 May 1940

Type of formations	Number of regiments
Army artillery (GHQ Troops)	
Army Field Regiments	6
Medium Regiments	10
Heavy Regiments	3
I Corps artillery	
Field Regiments	2
Medium Regiments	2
Survey Regiment	1
II Corps artillery	
Field Regiments	2
Medium Regiments	2
Survey Regiment	1
III Corps artillery	
Field Regiments	2
Medium Regiments	2
Survey Regiment	1
Divisional artillery	
I Corps (3 divisions)	9 Field Regiments
II Corps (4 divisions)	11 Field Regiments
III Corps (2 divisions)	6 Field regiments
Other divisions (2)*	5 Field Regiments

*) Employed in the Saar Region and south of River Somme

Fig. 16-3 The Gort-Line in the winter 1939/1940. The British used the time well for reinforcement of the border between France and Belgium waiting for a German attack (©Imperial War Museum O 844)

tions too. But the few heavy regiments were all regular regiments.

An important decision was made in January 1940 implying that each division was to have two regiments equipped with 18/25-pounders and one regiment with 18-pounders and the vintage 4.5-inch howitzer. The background was that this would facilitate ammunition supply when the divisional armament became standardised. Another reason was that no division would be in a worse situation than others when it came to the firing range of available guns. After all, the 18/25-pounder was better in this respect than the oldest guns (the 18-pounder had a maximum range of around 9km and the 4.5-inch howitzer not more than 5–6km).[192]

Preparations for the coming battle included extensive storing of spare parts and other supplies of all kind. **Fig. 16-2** shows stockpiling of artillery ammunition.

The gunners had to undertake tasks that were not possible for them to train for very much in peace time, namely full-scale digging of trenches, gun pits, command posts etc., and construction of fortified positions, anti-tank ditches, setting up barbed wire defences and much more.

Artillery units were quartered initially a distance from the Belgian border, as most units were. They were engaged immediately in reconnaissance and preparation of battery positions to be used once the fighting began, battle positions. Alternative gun positions and other temporary positions were reconnoitred and prepared as well. Gun pits and other fortifications were prepared as were observation posts; everything was well camouflaged. **Fig. 16-3** is a unique photograph from the 'Gort Line' as it was known; it is well illustrating battle preparations made over the winter 1939/1940 with fences, wire hindrances, anti-tank ditches and so on. The name emanated from the C-in-C BEF, General Gort.

The 3rd Infantry division, commanded by Major General Bernard L. Montgomery, took over a front sector north of Lille in October 1939 and prepared itself for immediately going into battle. The divisional artillery headquarters issued already on 10 October its first operational order, Operation Order No.1. In this order, it was informed that the division would deploy with two brigades beside each other and the third brigade

Fig. 16-2 Large amounts of artillery ammunition for the BEF artillery were stockpiled during the autumn 1939 in France (©Imperial War Museum F 2410)

as reserve behind them. Each brigade would deploy their three battalions beside each other. The order gives details also about the boundaries between the units. Furthermore, it was stated that the II Corps artillery commander for medium artillery, CCMA, would command two field regiments and two medium regiments, which were to be engaged for counter-bombardment tasks and harassing fire.

The details for the divisional artillery were given in an additional order, the Operation Instruction No. 1.[193] From this, it is seen that 25 Field Regiment RA was to support 8 Infantry Brigade, 33 Field Regiment RA 5 Guards Brigade and 7 Field Regiment RA the divisional reserve, 9 Infantry Brigade. The latter regiment was ordered to support the front brigades. With a series of map sketches, the deployment area for the divisional artillery units, the Corps artillery and wagon lines were given. Fire zones and observation zones to be prepared were also presented.

Much space in the order was used for instructions on local defence and protection of own artillery deployments. Each regiment was ordered to prepare direct fire from ordinary gun positions against enemy tanks within specified zones. It is of interest to note that the regiments were ordered also to assign two troops each for just anti-tank tasks in depth of the divisional deployment area, i.e. in total 24 guns of the division's 72. It is stated explicitly that the guns should be deployed on an individual basis and not to be given any other fire order. The fact that one third of the divisional artillery thus was withdrawn from the primary task, indirect fire, illustrates how important direct anti-tank fire from the divisional artillery was considered to be during the initial phases of the war.

Another observation is that the batteries were ordered also to reconnoitre gun positions, not more than 3,000 yards from the front line, for one or two guns (a Section,) to be used for harassing fire and fire against opportunity targets at an early stage of the battle to come.

Regimental headquarters were to be reconnoitred with care and be fortified with the help of Sappers.

The 'Operation Order' contained a regulation which was directed to the entire BEF and which had been ordered by the French, namely, that all units should observe strict radio silence. Communication was to take place by means of telephone lines and dispatch riders only. From observation posts visual signalling should be prepared as backup.

The stipulations regarding radio silence remained in force right up to the break out of the fighting in May 1940. Only minor exemptions for exercises were allowed; a unit could occasionally get a 'radio day' for training purposes. But on the whole, this implied that the units had not got enough training when the German attack came, and this with severe consequences.

The next step in preparation for battle was to prepare for marching and redeployment. Detailed orders for such scenarios were prepared. Stipulations were included regarding alertness to be implemented when the crisis emerged.

In parallel with all these preparations, systematic training from the individual level to collective training of troops, batteries and regiments took place. This training encompassed marching and deployment procedures and much more. Practice firing with live artillery ammunition could be organised in France to some extent, but 'dry firing' seems to have predominated as far as gunnery training was concerned. The Commanding Officer, Major General Montgomery, known to be much interested in training, organised a number of divisional exercises. These comprised in particular marches and redeployment of the entire division, which was to prove a great advantage in May 1940.

But now to the big principal question: Where to take up the battle against the invading Germans? Should it be near the Belgian border where so much of preparations had been carried out on the 'Gort Line'? The French had early made absolutely clear that an allied offensive was out of the question. They were stuck in the same type of defensive thinking that prevailed during the Great War. The only thing the allies could do, according to the French view, was to meet and stop the German offensive, which all were convinced would come. A possible allied offensive would have to wait until the allies were sufficiently equipped and prepared for this, which was deemed to be a matter of a couple of years.

Different opinions prevailed between the allies as to where the German attack would be concentrated. The French thought the Germans would advance through the Netherlands and Belgium, as was the case during the previous war. Hence, a repetition of the 'Schlieffen Plan', and they considered that the best way to meet the offensive was to meet it frontally in Belgium as early as possible. And here, the German forces would be tied down for a long time, as it was thought.

The plan called for decisive allied counter-attacks where strong German forces would cross the river and where the main defensive line would be established. The problem was that this line could not be prepared and fortified in peacetime in respect of the Belgian neutrality. A request for help must first come from the Belgian Government.

The British on the other hand were more inclined towards mobile battles during the interwar period as we have seen, and also trained for that, albeit at a small scale. The British did not like having to have to abandon the well-prepared positions at the Belgian border. Being forced to re-deploy to unprepared positions in Belgium was not considered an attractive strategy.

The British CIGS, General Edmund Ironside (later Field Marshal Lord Ironside), felt more convinced that the attack would come much more to the south than the French thought. He believed the Germans would attack the shortest way through Luxembourg to the English Channel and thereby cutting off the allied forces to the north. This must, it was considered, be met offensively. As it was to be shown, this British view on the likely course of the battle was to prove more in line with the course of the real battle in May 1940.

After discussions during the autumn 1939 regarding various potential defence lines in Belgium, the choice eventually made was to deploy BEF along the river Dyle. This river runs in a north-southerly direction east of Brussels. The plan was given the name *'Plan D'*. The British would have preferred a 'Plan E' which implied a defence line to be established along river Escaut further to the West (its northernmost section called the Schelde), this if the allies were to be ordered to march into Belgium.

The autumn of 1939 saw more of a concentration of forces and training, both individual training and later on, as mentioned, collective training at gradually higher unit levels. The winter 1939/1940 proved to be very cold and snowy, which made training almost impossible for some periods. With heavy rains during the autumn and thawing of snow after the winter, the troops experienced almost the same conditions as prevailed during the Great War in the Flanders: everything becoming wet, wet and wet, and fields and roads transformed into mud. Many exercises had therefore to be cancelled, as most troops were ill prepared for such adverse weather conditions. But units did what they could and practiced whenever possible despite snow and conditions they were not accustomed

Fig. 16-4 The winter in France 1939/1940 was extremely cold and snowy as well as in England. But the British soldiers had to accept it and tried to get used to it. They continued training and exercises as much as possible. Here are gunners with their 18/25-pounders (RAHT)

to. Training continued also in England for units to be dispatched to France (**Fig. 16-4**).

Operative and tactical training were adapted to the defensive strategy and not to mobile warfare with armoured units. By means of specific exercises, the redeployment to river Dyle was prepared as were the tactics for the defensive battle to come there. The gunners spent much time on preparation of complicated fire plans including covering fire for counter-attacks. The latter being both such based on timed concentrations on fixed targets and such comprising creeping or rolling barrages against line targets. The ordered radio silence, however, made the signallers less efficient in radio communication. In particular they lacked the skill that was needed in mobile battles and when concentration of artillery fire above the regimental level would be tactically sound.[194]

A threat causing more and more concern during the winter was the risk for German air landings, both as regards small groups of saboteurs and larger units.

9 Field Regiment RA issued in January 1940 Operation Instruction No. 12, which stipulated how this threat should be met by the regiment. This was related to the area, which was to be controlled by the regiment in accordance with an order from the artillery headquarters of the 5th Infantry Division to which the regiment belonged. The regiment should send out patrols in this area upon code words when immediate threats for air landings emerged. ('HOPPER' when air landing was imminent, 'LOCUST' if such a landing already had taken place). A patrol would comprise one officer and five other ranks equipped with two light machine-guns. When alerted, one patrol would immediately move to a certain important bridge, the others should be prepared to systematically survey the whole area. One patrol would be ready to go within ten minutes, and two more not later than 30 minutes after the alarm. A rolling scheme was prepared in the regiment for this type of service.

The instruction also stipulated that landing parachutists should immediately be fired at before they disappeared towards their goals. In particular, it was stated that 'There must be no question of it being 'unsporting' by firing at descending parachutists!'

For communication with the regimental headquarters, the patrols had to use the French public telephone service. Special regulations were issued regarding the procedures for this, including presentation of a card by the soldiers to prove that they were authorised to avail themselves of this service.[195]

End of the respite – April 1940

After the trying winter, preparations for 'Plan B' were resumed and training activities geared up at all levels. Although inactivity was not a problem, it was important for morale that recreation and entertainment were organised for the troops; as was a programme for leave at home. Football tournaments between the units were another popular break from active service. Unit commanders had a big responsibility arranging suitable activities for their men and keeping them alert and motivated.

Another sphere of activities, in particular for officers, were lectures and study tours. So, for instance, the war diary of 7 Field Regiment RA has this entry for 8 April 1940:

> Captain B.B. Storey and 2/Lieut. R.E. Candlin went to ABBEVILLE on a 4-days attachment to No .2 (A.C.) Squadron R.A.F. P.O's Cox, Mason & Watts No. 2 Squadron R.A.F. arrived for a 4 days attachment.[196]

This particular air squadron was one of those organised for cooperation with ground forces. It was equipped with Lysander aircraft. I will come back to them later.

Other objects for study visits for the gunners were the recce units of the divisions, where they could admire the light scout cars, Daimler Dingos. And sound rangers organised demonstrations of their equipment and methods. Many gunner officers had their own battle experience from the Great War and acted as guides at some of the battlefields of this war. One of the qualified guides was the commanding officer of 7 Field Regiment RA, who as late as 21 April 1940 organised a visit of this kind. The war diary gives the story:

> A Battlefield Tour to parts of the SOMME Battlefields was conducted by the C.O. All available Officers, Warrant Officers and senior N.C.O's attended. To give officers a chance of a long run as many as possible rode motor-cycles. The day was brilliantly fine and warm, and everyone enjoyed the tour, and gained new ideas from it.

On 28 April, he made another tour. This time he guided officers from 76 Field Regiment TA.

More serious things had, however, happened before these tours were done. It is of interest to me as a Scandinavian observer to see how the artillery units reacted on messages about the German invasion of Denmark and Norway on 9 April 1940. It seems that they were not really upset about the news, had they at all been informed! Montgomery's artillery headquarters (3rd Division) wrote in their war diary for this day: 'Major Brooks visited the HQS to discuss fuel transport. Representatives from various divisional units participated.'[197]

When we look into the war diary of 7 Field Regiment RA, we can read about another meeting taking place at the same headquarters:

> A conference was held at H.Q.R.A. 3 Div at 1015 hours to discuss problems in connection with Recrational and Physical Training. A helpful and interesting meeting. In the evening 16/43 Bty held a cocktail party.

But it has been added that:

> It was learned in the morning that Germany had invaded Denmark and was at war with Norway, and that a Naval engagement was taking place off the Norwegian coast.

99 Field Regiment RA has a very short note for that particular day saying, 'individual training was organised'.

However, the following day, the 10th, things began to happen. All leave was cancelled and units were alerted. The next day, the 11th, all units were ordered to be ready to leave at 14 hours' notice and packing and loading of vehicles commenced as were other preparations for a quick departure. Montgomery raised the alertness further on 13 April for an advance detachment to which the artillery commander and his headquarters were attached. Departure would take place at four hours' notice. The headquarters staff prepared themselves by packing as much as they could. Paperwork was reduced to a minimum, the war diary says.

After the raising of alertness and preparations for departure to Belgium, things calmed down a little and a period of waiting followed suit. On 19 April, alertness was further reduced and units could revert to their training plans. Night marches and redeployment exercises were again on the training agenda. Exchange and study visits resumed. The war diaries reveal no indications of a pending crisis, but a rough awakening was not far away!

An interesting observation is that the 5th Division was redeployed towards the end of April to prepare itself for transport to Norway. I will come back to this plan later.

'David 6 – David 6 – David 6'

Yes, here is the code word that was to be given to all divisional units when 'Plan D' was to be launched. The number '6' was the number of hours when this was to take place after the code had been received by units, i.e. the 'Z Hour'. The plan had a time schedule in hours and days to which all activities were related. The first day was called 'J.1', the second 'J.2' and so forth. 'Plan D' had, as mentioned above, been followed by production of detailed orders at all levels, and these had been continuously updated during the spring 1940. We can study the presumably final version of the 'Operation Order' for I Corps[198] and a late version of the artillery 'Operation Order'.[199]

A few extracts from these orders will illustrate how the initial phase of the battle against the invading German forces was planned to be undertaken. The Corps order comprises 17 pages and the equal number of Appendices. It deals partly with the march to river Dyle and partly to the deployment of forces along and behind the river. A complementary administrative order for all supply issues had also been prepared. It is interesting to note that all units were informed that they must also be prepared to engage in line with 'Plan E', i.e. marching only to river Escaut, should this be ordered.

The first recce unit was to cross the Belgian border at 'Z Hour'. This unit was a cavalry unit, 12th Royal Lancers (Prince of Wales'), abridged '12 L'. This was a GHQ unit and was to establish itself as soon as possible along a line 7–15km east and northeast of river Dyle.

The 'Plan D' required the forces to redeploy towards river Dyle in four phases. They must, however, be prepared to meet changes of plans for the last three phases. The four phases were:

Phase 1 Advance of I Corps (except 48th Infantry Division) to the right and II Corps

(except two divisions) to the left, Z to Z + 90 hours.
Movement day and night.

Phase 2 Advance of the 48th Infantry Division in the period J.5 to J.9, and one division from II Corps in the period J.5 to J.9.
Movement during nights only, if possible.

Phase 3 Advance of the third division from II Corps in the period J.8 to J.10. Deployment behind the division deployed in Phase 2. At the same time adjustment of boundaries between the two Corps close to river Dyle.
Movement during night only, if possible.

Phase 4 Advance of III Corps as GHQ Reserve at the time decided later.
Movement during night only, if possible.

It was furthermore decided that the French 1st Army was to deploy to the right of I British Corps, front Namur–Wavre, with the French III Corps nearest BEF. Its advance was to be protected by a cavalry Corps comprising a number of light mechanised divisions.

The operational order had been devised on the assumption that BEF would be in place within ten days and that fighting at the river Dyle would commence after fourteen days at the earliest. Reality was to be something else. The foremost units were in battle after only a few days.

The frontal divisions would, as understood from the Phase 1 plan, start their advance towards river Dyle immediately. They were to advance just behind their own recce units with an advance force of brigade strength reinforced with artillery. As far as I Corps was concerned, the 1st Division was to march to the left along a given route and the 2nd Division to the right of it. For the latter two routes were allotted. A third route was reserved within the Corps boundaries for other transport.

The cavalry units (recce) of the divisions were to cross the start line one hour after 'Z Hour', They would upon arrival at river Dyle replace 12 L east of the river. Detachments from the advance brigade with machine-gun and anti-tank units would follow suit. These units would secure the Dyle defence line within 48 hours, according to the plan. The main parts of the divisions would follow suit and be deployed within Z + 84 hours. Infantry was to move forward with buses (from RASC transport companies).

13 Air-cooperation Squadron RAF, which was attached to I Corps, was ordered to survey the area east and north of river Dyle. They would also survey the transportation area, this in order to assist in traffic control and in time detect sabotage attempts, risks of ambush, etc.

A tactical Corps headquarters was to be established during the second day and the main part of the headquarters would come later and be established south of Brussels on the fourth day. The Corps commander with his artillery commanders, CRA and CCMA, and reconnaissance detachments would leave the first day.

The divisional commanders with their artillery commanders, would leave as soon as possible and have their tactical headquarters in operation the second day, while the main staff resources were ordered to be in place the third and fourth day.

The Corps order included numerous details in the main document, but most of detailed directives were given in a number of voluminous annexes and the special 'Administrative Order', which were issued at the same time.

Now, what is said about artillery in the Corps Operation Order? First, it is noted that it does not include any provision regarding the march forward and deployment of divisional artillery. It is focused on the Corps artillery and GHQ units that were attached to the Corps. As is the case for the other arms, the order contains provisions regarding the marching and deploy-

Table 16-2. Army and Corps formations under command during march to River Dyle

1 Infantry Division
140 Army Field Regiment RA
1 Medium Regiment RA
3 Medium Regiment RA

2 Infantry Division
61 Medium Regiment RA
4/7 Medium Battery RA
3 Heavy Battery RA

Under CCMA I Corps command
27 Army Field Regiment RA
98 Army Field Regiment RA
5 Medium Regiment RA
1 Heavy Regiment RA (except 3 Battery RA)

Under CCRA I Corps command
115 Field Regiment RA

Table 16-3. Employment of Army and Corps artillery at River Dyle

Under command of 1 Infantry Division
140 Army Field Regiment RA
1 Medium Regiment RA

Under command of 2 Infantry Division
61 Medium Regiment RA

Under command of CCMA I Corps
27 Army Field Regiment RA
98 Army Field Regiment RA
3 Medium Regiment RA
5 Medium Regiment RA
63 Medium Regiment RA
4/7 Medium Battery RA
1 Heavy Regiment RA
3 Super Heavy Battery RA (if and when ordered forward)

Table 16-4. Coordination of observation and fire areas

1 Infantry Division artillery	Between coordinate lines 37 and 47 North
2 Infantry Division artillery	Between coordinate lines 43 and 56 North
Medium/Heavy Corps artillery	Between coordinate lines 38 and 48 North
The Heavy Regiment should cover the entire Corps front line	
French 3 Army artillery	Up to coordinate line 42 North (at least)

ment of these artillery units behind river Dyle. For the march, the artillery units were allotted to formations as listed in **Table 16-2**.

The 1st Infantry Division was ordered to reserve space in their columns for reconnaissance detachments from the Corps artillery, some 85 vehicles. The 2nd Infantry Division similarly was to reserve space for the 89 vehicles of 1 Survey Regiment RA and 11 vehicles from 13 Survey Company RE, the latter now being attached to the Survey Regiment.

The reason why these divisions were made responsible for several Corps and GHQ artillery units was not only a matter of traffic control. Another reason was that the divisions would be well equipped with artillery at hand if they were attacked and had to stop marching. By this arrangement, the Corps could also take advantage of units with the longest range and the opportunities for these to deploy early if needed.

When the Corps and GHQ units had arrived at river Dyle they were to be grouped as shown in **Table 16-3**.

Deployment areas where the units under CCMA command would have priority were specified in Annex Z of the Corps Operation Order.

It is interesting to note that no units would be under command of CCRA, the Corps artillery commander, but under CCMA, the commander of Corps medium artillery. This meant that the latter would be commanding not only medium and heavy regiments as was his normal duty, but also a few field regiments. It was to take a few years until a less fragmented command structure at the Corps level had been introduced.

We have now briefly studied the main features of the 1 Corps Operation Order for 'Plan D'. Based on this, a specific artillery order was prepared and issued by the Corps artillery commander, CCRA. This order deals with all artillery, hence also anti-tank artillery and how these resources were to be used in a coordinated way for the protection of all the units marching towards river Dyle. When it comes to ground artillery, we may notice a few specific issues of principal interest.

All reconnaissance in the forward area was to be well coordinated under the CCRA, who was to have a staff conference with all the CRAs, the CCMA and the commander of 1 Survey Regiment RA. This was to take place at 17.30 hrs the second day. One intention was to make sure that the units with longest range could be deployed as early possible. Fire and observation zones were coordinated as well, **Table 16-4**.

The artillery units were to deploy as soon as possible, but when it was dark. Furthermore an 'Active Artillery Policy' was to be applied while all defence preparations were forthcoming behind the river. This meant that temporary gun positions, Active Positions, were to be used. Single guns 'roving' firing from site to site were also to be used. At least 50% of the guns at the primary positions, the Battle Positions, were to remain silent. When these positions were completed gradually with fortifications and camouflage, this share could be reduced and more and more guns open fire.

The explanation of the fact that the firing zone for the medium artillery was limited to the northern part of the Corps area, apart from the assumptions that French artillery was expected to help in the southern sector, is found in the counter-bombardment provisions in the order (Paragraph 7). There, it is stated that it had been found from map studies that the most likely deployment area for the enemy's artillery was in the valleys between the latitudes of North 38 and 48. Units allotted for counter-bombardment would therefore be deployed and directed in such a way that they could combat enemy artillery in this area.

The importance of harassing fire in depth is stressed and this task will be coordinated by the CCMA. The CRAs should, however, themselves plan for 'Defensive Fire' and 'Counter Preparation Fire'. These plans were to be well coordinated with brigade commanders and then presented to the CCRA for final coordination. Requests for inclusion of Corps units in the divisional fire plans should be addressed to him. It was stressed that survey was to commence as soon as possible.

It was still believed before the war that fire observation and control from the aircraft of RAF Army Cooperation Squadrons would be an efficient complement to the ground resources. This was therefore much dealt with in the artillery order. Areas where to fly, call signs, frequencies are regulated as were the types of target to qualify for this type of bombardment (artillery positions, large marching columns, tanks, infantry assembling for attack, etc.), all provisions to be found in a separate Appendix. It is also stipulated how much artillery that was to be ready to respond on calls from the aircraft. Generally, it was a matter of 2–3 troops per division equipped with 18/25-pounders and one troop equipped with 6-inch howitzers or 60-pound guns. Sometimes even a section (2 guns) of the heaviest guns could be made available.

The detailed order for the march and deployment implied that all Corps and attached GHQ artillery was to be ready to fire latest the night between the fourth and fifth day, about half of the regiments one day earlier.

At 04.00 hrs on 10 May 1940, the Germans attacked the Netherlands and Belgium. German reconnaissance aircraft could soon be seen over the British positions around Lille and other places in Northern France where the BEF was deployed. Around 07.00 hrs the code word 'David 6' was transmitted to all BEF units. Reconnaissance detachments and scouts were alerted to be ready to go on two hours' notice. The 'Z Hour' was determined to be 13.00 hrs this day.

'Impress on the troops that this is the real thing and not a Divisional Exercise'

The 'Phoney War' was over and it was followed by a *Blitzkrieg* quite different from the one all had prepared for. The heading of this section refers to Montgomery's concluding words when giving his orders at his headquarters at 10.00 hrs on 10 May for the launching of 'Plan D'. The course of events had so far followed the 'manuscript'.[200]

After the German plan for the attack, *Fall Gelb*, had been revealed when a German officer had crashed in Holland with the plan in his briefcase, the French had been strengthened in their belief that the German concentrated attack would come towards this country and Belgium. They did not see the neutrality of these countries to be any protection against a German attack. A request from the Belgian government to the allies to put 'Plan D' in effect was expected to come at once, when the Germans crossed the border.

What they did not know, however, was that the plan had been changed on initiative of the chief of staff at von Rundstedt's Army Group A, General von Manstein. He had proposed that the attack came through the Ardennes with the purpose to strike south of the allied main forces the shortest way to the Channel. Hitler found the revised plan attractive and immediately approved it. The risks were high, but were deemed to be acceptable if the allied forces first had been tricked into the trap, and actioned a quick redeployment into Belgium. The plan was based on surprise and speed. Surprise was to be accomplished by the launching of a first attack into Holland and the northern part of Belgium, which would at the same time make the allied to move towards river Dyle. The main attack would then follow suit through the Ardennes.

The speed necessary for this main attack was to be achieved by having panzer divisions and motorised infantry divisions in the lead, while the majority of infantry divisions would come later. These were to a large extent equipped with horses and thus unable to keep pace with the mechanised forces. Another step for reducing the risks was close cooperation between the army and the air force, the *Luftwaffe*, in particular their JU 87 *Stuka* dive-bombers. These had to replace initially artillery during the fast advance towards the Channel.

If reaching the Channel quickly, the allies in the North would be deprived of all their supply. The British supply lines, which came from ports south of river Somme, in particular Cherbourg and Le Havre, would be cut off. The German High Command believed that they would quickly encircle the allies. These would then have to give up the battle due to lack of ammunition, fuel and other necessities. The Germans could never imagine an evacuation to England to be a strategic option on the part of the allies.

For the German assault in the north, Army Group B under General Feder von Bock had been assigned. It comprised 29 divisions, of which three were panzer (armoured) divisions. The divisions were grouped in two Armies, the 6th and 18th Armies. South of these undertaking the main thrust was Army Group A under Generaloberst Gert von Rundstedt. At his disposal were no less than 45 divisions, seven of them panzer divisions, i.e. the major part of the armoured resources. The divisions were grouped in three Armies, the 4th, 12th and 16th Armies. Further to the South, finally, was Army Group C under Generaloberst Wilhelm Ritter von Leeb. He had no panzer divisions but 'only' 19 infantry divisions grouped in two armies, the 1st and 7th Armies.

It should be particularly noted that von Rundstedt's seven panzer divisions were grouped in three Armoured Corps. Of these, the XIX Corps with three divisions was under command of the creator of the German armoured strategy, General Heinz Guderian. Another well-known armoured specialist was Major General Erwin Rommel who commanded the 7th Panzer Division, which belonged to XV Armoured Corps under General Hoth. The XLI Armoured Corps was commanded by General Hans Reinhardt.

On the allied side, the Belgian Army was deployed in the North along the Albert Canal. Along the northern border of France was, as mentioned, the French 7th Army deployed in the north-western sector beside the BEF which on its right side had the French 1st Army. Then followed the 9th and 2nd Armies. These armies, and the BEF, were commanded by the commander of 1 Army Group, General Bilotte. Further to the right along the border down to Switzerland four more French armies were deployed, the 3rd, 4th, 5th and 8th Armies, which were grouped in 2 and 3 Army Group. These armies were deployed behind the Maginot Line.

When 'Plan D' was put in operation, the 7th French Army would march to the area between Breda and Antwerp while at the BEF at the same time moved to river Dyle. South of the BEF the 1st French Army would deploy by turning right, having its left flank beside the British I Corps and the right flank close to river Sambre, just north-east of the city Charleroi where the 9th Army then came. The other French armies were to remain in their initial positions.

This was the situation when the game commenced in the morning of 10 May. This is illustrated at large in **Map 16-1**.

No political decisions were needed for this redeployment of the allied forces, the BEF was free to immediately cross the Belgian border, and everything was well prepared in advance. As we have seen, reconnaissance units and units for protection including advance guards, were the units to go first. These were followed by headquarters detachments and resources for reconnaissance of artillery deployment. The BEF was deployed with the 1st, 2nd and 3rd Infantry Division beside each other behind river Dyle. The 4th Infantry Division was after some time deployed within the area given to II Corps further to the north as a Reserve just northwest of Brussels. The 46th Infantry Division was deployed as Corps Reserve within the area given to I Corps. Further back the 5th and 50th Infantry Divisions, which belonged to Brooke's II Corps, were deployed as GHQ Strategic Reserve. Even further back, the two TA divisions, the 42nd and 44th Infantry Divisions, were deployed in accordance with the plan. They belonged to III Corps and deployed near river Escaut to increase the depth of BEF defence.

The respite of two weeks assumed for 'Plan D' never materialised. The fighting was in full swing before all units had been redeployed.

Montgomery's headquarters (the 3rd Infantry Division) sent a message at 07.00 hrs on 10 May to the artillery commanders' headquarters that Holland and Belgium had been invaded by German troops the same morning. The division had been alerted and ordered to be prepared to march at four hours' notice. The advance detachments were to leave at two hours' notice.[201] At 10.00 hrs followed a staff conference, when Montgomery gave his orders to the commanders of subordinated formations including the divisional artillery. It was now decided that the advance staff detachments were to cross the borders at 14.30 hrs. Much activity followed with packing up of vehicles and personal kits and disbandment of unnecessary equipment. Documents not to be kept by the staff were burnt or destroyed. Exactly at the time ordered, Montgomery with his group of staff and liaison officers and his artillery commander crossed the border. The latter was accompanied by his chief of staff, the Brigade Major RA, and dispatch riders on motorcycles from 7, 33 and 76 Field Regiments RA and from 2 Field Regiment RHA, the latter regiment attached to the division. This group crossed the border at 16.00 hrs. The main part of the artillery headquarters left together with divisional headquarters at 20.00 hrs.

Montgomery established his Tactical HQS at Everberg just west of Louvain at 23.30 hrs. The advance guard was deployed with a mobile detachment on the high ground east of the river Dyle and the main part west of the river. 2 Field Regiment RA, which was to support the advance guard, which was deployed near the river northwest of Louvain and arranged observation posts together with detachments from the reconnaissance units east of the river.

Early in the morning of 11 May, Montgomery and his artillery commander reconnoitred gun positions for the forward units but also the rest of the divisional artillery. The order was given to 76 Field Regiment RA to support 9 Infantry Brigade to the right and 33 Field Regiment RA the Guards Brigade to the left. Montgomery deployed 8 Infantry Brigade as his divisional reserve behind the two forward brigades. To 7 Field Regiment RA was given the order to prepare support along the whole divisional front as reinforcement of the other regiments.

Next day, 12 May, 2 and 53 Medium Regiments RA came under command of the division as was a battery from 60 Field Regiment RA, the latter a GHQ unit. The task assigned to the battery was anti-tank defence, i.e. direct fire from suitable gun positions.

Everything was a bit more chaotic than the above indicates. This was due to the fact that Montgomery on arrival found that the Belgian 10th Division already was in the area. Hence, it was found that several of the battery positions selected after map study were already occupied by Belgian artillery. Montgomery offered to become subordinated the Belgian commander and hoped that the latter would find this to be too big a responsibility and therefore would prefer to continue the Belgian retreat. However, the two generals agreed that the British artillery was to provide some support for Belgian front units. On 13 May, the British received from the Belgian divisional HQS an order to this effect, *'Ordre pour l'Emploi de l'Artillerie'*. But the Belgian division began already the same evening to leave the area. This retreat in combination with large refugee columns on their way from Louvain blocked the roads westwards, which had a severe impact on the BEF:s transports.[202] By and by, however, all the divisional artillery and units under command arrived and got deployed.

The other divisions, with their artillery, came forward and deployed during the period 11–13 May.

The artillery commander of the 2nd Division accompanied the divisional commander and his forward headquarters detachment and crossed the Belgian border at 23.00 hrs the first day. The first field regiment from this division to arrive was 16 Field Regiment RA, which was in place the next day. 99 Field Regiment RA sent its reconnaissance detachment at 08.30 hrs on 11 May. The rest of the regiment marched during the night and was ready for fire at 10.00 hrs on 12 May near river Dyle.

Often the artillery units had to get off the road and wait for the reconnaissance to be completed and the road cleared. Reconnaissance comprised 'Silent Battle Positions' and some 'Active Positions' nearer to the front line for a battery or a few troops. Some gun positions for alternate tasks were also reconnoitred.

As regards observation posts, two per battery were established, east of river Dyle and near the main battle positions west of the river. The OPO/FOO immediately began drawing panorama sketches over their observation zones and making 'silent registrations'. Telephone lines were laid and the posts camouflaged. All preparations were made as had been trained many times during the 'Phoney War'.

Apart from minor skirmishes between patrols and reconnaissance units east of river Dyle no major fighting took place until 13 May in the northern sector, and not until a couple of days later in the southern. But it was already clear that the war tempo was much higher than anticipated when 'Plan D' was devised. Redeployment of the BEF to the Dyle position had, however, followed this plan almost to the letter.

The artillery deployment at large is illustrated in **Map 16-2**, where also the nominal number of available guns is presented. Thirteen field regiments, out of which four were GHQ reinforcement units (Army Field Regiments), were deployed near the main defence line at river Dyle. This was about one third of the BEF field regiments. Furthermore, nine medium regiments were deployed forward, which were two third of the total number in the BEF. The few heavy regiments were, however, deployed far back from the front. The allotment of GHQ and Corps regiments did not exactly follow 'Plan D'. But it can be seen that the divisional artillery of all the front divisions had been reinforced with such artillery including artillery for counter-bombardment against enemy artillery positions.

As most of the medium guns were the vintage 6-inch howitzers with limited range, around 10km, the possibilities for effective counter-bombardment in depth were limited. Only a few 60-pounders with a range up to 14–15km offered better opportunities in this respect. But we can see that efficient counter-bombardment programs against likely enemy artillery deployment areas were planned to the extent possible.

Before we begin to look into the details of the engagement of British artillery units, from the commencement of the fighting near river Dyle to the end of if at Dunkirk three weeks later, it seems worthwhile first to look at the course of the war at large as a general background.

The BEF outflanked but avoids encirclement

The Germans met a much tougher opponent at river Dyle than the one they had encountered during the initial fighting. This was obvious during the few days the battle was raging here. In particular during 14 and 15 May, the Germans made several fierce attacks against the British lines without success.

While the BEF was on the march towards the river Dyle and deployed there and the battle was going on in Holland and near the Albert Canal in north-eastern Belgium, the German Army Group A worked its way through the Ardennes, not without difficulties, but decisively, purposefully and energetically. The allies had as planned entered the trap and it was important to take advantage of the situation. On 13 May, the first units crossed river Meuse at Dinant. It was Rommel's 7th Panzer Division that was in the lead. Soon Guderian's panzer divisions came to the south of Rommel at Sedan. On 14–15 May large forces crossed the river and were attacking westwards. But after this initial success, the German High Command became nervous and was afraid that Guderian had taken too a big risk by exposing his southern flank and deliberations about this caused delays to the advance towards the Channel. We will, however, not look into this just now.

The Germans encountered the first serious French counter-attack on 17 May. This was launched south of the city of Crècy-sur-Serre by a French armoured division under command of Colonel Charles de Gaulle, who now became a known figure for the first time. His attack failed, however, and he had to withdraw.

The rush towards the Channel regained its speed and soon it became clear that the French the 2nd and 9th Armies could not prevent it. The risk increased dramatically that the allies in the North with the 1st and 7th French Armies, the BEF and the retreating Belgian Army would be cut off and encircled by Army Group B from the north and Army Group A from the south. **Map 16-3** illustrates schematically the German rapid advance towards the Channel.

It was decided already on 15 May that the British would leave their positions at river Dyle and re-deploy at a new defence line along river Escaut (the extension southwards of river Schelde). This would be accomplished by performing delaying actions at the rivers Zenne and Dendre.

There were, as we have seen, two divisions deployed by the BEF as a strategic reserve under GHQ, the 5th and 50th Infantry Divisions. These could be used for a counter-attack southwards with the purpose to cut off the foremost German panzer divisions before the slower infantry divisions would be there to interfere. This would be an option if the French could attack simultaneously from the south, they too with two divisions at least.

Such an initiative was also planned by the French Commander-in-Chief General Weygand. His plan was under discussion up to 26 May, but then it was too late. The plan could not be implemented. Chaotic command structures on the French side and lack of efficient communication means between the armies and concerned Corps (the partly destroyed telephone systems in France and Belgium) made the necessary coordination impossible. Things were not better when the French commander of the 1st Army

Group, to which the BEF was attached, was seriously injured in a car accident on 21 May and eventually died a short while later.

The foremost units of Guderian's panzer Corps had already reached the Channel on 20 May; thereby cutting the British supply lines.

The confused situation on the French side made the British to launch a counter-attack on their own on 21 May at Arras. This became something more than an attack by two divisions. It was decided to have two temporary battle groups attacking in two independent columns. Each one was to comprise one infantry battalion from 151 Infantry Brigade of the 50th Infantry Division. Attached to them each were one tank battalion and one artillery battery and one antitank battery. A few French units were also to take part in the attack.

At the beginning everything went well and the attackers soon reached the area west and south of Arras and turned eastwards. But resistance stiffened more and more and finally the advance came to a halt at Wancourt through overwhelming artillery fire from Rommel's panzer division and the SS *Totenkopf* division. After bitter fighting, Lord Gort decided to cancel the attack and ordered the survivors to withdraw.

The Germans, however, misjudged the strength of the British attack and became very concerned. It was a reminder that armoured units at the head of advance could be cut off, a risk that should not be neglected. But soon the Germans regained confidence and pursued their advance in force.

Lord Gort was after this phase of the battle convinced that the BEF had to retreat towards Dunkirk and be evacuated. But as yet, it was not finally clear as to whether another attempt to break the German lines by attacking together with the French would be made. Hence, the 5th and 50th Infantry Divisions remained in the area north and west of Arras for a few more days. Some reconnaissance was ordered as late as on 25 May, but it had hardly begun when the order was received in the evening that day that the whole operation had been cancelled. Instead, a new order was given at midnight to both divisions. They were immediately to re-deploy northwestwards to the vicinity of Ypres, where the tactical situation now had deteriorated seriously.

The British were soon forced to abandon the Escaut-position and continue the delaying fighting northwestwards. This was done in fairly good order albeit that the BEF units were under pressure from all directions.

On the southern side, the 1st and 2nd Infantry Division made a stand just east and north of Lille. Other divisions also resisted the German attacks fiercely, amongst them the 3rd and 4th Infantry Divisions farthest to the north and the 42nd and 46th Infantry Divisions southwest of Lille near the French 1st Army. The British III Corps was now made responsible for the defence along the Aire-canal with the 44th, 46th and 48th Infantry Divisions. Some help was expected from the less trained 12th and 23rd Infantry Divisions, although they had no artillery.

In the northwestern sector, where the BEF had the Belgian Army as flank protection, the situation became, as mentioned, extremely serious on 26 May and the subsequent days. The Belgian Army began to dissolve and retreated southwestwards. No organised resistance seemed possible any longer. Fruitless attempts were made to get the Belgian king to order his army to establish strong defence along the river Yser from the coast to Ypres.

Should a Belgian collapse take place, a very serious situation would emerge for the British divisions located far to the south in the Lille area. The German divisions could quickly advance towards Dunkirk and completely cut off the BEF from the coast.

When this situation became obvious, the 5th and 50th Infantry Divisions were ordered to re-deploy as quickly as possible to the area around Ypres. This was for the survival of the BEF a decisive and critical decision was taken by Lord Gort on 25 May. The two divisions came gradually in place and were already engaged on 26 May in heavy fighting which increased and culminated on 27–28 May. The imminent Belgian collapse came on 28 May when the king capitulated which necessitated direct action on the British side.

The first step was to withdraw Montgomery's division and re-deploy it to the northernmost sector, moving behind the two aforementioned divisions, which now were involved in most heavy fighting against the Germans without any help from Belgian forces. The intention was to extend the British front from Ypres to river Yser. This redeployment was carried out over the night of 27 and 28 May. This was a hard task, but successfully achieved by the 3rd Division. Obviously Montgomery was proud of this operation, which he saw as a quality mark for his division. But he wrote in his memoirs: 'If this move had been suggested by a student at the Staff College in a scheme, he would have been considered mad. But curious things have to be done in a crisis in war.'[203]

The situation on 26 May is summarised in **Map 16-4**. I will discuss the fighting at Ypres a bit further on when the role of the British artillery is being analysed. The fighting here turned out to be of utmost importance for the chances of the BEF to avoid annihilation.

When this battle was raging, Operation Dynamo, the evacuation of BEF from the beaches at Dunkirk had been organised and commenced. In order to make it work, all units had to withdraw to a final beachhead, some 35–40km wide and 5–7km deep. A firm organisation was also necessary for controlling the process. In addition the beachhead had to be firmly defended to the last, a task first given to III Corps.

In the final phase, the beachhead was divided into three sectors and the defence to the southwest was assigned to a French division, and east of this to I Corps and then in the northeastern sector to II Corps. French units employed in the beachhead were also incorporated in the defence as well where it was possible.

The evacuation started with shipping of non-combat personnel.

Before the final consolidation had been organised in the beachhead, the French 1st Army was encircled and forced to surrender. The two British divisions without artillery, the 12th and 23rd Infantry Division, had also been encircled and ceased to operate as coherent units. But they were not completely without artillery. Not least through individual initiatives. Batteries were organised with a few 18-pounders, which were in store as reserve guns. They were brought forward but lacked dial sights and spare parts. Yet it was possible to improvise and use them for direct fire to the end.

The third division without artillery, the 46th Infantry Division, played an important role in the defence along the canal in the west and was 'up-graded'. The commander of 16 Field Regiment RA was nominated divisional artillery commander and his regiment was subordinated the division together with remnants of a few other units.

Another event, most likely of immense importance, when it came to getting the beachhead stabilised and making it possible to pursue the evacuation successfully, was Hitler's decision on 24 May to halt the advancing panzer divisions; that was his *Haltbefehl*. The destruction of the beachhead, it was thought, should be a matter for the infantry divisions and – foremost – the *Luftwaffe*. Hitler's decision, which gave the British and the French a few days well-needed respite, may have decided the outcome of the campaign in France. This is still a subject for many discussions and controversies.

Thanks to the successful delaying during the critical days 26–28 May of the attacks made by German forces, both along the canal defence line in the west and along the Ypres-canal in the east down towards Comines, all British divisions further south were able to withdraw back towards the beachhead. A 'half-halt' was made along the river Yser, by which divisions there could help others to withdraw into the beachhead. So, for instance, the 4th Infantry Division held the Yser line in the east while the 5th and 50th Infantry divisions withdrew during the night between 28 and 29 May.

The whole retreat from river Dyle had been undertaken under appalling conditions. The BEF units were all the time exposed to enemy air attacks from bombers, dive-bombers and fighters all of which could benefit from excellent weather conditions. Initially the Germans enjoyed almost complete air superiority. This changed somewhat, however, towards the end of the campaign. The air battle over the beachhead then included much more RAF engagement.

Hard fighting day and night and constant fire from German artillery and mortars and constant movements and redeployment gave few chances for rest and sleep. Shortage of food and water further reduced strength too. The speed of the battle activities also opened up for enemy infiltration and attacks from unexpected directions. All this put the soldiers' nerves to a real test.

If this had not been enough, there was another troublesome problem - fifth columnists. This problem had in particular been experienced during the fighting in Belgium. It was found that enemy agents made markings on the grass in fields to show German aircraft where headquarters, guns and various units were deployed. Even snipers were found. But when these enemies were caught, the process was short. The war diary of 7 Field Regiment RA from 15 May 1940 gives an example:

> An order was issued that all civilians were to leave by midnight. During the morning a civilian was apprehended on suspicion, sent to 9 Inf Bde for interrogation and released by them [...] In the evening the suspected civilian who had been apprehended in the morning was again found in the village, and it was discovered that he had been cutting marks in the grass. He was again taken to 9 Inf Bde for interrogation, and 5 minutes later was, by order of the Brigadier, taken out and shot.

On 20 May the war diary had a similar story:

> 9/17 Bty caught a civilian snooping round their area in the early hours of the day. He ran away when challenged, was caught and shot.

The evacuation beachhead was exposed to continuous artillery fire and attacks from the air. The latter were restricted mainly to daytime, but still they were very wearing. The casualties on the shores and among ships and boats just off the beach were heavy. But the fact that the area now could be covered by RAF fighters from bases in England changed the air battle although *Luftwaffe* could still retain the initiative.[204]

From the final beachhead which became smaller and smaller every day, most units were evacuated under amazingly good and disciplined order. After a slow start, the evacuation was speeded up on 26 May and went on to 4 June as far as the British were concerned. The width of the beachhead was on 1 June still as much as 20km and it was around 5km deep. After 4 June, evacuation of some French units went on for another day, but on 5 June all was over; no more allied soldiers could be rescued.

Strong management had made it possible to pursue the evacuation without disorder or panic. This does not exclude many examples of units that found conditions on the beaches chaotic and also found the long waiting for embarkation very nervous and tedious. In London it was thought that some 45,000 men as a maximum could be rescued from France. When the operation was over 338,000 British and French soldiers had disembarked in England from the numerous ships and boats that had taken part in Operation Dynamo, indeed a remarkable success! About half of the BEF had been rescued, albeit without any heavy equipment and guns.

What role did the British artillery play?

What did the artillery units go through during the three weeks of fighting up to the evacuation at Dunkirk, and what tasks did they face? How were these resolved? We will now return to the beginning of the battle at river Dyle.

As we have seen, the march to river Dyle could be done without any major complications. After all, this had been trained so many times and the Germans wanted to get the BEF into the trap as soon as possible, hence air attacks were almost non-existent. The planning of the march and traffic control worked well and no streams of refugees along the roads had yet commenced. But the advance of the BEF was a tiresome a task on the part of the drivers. They had to drive in the dark and without any lights ahead of the vehicles, only a minor rear light on the vehicles was allowed. 10 Field Regiment RA still managed to cover 200km in 42 hours without any major accidents or breakdowns.[205] The artillery units were deployed beginning 11 May and it was completed a few days later. This was also the case as regards the Corps artillery to be deployed at forward gun positions.

In the northern sector, where the 3rd Infantry Division was deployed, the reinforcement regiment, 2 Field Regiment RHA, which had been put under command of the division, was in position and ready to fire early on 11 May. It was thereby prepared to support advance protecting units and reconnaissance detachments which had crossed river Dyle to the eastern side of it. The regiment had been allotted an advanced deployment area for this task. The main part of the divisional artillery had their gun positions 5–6km west of the river. From the latter there were another 1–2km eastwards to the area where the first fighting was to commence. In order to get a shorter range initially, temporary gun positions would be used for single batteries, or more often, a few troops. They were reconnoitred only 2–3km behind the front line (See also **Map 16-2**).

As we have seen, one field regiment was allotted for support to each of the forward brigades, i.e. they were under command of these. The third regiment of the division was to cover the front of both brigades when necessary. The possibility for concentration of all divisional artillery towards the same target, either a Corps target or a divisional target, was not a viable option. Short ranges and lack of adequate communication means were amongst the reasons for this.

Stockpiling ammunition close to the guns was included in the battle preparations. The artillery of the 3rd Infantry Division was ordered to prepare 100 rounds per gun and day although initially only 30 were to be used. Obviously one was expecting a fairly moderate firing, still influenced by peacetime requirements.[206]

All artillery units were surveyed into the same grid by 13 May; DF and SOS targets were prepared in cooperation with the infantry. Observed fire organised from Forward Observation Posts (FOP) against advancing German columns began taking place this day. The foremost units east of river Dyle were ordered to withdraw west of the river and towards the evening, the first German units entered Louvain.

The next day, 14 May, the fighting became more intensive as was the artillery fire. But at this stage the batteries had to be restrictive as regards ammunition expenditure. The war diary of HQRA 3rd Division tells:

> Fighting general all along the R. Dyle. Enemy held. A certain amount of German aerial activity with bombing attacks on LOUVAIN and targets to the rear. Arty activity restricted owing to limited number of rounds being allotted for ordinary observed shooting. During the night, regts had a number of defensive fire tasks and concentrations.[207]

7 Field Regiment RA also tells us about the initial fighting:

> About 2100 hours the sound of heavy firing was heard on the front and at 2140 hours the S.O.S. and defensive fire tasks were fired almost continuously until midnight on the left of 9 Inf Bde front, held by 2 R.U.R. Several times a report was received that the situation was critical. It was later learned that the whole affair was a 'flap' caused by conflicting reports, and, possibly, the natural nervousness of troops under fire for the first time. About 700 rounds were fired during the 'flap', and the infantry stated later that the expenditure had been worthwhile if only for the additional confidence it had given the troops.[208]

The German air force was not any longer satisfied with just reconnaissance sorties. Everything was now done to destroy the allies. Two troops of 76 Field Regiment RA were attacked this day by dive-bombers for the first time. The troop positions and the nearby road with refugees were strafed with machineguns from the air.

On 15 May, the task given to 2 Field Regiment RHA to support advance units east of river Dyle was over. The Divisional artillery commander decided to put the regiment under command of 33 Field Regiment RA. 7 Guards Brigade was, thereafter supported by the '33rd Artillery Group'. This way of delegating artillery resources to a lower level and to commission a regimental commander to act as 'Group Commander' was quite common during the first years of the war.

The order to withdraw to the area north and west of Brussels was given to the 3rd Infantry Division on 16 May. The artillery regiments were ordered to leave at 20.30 hours. 7 Field Regiment RA and 33 Field Regiment RA would leave one troop each to cover the divisional withdrawal. The troops were put under command of respective infantry brigade.

At the right flank of the BEF, where the 2nd Infantry Division was deployed, several regiments were also deployed, amongst them 99 Field Regiment RA and 10 Field Regiment RA. The initial fighting resembled that on the left flank. 10 Field Regiment RA, under command of Lieutenant Colonel Jack Parham, had been ordered first to deploy one troop on the eastern side of the river, this in order to be able to answer calls for fire from the foremost observation party, which was positioned around 8km east of river Dyle in support of recce detachments. Wireless sets for communication with army-cooperating aircraft (Lysanders) were taken with them. The troop was ordered back west of the river in the evening for better protection. Besides these activities, reconnaissance of various gun and HQS positions had taken place, as had been done by their colleagues further to the north.

On 13 May, enemy artillery fire reached the artillery positions and retreating Belgian and French tanks were be observed. The fighting was in full swing on 14 May. 99 Field Regiment RA reported that it had been engaged in heavy firing against prepared S.O.S. targets. The regiment also fired against many unprepared targets, i.e.

observed fire against opportunity targets on requests from infantry commanders.

Harassing fire was fired during the following night. The battle intensified on 15 May and the Germans made repeated attempts to break through, but the war diary of 99 Field Regiment RA was confident: 'Action continues with increasing intensity. The enemy attacks were generally repulsed and when he had any local success he was driven back by 6th Inf Bde. With arty support.'[209]

Civilians were in full flight westwards having had to leave houses and farms just as they were. Jack Parham wrote about his feelings:

> The weather all this time was perfect and the country looked lovely. The only abnormal feature, when the guns were not firing, being the continuously lowing of cattle left unmilked and unwatered; the barking of abandoned dogs, many of them still chained up, and the noise made by poultry shut in fowl runs without food or water. Cattle and loose horses wandered about the place, mixed up with army vehicles and odd groups of refugees.[210]

Jack Parham wanted to concentrate artillery fire and he had prepared his regiment for this by arranging efficient radio and telephone communication means. Here, at river Dyle, he suddenly got his chance:

> I was back at RHQ after tea when a call came through from B Bty's right OP overlooking Wauvre to say that John Moulton had spotted enemy tanks in a wood across the valley. It sounded a really super target (A signaller actually spotted the target, a good piece of observing) and for fear of spoiling the show by disturbing the 'game' I rang 2 D A to ask if they would like a Divnl concentration – I was told to take it on with the Regt. I gave out the full orders as per book 'Regtl Tgt M1, Ridge (map ref) Ledge (map ref) Engage from Z to Z plus 5 rate intense. Amn HE – Zero hour ....' (giving ten minutes I think to prepare).
>
> The OP reported the tanks still there and at the appointed time the whole Regt (less the forward Tp) cracked off. A delighted message from the OP confirmed that we were plumb into the wood, that big fires resembling petrol fires were started. The wood continued burning for some hours and it seems that our shoot of some 400–500 shells in 5 minutes may have destroyed a tank unit of some sort. It was all very satisfactory and a good advertisement for the new organisation.'[211]

It was later believed that it had been a tank unit that had stopped for refuelling. The event has in literature been stated to be the first, and maybe only, radio-communication controlled shoot against a regimental target during the campaign in France, and that it was made possible thanks to the use of radio communication.[212]

Everything was done by the BEF to stop German attack preparations east of river Dyle. The British artillery fired both harassing fire and 'counter preparation fire'.

The situation further to the south deteriorated quickly and when the right flank of the 2nd Infantry Division was threatened, it was ordered to withdraw. This was one day earlier than the retreat in the northern sector was ordered. Just after midnight, 99 Field Regiment RA began redeployment. The batteries continued firing extensively till the moment they had to leave. They were concerned about their vehicles. Would they succeed to get them forward in the massive traffic westwards? At 04.00 all guns were, however, on their way to a temporary RV. After subsequent reconnaissance and rest, they deployed and were ready to fire from 14.00 hours. In the evening, around 18.00 hours, they fired for 45 minutes 300 rounds against enemy concentrations. Reality had now shown what ammunition expenditure was really like in a modern war.

Withdrawal under artillery protection

The retreat towards Dunkirk now followed step by step under intensive delaying fighting. A new main defence line would be established along river Escaut at first. But the artillery units could not go direct to this river. They had first to deploy behind the easterly rivers Zenne and Dendre; some units at the Brussels–Charleroi Canal. Most units were in place behind river Dendre on 17 May after having had to wait at temporary locations until reconnaissance had been completed. It was necessary to impose strict traffic control, which certainly was not easy due to heavy unorganised streams of refugees from time to time. An impression of this human tragedy is given in **Fig. 16-5**.

7 Field Regiment RA was ordered at 16.30

Fig. 16-5 Belgian refugees heading westwards away from the battle area. In the opposite direction BEF strived towards its planned positions at River Dyle in Belgium. The competition for road space was most often hard (©Imperial War Museum F 4403)

hours, on 16 May, to prepare for deployment west of Brussels in connection with the 3rd Infantry Division withdrawal. The regiment was to re-deploy troop-wise and first go to a hiding place and there await further orders. Two troops and the regimental 'B Echelon' left the river Dyle positions at 18.30 hours. The other troops continued firing. They supported the holding actions by the infantry, and also had to expend all dumped ammunition that the regimental units could not take with them.

The Regimental HQS and three more troops left at 20.30 hours. Still in position was D-troop supporting the rear guard. The withdrawal went well without any major problems. At 04.00 hours these units were at the RV, resting and carrying out equipment maintenance with exception for D-troop that did not arrive until around 11.30 hours. The artillery units received the 3rd Infantry Division Operation Instruction No. 15 this day. This showed that the entire division was to deploy behind river Dendre just south of the city Alost (northwest of Brussels) with its brigades beside each other. Farthest to the south, 7 Guards Brigade was to deploy and be supported by 7 Field Regiment RA. The two other brigades were to be supported by 76 Field Regiment RA and 33 Field Regiment RA respectively.

As soon as darkness had fallen, 7 Field Regiment RA began its redeployment to battery positions west of river Dendre which now had been reconnoitred. The regiment was here ready to fire at 06.00 hours on 18 May. A simple telephone network had then been built between the regimental headquarters and the brigade headquarters via the two batteries.

The 4th Infantry Division covered the retreating 3rd Infantry Division with its artillery, which included a medium regiment under command before the former division itself withdrew to positions behind river Escaut. A much used tactic was to let a retreating division pass through another division which had already established a strong defence line, and then to deploy the former in a new defence line further back.

The most forward German units reached river Dendre around 12.00 hours, but here the battle would not last very long. At 13.00 hours the next order came for the artillery to move again and deploy towards river Escaut. This time too, it was necessary to have the artillery waiting near the river. The march was to continue when the roads were free enough for further transport.

In this phase the vehicles of the artillery units were put at disposal of the infantry to speed up their retreat. The eventual deployment of the artillery behind river Escaut is illustrated on **Map 16-5**.

The artillery remained in positions here during the afternoon and evening. It was decided at the divisional headquarters at 22.30 hours that 7 Field Regiment RA was to stay where it was during the night to perform harassing fire and, if necessary provide S.O.S. fire, up to 08.00 hours on 19 May. The regiment would then re-deploy nearer the coast. Two troops would be left until 12.00 hours in support of retreating infantry. The situation became more serious during the night and the two troops were ordered at 01.00 hours to leave their positions one hour earlier than ordered during the evening, i.e. at 11.00 hours. The main parts of the regiment were at 02.00 ordered to leave two hours earlier than had been planned, i.e. 06.00 hours. The other regiments of the division were to re-deploy during the day. 8 Infantry Brigade would act as the rear guard and be supported in this task by one troop per battery of these two regiments. 2 Field Regiment RHA was also given that role.

7 Field Regiment RA worked its way back during the morning of 19 May along roads filled with refugees, horses, wagons and other vehicles but eventually reached Estaimburg at the western side of river Escaut around 9km northwest of Tournai. After reconnaissance the regiment was deployed later during the day in an area around Dottignies 5km further to the north and was to support 8 Infantry Brigade which was to arrive during the following night. All the divisional artillery units were gradually brought to the same area where the entire 3rd Division was to take up the defence along the river.

That division was to get the 4th Infantry Division as it neighbour to the left and the latter was to have the 46th Infantry Division deployed at its left as the BEF's flank division. The 3rd Infantry Division was to have the 1st Infantry Division on its right side. Further to the right followed the 42nd Infantry Division, 2nd Infantry Division and 48th Infantry Division, the latter then being BEF's right flank division south-east of Tournai. After these arrangements, there was a new complete defence line with extended width along river Escaut.

7 Field Regiment RA received a medium battery from 53 Medium Regiment RA under command from 03.00 hours on 21 May.

The artillery of the 2nd Infantry Division began, as mentioned, its withdrawal from river Dyle during the night between 15 and 16 May. 99 Field Regiment RA deployed that afternoon at a temporary position south of Brussels and fired from 18.00 hours to 18.45 hours 300 rounds against enemy concentrations before continuing south-westwards to river Dendre. The first stop was a halt at Moerbeke, which the regiment reached during the night. The regiment deployed the next morning west of the river and was ready to fire at 14.00 hours. A day later, it redeployed again, this time near La Glaneri, around 10km southwest of Tournai. This position was behind river Escaut, but on the 19 May the regiment moved closer to the river, where it was ready to fire at 20.00 hours about 4km south of Tournai.

In this position, one of the regiment's batteries was attacked from the air by dive-bombers on 21 May, but was spared any casualties; only one gun was destroyed. This lucky outcome was considered to be due to the fact that the gun crews were well protected in foxholes and trenches, which they had started to dig immediately after arrival.

10 Field Regiment RA from the same division had also a troublesome move from river Dyle to the southwest. Redeployment section-wise, night marches, a few hours rest and sleep here and there, often exposed to enemy fire from ground forces and from the air. The commander of one of the batteries, Major R. Gordon-Finlayson, wrote in his diary for the night between 18 and 19 May:

> 0018. Column starts for TOURNAI. We are told to join in and get to TOURNAI somehow. All goes well until Infantry trucks etc. begin to overtake us, then tremendous jam ensues.
>
> 0400. It is light and we are still jammed up in road North East of RENAIX. How we escaped bombers don't know. S.R.N.S. and I most of night trying to sort out traffic and wake up drivers.
>
> 05.00 O.C. comes back along column. Sees me and tells me to get all our vehicles out of the column and formed up in a suitable place.[213]

The diary then gives a detailed account of all the

difficulties encountered almost hour by hour when Gordon-Finlayson did his best to get his battery to the goal just southwest of Tournai. Around 10.00 hours Gordon-Finlayson himself crossed river Escaut but due to taking wrong turns, air attacks and other mishaps it took another three hours before arriving at Tournai. All the afternoon and evening was required for getting all in place for the night near Ere about a kilometre south-west of the city.

The gunners now got a well-earned rest and during the next day, 20 May, a battery position and observation post were reconnoitred. This was done at 16.30 hours, even if the location of the OP was not the best, in particular as the infantry was not yet in place. With whom to cooperate and where had no answers. Reconnaissance was continued during the evening. During the night the observation party prepared for the coming actions by camouflaging, digging and improving their positions.

Despite all difficulties observation parties continued preparations for firing. In his diary entry for 10.00 hours he writes that 'Banks' [the FOO/OPO] made a panorama sketch including silent registrations. In addition to his binoculars, Gordon-Finlayson had a telescope to make observation less exposed. During the afternoon, communication with the battery command post ceased. The telephone line had been cut and the telephone batteries discharged. The latter could, however, be replaced around 16.00 hours. The fighting was intensive all the day and the gunners were all the time exposed to shelling.

They managed to survive due to the dug-in positions, but found the telephone line cut again and again. A signaller crawling backwards to mend it was killed. The observation team had its remote control for the wireless set, but it did not work well. The batteries had to be charged but this could not be performed. In addition to insufficient training this turned out to be a general problem during the campaign in France. Due to such deficiencies radio communication was not used much. An exception was Jack Parham's regiment, 10 Field Regiment RA. He had long before the battle been very interested in wireless technology and the possibilities it offered. As mentioned above, he trained his regiment in using it properly.

Fatigue takes its toll
The battle at river Dyle and the hard retreat to river Escaut with its constant delaying actions had been extremely onerous for all and many accounts of completely exhausted drivers falling asleep at the driving wheel were recorded. Many lost control and went into ditches, others managing to keep awake but immediately falling asleep when the column halted.

Tiredness of course also fell upon commanders. Jack Parham is commenting on this in his account. During the retreat from river Dyle, the commanding officer of the 2nd Infantry Division, Major General Loyd, collapsed due to lack of sleep and overwork; a temporary successor from his HQS had to be nominated. At a meeting with the divisional artillery commander during the chaotic situation between the rivers Dyle and Escaut Jack Parham was in a critical state and was told by his commander: 'Jack, you are no damn good for anything more – I'm going to get Tubby Tyler (Comdr 16 Fd) to relieve you.' He had fallen asleep a dozen times during this rather dramatic staff conference. He also writes:

> I think it was a bit after 0200 hrs that I was relieved, I think I must then have lain down on a rather untidy heap of blankets there were in the room and got a bit of sleep.

But he had to leave after an hour:

> About 0300 hrs MacRae and I started off, he travelling in my car with his own following, He drove and I tried to keep awake but was only partially so!![214]

In his article in the Royal Artillery Journal about experience from France, which Parham wrote after his return to England, he further commented on the problem with exhaustion: 'Here let me say a word about the vital necessity for the conservation of energy by every legitimate means. One must have an absolutely 'cast iron' system of reliefs, particularly of officers and one must stick to it!'[215]

Those readers, who have tried to be effective after a week without, or just with a few hours' sleep, know what Parham is talking about!

Lysanders – not suitable for air observation
Jack Parham was, as we have seen, one of the pioneers as regards fire observation and control from aircraft. The BEF artillery could not yet use any of their own aircraft but were directed by the

RAF army-cooperating squadrons, in particular those which were equipped with Lysander aircraft. At the outbreak of war, there were four such squadrons; another four had Blenheim aircraft.[216] Parham was determined to take advantage of the possibilities they offered and made sure that the necessary radio equipment was at hand near the front. Certainly, he had trained his batteries for this type of cooperation.

The foremost task on the part of the Lysanders was photoreconnaissance, then artillery reconnaissance and fire control. In France some tests were also done to use them as bombers equipped with small bombs under the wings. It was soon found that the aircraft was unsuitable for all these tasks. It was too vulnerable. Major Gordon-Finlayson reports that one aircraft was shot down close to one of his troop positions on 15 May. An entry in his diary for 04.00 on 17 May states that two Lysanders were shot down that morning by *'Messerschitts'* (note his spelling).

Jack Parham had a similar observation:

> There was some heavy air fighting this day and it was about the last day [16th May?] we saw any quantity of friendly planes. Several Lysanders were shot down. Apropos of this, the Regt only attempted two air shoots, neither of which was completed as on both occasions the aircraft was shot down almost immediately.[217]

Parham was, as we have seen, convinced that the artillery should have its own air observers and have quite a different plane. He wrote in his account on 27 May:

> There had been repeated reports of tanks between La Bassee and Givenchy earlier but they were hard to verify and hard to observe. Here was a perfect example of the need for an Air O.P. Had we only one and could it have popped up for 2 to 3 minutes only, to a height of not more than 400 feet, any time this day, before the Boche attack, we should have known what was going on between the canal and the low GIVENCHY – VIOLAINES ridge. The high-flying Lysanders (had there been any left) would never have got there. We could have picked a quiet moment and done the job.[218]

Maybe it was the irony of fate that one of the first trials with adequate planes and with gunner officers as pilots had been allocated to France and beginning just before the breakout of the war. It became a quick return to England on 20 May (See also Chapter 6).

The artillery is once again concentrated

The entire BEF was in place behind river Escaut on 20 May. The deployment at large has been illustrated on **Map 16–5**, which also roughly shows where the artillery was positioned. We have followed a few of the regiments on their onerous way to the Escaut-line. Most of the other army units had experienced about the same struggle as the gunners had been through.

It was not yet clear that a retreat to Dunkirk for evacuation would be unavoidable, but some thoughts in that direction gradually emerged. In an additional piece of paper to the war diary of 7 Field Regiment RA for 21 May it is said:

> This morning C.O. warned senior officers to have in mind future course of operations. Might involve falling back on coastal bridgehead – CALAIS – NIEUWPORT. Choice might arise between heroic annihilation and evacuation of personnel. National eugenics and public opinion would probably demand latter. Officers to look out maps and consider order of priority for jettisoning stores if ordered.

The Germans had reached the Escaut-line in the afternoon of 20 May already, but the British gunners were ready. They had managed to get there despite enemy interference, traffic jams and lack of efficient traffic control. They had rarely arrived as coherent regiments. Instead batteries arrived, fairly well united, sometimes single troops came, sometimes only a group of a few guns. There are many good examples of young subalterns and NCOs acting independently and decisively to get the artillery in place.

As we have seen, single troops were often left behind to support the last infantry units retreating. Hence, when artillery fired, it was often a matter of just firing on troop targets, sometimes also on battery targets, seldom were regimental concentrations fired. A problem was that the units often had to fire somewhat at random without appropriate ballistic and geodetic data. Jack Parham gives a striking example:

> Finally, we had to face a night 'get-away' over unreconnoitred country roads of the most intricate

nature. It was the most depressing evening I have ever spent in my life. (The whole area round Bde HQ was well and truly blocked with traffic and I could not get the vehicles I wanted up to my forward HQ.)

However, thanks largely to magnificent determination and 'drive' on the part of Capt Lamont and of the other FOO (Tom Mead I believe) we got something sorted out. About 2300 hrs there was a call from the Infantry for defensive fire – There was a long and ominous silence from the guns!! … this the worst thing that can well happen to a gunner….The Brigadier asked what had gone wrong – I couldn't say.

Then, *very* late but incredibly welcome, came the sound of one Troop firing over our heads at Gun Fire. It was the best noise I'd heard for years.

Lamont, faced with the problem of an SOS with a Bty which hadn't really got settled in, had taken a chance off the 1/50 000 maps and was pushing it over – I waited anxiously fearing the frightful news that we were shooting into our infantry…. Or at best that they would say that the shells were miles plus and ineffective. The phone from the Bn's leading Coy buzzed and they said that the fire was grand and just where required – It was a relief almost beyond words![219]

When arriving at river Escaut, the artillery was immediately engaged in new fighting. And now there was shortage of ammunition, at least at the regiments supporting the frontal divisions at the river Dyle. For the regiments of the 3rd Infantry Division, ammunition expenditure was restricted to 5 rounds per gun and day! They were ordered not to fire at SOS targets with more than two rounds per gun from one troop per battery during the night, indeed not much for stopping a decisively attacking enemy.

Artillery units belonging to rear divisions of the BEF had on the other hand plenty of ammunition and also took advantage of that.

The counter-attack at Arras – no role for the artillery

The counter-attack at Arras was launched some 50km southwest of river Escaut. As we have seen this was not big an event for the British artillery. Only one battery was attached to each of the two attacking battle groups. They were allotted from 92 Field Regiment RA. No overall artillery plan was produced, neither at divisional nor brigade level. It is striking what is said in the regiment's war diary for 21 May, 13.00 hours:

> Regt. Supported 150 I.B. in quickly planned attack round S.W. of ARRAS. […] Advance went well at first, but French on right withdrew and allowed a German tank on our right flank to pass. Btys not called on to fire until late in day.[220]

The coordination with French units that were to participate in the area was not effective, at least not as far as the French artillery was concerned. The weak artillery support probably was the reason why the British attack slowed down and eventually was stopped and the attackers forced to retreat. This shows again that commanders at the beginning of the war hardly had their thoughts on availing themselves of heavy artillery concentrations. Later during the war it became normal practice to take advantage of the artillery forcefully.

Farndale's opinion about the role played by the artillery is not either merciful:

> The guns were not used well; not enough was assembled and there is no evidence of a major fireplan or plans for subsequent artillery attacks.[221]

Farndale is also quoting Rommel who is believed to have said: '…The British attack seemed to lack any co-ordinated artillery fireplan.'[222] But he is giving the credit for his own success when stopping the British attack to his own artillery.

The divisional artillery commander of the 50th Infantry Division issued an operational order after the withdrawal on 22 May by which he tried to include French artillery in the divisional plans. The Commanding Officer of 92 Field Regiment RA became the leader of an artillery group in which no less than three French regiments were included. The group was to support the defence operation of 17 Infantry Brigade. In the middle area an RHA battery, together with a few French artillery detachments, was given the task to support 'Petreforce' – the garrison in Arras. To the right, 150 Infantry Brigade was to be supported by the 72 Field Regiment RA-Group, which included 9 Field Regiment RA.

In the order, the Group Commanders were assigned the task to prepare fireplans in cooperation with the respective infantry commander.

No role for the divisional artillery commander and his staff was foreseen. The defence in this area did not last long. The following day, 23 May, Lord Gort had to order the Arras garrison to withdraw westwards in order to avoid encirclement.

BEF under extreme pressure but holds the right flank thanks to its artillery

The two British divisions, the 5th and 50th Infantry Divisions, still prepared a new larger attack southwards, as we have seen. In the evening 25 May the divisional artillery commander of the 5th Division had called all his regimental commanders to his HQS near Douai to give order for reconnaissance related to this attack. But when the concerned officers arrived, they were met by the message that the operation had been cancelled.[223]

A few hours later, at midnight, the artillery commander received order from the divisional commander that he should immediately bring his artillery up to the Ypres area, this was due to an imminent Belgian collapse. Two field regiments, 9 and 91 Field Regiment RA, had not left the division as the third regiment, 92 Field Regiment RA, had, but now two other regiments were attached, 18 and 97 Field Regiment RA. The former came from the 48th Infantry Division whereas the latter was a unit from III Corps.

A warning order regarding reconnaissance and deployment was immediately issued to get the units moving. At 04.00 hours on 26 May, the final order was given by the divisional artillery commander. This took place just west of Ypres Canal, to be more specific at Ploegsteert north of Armentières. Around 12.00 hours most artillery units were in place there and ready to fire. The attacking German units had not as yet reached the area, so the gunners could take advantage of the afternoon for fire planning and improving the protection of their positions.

Soon, however, they were all dragged into heavy fighting, which culminated on the 27–28 May. Not least due to strong action by the Corps commander himself, the old ex-gunner Alan Brooke, and the two divisional artillery commanders, everything possible was done to close the gap against the attackers at this sector of the front. This was to be accomplished by employing a few medium regiments as reinforcement and organising efficient re-supply of ammunition.

So here for the survival of the BEF, a most vital concentration of available artillery resources was arranged. The war diary of HQRA 5 Infantry Division and a number of preserved operation orders testify the forceful engagement by, in particular, the divisional artillery commander and his staff to arrange an efficient use of the artillery resources, which saved the situation. As an example, we can look at the fireplan for defensive and counter preparation fire produced at the divisional level, which is graphically illustrated in **Map 16-6**.

I have based this map on the written fire plan with its attachments that the divisional artillery commander issued to subordinated units in the evening of 26 May.[224] From this map, we can see that the 5th Infantry Division took up defence with four infantry brigades between Ypres and Comines. The forward line followed the canal and the railway close to it. A fourth brigade had now been attached to the division, the 10th Infantry Brigade, which belonged to the 4th Infantry Division. The sources are not consistent as regards the deployment of this brigade, which maybe is due to the fact that it was engaged in a counter-attack as divisional reserve, when the situation became very critical. In **Map 16-6** it has been placed in accordance with the divisional artillery order mentioned above.

Closest to the front line, we can see a series of 'DF' targets (Defensive Fire) marked 'DF' plus a number. Further to the east, 2–3km, a number of 'CP' targets were prepared (Counter Preparation Fire), these also with a number. The former are 'line targets' where the fire from batteries are placed beside each other. The artillery order stipulated that medium regiments were to plan their fire 300 yards beyond the fire of the field regiments, which could be closer to own infantry positions. As we can see, it was not an unbroken line of defensive fire as would be normal practice later during the war.

Turning to the 'CP' targets, these were planned for concentrated fire from all guns of a regiment towards the same point. Most of the targets were registered along a road stretching north south in parallel with the canal where farm buildings and small woods were located. Places where the enemy was expected to assemble attack forces or deploy artillery etc., had been selected.

I have in the map indicated which regiments that were to prepare fire against the various targets. We can identify three medium regiments besides the field regiments, 1, 5 and 63 Medium

Regiments RA. These were not under command of the division but were still under command of the Corps CCMA (Commander Corps Medium Artillery). The latter had, however, ordered them to take part in the planned firing. Coordination had thus taken place between Brooke's Corps artillery commander (CCRA), the CCMA and the divisional artillery commander (CRA). There are despite this no signs of planning for a concentration of all Corps artillery against the same targets.

How much ammunition was to be fired? The order says that any call for fire should be answered by two minutes gunfire, this for both types of target. This implied an impact of 400–500 shells when two regiments engaged the same target. Defensive fire should be fired when three green flares from Very signal pistols were fired by the infantry, this if not the attached FOO could give the order over telephone or radio.

The fighting on the eastern flank became as mentioned very intense for several days, in particular over the 27–28 May. This meant that the gunners had to fire again and again on registered, pre-planned targets. 91 Field Regiment RA received a fire plan at 14.00 hours on 26 May and made preparatory ranging during the afternoon, which ended at 17.00 hours.

Infantry made contact with enemy patrols during the night and in the morning of 27 May and the decisive battle began. 91 Field Regiment RA records the story in its war diary. Here is an extract:

> Considerable air activity throughout morning. The Regiment fired on D.F. and C.P. tasks. Heavy attack by enemy infantry on right and left flanks. At one time it looked as though both flanks were going. Orders received that the Regiment will remain in present position until otherwise ordered. Enemy infantry continued their attack throughout the day, and our guns fired continually on D.F. and C.P. tasks.[225]

And the hard fighting continued all the evening and night. At around 22.00 hours, the regimental commander ordered a special control of the guns as the enemy now was up to the own infantry lines and friendly fire against own infantry must be avoided at all costs. The regiment was ordered at 03.30 hours to re-deploy backwards. The enemy had pushed the British infantry back and infiltrated their positions. Hence, there was a severe risk that the battery positions be overrun. D-Troop did not manage to get away in time and lost two guns when trying to winch the guns out of their gun pits.

The general order for withdrawal northwards to river Yser came on 28 May. All unnecessary stores and equipment should be destroyed including all vehicles not needed. It was made clear again that no 18-pounders or medium guns should be taken to the beachhead.

The successful concentration of artillery and the coordination of the fire planning at a most severe phase of the battle leave us with an impression of a very strong and effective divisional artillery commander of the 5th Infantry Division. The impression is also that his staff worked with calmness and efficiency despite the very pressing situation. The artillery was led with relevant, well-prepared orders and instructions through the tough battle.

Another indication of the efficient management of the 5th Infantry Division's artillery is that four almost intact field regiments could be brought into the beachhead with a total of 79 guns. Due to shortage of ammunition, they could, however, not all be used. There were only 40 rounds left per gun. It was now decided that the artillery of the 5th Infantry Division would be attached to the 50th Infantry Division, and furthermore, it was also decided that only two of the four field regiments were to continue the fighting. The two others were to destroy their guns and other equipment and march down to the beach for evacuation.

Typically British maybe, the choice of the regiments to leave was decided by tossing a coin. The result was that 18 Field Regiment RA and 91 Field Regiment RA would remain fighting. 9 Field Regiment RA and 97 Field Regiment RA abandoned their equipment and went to the beach for embarkation.[226] We may here recall that 18 Field Regiment RA had belonged to the 48th Infantry Division and 97 Field Regiment RA had been a GHQ/Corps unit of III Corps. It is an illustration of the ability to improvise and make good use of resources during those critical days.

Brooke wrote in his diary the 28 May 1040 that the medium guns of I Corps had fired 5,000 rounds in 36 hours. By this, the front was held, otherwise the 5th and 4th Infantry Divisions would have been lost and II Corps rolled up.[227] In his diary on 30 May he furthermore wrote that the 5th Infantry Division had only two brigades of 600 men each left after these final days. The 50th Infantry Division had also been mauled and was down to two brigades with 1,200 men each (the nominal strength of an infantry division at the time which was some 14,000 men). Alanbrooke's conclusion was clear: He wrote that it was no doubt that 5th Infantry Division and its artillery saved II Corps and BEF.[228]

Fragmentation – the 'indirect fire system' put out of order

We will now return for a moment to the south-western front along Aire (Aa) Canal. It was here the artillery, the little they had, was to be used in particular for direct fire at critical bridges and other vital passageways. Seven guns from 98 Field Regiment RA were, for instance, deployed like this on 22 May and fought heroically, although it was a losing battle against a superior force. The fate of these gunners is described in the official story of the campaign, but also in the history of the Royal Artillery, Farndale: The Years of Defeat. From the latter an extract illustrates what they had to endure. It is about the gun deployed at Renescure (an 18-pounder):

> Enemy-held houses across the bridge were destroyed by gunfire, and though two of the detachment were wounded the gun remained in action till the late afternoon. An enemy attack then developed from the flank. One enemy tank was knocked out but accurate mortar fire was put down on the gun position and under cover of this the enemy closed in. It was decided that the gun must be saved, but as it was limbering up the tractor was put out of action. Before anything could be done the position was overrun.[229]

A person really disliking this way of using the artillery was Jack Parham, who wrote in his account from 25 May:

> The 'Boche' were pretty active, both with aeroplanes, 4.2 inch guns and trench mortars. We had one Tp in a purely Anti-Tank role with it's guns scattered along behind the La Bassee Canal (2 in Givenchy and 2 nearer La Bassee). It was a *rotten job* [italic by author], very difficult to feed the men and I hated the idea. This was F Troop of 51/54 [Battery] with MacGregor and Epsom. They got shelled but never got a shoot and were withdrawn before the Boche tank attack on 27th [May]. Had they stayed perhaps 2 guns would have done some execution if not knocked out beforehand.[230]

The heavier guns were not employed in the final phase of the battle, i.e. those of 52 Heavy Regiment RA and the two No. 1 and 3 Super Heavy Batteries. The gunners made however a good fight as infantrymen along the front from St Omer to the coast.

Before following the surviving artillery units into the beachhead, we will look at the Survey Regiments and their efforts from 10th May to the end.

The unremitting work of the surveyors

1 and 2 Survey Regiment RA came along with the first BEF divisions to France. The former was put under command of I Corps and arrived already in September 1939. The latter became a Corps unit too, attached to II Corps. The regiment was on French soil in October. During the final phase of the build-up of the BEF, 3 Survey Regiment RA arrived and consequently was put under command of III Corps. This was in April 1940.

The three regiments had the pre-war organisation with Commander and regimental HQ's and three batteries, one Survey Battery, one Flash Spotting Battery and the third, a Sound Ranging Battery. The batteries had the same numbers as their 'parent' regiment, i.e. '1 Flash Spotting Battery', etc.

The first two regiments had plenty of time to survey gun positions and observation posts at the Gort Line; sound ranging and observation bases had been surveyed as well. The third regiment could not do much before the battle started.

It was stipulated in the artillery order attached to 'Plan D' how the survey regiments were to be employed. When coming back to the related I Corps artillery order, we can see that 1 Survey Regiment RA was to leave the first day together with the Corps artillery commander and his staff, this in order to take part in the initial reconnaissance of gun positions near river Dyle. As we have seen, the entire survey regiment was to march in a forward position of a divisional column. By this they were to commence the field survey work as early as possible. Late the second day, the regiment had been informed about the gun positions and could begin surveying them in to the Corps grid. The order from the Corps artillery commander was to undertake the survey in the following order of priority:

- Battle Positions surveyed into the permanent grid
- Survey of likely target positions including likely enemy gun positions, this in accordance with directives of CRAs and the CCMA
- Survey of alternative battery positions and temporary gun positions

A survey section from Royal Engineers, Topographical Section 13 Survey Company RE was attached to the regiment. This arrangement was to last until the two first mentioned tasks had been completed.

The Flash Spotting Battery and the Sound Ranging Battery ' were ordered to prepare for observation along the entire front of the two divisions of the Corps with emphasis on likely zones for enemy gun positions, i.e. the northern part of the Corps front. In a similar way engagement of 2 Survey Regiment RA was planned in II Corps area near river Dyle.

A number of Trig Points, and other easily recognisable reference points such as church towers, large buildings, etc., had to be used as a basis for the survey. A register of Trig Points had been prepared already before the war. This was now of much help.

This was the plan at large, but changes were to come. Around 25 April, Y Troop, a section from 13 Survey Company RE and 1 Sound Ranging Battery were ordered to go to the 51st (Highland) Infantry Division deployed behind the Maginot Line north of Metz where they were to come under command of that division. The divisional artillery had been reinforced there by a GHQ unit, 1 Field Regiment RHA, and a battery from 97 Field Regiment RA and 51 Medium Regiment RA, all of which had to be surveyed into a common grid.

The reduction of resources from 1 Survey Regiment RA was thought to be temporary. When the survey at the Maginot Line was finished, the detached resources would return to river Dyle. When arriving in the Saar region, the survey for all regiments was commenced immediately. The positions of a sound ranging base were also fixed and the base was ready for measuring on 3 May.[231] The base was in operation for the first time on 5 May 1940 and by this, they claim to be the first battery to measure against German artillery during the war. They also claim to be the first unit of I Corps to take up the fighting in France.

A second sound ranging base was prepared beginning on 8 May. It would have an unusual curve form for six microphones positioned 2km from each other. Two 'Advance Posts' were employed.

There was more of rumbling sounds further to the north and eventually it was decided that a third base would be established with its zone of ranging in that direction. The microphone positions were surveyed beginning on 10 May, this with the assistance of 'Y Troop'. When the German attack came on 10 May the units began preparations for a quick return to I Corps and stopped surveying the third sound ranging base, and also stopped measuring at the two other bases at 20.00 hours. Retrieval of microphones and cables started during the night and was continued on 11 May. The RE Section was ordered back this day and left the area. But the same day new orders were unexpectedly received, two new sound ranging bases should be surveyed.

One of these was to be surveyed by 'Y Troop' and was to be 10km wide with six microphones. The other one should be surveyed by the sound ranging battery itself. It would be 8km wide and have five microphones. The survey continued on 12 May and when extensive enemy artillery firing was encountered in front of the division, it was decided that the two bases should be put in operation immediately. The battery managed to reel out 80km of telephone cables! The next day, 14 May, measuring could start and the results were soon found satisfactory. Ranging up to 18,000 yards from the base was said to be possible. This was much longer than the range of the available artillery.

The same day came, however, the order that 1 Sound Ranging Battery should return to I Corps at the Escaut Line. All cables were taken in the following day and during the afternoon; the battery was ready to leave. It could report to the commander of 1 Survey Regiment RA just west of Tournai on 17 May. The 'Y Troop' stayed on, however, to support the divisional artillery when the 51st (Highland) Division began its retreat westwards. Before leaving the area, the troop had surveyed and registered 25 'Bearing Pickets', with bearing and coordinate data for the artillery units being provided by the surveyors. The troop had also participated in survey of the two new sound ranging bases.

Now, going back to the 'parent unit', 1 Survey Regiment RA, which had been ordered to be prepared to march across the Belgian border at two hours' notice on 10 May. Its reconnaissance detachment actually crossed the border at 07.15 hours on 11 May. At 12.00 hours the main body of the regiment followed suit. The next day, 12 May, the regiment was ready to commence surveying near river Dyle.

But, at this time there was no sound ranging unit available and the resources for ordinary survey of artillery units continuously arriving had been depleted by the redirection of 'Y Troop'. This made it necessary to use the Flash Spotting Battery instead, thus giving establishment of observation bases lower priority. This battery had to organise a replacement troop for survey work as replacement for 'Y Troop'. On 12 and 13 May survey went on. After this, it was possible to move the surveyors to the planned defence line along the Brussels – Charleroi Canal.

On 17 May, the order came that the entire regiment would be redeployed to the area behind river Escaut, where they would meet 1 Sound Ranging Battery coming back from the Saar area.

It was now out of the question to prepare for sound ranging. The sound ranging battery was instead ordered to organise a number of survey sections near the river. These were to assist in surveying in arriving artillery units to the grid. Besides fixing battery positions and observations post, they would also survey likely targets at the south-eastern side of the river such as groups of farm buildings, woods, road junctions etc.

The survey started from a number of available Trig Points and was done by triangulation in open landscape and in more woody terrain by 'resection' towards places with known coordinates, in particular church towers and so on. But also angle measuring by traverse and measurement of distances had to be used when fixing artillery positions. A beautiful example of such a survey record is shown in **Fig. 16-6**.

The triangulation seems to have started from the top line marked 'RE'. 'Bearing Pickets', with bearing and coordinate data for the artillery units, were delivered by the surveyors, 'Bearing Picket Cards'.[232]

When the surveyors had finished at river Escaut, they were ordered northwards to prepare for repeated redeployments towards the coast. They were engaged near river Lys between Armentières and Comines on the 25 May when the order was given to them to immediately cease surveying and to go to Dunkirk for evacuation. This was done already on 26 May in good order and without having to leave instruments and other vital equipment behind.

We have now followed the events of 1 Survey Regiment RA, but what had 2 Survey Regiment RA been through? We can get a glimpse of that by studying the regiment's war diary. First, we can see that this regiment also went to river Dyle early. 2 Survey Battery RA crossed the Belgian border at 00.30 hours on 11 May and the main body of the regiment later the same day. Upon arrival at river Dyle, units were engaged gradually and on 13 May all units were

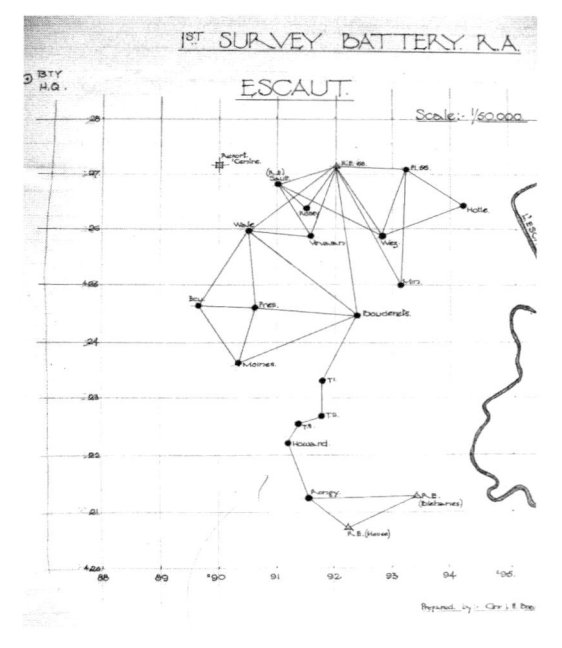

Fig. 16-6 1 Survey Regiment RA prepared the survey of all artillery formations to be deployed behind the Escaut-line into a common grid by means of triangulation and traverse to fix a number of Trig Points (Control Points). From one of these each unit should carry survey data to its own position (The National Archives WO 167/571)

in action. Probably all artillery regiments were surveyed and maybe one observation base fixed as well. No notes on deployment of any sound ranging base are found in the diary.

On 16 May the regiment was ordered to withdraw and on 18 May it was back behind river Escaut. The regiment did not stay here for long before again ordered to withdraw to the Dunkirk beachhead. On 26 May the order had been given to destroy all supplies and unnecessary equipment except instruments. Several attempts were made during the subsequent days to evacuate from the beach, but to no avail. In the morning of 29 May, the regiment walked to the pier at Dunkirk where they could embark on destroyers. On their way across the Channel, one of the ships with personnel from the regiment was torpedoed which led to a great loss of life.

What happened to 3 Survey Regiment RA? Well, the regiment commenced survey at the Gort Line as soon as it was fully equipped and ready in the middle of April 1940. As late as 8 May, they had actually completed a sound ranging base close to the Belgian Border just north of Lille. The regiment went into Belgium on 12 May for survey along river Escaut where III Corps, to which it was attached, was to be deployed as of 'Plan D'. The regiment was reinforced by two survey sections from '514 Survey Company RE'. The first task was to fix bearing pickets for the artillery of six divisions, which was to be completed in a week, it was hoped. In addition to that, observation bases for Flash Spotters and Sound Rangers would be established. No sound ranging bases materialised, however. A fairly small observation base for three observation posts was arranged east of Escaut and this was ready to register targets on 17 May. The southernmost observation post was located at the 145 m high Mont St. Aubert, which is a dominating hill just north of Tournai, a few kilometres east of the river.

The divisions of the two other Corps were at this time in full retreat westwards and those of III Corps had to move backwards as well. 3 Survey Regiment RA was now also forced to withdraw stepwise from one position to the other. The regiment was at Ploegsteert just northwest of river Lys on 21 May. Here, it was ordered to send a large detachment to the 46th Infantry Division which was to be up-graded with some artillery resources giving it better prospects for defending the canal front to the west. But the regiment was not to contribute with survey resources, but with equipment and personnel for radio and telephone communication.

Then, on 22 May, parts of the regiment was ordered to go to Dunkirk and left St. Omer at 14.30 hours, which place the regiment had reached the previous evening. Still in the area was 3 Survey Battery RA and the detachment sent to the 46th Infantry Division. Those sent back to Dunkirk were ordered at 15.45 hours on 25 May to evacuate at 18.00 hours, which they did, bringing with them 'a large amount of technical stores which were saved'.

The survey battery and the left detachment were later also evacuated, the former on 28 May and the latter on 29 May.

In summary, all survey tasks could be fulfilled despite the quick retreat towards Dunkirk. In particular along rivers Dyle and Escaut extensive survey of artillery positions were made. There was time for quite a lot of fixing of potential targets just in front of these major defence lines. This could also take place near temporary delaying lines to the advantage of retreating infantry and FOOs. But, as noticed, no sound ranging bases could be established apart from those brought into action in the Saar region [51st (Highland) Division].

The last shots – the gunners fire to the end
Jack Parham has described how he received the evacuation order, and how he experienced the unavoidable end of the campaign in France:

> The G.1. de Fontblanque came along and told me we were to throw away and destroy all vehicles other than the guns, wireless cars and essential fighting vehicles, otherwise the force would never get back to embark —— So it was as bad as that, was it! It is difficult long afterwards to remember what ones feelings were on hearing this, for it meant, if not that the capture of the British Army was imminent, that the whole British effort on the Continent was more or less finished for the time being.[233]

The last deployments of artillery became more and more difficult as all roads were jammed with not only retreating British, but also French units coming from the North and which were crossing the British routes. Many angry comments about the complete lack of traffic discipline on the part of the retreating French units can be read in many war diaries.

When the final orders for withdrawal to the last beachhead along the Bergues – Furnes Canal came on 26 May, the units were also ordered, as we have seen, to leave and destroy vehicles and equipment at the sides of the roads when approaching the bridgehead. The gunners were to proceed on foot once their vehicles had been destroyed. It had also been decided that no medium and heavy guns should be brought into the beachhead but be destroyed. This was also the case as regards the oldest light guns, the 18-pounders and 4.5-inch howitzers, from Territorial units. The personnel of these units were to fight as infantry until they could be evacuated. But despite these orders some crafty Gunners still took some 18-pounders with them into the beachhead, and they were of much help, in particular when the northern part of the front towards Nieuwpoort had to be stabilised.

Certain artillery regiments were more and more split up during the last few days, others were thanks to skilful leadership kept together, albeit not always with all their guns. But whatever the status was, the gunners kept on firing there guns as well as they could. Patrols were sent out to collect abandoned ammunition and at the end remaining guns in action were quite well supplied with ammunition. Yet disasters everywhere could not be prevented; some regiments were overrun and annihilated.

The bridgehead was defended by remnants of II Corps in the northeastern sector during the last few days, by I Corps in the centre and by the French 68th Infantry Division west of Dunkirk. A few more French divisions, or more correctly small remnants, were mixed up with British units inside the bridgehead. Out of the original 40 field regiments of the BEF, there were now complete, or remnants of, 16 regiments left to the end. One medium regiment, 59 Medium Regiment RA, was still relatively intact inside the bridgehead.

Actions during these final days were rather chaotic but everything was done to use the remaining artillery resources as efficiently as possible. Several divisional and regimental headquarters still worked as they should and, for instance, as late as 30 May, the HQRA of the 50th Infantry Division issued an operation order to subordinate units: one of the original divisional regiments, 92 Field Regiment RA and three regiments from other divisions. Regimental headquarters went on producing written orders to the last, though these were normally confirmation of already given oral orders. They were short and distinct and stipulated which unit that was to support which infantry unit or to be put under command of it. The location of the headquarters was also confirmed. Sometimes such orders could include administrative directives regarding supply of ammunition, fuel, food and water etc.

One gets the impression from the war diaries and personal accounts that the actions were much focused on independent engagement by lower units, batteries and troops, sometimes even sections (2 guns). This was all done in a well-disciplined way, albeit there were some exceptions, and was generally initiated in line with the 'Intentions' of higher command. A couple of examples follow further below.

An overview of the final deployment is illustrated on **Map 16-7**.

I have taken the first example from the account of one of Jack Parham's officers, Captain R.B. Taylor. It is about a troop of 10 Field Regiment RA:

> All four guns of 'A' Troop got back into the Dunkirk area. Two escaped from the roadblock under Sgt. Smith D.C.M., joined Capt Moulton later. These were the two concerned in Major Sheil's party. The other section I brought back myself and we remained in action two miles east of the mole and within 100' of the beach until 2300 hrs on Sat June 1st, when the general order to upsticks was given.
>
> This section attached itself to 27/72 Bty R.A. 16th Fd Regt R.A. who had 11 guns with them, the lay out being 5 on Z.L. [Zero Line] due East, 8 due South, a tremendous amount of firing was done during the last two days to the South in the form of concentrations chosen from the map at random, as there were no communications, down to the range of 6000. We did not however have to fire to the East as no Boche came within 1,000 [yards] of us from this direction, at any rate, not until the order to withdraw had been given.[234]

Turning then to 7 Field Regiment RA that we have followed above. This regiment was in the beachhead when receiving the evacuation order on 31 May. One of its batteries, the 9/17, was to leave two sections and the second battery, the 16/43, one. The six guns were to support the three battalions of 8 Infantry Brigade by means of two guns each. The regiment still had another 13 intact guns and brought back to England the dial sights, but were required to dump the gun mechanisms in a nearby little stream. This was the instruction of what to do with all guns left behind when their crews embarked. Before the guns were finally destroyed however the Gunners continued to fire them. Some 3,000 shells had been collected from abandoned guns, which all were fired towards enemy positions. They availed themselves of some pre-registered targets, but also fired on opportunity targets. The accuracy was probably not the best as good maps were missing. Only one 1:250,000-scale map was available instead of the normal 1:25,000 or 1:50,000 required.

The divisional artillery commander gave at 17.30 on 31 May the order that the remaining six-gun crews should embark when ordered by 8 Infantry Brigade HQS. From this headquarters, the guns were notified that they were to close down at 22.30 hours, but the guns should continue firing until 02.30 hours on 1 June. At this time, the last soldiers of the brigade would leave their positions along the Bergues – Furnes Canal. The commander of 7 Field Regiment RA and his remaining staff officers left for the beach at midnight. All their telephone lines had then been destroyed by German artillery fire and nothing more could be done.

The supply situation had seriously deteriorated for all units still in the beachhead during the final days. The shortage of food and, in particular, water was critical. The regimental war diary however allows itself a small joke on 31 May:

> Regtl H.Q. Water trailer had been abandoned on the journey from Oostvleteren, and by the start of the day the water situation became precarious. The Officers Mess had a fairly large supply of whiskey and gin left, and this was used for washing and washing up. This procedure was started by the M.O.; a strange thing for a true Scotsman!

One of the last artillery regiments, not to say the last, to leave Dunkirk was 27 Field Regiment RA, which was a I Corps regiment. The Command Post Officer (CPO) in 37/47 Battery was Lieutenant (later Brigadier) E.R.D. Palmer. His regiment was intact apart from one gun that had been positioned for anti-tank tasks. He could thus prepare, in accordance with the book, a fire

Fig. 16-7 While waiting for evacuation at the shores at Dunkirk the soldiers were continuously exposed to attacking German aircraft strafing them with machine-guns and dropping bombs on the beaches (AWM No. 101172)

plan during the last night for the three troops in the battery. It comprised five tasks for each one of the troops, each target to be engaged for 15 minutes. The first task was at 19.00–19.15 hours. The battery had registered three DF targets (Defensive Fire) close to important bridges towards the beachhead and also a number of enemy mortar positions.

In accordance with Palmer's plan, the regiment fired between 19.00 hours and 21.00 hours. Palmer added a sort of 'goodbye salute' in connection with the destruction of their guns. He ordered the E Troop to destroy their guns at 21.40 hours, D Troop at 21.45 hours and at 21.50 hours, finally, the F Troop. But Palmer had ordered also each gun to fire ten rounds gunfire, the first round of which to be fired as a troop salvo exactly five minutes before the time ordered for destruction of the guns. Palmer reported after all rounds had been delivered: 'The result was most impressive as the flashes lit up the night sky, and it gave our morale a boost.'[235]

When the war broke out, they had been 70 men in the Battery Headquarters, now 11 besides Palmer himself remained. He tried to boost their fighting spirit and saw to it that they would leave France with dignity and in a way befitting a fine regiment.[236]

While waiting for transport, the survivors were attacked by *Luftwaffe* every day and did what they could to meet the threat by digging in and using anti-aircraft guns but also personal weapons (**Fig. 16-7**).

Discipline was strictly enforced on the beaches, which was a prerequisite for avoiding panic and securing the planned boarding (**Fig. 16-8**).

Fig. 16-8 Despite repeated air attacks and artillery fire panic rarely occurred and men patiently queued on the beach for their turn to get evacuated (RAHT)

The battle is over – but not south of Somme!

The campaign in Northern France was over and all the BEF artillery equipment north of river Somme had been lost. Pemberton (1950) has given a summary of the losses; anti-tank and anti-aircraft guns here excluded:

- 18/25-pounders, 704 guns (including 72 reserve guns)
- 18-pounders, 216 guns
- 4.5-inch howitzers, 96 pieces

Hence, in total 1,016 guns lost.

In addition to lost light guns came the loss of medium guns:

- 6-inch howitzers, 221 pieces (including 45 in reserve)
- 60-pounders, 51 pieces

Hence, in total 272 medium guns.
To all these losses came 59 heavy and super heavy guns with different calibres.[237]

The campaign in Flanders became a setback of immense magnitude for the British. They had met an opponent superior in everything, except numerical strength, and lost the battle. But the British were not defeated! Confidence and spirit to fight were not broken. The gunners returned to England with retained, not to say, improved self-confidence!

The fighting was to continue for some more weeks south of river Somme. The 51st (Highland) Division left the Saar Region when the German break-through at river Meuse came. The division was engaged in the battle further to the South when the bridgehead at Dunkirk had been eliminated and the river Somme could be crossed. The British 1st Armoured Division which had been landed at Cherbourg and Le Havre around 20 May was now engaged. Both British divisions were attached to French armies.

As a consequence of the political decision not to let down the French after Dunkirk, a new, second BEF was organised in England. It was under command of General Alan Brooke and was to be sent to France over the 11–14 June. Besides the two divisions already in France south of river Somme, the 52nd (Lowland) Division and Canadian 1st Infantry Division were also to be dispatched from England.

Soon it was obvious that the allies could not stand up to the German onslaught. The 51st (Highland) Division was pressed towards the coast where it could not be evacuated and had to surrender on 12 June 1940 at St. Valery en Caux. With it followed one of its field regiments, 23 Field Regiment RA, 1 Field Regiment RHA (except one battery) and 51 Medium Regiment RA.[238] The 1st Armoured Division was released from the fighting and taken home via Le Havre. Brooke managed also to get the political leaders to accept a total British evacuation from France. There should be no BEF II! Units already arriving were quickly evacuated and those under way to France were ordered to return. In total 192,000 men were evacuated from Le Havre, Cherbourg, St. Nazaire and other ports further to the South before the truce between France and Germany was signed on 22 June. Around 332 guns of different calibres were saved back to England.

Summary of the role of British artillery in France 1940
It has not been possible to follow the use of BEF artillery in every detail. Numerous documents including war diaries, plans, written orders, etc. were destroyed on the beaches at Dunkirk. Much of written documents about the events and participating units and headquarters were produced after the return to England, most often during the summer 1940, but often much later. Hence, there can be mistakes and errors as well as critical gaps in reviewed documents. I feel, however, that I can summarise my impressions and findings as follows:

- The BEF had much artillery, but a large part of it was obsolete and not adapted to the requirements of a *Blitzkrieg*.
- Engagement of artillery was generally delegated to brigade and battalion level. Concentrated fire by regiments took place, but not very often. Concentration of fire from divisional and even higher levels took, probably, never place.
- Physical concentration of artillery resources was organised during the hard fighting on 27–28 May by II Corps at Ypres, in particular. Here, the divisional artillery was reinforced with several field regiments, some medium regiments and one heavy battery. This might have had a decisive impact on the outcome of the battle when the attacking German forces were prevented from cutting off the BEF from the beaches.
- No fire planning at higher levels other than regimental headquarters seems to have taken place. An exception might be HQRA of the 5th Infantry Division. The role of divisional artillery headquarters was to delegate artillery resources primarily to coordinate marches and redeployments. Sometimes, however, planning of harassing fire was coordinated at higher levels.
- Planning of 'Defensive Fire', 'SOS Fire' and 'Counter Preparation Fire' dominated fire planning in addition to observed fire on 'Opportunity Targets' and 'Covering Fire' in support of counter-attacks. The latter generally at battalion level, never attacks by higher formations.
- The limited range of vintage guns made fire concentrations at depth, for instance against enemy artillery positions, difficult, not say impossible.
- Support of armoured units was never required, as no such units had arrived in France before the evacuation.
- Smoke was rarely used.
- The battery or the troop was normally the fire unit, in particular during the delaying battles back from river Dyle. During the last days before evacuation, even sections (2 guns) and single guns became fire units.
- Field artillery units were often given anti-tank tasks based on direct fire, i.e. an important deviation from the main task of field artillery, i.e. 'indirect fire'.
- Ammunition supply varied between units. There was plenty at river Dyle, whereas it was down to a critical level at river Escaut at the forward units retreating from the river Dyle. Regiments belonging to divisions in the rear reported no shortage of ammunition.
- The ordered radio silence during the whole 'Phoney War' made efficient training in radio communication impossible. In combination with inferior wireless sets that made concentrations above the regimental level very difficult to arrange.
- The dispatch riders were invaluable as a means for communication and liaison as replacement for bad radio equipment and

telephone lines cut off. They were also invaluable when traffic control and directions of redeployments had to be improvised.
- The swift changes of the tactical situation made it impossible for the three survey regiments to establish observation and sound ranging bases. As Pemberton (1950) wrote: '[they] were soon brought to impotence'.[239] Problems in getting time enough for the laying of extensive lines added to the difficulties. The huge battle noise hampered the possibilities for the sound rangers to use their equipment. A few sound ranging bases could, however, be established and brought into successful operation where the 51st (Highland) Infantry Division was deployed near the Maginot Line.
- Artillery reconnaissance and fire observation from the air by means of RAF Army-cooperating Squadrons failed. The Lysander aircraft used proved to be too vulnerable. Most of those available were shot down.
- When required, gunners acted well as infantry. This became necessary many times during the final days of the campaign.
- Artillery units were skilled in marching and redeployment even when roads were jammed with streams of refugees, retreating French units, own infantry, supply vehicles, etc. Young officers and NCOs proved to be energetic; often acting with great flexibility when units had been dispersed or had taken wrong roads.
- The poor structure of artillery command at the Corps level with both a 'Commander Corps Royal Artillery' (CCRA) and a 'Commander Corps Medium Artillery' (CCMA) was clearly demonstrated. The unsuitability of the regimental organisation with two 12-gun batteries became obvious too. A better conformity with the infantry's three-pronged organisation was needed. The shortage of FOOs/OPOs when supporting the infantry was another weakness of the battery organisation. Leading such big batteries was difficult too; in particular when the battle was mobile and the tactical situation changed frequently.
- The basic skills of the gunners acquired in peacetime training and during the 'Phoney War' drills resisted all challenges. Shooting, they could always do!

Despite the fact that the artillery could not generally be concentrated physically nor to produce concentrated fire, but had to act in lower formations, batteries or troops, in support of the withdrawing infantry, the engagement should not be underestimated. The willingness on the part of all gunners to assist with artillery fire to the last round was deeply rooted. The gunners were often the last to yield to the pressure from superior enemy units. The fact that it proved possible to keep so many artillery units in operation all the way into the final beachhead is a proof that the spirit and discipline of the Royal Artillery units were first class. Thanks to this, the gunners could protect the evacuation during the very last days until almost no soldiers were left. They did what was expected from them and more so, despite continuous shelling and bombardment from the air. Without its artillery, the BEF would likely been annihilated.

At a meeting with the French and Belgian leaders on 31 May 1940, Churchill stressed that Britain had lost 1,000 guns and thousands of vehicles and other equipment. There were only some 500 guns left at home, he said. This was extremely serious in respect of a possible German invasion. He meant that if a German force, well equipped with artillery, landed in England, it could not be met by an equally strong force. But in his typical way, he added, that if this took place, 'the civil population would fight with desperate energy and unconquerable resolve.'[240]

17. Failed Intervention in Norway

We have in the previous Chapter seen how the 5th Infantry Division had a decisive role in the battle at Ypres-Comines 26–28 May, an engagement that probably saved BEF from being completely encircled at Dunkirk. But the division could have had quite a different role. On 29 April 1940, it was ordered to march to Le Havre for transport to Norway.

While waiting for embarkation, it suddenly became known, however, that the plan had been cancelled, and the division should return. Again it was attached to BEF just before the German attack on 10 May.[241]

Maybe the redeployment order for Norway had not been a complete surprise. After all, one of its brigades, 15 Infantry Brigade, had already at the beginning of April been relieved and transported to Norway.

Norway a country of strategic interest

Both sides had their eyes on Scandinavia, in particular Norway, already when the war broke out in September 1939.

As to the Germans, the Norwegian coast was of interest as a potential base area for its naval forces, the *Kriegsmarine*, in the coming battle against the Royal Navy. The warfare against the transatlantic transports to Britain, which were so important for the allies, could be much easier with submarine bases in Norway.

From British military point of view, control of the Norwegian sea lanes would also be an asset. It would make a blockade of German ports easier to maintain and also be a benefit as to the defence of the Homeland. The most serious, urgent problem to the British political leadership was, however, the sea transport of Swedish iron ore from Narvik to Germany. These took place particularly during the winter months when the port of Luleå in Northern Sweden was difficult to use due to widespread ice cover in the Baltic Sea. Sweden was one of the neutral countries of Europe at the time.

The British regarded the iron ore transports as very important for Germany's ability to sustain a long war as the country lacked own ore resources. As the transports from Narvik took place on the sea-lanes of neutral Norway it was seen crucial to stop them by mining the corridor used, irrespective of Norway's neutrality. But even better would be landing of a strong force at Narvik and having this to cross the Swedish border to capture the Swedish ore fields at Kiruna and Gallivare. If that proved to be unrealistic a strategy, mining of the port of Luleå from the air from Norwegian bases to stop the summer transport to German ports might be an alternative. Churchill argued during the whole autumn 1939 for some action in Scandinavia. But he faced much opposition from other politicians who were against military actions against neutral countries.

When the Soviet Union, with the support of the Ribbentrop-Molotov Pact, attacked Finland on 30 November 1939, a completely changed strategic situation arose. Britain and France reacted strongly and began contemplating if and how they could intervene in support of Finland. The League of Nations told member countries to intervene. This seemed reasonable in respect of the fact that Britain and France had declared themselves as protecting nations in 1920 following Mannerheim's diplomacy in connection with the Finnish declaration of independence (France had already in 1918 and Britain in 1919 officially recognised Finland as an independent nation).

The British now saw an opportunity for capturing the Swedish ore fields by requesting permission from Norway and Sweden to transport an intervention force to Finland from Narvik via Luleå in Sweden to Finland. A good excuse, thought Churchill and some other politicians in Britain and France. He had the idea that two British divisions would be used.[242] But while this prospect was discussed, probed and negotiated, the war between Finland and the Soviet Union ended with a truce on 13 March 1940. The two British divisions were instead now sent to France and BEF, but still in England were ten infantry battalions intended for intervention in Norway. However, the planning for their transport to Norway went out of sequence, not least due to shortage of resources for transport of equipment, ammunition and stores.

In France there was a strong political pressure for engagement against Germany, preferably outside French territory. To arrange this together with the British in Norway was seen as an attractive alternative, and the planning for this commenced.

Planning of the attack

In Britain planners reverted to the initial scope, mining of Norwegian waters. The political reluctance to do this disappeared quickly later in March 1940. On 3 April the British Government decided to put the plans in operation on 5 April, a date that due to some controversies was postponed until 8 April. The French acknowledged the decision.[243]

Mines would later be dropped also outside the Swedish port Luleå to stop the shipping of iron ore to Germany during summer months, as it was thought.

In respect of the risk for a large-scale German intervention in Norway, it was decided that a British infantry brigade and a French unit would be landed in Narvik to secure the harbour and then proceed to the Swedish border. Landings of ground forces were furthermore to take place in Stavanger, Bergen and Trondheim. By military presence near the latter city, one would be better prepared to provide help for Sweden should Germany decide to meet the British-French actions with invasion of Sweden.

Again, the focus was on landing at Narvik, but with more limited scope than capture of the Swedish ore fields. If Sweden was not willing to accept help with allied 'protection' of the fields, the allies could at least prevent iron ore export via Narvik, this preferably with Norwegian consent. The British view on Sweden's position had been fairly moderate before the war broke out, even with Churchill, who had said: '…it is far from our wish to quarrel with the Swedes.'[244] Now it became harsher.

Through the British decisions on action in Scandinavia, the Norwegian neutrality was lost, and Sweden was brought into acute danger.

As for the Germans, the planning for an invasion of Norway had started on 14 December 1939 upon a directive from Hitler. The final decision to launch the attack, Operation Weserübung, was made by Hitler when the so-called Altmark Incident took place. This was the action ordered by Churchill to free 300 captured British sailors on board the German steamer *Altmark*, which took place in the night between 16 and 17 February 1940 in a Norwegian fjord. The action was a clear violation of the country's neutrality. The British excuse was that the Germans had violated neutrality by taking prisoners of war into Norwegian waters. The event convinced Hitler that the British did not respect Norway's neutrality and that further actions on Norwegian territory could be expected. So the respect for this neutrality was lost also on the German side. Strategic interests on the part of larger countries had definitely taken over.

The British planning was hastily done with too many political and military 'cooks' involved, the result of which would prove disastrous. The German planning, on the other hand, was meticulously done, characterised by professional skill and determination. Operation Weserübung was to be one of the largest and most daring surprise attacks on any nation. By means of timely coordinated attacks troops were to be landed in the morning of 9 April 1940 in Oslo, Kristiansand, Arendal and Egersund in the South, and in Stavanger, Bergen and Trondheim in the middle part of the country and in the so important city Narvik in the North as well. The invading soldiers were to be landed primarily from ships, but some also with parachutes and some units were to be landed with aircraft.

It was not only the quality of planning that differed dramatically. Also the choice of troops, their equipment and, not the least, their training differed. The British decided to use some regular forces with adequate training, but also untrained territorial units were engaged. They had no personal kits and training for the terrain conditions meeting them; and they were not used to the weather prevailing this time of the year in Norway with deep snow and low temperatures. The British did not plan for offensive actions, at least not at the beginning of the campaign.

On the German side, adequate units with the right equipment were landed. First, two infantry divisions with its own artillery, anti-tank guns, etc and a mountain division were to be landed. Another three infantry divisions would later follow suit. In addition, large reserves were available in Germany, for instance an infantry division, more artillery and light tanks. German strategy and operation plans were well conceived, and allotted resources, by strength and types, sufficient for securing success, albeit large risks were taken.

To forestall or be forestalled – the battle begins

Plans were on both sides put into operation through final decisions by top war leaders during the first week of April 1940. The British and the French had avoided getting dragged into war with the Soviet Union, and had put plans for occupation of the Swedish ore fields on the shelf for the time being. Now the objective was mining of Norwegian water lanes, and in combination with this a limited landing of ground forces on Norwegian territory to forestall a possible German counter-action. As a start, mining would commence on 8 April to be followed later by landings at Narvik and cities to the South, provided the Norwegians would be in favour of the plan. Acquisition of permission to do the mining was not an issue.

For Hitler the challenge was a matter of forestalling the allies and he gave the final order for the launching of Operation Weserübung. The German surprise attack was to begin in the early morning on 9 April.

Both sides thus commenced operations against Norway within one day from each other. And they were equally surprised to encounter the action of the opposite side. On the British side, the surprise came despite information from various sources several days beforehand, including from Sweden, that military units and supplies had been loaded and that columns of ships had started to leave German ports and were on their way northwards.

The British had dispatched three groups of naval ships towards Norway for the planned mining and escorts (**Fig. 17-1**). They were in place when the German invasion groups came closer, but initial armed contacts on 7 April were not interpreted as the prelude of an invasion. Intelligence reports from reconnaissance aircraft and submarines were also misinterpreted. The British had met *Marinegruppe I* on its way to Narvik and *Marinegruppe II* heading for Trondheim, but they thought it was a matter of breakout to the Atlantic and not an invasion.

The result of this was a decision to get the troops already on board numerous ships to disembark and get Home Fleet to leave for a chase of those 'breaking out' westwards. For logistic reasons it was necessary for Germany to simultaneously capture also Danish territory. This country surrendered on 9 April in a couple of hours. The Germans seems to have hoped for something similar in Norway, but this was not to happen. Norway mobilised its army gradually and took up the fight against advancing German units. As usual, the politicians had not dared to give the mobilisation order in time for meeting the invaders right from the beginning. A quick build-up of German strength, both ground forces and air forces, could thus take place. This made the situation for the Norwegian army very difficult. Formations reacted with mixed feelings of defeat and resolution to resist. Certain units gave up almost immediately, whereas others only reluctantly retreated northwards under the pressure of hard delaying fighting. To avoid annihilation, the major part of a Norwegian division crossed the border to Sweden where it was interned. Other resources were to some extent also moved to Sweden in order to prevent that they came into German hands (**Fig. 17-2**).

The allies had forestalled the Germans with one day when starting the mining on 8 April, but they were deeply forestalled by Hitler when it came to landing of ground forces in Norway. The much-divided allied war leadership was now hesitating about what to do in the new situation; the initiative had definitely passed to the Germans.

The result was a half-measure although the decision to land ground forces remained in

Fig. 17-1 Royal Navy played an important role in the battle of Norway. British ships attacked German warships already from the first day. Much needed artillery support for the allied ground forces was also provided till the end. Here is the British destroyer HMS Southampton (AWM No. 001990)

Fig. 17-2 During the chaotic first days after the German invasion a Norwegian division crossed the border to Sweden where it was interned. Further to the North some other Norwegian resources were transferred to Sweden thus preventing the Germans to get their hands on them. Here is long column of Norwegian lorries waiting on the Swedish side of the border (RAHT)

force. A well-conceived strategy lacked. No ability to thoroughly revise plans for the new situation was at hand. This led to allocation of too small resources and these lacked proper training and equipment for the tasks assigned to them in Norway; altogether this made things even worse.

This was in particular true as regards the British part of the allied Expeditionary Force. French units and the Polish attached to them were to prove more suitable and better trained for the fighting to come.

Now, in this situation, what were the decisions made and what could be done?

The allies give priority to northern Norway
Norway was to be given help, but where and how was basically determined by the earlier strategy. Narvik must be the prime target! It was here that the iron ore traffic to Germany must be stopped. And in the background were still hopes that the Swedish ore fields could be occupied, or at least brought under allied control. Soon a new reason for a thrust in the North arose. The Norwegian King and Crown Prince were on flight northwards together with the Government and eventually arrived at Tromsø. Therefore the allies should try to prevent the Germans from occupying the northernmost part of the country. Hopefully this part could be kept as a free zone, from which the King and Government could continue fighting for their country.

The task for retaking Narvik was assigned to the retired British Admiral William Boyle, 12th Earl of Cork and Orrey, here further on called Lord Cork. He was to be assisted by Major General P.J. Mackesy as commander of the British ground forces. Brigadier Antoine Béthouart was appointed commander of the French forces.

With Lord Cork, the Expeditionary Forces got a strong and energetic commander inclined towards offensive actions. He was a worthy representative of a several hundreds of years long tradition in the Royal Navy to act offensively and boldly. Mackesy was a different personality. He was not willing to take risks and was definitely not a man who wanted to catch a moving opportunity.

While Lord Cork wanted to recapture Narvik as soon as possible with resources available, Mackesy first wanted to establish a strong base at Harstad. When this was done, an attack could be made from this place. Furthermore, he was also of the opinion that the allies should wait till the snow had melted away nearer the pending summer.

Orders were given in England to the units that had disembarked to get on board again for transport to Norway. As mentioned, one of the brigades of the 5th Infantry Division in France, 15 Infantry Brigade, had left BEF to be attached to Expeditionary Force for Norway. [245] From England 24 Guards Brigade was sent to Harstad with its three regular battalions, consisting of the 1st battalion Scots Guards, 1st battalion Irish Guards, and 2nd battalion South Wales Borderers. A Territorial Brigade, 146 Infantry Brigade, was to be shipped to Harstad as well. Other units were prepared for transport, amongst them 147 Infantry Brigade, which was another Territorial formation. In parallel with these troops, transports, equipment, supplies, ammunition and much more were shipped together with supply units for the larger force to be built up gradually with Harstad as its main base.

In France, the 1st Light Division, with two Half-brigades each comprising three battalions of *Chasseur Alpins*, mountain infantry, and a Half-brigade from the Foreign Legion, was alerted and had been ready for the intervention in Finland since the planning for this engagement had commenced. Attached to the division was also a Polish Brigade with four battalions divided into two 'Half-brigades'. These units were ready also to go to Norway without delay. In the French force were also a few batteries with important 75-mm mountain guns included, *2e Groupe Autonome d'Artillerie Coloniale*.

While these forces were on their way to Norway another confusing discussion broke out in London. The new Norwegian Commander-in-Chief, Major General Ruge, argued that the allied intervention should in the first place be done in the Trondheim region. Here the chances were best for halting definitely the German advance northwards.

Ruge's arguments made an impression. Eventually even Churchill, at first a bit reluctantly but later with more enthusiasm, accepted the idea that Trondheim should be captured. The city should be held and all communication lines northwards and to the east towards Sweden should be secured.[246] Taking Trondheim would not only give best opportunities to stop the Germans as Ruge argued, it would also mean that the allies got hold of a harbour large enough for supplying an Expeditionary Force of at least 50,000 men. At the nearby airfield, large air resources could be based by which the German air superiority could be broken, so was the argument.

There were definitely good reasons for taking Trondheim, but against it was the negative effect of dispersion of resources which would be a consequence. Additional resources required were lacking, at least in the short term. Resources aimed for the Narvik campaign must be reduced.

Now it was necessary to quickly devise a plan for the capture of Trondheim. It was decided that the attack should come from the sea. The Royal Navy was to land two Canadian battalions to silence the coast artillery batteries outside the city. Then, the forces would proceed towards the city itself where 15 Infantry Brigade would be landed. 147 Infantry Brigade would be the reserve in England. At about the same time the 146 Infantry Brigade and a half-brigade of French mountain soldiers would, as it was said, make a deceptive attack at Namsos further to the North, the *Mauriceforce*. This attack was implemented on 17 April. The infantry brigade had been on its way to Narvik but was suddenly redirected towards Namsos. A small detachment of marine infantry had already landed there on 14 April in order to establish contact with the Norwegian forces.

The transport with heavy equipment for the brigade and vehicles could not be redirected, unfortunately. But even more critical: no anti-aircraft or artillery units were available for support of the brigade in the coming battle.[247]

On 17 April, 700 marine soldiers and a body of other soldiers were landed south of Trondheim at Åndalsnes. They were soon followed by 148 Infantry Brigade, a Territorial brigade. Even here neither artillery nor anti-aircraft guns were accompanying them. The force was given the name *Sickleforce*.

The plan was now to launch a pincer manoeuvre against Trondheim. This operation was called Operation Hammer to be effected on 22 April.

Everything began 'swinging' already before the first landings north and south of Trondheim had commenced. The Royal Navy got cold feet after having experienced unceasing bombings by *Luftwaffe* on ships near the Norwegian coast. It was concluded that the risks on ships and landing infantry would be too large, and it was recommended that Operation Hammer would be cancelled. An additional factor affecting the decision was that British Press had started to write about a coming operation against Trondheim. Hence surprise was definitely lost. On 19 April the formal decision to cancel the operation was taken by the Cabinet. It was now instead hoped that the pincer operation would be able to pursue and Trondheim thus to be retaken. However, the southern leg got other things to attend to. Upon Norwegian request, the brigade turned southwards into the Gudbrand Valley in order to halt the German onslaught in cooperation with Norwegian forces. 15 Infantry Brigade, not any longer required for Operation Hammer, was landed at Åndalsnes and rushed southwards into the Gudbrand Valley.

In the North, the *Mauriceforce* was stopped halfway towards Trondheim. Against well-trained German mountain warriors, and lacking own artillery and anti-aircraft guns, nothing could be done, in particular as the Germans maintained absolute air superiority.

The details of the fighting that followed will not be discussed here; we may just notice that the allies soon were forced to realise that Trondheim could not be recaptured, neither could the German advance be halted nor encirclement avoided. At last what remained to do was to retreat and save the remnants of the forces by evacuation. This was organised, and was done successfully on 3 May.

Now the battle for Narvik remained, but before leaving the middle sector we will notice how lack of artillery was experienced by one of the front commanders, Lieutenant Colonel E.E.F. Cass, commanding a battalion in 15 Infantry Brigade. He was to meet the Germans in the Gudbrand Valley. After the evacuation he wrote about this. Lack of artillery was one of the greatest mistakes in this campaign (see Farndale (1996), p. 27):

First came tanks and about 50 lightly equipped infantry. Behind came more infantry on foot, motor-cyclists, machine guns in side-cars and towed guns. Behind again came motor vehicle after motor vehicle . . . It was a target that Gunners would dream about – three quarters of a mile of confined road, crammed with troops and vehicles, all clearly visible from our observation post. Just one battery of 25-pounders [12 guns in a battery] could have blown the enemy off the road. [Farndale: 'but there were no guns']

But where was the artillery?

If the British-French intervention in Finland had taken place, two British divisions had been sent to Narvik for transport via Sweden to Finland; 42nd and 46th Infantry Divisions were allotted. Both of them had most likely come with all their divisional artillery, i.e. 2–3 field regiments each.

When the adventure went to the grave with haste after the Finnish truce on 13 March 1940, the two divisions were dispatched to France. But only the 42nd Infantry Division brought artillery to France. The 46th Infantry Division was to protect BEF supply lines and left its artillery at home in England. Here was now a resource for Norway.

In France, 15 Infantry Brigade left BEF in early April for engagement in Norway. Normal support for a brigade was one artillery regiment (24 guns), but no artillery was accompanying the brigade. Maybe, one thought it could come later.

When the whole British 5th Infantry Division on 29 April prepared itself for transport from Le Havre to Norway, no exception for its three artillery regiments was envisaged. They would go to Norway, all three of them.

When the evacuations of British troops from Åndalsnes and Namsos were finished, a contra-order was issued to the division: Stop embarking, return to BEF! With this order valuable resources disappeared from the Norwegian scene.

We will therefore now take a look at the artillery of the 46th Infantry Division left in England. One of the divisional regiments was 51 Field Regiment RA. What does its war diary tell us?[248]

The regiment was organised at the time in a regimental headquarters and two batteries, each with twelve guns divided in three troops, as were other regiments after 1938. The batteries were 203 and 370 Battery RA.

The regiment was a Territorial formation, which had been mobilised in September 1939 and was then gradually equipped and trained during the winter. The intention was to join BEF in France during the spring 1940. Certain reconnaissance work there was done in February. Nothing in the war diary hints at engagement in Norway or Finland.

In March 1940, the regiment was a given a 'warning order' that it should be made ready for transport overseas. The order was received when several regimental exercises were going on (Easter Sunday this year was on 24 March). Immediately after the Easter holiday, equipment maintenance was performed and packing commenced, activities that continued over the end of the month. On 9 April the regiment was ready to leave its quarters at Aldbourne and Ramsbury (around 40 miles north of Plymouth). But two days later something strange happened. It was suddenly made clear that only one of the batteries was to leave; the choice was 203 Battery RA.

On the following day, 12 April, the battery was ordered to be ready to go upon six hours' notice. At 17.00 hours, the order came that a 'road detachment' should leave at 11.00 hours the next day. A 'railway detachment' should leave the following day, 1 April. The former comprised three officers and 125 other ranks and was directed to a port in Southern England. The detachment brought all guns and vehicles that would be loaded on a ship. The rest of the battery was to travel to an unknown northerly port, which later turned out to be Glasgow.[249]

The main body of the regiment (now without 203 Battery) was ordered on 14 April to be ready to go, certain parts of it on 15 April. On 16 April a 'railway detachment' arrived in Glasgow and on the 17 April the regimental HQS and 370 Battery RA embarked on the troop carrier RMS *Lancastria*. Later during the day, the 'road detachment' arrived and embarked. The regiment could however not get all its vehicles on board. Still nothing was known about the destination.

On 19 April it was suspected that it was not France but Norway as winter kits were distributed to the soldiers on this day. The convoy to which they were attached assembled the same day with escorting ships outside Greenock; but still no departure. On 23 April, they are all back in Glasgow again and disembarked! Short leaves were permitted for some; the others were engaged in drills and marching. And on 25 April a final order was received to leave the port and the ship. The order was to go to Leith where the regiment (except 203 Battery) embarked on the troop carrier *Ulster Monarch*, which at 22.45 hours on 26 April hoisted its anchor and sailed northwards along the eastern coast of Scotland. Most of the personnel believed now Norway to be the destination.

Ulster Monarch arrives the next day at the naval base Scapa Flow after an adventurous passage; 'the boat very crowded' the war diary tells us. The day after arrival, the regiment left the ship and went to quarters ashore at the naval base. Again, there were doubts as to whether Norway was the destination after all, because on 29 April they embarked on the troop carrier *Orion*, which on 1 May at 20.15 hours sailed southwards and eventually anchored the following day close to the Forth of Firth Bridge. On 3 May, they went ashore at last in Leith and were given quarters at Marine Gardens Portobello. After recovering and having got complementary equipment, training was resumed. Having been 'shuffled' here and there on crowded ships and unclear instructions about the purposes of the movements quite a lot was needed for restoring good spirit and discipline.

On 11 May it was time for next transfer, now to new quarters at Jedburgh where the regiment remained until June 1940. In September, finally, the regiment went overseas, now complete with both batteries. Egypt via Cape Good Hope was the destination.

The account indicates that the intention in April never was to engage the regiment in France, nor at Narvik, but in the Trondheim area. Probably the plan was to support the reserve brigade, 147 Infantry Brigade, when this had been landed. When the attack on Trondheim was cancelled, it seems that the intention changed again, now landing at Åndalsnes for the support of *Sickleforce* was the plan. But this force had to be evacuated, as we have seen, and this caused the final disembarkation of the regiment. In hindsight, one might wonder why the regiment was not instead redirected to Narvik; maybe they were a victim of chaotic leadership and frequently changing plans?

The only artillery unit

As a consequence of events, the only artillery unit sent to Norway was 203 Battery RA from

51 Field Regiment RA. The battery left its quarters on 13 and 14 April, as seen above. The port to be used for loading guns and vehicles was Southampton. One officer and 20 other ranks were to accompany the ship, the *Empire Ability*. On board were also 4,000 high explosive shells and 1,200 smoke shells loaded. For the infantry mortars 1,000 bombs were taken aboard besides a lot of other supplies.[250] The ship sailed on 16 April and arrived at Harstad, Norway on 27 April.

Most of the staff in the battery 'road detachment' returned to the battery quarters after having loaded the ship in Southampton. Here they accompanied the 'railway detachment' leaving for Glasgow and arriving on 14 April at 12.10 hours. After parade on the quay, they immediately embarked the troop carrier *Lanconia*. All were on board at 14.00 hours and the ship sailed at 16.00 hours; the weather was fine and the travel went well without any major problems. Arctic clothing was handed out later the first day and lifeboat exercises took place. The ship went to the mouth of Clyde to enter its place in a larger convoy.

In the early morning on 16 April, they weighed anchor. They were accompanied by a number of French troop carriers and escorting French destroyers. The following days passed fairly uneventfully. Parades, inspections, lifeboat exercises etc., kept the men active. Quite thrilled they were on 18 April when a British 'C Class' Cruiser was observed and later also a Battle Ship with destroyers escorting them. These ships made an attack on a suspected submarine with depth charges.

It is noted in the war diary of 19 April that the French ships left the convoy that day. Probably it carried 5 Half-brigade of the French mountain division with its three battalions *Chasseur Alpins* that were to be landed at Namsos and join *Mauriceforce*.

On 21 April at 03.00 hours reveille sounded. The ship had arrived at Harstad and weighed anchor in the bay. At 05.30 hours disembarkation and unloading of equipment and stores to small vessels and boats in shuttle traffic to the quay commenced. This went on the whole day and now the gunners also experienced *Luftwaffe's* undisturbed bombings, which were repeated several times. Every time the alarm sounded they had to go below deck; no one was hurt. What it looked like when the bombs fell is seen in **Fig. 17-3**.

Disembarkation and unloading the ship was, as far as the battery was concerned, finished in the morning on 22 April and the battery went to its given quarters at Ervik, just north of Harstad. Here the gunners tried to make it as comfortable as possible, but snow and icy winds did not make it a hilarious happening. Spring was late this year, 1940.

The gunners had arrived without guns and vehicles. The only thing to do was to wait and organise their own local defence and take part in alarm exercises and daily parades etc. After a few days, parts of the battery were detached for stowing work in the harbour of Harstad.

On 27 April, contact was made with batterymates on board *Empire Ability* which now had arrived too. The ship was immediately exposed to several bombing attacks but was lucky enough not to be hit. Indeed important, as all the guns and vehicles of the battery were on board this ship. The gunners first had to assist in disembarkation of the French mountain soldiers with their kit and equipment before the unloading of their own equipment could commence. On 30 April at 12.30 hours the first vehicles and guns were at last onshore; and at 16.00 hours the last one. After a week of waiting, the gunners could now again act as a coherent artillery unit.

But one might now wonder what type of gun they brought to Norway? The official version, for instance in Farndale (1996) and in many other books, is that the battery was the very first in the Second World War to go into battle with 25-pounders. At guns on display in museums, for instance, at Imperial War Museum in London, this is stated too. I will however for now raise a question mark for this. More likely is that the battery had 18/25-pounders, which in daily speech often were called '25-pounders' as its nominal name was QF 25-pounder Mark I.[251] This might be just an obscure observation in artillery history. More important is to see how the guns actually were used in Norway. Before proceeding with that, we will first look at the course of the campaign at large.

Positions are taken in the Narvik area
The allied build-up of forces in the Narvik area took place during the second half of April 1940. The British contribution to the Expeditionary Force was 24 Guards Brigade with three battalions. The first to arrive was the 1 Battalion Scots Guards, arriving 14–15 April and quartered at

Fig. 17-3 The few British gunners sent to Norway went ashore at Harstad beginning on 19 April 1940. The 203 Battery RA was given quarters at the village Ervik just north of Harstad. This small city was the centre for supply of the British Expeditionary Force to Northern Norway. The many ships with supplies were daily attacked by German bombers (©Imperial War Museum N 204)

Harstad, where also the brigade HQS was located. On 18–19 April the 2 Battalion South Wales Borderers arrived and was quartered at Skånland. Finally the third to arrive was the 1 Battalion Irish Guards, which landed at Bogen on the northern side of the Ofoten fjord.

On 26/27 April, the South Wales Borderers moved to Ballangen and a couple of days later they landed at Håkvik on the Ankenes peninsula closer to Narvik. From there, they advanced eastwards to Båtberget where they met a German mountain regiment.

The French formations arrived a bit later than the British. On 28–30 April two battalions of mountain infantry and one artillery battalion arrived in Gratangen (60km north of Narvik), and advanced southwards towards the Laberg Valley, where they on 4 May attacked German positions. On 6 May, two battalions of the Foreign Legion arrived at Ballangen from Harstad, where they had landed on 3 May. The four battalions of the Polish Brigade arrived on 9 May at Ballangen. The same day a battalion of French mountain infantry (*Chasseur Alpins*) was landed at Håkvik.

Lord Cork had been very active from his arrival in the area already. He wanted to attack Narvik as soon as possible with the Scots reinforced by detachments of sailors. He believed that only only a weak German force initially defended the city. But General Mackesy refused. Similar controversies between the two commanders went on towards the end of the month and continued into May. On 3 May, Lord Cork made his last attempt to get the General to attack Narvik. The commander of the Guards Brigade, Briagdier William Fraser, however now supported the latter and the plan fell. But the battle raged during the first week of May at the northern side of the Ankenes peninsula.

At this time, the strength of the allied Expeditionary Force peaked at 25,800 men, out of which 14,100 were British and 11,700 French and Polish.[252] But much artillery was not coming with them!

If the cooperation between the commanders on the British side did not work well, it was easier with the French. Lord Cork and General Bétouart were in tune. It was the latter that later came up with the idea how Narvik could be recaptured, a plan which was a compromise between Lord Cork's offensive ambitions and the cautious attitude of Generel Mackesy.

While this was going on in Norway, it became clear in London that fighter squadrons had to be deployed in Northern Norway and that their fighting must be coordinated with that of the ground forces. This would in its turn require a strengthening of the command structure. It was realised also that the cooperation between Lord Cork and General Mackesy did not work, which was another reason for a change.

An experienced mountain warrior takes over

In England the IV Corps prepared itself for deployment in France as the fourth Corps of BEF after having finalised training during the winter and spring. The Commanding Officer was Lieutenant General Claude Auchinleck, who for most of his career had served in India.[253] He had extensive battle experience and, not the least, experience from leading military forces in tough mountainous terrain at the Indian northwest frontier. In January 1940, he was called back to England to take command of IV Corps. At this time he was not particularly well known at home, but was later to be one of the most written about and controversial British commanders in the Second World War.

After the Norwegian campaign, he submitted a lengthy report in which he described in detail the course of the battle and his own considerations and decisions.[254] We will first look at a quotation from the report where the General recalls how it all began on his part:

> On the evening of April 28th I was summoned by the Chief of Imperial General Staff (General Sir E. Ironside) to the War Office and informed by him that I, with part of the 4th Corps Staff, would be required to go to NARVIK in the immediate future. I returned to my headquarters at ALRESFORD and arranged for an advance headquarters to be established in the War Office. [. . .] For the next week, my staff were fully employed collecting and collating information concerning Northern Norway and the existing situation in that theatre.[255]

On 6 May he received his final instructions from the Minister of Defence. It was to secure and maintain a base in Northern Norway from which it would be possible:

1. To deny ore supplies to Germany via NARVIK.
2. To interfere with ore supplies to Germany from LULEA in Sweden.
3. To preserve a part of Norway as seat for the Norwegian King and Government.

He was now appointed General Officer Commander-in-Chief of the Anglo-French land forces and of the British Air Component in the theatre of operations. Initially he was subordinate of Lord Cork.

The General was requested to submit information, in conjunction with Lord Cork, of the forces deemed necessary for attaining the three objects, and also the area, which should be occupied. A special task was to investigate the possibilities for shipping iron ore from Narvik to United Kingdom and resuming a supply of iron ore from Swedish mines at GALLIVARE [Author's note: Why was not the largest mine field at Kiruna mentioned?].

On 13 May, General Auchinleck assumed command of land and air forces of what was now called North-Western Expeditionary Force (NWEF) and began dealing with the tasks that had been assigned to him. His headquarters was located at Harstad. He had understood that Lord Cork and General Mackesy for personal reasons could not work together and decided, with the consent of the Lord, to sack the latter.

The Commander of the Guards Brigade, Brigadier Fraser, was ordered to take the brigade headquarters and the Irish Guards battalion to Bodö, where he was to hold the city 'permanently'. He should as long as he could defend also the small city Mo further to the South. Since the beginning of the month, the Scots Guards battalion of the brigade and an Independent Company were operating in that area.[256]

Auchinleck's assessment

Next on the programme was to analyse the resource requirements, as Auchinleck had been instructed. This was done and on 16 May his findings were dispatched to London. But the General had a reservation. The estimated strength would be sufficient for holding Northern Norway provided the country was not invaded by the Soviet Union through Finland or Norway was attacked by Germany via Sweden.[257] His estimate included air and naval resources. Looking at land forces, this is what he considered necessary for the tasks given:

- One divisional cavalry regiment
- One squadron armoured cars
- One mounted infantry unit (Lovat's Scouts)
- Five field artillery batteries (60 guns)

- Two medium batteries (16 howitzers)
- Thirteen heavy anti-aircraft batteries (104 guns)
- Eight light anti-aircraft batteries (96 guns) [i.e. Bofors]
- Five companies engineers;
- Seventeen infantry battalions
- One machine gun battalion

It is noted that Auchinleck does not speak in terms of higher formations (Corps, divisions, brigades) and as regards the artillery not in terms of regiments. Maybe his experience from the outskirts of the Empire had influenced him here.

Converted to higher formations, the numbers above would be equal to two infantry divisions and two and a half field regiments and one medium regiment. In other words, a fairly weak artillery force as compared with BEF where each division alone had two, sometimes three, field regiments, here thus about half that strength.

It is also amazing that Auchinleck did not foresee a need for any anti-tank resources.

If the importance of artillery in a modern war still was not clear to all, the importance of anti-aircraft guns was already obvious, as we can see from the list above.

Auchinleck furthermore stressed that Bodö, Narvik and Tromsö must be seen as strategically interdependent. Hence the defence of them must be well coordinated. Not least Tromsö was needed as a base besides Harstad.

Looking again at the three tasks assigned to Auchinleck, the first was already settled, i.e. stopping the iron ore export to Germany from Narvik. The Royal Navy and the Germans themselves had already destroyed the port facilities. The second task, interference of ore export from the Swedish town Luleå, was not 'a practical proposition unless the active and full cooperation of the Swedish armed forces could be assured'. With these statements, only the third task required immediate consideration, Auchinleck concluded.

Auchinleck was notified by London already on 17 May that due to the battle in France he could only have twelve French battalions and three British. In addition to these he would be allotted ten independent British companies. Some support from Engineers and artillery would come as well. To what extent, nothing was said.[258]

Auchinleck could do nothing but to accept the situation and make the best out of it.

The southern front a great concern

Béthouart's plan for the recapture of Narvik was fixed. The attack was to be done across the Rombak Fjord the night between 24 and 25 May, but was postponed to 27 May after a decision made by Achuinleck. The reason was that the first Hurricane fighter aircraft would not arrive before that day. Their role was to protect the attackers when landing on the southern shore of the fjord.[259] Besides the date, the General felt confident with the plan, although he considered the operation to be an extremely risky business. It was to be executed by French, Polish and Norwegian forces.

Auchinleck himself now concentrated on the southern front, i.e. Bodö and Mo. How to efficiently stop the German advance there? They were advancing in force since the arrival of the German 2nd Mountain Division, which recently had landed in Trondheim, thus reinforcing a mountain regiment landed there already on 9 April. The German force now available for advance northwards amounted some 5,000 men.[260] With a battalion from 137 Mountain Regiment in the lead, the Germans now moved quickly northwards aiming at reinforcement of General Dietl's 3rd Mountain Division in the Narvik area.

In their way was the Scots Guards battalion from the Guards Brigade since the middle of May. It was deployed far to the South near Mosjöen together with three independent companies. One of the companies of the battalion was still in Bodö where two more independent companies had also been landed.

Auchinleck ordered the two other battalions of the Guards Brigade and the brigade headquarters to go to Bodö. Due to bombing and sinking of the troop carrier used by the Irish Guards battalion and grounding of the ship transporting the South Wales Borders battalion only a portion of the brigade could get into the battle down south as planned.

As a result of the measures taken, no British fighting units were left in the Narvik area from around 20 May, only many supply and depot resources and part of 203 Battery RA. Recapturing Narvik thus became a true French-Polish-Norwegian affair.

The situation at Mo and Bodö became hopeless in the last week of May, not least due to shortage of artillery. The British units were under heavy delaying fighting forced back to Bodö, where evacuation was the final option.

This was completed on 31 May; the road to Narvik was now laid open to the invaders.

How to employ 203 Battery RA?

As we have seen, the battery was complete again on 1 May after having received guns and vehicles after one week of waiting. Ammunition was plentiful, around 400 shells per gun. And more was under way. The ship *Ciscar* arrived with a large load of ammunition on board; 34,920 high explosive shells and 7,200 smoke shells were unloaded for the artillery, a clear indication that there had been plans for much more artillery later on than the single battery hitherto landed.[261]

But with whom to cooperate and give support? Of course the Guards Brigade was a natural alternative, but was the battery to operate as one 12-guns unit or were the resources to be delegated out to the three battalions? These were not deployed together and much indicated that they would be given quite different tasks. Hence, this indicated a forthcoming delegation, not to say fragmentation, of the only artillery available.

The battery commander was already the first day ordered to prepare the battery for movement and to allocate one FOO with assistant and signallers to the South Wales Borderers battalion still in quarters at Skånland, but to be engaged on the Ankenes peninsula west of Narvik.

Captain Sabrum, commander of F Troop, was given the task. Next day, 2 May, he was ordered to take a section of two guns to the port of Harstad for loading on board a vessel to take them to Ankenes. This was done around 20.00 hours this day. They arrived at Bogen on the northern side of Ofoten Fjord around 04.00 hours on 3 May. The transport then continued across the fjord to Skjomnes where they were transferred to two smaller landing craft. It was unclear during the day as to where to be landed, resulting in inactivity, but eventually they were landed at Meieri.

In the morning 4 May, British artillery opened fire for the first time in Norway, let alone at a small scale. Ranging against a target near Narvik with 12 rounds per gun took place. The weather was pleasant and it was fairly warm in the sunshine. Towards the night, however, the temperature dropped below zero. The ranging was not only the first artillery fire in Norway; it seems likely that it was the very first time during the Second World War that British artillery of any kind became engaged in battle!

The battery commander and his subordinates at Harstad were engaged the following days in reconnaissance of new quarters and possible gun positions. Reinforcement of the section from F Troop now deployed at the Ankenes peninsula was also prepared. RASC stocked more ammunition at Liland for that section. The two guns now supported the French battalion that had been deployed at the peninsula. Observation zones were excellent and most of Narvik could be well observed and fired at, which the gunners did already on 8 May.

The rest of the battery still had not been engaged, no task had been assigned to them, so on 9 May an exercise with D and E Troops was arranged in the neighbourhood of Ervik. The war diary tells: 'This was practice for working as detached troops under the conditions prevailing in Norway.'[262] This is another confirmation that one was not thinking in terms of concentration of resources, nor fire. Was the historical heritage a 'ghost'?

The diary says the same day that the planned move of the remaining F Troop section to Ankenes had been postponed. On the other hand, next day D Troop was placed on two hours' notice to move to Bodö via Harstad. The loading was completed at 22.00 hours. The task was to support the Scottish battalion down south at Moesjöen.

Day after day then passed and no tasks were given to the remaining half of the battery. In the afternoon 13 May, it was placed on two hours' notice for movement, but soon this was cancelled and the gunners had again to continue their waiting. One can imagine that General Auchinleck was met with frustration when he came to the battery on 19 May at 09.00 hours for inspection. It was now requested permission for the battery to, at least, practice some shootings on their own, which the General accepted, and later the same day the battery commander and the commander of E Troop reconnoitred for such an exercise. But it was to last a week until the exercise could be done.

The days in between were used for other types of exercise, which was not that easy as the gunners had to experience daily air attacks as well. The Battery sent spare wireless batteries and cables etc, to the section at Ankenes. The battery commander and other officers visited their fellow-gunners across the fjord. Even contacts with D Troop south of Bodö were tried to some extent.

Not known to the battery was that Auchinleck in a written order to the commander of Guards Brigade on 13 May had said that 203 Battery was to be put under his command at Bodö. It was furthermore said that it was 'hoped that this could be arranged the next day'.[263] This did not happen because the brigade had been forced to halt the transport to Bodö due to bombing and ship grounding. The survivors had returned to Harstad without their equipment.

On 20 May, brigade headquarters managed to be back in Bodö and both the Welsh and the Irish battalions were also on their way, albeit at reduced strength. Also two Norwegian battalions were now in the area. Therefore more artillery was needed than the four guns of D Troop already engaged down at Moesjoen and Mo supporting the Scottish battalion.

Auchinleck made the decision at his daily staff conference on 22 May that the battery commander with a headquarters detachment and one troop would be placed on six hours' notice for transport to Bodö.[264] But again no movement was ordered. It has been said that only one vessel with capacity for transport of guns and vehicles existed, and other tasks for it had been given higher priority.

One troop would be left at Harstad. It may have been the intention to transfer the two remaining guns of F Troop over to the Ankenes peninsula and reunite them with the section that had been there since 4 May. The war diary reveals that this transfer never materialised. Further problems again in finding suitable vessels?

The Minutes from General Auchinleck's conference on 26 May breathed hesitation: 'C in C [Auchinleck] said remainder 203 Bty may need to be sent south.'[265] A reason for this might be the fact that Auchinleck the day before had received London's decision that the Expeditionary Force would be evacuated. More about this later.

The gunners at Ervik could do nothing but wait, until on 29 May at 08.30 hours it was at last possible to perform the shooting exercise organised a week ago. The war diary explains that 'link shooting' was practiced by E Troop and the remaining section from F Troop.

On 31 May, a rumour reached them that D Troop had returned from Bodö and the next day 2nd Lieutenant Clapham arrived informing the battery commander that the troop had been evacuated by a destroyer without the guns. He and the others had been put ashore at Borkenes. **Map 17-1** shows where the various parts of 203 Battery were deployed and the dates and times when they were evacuated.

We will now go back one week to have a brief look at the course of the battle around Narvik.

Narvik recaptured

After a successful landing at Bjerkvik on 13 May and subsequent fighting north- and eastwards, and at the same time Norwegian advance southwards, the allied attack against the southern shore of Rombak Fjord at Orneset was launched at midnight 27 May. As usual up here it was preceded by intensive fire from many naval ships. The French artillery battalion and a Norwegian mountain battery took part. These artillery units were now deployed at the Öyjord peninsula. After hard resistance, the German garrison in Narvik retreated and the city was recaptured finally on 28 May.

At the same time as the battle on the eastern side of Narvik went on, the battle of the Ankenes peninsula was initiated too. After the British and French units had been relieved in the middle of the month, the fighting was done by two battalions of the Polish Brigade under General Bohusz-Szyszko.

The Polish brigade was well trained and its fighting spirit first class. They had now been given the opportunity to take revenge for the German attack on their country the previous autumn!

The Polish 2nd Battalion would attack Ankenes in the night between 27 and 28 May and push the Germans into the sea, so was the final plan. In a coordinated attack the Polish 1st Battalion would concentrate on Skuvtua and Hestefjell and push the Germans away here but also from Beisfjord, by which a retreat by road from Narvik would be prevented. One company would simultaneously by a flank attack capture Tvedalsryggen.

A French battery with four 75-mm guns and the two British guns from F Troop of 203 Battery RA were supporting the Poles. The attacks were also to be supported by heavy fire from the cruiser HMS *Southampton* equipped with 6-inch guns.

In the official Royal Artillery History (Farndale (1996), *The Years of Defeat*) it is said that besides the two guns from F Troop also the rest of the battery, except D Troop that had been sent to Bodö, had been engaged on the Ankenes peninsula supporting the Poles.[266] This is however not verified by neither the battery war diary nor General Auchinleck's report. Only two British guns were engaged, likely supporting 1st Battalion in its attack towards Beisfjord. The mistake is repeated in other books.

The allies entered Narvik on 28 May beginning at 11.00 hours. The same morning the Poles took Beisfjord, but the Germans had already escaped the trap.

The large evacuation – a failed campaign is over

Lord Cork and General Auchinleck were informed by London on 25 May that the Norwegian campaign must be ended. All allied forces were to be evacuated. It was now obvious that BEF in France was in a very critical position and must be evacuated from Dunkirk. Preparations must then be made for meeting a German invasion on the British Isles, which in its turn would make it impossible to build up the forces in Norway required for meeting the set objectives there. All resources were needed at home.

When the evacuation orders eventually were given, equipment and stores not needed any longer were shipped away. All was done with the pretext that the troops at Bodö and Mo must be reinforced. It was also said that much material was needed for a new base at Tromsö. Those aware of the true reasons spread false rumours and information with the intention to reduce risks for revelation that a total evacuation was prepared, and it worked!

A critical decision was as to whether the attack on Narvik still would be made, despite the evacuation order. As we have seen, the order was to pursue the offensive as it was considered vital to conceal the preparations for the evacuation.

Intensive staff work was initiated to organise the evacuation immediately upon reception of the order. It was soon decided that the evacuation would be made during a period of five days, 2–7 June. It was later postponed for 24 hours.[267] Each night 5,000 men were to embark troop carriers taking as much as possible of equipment with them, even heavy equipment. About half of the total force amounting around 27,000 men was to embark at Harstad. The French and Polish forces engaged in the Narvik/Ankenes area would be taken by fishing boats and other small vessels from the beaches to waiting destroyers. From the latter, the troops were later to be transferred to troop carriers.

And what about the gunners? How and when would they be evacuated?[268] From the plan we can see that the section of F Troop at Ankenes would embark first, the second day (Series No. 47 in the plan). Their two guns had to be left ashore. Some signallers and other ranks were to stay on until the fourth night before being evacuated (Series No. 97). The main body of the battery at Harstad (Series No. 75) would be taken aboard the third night along with their six guns with vehicles (Quads), but they would have to leave the remaining around 50 vehicles and 13 motorcycles.[269]

When the evacuation order/plan was devised, it was not known that D Troop arrived at Borkenes from Bodö on 31 May. This contingent is not included in the plan as a separate series. An uncertain, however not unreasonable, note in the war diary says that the troop boarded a ship with unknown destination on 4 June.

Auchinleck mentions in his report that all special vehicles including tanks, 28 ambulances, a large number of lorries and motorcycles were taken aboard various ships. Some 20 passenger cars were also loaded. In total, he states, 390 vehicles were brought back to England, but some 400, mainly 15-cwt trucks, had to be left behind and were destroyed where they were. The French could take 400 vehicles aboard their ships. By means of a special ship, the mountain units could take some 340 mules with them!

In Auchinleck's summary it is mentioned that '6 25/18-pdrs' were loaded as were 5 heavy anti-aircraft guns and 21 Bofors 40-mm guns.[270] Air protection was a priority to the end. Much ammunition had to be dumped too. Auchinlech reports that 4,000 shells for '25/18-pdrs' were left behind and not less than 10,000 shells for heavy anti-aircraft guns and 8,000 for the Bofors guns.

The loaded ships were assembled in two convoys for the travel to England, one slow and one with more fast moving ships. They all left Norway on 8 June and this with a minimum of escorts. Thanks to almost an unbelievable luck they reached the homeland without any losses. Luck was also on the side of the Norwegian King and Government, who left Tromsö in Northern Norway on board the cruiser HMS *Devonshire*.

After arrival home, the gunners of 203 Battery RA marched to Jedburgh, entering on 11

June, and again joined their regiment, 51 Field Regiment RA. They came without guns and vehicles and were quartered at nearby Hawick. A rear detachment of 40 men returned two days later. They were all granted 48 hours leave. The Norwegian adventure was over.

General Auchinleck wrote his extensive report after his return. I have included a number of quotations from it, and will end by extracting a few lines illustrating his fairly harsh judgment regarding the quality of the British forces he had commanded in Norway:[271]

> I regret to have to record that my considered opinion is that generally the morale of our own troops was undoubtedly lower than that of the enemy. It is considered that this was due, first, to our inferiority of resources as compared with those of the enemy, particularly in the air. Secondly, it was due to the lack of training of the men as soldiers and a lack of adaptability, which induced in them a feeling of inferiority as compared with the enemy. Thirdly, their flanks and rear were continuously threatened and they were under a continuous probability of being surprised owing to our having no means of carrying out aerial reconnaissance. Nevertheless the comparison of the standard or morale of the two armies is disquieting. No such lowness of morale was discovered among the French troops.

Indeed a testimony remarkably different from those seen about the quality of BEF. Was it fair?

Summary of the (limited) role of artillery in Norway
- Artillery was a resource of which not enough was allotted in Norway. This might have been the result of poor planning of the campaign, frequent changes of plans and mixed up political and military command structures. Maybe there was a lack of belief that artillery could play an important role in the mountainous terrain, maybe it was due to logistic constraints. Maybe Mackesy, and later Auchinleck, was stuck in peacetime thinking with artillery seen as just a complement to infantry, and not a resource for operative and tactical decisiveness.
- It is particularly remarkable that the landed forces for recapture of Trondheim came without any artillery resources for indirect fire whatsoever. Against a well-trained mobile opponent like Germany with own artillery resources the outcome of the battle could be just one, an embarrassing defeat.
- The planners did not think in terms of concentration of artillery, neither physical concentration nor concentration of fire. The Royal Navy on the other hand delivered concentrated fire in support of land forces several times in the Narvik area.
- Concentration of fire could not be arranged in Norway as battalions or companies and not higher formations fought the battle. The distance between the fighting units was often substantial. Fragmentation of the resources as in the past therefore took place. Just one troop (4 guns) or even just a Section (2 guns) was in support of an infantry battalion, never more than that.
- At the operative level no artillery commander for securing concentration of fire existed.
- Hardly any resources existed for counter-bombardment against enemy artillery. Hence, the German artillery could be employed freely in the absence of the risk for counter-bombardment.
- It is remarkable that half the British battery in the Narvik area never was engaged (The official history of the Royal Artillery tells a different story). Intentions to use this resource at Bodö/Mo never materialised due to transport setbacks. An alternative use, for instance support of the attacks at Bjerkvik and Narvik, does not seem to have been on the planners' agenda. Coordination of British and French artillery resources neither took place.
- No notes have been found in available sources that smoke ammunition, despite plentiful, ever was used, neither at the Ankenes peninsula nor at Bodö/Mo.
- Wireless Set No. 11 used by the gunners proved to imply good communication, but General Auchinleck considered the gunners 'insufficiently trained' in the use of 'heliographs'. Maybe a natural observation by an old India veteran?

We have seen that Norway did not imply a large and efficient use of artillery resources. This was largely due to mismanagement by others. The few gunners did what they could.

18. From Imminent Invasion Threat to Offensive Training

Restoration

After the remarkably successful evacuations from Dunkirk and ports further to the south in France and also from the Narvik area, the time had come for preparing the country to counter a likely invasion of the British Isles. All were convinced that this was imminent. Inspired by Churchill's words about a never failing resistance, *on the beaches, in the fields, on the hills* etc., the work began hastily. And one had to get on also with new challenges; not unexpectedly, emerging in other parts of the Empire. On 10 June 1940 Italy declared war on Britain. British interests in the Mediterranean and Egypt and other countries in the region were attacked. The Japanese threat in the Far East began more and more casting its shadows over the British Empire.

It became necessary first to restore the forces that had left France without their heavy equipment; a loss particularly serious on the part of the Royal Artillery. As we have seen, some 60% of Britain's all available guns and tractors had been left behind, as had all other motor vehicles and heavy equipment, all radio equipment included. The BEF soldiers had been brought back to many harbours in England and had had to be dispersed to numerous temporary camps around the country for reorganisation. They were amazed to notice that they were received as heroes by the general public; and after having got something to eat and rest, and in many cases also granted 48 hours leave, restoration of all units commenced with determination. From the camps soldiers were returned to their units wherever quartered. Replacements were gradually provided for those lost in France and Norway.

The newspapers of course had been interested in covering the retreat as best as they could, **Fig. 18-1**.

The morale and fighting spirit left nothing to bother about. This is how 16 Field Regiment RA saw it on 7 June:

> Parties still arriving from all over U.K. Spirits high. Looking forward to re-equipping. The anxious inquiries after friends, the genuine pleasure displayed on meeting again indicated the spirit of comradeship in the Regiment. The kindness of the people of Halifax could not be excelled. Warm and sultry.[272]

A general comment in the war diary of 92 Field Regiment RA leaves us with the same impression:

> A difficult period as the regt. cannot fulfill its proper role: that of a field artillery regiment, through lack of equipment. Men are enthusiastic, and it is necessary to keep them interested in constant infantry tactics, etc. Redrilling classes and general smartening up is the order of the day.[273]

Fig. 18-1 The evacuees from Dunkirk were received at home as heroes and quickly and efficiently transferred to a number of collection camps around the country for recovery and reorganization. *Daily Express* had quite a correct description of what was going on 31 May 1940 although not yet knowing that the number of British and French soldiers rescued would exceed 300,000 (RAHT)

However, it took time, until the end of June, before units again began acting coherently and with normal capacity. This did not mean that the nominal strength was back everywhere. Much vital equipment was still lacking, including personal kits and weapons on many hands. The vintage guns still available in the Empire amounted to some 400 field guns and around 160 medium guns.[274] These were already in use by units under training, which had now to transfer parts of their stock to units under restoration, a process quickly initiated.

Deliveries of the new field gun-howitzer, the 25-pounder Mark II, had begun in April 1940 but only around 30 could be delivered in June. Deliveries then increased gradually as we have seen in an earlier chapter and reached its target 350 pieces/month in the middle of 1941.

Another important addition was some 900 75-mm guns of French First World War design, which Britain in haste 'borrowed' from America as a temporary solution while waiting for 25-pounders. They were of no immediate relief, as the first did not arrive before August 1940.

The distribution of guns seems to have been directed towards provision of at least 8–12 guns per field regiment. These could be of different types depending on availability. The process implied that regiments better furnished than others sometimes had to transfer some of their guns to regiments less lucky. Let us have a look at some examples.

One of the Royal Horse Artillery field regiments, 2 Field Regiment RHA, recalls in their war diary that the regiment had no guns at all during the period 12–28 June 1940, but then four 25-pounders Mark II arrived directly from the factory of Vickers Armstrong at Newcastle-on-Tyne. More followed, and on 30 June they had a complete stock (24 guns). A problem was, however, that no dial sights had been delivered; and only eight tractors (Quads).[275]

16 Field Regiment RA mentioned above says that the regiment on 15 June expected their first 25-pounders. The first arrived the next day and a couple of days later two more. It is noted in the war diary that they on 30 June still had only these three guns.

A regiment quite well favoured was 76 Field Regiment RA. This regiment was given eight 18/25-pounders from 7 Field Regiment RA along with twelve tractors, sixteen ammunition trailers and other technical articles; this took place the first week after the regiment had been evacuated from Dunkirk. On 20 June, five 25-pounders arrived, but the regiment had to transfer two 18/25-pounders to another regiment on 26 June. Eventually, seven more 25-pounders arrived on 30 June, but then their remaining six 18/25-pounders had to be handed over. So the regiment now had twelve modern guns, half the nominal strength. They were distributed on four troops with three guns each. Two troops still had no guns.[276]

A motley set of guns were provided for 99 Field Regiment RA. On 23 June, the regiment had eight 18/25-pounders, however without dial sights. That problem was resolved quickly. Near the regimental quarters was 125 OCTU. Dial sights could here be borrowed temporarily and also directors as the regiment had lost all such instruments in France. Three 4.5-inch howitzers were also gently put at the regiment's disposal by the OCTU. At the same time the regiment received six 25-pounders.[277] Hence, they had seventeen guns of different types.

74 Field Regiment RA told about an odder inventory of guns. On 27 June, 60 Army Field Regiment RA handed over two German 105-mm howitzers, complete with dial sights, tools, ammunition, etc. They had been captured in France by a medium regiment and transported to England before the final critical days (via Le Havre?).[278]

The evacuated medium regiments could not get any guns during the first few months. 69 Medium Regiment RA, for instance, received guns on 4 August, eight vintage 6-inch howitzers.

Another big problem was replacement of lost vehicles. Without them, no deployment nor ammunition transport could be done. One had to improvise by renting or buying a few civil lorries until proper army vehicles could be provided. Some officers were granted permission to use their own private cars, however without being paid for it! Neither would they receive any petrol from the Army. Longer transports had to be done by train or civil buses rented by the authorities. Buses were the only possible option for the mobile reserves set up as part of the defence against an invasion.

Personal equipment, communication equipment (radio and telephones), special equipment for various purposes, instruments, spare parts and, not the least, personal weapons had to be provided before the restoration of the units could be considered complete.

Besides restoration, re-equipment, training and much more that was going on, the artillery units had to assume the role of infantry, which they had no training for, (**Fig. 18-2**).

Fig. 18-2 Most of the gunners had to become infantry soldiers in the invasion defence after their return from Dunkirk while waiting for replacement of guns, vehicles and other types of equipment that had been lost in France (©Imperial War Museum H 4741)

The limited number of guns they had would of course be engaged in invasion defence, at first with static tasks only. Artillery fire as of the 'higher school' was not a realistic issue.

The 5th Infantry Divison, which had done so well in France but had suffered great losses, was reassembled in Scotland and given the task to defend against invaders and air landings in North-Eastern Scotland. Its artillery regiments were ordered to organise and train an infantry company each. The divisional artillery headquarters described the situation in its war diary:

> During this period Div H.Q. was at Enverurie. Guns, equipment and vehicles were arriving spasmodically. Had the Div Arty been required to go into action during the first 10 days in Enverurie, it would have consisted of 15 rifles. Immediately before moving to Perth on 30 June, it could have produced the fire power of some 10 guns, but owing to shortage of essential equipment and gun stores, only bow and arrow methods would have been possible.[279]

Not only the evacuated units faced difficulties. There was still a severe shortage of equipment for mobilised new Territorial units under training. Captain G.W. Robertson of 136 Field Regiment RA gives an illustration of the situation in his regimental history:

> [...] Meanwhile 348 Battery down south of the River Alde at Sudbourne Hall were split up into small detachments and posted as infantry at various points considered to be danger spots along the river. Rifles were still in short supply in the Regiment and those available were only enough to arm one man in three. Ammunition was equally short – five rounds a man. Those without rifles were told to provide themselves with pieces of wood, which were to be fashioned into clubs. Shortly afterwards, to the great amusement of all, there was an issue of pikes! These were bayonets of Great War pattern welded into the lengths of steel tubing. They proved quite dangerous to the user. The wags claimed that the idea was to show the pikes to the invading soldiers who would then die from laughing.[280]

British humour in a very critical situation!

Not only lack of equipment made the task difficult but also other problems influenced the situation. This is illustrated by the task given to 72 Field Regiment RA in the evening of 26 June. The regiment was ordered to move to the Weymouth area on the southern coast where the regiment was to come under command of 151 Infantry Brigade (one of the brigades of the 50th Infantry Division). The brigade was to defend a sector of the coast near Weymouth and to Lyme Regis, the latter around 40km west of Weymouth. Here 285 Battery RA was assigned a 5km wide sector west of Weymouth and the second battery, 286 Battery RA, a sector east of the city, around 3km wide. The batteries should each deploy one infantry company with three platoons in respective sector and in addition to this, they should have one infantry company in reserve. It is stressed in the war diary that the armament was one rifle per gunner![281]

Artillery units engaged for the defence of a coastal sector like this began immediately to build fortifications. Trenches, foxholes and shelters protected by wired fences were built wherever possible. Observation Posts, preferably in high buildings, water towers etc. were arranged. Numerous sand bags were filled and in true British sports tradition competitions between units were arranged to see who could fill most sand bags at a given time. Competitions in carrying sandbags on ladders up from the beach were also arranged.

When resources from Royal Engineers became available, provisional constructions protected by sand, soil, wood etc. were replaced by new ones made in concrete, some still to be seen today. Gun pits were also built the same manner, often placed in such a way that enfilading direct fire could be fired by the guns along the beaches.

In order to strengthen the invasion defences, a fast-track programme for construction of coast artillery positions near harbours was launched quickly. The Royal Navy provided already in May no less than 150 6-inch guns to be used in the programme. These had long been in store for use on merchant ships in case of war, but were now to be used for other tasks. Later even more guns of different calibres were made available. During the three summer months, a coastal defence line with more than 600 guns was constructed, indeed an impressive achievement![282]

The shortage of field artillery for fire against potential invasion beaches made inclusion of old naval guns in the field artillery necessary. Even a few old salute guns were deployed! It became an important task on the part of Royal Engineers to construct suitable foundations of concrete for these guns and also protective structures for them and the crews. But it was not obvious how to man them. Initially it became the responsibility of field and medium regiments still waiting for new guns as replacement for those lost abroad. A good example is 69 Medium Regiment RA deployed near the southern coast. In August 1940 the regiment had in its arsenal:[283]

- Eight 6-inch howitzers (received on 4 August)
- Two 2-pound naval guns
- Two 100-mm naval guns for shells where shell and cartridge was one entity
- Two 100-mm ship guns for shells where shell and cartridge were loaded separately
- Two 3-pound naval guns
- Sixteen 6-inch mortars
- Five light machine guns (Spandau)
- Three heavy machine guns (Hotchkiss)

It is furthermore stated in the war diary that the regiment had six Campbell armoured cars.

Attaching artillery units to fixed positions like this was not what these units wanted. They wanted to be free to assume normal duties and be ready to re-deploy quickly when the tactical situation so required. Meeting the needs for gun crews for the coast artillery positions was therefore transferred gradually to new Defence Regiments; eventually ten were constituted. As we have seen, some were later reorganised to become field regiments; others were disbanded. The process was concluded in 1942 when no invasion threat existed any longer.

Further tasks on the part of gunners in the summer 1940 were to build road blocks across roads leading to the coast, an undertaking requiring lots of men for filling sand bags, collecting timber, stones etc. They also assisted in removing road signs, name signs at villages and railway stations, everything in accordance with a Governmental decision on 31 May 1940.

A new regimental organisation is born

The Royal Artillery was a learning organisation. Lessons learned during the initial campaigns were to be taken care of. Soon after the evacuation, a lively discussion followed regarding what had been good and what must be changed. As seen, one of the most important lessons was that the battery organisation with two 12-gun batteries from 1938 had several disadvantages. It was too 'heavy' and difficult to lead in a modern mobile war. Neither did it fit well with the three-pronged organisational structure of the infantry. It was normal practice in a division to have one field regiment to support one brigade. With three regiments this was not a problem, but it was also required that each one of the three battalions in a brigade could be supported by a battery, and this was not possible when a regiment had two batteries.

The solution was obvious. The resources available in a regiment should be split up in three batteries instead of two, each one with two instead of three troops. In total the battery was to have eight guns in two troops and the regiment three batteries with, as before, 24 guns. (Cf. Chapter 5)

A division that made the change early without asking for permission was the 2nd Infantry Division. Its three field regiments (10, 16 and 99 Field Regiment RA) were reorganised directly after their return to England. Who took the initiative? Was it the divisional artillery commander? Or was it one of the regimental commanders? A good guess is that the commander of 10 Field Regiment RA, Lieutenant Colonel Jack Parham, is the most likely candidate. He was untiringly working to make the best out of the artillery resources, as we will see more of later on.

The new organisational structure was not controversial and was quickly adopted by others, though it was not officially confirmed by a revised War Establishment until the spring of 1941.

The structure of medium regiments could be retained. Such a regiment had 8-gun batteries (two) already. Neither was there a need to change the organisational structure of heavy regiments. Four 4-gun batteries had proved efficient and adequate. The problem on the part of medium and heavy batteries was instead the guns. So far the batteries had had to use vintage guns and howitzers. These were not up to modern requirements in terms of range and mobility. Modern pieces were still pending.

Now we turn our attention to the invasion threat at large as it was interpreted in the summer 1940.

First phase of invasion defence – the threat and need for improvisation

The rapid German victory in France meant that a threatening invasion of the British Isles across the Channel was felt to be imminent. People were afraid of sudden air-landings of troops and also various subversive actions through fifth columns and enemy agents. But there was no doubt that the public support of Churchill was strong. The Government decided in May 1940 to organise voluntary forces to support the armed forces by establishing Local Defence Volunteers (LDV). When the decision was announced by Anthony Eden on 14 May it got an overwhelming response. People rushed to the recruiting offices; soon more than 300,000 men at ages up to 65 years were enlisted, with even many above 80 years of age attempting to enlist! The number increased all the time and in August it was over one million.[284] The willingness to help was magnificent. Thousands of women also wanted to be armed, but that was not accepted.

A great problem initially was the lack of an established organisation to take care of the volunteers. Neither were uniforms and weapons available. Membership was shown in classic style by means of armlets. Weapons of all kind were supplied by improvisation. It could be anything from private hunting rifles to axes, wooden clubs and spears. But the situation gradually improved. Uniforms and steel helmets were soon distributed and a more efficient Home Guard (as it was later called by Churchill in a speech in July 1940) was developed and the denomination was to last as the official one.

How was the army to counter an invasion? The Commander-in-Chief Home Forces, General E. Ironside, decided to apply a defensive strategy in respect of lacking resources, **Map 18-1**. He decided that all the southern and eastern coasts of England, some 800km (!), were to be defended at the beaches by fairly weak forces, as these could not be concentrated due to the length of the defence line. Hence, Ironside did not expect the defenders to be able to prevent the enemy from getting ashore. They were to fight as best as they could and then delay the enemy's inland advance. The General deployed two infantry divisions between the Thames estuary and Southampton: 1st Infantry Division adjacent to Thames, and to the right of this 45th Infantry Division towards Southampton. Later further divisions were deployed all the way towards Devon.

Ironside first deployed three infantry divisions north of the Thames in Essex and Suffolk: the 15th, 18th and 55th Infantry Division. None of the divisions, perhaps with the exception of the 45th Infantry Division, had more than half their nominal strength during the summer 1940; the shortages of equipment and, not least, transport resources were critical.

These five divisions along the coasts had a very limited stock of artillery. The resources were deployed closely behind the beaches. In the northern sector there were only 62 guns and in the southern 53.[285] This meant less than one third of nominal strength. Furthermore, many different types of gun had to be used – most of them obsolete.

If we in the northern sector take the distance between Southend and Great Yarmouth in the north, which is roughly 150km, the artillery density was not more than one gun per 2.4km (one per 1.5 miles). In the southern sector the situation was even worse. The front from Ramsgate to Southampton to be defended was about 200km, which implied a density of one gun per 3.8km (one per 2.4 miles). The old naval guns deployed gradually along the coast during the summer did not significantly improve the situation. So one has to conclude that the artillery had not been capable of decisively interfering on large-scale invasion forces during the summer 1940.

Part of the defensive strategy was the establishment of a fortified defence line further back, the *GHQ Defence Line,* shown on **Map 18-1**. The intention was to finally stop the invaders along that line. Besides fortifications, all available anti-tank guns would be deployed here, basically 2-pounders.

The offensive component was a mobile reserve comprising three, relatively untrained, infantry divisions, the 43rd (Wessex) Infantry Division, the 52nd (Lowland) Infantry Division and the Canadian 1st Infantry Division, together with two armoured divisions, 1st and 2nd Armoured Division. The latter two were also weak and had together only 170 light tanks.

Around the nation, further divisions were under restoration and training, for instance in Scotland.

Ironside's strategy was criticised as being too static and implying unacceptable risks. The General himself had wanted a more offensive strategy, but he saw no possibilities for that just after Dunkirk. Severe shortage of equipment, transport resources, armour and artillery in combination with the insufficient level of training made this impossible, he thought.

On 20 July, Ironside was replaced by General Alan Brooke as Commander-in-Chief Home Forces. He thought the time was ripe for a more offensive strategy. He believed it vitally important to try stopping the invaders right at the beaches and thus preventing them from establishing a strong beachhead. If they were to succeed in that, a continuous build-up of resources with artillery, armour and more infantry would make any British counter-attack much more difficult. As a consequence, Brooke redeployed the anti-tank units to the beaches.

He also saw to it that the artillery, now becoming stronger and more mobile, was not tied up in the local beach defence. The artillery units would be ready for quick redeployment and concentration to sectors where the main landings had taken place. It was here that the mobile strategic reserve was to counter-attack with strongest possible artillery support. Only if this could be done, there was a real chance of defeating the invaders, Brooke thought.

General Brooke also redeployed formations to make the defence in the southern sector stronger and deeper behind the beaches. He furthermore pressed on rearmament and training. But all-arms training at higher operative levels were not yet possible. Possibilities for well-coordinated counter attacks were thus still not the best.

In June and July political uncertainty prevailed. Churchill was not at all willing to compromise with Hitler. The latter should be militarily defeated and his Nazi regime completely annihilated, even if it was to take time and require severe sacrifices. But behind the scene, there was a group of politicians who were not reluctant to probe opportunities for peace with the enemy. Hitler learnt about this, which was in line with his own wishes.

Hitler wanted to accomplish a separate peace agreement with Britain with or without threats. His overriding aim was not the elimination of the British Empire. Hence, he waited with directives to his armed forces to prepare for an invasion of the British Isles. It is beyond the scope of this book to review the political game in Britain and Germany during the summer 1940. Neither will the considerations made by the German High Command regarding how best to perform an invasion be discussed here, nor how Hitler intervened. We can only observe that the planning commenced actively when Hitler issued his 'Directive No. 16' on 16 July.

Hitler gave his generals four weeks for planning the invasion, the much written about Operation Seelöwe. This was to engage not less than 41 divisions directed towards South East England. An air-borne division was also to be used. The logistic problems were however enormous.

A prerequisite, as seen from the German side, was complete air superiority. Hence, the Royal Air Force had to be defeated. It was also necessary to hold off the Royal Navy from the invasion lanes by means of mines, coast artillery and air attacks. Weather and tide must also be right. D-Day was thus postponed several times in respect of all difficulties, the last time on 27 September 1940.

The battle of Britain, the gigantic struggle between the *Luftwaffe* and the Royal Air Force aiming at German air superiority over the invasion area, began on 7 August 1940 on a limited scale. But it was in full force from 13 August, *AdlerTag*. As known, it did not result in an easy victory for Germany within four days as Marshal Göring had promised. The fight continued into October. At the end of September *Luftwaffe* had realised that it could not annihilate the fighter squadrons of the Royal

Air Force and changed tactics towards terror bombing of London and other large cities, the so-called *Blitz*.

The Royal Navy had embarked on an offensive strategy right from the beginning including daring attacks into the ports where invasion vessels and barges were assembled, thus demonstrated that another prerequisite was denied the Germans. British naval ships could not be kept away from the planned invasion lanes.

When neither *Luftwaffe* nor *Kriegsmarine* had succeeded, Hitler had to cancel the whole operation on 17 September, at least 'for the time being'.

With this decision, the first phase of invasion defence ended, thanks to the Royal Air Force and, even more, the Royal Navy. They had saved the country.

The British Army was now much stronger than it had been just after Dunkirk. All had been done to restore fighting strength, but although British industry after the summer was working flat out, it would take a long time until the Army had compensated for what had been lost in France (and Norway). Replacing lost heavy equipment and armament of numerous new Territorial formations and other new formations was still a process to take several years.

In September 1940, the Army had 26 divisions and 16 independent brigades, amongst them a few armoured brigades. Contingents had also arrived from Australia and New Zealand.

The divisions were grouped in twelve Corps, two of which were mobile forces. One was IV Corps in which the 2nd Armoured Division was grouped along with two infantry divisions. The second 'mobile' force was VII Corps with the 1st Armoured Division and the 1st Canadian infantry division. The two armoured divisions were the only so far existing of this type.

Looking at the artillery we can now see that a significant force had emerged. In September there were 94 Field Regiments, out of which 22 were Army Field Regiments attached to the five regional commands, Western Command etc., which constituted the national military structure of the time. The bulk of the regiments were divisional artillery. In Northern Command there were also three light batteries, the embryo of the airborne light regiments to be established later.

Twenty-seven medium regiments were in place; 17 of these were army units, the rest Corps units. Five heavy and three super heavy regiments added to the national artillery force.

In terms of regiments, it was indeed an impressive force built up till September 1940. But…still a very troublesome shortage of modern guns prevailed. The number of field regiments mentioned plus training units would need around 3,000 guns, reserves for damages and war losses included. What they had were 400 obsolete guns and some 500 modern 25-pounders. To this stock a few hundreds of the American 75-mm guns 'on loan' must be added.

The medium regiments would nominally have together 500 à 600 modern guns but after Dunkirk only 200 obsolete guns were available in England. No production of the new generation of medium guns had as yet commenced. Searching 'in the barns' for more guns had to be pursued. Those then found had to be brought into order as soon as possible. Important too, was to get the guns modernised without delay. Other Commonwealth countries were also asked to help. Even if the British Army now in September was much stronger it is, in respect of remaining deficits, hard to believe that it had been able to quickly enough concentrate a force needed to defeat the nine well-trained German divisions that were to land in England in the first wave, had Operation Seelöwe been launched successfully.

The necessary redeployment and concentration of the British artillery to counter a large-scale invasion, wherever it was to take place, stood small chances to succeed. Not only the equipment shortage would make it difficult, but also the command structure was a problem.

In September 1940 large contingents from other countries, in particular from those occupied by Germany, had been assimilated in the British Army. The largest was the Poles, around 18,000 were already serving with the British Army. Their number was to be doubled many times during coming years. Second largest contingent was the Norwegian.[286] Some of these were gunners and early photographs show the Norwegians training in Scotland and other places with the French-designed 75-mm guns, when such had arrived from America in accordance with the 'loan agreement'.

Second phase of invasion defence – continued rearmament, training, development of new methods

The first Phase can be said to have ended when Operation Seelöwe was cancelled and the most imminent invasion threat had disappeared. It was in September 1940 that the war in North Africa required more attention and more resources than those available in the British Nile Army. A few divisions with their artillery were now detached to Egypt by sea transport via Cape of Good Hope. Amongst these was 51 Field Regiment RA. For the gunners of 203 Battery RA, it was to become a dramatic change from having fought in snowy mountains in Norway to preparing for battle in the deserts of North Africa. They had to stand up for the motto of the Royal Artillery: 'Ubique – Quo Fas et Gloria Ducunt' (cf. Chapter 2). Gunners had to act 'Ubique', i.e. 'Everywhere'. We will in the next Chapter see what this meant to them.

At home rearmament went on decisively and at ever increasing speed. There was a worry that Hitler might again try to launch an invasion in the spring 1941. Preparations were made over the winter to meet such a threat in line with General Brooke's strategy. In parallel with upgrading of units with new guns and training, exercises were run intensively and systematically. It was a matter of providing individual training but also collective training at troop and battery levels to become better prepared for defensive tasks. Numerous recruits and conscripts were to bring up the strength of formations to nominal level, and they must be given basic skills and become proficient gunners as soon as possible. The respite should not be given up!

In the battle preparations, deployment and firing exercises with live ammunition at battery and regimental levels became an important ingredient on the part of restored and new artillery units (**Fig. 18-3**).

It implied a great challenge for unit commanders to plan and run all training and firing exercises. These were, as we have seen, arranged at the five permanent large training ranges but also to places near those where units were deployed for invasion defence. One such area was South Downs near the southern coast of England. Firing with live artillery ammunition

Fig. 18-3 The British artillery gradually recovered mobility and fire strength. The invasion defence was trimmed and improved through more and more large exercises, often with live ammunition (RAHT)

and other exercises were here arranged throughout the war. About such practice firing, unthinkable in peacetime, Major Douglas Goddard has written:

> The South Downs behind Lewes, Brighton and Shoreham became one vast training and firing range which must have caused great discomfort and nervousness to the people of the towns and villages in the area; who were already suffering from regular enemy air raids and who now had the constant noise of war weapons and sadly the odd random rounds landing dangerously close. The artillery seemed intent on sinking the Downs under the weight of bombardment.[287]

Running firing exercises across the land of heaths in Scotland was another popular and efficient type of training.

Practicing indirect fire was of course the main task, but also direct fire against moving targets, i.e. potential tanks in particular, had to be practiced (cf. **Fig. 10-1**). With departure from peacetime conditions this could also be arranged at a nearby beach. For Douglas Goddard and his mates from 112 (Wessex) Field Regiment RA this often meant shooting at the Lydd peninsula between Folkestone and Hastings.

In 1941, larger exercises with higher formations could be arranged as preparation for a more offensive action against an invading German force than had been possible in 1940. Many exercises at divisional and Corps levels thus took place. As had been the case in France these large-scale exercises were short in time, not more than 3–4 days. The difference, however, was that it was not any longer primarily defensive operations that were in focus. The training aimed now at improving the ability to act offensively for the defeat of the enemy, should he invade the country.

In the autumn 1941, one of the greatest military exercises ever held in Britain took place at the turn of September/October, Exercise *Bumper*. According to one report, albeit a bit uncertain, 250,000 men were engaged directly or indirectly. The Royal Air Force took part with some of its army-cooperation squadrons as well.

In that exercise, two armies, the 'South Army' and the 'East Army', had both been given the task to defeat an invading enemy army. Supreme leader of the exercise was Lieutenant General Bernard L. Montgomery, now promoted Corps Commander. To his assistance, several groups of umpires and instructors had been established. On the artillery side the chief umpire was Brigadier (later General) Sidney Kirkman; an individual who will be encountered elsewhere in this book.

Kirkman had been the commander of a medium regiment in France and had made a rapid career after the evacuation from Dunkirk. He was first appointed divisional artillery commander (CRA) of the 56th Infantry Division and then artillery commander of three Corps in turn, I, VIII and XII Corps. He was to be appointed artillery commander of 'South Eastern Command' in 1942 before being assigned the position of Artillery Commander the 8th Army in Egypt.

An officer who had become much impressed with Kirkman's qualities was Montgomery, who in 1941 was commander of XII Corps. It is therefore not surprising that he nominated Kirkman as his chief artillery umpire for 'Exercise Bumper'.

This enormous exercise proved to be very important for the development of artillery battle techniques and tactical use of artillery resources at large. Not least, it led to a better understanding of the need for concentration of artillery fire. How direct cooperation between infantry and armour on one hand and the supporting artillery on the other hand was to secure concentration of fire was made clear by this exercise. At last, two years after the outbreak of the war, new thoughts had taken root.

Concentration of artillery resources and fire is a matter of principles about leading and employing resources in the right way. Efficient gunnery procedures are required when to accomplish fire concentration with speed and accuracy. If Kirkman was the man for the first issue, Jack Parham was one of the leading inspirers and developers regarding the second. He had in the autumn 1941 been promoted Brigadier and divisional artillery commander (CRA) of the 38th Infantry Division. A real breakthrough as regards new methods for accomplishing rapid concentrations of artillery fire came with demonstrations made by him in late 1941.

The pioneering contributions made by Kirkman and Parham in 1941 had probably not materialised had they not been supported from higher ranks. Amongst gunners one of the key figures was the artillery commander 'Home Forces', Major General Otto M. Lund. His superior, the old gunner General Alan Brooke, the Commander-in-Chief of 'Home Forces', was another. Amongst non-gunners understanding what it all was about, and giving his strong support was, not surprisingly, Montgomery. He is said to have declared that, 'The business of the Gunner Commanding Officer is first to train his Regiment and then to train infantry (and armour) brigadiers to use it properly.'[288] What he meant was that concentration of artillery forces and fire should be ensured by close cooperation between the infantry/armour commander and his artillery commander. The artillery plan should be an integral part of the operation plan of the supported formation; hence joint planning must be the rule.

Now back to 'Exercise Bumper'. We will look at some of the observations made by Kirkman and presented by him at the general briefing after the exercise that was held at the School of Artillery at Larkhill on 3 October 1941 and which was chaired by Alan Brooke.[289]

Kirkman started with a presentation of the employment of Army and Corps artillery, i.e. those formations not belonging to any division. He had found that the command of these regularly had been delegated to levels too low. The consequence was that these units had not been employed where best needed, and sometimes even remained idle. No tactical concentration had been possible. Another consequence was that some divisional artillery headquarters had been overloaded by having to lead more units than their capacity allowed.

Kirkman criticised also those artillery commanders who had not been close to their Corps commander. One had been away for two days. He wrote in his report:

> It must be wrong for Cs.C.R.A. [Commanders Corps Royal Artillery] to move and remain away from their Corps HQ. Cs.R.A. can control the movements of their artillery from a distance by D.R. [Dispatch Riders], W/T or periodical visits, but they cannot be consulted by their Corps Commander, know what is in his mind, or be in the tactical picture so as properly to position his artillery and anticipate the Corps Commander's plan, if they are permanently away from Corps and HQs.[290]

Then Kirkman turned to one of the strongest parts of criticism in his report, the miserable use of divisional artillery, i.e. most of the field regiments. He had noticed that the CRAs by routine had decentralised their artillery to the brigades of their division. They had often put regiments under command of brigade commanders and sometimes even split them up by putting single batteries under command of infantry (armoured) battalions. Kirkman had noticed that one CRA, when having got external regiments put under his command, had put the whole lot under command of a single brigade.

It was not acceptable to use artillery resources like this, Kirkman energetically stated:

> As soon as the Div front is stabilised, Arty should revert to the C.R.A., who can then establish communications with his Regts and locate them so that the maximum amount of fire can be concentrated on the front of any Infantry Bde which is to attack.

Kirkman had found that despite the regiments were regularly put under command of brigades they had not even there been used properly. He illustrated with thirteen examples how brigades had attacked without having had the artillery plan coordinated with the brigade commander's plan. Artillery fire could therefore only be delivered by improvisation as observed fire on 'opportunity targets' with an inferior number of barrels. Brigade commanders had generally overlooked, Kirkman said, the need for well-planned barrages or concentrations in support of their attacks, and they had also been reluctant to give the gunners the time needed for necessary preparations. He concluded quite harshly:

> Attacks were normally organised so quickly that even if there was time for adequate orders being given to the Inf, insufficient time was available for the gunner, particularly as two or three Regts were often grouped under one Arty Regtl Cmdr. The speed at which attacks were staged is perhaps inevitable on manoeuvres. In real war enemy bullets would make the necessity for Artillery support obvious. Umpires report that in the Cdn Corps cooperation between Arty and Inf hardly exist.[291]

More was to come. Kirkman had many words to say about counter-bombardment, i.e. how to combat enemy artillery. He criticised that officers responsible for this and other key tasks, often were ordered out on the roads to control and direct traffic by which they were prevented from doing what they should do. Unclear lines of command contributed to bad use of available resources. In particular, he criticised the Canadians:

> No C.B. [Counter-Battery] work was apparently attempted in the Canadian Corps.[292]

Before Kirkman turned to the use of anti-aircraft and anti-tank units, which we will not look at here, he urged commanders to avail themselves as much as possible of liaison officers to improve exchange of information and to ensure efficient coordination between headquarters.

Kirkman's report had a great impact. The British doctrine had now been clarified for the rest of the war on the best use of artillery resources. Rapid concentration of firepower over the battle area should be ensured. This would, as Kirkman saw it, be accomplished by adhering to the following rules:

- Avoid fragmentation of resources by instead allocating Command of artillery resources to the highest tactical level practicably possible, normally the divisional and Corps level. Tactical concentration of all resources to places and time where they are best needed then is secured
- Make sure that the artillery will be a strong, not to say formidable, resource for supported infantry (armour) commanders by creating a close and trustful cooperation between supported commander and his artillery chief. They are to ensure together that the artillery plan is a well-conceived part of the overall operation plan
- Decentralise Control of fire to the lowest possible level

With this, a debate that had been going on since Dunkirk was closed. Some had argued that artillery resources should be decentralised to brigades. Command of artillery resources above the brigade level was unnecessary, they thought. That would mean that no CRAs were needed. Luckily enough, in respect of coming battles, this group lost the debate as a consequence of Exercise *Bumper*!

Now, if it was made possible to concentrate fire from multiples of ten, not to say hundreds, of guns by adoption of an appropriate command structure, how should it technically be accomplished in shortest possible time? This had long been the challenge to Parham and other foresighted gunner officers. He had worked on it since his return from Dunkirk. There were two aspects to be recognised, he thought (**Fig. 18-4**).

The first one was that one had to accept that artillery was not a precision weapon. It was a weapon for fire against an area, and not against a distinct point. Area-covering fire was normally needed tactically and one should not bother about the lacking precision and large dispersion of the fire along the line of fire. Waiving of precision could be done if compensated by a larger number of guns and after rearmament these would be available. Another requirement was availability of much ammunition. Strategi-

Fig. 18-4 After return from Dunkirk Brigadier (later Major General) Hetman Jack Parham became one of the most important and influential reformers of Royal Artillery gunnery methods and battle techniques (RAHT)

cally, this was not a problem either. When industry had geared up, there would never strategically be a shortage of ammunition on the British side. In certain tactical situation a shortage might appear locally, but this did not change the general picture, as Parham saw it.

His second point was 'SIMPLICITY'! He used to write it like this, in capital letters, whenever he talked about gunnery procedures and the need for reforms. One of his ideas was a simple categorisation of targets, or rather the number of guns to be employed against a specific target. If a FOO wanted all the 24 guns of a regiment to be employed, he was to order 'Mike Target', and if it was an even larger target he ordered 'Uncle Target', meaning that all the divisional artillery was wanted, i.e. 72 guns. And the real 'club' was 'Victor Target' implying fire from all available guns of a Corps, i.e. several hundred guns. It was realised by all that this was an elegant method for simplifying communication between FOOs and batteries, so it was soon adopted officially.

It was also necessary to have a simple system for radio communication. A minimum requirement was to have all batteries of a regiment connected to the same network, i.e. using the same frequency. Parham even argued that all three regiments of a division could be signalling on the same network provided all adhered to strict traffic rules and standardised ways for communication, e.g. when fire was ordered and observed. Much training was needed to get through with messages in particular when transmission for any reason was hampered. One-way around difficulties was relay signalling, for instance when transmission distances exceeded the range of the wireless sets. This could be arranged by having an extra signaller with a set on the same frequency as the sending and receiving party. He could receive a message from the sender and then transmit the message by calling the receiving station. Relay signalling could also be arranged when sending and receiving parties used wireless sets No. 22. Two sets could be connected together via a short cable. When one of them received a message, this was transmitted automatically by the other set to the ultimate receiver. But innovative signallers and their officers were capable of finding other tricks to overcome transmission problems. Jack Parham was a strong believer in radio communication as a means for concentration of firepower.

The technical procedures at troop and battery command posts also had to be developed and made simpler and more efficient. This took place these years. And much practice gave good results.

A procedural area where Parham's quest for simplicity did not work well was his idea that the same procedure for changing the point of impact as used when a troop or battery was ranging, could be used also when many units were engaged. Ordering for instance 'plus 2 degrees, add 300' to all would not work when units were deployed far from each other. Parham had experienced that himself when running one of his demonstrations of rapid concentration of the fire from all guns of his division, which he made for many spectators in 1942. After having ordered a change, the next rounds from one of the batteries fell very close to a group of high-ranked spectators and splinters hit ground very close to himself.

Instead of giving changes relative the zero line and range of one battery irrespective of the position of all other guns, a better method now found necessary was the 'cardinal method'. As we have seen in one of the previous Chapters, this meant that changes of impact should be given using compass bearings, for instance all guns were ordered to go 'west 200, north 300'. What it meant for the individual gun was left to the command posts to calculate. This method became standard for the rest of the war when many different units were employed.

Parham wrote a report about the very first, as he believed it to be, large concentrated fire based on simplified procedures. It took place during an exercise on 15–16 December 1941 with the divisional artillery of the 38th (Welsh) Infantry Division, around 70 guns. According to the plan all three regiments marched in the evening to the range and were deployed at 22.00 hours. He wanted to train the regiments in disciplined march with much reduced lights and deployment in the dark so that a surprise barrage could be opened at 07.00 in the morning next day, 16 December. The barrage was prepared during the night by command posts and was executed to the satisfaction of Parham. Opening of fire at the right time was an important indication of quality. Anything else was inexcusable, but here his gunners did not let him down.

Later in the morning Parham wanted to test his ideas about rapid concentration of fire in connection with ongoing observed shooting. Fire from all the 70 guns against the same target was ordered and repeated several times. The result again was to his satisfaction. Accurate fire fell against three different targets within 5–7 minutes from being ordered.

Parham hoped that this example would lead to general acceptance of his methods for the rest of the war, and so it was. Montgomery liked to talk about divisional artillery as a '72-guns battery' and that it should be employed like that as often as possible.

In the summer 1942, Jack Parham was promoted again, now becoming artillery commander of the new 1st Army (Brigadier Royal Artillery), which was to land in North Africa in November that year. At a conference on 8 June 1942 at the Royal Artillery School, Larkhill, he again lectured about his fundamental principles for the mass use of artillery resources, in particular gunnery procedures.[293] Of six principles discussed one was this:

> There is now practically no limit to the number of guns which can be shot by one commander. This commander can be carried in armour or in the air. His fire orders can be of the simplest. [Principle IV]

Another of his main principles was the need for securing the same geodetic data for all units as soon as possible:

> The rapid building up of the largest possible fire unit is of paramount importance. Hence the vital necessity of concentration on quick and simple survey. [Principle V]

His last main principle in his paper was just this [Principle VI]:

'AT ALL COST BE SIMPLE!'

The capital letters showed again that this was his real mantra.

As we have seen above, a prerequisite for accomplishment of rapid fire concentrations was completed survey of all units into the same grid. When this now was recognised, a survey detachment in regimental headquarters was reintroduced.

During this second phase of preparations for war at home, invasion had been seen as a real threat. Absolute certainty that it would not come was not experienced until Germany had got stuck in Russia and it was obvious that the Soviet Union could not be defeated. Britain could thereafter leave the defensive strategy behind and direct further actions towards preparations for an offensive, including landings on the European continent.

The third phase – preparations for an offensive overseas

During the second phase, more and more formations had been transferred to North Africa (Egypt) and the Far East, but the bulk of forces were still at home. And the rearmament went on. At the end of this phase, around the turn of 1941, some 5,000 25-pounders Mark II had been manufactured. Rearming of the field regiments could now be completed. The provision of the new guns made it possible to transfer some of the obsolete guns to the 'Home Guard' and local defence batteries.

But still more 25-pounders were needed. Besides the own regiments at home, now around 130 field regiments plus training regiments, Commonwealth regiments would also be supplied with new guns (in particular India, Canada, Australia and New Zealand). War losses had to be compensated as well. At the beginning of what I call the 'third phase' for instance the surrender at Singapore took place (15 February 1942); the largest British defeat ever. Besides more than 80,000 men becoming prisoners of war, around 150 25-pounders seem to have been lost.

Manufacture of the new medium guns (4.5-inch and 5.5-inch guns) had gained momentum, but still only some 250 pieces had been delivered. These were enough for the rearming of about half the number of medium regiments only.

An area of much concern was the supply of guns to heavy regiments. No new design existed, just a modernisation of the obsolete 8-inch howitzers. Using the carriers and new barrels 7.2-inch howitzers were provided for these regiments. As we have seen, the Americans later gave a hand and supplied 155-mm guns, the 'Long Tom' (cf. **Fig. 4-7**). During the second half of the war, heavy regiments thence had two 4-gun batteries of the former type and two 4-gun batteries equipped with the latter.

Self-propelled guns (SP) were provided

from 1942 onwards. The less versatile 'Bishop' came first; soon to be followed by the American 'Priest'. The former was armed with a 25-pounder and the latter with a 105-mm howitzer. FOOs of regiments equipped with SP guns had to be provided with better vehicles than the light 'Bren Carrier', or more correctly the 'Universal Carrier', that was normal practice. A natural step was to give them tanks for the sake of speed and protection, but also half-track vehicles became a common alternative.

Efficient radio communication was an important prerequisite for Kirkman's and Parham's ideas to work. Better wireless sets were gradually manufactured and supplied to artillery formations. The number of sets was also increased quite rapidly.

At this time, RAF Army-Cooperating Squadrons had at last got a modern suitable aircraft, the American Mustang. And Air Observation Officers (AOPs) were now operative with their Auster aircraft.

With all these improvements behind them, and no longer with an invasion threat to meet, the forces at home on the British Isles could turn their full attention to preparations for offensives. Of course gunners had to refine their gunnery abilities all the time through training and special exercises. They must be first class professionals in the art of 'firing the gun', and that at all levels irrespective of the task whether it was fire observation and control or command post procedures, signalling, survey, sound ranging, vehicles maintenance, transport or whatever. Organising everything was the responsibility of the commanding officers, even if they sometimes could be assisted by, for instance, instructors from School of Artillery at Larkhill. Officers were as we have seen from Peter Wilkinson's account, sent also to various central courses.

But it was not enough to just maintain a high level of individual training. Collective training of units must also take place, i.e. boosting teamwork of a troop, a battery or a regiment. It was first a matter of improving the skills in marching and deployment, in particular in the dark, fire preparations and firing with all the guns of the unit. When all this worked well, training with other units would follow, as would all-arms training.

A special problem bothered commanders constantly. Once they had trained their gunners to perfection, they had often to send away some of them as replacements to other units, at home to new formations set up or overseas to compensate for war losses.

The problem was serious, in particular when officers, warrant officers and specialists had to leave. Losing skilled signallers, e.g., could become a nightmare for any regimental commander.

Albeit many problems and difficulties were burdens to carry, much enthusiasm also emerged as a consequence of the course of the war. With no invasion threat, Germany stuck in Russia and America having entered the war, it became clear that Churchill's vision about a complete defeat of Germany was realistic. Not yet known, however, was that the fight against Germany across the Channel could not commence for another two years. Not only a gigantic build-up of allied resources took time, but also the need for more large-scale training, training and again, training must be met.

Large exercises with offensive objectives became very frequent, not to say daily undertakings. As before, exercises were short, a few days, maximum a week, but they were tough, at least if the chief initiator was Montgomery.

It was not difficult to keep up enthusiasm at the beginning, but as things dragged on, people became bored, and also felt that they knew everything and had the required skill for any action. For some commanders, it became a tough challenge to maintain and boost morale and discipline. When the D-Day eventually came closer, a fear spread among the troops that they might not be engaged in the coming final battle: 'We have now trained for four to five years and we might not get the chance to fight!' This was another challenge for commanders to meet.

At the beginning of 1944, it became obvious that D-Day was not far away any longer. Douglas Goddard writes:

> In January, Gen Montgomery, who had left England in 1942 to command 8th Army in the Desert, returned to command 21st Army Group of which 43rd Div had become part. That the invasion of the Continent was imminent was now clear to all. He inspected the Div at Rye on 4 February in an early winter dawn with snow falling steadily and called on the troops to 'embark on a crusade'. He completely captivated the audience.[294]

The exercises eventually were extended for many units also to include amphibious training, i.e. attack from the sea against a fortified coast. Such exercises were, with preference, done in Scottish fjords and with live ammunition. It was during the final months of training that some gunners in SP regiments to be landed in Normandy developed firing procedures to be applied when the landing craft were on their way to the shore. It was called 'run-in-shoot'. We will see more of that in a later Chapter.

Preparations were done to the last by all units to take part in the Normandy landings. Douglas Goddard has recalled the final training programme for his regiment, 112 (Wessex) Field Regiment RA:[295]

March	26 to 31	Took part 12 Corps Exercise 'Shudder'
April	01 to 03	Firing practice at South Downs at Alfriston
	05 to 07	43 Div Exercise 'Sabre 1'
	13 to 15	43 Div Exercise 'Sabre 2'
May	01 to 06	Final firing camp at Lydd, for field firing at Dungeness

The night between 23 and 24 June, Douglas Goddard's regiment landed in Normandy and engagement in real battle became a reality for the gunners after four years of waiting and training. For others, serious business had begun on D-Day itself, i.e. 6 June 1944.

For many other gunners, the battle baptism came much earlier, at the beginning of the now ended 'third phase'. We will now turn our attention to those who became engaged overseas in the summer and autumn of 1942 already.

19. 'It will be a killing match' – El Alamein

> This battle for which we are preparing will be a real rough house and will involve a very great deal of hard fighting. If we are successful it will mean the end of the war in North Africa, apart from general 'clearing-up' operations; it will be the turning point of the whole war. Therefore we can take no chances.
>
> Morale is the big thing in war. We must raise the morale of our soldiery to the highest pitch; they must be made enthusiastic, and must enter this battle with their tails high in the air and with the will to win.

The new commander of the 8th Army in North Africa, Lieutenant General Bernard L. Montgomery, informed in a memo dated 14 September 1942 how he intended to defeat the German-Italian forces by launching Operation Lightfoot. The quotation is retrieved from this memo and illustrates how important it was for Montgomery to strengthen the fighting spirit and self-confidence in the army.[296] If this failed, it would not be possible to match an opponent like Rommel. We will look at the plan and Montgomery's measures taken, but first a few words about what had passed before his arrival.

Varying initiatives

As we know, Mussolini had imperial dreams in the 1930s and commenced his fight for it by attacking Abyssinia (today Ethiopia) in 1936. When the British were forced out of France and could not resist the German assault, he found the time ripe for challenging the British in North Africa. As seen, the declaration of war came on 10 June 1940. His objective was to force the British out from their protectorate Egypt, this as part of his grand strategy, control of the whole Mediterranean region.

He was not that successful at the beginning. He suffered a decisive defeat at the hands of the British general O'Connor in December 1940. This was followed by a number of British victories in January and February 1941. The Italians were forced back all the way to El Aghelia, some 600 miles to the west. The British, however, failed to avail themselves of this advantage. A historical mistake was done. Resources were dispersed by sending a large force in springtime 1941 to Greece – a country threatened by an attack from Italy. This caused a strong reaction from the German side.

By means of a more successful invasion of Greece than the Italians had launched earlier, the *Wehrmacht* quickly pushed the British out of the country, at first to Crete and then eventually to Egypt. They also sent Rommel with his Africa Corps to North Africa to support the Italians, whom they did not have any better thoughts about. Further on, the Germans also were strategically attracted by the oil fields in the Middle East. These could be captured if the British were defeated in Egypt and Palestine at the same time as a German thrust through the Soviet Union to Iraq and Iran took place. Conquest of the Suez Canal and cutting the British lines to India was also an attractive strategic objective.[297]

During 1941, the battle in North Africa raged back and forth along the coast and at the end of the year, the British were again at El Aghelia. They had relieved the besieged town of Tobruk. However, the initiative went again to Rommel who in 1942 forced the British back to El Alamein. On his way, he also forced the British garrison at Tobruk, some 30,000 men, to capitulate on 21 June. Large stocks of petrol, vehicles, heavy equipment including artillery and ammunition were lost. The shock in Britain over this defeat was immense. It became a huge national burden just four months after the largest British defeat in history, the capitulation in Singapore on 15 February.

But the British could stand much and never gave up. The British Commander-in-Chief, Auchinleck, whose lack of leadership qualities had contributed much to the sad outcome of the war during the first half of 1942, managed to just stop Rommel at El Alamein in July 1942. Churchill and the CIGS Alan Brooke were not satisfied with what they had seen and heard about Auchinleck's way of waging war in North Africa. He was sacked as C-in-C Middle East at the beginning of August and was replaced by General Harold Alexander (Later Field Marshal Earl Alexander).

Auchinleck has remained a controversial person up to these days. On the one hand, this was due to his skills and on the other hand to his weaknesses. This will not be discussed in detail here, but it might be relevant to raise the question as to whether he lacked one of the most important qualities of leadership, so important both in the civilian life as in the military sector, namely the ability to recruit good subordinates and with them establish a strong managerial team. We had an early indication of this already when looking into his role in Norway 1940. This became even more obvious in North Africa. But, to his credit, he was the man who stopped Rommel at El Alamein in July 1942.

The intention of Churchill was to get one of the Corps Commanders of the 8th Army, General Gott, to replace Auchinleck as army commander. However, he was killed when his aircraft was shot down by a German fighter. The order then went to Montgomery, at the time commander of XII Corps in England. He was to replace Auchinleck on 15 August 1942, but as was typical, he took command on 13 August. This, he told London by means of a short message, and this just had to be accepted.

Qattara Depression – its historical importance

El Alamein was small a village with a railway station and a few buildings near the Mediterranean coast. Despite this, the location has received a place in world history due to the battles that took place there in 1942. But the fact behind this was not the place as such but the terrain at large and the decisive importance of the Qattara Depression. This formation has its northernmost part some 50–60km south of El Alamein. To the south, the Depression extends 140–160km. The width of it in west-east direction is of the same magnitude. The Depression is situated around 10–50m beneath the sea level in the northernmost part and falls to around 100m below the sea level in the southernmost section (the lowest point is said to be -133m).

The Depression is comprised of salt marshes and sand dunes and was regarded at the time to be impossible to cross with motor transport and large military formations.

Between the Mediterranean and the Depression, the terrain can be characterised as a plateau 10–50m above sea level in the North rising to around 100–150m in the southernmost part. There are several large hills in the latter part with heights up to more than 200m above sea level. Several fairly distinct ridges exist in the northern part. These became important during the battles to come. To the east, the Alam el Halfa ridge dominated, southwest of this down towards the Qattara Depression was the Himeimat Ridge and northwest of this the Ruweisat Ridge. In its turn this had another ridge, which was to play an important role, the Miteiriya Ridge located northwest of it. And when we look further northwest from the latter, we have the smaller Kidney Ridge (its shape reminiscent of a kidney!) and west of this the important the Rahman Track which went from the sea southwards. Close to the latter in the northern sector was another hill, Tell El Aqqaqir.

The ridges had a hard surface made up of stones. It was practically impossible to dig in and arrange battle positions with shelters and trenches. This was easier between the ridges and hills where the surface generally was covered with sand.

A distinct difficulty in this terrain was difficulty in navigating. Lack of dominating features and other distinguishable features made this very difficult. Dust clouds from numerous military vehicles and bursting shells made observation even more difficult. A few methods used to overcome this problem will be discussed later.

Due to the existence of the Qattara Depression, all major military movements had to be 'channelled' into the narrow area between the Depression and the Mediterranean at El Alamein. It was a natural choice on the part of the British to establish strong defence positions here; it was here that an outflanking movement by the enemy could be prevented. **Map 19-1** illustrates the area at large where the battles of El Alamein took place. Germans and Italians were on the western side of the front line and the British east of this.

When Auchinleck had stopped Rommel in this particular area, a static battle between the two opponents followed, and this behind huge minefields and barbed wire fences. The British defence was strongest in the northern part and did not cover the whole distance down to Qattara Depression. The depth of defence eastwards here was around 100km (as far back as Alexandria) and to Cairo the distance was around 200km.

The British supply lines were short, but for Rommel and his Italian allies it was the other way around. To the most important harbour, Tripoli, it was as much as 1,600km and to the nearest harbour with capacity, Tobruk, it was some 500km from the front. Added to this problem, were the frequent attacks by the Royal Navy & the Royal Air Force on the seaborne transport across the Mediterranean. The Royal Air Force also frequently attacked the transport routes on land. The huge logistic challenges would discourage the German High Command, one might expect, but this was not Rommel's nature.

How had the artillery resources been employed before El Alamein?

During the fighting in North Africa in 1940–1941 the availability of artillery was limited. As in other theatres obsolete guns were a huge disadvantage. Divisional artillery had 18-pounders and 18/25-pounders, later being replaced gradually by the 25-pounder Mark II. At the time of the great offensive in October 1942, all the vintage field guns, however were gone (**Fig. 19-1**).

The situation was really bad as regards medium guns. A few medium regiments had 60-pounders and obsolete American 150mm howitzers. No heavy artillery existed at all. When the first few months of 1942 had passed, the old medium guns were replaced by new guns. In June 1942 the two medium regiments in place, 7 Medium Regiment RA and 64 Medium Regiment RA, had been rearmed. Each received one battery with 4.5-inch guns and one with the 5.5-inch gun. Later 69 Medium Regiment RA was allotted to 8th Army also. That regiment was equipped with 4.5-inch guns only.

> The Eighth Army had in this period thrown every rule for the correct employment of field artillery out of the window, and was paying for it.

This was written by one of the true experts on British artillery development, Brigadier R.G.S. Bidwell, in an article about the employment of British artillery in the Desert War before the great offensive in October 1942.[298] What was on his mind?

His primary criticism was about dispersion of resources. The battles were generally fought at the brigade levels, often by temporary battle groups, so-called 'Jock Columns'.[299] Such battle groups normally comprised infantry and tank units to which were attached an artillery battery, in some cases a regiment. Sometimes could not more than a troop (4 guns) be made available.

Fig. 19-1 Once British artillery resources were less dispersed, and fire could be more concentrated in battles, artillery had a much more decisive role than before. One of the first examples is when the besieged British forces prevented Tobruk to fall in 1941 and eventually managed to break out. This 25-pounder took part in that battle (RAHT)

The limited artillery resources made strong concentrations of fire impossible.

Dispersion, and the fact that initiative almost every time was lost in battle, made pre-planned concentrations of firepower an art that was completely neglected, as Bidwell saw it. The same could be said about counter-battery fire. That was almost never applied. Lack of long-range firing guns and less understanding on the part of commanders of units to be supported regarding the importance of such fire led to negligence.

The British Army had before the war largely neglected the importance of close cooperation between infantry, armour and artillery. This was particularly the case as regards armoured formations. These considered it best to run their own battle; their own weapons would do what was needed in the context of firepower. That seems to have been the general opinion. The result in the Desert War was that tank formations ran into traps arranged by the Germans again and again. The traps were the result of carefully employed tank units cooperating with lines of anti-tank guns, cleverly positioned. To the latter were several of the famous '88' anti-aircraft guns often added. They were then used as a long-range anti-tank gun. It is amazing to note that the British so often accepted great losses due to erroneous use of tank resources. The situation did not become better by the absence of high explosive shells for the British tank guns. Solid armour-piercing shells were quite useless against anti-tank positions. Bidwell again:

> Our armoured doctrine of the day, which was quite opposite of the German, was that to exploit its full potential armour must operate in its own, untrammelled by any need to seek or lend support to the infantry and artillery. [. . .] British armour seldom, if ever, used its artillery correctly in a coordinated plan. Nor did it discover how to cooperate with anti-tank guns, in the German manner.[300]

See also **Fig. 19-2**.

Bidwell raises the interesting comment also that the frequent disruption of the ordinary organisational structures, when establishing temporary battle formations including changes of commanders, contributed to the fact that artillery resources were not properly used. A trustful relationship and cooperation between the gunner and the commander to be supported takes a long time to establish. Much exercising together was needed. Personal relations must also not be underestimated. The understanding of this was lacking during the first years of battle in North Africa, according to Bidwell.

But changes were to come, and this not only regarding the discussed deficiencies! A new situation emerged when Montgomery arrived and took command of 8th Army. He had the will, the self-confidence and the visions regarding what was needed.

Montgomery in command

'Monty', as he was called, took command of the army with a clear task given by Churchill. He should not only prevent Rommel from occupying Egypt, he should also once and for all destroy the German-Italian army, now called the *Panzerarmee Afrika*. With this in mind, he at once initiated a number of measures.

Montgomery was concerned when he found that the morale of the 8th Army was low. People lacked confidence in the High Command. A widespread practice existed at various levels of command to question orders and plans. Authority of command was missing. He also recognised a large need for training. This must include improvement of personal skills related to individual tasks but also collective training at different unit levels. An offensive was out of question until 'we are ready', he stated. This

Fig. 19-2 Montgomery and his artillery commander Kirkman failed to change the bad habit rooted for long amongst many commanders of armoured units to attack without proper, planned artillery support. Losses were large when their tanks ran straight into the well-planned German anti-tank shields. This Sherman tank may be seen as a representative of such armoured units (AWM No. P01614.017)

could not take place in September as Churchill wanted, rather in October at the earliest.

Some of the immediate measures taken by Monty were the following:

First, he stated emphatically that no retreat whatsoever from El Alamein should take place. The army should stay on where it now was, to victory or death. Retreat towards the Nile Delta from now on, was out of the question, all planning for this should cease immediately. Plans prepared earlier for this should go into the wastepaper basket! This first message alone gave a distinct boost to morale and fighting spirit.

Montgomery's next step was to replace high-level commanders. He recruited Brigadier Francis de Guingand from the General Staff at Cairo as his own Chief of Staff, this after having interviewed him and established his view on the overall military situation. This choice proved to be fortunate. De Guingand (later Major General Sir Francis de Guingand), known as 'Freddie' by Montgomery as well as others, was to serve under Montgomery until the end of the war.

Montgomery wanted to replace also all Corps Commanders, but had to retain one, Lieutenant General Lumsden. With great appreciation, he managed to get Brian Horrocks released in England to come to Egypt and assume command of XIII Corps. An already close relation between the two Generals was here further strengthened. Horrocks remained one of Montgomery's favourites as Corps Commander through the war, which we will see more of later on in the book.

Another important change was his nomination of an army artillery commander. Montgomery knew the importance of artillery and how it should be employed. To make sure that this was to take place in the coming offensive, Montgomery requested that London gave him Brigadier Sidney Kirkman (**Fig. 19-3**).

They knew each other very well; Kirkman had as we have seen been divisional artillery commander (CRA) and Corps artillery commander (CCRA) under Montgomery. The latter used to say that Kirkman was 'the best gunner in the British Army'. We may recall his most important role as chief artillery umpire under Montgomery when the huge Exercise 'Bumper' was run in October 1941 in England.[301]

Montgomery made clear from the beginning that the fighting onwards should be done by coherent divisions. There must be an end to 'Jock Columns' and other types of fragmentation of high-level resources. The artillery should be given a prominent role and be used in a concentrated manner.

When he visited various units in the field, he became angry when finding commanders who did not train their people continuously. This was another reason for re-shuffling of commanding officers.

We may also observe another important change in the army. Montgomery demanded that everyone was well informed about the battle they were to conduct. Everyone, irrespective of rank, must know exactly what their personal role would be in the coming operations. He checked through numerous visits to units that this order was adhered to when the time came for engagement.

Furthermore, Montgomery made it clear to all officers that no objections to given orders were tolerated henceforth. Orders were not intended for discussion, they were to be strictly

Fig. 19-3 Brigadier (later General) Sidney Chevalier Kirkman was another of the most important reformers of Royal Artillery after Dunkirk. Montgomery considered him to be 'Britain's best Gunner' and wanted to see him as artillery commander of 8th Army. Kirkman became his principal artillery advisor when the plan for the battle of El Alamein was prepared (Portrait by S. Morris Brown, RAHT Collection)

obeyed, to the point. 'Belly-aching' was no longer tolerated!

Finally, Montgomery also made clear that the army and the Royal Air Force were not to wage separate wars. The forces were to be well coordinated for maximum effect. In order to make this easier, Montgomery moved his headquarters to the location of the RAF:s headquarters close to the Mediterranean coast and made arrangements for the staff officers to work together and get well acquainted with each other.

Recovery and then – a new battle

Not only were the structural changes mentioned above important in August 1942. What has been called the first battle of El Alamein was concluded on 27 July 1942 and prevented Rommel from reaching the Nile Delta. After this, both sides started to consolidate their positions. There was need for recovery and replacements for those lost had to be arranged; lost or damaged equipment had to be compensated for as well. On the British side new resources were provided also besides replacements.

A new infantry division arrived from England, the 44th Infantry Division, which had no previous battle experience, but was to prove a most valuable reinforcement during the coming battles. A very important addition came on the equipment side, namely some 300 American Grant tanks. These had both a 37mm and a 75mm gun. The latter was not a turret gun but was placed to the right in the hull in a sponson. With this tank, the British had a resource capable of matching the German tanks of the time. A disadvantage was however that the 75mm gun had a very limited field of traverse. If targets suddenly appeared to the left or right of the tank it had to turn completely towards the target before firing could commence. The Grant was not a tank for mobile battles in open terrain and the emerging duel situations with enemy tanks.

Further reinforcements were expected in September, amongst them the 51st (Highland) Division but also more equipment. 300 American Sherman tanks and a few self-propelled 105-mm howitzers, *'Priests',* provided a great reinforcement of the 8th Army. The 'Priest' was a modern SP gun that quickly replaced the out-dated 'Bishop' as the prime weapon in field regiments attached to armoured divisions. As we have seen, it remained in service until 1944 when being replaced gradually by 'Sextons'. At El Alamein, 11 (Honourable Artillery Company) Field Regiment RHA was rearmed with 'Priests' just in time for the great offensive to come. This SP gun could easily follow fast moving tank battalions.

The artillery intelligence resources were not abundant in the Desert War. The 8th Army had only one survey regiment, the 4th (Durham) Survey Regiment RA. This came to North Africa with the type of organisation prevailing when the war broke out, i.e. beside the regimental headquarters there were a 'Survey Battery', a 'Flash Spotting Battery' and a 'Sound Ranging Battery'. It was, however, reinforced by an independent survey troop. This structure was soon to be found to be unsuitable when fighting formations were deployed over large areas and fighting was going on at many places simultaneously. As we have seen this led to a revision of the regimental organisation in 1942, by which a new structure that survived the entire war emerged.

The resources were grouped into two 'Composite Batteries', each comprising a survey troop, a flash spotting troop and a sound ranging troop. A survey troop was attached to the regimental headquarters.

The new organisation quickly proved to be very versatile and efficient. But the regiment was struck by a serious loss. The 2nd Composite Battery, in June 1942 was deployed in the Gazala Line and was amongst those units driven into Tobruk by Rommel's offensive and forced to capitulate on 21 June 1942.[302]

Going back in time, the Regiment had in the Spring 1942 been transferred to Syria in order to undertake survey work for the 9th British Army, which prepared itself to meet a possible German attack from Turkish territory.

When Rommel continued his advance from the Gazala Line to El Alamein, 4th Survey Regiment RA was called back to the Nile Delta.

The regimental commander, Lieutenant Colonel Whetton began to immediately rebuild his regiment after the loss of one of his batteries at Tobruk. He made it by carefully recruiting skilled individuals from England. In order to speed up the process, an independent survey troop from Syria was transferred to the regiment and included in the new 2nd Composite Battery.

The regiment was used for survey of

planned artillery deployments in the Nile Delta, but for operation of a few observation and sound ranging bases as well. In July, the 'A' Troop (Flash Spotters) and the 'R' Troop (Sound Ranging) from 1st Composite Battery were employed at El Alamein and were positioned in the XXX Corps area. The re-established 2nd Composite Battery was ready for action towards the beginning of October. As we will see, the battery was then put under command of XIII Corps.

When Montgomery after his arrival gave the order that all preparations for a battle in the Nile Delta would be terminated, the remaining resources of the 4th (Durham) Survey Regiment RA could be transferred to El Alamein where they were better needed. In this area, a survey company of South African Engineers was now also engaged with production of maps for the whole area down to the Qattara Depression. With this company the British surveyors established a fruitful cooperation.

Montgomery had his thoughts correct from the beginning on the strategy for his offensive against Rommel – aiming at a final annihilation of his forces, but it would take some time to prepare for it. He realised that he first must meet another strong attack by Rommel which could be expected to come around 1 September. His judgment was that Rommel by that time had recovered and restored his force for a new attack. At this date, the attack could be launched during the night, as full moon conditions would provide some light for the attackers.

His considerations proved to be correct. Rommel himself had realised that he must make a final attempt to destroy the 8th Army at this date. In the middle of September and onwards, the British resources would be so strong that the 8th Army could not be defeated, as he saw it.

Rommel's plan was similar to what the British had experienced before. He intended to take his armoured units in a swift move around the British southern flank and then turning northwards towards the coast. When the main part of the 8th Army had been encircled and its supply lines been cut off, he would direct one of his armoured divisions towards Alexandria and another towards Cairo. Succeeding infantry divisions would complete the destruction of the enclosed British forces. A prerequisite was, however, that large supply stores needed to be captured; petrol being the most important commodity.

The British had well understood the tactical situation and prepared themselves for this scenario. Montgomery decided to deploy the British armoured units for defence with the tanks well protected behind hillcrests or dug in 'hull down' in positions where they could fire at the attacking German tanks. This time the tanks were not to be lured out into open terrain where they would fall easy victims to Rommel's tanks and numerous anti-tank guns.

The British tanks were to be assisted in the German manner by a line of anti-tank guns. And now a modern, effective gun had been provided, the 6-pounder. During the first years of the Desert War there had been a shortage of modern guns. Only obsolete 2-pounders with inadequate armour penetration capability against German tanks were available. As a consequence, 25-pounders of the field artillery had to be used often for direct fire against attacking tanks instead of being used for concentrated indirect fire.

The shortage was eliminated in October 1942. A large number of the new anti-tank gun had been delivered to the 8th Army just before the great offensive, and they could match any German tank. With this the 25-pounders could be relieved from anti-tank tasks, except when protecting their own deployments.

For the expected attack defence positions had been selected at the Alam el Halfa Ridge and its extension southwards to the Bare Ridge. That location was a distinct advantage as it was to be seen. The newly arrived 44th Infantry Division was deployed here, and southwest of this the 10th Armoured Division. Other infantry divisions were to hold the front further to the west.

Montgomery had decided that the artillery this time would be used for concentrated fire; the resources were not to be fragmented. Furthermore, RAF bombers and fighter-bombers should attack the German advancing tanks and, not the least, the German supply transport.

This battle, which commenced on the night between 30 and 31 August 1942, resulted in success for Montgomery, albeit the 8th Army suffered great losses. After a week of hard fighting Rommel had to give up and break off this his last offensive on 6 September. The result strengthened Montgomery's position and reputation.

This battle will not be described in detail here. Reference is made to the numerous books available, in particular the one written by Jon Latimer (2002). His book is to a large extent based on original sources. I have therefore found it being of special value.

Montgomery's plan for his own great offensive

The preparations for the great British offensive geared up when the battle at Alam el Halfa had petered out. For the gunners of 64 Medium Regiment RA there was no time for rest. They had to fire against enemy transport and artillery positions every day and were often called out to counter enemy patrols and smaller reconnaissance attacks. One troop (4 guns) was sent to the south to act as a 'roving unit' for harassing fire. After having been active as such for a week or more, it was replaced by another troop of the regiment. A battery of the newly arrived 69 Medium Regiment RA was put under command of the former regiment in September. There were then six troops alternating (**Fig. 19-4**).

A typical day is recorded in the regimental war diary, 21 September:

> A fairly busy day for the guns. C Tp were ranged by sound rangers on hostile battery, but conditions were against a final accurate result. Captain Wilson at the O.P. also engaged enemy vehicles and gun area. A Tp, Lt. D-Young at the O.P., twice engaged a hostile battery and Lt. McKillop later in the day, engaged an infantry gun using 37 rounds and causing it to retire. He reports the enemy frequently run this gun forward, in full view, and use it to harass the O.P. area.
>
> Captain Whitworth-Jones, at the O.P., used B Tp to engage, on six separate occasions throughout the day, a number of infantry, appar-

Fig. 19-4 Just before the battle of El Alamein in October 1942 the few British medium regiments had been rearmed with the new modern 4–5-inch and 5.5-inch guns, which implied a dramatic improvement of the British firepower. One of these new guns is here seen firing during the battle of El Alamein (RAHT)

ently working around 3 vehicles South of the Minassib Depression. The Regiment used 147 rounds in all. D Tp is still down South.

In his headquarters, Montgomery prepared his 'Master Plan' for the great offensive. This is how he always worked. He wrote in his memoirs that he always prepared his 'Master Plan' himself. He was the 'Master' and therefore 'I could not have my headquarters prepare it'. As to the offensive at El Alamein, he produced a plan of 42 points.

Several such plans with many numbered sections were to come later on during the war.

The plan for Operation Lightfoot was aimed at complete destruction of the enemy forces opposing the 8th Army. Montgomery adds that if 'minor elements' flee westwards they would be pursued and taken care of later. In respect of what was to happen this is of interest to note.

Montgomery had decided that XXX Corps would launch a direct attack in the northern sector with four infantry divisions beside each other with the object to capture a large bridgehead through which X Armoured Corps later would pass.[303] The four divisions assigned for the task were the 9th (Australian) Infantry Division in the north, the 51st (Highland) Infantry Division and the 2nd (New Zealand) Infantry Division and south of the latter the 1st (South African) Infantry Division. The bridgehead which these divisions were to establish would cover all the enemy main front positions and, as it was hoped, the majority of his artillery positions. It would include the important Miteiriya Ridge.

Through a northern corridor, the 1st Armoured Division would pass, through a southern the 10th Armoured Division.

The New Zealanders, who nominally were part of X Corps, would initially be under command of XXX Corps as one of four divisions. When the armoured Corps broke through, the division was to revert to this Corps and turn in behind the Italian-German units cutting off their supply lines. See **Map 19-2**.

In the southernmost sector Horrock's XIII Corps was to attack with the aim to tie-up the German and Italian armoured reserves. A further objective was to launch a number of brigade attacks to create uncertainty on the part of the enemy as to where the main thrust of the offensive was to be directed. A few diversionary attacks were also included in the plan for the first night and day. A special role was given to the 1st (Free French) Infantry Brigade, which would make an attack, well coordinated with the main attack, against the dominating high ground at Heimimat and Hunters Plateau in the South.[304]

When Montgomery devised his 'Master Plan', he had in mind also a sea landing to take place in the enemy's rear. This force was to work its way eastwards to join up with the advance units of XXX Corps.[305] This operation was, however, deleted from the final plan.

Map 19-3 illustrates the main attack in the North with first-hand and final objectives indicated. We can see that the envisaged bridgehead included the wide and dominating – albeit not that high – Miteiriya Ridge. Some of the succeeding operations, which will be discussed later, are indicated on the map as well.

Montgomery stressed that success of XXX Corps' attack into the main enemy positions was critical for the outcome of the whole operation. This will in its turn depend on correct use of the artillery resources. He writes:

> Up to 400 guns will be available and the concentrated use of this great fire power should ensure success.

He adds that all the Corps artillery resources should remain under command of the artillery commander (CCRA) XXX Corps to secure concentration. Decentralisation was not to be allowed. When the bridgehead had been established, artillery should be ready to fire into the depth of enemy positions and also to meet strong counter-attacks.[306]

An important part of the plan was cooperation with the Royal Air Force. Besides night bombardment of air bases at the full moon towards the end of September violent air bombardment of enemy tank columns and artillery deployments should take place through the first night of the operation.[307]

The fact that it must be a frontal attack could not be concealed. But on the other hand, Montgomery wanted to, and could, surprise his opponent as regards the date and time of the operation, and also where the main attack would come. He therefore gave detailed instructions about deception measures to be taken, and also how to minimise the risks of such information getting into wrong hands.[308]

After these provisions, he issued clear directives as to the training programmes to be run at all levels including full-scale rehearsals with the concerned divisions. It is interesting to see that he emphasised the importance of getting the soldiers used to advancing close behind a creeping barrage. Exercises with live artillery ammunition thus would be arranged, even if this might imply certain losses (which he stated he would assume full responsibility for).[309]

The 'Master Plan' is concluded with several statements regarding the importance of the strengthening of morale and fighting spirit. All commanders here carried a large responsibility, Montgomery stressed. 'The German is a good soldier and the only way of defeating him is to kill him!'

'It will be a killing match,' Montgomery went on. The soldier must be tough and hard. In that context, he also ordered all commanders and soldiers to commence physical training.[310]

Montgomery gave the order that his plan from now on should become the basis for all detailed planning and preparations for Operation Lightfoot. His authority was well founded and now undisputable and all went on without any 'belly-aching'. The 'ball' was now passed to the Corps commanders and their subordinates.

The planners arrived at the conclusion that the attack in the XXX Corps area should be conducted in two phases. The first phase would see advance through the main minefields and capture the foremost enemy positions. After consolidation and mopping up, which was assumed to take one hour, the attack would in a second phase proceed until the final objectives had been captured. The brain behind this concept was the experienced commander of the 2nd (New Zealand) Division, Lieutenant General Bernard Freyberg. In a personal letter dated 21 September 1942 to 'My dear Oliver' (the Corps Commander, Lieutenant General Oliver Leese) he elaborated his view in an attachment on how they were to conduct the coming battle.[311] In this, he also expresses some interesting suggestions as to how the artillery must be employed.

According to Freyberg, the enemy artillery out of reach of most of the 25-pounders would seriously affect his troops when they had reached the Miteiriya Ridge, in particular as the stony soil made it impossible for them to dig in. He therefore wanted his divisional artillery to be reinforced by another field regiment (25-pounder) and a medium regiment to conduct counter-battery fire when the divisional artillery was firing their barrage. He wanted also the artillery to re-deploy forwards during the first night into no-man's land. This would secure best possible firepower when counter-attacks would come in the morning.

As regards the covering fire during the attack, Freyberg argued, this should be planned as timed concentrations against all located enemy positions, and not as a barrage.

Freyberg's ideas became the norm for all the four attacking divisions within XXX Corps and thus influenced the detailed fire planning, as we will see. Obviously he was in tune with Montgomery, who accepted his suggestions.

The situation before the great offensive

Detailed planning of Operation *Lightfoot* and production of orders gained momentum in the second half of September. On the artillery side, Brigadier Sidney Kirkman became army artillery commander on 15 September 1942[312] and immediately felt the strong support from Montgomery. He found, with relief, that most of the divisional artillery commanders shared his and Montgomery's opinion about how to use the artillery resources. One of these was Freyberg's artillery commander, Brigadier Weir, who all the time had been against dispersion of the divisional artillery in the earlier battles.

The extensive exercises that were conducted towards the end of the month and later gave important lessons that were to influence both Montgomery and other senior commanders. Successive changes of the plans and orders were made, one of these was the important change that came on 6 October when it was decided that an intermediate gap between the initial attack and the final outbreak by the armoured units should be accepted. Emphasis was placed on meeting repeated strong counter-attacks from the Axis units and to clear the bridgehead of enemy units. The overriding aim of this was to wear down the enemy before the final out-break took place. A few minor operations to consolidate the army positions were also to be conducted. Montgomery called this the 'dog fight'.

We can note that all major orders were complete by 20 October 1942.

The four divisions of the *Afrika Korps* and the independent parachute brigade under General Ramcke were now deployed along the

German-Italian frontline, as were some support units. As Rommel was in Germany, all Axis forces were under command of General Georg Stumme. Lieutenant General Wilhelm Ritter von Thoma had assumed command of the *Afrika Korps* in mid-September.[313]

Deployed together with the German formations were the three Italian Corps, the X, XX and XXI with in total eight divisions, of which two were armoured divisions: the *Ariete* Division and the *Littorio* Division. Another strong force was the 185th *Folgore* Parachute Division. The combined German and Italian forces were named *Panzerarmee Afrika*.

In June, Rommel (now promoted General Field Marshal), did not have much faith in the capability of the Italian formations to resist a decisive British attack. He therefore created a number of hybrid units comprising both German and Italian battalions.

The responsibility for the northern sector of the Axis front was given to the XXI (Italian) Corps and the southern sector became the responsibility of the X (Italian) Corps. The armoured units were kept in reserve, in the North the German 15th Armoured Division and the *Littorio* Division, in the south the German 21st Armoured Division together with the *Ariete* Division.

Each division had an artillery regiment comprising 2–3 artillery battalions. The Italian armoured divisions had an additional SP battalion. A capable artillery group of five independent artillery battalions were under Rommel's direct command. The total number of guns was around 500, out of which 70 were medium guns and 14 heavy. Their positions had all been located by the British sound ranging and flash-spotting troops of the 4th Survey Regiment RA assisted by air reconnaissance and ground patrols.

This meant that Rommel was inferior to the British as regards the number of guns. In terms of medium guns the resources were about equal, and as to heavy guns he was stronger as the British lacked this type of resource.

Turning to the British side of the front line, this was covered by two Corps, in the North XXX Corps (Leese) and in the South XIII Corps (Horrocks). Behind the former, 80–120km to the East stood X Armoured Corps.

South of the four attacking divisions of XXX Corps, the 4th Indian Division was deployed at the Ruweisat Ridge.

XIII Corps deployed the 50th Infantry Division in its northernmost sector along with the 1st Greek Brigade. Further to the South, the 44th Infantry Division and 7th Armoured Division were positioned. The 1st Free French Brigade was deployed in the southernmost sector. A second French Brigade was also available to Horrocks. All formations can be seen on **Map 19-3** and **Map 19-4**.

The British artillery resources comprised three regiments per infantry division. In the Northern sector an Army Field Regiment was allotted to an independent armoured brigade as well. There were thus a total of 16 field regiments available to XXX Corps. Four of these had however only two batteries, i.e. 16 guns instead of the normal 24 guns. There were still 352 field guns (25-pounders) in this sector. To these can be added the 48 medium guns (4.5-inch and 5.5-inch guns), which were employed.

The two armoured divisions of X Corps had five and four regiments respectively, this when we include artillery resources of the *Hammer Force* (remnants of the disbanded 8th Armoured Division), which had been attached to the former. One of the regiments was 11 (HAC) Field Regiment RHA, which was the first one equipped with the Priest SP guns. In summary, this Corps had 216 guns (25-pounders and 'Priests'). This allotment was much larger than that to be the norm later for armoured divisions (one regiment with towed and one with SP guns).

It should here be noted that 18 troops (18x4 guns) from X Corps were temporarily put under command of XXX Corps. They were there organised as a third troop in the same number of batteries, which by this became 12-gun batteries. This arrangement was to remain in force during the first five hours of the offensive until the attacking divisions had captured their final objectives. The troops would then return to X Corps and respective armoured division.

With some Army Field Regiments included, 14 field regiments were ready in the south, i.e. XIII Corps deployment area. Six of them had only 16 guns. One regiment was attached to the 1st Free French Brigade. This Corps had a total of 288 field guns at its disposal.

The availability of medium guns in the 8th Army was limited in comparison with the allotment later in the war. Here were, as seen, only three medium regiments in place in October 1942 in the northern sector. And as mentioned, no heavy guns at all. Scarcely observed in literature is that the regiment of the 1st Free French Brigade in the South had an extra troop of four 5.5-inch guns.[314]

We can now provide a summary of the British artillery resources available to the 8th Army when the major offensive was launched on 23 October 1942:

832 25-pounders
24 'Priest' (105-mm guns)
32 4.5-inch guns
20 5.5-inch guns
i.e. in total 908 guns.

In addition to the guns listed, there were another 31 guns in reserve or in repair. It can be noted also that the new 4.2-inch mortar had been provided for the first time. These were operated by an RE sapper company and organised in three sections with six mortars each. Two of the sections were allotted to the Australian division. This was on an experimental basis and it would be a long time before these mortars were given their definite place in infantry units, and an even longer time before the use of mortars was systematically coordinated with that of the artillery.

The artillery Order of Battle is presented in **Appendix 2**.[315] The geographical dispersion of deployments in the evening of 23 October 1942 is illustrated in **Map 19-4**, along with the German-Italian artillery resources, as had been located by the British. We can see that the British had a superiority of 2:1 in terms of field artillery, but as mentioned above, in terms of medium and heavy guns the superiority was on the Axis side. Looking at the area in the North where the main attack was to take place, the British superiority in field guns was approximately 3:1.

As we have seen above, the British survey and intelligence resources were limited; only one survey regiment was available at El Alamein. We will later see how the scarce resources actually were employed. Later in the war, normal standard to be was one survey regiment allotted to each Corps.

The artillery of the four attacking divisions of XXX Corps were deployed as close as possible to the front line due to the limited range of the field guns. The location is shown in **Map 19-6**. The positions of the three medium regiments are also shown on the map. The enemy's light artillery (75–105mm) was in range of these but also from some of the field regiments. As the range of the field regiments only was up to around 10–11km, the enemy medium and heavy batteries were out of range from the initial positions of field regiments. Only British batteries with 4.5-inch guns could in most cases be used for counter-battery fire against such artillery.[316] This made the participation of the RAF in the battle even more important.

The planned deployment of artillery could not be revealed too early, but was prepared in advance by the surveyors and through preparation of gun pits. Work had to be performed at night. Ammunition was stocked in the gun pits by the gun crews.. Telephone cables were laid and dug in. All preparations were carefully camouflaged. Final deployment forwards could only be performed the day before the attack.

Intelligence status good

During the battles that took place at El Alamein, in August/September 1942, the survey resources were not used at all. When the battle was over, however, a period of intensive work commenced to collect information about the location of the German and Italian positions, in particular artillery positions. Besides extensive patrolling by the infantry, the intelligence resources of the artillery were used, as were air resources.

1 Composite Battery RA established a 'Long Base' along most of the XXX Corps front line. A 'Short [observation] Base' was also established in the XIII Corps area to be taken over by 2 Composite Battery RA when that battery had been reorganised and was ready for action. A sound ranging base for six microphones was established in the North from the coast southwards. For unknown reasons it was a fairly short base, around 6km.[317] The accuracy when measuring against most of the German and Italian batteries was not very good with such a short base. Only a few locations were found with the accuracy needed for counter-battery fire without preceding ranging. But when approximate location had been made, the locations could be fixed exactly from air photographs.

1 Composite Battery opened a sound ranging base in the XIII Corps area. This too, was later to be transferred to 2 Composite Battery. The length of the 'Long Base' and good

observation conditions made locating here more accurate than in the North.

2 Composite Battery took over the Long Base in the South established by 1 Composite Battery in September. It was then extended with two new observation towers/posts and one of the first towers was relocated.[318] Good observation opportunities towards the enemy batteries in the South had now been arranged.

The sound ranging base established in the South by 1 Composite Battery in support of XIII Corps was taken over by 2 Composite Battery on 18 October 1942. The 'S' Troop was made responsible.[319] The troop had been trained a little on a sound ranging concept based on radio link communication instead of traditional use of telephone lines between the microphones and the evaluation centre. The troop was now ready to use the new technique.

We can on **Map 19-7** see the location of the various observation bases. They covered the whole front line from the coast in the North down to the southernmost deployments. In this context we will not forget that in addition to these qualified intelligence resources we had also all the ordinary fire observation posts (FOO/OPOs). These were very important sources for information about the enemy's actions and deployments, not least the artillery deployments. Besides direct observations into enemy-held territory, the firing against enemy targets, which were going on almost all the time, was a good source for intelligence.

Observation posts established by the Flash Spotters were in most cases arranged in high towers built by the sappers. This had become normal practice in 1941 at Tobruk and the results were so good that such towers were used at El Alamein as well (**Fig. 6-10**).

The open terrain and the good observation conditions made possible by means of these observation towers made it easy to locate enemy artillery. The Italian-German guns were at the time normally using a propellant, which created a distinctive muzzle flash, which acted as a distinct advantage to the British flash spotters. A change to flash-less propellant was, however, already under way.

In order not to get the enemy batteries already located to re-deploy as a consequence of counter-battery fire, a 'silent policy' was enforced during the final two weeks before the offensive. The implication of this policy was that British artillery should not be engaged in counter-battery programmes unless this became absolutely necessary.[320]

Air reconnaissance was also an extremely important intelligence source. Numerous air photographs of German positions were taken. As mentioned, these photographs in combination with the locations fixed by the observations resources of the Composite Batteries gave a complete picture of all the enemy artillery deployments.

Improved routines for submission of evaluated air photographs made it possible eventually to give the gunners correct data for counter-battery fire within 4–5 hours as compared with the previous 36 hours.[321]

For collection of intelligence data when the battle was already going on, it would have been necessary to have army-cooperation resources with adequate aircraft (Arty/R procedures), but such resources were as yet not available. Neither were enough fighter resources available for protection of such aircraft.

Air Observation Posts were not provided. Such resources were implemented for the first time by the 1st British Army when advancing into Algeria in November 1942 after Operation Torch landings. Jack Parham was, as mentioned, artillery commander and was a strong advocate of the use of AOPs with suitable aircraft.

During the coming battle, the communication systems of the artillery would as usual assume an important role for collection and distribution of information of a tactical nature. Besides telephone lines, built with threefold or sometimes fourfold redundancy, the gunners had two modern wireless sets, the WS No. 18 and WS No. 19, as a complement to the older WS No. 11 used for basic artillery communication. With these resources at hand, the possibilities for good communication between the gunners and the infantry and armour commanders to be supported by artillery fire were improved.

In summary, the intelligence status was extremely good when the offensive was to be launched. The accuracy of located enemy batteries was good enough for the counter-battery programmes planned. All enemy positions from the front line to a depth of 5–6km were known exactly.

Surveyors were to be delegated to the New Zealand Division and the Scottish Division when the battle commenced. The task was given to 'Y' Troop of 1 Composite Battery RA which was split into two sections. The intention was to allot these sections to the armoured units when passing through the infantry, one section to the 1st Armoured Division and one section to the 10th Armoured Division. By this arrangement, survey of the divisional artillery into the same Corps grid when redeploying forwards could be facilitated. As a starting point, the surveyors would themselves fix their positions by measuring against two or several observation towers backwards. Certain 'trig points' with known coordinates were made available also for this kind of initial survey. Once this was done, the surveyors would extend the Corps grid westwards by triangulation, and survey the field artillery when redeployed forwards. It was considered possible to fix the batteries with an accuracy of 2–3 yards (**Fig. 9-1**).[322]

No ammunition shortage

The week before D-Day, 23 October, large amounts of artillery ammunition were dumped at the prepared gun positions and nearby depots. This was camouflaged by various means. The volumes were large:[323]

- Divisional artillery 400–760 rounds per gun
- Artillery from 10 Corps 500–920 rounds per gun attached to attacking divisions of XXX Corps
- Medium artillery 400–500 rounds per gun

In addition to these volumes, several hundred rounds were loaded on supply trucks and at rear depots. It would by this arrangement be possible to re-deploy the artillery quickly without having to wait for ammunition.

For the divisional artillery, i.e. the 25-pounders, percussion fuzes as well as fuzes for smoke rounds were available. In the numbers given above were included 50–100 smoke rounds per gun. The medium guns had time fuzes (20%) besides the ordinary percussion fuzes (80%).

The highest numbers above applied for the artillery of the Australian division inclusive the troops attached from X Corps. The smallest volume was dumped for the 4th Indian Division at the southern/left flank of XXX Corps.

This huge stocking of artillery ammunition before a major attack was to become the norm for the rest of the war.

We will later see the real ammunition consumption during the twelve days of battle at El Alamein.

The coordinated fire plan

The artillery commander of XXX Corps was to retain the overall command of the artillery resources in the area of attack. With this arrangement, he was responsible for coordinating the fire planning by the divisions to secure concentrated firepower.

Assisting him temporarily was a Counter Battery Officer with staff assigned to his headquarters. With the older denominations he was to act as Commander Corps Medium Artillery (CCMA) albeit with extended authority to include all artillery irrespective of calibre to be used for counter-battery fire. In reality, this was a precursor to the Commander of an Army Group Royal Artillery (AGRA) to come later.

It was a joint undertaking by the CCRA, CCMA and the CRAs to lead the preparation of fire plans with the CCRA as coordinator, the latter having the ultimate responsibility.

The fireplan for the main attack was influenced by the aspects put forward by Freyberg and had the following conceptual design; times given are relative the time of attack on 23 October 1942, i.e. Z hour:

Z-20 to Z-5 min: All artillery take part in counter-battery programmes under CCMA.

Z to Z+7 min: All artillery combat the enemy forward positions. 7 Medium Regiment RA and one battery from 64 Medium Regiment RA support 9 Australian Division (in addition to the divisional artillery). The artillery regiments of the three other divisions were reinforced by one battery each from 64 Medium Regiment RA and 69 Medium Regiment RA.

Z+7 to Z+115 min: All field artillery (25-pounders) are engaged in divisional covering fire programmes under respective CRA. Medium batteries continue combating enemy artillery positions under CCMA.

Z+115 to Z+175 min: Divisional artillery firing at enemy positions in accordance with CRA plans during the attackers' pause. The medium regiments and four field regiments conduct counter-battery firing under the CCMA.

Z+175 to Z+185 min: All artillery firing at the enemy's main positions.

Z+185 min and onwards: Continued firing under respective CRA. Continued counter-battery firing with 64 Medium Regiment RA, 69 Medium Regiment RA and 2/8 Field Regiment RAA. 7 Medium Regiment RA supports 9 Australian Division.

Phase I of the attack, as proposed by Freyberg, was to conclude at Z+115 min at which time a pause of one hour was to follow for reorganisation and preparations for the next phase of the advance, Phase II. The field regiments were to continue firing during the pause, but at low intensity, 1–2 rounds/min. Counter-battery firing was to continue by the medium batteries at normal fire intensity.

The fact that priority was given to the northernmost sector is indicated by the order to concentrate counter-battery firing against enemy artillery north and west of the Australian division. This engagement was to take place when the armoured divisions were expected to pass through cleared lanes in the minefields.

The time for the attacking divisions to reach their final objectives varied a little depending on the dispersion of enemy positions. On an average, it was assumed that it would take about five hours. The artillery was to fire continuously during the whole period, albeit at varying intensity.

To meet expected counter-attacks when the final objectives had been captured DF targets were prepared in front of these as usual. The Corps artillery order gave directives as to how the resources for such firing would be employed.

In the area allotted to the Australian Division one regiment from the 51st (Highland) Division and one from the 2nd (Ns) Division were to be engaged in addition to the division's own regiments. Furthermore, CCMA was instructed to prepare defensive fire with one medium regiment in this area.

Three to four regiments from neighbouring divisions were to plan in the same way defensive fire in addition to the divisional artillery of respective division. The CCMA was to prepare defensive fire with one medium regiment in front of each division. DF targets were to be engaged for two minutes with highest intensity to be followed by normal intensity for another three minutes. In accordance with the book, fire against the most critical target, denominated 'SOS', would be prepared and guns not otherwise engaged were to be laid on this. Fire could be ordered via line (telephone) or radio but also by using signal pistols (Very flares). The latter was planned to be one signal comprising three white 'stars'. Such requests for SOS fire were to be answered by respective divisional artillery only.

Where are we? Finding the way ahead

Although the attack was to take place in moonlight, it was not easy due to the flat terrain and lack of distinct identifiable objects to know exact positions in respect of the planned direction of advance. Clouds of dust from numerous vehicles and bursting artillery shells did not make it easier. Besides keeping track of direction, it was also necessary to identify the attack objectives and terrain sectors where to pause to allow units regain order once again. It became a task on the part of the gunners to assist in the navigation. This was to be achieved by different methods.

Artificial light

It was not just a matter of direct illumination of the battlefield. Anti-aircraft searchlights with known coordinates were used to send a vertical beam upwards into the sky. By means of intersection of lights, the exact position of (for instance) an advancing infantry unit could be found on a map. It was also decided that crossing beams from two searchlights would indicate the time between Phase I and Phase II.

As we have seen, another practice was to have towers of the observation bases illuminated from time to time, this giving opportunities also for finding position by simple survey methods. The observation posts could be used the other way around. These could determine the direction of flares from Very pistols fired by the infantry. Combining the results from different towers/observation posts would give the coordinates of the infantry location, which could then be transmitted to them by radio.

Smoke

The possibilities on the part of the gunners to fire smoke were used in many ways. One method was indicating boundaries between attacking units by firing a smoke screen or a few smoke rounds at certain intervals. Smoke could be fired also in front of the advancing infantry, for instance, to indicate objectives or just a line in the terrain to indicate roughly the position of the advancing unit. More about this later. Firing smoke was dependent on the prevailing weather conditions and could be disturbed by clouds of dust or smoke from burning vehicles. The methods had to be applied with due considerations of possibilities and restraints.

Tracer firing
A very useful method for indicating boundaries between units or the correct direction for their advance was firing of tracer bursts from Bofors guns (40-mm semi-automatic anti-aircraft guns). Often a few rounds or a couple of bursts would be sufficient help to the advancing infantry. When two brigades were attacking in parallel, this method proved to be very helpful when indicating directions but also to keep them apart within the divisional boundaries.

This method as it was here applied in grand style became the norm for the rest of the war when attacks at night took place with large formations.

Creeping artillery fire
A creeping or rolling barrage with artillery fire on line targets shifting forwards at given intervals and fixed distance between the targets was an efficient way of guiding the infantry. At El Alamein, it was decided that barrages were not to be used in general as we will see below, but exceptions were accepted. In the sector for the advance of the New Zealanders, it was decided that one field regiment was to fire a creeping barrage for the purpose of helping the attackers in their navigation on the battlefield, this while all the other field regiments were firing timed concentrations against well located enemy positions.[324] The regiment used for the barrage was also assigned the task to fire smoke when needed.

A smaller version of this method was also utilised by the Scottish division. In the fire plan for this division, a number of 'print out lines' had been included in the fire plan. These were to cover the whole divisional front and were positioned forward of the infantry's pause lines. Smoke rounds were fired for two minutes against these lines just before the planned arrival time of the infantry at the pause lines. When the advance was to be resumed, fire with high explosive shells was released for two minutes along the whole 'print out line'.

Intensive covering fire – but no barrages
In the overall planning of the artillery fire plan, it was decided that the covering fire in assistance of the attacking divisions was not to be fired as barrages. It should instead be planned as timed concentrations against located enemy positions. After opening, the fire was to move forward in pace with the advancing infantry with the aim to neutralise the enemy before the infantry broke in.

The reason for this concept was twofold. One was that the Corps lacked resources for a barrage covering the whole front and the large area to be crossed by the infantry. Each division had a front of around 4km and the final objectives were located about 6km from the start line. The second reason was, as has been indicated previously, the fact that for once a complete knowledge of the location of the enemy positions was in hand. Why then to waste large amounts of precious artillery ammunition on terrain where the enemy had not deployed any soldiers?

The different targets were of course not located symmetrically, which made it necessary to have different length of the fire against them. The time was dependent on the time for the infantry to advance. Ideally, the fire would be lifted when the infantry reached the safety distance. The varying sizes of the targets required different width and depth of the fire.

As the basic conditions regarding the enemy's positions varied between the divisions, it was natural to have them to design and plan their own covering fire. However, the time to commence the attack in Phase I should be the same for all, and the same would apply for Phase II. The advancing pace should also be the same, 100 yards per minute.

Principally the fire plans of the four attacking divisions were about the same even if the targets were of different location, size and character. The timing of fire concentrations thus varied as well. A typical example is the fire plan prepared for the attack by the 51st (Highland) Division. **Map 19-5** illustrates the targets to be engaged, some of them by a battery only, others by one or several regiments. Some were concentrations against the same point; others required a wider and deeper fire pattern as we can see.

The trace is an example as to how all concerned units were informed graphically about the fire plan at large. The different objectives have been indicated on the trace by means of broken lines. The 'print-out-lines' are clearly labelled. All timing data for fire and pauses are given. The final objectives were to be reached at Z+291 minutes in the left sector and at Z+310 minutes on the right. A number of pause lines of 15 minutes duration were planned in order to get it easier for the infantry units to reassemble before proceeding. A gap between the moving fire (100 yards/3 min) and the advancing infantry must be prevented. A related written fire plan gave all the details needed by the guns for all the shifts forward.

In XIII Corps, fire plans were prepared for the different brigade attacks. These often were quite simple and designed for several phases. Some included simple barrages in combination with timed concentrations against targets in the direction of attacks or at the flanks.

21.40 hours on 23 October 1942
At this time the thunder of the guns broke the silence when all the artillery in the northern sector opened fire, see **Map 19-4** and **Map 19-6**. With Montgomery's words: 'We are now ready'. One and a half month of preparations after the second battle at El Alamein was over, and the troops and equipment were in the best order and readiness. The extensive exercises and rehearsals with live ammunition had raised self-confidence. The large deception programme, Operation Bertram, seemed to have worked well. Advancing lanes were in good order; the battle positions were prepared during many nights and were well camouflaged and had now been occupied by their units, ammunition stores were complete etc. The Game could commence. And the attack surprised the enemy.

At the time given above, artillery opened fire from the Mediterranean coast to the Qattara Depression in the South. The sky was illuminated by muzzle flashes and the noise was deafening, everything almost unreal to those present (**Fig. 19-5**). Never had anyone experienced such a violent artillery bombardment during the first years of the war. After three years, the British Army had gained this capability.

The commanding officer of 11 (HAC) Field Regiment RHA who moved forward with his new 'Priests' at the end of one armoured battalion column of the 1st Armoured Division gave later his account of what he experienced this night:[325]

> Waiting in the 'deception' leaguer under no movement orders was hot and boring, but by the early evening of 23rd October we were all set. Peter Thompson Glover (G. Troop) and Tom Butler Stoney (H. Troop) and myself went over to a brief orders at the 9th Lancers and had a quick drink – back to the Battery with orders to move into our positions in the 9th Lancers column at 19.30 hours. Last minute personal preparations, and curious and apprehensive quiet pervaded, still no movement from our 'hides' was permitted for even now a Boche recce plane might put in an appearance – waiting as the sun went down in its usual glorious technicolour came that old hollow feeling in the stomach! Engines were warmed up and as the full moon rose in the cloudless sky, a great orange red ball until it cleared the lower atmosphere, when it and the desert turned silver, the air was filled with the deep throb of the hundreds of diesel engines. The long lines of tanks and guns moved forward towards the start line, an ominous black frieze against the light of the desert. Then above the engine noise came the familiar drone of Boche plane, followed by the whistle and crump as a

Fig. 19-5 The offensive at El Alamein commenced at 21.40 hrs on 23 October 1942 with an unusual, forceful counter-battery artillery program fired by some 400 guns within the sector where the main attack was to take place (Wikimedia)

single bomb was dropped – a suitable reminder this was not a practice run!

As the column advanced we passed battery after battery – guns dug in, piles of ammunition – the gunners resting waiting for Zero hour, many gave us cheery greetings – as we reached the start point it was Zero hour – the moon now high, visibility surprisingly good – the distant blackness erupted in a vast curtain of fire from right to left as far as the eye could see, a thunderous explosion of noise as some 800 guns along the front opened up – the fire plan had started. The middle distance was filled with flickering flashing of the guns, the horizon aglow with small bursts, the glare of searchlights reaching up in cross lines forming 'trig' points for directional aids, Bofors firing on fixed lines streams of tracer marking boundary lines – Brocks famous fireworks were not in it! A halt to top up diesel and petrol, and take off gun covers – so far not a single shell had come from the Boche – the barrage had lifted and it was now bitterly cold as the column started forward again – as a 9th Lancers said '2.0 am is not a time to feel particularly brave!'

As we moved on we could hear the crackle of small arms as the infantry and R.E. Minefield clearing taskforce fought their way through the Boche lines. We passed through our own minefield directed by the Military Police until across the 'neutral' ground we reached the first Boche minefield – the entrance marked with shaded red and green lights and white tapes. Our eyes tired and strained by the dust despite goggles, made out dim shapes of smashed gun pits, tangled wire and minefield Crossbone signs, then a few bedraggled and dazed prisoners – almost no shelling, our counterbattery work had been good!

A detachment, which has experienced hectic work, was the Counter-Battery Officer and his staff. This is how he experienced the start of the offensive:

The whole C.B. Staff take up position on high ground in front of the C.B. Office to watch the labours of the past week put into effect. There was a tenseness and expectancy over the desert but almost instantaneously this was replaced by a shattering roar as the horizon was lit from end to end by the flashes of 372 Field and 48 medium guns all firing C.B. Tasks [in XXX Corps sector].[326]

In the sector where the main attack was launched some 400 guns now opened fire against enemy batteries located earlier. The fire was concentrated in time over these in such a way that a superiority of 20:1 was accomplished if possible, but it should never be less than 10:1.[327]

In the southern sector, the counter-battery fire was commenced ten minutes earlier, i.e. at 10.30 hours, here too by several hundred guns. No medium guns were available there apart from the four French guns.

Ranging was as mentioned not to take place for security reasons. It was still important to do as much as possible to ensure accuracy of the fire. Correct fixation of gun positions and targets was of course important and the required survey must have been performed properly. Availability of good weather data was equally important. This was accomplished by having a medium regiment to fire airbursts one and a half hour before the main opening of fire; the bursts being measured by the surveyors from their observation posts. This gave sufficiently good data to remain valid for a few hours ahead, it was hoped. Met telegrams were then distributed every second hour, sometimes in shorter intervals.

This was very important. Wind conditions on the actual day were such that the fire impact would deviate from the correct position by some 700 yards had not the correct 'Correction of the Moment' been applied.

All fire plans across the two Corps areas were, as we have seen, carefully coordinated in terms of fire intensity and timings. This was new in the Desert War and aimed of course at accomplishing best possible concentration of firepower as Montgomery had requested. Work at command posts was very demanding.

The initial attack – success and setbacks
The four divisions in the North started their offensive at 22.00 hours with great self-confidence. Not least, this was the case at the 51st Highland division under their charismatic commander, Major General Wimberley. He led his division with seven battalion battle groups in parallel. In accordance with their tradition, bagpipers were leading at the front.

Extensive mine-clearing operations had to be undertaken the first night. A large number of passages through own and enemy minefields had to be cleared and marked. White tape and respective green lights were used as guidance along the boundaries of the cleared lanes (**Fig. 19-6**).

Resistance was of varying strength initially, lightest against the Australians in the North and toughest, probably, against the Highland Division. The plan to have all four divisions on their final objectives after five hours did not work completely. Tough fighting through the night and following day was required until all brigades had captured their objectives.

The subsequent armoured attacks caused trouble for Montgomery. The units had difficulties in getting through the minefields, passing the infantry and preparing for the final break-out. Enormous traffic jams and intensive enemy fire were the reasons. Montgomery had to 'push on' the armoured commanders several times during the first night and day and threatened to replace them if they did not follow the initial plan.

During the evening 24 October everything was close to a collapse in the North, which caused Montgomery's Chief of Staff, Brigadier de Guingand, to call the two Corps Commanders, Leese (XXX Corps) and Lumsden (X Corps) to a meeting with Montgomery at 02.30 hours 25 October. This was one of the very few occasions during the war when Montgomery allowed being wakened up from his sleep. He had the habit of going to bed early every day, around 21.30 hours, and normally did not allow

Fig. 19-6 The El Alamein offensive required extensive mine clearing programs resulting in lanes that were well marked day and night on which the attacking infantry and armoured units could pass when attacking enemy positions (©Imperial War Museum E 18617)

anyone to wake him up during the night. But in this situation, de Guingand dared to challenge the rule.

It became a tense meeting during which the Corps Commanders in turn gave their view on the tactical situation and recommended Montgomery stop the advance and withdraw the forward armoured units. After having listened to them, Montgomery stated that the plan was to remain in force, despite the difficulties and losses encountered. He mobilised all the authority he could demonstrate. After the fairly short meeting, he took Lumsden aside; he was the main problem not Leese. Montgomery once again made it clear to Lumsden that he was to be relieved from his command if he did not believe in the plan and hesitated in delivering his part of it.

It has been said that Montgomery became very angry when he learnt that the commander of the 10th Armoured Division, Major General Gatehouse, began to weaken his position and, furthermore, was leading the battle some 10 miles behind the front. At the request from Lumsden, Montgomery called him, and in 'forceful' words ordered him to move up to the front to lead the battle from there.

After the nightly meeting, de Guingand wrote short Minutes, which had three parts (he writes that the meeting took place on 25 October at 02.30 hours):[328]

1. The tactical situation at the time of the conference
2. The Army Commander's view on the situation
3. The tasks of the two Corps

Under the first point, it is noted that the 1st

Fig. 19-7 After the initial attack on 23 October 1942 much fighting remained to maul down German/Italian resistance before the final break-out could take place. Montgomery called it the 'dog-fight'. Here Australians are attacking a German stronghold (Wikimedia)

Armoured Division had got through the minefields whereas 24 and 8 Armoured Brigade from the 10th Armoured Division and 9 Armoured Brigade from the New Zealand Division were struggling to get through. In the south, the 7th Armoured Division (XIII Corps) was moving westwards and had passed minefield 'JANUARY'.

It is also noted in the Minutes, maybe to show some understanding of Lumsden's difficulties, that a new 'element' was heavy attacks by enemy bombers against forward areas and against areas further back as well. These had caused a certain amount of 'disorganisation' in the forward area. Gaps in minefields were also continuously shelled by enemy artillery.

In the second point of the Minutes clear directives are given:

> The Army Commander gave as his opinion that the situation was developing as well as could be expected, and that there was a great need for determination and resolution, and that he was quite decided that the original Army plan of battle should be proceeded with.

After this clear statement the two Corps were given the following orders:

XXX Corps to:
(i) Re-organise and hold the bridgehead gained.
(ii) Operate with N.Z. Division southwestwards from the MITEIRIYA Ridge in accordance with the original Army plan.
(iii) Endeavour to reduce transport in the forward battle area in order to minimize casualties from bombing and shelling.

X Corps to:
(i) Get the armoured divisions clear of the minefield area and out into the open where they can manoeuvre, using whichever gaps are most suitable for the purpose.
(ii) Recce. Find and manoeuvre with a view to destroying the enemy's armoured battle gps.
(iii) Ensure that the NZ Div operations southwest from Miteiriya Ridge are not interfered with enemy armoured action from the west.

The fact that Montgomery at this critical moment did not give way had decisive importance. He had once again shown that final plans and set goals were fixed.

If plans were to be changed, only the Army Commander and no one else could do that.

Once again on the same day, Montgomery met the two Corps commanders, this time at the headquarters of the New Zealand Division and gave new orders.[329]

The 'crumbling' Operations should now be directed towards the north. The 9th Australian Division was to attack towards the coast. The remaining formations of XXX Corps should hold the Miteiriya Ridge firmly, and the New Zealand Division should not try to attack in southwesterly direction.

X Corps with the 1st and 10th Armoured Divisions was still expected to attack westwards and in northwesterly direction from the bridgehead. This attack was to be slightly delayed however. Montgomery ordered all three Corps to patrol actively enemy-held land in order to find out as to whether the enemy had begun to withdraw.

The fighting became hardest in the north and northwest during a week. The Australians managed to extend the bridgehead to the north, although not as far as to the coast (**Fig. 19-7**). It was here the strongest German-Italian counter-attacks had to be met.

An early breakout to the west did not materialise. Instead Montgomery withdrew the New Zealanders and the 1st Armoured Division for rest and recovery in order to later use them in the definite attempt to break out.

In the South, the 7th Armoured Division also failed to break through as had been planned. Various other attacks including diversionary attacks by the 44th and 50th Infantry Division did not improve the situation. XIII Corps was ordered to stop its offensive in order to reduce losses, in particular tanks. Later the 7th Armoured Division was withdrawn for recovery and to become part of the reserve before the final breakout in the North.

Montgomery demonstrated his exceptional leadership by stopping the attempts to breakout to the west as originally planned. When the situation made this impossible he attacked instead northwards with the Australian Division, this without losing the initial goals.

The final breakout was to take place between the German formations in the north and the Italians with Freyberg as the main actor. Besides his own division, he was allotted a brigade from the Scottish division and another from the 50th Infantry Division, the latter being part of XIII Corps.

Fig. 19-8 The Commander of the German Afrika Corps Lieutenant General Wilhelm Ritter von Thoma was taken prisoner on 4 November 1942. Here he is seen when having been brought to Montgomery's headquarters. Over a dinner the two commanders discussed the battle that had just been concluded (AWM No. 014071)

The breakout operation was given the name Operation Supercharge and Montgomery's order for it was given on 30 October 1942. More time was needed for the preparations, so the start was postponed until the night of 1 and 2 November. The attack was supported by a huge artillery concentration. More details about this later.

The fighting raged until 4 November. When the 8th Army finally broke through the German-Italian defence at last and Rommel, who had returned from Germany, ordered full retreat in order to avoid encirclement and annihilation of his remaining forces. The British superiority in equipment and men had made the decisive victory possible.

This day, the British also managed to capture the commander of the *Afrika Korps*, General von Thoma. He was taken to Montgomery's Tactical Headquarters, where he was well received (**Fig. 19-8**).

The two Generals exchanged views on the battle just fought over a dinner, or was it tea and sandwiches? Montgomery later wrote that he found von Thoma being 'a nice chap'.

We will now go back and see how the artillery resources were used during the now concluded battle of El Alamein.

Continuous artillery fire for twelve days

After the initial counter-battery fire and covering fire, the British artillery went on intensively. The medium guns fired almost continuously for the first 20 hours, a demanding performance. Subsequently the fire lessened, but went on the next twelve days. It was a tough undertaking, for the equipment and the gunners.

Teething problems emerged with the new medium guns. In particular the buffer/recuperator mechanisms, which proved to be too weak, were affected. Guns had to be taken out of service for repair. 64 Medium Regiment RA notes in its war diary on 24 October that half of its guns were taken out of service for a certain period.

It was also found that the wearing of barrels was a quicker process than expected. This meant a gradually decreasing muzzle velocity, which in its turn implied reduced range. In several cases rounds dropped too short and landed on advancing friendly troops with casualties as a consequence. This was of course not good for the morale of the troops.

Kirkman made a comment on the problem

in his report after the battle and stressed that calibration of all guns should take place before any major battle and that this should be repeated every third day as long as the battle went on.[330] He also noted that seven out of eight 4.5-inch guns and five out of eight 5.5-inch guns per battery could be used on average during the first 24 hours.

The 25-pounders were affected by technical problems too during the long period of engagement. An interesting comment regarding the need for spare guns is found in the report by the artillery commander of the Australian division, Brigadier Ramsay, who wrote after the battle:

> At the commencement of the engagement on 23 Oct, one 25 pdr was available at No. 1 Rec Sec as a 'pool' for replacement purposes. Another 25 pdr was made available next day from 2/1 AFW. These two guns were of immense value. Between Oct 23 and Nov 3 eighteen (18) 25 pdrs were taken out of the line for various purposes and evacuated beyond LAD's. Only six (6) replacements for these guns were asked for. […] By using the two pool guns to replace guns pulled out for repair (the number rose to three with the return of one repaired gun from Wkshops) there were only two occasions during those operations (one on night Oct 23/24 and one on night Nov 2/3) when the divisional arty did not have all 96 guns in action.
>
> It is most strongly felt that the holding of one gun per regt by a rec sec, to be used as replacement for guns put out of action, is essential if the fire power of the Div Arty is to be kept up during a prolonged engagement.[331]

British attacks and the repulsing of enemy counter-attacks required intensive firing. The gunners were now good masters of the art of concentrating fire quickly and efficiently. Kirkman tells us that in one of the divisions more than 50 regimental concentrations (72 guns) were fired. In addition to these each of the three regiments fired 20–40 regimental concentrations. And the fire came quickly! Kirkman said that it did not take more than 10 minutes to get a divisional concentration onto the target from first order, sometimes not more than 4–5 minutes.[332]

Montgomery wanted to see divisional artillery used as a '72-guns battery' whenever possible. This was what the gunners could deliver! The preparatory training and all exercises during September and October had been a success, not least thanks to Montgomery's support and encouragement. No one wanted to let him down!

In respect of the fairly short range of the 25-pounders, concentrations required quick redeployments forward when the situation demanded this.

The artillery mastered the art of planning and executing huge barrages and timed concentrations. This was demonstrated in particular during the final days of the battle. When the 20th Australian Infantry Brigade attacked during the night between 28 and 29 October, no less than 360 guns supported the brigade, i.e. almost all the artillery of the Corps. When 26 Australian Infantry Brigade continued the divisional attack during the night 30 to 31 October this brigade was also given massive support.[333]

Operation Supercharge was launched under heavy artillery support. A remarkably large rolling barrage covering the whole front, around 4,000m, of the two brigades attacking beside each other was covered, and to about the same depth. The fire was shifted forwards with the speed 100 yards per 2.5 minutes. For this programme that commenced at 01.05 hours on 2 November 1942, eight field regiments were engaged, i.e. 192 guns. But in addition to these, another five field regiments and three medium regiments took part firing on located enemy positions and artillery deployments. Their fire plans included targets also along the flanks of the attacking brigades up to around 2km from the barrage lanes. In summary, this meant that the artillery fire covered a width of around 8km and a depth of 4km! With this huge artillery programme, Freyberg succeeded in reaching all his objectives. But more was needed.

After a few hours break the barrage rolled on another 2km in support of the attacking 9 Armoured Brigade aiming for the Rahman Track. The problem was that a strong anti-tank screen was situated west of the final barrage line target, which in combination with strong enemy artillery fire almost annihilated the brigade (more than 70 of the brigade's 90 tanks were destroyed!).

At the final stage of the operation, two days later, 5 Indian Infantry Brigade attacked in a more southerly direction supported by 270 guns, which resulted in success. The 8th Army was through the enemy positions at last.[334]

Despite the massive artillery employment in connection with the various attacks, the victories were not easy. The losses were significant. The reasons for this can be found in several areas.

First, the British met an opponent who was skilled, experienced and motivated and was well equipped. To destroy such an enemy psychologically was not easy. Secondly, the British had plenty of artillery, but most of the available resources were light guns of small calibre. The 25-pounder was not a gun for destruction of an enemy who had fortified battle positions and strong shelters. The doctrine was that a large number of light shells would keep him neutralised while the attacking infantry advanced. Destruction/annihilation of the enemy units could not be done by the gunners, the infantry had to do this job.

A lesson bitterly learned at El Alamein was that neutralisation of an enemy worked only whilst they were being fired on. The enemy soldiers were up fighting again within a few minutes after it had ceased. This meant that the attacking infantry had to advance as close as possible behind the moving barrage if this was to provide any protection against enemy fire. If the advance were delayed, severe casualties could be the consequence.

A technical detail in this context is the observation that a barrage against line targets normally implied shorter safety distance to the incoming rounds than was the case when the covering fire comprised timed concentrations with a large number of guns firing against the same spot. The random dispersion of shells around the planned point of impact was much larger in the latter case. This meant in its turn that when fire was shifted forward, the infantry had to cover a longer distance before breaking in on the enemy positions. When medium guns were included in the plan for covering fire their longer safety distance had to be taken into account as well.

The problem with neutralising fire and different types of covering fire was to remain a topic for repeated discussions through the war. Different schools of thought existed and prevailed. Freyberg and his artillery commander generally preferred barrages and the New Zealanders proved to be very good at advancing close behind the barrage and remained so through the war, maybe the best example in the British Army.

The British artillery fire had best effect when counter-attacks were to be stopped and held. Quick and violent concentration of firepower from a large number of guns against the wider area, over which the attackers came, could stop even very strong German-Italian counter-attacks. The 25-pounder was superb in such situations and the gunners were now masters of the art.

The British artillery could also have a good effect against the enemy anti-tank screens, as these often were less well protected. The commanders of British tank formations inability, or lack of interest, to take advantage of this possibility caused unnecessary losses, as shown during the last phases of Operation Supercharge'. Interesting in this context is to note what General von Thoma said after his capture. He stated that the final collapse on the German side was due to the fact that British artillery had destroyed 50% of his anti-tank guns.[335]

A general lesson learned at El Alamein was that airbursts should be applied much more than had been the case. But there was as yet a shortage of time fuzes for the 25-pounders. Observation Post Officers often lacked training in control and direction of fire with time fuzes. It was realised that more of these fuzes should be requested now and that training in their best use must be arranged.

The counter-battery programs, which marked the start of the offensive, was another novelty aiming at neutralisation of all located enemy gun positions. Combating enemy artillery systematically with a superiority of up to 20:1 had not been normal practice in the army.

In the northern main attack area, the Axis had 240 field guns, 70 medium guns and 13 heavy to be countered (cf. **Map 19-4**). A problem was that the 25-pounders did not have enough range to reach the medium and heavy guns. This became the task for the fewer medium guns and the RAF.

The shortage of medium and heavy guns made it impossible to destroy all enemy guns. The huge intensity of the British artillery fire led, however, to keeping the German/Italian artillery silent during the night of the main attack and until the morning of the second day of the offensive. Bomber attacks contributed to this during the night.

It has been estimated that some 70–80% of planned German/Italian defensive fire never materialised, which can be seen as a good result of the initial counter-battery programme in the North although this was of short duration – only 15 minutes. Later in the war such programmes would often take several hours to complete.

The intelligence data on which the initial programme was based was extremely good. During the course of the battle available data became of worse quality and the result of counter-battery programmes was thus not as good as during the first night. Best results were obtained when counter-battery fire could be executed quickly after the fixation of gun positions. In some cases this could take place within 3–5 minutes.[336]

When the covering fire had ended and the infantry were at their objectives, it became necessary to fire quickly against pre-planned DF-targets when the counter-attacks came. The FOO/OPOs also had to assist the infantry with fire against emerging opportunity targets. Brigadier Ramsay presents an impression of the situation in his report:[337]

> By 07.00 hrs 26 Oct counter attacks by tanks and inf were being engaged by observed fire from 2/7 and 2/12 Fd Regts. At 08.07 hrs, counter attack was met by firing Div DF Tasks Lorne and Newcastle with two Fd Regts on one, and one Fd and one Med Regt on the other.
> At 09.00 hrs, four Div DFs were fired, 51 Highland Div assisting.
>   At this stage 2/7 Fd Regt was moving one battery at a time to its forward position.
> Numerous heavy enemy attacks on Trig 29 were made throughout the day by both tanks and Inf, and were engaged by both observed fire and Div DF tasks by Div arty and 7 Med Regt RA. One OP team of 2/7 Aust Fd Regt was killed or wounded, the FOO from 7 Med Regt had his line and W/T set knocked out, and at one stage an FOO from 2/12 Aust Fd Regt with his team were the only tps actually on Trig 29. Besides shooting his own Regt, this FOO at 14.30 hrs engaged an enemy attack with 7 Med Regt.

The twelve days of hard fighting implied tough work not only on the part of the fire observers and command posts, but also signallers and those laying telephone lines, ammunition suppliers and others had much to do, day and night. Brigadier Ramsay wrote that the larger attacks carried out by his division required 6–6.5 hours for production of orders. This required good cooperation between commanders and the staffs of supported units. Work at regimental headquarters and battery command posts must also be well organised and be efficient. At the latter detailed fire plans and orders for all guns must be produced within two hours, and this with the usual double-checking of gun data.[338] When large covering fire plans and numerous observed firing were required, they also had to manage harassing fire plans through the night, i.e. fire against targets in the depth.

The skilled divisional artillery commander of the New Zealand Division, Brigadier Steve Weir, who in reality became Corps artillery commander during Operation Supercharge had no time to follow normal procedures with written orders before the operation when the Indian Brigade was to make their final decisive attack on 4th November. He ordered via radio fire against the foremost line for 90 minutes, this with the aim of showing the infantry where the start line was in relation to the terrain. Then he gave the coordinates for the barrage via telephone to all participating regiments, a procedure never applied before. It became one of the first examples of a 'Quick Barrage', a method to be used many times later during the war.[339]

The surveyors, who had contributed so much to the locating of enemy positions the last month before the offensive, would remain active also during the battle when this commenced. The Flash Spotting Troops of the Composite Batteries were fully engaged to fix enemy batteries coming back to life after the initial counter-battery fire when they again opened fire. It was endeavoured to respond on that forcefully and quickly with fire from the medium guns. The observation bases were needed as assistance also to the infantry for fixing their positions. Long bases were moved forward early which was of particular importance in the northern sector.

Sound ranging troops could not, however, be of any real help. The intensive battle noise and the almost continuous firing by own artillery made measurements impossible. In the north it was decided already on 22 October to cancel all further sound ranging activities. It would last until 4 November before sound ranging bases could be employed again.

In the southern sector the situation was different. Here, the sound rangers wanted to try measuring and recording. It was here that trials were made to connect microphones with the evaluation centre via radio links instead of the normal telephone lines. On 23 October 1942 at 13.30 hours the 'S' Troop was ordered to establish such links for measurement in south-westerly direction. The base was ready to measure at 06.00 hours on the following day, 24 October. The results were not good enough: only four batteries were located. The troop was ordered already on 25 October to return to its previous line-based sound ranging base.

But the following day, 26 October, high command wanted them to make another attempt. However, this time they had to cancel their operation the following day, 27 October, due to empty batteries. A new base using telephone lines was established, now closer to the original front line. It was ready to measure at 18.00 hours and remained there until 4 November, but no enemy batteries could be located from this base due to the battle noise. We can see the four bases discussed on **Map 19-7**. It should be noticed that the exact location of the two radio link bases are unknown. The war diaries obviously report wrong locations to some extent. The bases are therefore indicated with broken lines on my map.

Although much now was better as regards the use of the artillery resources, one problem bothering Montgomery and Kirkman remained. The commanders of armoured formations were, as seen above, not interested in coordinating their battle with that of the infantry and artillery (cf. **Fig. 19-2**).

Kirkman included in his report a section where he discussed this problem and stated that the infantry could capture their objectives without large losses when a carefully planned artillery support was implemented, and this without support from tanks. He added: 'Unfortunately no occasion arose when the action of armour was supported by heavy concentrations of artillery fire.'[340]

Kirkman also blamed Lumsden for moving out on the field of battle without taking his artillery commander (CCRA) with him, this also symptomatic. This meant that the CCRA did not know what was going on, and could not advise on how best the artillery could support the armoured formations. When Montgomery heard of this, he immediately ordered Lumsden to take his artillery commander forward and start cooperating with him.

Montgomery also wrote in his diary about the problem with lacking all-arms cooperation: '…there is no doubt these RAC Generals do not understand the cooperation of all arms in battle. I have had many examples of this since the battle started.'[341]

What about 'simplicity'?

As we recall, Jack Parham had stubbornly insisted that the employment of artillery must be characterised by simplicity, both as regards tactics and technical procedures. What about that at El Alamein? Well, the question is best answered by both 'yes' and 'no'.

Large barrages with a simple configuration with straight lanes and right angles to these can be said to meet the criteria of 'simplicity'. Large concentrations with regiments, and predicted concentrated fire with all the divisional artillery, could quickly be planned and implemented, as they were not complicated.

The covering fire plans implemented at the beginning of the offensive were, on the other hand, very complex. They included a very large number of targets of varying width and depth that would be engaged at very varying length of time, and this sometimes with regiments, sometimes with batteries and even single troops. Such plans cannot be said to represent 'simplicity'.

Most complicated were the fire plans for units whose fire over-lapped the barrages, either against targets in the same area, as the barrage was to proceed over, or along the flanks of the advancing infantry. As an example, we may look at the fire plan prepared by one of the Australian field regiments, which together with four other field regiments and three medium regiments were to fire such overlapping fire in Operation Supercharge.

The plan was prepared for 2/7 Australian Field Regiment RAA and all the others fired in a similar way during the nearly three hours (165 minute) during which the attack went forward.[342] The fire plan is summarised graphically on **Map 19-8**. We can see that the firing included troop, battery and regimental targets. The targets were dispersed over a large area, and the firing was to vary much in time. As seen, a few barrages were also part of the plan and these were to be executed at two different times. And to make life even more difficult for the command post, one of the targets was to cover a circular target area with the radius 400 m!

But this was not enough. Most of the targets

were to be engaged with varying intensity, and the impact area was to be modified by changes of line and range by the guns (the command was for instance 'sweep 10' and/or 'search 100 yards'). For some targets, the plan called for one gun per troop to fire smoke rounds, which required these guns to be laid differently compared with the other three guns of the troop. So, farther from 'simplicity' one could not come!

A special problem was all the DF tasks to be prepared around captured objectives. This had sometimes to be quickly improvised. Simplicity was then a must, but at the time of the offensive, good methods for this had not yet been introduced.

DF targets/tasks were recorded as rectangles and each corner had to be fixed with coordinates in twelve digits. This at concerned field and medium regiments, and the latter must register points of impact a bit further away from the infantry positions due to longer safety distance. Batteries and troops had to disperse the fire such that the whole rectangle was covered. All the calculations were time consuming; in particular as meticulous controls should be done in order to make sure that no shells fell on friendly troops.

At El Alamein a new procedure for handling of DF tasks was invented, the 'Stonk'. The idea was to record the position of a DF target with one coordinate only, and by a bearing order the direction of the rectangle. The fire was to cover a length of 1,000 yards and a depth of around 200 yards.

Different units had initially their own size of a 'Stonk', but this was standardised in 1943. A regimental 'Stonk' should thereafter have a length of 525 yards and a depth given by the natural dispersion. This meant that two batteries would have their fire beside each other and that of the third battery was to be superimposed over the whole length of the 'Stonk'. The direction of it was now to be at right angle of the direction ordered. At El Alamein, the rectangle was still to be oriented in line with the ordered bearing.

Many lessons were certainly learned at El Alamein as to how procedures could be made simpler and implementation speeded up.

One million shells

Contrary to their opponents the British had an almost unlimited supply of artillery ammunition. This does not mean, however, that supply problems would not happen in given tactical situations. Difficulties in transporting ammunition due to terrain conditions and enemy shelling could severely hamper the supply. Such interference made it necessary during the first two days of the El Alamein offensive to limit consumption in the central and southern sectors to 40 rounds per gun per day and give priority to the northern

Fig. 19-9 More than one million cartridge cases had to be taken care of after the extensive firing by the 25-pounder guns during the twelve days long battle at El Alamein (©Imperial War Museum E 19077)

sector.[343]

The field regiments fired an average for all three Corps of 317 rounds per gun during the first 24 hours. In XXX Corps area, where the main attack was launched, the consumption was as high as 577 rounds per gun as shown in Kirkman's report, **Appendix 3**.[344] The consumption went down during the following days, but on 2 November (during Operation Supercharge) the artillery of X Corps fired on average 309 rounds per gun and their colleagues in XXX Corps 314 rounds per gun.

Looking at the whole period, the 25-pounders of X Corps fired on average 87 rounds per gun and day. XIII Corps artillery fired 48 rounds per gun and day on average, whereas the guns of XXX Corps fired 159 rounds per gun and day. As an average for all 25-pounders of 8th Army, in total 832 guns, 102 rounds per gun and day were fired. In total the 8th Army artillery fired about one million rounds during the 12 days the offensive lasted. A lot to handle! Firing a large amount of ammunition also required many cartridge cases to be retrieved as salvage (**Fig. 19-9**).

The medium guns fired a large number of shells too. The war diary of 64 Medium Regiment RA says that the regiment fired 4,844 rounds up to 15.00 hours on 24 October, which equates to approximately 303 rounds per gun. The consumption then decreased, not only due to the course of the battle as such, but also due to technical problems that affected many of the guns. Kirkman tells us that despite such problems the 4.5-inch guns fired on average 133 rounds per gun and day during the twelve days and the 5.5-inch guns 157 rounds per gun and day.

Summary of the role of artillery at the last battle of El Alamein

- The British had superiority over Rommel in tanks and artillery, about 2–3:1. Looking at technical performance and quality, the balance was probably a bit more even, if not to say to the advantage to the Germans and Italians.
- The rearmament of the British divisional artillery to 25-pounders was complete. Several field regiments could not, however, be provided with guns for more than two batteries instead of the nominal three. A shortage of SP guns for the armoured divisions had not been completely eliminated.
- A large shortage of artillery for reinforcement, i.e. medium and heavy guns, prevailed through the offensive. This hampered an effective counter-battery bombardment in the depth. Neither could the 25-pounders firing covering fire during the main attacks be reinforced by such artillery, as was to become normal practice later in the war. It was difficult here to combat enemy tanks with artillery except when these had stopped for re-supply of fuel and ammunition etc.
- A distinct drawback was that the new guns, in particular the medium guns, proved to suffer from various teething problems. These were first discovered at El Alamein as a consequence of the intensive and long firing required. Thanks to an efficient repair organisation the consequences of these failures could be reduced.
- Suggestions began to emerge that the 5.5-inch gun should use a lighter shell than the 100lb shell. An 80lb shell would reduce the mechanical strain and at the same time add to the maximum range by 2km. The matter was under discussion into 1943, when the definite decision was made to introduce this lighter shell.
- Strategically, there was no shortage of artillery ammunition, a situation that prevailed through the whole war. This was a distinct advantage on the part of the British over the German/Italian forces that suffered from shortages of most types of supply. This favourable situation did not exclude tactical situations where the British artillery encountered a shortage of ammunition for some time.
- The available artillery resources were used efficiently. Concentration of firepower was now an art well within the capability of the British gunners. Whatever the targets were, they could be covered with fire from hundreds of guns within a short time from order. This could be pre-planned engagements or just be improvised at a given moment, for instance as observed fire to support an attack or to meet an enemy counter-attack. The British benefited in this context from their doctrine that 'Command', i.e. how tactically to use the resources, should be centralised to the highest possible level, whereas 'Control',

- i.e. technical employment of fire, should be decentralised to the lowest possible level. The foundation laid by Kirkman and Parham in 1941 proved now its worth (cf. the huge Exercise *Bumper* in England in October 1941).
- El Alamein marked a new trend for the British artillery. It might even be correct to talk about a paradigm shift. But much work remained in order to get all concerned to understand the implications and how best to employ artillery, not least the many commanders of infantry and armoured units. Time for necessary all-arms training had so far been too limited. The consequence at El Alamein and later was that the artillery as a vital resource was not used as best as it could, and the price for this proved to be high. The problem diminished gradually but deficiencies remained throughout the war.
- Cooperation between the Army and the Royal Air Force developed favourably at El Alamein. The result of this can be seen as a final change of an earlier trend. But resources still lacking for Montgomery were army-cooperation aircraft for reconnaissance and observation and direction of artillery fire at depth. He had not yet received any AOPs equipped with Auster aircraft.
- The efficient acquisition of intelligence data was to the credit of 4 Survey Regiment RA. This was much due to the new organisation with 'Composite Batteries', initiated by the regimental commander Lieutenant Colonel Whetton. Best results were obtained from 'Long Bases' established by the Flash Spotting Troops of these batteries. They were effective also when the offensive had commenced, whereas sound ranging bases could not work at that stage, due to the battle noise. Beforehand they had, however, been most useful.
- The British were very skilled throughout the war to implement large deception plans. El Alamein is a good example of what could be accomplished by creative and interested officers and men. All attack preparations were efficiently concealed. They were performed in the dark. All artillery positions including dumping of large amounts of artillery ammunition were for instance prepared during the nights before the offensive commenced. Everything was well camouflaged before the dawn. This made it possible to keep the immense concentration of firepower concealed, which was a prerequisite for success during the offensive.
- Another feature of the deception plan was to arrange deception attacks under participation of artillery, which was an effective means for binding enemy armoured reserves. This was not part of the overall plan in the northern sector, but one might see the whole operation in the south by XIII Corps as a series of deceptive attacks under artillery participation.
- The massive, and at the same time flexible, employment of the large artillery resources at El Alamein had not been possible without well-functioning communication systems, both telephone networks and radio systems with several different types of wireless sets being used. The necessary equipment was in place as were well-trained signallers. And without these and adequate traffic procedures and observation of strict traffic discipline when using the communication resources, the course of the battle most likely could have ended in disaster. The high standard was a result of innumerable exercises, a need of which that was never overlooked by the Royal Artillery.

A large-scale frontal attack as conducted by Montgomery at El Alamein had not been possible without the massive artillery support that the Royal Artillery now could deliver. Neither the following battles of attrition, 'the dog fights' in Montgomery's terminology, in which the British had to meet countless heavy decisive counter attacks launched by Rommel's forces, had been possible to bring to a victorious end without the artillery resources being employed skilfully.

Those stating that the Royal Artillery from El Alamein onwards was a 'Battle Winner', have a good point. The previous poor deployment and use of artillery had finally been ended.

20. A New Front is Opened – Normandy

Rarely has a single human been under such pressure as the allied Commander-in-Chief, General Eisenhower, was during the morning hours on 5 June 1944. At least when one is looking at the consequences of the decision he had to make. As we know, the decision was 'We will sail tomorrow'! [de Guingand, but other sources have other versions] The invasion in Normandy was to be launched on 6 June. The bad weather during the past few days would improve a little during that day. All preparations were finished, troops had been loaded on-board the transport ships, naval ships and air forces were ready to go since one day back.

Beginning at dawn the landings were to take place at two American sectors, Utah and Omaha, and three British-Canadian, Gold, Juno and Sword. Three infantry divisions were to land in the western American sectors and three also in the eastern British-Canadian sectors. These landings were to be preceded by the landing of two American airborne divisions on the western flank and one British on the eastern. They were to seal off the main landing area and by that impede German attempts for early counter-attacks. We can see the operation area at large on **Map 20-1**, where the planned extension of the bridgehead at some dates is indicated.

The American divisions were part of the 1st US Army under General Bradley and the British-Canadian part of the 2nd British Army under General Dempsey. The armies constituted together 21st Army Group commanded by General Montgomery.

To make the operation a success, a logistic planning was required that might be the most demanding and extensive one humanity ever had experienced then and later. And to make the plan work, a most skilled transport management must be at hand, as well as prepared and trained units of all kinds.

The presentation of the battle of Normandy now following is limited to the British sector.

Preceding bombardment – the task of the navies and air forces

An extensive bombardment was to precede the landings aiming at the destruction or neutralisation of known coast artillery batteries and field artillery deployments. Another aim was destruction of fortified beach defence positions. Hence, it was the 'Atlantic Wall' that was the objective. The programme started months before the D-Day and was coordinated with extensive bombings further to the east and north for deception purposes. The day before the landings, the bombardments near the landing beaches were intensified and just a few hours before the first landings, the Royal Navy commenced an intensive bombardment.

Thirteen ships were engaged in the British-Canadian sector with its three landing zones. We summarise the number of guns of different calibres of these ships:[345]

1 Monitor	2 x 38 cm (2 x 15 inch)
2 Battle Ships	16 x 38 cm, 20 x 15.2 cm, 16 x 10.2 cm (16 x 15, 20 x 6, 16 x 4 inch)
1 Heavy Cruiser	7 x 19 cm, 9 x 10.2 cm (7 x 7.5, 9 x 4 inch)
1 Dutch Gun Vessel	3 x 15 cm (3 x 5.9 inch)
A strong reserve was available:	
1 Battle Ship	9 x 40.6 cm, 12 x 15.2 cm, 6 x 12 cm (9 x 16, 12 x 6, 6 x 4.7 inch)
1 Monitor	2 x 38 cm, 8 x 10.2 cm (2 x 15, 8 x 4 inch)

If we group all these guns in accordance with land artillery principles we can see that the Royal Navy made available the following resources for the preceding bombardment and later direct support:

Light artillery (cf. divisional artillery)	93 pieces
Medium artillery	24 pieces
Heavy artillery	93 pieces
Super Heavy artillery	29 pieces

The total number of guns, 239, can be compared with the artillery resources normally being available to a Corps, which were 300–350 guns.

The air attacks began when the airborne troops had commenced their landings at 01.30 hours and continued until dawn when the naval ships took over from positions outside the landing beaches at 05.00–05.30 hours. Their bombardment covered the transport of assault units towards the beaches and was aimed at continued destruction and neutralisation of artillery that could fire at the transport ships and all landing craft. Initially observation and control of this fire was the task of RAF Army-Cooperation Squadrons. As soon as possible direct fire control was to be taken over by landed Observation Parties, Forward Bombardment Observers (FBO). These parties could communicate directly with the artillery ships but also with artillery commanders of landed infantry units.

The detailed planning of the artillery programme preceding the landings was the responsibility of the artillery headquarters of the 2nd British Army. The artillery commander of this army was Jack Parham, who afterwards expressed how strange it was to have an artillery headquarters at this high level to prepare detailed fire orders for the participating ships and air force units. But…Operation Overlord was certainly not an ordinary type of operation!

In the British-Canadian landing zones, the first units were to disembark their landing craft at 07.25 hours on D-Day, 6 June 1944. Before this, disembarkation of transport ships into the small landing craft and their ranging was a time-consuming process. Upon this followed the rush towards the beaches, in all 3–4 hours were required for the whole process, a very tough and demanding time for the infantry in the dark, and exposed to heavy sea as they were.

The final phase of covering bombardment in the British-Canadian sector was made by 37 destroyers moving at the flanks of the columns of landing craft and firing continuously at the beach defences. The fire from guns on-board the landing craft themselves, must also be mentioned. We will come back to that below (**Fig. 20-1**).

Fig. 20-1 Destroyers of the Hunt Class moving towards the Normandy beaches on the flanks of the invading forces fired continuously towards targets near the beaches (RAHT)

Large amounts of artillery landed

At Gold beach, XXX Corps was to land the 50th (Northumbrian) Infantry Division. At Juno beach, I Corps was to land the 3rd Canadian Infantry Division and at Sword beach the 3rd British Infantry Division. The two former divisions were each to land two brigade groups beside each other, the latter one brigade group. The three divisions were reinforced with one armoured brigade each and some special additional units for clearing the beaches close to the German beach defence positions including mines. Special attacks were also planned for some brigade groups with Commando units from the Royal Marines and army commandos. These units were among the first to land on D-Day (see **Map 20-2**).

It was important to get much artillery on shore the first day. It was deemed difficult to land the normal divisional artillery under the chaotic conditions expected, i.e. towed 25-pounders. It was therefore decided that only SP guns should be landed during the first eight hours. This meant that the divisions had to exchange on a temporary basis their normal regiments with towed guns to such with SP guns. The grouping thus became as illustrated on **Map 20-3**:

50th (Northumbrian) Infantry Division
    86 Field Regiment RA, 90 Field Regiment RA and 147 Field Regiment RHA
3rd Canadian Infantry Division
    12 Field Regiment RCA, 13 Field Regiment RCA, 14 Field Regiment RCA and 19 Field Regiment RCA
3rd British Infantry Division
    7 Field Regiment RA, 33 Field Regiment RA and 76 Field Regiment RA

The three first mentioned regiments had 'Sexton' SP guns (25-pounders) and all the others 'Priest' SP guns (105-mm).

Rearmament of British regiments to 'Sextons' of all regiments with SP guns had been commenced before the D-Day and was to continue during the summer and autumn 1944. But some of the regiments above were to get towed 25-pounders instead of their 'Priests' later during the summer, i.e. back to normal practice for the divisional artillery of infantry divisions. This change was to take place when the 'Priest' ammunition allotted for the invasion and the subsequent battle of Normandy had been consumed. Their 'Priests' were then to be stripped of their guns and become open tracked vehicles for transport of infantry; they were thereafter called 'Kangaroos'. That process started at the end of July 1944.

Besides the field regiments, 5 AGRA, which supported XXX Corps, was to land an American battalion, which had been placed under command of this AGRA.[346] The artillery plan called also for landing of a first medium regiment with towed 5.5-inch guns late on D-Day. It was 53 Medium Regiment RA that belonged to 4 AGRA, which was in support of I Corps. The American battalion and the British medium regiment were to be followed by other units from these AGRAs during the subsequent days.

A special artillery resource, also landed during the first day of the operation, was the Royal Marines Armoured Support Group. It comprised 1 Royal Marines Armoured Regiment under command of XXX Corps and 2 Royal Marines Armoured Regiment allotted to 1 Corps. To the latter was attached an independent battery, 5 Independent Royal Marines Armoured Battery.

This support group was equipped with 80 Centaur tanks armed with a 95mm howitzer divided into 20 troops of the group's five batteries. Twenty Sherman tanks used as command posts were included. The batteries were to be used for direct support of the Commando units and had no observation parties for indirect fire. They could, however, link up with field regiments and participate in indirect fire to some extent that way. See **Fig. 20-2**.

If we include the Centaur guns no less than 352 SP guns were to be landed during D-Day up to the late afternoon, indeed a remarkable resource and an impressive achievement.

These were the guns landed from the sea, but we will also note that another unit came by air. The 6th Airborne Division had a light regiment attached, 53 Air-Landing Light Regiment RA. This was trained for transport to the battlefield in Horsa gliders. But a significant shortage of such gliders still existed which made it impossible to transport more than one of the regiment's three batteries to Normandy on D-Day, i.e. only 8 guns were landed.

The latter resource was of course not sufficient for support of the whole airborne division.

Hence, it was planned to take advantage of the three field regiments of the 3rd Division as reinforcement as these were to be landed the first day. From their initial deployment just inside Sword beach, these regiments would be able to protect the bridgehead of the airborne division against counter-attacks from the East and South. In order to facilitate this kind of support efficiently, extra observation and liaison resources had to be provided for the airborne division. A unique fire observation unit was therefore organised in haste, 2 Forward Observation Unit (FOU). FOPs could be allotted to all airborne brigades from that unit. They could communicate with liaison detachments at the field regiments of the 3rd Division by means of wireless sets. 76 Field Regiment RA was the regiment to give support first to the 'Red Berets' under this arrangement. This organisational model was to be applied for other airborne operations later as we will see.

To further increase opportunities for efficient observation and control of artillery fire it was an endeavour to fly AOPs from England to Normandy as early as simple landing strips had been secured. It was hoped that this could take place on D-Day and that each Corps would have a minimum resource of at least one Flight, i.e. four Auster aircraft. Observation of fire from ground OPs was not easy due to the terrain and dense vegetation, in particular hedges. Counter-bombardment against enemy artillery and mortars would thus be severely hampered without the AOPs. As things developed, the first Austers arrived on D + 2.

It is to be noted that the artillery intelligence resources, 'sound rangers' and 'flash spotters', had to wait for the bridgehead to become enlarged after a couple of days' fighting, before they could be deployed. Survey into a theatre grid for landed batteries was, however, given high priority and the first surveyors went ashore about one and a half hour after those soldiers landing first. Another priority task for them was to provide Landing Craft Guns with necessary survey data when running towards the beaches.

The surveyors could avail themselves of a large number of easily identifiable 'Trig Points'.[347] The British soon got access also to a German grid covering the whole of Normandy, which could be used as a 'theatre grid'. Fixation of bearings was initially done by measurement against the sun.

'Flash Spotting Troops' and 'Sound Ranging Troops' were landed gradually during the first two weeks.[348] A first 'Short Base' was established by 4 Survey Regiment RA near the village St. Leger at the road between Caen and Bayeux on D+2 already. A few days later a first 'Long Base' with four observation posts was established. The first 'Sound Ranging Base' was in action from 10 June.[349]

Now back to the landings on D-Day.

Fig. 20-2 One of the 80 Centaur tanks equipped with a 95-mm howitzer that were landed for direct support of the Commando formations and the infantry divisions. Occasionally they were attached to Field Regiments as reinforcement; the Marine Support Formations, to which they belonged, lacked own resources for observation and control of indirect artillery fire. Note the ammunition sledge which all landed SP guns towed when landing on the beaches (Wikimedia)

Covering fire after the initial bombardment
When the assault troops moved towards the beaches a violent and sustained covering fire was needed. Several resources were available for this kind of support. We have mentioned already the destroyers of the Royal Navy moving in parallel with columns of landing craft continuously firing until around 2,000 yards from the beaches. A brigade group in their landing craft covered an area with a depth of around 10,000 yards outside the beach. In the columns were armed landing craft, designated Landing Craft Gun (LCG), of different types and with different types of gun. They were moving in the middle of the columns where also the assault troops were in their landing craft.

Further back, a few landing craft with rocket launchers were deployed. They could each fire about 1,000 rockets against targets just beyond the shores. The rocket salvoes were not very accurate and the impact dispersions were quite big, so their importance was thus more psychological – for both sides!

Towards the end of the columns came the 'Priest' and 'Sexton' SP guns of the field regiments. As we have seen, ten regiments equipped with these guns were to land on D-Day. They had trained during the winter for firing from their landing craft, Landing Craft Tank (LCT), against beach defences. That was known as a 'run-in-shoot'; it was planned to begin around 10,000 yards from the beaches and continue until the guns were around 2,000-3,000 yards from the beach. In order to make this possible, a smaller boat with radar fixed the starting range and line of fire. Based on this data and a fixed speed of 6 knots, the LCT captain had to move towards the beach. By using a special timepiece, artillery officers then ordered change of the firing range (elevation) every, say, 200 yards.

How were the guns and ammunition transported to make this type of shooting possible? The allotted landing craft, 'LCTs', were big enough to transport a troop, i.e. four guns, and a few tanks or half-tracks for observation parties and command post personnel (**Fig. 20-3**).

Two guns were placed towards the bow beside each other, and then came the tanks and/or half-tracks and maybe a couple of jeeps, then the two remaining guns. With this arrangement the latter could fire over the former.

Fig. 20-3 During the D-Day only self-propelled guns were landed. They were transported troop-wise on tank landing crafts (LCT) with the guns on deck two by two. The rear pair of guns fired over the forward pair during the advance towards the shore. This firing by the four guns was known as 'run-in-shoot' which commenced around 6–7 miles from the shore and continued until they were a bit more than a mile from the shore. This technique had been much tested in exercises at home (Painting by David Rowland for RAI, RAHT Collection)

For the battle on shore, the guns brought 300 rounds each. Some of these were carried on a towed sledge, called 'porpoises' (cf. **Fig. 20-2**). For the 'run-in-shoot' 200 additional rounds were provided for each gun.[350] All the ammunition was not to be consumed; a reasonable reserve stock was to be kept. It was planned that each regiment would fire around 1,800 rounds, i.e. 75 rounds per gun.

This special type of firing was not done blindly. At the front of each brigade group, a group of small support boats moved. On-board one of these followed a battery commander from one of the field regiments to be landed who could observe the fall of shots. With radio communication, he could to some extent correct the firing when needed. Many indications seem to prove, however, that the material effect of the 'run-in-shoot' was limited. On the other hand, many accounts suggest that the assault troops experienced the fire psychologically very positive. Certainly the fire here and there had good neutralising effect on enemy soldiers in open positions.

An officer who wrote down his account of this type of firing was Lieutenant Sidney Beck, who served with 341 Battery, 86 Field Regiment RA. An extract from his excellent account may illustrate how it was to approach the beach while firing this morning in June 1944. Besides, we will come back to him several times later in the book. But now Normandy:[351]

> Reveille on the L.S.I.s was 0230. Breakfast at 0300 on eggs and bacon. In the bowels of the ship, lit only by weak orange lights, sleepy soldiers loaded into L.C.As. At 0345 the tiny L.C.As were lowered in the darkness into a vicious sea, which tossed the 25-foot craft about like corks. A Tp O.P. party set off independently in their L.C.S. to position themselves to observe the run in shoot. B Tp O.P. party continued with the leading company of the 7 Green Howards. It was a 7-mile journey to the Normandy coast – a three-hour journey of acute abdominal discomfort to one and all.
>
> On board the L.C.Ts the long uncomfortable night came to an end at 04.30 when preparations were begun for run-in-shoot. Blankets stowed away, a hasty breakfast snatched by those who felt capable of eating, ammunition prepared and guns checked. Wireless silence which had been maintained for more than 10 days was broken at 0530 assets were switched on and communications checked. By now it was light enough to see the most amazing sight. The sea was literally alive with ships of all shapes and sizes as far as the eye could see. Just ahead were the small L.C.As of the 7 Green Howards and on either side were long lines of DUKWs, all heading in the same direction, all intent on the strip of beach still out of sight. The run-in-shoot began at 0645 hrs while the L.C.Ts carrying our guns were still 7 miles from the coast. It was the signal also for the Navy to open up. Fast destroyers raced past the L.C.Ts firing their guns at the coast and even drowning the noise of our own guns.
>
> H hour, the time for the first troops to set foot on the beaches was 0720. As the L.C. As approached the coast they were greeted by spasmodic fire from the German coast defence battery of 150-mm guns at Mont Fleury and the rattle of Spandaus. A great pall of smoke drifted along the coast line, the remains of the smoke screen laid by our aircraft and the smoke from the burning buildings from the bombardment and bombing.
>
> A few L.C.As were seen to go up on mines but the majority picked their way through the mines to land safely. As the L.C.As ran the last 1,000 yards to the beach the Regiments guns, still firing from the L.C.Ts and doing great work on the causeway, shifted their attention to the lighthouse area.
>
> The 7 Green Howards landed at 0750, ahead of schedule. Their first objective was the capture of the Mont Fleury battery, which dominated the coast. Although they landed on the wrong beach, B Tp O.P. party, after trudging across the sand, joined up with the attacking Company and pushed towards the enemy Battery.
>
> Meanwhile the L.C.Ts carrying the Regiments guns were steaming up and down off the coast waiting for their turn to beach. The three craft carrying A, C & T Tps beached first. A Tp went into action immediately on the narrow strip of beach with water lapping round their tracks. Enemy infantry and tanks were worrying the 7 Green Howards attacking the Mont Fleury Battery. The fire of the guns was directed on to the enemy by Capt Perry and Capt Greig (an F.O.O. attached to the Battery for the operation). With this support the Green Howards rushed and overpowered the enemy battery, the enemy gunners being demoralized by the very heavy

bombing and naval bombardment during the assault.

By this time (0845) the second half of the Regiment were due to land. It was getting difficult to find a clear spot on the beach. The strong wind and tide had made the first boats ground almost sideways to the coast instead of head on and far too much of the beach was covered by ships' sides. Also boats which should have pulled away after unloading had been damaged or stuck and the beach was fast becoming jammed.

The regiments came ashore and were immediately engaged in the fighting beyond the beaches. At the beginning, it was a matter of support of battalion and company attacks by single troops or a battery; soon enough also support with divisional artillery concentrations. As far as Beck's regiment was concerned, this happened the first time on 9 June when an important road junction was the target. And it was reported on 12 June already that 'Victor' targets were engaged, i.e. concentrated fire by all available artillery of a Corps. This took place when heavy German counter-attacks were to be met in particular. Sometimes fire was opened before the attack was staged and the enemy was forming up his forces for the attack, i.e. 'Counter Preparation Fire' as it was called.

Now, how was the build-up of artillery resources at the beachhead organised?

Continuous landing of artillery resources

As we have seen much artillery came ashore already on D-Day despite the chaotic conditions on the beaches and much more was to follow. The artillery headquarters of 2 Army had under Jack Parham planned in detail how the further build-up of resources was to take place. We can from this plan get a view graphically as to how field, medium and heavy guns would be available in Normandy during the first month (**Fig. 20-4**).

It is noted that after two weeks already, the total number of guns was well over 1,000; anti-tank and anti-aircraft guns excluded. The further increase was mainly medium and heavy guns. It should also be noted that a continuous inflow of anti-tank and anti-aircraft guns had also been organised for the first six weeks. Many heavy anti-aircraft guns were later to be used more for ground tasks than against aircraft.

According to the plan, all artillery for twelve divisions of I, VIII, XII and XXX Corps would be available in Normandy on D+17. Each Corps was reinforced by an AGRA. Around D+30, XII Corps was to get a second AGRA. Even more artillery was later provided in the bridgehead when the II Canadian Corps had landed.

The AOP Squadrons would, as we have seen, be redeployed to Normandy from England as soon as possible. Within two weeks, all would be available according to the plan. A similar plan was applied for intelligence resources. They were all in action after about two weeks.

In this context we must remember all mortars that were brought ashore. The largest ones were the 4.2-inch mortars, the fire of which now preferably was coordinated with that of the artillery (**Fig. 20-5**).

These were the plans made by Jack Parham and his staff.[352] But the situation and how it changed made certain adaptations necessary. The severe gale around 20 June made landing of artillery units impossible during the period 20–24 June. Among those affected were three regiments of the 43rd (Wessex) Infantry Division, which had to wait outside the beaches these days in the very rough sea. With mines drifting around, it was not only the stormy weather as such that made the waiting extremely

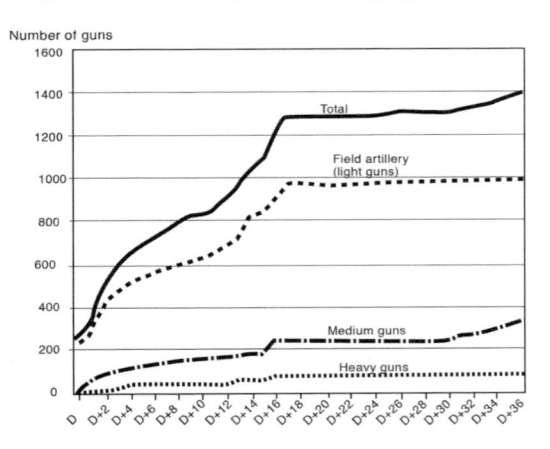

Fig. 20-4 The planned build-up of artillery resources for 2 British Army in Normandy shown for different types of artillery formation. The divisions landed the first day should be complete with divisional artillery already this first day. Within about two weeks the army should have enough artillery on shore for attacks by one or several Corps. 'Field Regiments' basically means 25-pounders and self-propelled guns with 105-mm howitzers (Author, data have been compiled from RAHT Collection MD/185)

Fig. 20-5 Besides all guns brought ashore in Normandy the British also used a large number of 4.2-inch mortars, the fire of which often was well coordinated with the artillery (RAHT)

tough (the troop carrier, on-board which the division's 'Recce' battalion was waiting for landing, was hit by a mine and went down with hundreds of men being drowned).

Another problem with the storm was that supply transports to the troops already deployed in the bridgehead must be halted, a consequence of which was an acute shortage of artillery ammunition during a few critical days.

Consolidation and enlargement of the bridgehead

The overall objective was to bring as strong resources into Normandy as were needed for a breakout that would be the initial phase of the dash into Germany. This could, however, not be accomplished unless supply problems were eliminated. Besides supply lines over the beaches and artificial harbour facilities, a large harbour with capacity to accommodate ocean-going ships was needed. The harbour selected was Cherbourg and the task to capture it and restore its capacity was assigned to the Americans. This in its turn required capture of the entire Cotentin Peninsula in the West.

While the Americans pressed for Cherbourg and eventually a breakout to the South, the British and Canadians had to consolidate their sector of the bridgehead and enlarge it gradually. Of particular importance was capture of Caen, which was hoped to be achieved late on D-Day. This plan failed and it would take a month before the city fell into the hands of the Allies. Before that, it had been bombed to ruins by an armada of strategic bombers killing more than 2,000 civilians. The bombing made it more difficult rather than easier for the Allies to push the Germans out of the city. The operation has since then been heavily criticised, not the least in France, where bitterness has remained to this day.

Montgomery's plan was to bind as much as possible of the German armoured reserves by actively attacking the German lines. Repeated offensives would facilitate an early breakout in the American sector, he thought.

Initially the resources were limited and allowed only minor offensives at brigade and battalion levels, but after two weeks from D-Day, offensives at divisional and even Corps levels were possible to launch. As we have seen, artillery resources strong enough for such operations were at hand. Initially, the main offensive was Operation Epsom and its successor Operation Jupiter. The objective was the capture of 'Hill 112' and the high ground between the rivers Orne and Odon southwest of Caen from which a large area to the South and Southwest could be observed. Another important operation was Operation Charnwood, the objective of which was to capture Caen after the bombers had done their part. After these came one of the most important operations, Operation Goodwood, which would facilitate an American break-out by enlarging the bridgehead south of Caen and also binding as much as possible of German armoured resources. After this followed several sub-operations before the battle of Normandy was over. An overview of the various operations and their locations and dates for execution is given by **Map 20-4**.

Operation Epsom was postponed several days due to the heavy storm of the 20–24 June, which delayed the landings of the 43rd (Wessex) Division, which was scheduled for this operation. Overall responsibility had been given to VIII Corps. The operation was finally launched on 26 June with the 15th (Scottish) Division in the lead. The division had the 11th Armoured Division behind. The intention was to grab, in several phases, terrain west and south of Caen. At the same time I Corps was to launch a smaller attack as the pincer of the operation around Caen. In Phase I, the 11th Armoured Division was planned to seize a bridgehead across river Odon, the westernmost river southwest of Caen.

When the first part of the attack had taken place, the 15th Division were to be replaced by the 43rd (Wessex) Division with the task of consolidating captured terrain.

The night before the operation, 25 June, an attack aiming at protection of the right Corps flank was launched by the 49th (Riding) Division of XXX Corps.

It has been stated that this massive operation by VIII Corps involved more than 180,000 troops.[353] At the disposal of the Corps Commander were 700 guns. Some 400 of these were from his own artillery units, whereas the rest came from I Corps east of Caen and XXX Corps operating west of VIII Corps.

This is not the place where the course of the battle will be presented in detail. We may, however, note that the massive artillery engagement started off with a barrage moving slowly forward over a front 3km wide. The battle became an extremely hard business and it turned out to be impossible to extend the bridgehead to river Odon as planned, except temporarily. The so important 'Hill 112' was captured, but the Germans managed to recapture it in a counter-attack thus forcing the British to withdraw. The offensive then slowed down and the Corps had to concentrate on meeting repeated strong German counter-attacks; but it was possible to keep most of the captured terrain thanks to well coordinated engagement of ground and naval artillery and fighter-bombers of the RAF.

The offensive was resumed on 10 July as Operation Jupiter. Again VIII Corps was responsible but this was changed already on 13 July when XII Corps was ordered to take over, this, as the former Corps was to plan Operation Goodwood.

Operation Jupiter had as its prime objective to finally capture Hill 112 and the vital area around it. Both sides considered it strategically extremely important to command this feature.

Again the fighting became extremely hard, maybe the hardest during the whole battle of Normandy, and went on for almost two weeks. The losses in lives and equipment were horrendous on both sides.

The task to finally capture Hill 112 was given to the 43rd (Wessex) Division. One of its field regiments was Douglas Goddard's regiment, 112 (Wessex) Field Regiment RA. We can read in the history of the regiment how the gunners experienced the initial barrage this day:[354]

> Zero Hour was 05.00 hrs on 10th [July] and the barrage started at 04.50 hrs. The arty included two AGRAs, the guns of 11th Armd and 15th Scottish Divs as well as the guns of 43rd Div.
>
> The delivery of this massive fire power will be remembered by all. The entire Corps Arty engaged at rates of up to 5 RPM [rounds per minute] with the guns having to be cooled with

water. The Regl Diary records Uncle Tgts of 1,260 RPM for 19 minutes. Between 8th and the 11th July C Tp fired 2,753 rounds of HE and D Tp 2,906 rounds. Bty ammunition expenditure on 10th was 3,400 rounds.

The attempt to capture Caen became an affair on the part of I Corps, who commenced Operation Charnwood on 9 July. The operation was launched after the city had been bombed by the strategic bombers during the night between 8 and 9 July. The result was that the northern part of the city up to river Orne was cleared from enemy defenders.

Then followed Operation Goodwood on 18 July, which had to be terminated on 21 July due to heavy rain, which made tank movements impossible.

Operation Goodwood – an attempt to break out?

This operation was larger than all those already executed. The prime role was assigned to VIII Corps, which now by a temporary grouping became an 'Armoured Corps'. This leads the thoughts to El Alamein where Montgomery had also established a temporary Corps of this kind by grouping three armoured divisions and one infantry division together.

The new armoured Corps was to attack via a 'left hand hook' east and south of Caen with the three armoured divisions in column. The 11th Armoured Division was to lead followed by the Guards Division, which in its turn was to be followed by the 7th Armoured Division (see **Map 20-5**).

At the same time, the left flank of the Corps was to be protected by I Corps attacking with the 3rd Infantry Division. Protection of the right (western) flank was the task of the 3rd Canadian Division from II Canadian Corps. This division was to attack through the southern part of Caen east and south of river Orne.

The major problem to face was the limited space east of river Orne, which made it necessary to launch the initial phase of the offensive through a very narrow corridor. But before that, all assault forces had to cross the river Orne from the northern part of Caen across the only three bridges available to get to the opening line. More than 6,000 vehicles were engaged. This was indeed to ask for trouble and traffic jam!

The prime objective was to capture the whole area south of Caen to a depth of 10–15km up to Orne-Laize. This would secure the whole city Caen and establish good opportunities for a later breakout towards Falaise. The operation has been much debated since the war; questions have been raised as to whether Montgomery had such a limited goal. Had he not planned for a direct full-scale breakout from the bridgehead in the direction of Falaise? Such visions were in fact on the agenda early during the planning stage.

When looking at the VIII Corps Operation Order for Operation Goodwood, and also the divisional order based on this, no direct guidance is provided. These orders are focused on the primary tactical objectives and how these would be reached. One can, however, not escape a feeling that unpronounced expectations existed that in a second phase success would be exploited southwards towards Falaise. When reading the report presented after the battle by the Corps Commander, General O'Connor, the same indication appears.[355] To the confusion about Montgomery's real intentions contributes his own unclearness on the subject. After the battle, he argued that the objectives were limited geographically, and that binding as much as possible of the German forces was the focus, thus facilitating a breakout by the Americans from their sector of the bridgehead.

A likely hypothesis is that Montgomery in view of the tremendous opposition he expected did not dare attempting a large-scale breakout. On the other hand, he may have wanted to establish a kind of mental preparedness on the part of his subordinate commanders for a breakout should the initial attack develop favourably. This is supported by the third point under 'Intention' in the VIII Corps Operation Instruction No. 4, where it is stated what will apply when the primary objectives had been secured:[356]

> If conditions are favourable, subsequently exploiting to the SOUTH.

Operation Goodwood was opened by the strategic bombers dropping their bombs on each side of the planned advance corridor east of Caen where the assault units would attack. After the bombing a rolling barrage followed, about 5km long, divided in two parts. Behind this the leading units of the 11th Armoured Division was to advance. This unit was 29 Armoured Brigade.

The brigade had been organised in three battalion groups supported by infantry and artillery.

In front of the attackers was open terrain, 'good tank terrain' as it was said, which dominates the whole area southeast and south of Caen. Spotted in the area were many villages including orchards, grown up trees and hedges. These were prepared for artillery fire later and are to be seen as targets beyond and on the flanks of the barrage.

For Operation Goodwood, 712 guns had been made available plus 48 heavy anti-aircraft guns to be employed in a ground role. **Appendix 4** has the details. These resources were to be used not only by VIII Corps but also by the two Corps on the flanks, the II Canadian Corps to the right and the British I Corps to the left.

A problem was the fact that most of the artillery units had to be deployed north and northwest of Caen. This implied long ranges from the start of the offensive for those units (the majority) that were to support the main attack. It was known that many regiments quickly would have to fire at maximum range and then had to see the attackers disappear out of range. Some units would be able to later re-deploy to the eastern side of river Orne, but it is obvious that the overall operation plan suffered from flaws as regards possibilities for the artillery to support in depth (see **Map 20-6**).

In order to make sure that the 11th Armoured Division in the lead would at least have some artillery close to the front its regiment equipped with SP guns, 13 Field Regiment RHA, was split up with one battery attached to each battalion battle group. By this arrangement they could at least avoid being stuck in traffic jams west of river Orne.

Strong fire programmes were implemented before the attack. The first one was firing to neutralise anti-aircraft batteries that were a threat against the strategic bomber armadas. Then followed counter-battery bombardment against enemy artillery deployments. Some 600 guns were employed for this task. The commander responsible for these programmes was not, as one might expect, the artillery commander of VIII Corps, but his colleague on the left, i.e. the artillery commander of I Corps.

The barrage in the assault area was to be opened at Z Hour across a 1.6km-wide front and was to continue until Z + 80. 192 guns from eight field regiments were engaged, firing two beside each other at four lines of the barrage. All fired during one and a half minute followed by a shift of 150 m to the next line. Several pauses had been prepared in the plan, one longer after the first phase during which the direction of the barrage would change a little in westerly direction (**Map 20-5**). Despite this pause, the advancing tanks had difficulties in keeping pace with the barrage as it moved forwards.

We can also notice that concentrations were to be fired at targets along the flanks. For that particular task, VIII Corps had allotted two field regiments, six medium regiments and four heavy batteries, i.e. in total no less than 160 guns. In parallel with all these programmes, various counter-battery programmes were included too in the overall fire plan.

As we can see on the map, barrages were to cover also the advance of the divisions attacking along the flanks of VIII Corps.

A critical situation developed when the advancing tank units left the infantry behind and became victims of a murderous anti-tank fire from well-positioned German guns.

The Germans were in general well prepared to meet the offensive and had skilfully deployed several lines of tanks and anti-tank guns in depth. With the long and effective superior range of all these guns the fight was uneven an undertaking. The British were to lose 300 tanks before further attacks were cancelled. The fact that the open terrain with its villages and orchards was not as 'good tank terrain' as expected became a harsh lesson.

If the British had better envisaged what would come, they had made sure that tank units and infantry fought together all the time. They had arranged also for a better employment of available artillery resources to combat anti-tank guns and tanks deployed in villages and behind concealing terrain formations. The lessons from El Alamein had obviously not been fully learnt.

It is also remarkable that no plans were made for taking advantage of the artillery option to protect advancing tank formations with smoke screens.

It might be of interest in this context to see what lessons the Corps Commander O'Connor noted. He wrote:[357]

> [...] a direct advance over open country on enemy tanks in position should be avoided, unless

they have been masked by smoke, or so heavily bombarded by bombs or artillery that they are unlikely to be able to shoot.

Obviously O'Connor after the battle believed much in the use of smoke. He added:

> No risk seems to me to be so great as to launch a number of tanks directly on the enemy tanks in position, without some arrangements being made to mask their fire.

French observers
A few French ex-officers happened to become witnesses within the battle area in Normandy and they could, based on their observations, provide interesting information to the British. By means of the regularly compiled RA Artillery Notes experience from the various theatres of war were distributed to formations and headquarters, and one did not fail to pass on these French observations. The summary of these, below, including some direct quotations, are taken from one edition of the 'RA Artillery Notes'.[358]

One of the French observers was positioned at the Cotentin Peninsula whereas two others were in or just outside Caen.

The former reported that the Germans were afraid foremost of the American artillery when that was firing airbursts or high velocity shells, which they could not hear before the shells arrived. He estimated that 70% of the German losses were due to these types of artillery fire.

He was very critical against the Allies for often destroying totally villages and cities by bombing and artillery fire. These actions lead to unnecessary killing of civilians and destruction of their houses and belongings. The Germans stayed outside villages and went in only when destroyed buildings offered them better protection and opportunities to meet the advancing Americans. This observation proved to be particularly correct when Caen was bombed to ruins in the night between 8 and 9 July 1944. That was a big mistake, which was unfortunately repeated before the end of the war.

A general observation made by this observer and also by the two others, was that the Germans were very skilled in quickly changing gun positions after firing, this in order to avoid British counter-battery fire. Redeployment to alternative positions had been trained on a drill basis. They were skilled also in taking advantage of pauses in the firing by British artillery for movement to new positions for tactical reasons.

One of the other French observers wrote about similar observations he had made:

> The German SP Arty is extremely mobile. As soon as the British fire has found the mpi [mean point of impact] they change position and I cannot help admiring the masterly drill and the rapidity with which they open fire again after moving (e.g. 150mm bty shooting again 10 minutes after changing position).

An observation made several times by the French observers was that air bursts often were too high above the target, and this was not corrected in time. One of them, located at Caen, made this observation on 18 June:

> At about 1800 hrs the British Arty opened fire for the first time on the — road [the name deleted in the RA Artillery Notes]. They ought to have started days before. About 50 air bursts were seen stretching along 500m of the road. They were well on for line but much too high (about 100 m above the target). The German vehicles were going along at 200m intervals and did not stop.

But on 14 June it was reported:

> At 1245 hrs there was well-sustained fire for 20 mins on – [name deleted]. The lower time bursts were at about 8 m height and were very effective. Over M – [name deleted] they were bursting at roof-top height. The firing was a bit wide and half the bursts were on percussion. The result was most effective: all traffic was completely stopped and it was turned back by the Germans.

The observers also discussed a frequently reoccurring problem, namely which battle technique that was the best: Should the FOO go for precision by ranging before fire for effect was ordered, or should he order predicted fire and compensate, when needed, poor accuracy with more shells?

One of them had a firm opinion:

> It is always the first shells, which have the greatest effect owing to the surprise they give. It is most necessary therefore to send as many as possible 'Time on Target'.

They had also noticed that the Germans were very skilled in quickly taking cover when they heard the whistling sound of approaching shells.

Throughout their reports, they are, in summary, praising the British gunners for most often firing accurately and efficiently (except for the height of air bursts).

'The scourge'
The Allies were shelled continuously by German artillery on the beachhead. It was not at the level of the British artillery in terms of intensity (not to mention what the Russian could provide at the Eastern Front). The Germans had given priority to the air force and armoured vehicles at the beginning of the war and never managed to compensate for the shortage of artillery later. What they could accomplish, however, was to add mortars in large quantities, both the ordinary type and rocket propelled, The latter was the much feared *Nebelwerfer*, or as it was also called by the allied soldiers, 'Moaning Minnies'. It was supplied in several versions. The most common one was, as mentioned before, a version of 150mm calibre, which could launch its projectiles up to around 8,000 yards (cf. Fig 12-7). Other types with calibres of 210mm, 280mm and even as big as 320mm were implemented. These could reach target areas up to ranges around 9,000 yards. They all had 5–6 launching tubes attached to a simple carriage.

The Allies were exposed to mortar shelling very frequently, which caused severe losses. The mortar threat became more serious than the artillery shelling. The Allies expected this threat and prepared to meet it as well as it was possible.

One objective was to improve the capability to locate mortars. The traditional 'heavy' sound ranging equipment had its limits and required a long time for deployment. The solution adopted was the 'light' equipment, the 4-pen recorder, which had been devised to meet this specific requirement (cf. Chapter 6). The microphone base was only 1,500–2,000 yards and the recording depth about the same. Evaluation of microphone data could be done much faster with this equipment. But during the battle of Normandy, only one prototype section existed. The first experience gained was very positive and it was decided to provide at least three sections to each survey regiment as soon as possible. We will in coming chapters see how this policy turned out later.

Another measure taken was of organisational character. It was decided that a special resource for counter-mortar combat should be introduced. Each division was provided with a Counter Mortar Officer (CMO) with a Captain's rank. Assisting resources were also provided for him. At the brigade level, it was endeavoured to provide an Assistant Counter Mortar Officer (ACMO). To speed up communication when combating enemy mortar positions, special communication resources were provided as well.

Finally – material superiority counts
After Operation Jupiter and Operation Goodwood, the British had secured such large a beachhead south of Caen that material superiority could be secured. It was possible to bind most of the German armoured resources and thus making a breakout by the Americans feasible. This was commenced on 25 July after a tremendous attack by strategic bombers.

The British continued with several large operations in their sector, one being the decisive Operation Bluecoat at the end of July and beginning of August. The objective of the plan was to attack with VIII and XXX Corps along the left flank of the American sector towards Caumont down to Mont Pincon, which was another dominating hill. The time of the operation did not allow for detailed planning of the artillery engagement; the operation plan was built on surprise.

The final operation in Normandy was Operation Totalize, which was commenced on 7 August. It was to become the northern arm of the pincer operation by which the Allies tried to enclose the Germans in the 'Falaise Pocket'. The southern arm of the pincer was the responsibility of the Americans. The operation was halted just before a complete closure of the 'pocket' could take place. By this, most of the German units managed to escape, but their losses were significant.

With this retreat by the German forces, their defence of Normandy collapsed, and by 17 August the battle of Normandy was over and the Allies began their rush eastwards and northwards. France lay open.

When the role of the British artillery in Normandy is discussed much focus is on the gigantic counter-battery programmes and the large rolling and creeping barrages, which were, integrated parts of operation plans. These engagements were of course very important and would justify in-depth studies. One should, however, not forget that between the major operations, the battle was raging all the time at a smaller scale. The gunners had to be in action almost continuously. They had to deliver fire at opportunity targets in connection with attacks, but also counter-preparatory fire and fire against DF targets to meet German counter-attacks. The Germans never failed to quickly organise and implement counter-attacks with great skill.

The firing in minor battles took place by means of single troops or batteries and sometimes as regimental concentrations. When meeting enemy counter-attacks, larger bounces by the entire divisional or Corps artillery sometimes had to be employed too. The procedures to quickly deliver fire from anything between the four guns of a troop up to 300–400 guns of a Corps always worked well, now a well-established routine.

As a complement to these general observations, it might be of interest to see how a FOO experienced his role when supporting a battalion. The unit to attack was 12 Battalion King's Royal Rifle Corps, which belonged to 8 Independent Armoured Brigade, which in its turn was under command of the 49th Infantry Division. The division was to attack southwards in protection of the VIII Corps attack in Operation Epsom. The objective of the battalion was the village Rauray, south of Fontaney-le-Pesnel west of Caen.

The FOO was the GPO of one of the batteries of 147 Field Regiment RHA, who had been ordered to replace the ordinary FOO this day, i.e. the troop commander. After having reported to the battalion commander, it was time for the attack. This is what happened, on 26 June:[359]

> Communication was not easy but I was through on the 19 set in the carrier and it would have been impossible with an 18 set so, as there was no other FOO with the battalion, I thought it best to remain by my carrier with the CO to control the fire support. The 4/7th were getting support from C Troop and the rest of the Regiment were engaged on some other task so I had to do the best I could with D Troop. The first thing was to range on the church. Using close target procedure I got onto the church and ordered 90 rounds of gunfire at 15 seconds interval to support the advance across the field. As they got bogged down I changed the interval to 30 seconds. The battalion attack was stopped in a fold in the ground not far from the church. I asked if I could have the support of the whole regiment to get them onto the objective. This was granted provided I ranged each battery separately as there were other troops nearby. This I did and was ready to fire a Mike Target when the CO said he wanted to withdraw the battalion, so I ordered the regiment to fire smoke instead of HE. Two rounds gunfire followed by six rounds gunfire at 60 seconds interval from the whole regiment concentrated produced the most wonderful smoke screen and the whole battalion was successfully withdrawn without any further casualties.

It was a tough time for all gunners, an indication of which, we can see from Douglas Goddard's diary:[360]

> At this relatively static stage our first priority was to dig in, including our sleeping trenches, and get below ground to minimize casualties from shells, mortar bombs and air attacks. The sleeping trenches were frequently water laden since we only had groundsheets for cover.
>
> First mail arrived. An illicit meal of suckling pig from nearby deserted farm. Rations meagre and appetite large. Moved again at night to dangerous spot in a suspected minefield. It really is the most trying experience careering into an unknown blackness with the prospect of mines blowing you up every yard.
>
> Bit of strain coping with Defensive Fire (DF) tasks nearly all night. Slept from 3 to 7 to the sound of our guns firing a few yards away. The ruination we are bringing to the country is incredible. One can't help feeling sorry for the French whose fields are being so desecrated, cattle slaughtered and homes ruined. Scare as enemy counter attack came in. Watched 250 RAF bombers dropping 1,000lbs bombs on enemy armour. Not sure what it achieved.
>
> Hun has moved up three SS Panzer Divisions for counter-attack and our offensive has been discontinued but bridgehead maintained. Our guns have been brought out of gun pits and in anti-tank positions against the armoured attack. Slept from 2.30 to 4.30 am – it's quite a

habit. Encouraging to see the tremendous firepower we have in tanks and artillery in this area. I feel confident we can deal with the counter-attacks.

Enemy armoured attack. Engaging Divisional target against the attack which was repulsed. Enemy shelling and mortaring, including air-bursts, fairly heavy for past two days and continuing. Heavy counter attacks all day. Regiment firing continuously. Some enemy tanks have broken through on right of Cheux. Infantry battle with own tanks counter-attacking.

Goddard's regiment fired almost continuously for two months from their landing until the final breakout from Normandy in August. It was a heavy job for gun crews and supply units to bring forward all ammunition consumed. Douglas Goddard made notes every day about the ammunition consumed by his battery (8 guns). From his notes I have made the graph in **Fig. 20-6**, which illustrates the daily consumption of HE shells and smoke shells during the battle of Normandy.

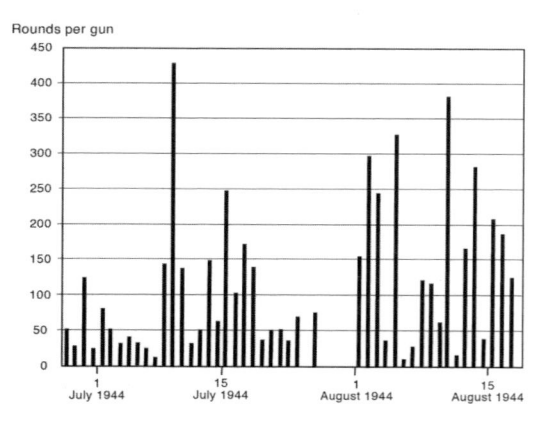

Fig. 20-6 Ammunition expenditure per gun and day (RPG) recorded for 220 Battery/112 (Wessex) Field Regiment RA in Normandy. During July 1944 the heavy fighting for Hill 112 dominated followed by a few days of recovery back from the front. During August the Battery was in particular supporting the advance towards Mont Pincon and the battle for the Falaise Pocket. Extensive smoke firing took place during the initial period to protect the flanks of attacking infantry (Author, the diagram is based on the records made by Douglas Goddard regarding the ammunition expenditure at his Battery during the Normandy campaign)

We can see that the peak came on 10 July when Operation Jupiter commenced.

The artillery intelligence resources played also an important role during the months before the breakout. AOPs (Auster aircraft) as well as flash spotters and sound rangers were busy all the time being engaged in locating enemy artillery and numerous mortars as a basis for counter-bombardment programmes. Whetton and Ogden state that during this period 4 Survey Regiment RA located 649 enemy guns, out of which 486 were located by the sound rangers alone.[361]

Finally, a voice from the opposite side. Douglas Goddard tells what a Prisoner of War from the 21st SS Panzer Division said when interrogated after the Hill 112 battle:[362]

> At Tarnopol we endured heavy Russian artillery but in Normandy we were hit again and again, day after day by British artillery that was so heavy the Frundsberg (10th SS Panzer Division) bled to death before our eyes. It was worse during an attack, theirs or ours. We would be terribly blasted. I saw Grenadiers struck dumb and unable to move and others made mad by the unceasing drumfire. Your artillery is my worst memory of Normandy.

Summary of the role of artillery in the British sector

- The Normandy landings were a tremendous logistic challenge. They were also unique when compared with the earlier landings on Sicily and at Salerno as they were made against strongly fortified and defended shores. The enemy defence at the Normandy shores could only be defeated through a coordinated attack by bombers, fighter-bombers and – not the least – naval artillery.
- Field artillery played but a small role in connection with the landings, albeit innovative. Logistically, however, it was an impressive accomplishment to land on the very first day, ten field regiments with 240 SP guns, and in addition to these landings the special support group of the Royal Marines with its 80 howitzers mounted on Centaur tanks. This meant that the landing divisions had a nominal stock of guns right from the beginning. As regards reinforcement artillery, the situation was

worse; only one American medium regiment (battalion) was landed in the British sector during D-Day.
- Landing of airborne artillery was not a big affair. Shortage of gliders restricted the transport by air to one battery. Fortunate was, however, the decision to provide additional fire observation resources to the 6th Airborne Division, which made it possible for the division to avail itself of the artillery of the 3rd Division already from the first day in battle. This became a model for future airborne operations.
- The build-up of artillery resources was well planned and was almost completed within two weeks. From then on, there was sufficient artillery available for support of divisional and Corps attacks. The build-up of artillery resources can be said to be complete after 4–6 weeks.
- Naval artillery was, procedure- and communication-wise, well coordinated with the field artillery and divisions to be supported. Fire observation could be done by observation detachments on land but also by means of AOPs and RAF Army-Cooperation Squadrons. Two cruisers and one monitor remained outside the landing beaches for several weeks and were included in divisional and Corps fire plans as a sort of extra medium regiments.
- The artillery units once landed all represented a high quality level in terms of training and combat value. They were able to adapt their support to any tactical requirement, was it a matter of large-scale operations or just minor attacks. Of particular importance was the ability of artillery to meet and stop German counter-attacks, even the strongest.
- Covering fire plans in support of attacks were planned as timed concentrations or rolling and creeping barrages. Experience showed clearly that the fire from 25-pounders, even when extremely strong, could not destroy defenders fighting from fortified positions. But even strong and battle-experienced units, such as the SS units, could be neutralised as long as the fire was over them. In order to make it possible for the attackers to take advantage of this, they had to move forwards just behind the covering fire. This was not always the case in Normandy. The consequence was that the attacking soldiers were met by murderous fire and had to stop; own large casualties could not be avoided.
- The British were skilled in concentrating artillery fire very quickly, say within 5–10 minutes, from hundreds of guns irrespective of unit boundaries. This had devastating effects on unprotected enemy units that were counter-attacking. Numerous counter-attacks could be stopped thanks to this important capability.
- The British doctrine to centralise Command of artillery resources to the highest practicable level and at the same time decentralising Control, basically fire observation and control, to the lowest possible level was a remarkable success. The skilled and experienced signallers needed for this doctrine to work were almost always at hand.
- The surveyors, well experienced too, surveyed quickly all firing units into the same grid, which was another pre-requisite for large fire concentrations. Other intelligence resources of the survey regiments provided data needed for large counter-battery programmes as far as artillery was concerned. It was not that good as regards locating mortar positions and *Nebelwerfers*, but the situation began to improve when the 4-pen recorders were introduced on a trial basis. It was not yet possible to use radar for locating mortar positions.
- A British dictum was the almost unrestricted availability of artillery ammunition. This meant that it was not necessary to be overambitious when it came to ranging of targets before fire for effect. Lack of precision could be compensated by spending more ammunition over a larger area. Ammunition supply took place over the landing beaches and the artificial harbour at Arromanches. On a few occasions the artillery units had to suffer from ammunition shortage, for instance when bad weather prevented a continuous re-supply.
- Tactically, artillery resources were used correctly when the artillery plan was well coordinated with the plans of infantry and armoured units. This was normally the case. A remarkable exception was

Operation Goodwood, one of the largest operations in Normandy. It is tempting to assume that the plan and execution of this operation had been much different if larger focus on all-arms cooperation had been prioritised and more distinct objectives had been formulated. If so, the artillery resources most likely had been in a much better position to contribute better than became the case.

- The battle of Normandy introduced a distinct shift of roles. The artillery lacked resources for combating targets at great depth from the front line such as enemy long-range artillery, armoured reserves etcetera. This now became the prime responsibility of heavy and medium bomber formations, not to mention rocket- and gun-armed fighter-bombers. These air resources got a particular important role thanks to the fact that the Allies managed to retain almost complete air superiority. The artillery became the prime actor closer to the front line, say up to 10–15km from this.

21. 'BERLIN tonight' – Arnhem

No, it was not about moving ahead towards Berlin. That was still beyond the capability of the Allies. The order issued on the morning 25 September 1944 was the final confirmation that Operation Market Garden had to be aborted, and that the evacuation of The British 1st Airborne from Arnhem should be done that night. Or more correctly: the remnants of the division. Nine days of extremely hard fighting had reduced the number of combatants from over 10,000 to little more than 2,000. What had happened, and what had the artillery meant for the outcome of the operation?

The remarkably quick advance by the Allies from the bridgehead in Normandy against comparatively weak German resistance had given hopes for a quick victory, hopefully by the end of 1944. The triumphant reception by the French and Belgian population added to the euphoric sentiments. But there were problems.

The great losses had, in particular on the British side, been difficult to replace. In August 1944 the British were forced to break up the 59th Infantry Division and a few reserve divisions in England in order to keep up the nominal strength of the divisions in Northwest Europe. The three field regiments of the 59th Division were, however, rescued temporarily and were re-organised as 59 AGRA.

A gigantic problem affecting all units during the quick advance after the breakout from Normandy was that all supplies had to come from harbours and beaches in Normandy. There were just not enough transport resources to cope with these long supply lines when five allied armies were advancing quickly. Several artillery units had to stop at river Seine for a couple of weeks to let the RASC use their vehicles, thus speeding up the preparations for the next large offensive. It is true that besides Brussels, Antwerp had been captured on 4 September, but the latter harbour could not be used as the German 15th Army still held the northern shore of river Schelde, which prevented any ships from approaching this large harbour. The smaller harbours at Boulogne, Calais and Dunkirk were still held by German garrisons. So, it became impossible to supply all the advancing armies with fuel, ammunition and other vital commodities, at least if the armies were to pursue their offensives at the same time.

This was the situation when Montgomery received Eisenhower's permission to launch Operation Market Garden. It was preceded by intensive discussions, debates and political pressure and where the rivalry between the highest allied commanders was obvious to all.

One might wonder why the Allies did not give priority to Antwerp to reduce the supply problems. A strategic mistake took place on September when the city was captured. In the course of capturing the city and meeting jubilant citizens, the 11th Armoured Division was ordered to stop its advance at the Albert Canal. Had the division proceeded only some 30km, they would have cut off the line of retreat for the German 15th Army. This army was just then crossing the outer parts of the river Schelde. It is estimated that up to 80,000 men, 600 guns, 6,200 vehicles and 6,200 horses avoided capture by the Allies before 23 September.[363] Nothing prevented the Germans from transferring huge resources to Northern and Eastern Holland, where they were to play an important role during the course of Operation Market Garden. At the same time strong forces were left at Schelde, making allied use of the harbour at Antwerp impossible.

That failure, and what caused it, is worth a separate study, but this is beyond the scope of this book. It might also be of interest to note that the commander of XXX Corps, Lieutenant General Brian Horrocks, when asked about it after the war, said that at the beginning of September all focus and thoughts were directed at crossing river Rhine before the Germans could establish a strong defence line along this river. That led to plans for Operation Market Garden. The strategic gain, if this operation would be successful, was presumed to be so great and tempting. The idea was to turn eastwards once Arnhem was in allied hands and capture the Ruhr with all its still fairly undamaged industry. This would have a decisive impact on the German capacity to wage war. With the Ruhr region captured the road to Berlin would be open, it was thought. The war would be ended before the turn of the year. Hence, one was prepared to take large risks to obtain the goal.

'A bridge too far'
The resources made available for Operation Market Garden were 1 Airborne Corps and VIII, XII and XXX Corps of the 2nd British Army. The airborne resources were under command of Lieutenant General Frederick 'Boy' Browning and were assigned the task to lay a 'carpet' from the Belgian-Dutch border via Eindhoven and Nijmegen up to Arnhem. This meant capturing all important bridges across the rivers Maas, Waal and Rhine (the Dutch call it Neder Rijn, and sometimes Lek) and a few canals between them.

The Airborne Corps assigned the task given to the 82nd and 101st U.S. Airborne Divisions. This would secure the route of advance for XXX Corps. The latter had been given the task to advance as quickly as possible to Arnhem and there reinforce the bridgehead established by the British 1st Airborne Division. The large bridge at Arnhem crossing river Rhine, **Fig. 21-1**, and the adjacent railway bridge should be taken and the whole city occupied by the airborne division. Possibly a pontoon bridge would still be in use and had to be taken as well. Further to the West a ferry was in operation, another potential objective that however does not seem to have been considered important by the planners.

The 1st Polish Independent Parachute Brigade was put under command of the 1st Airborne Division. **Map 21-1** illustrates where the different airborne divisions had their objectives. This was 'Market' in the operation plan. It can be noted that the American divisions were assigned tactically important tasks, but the most important one was assigned to the British airborne division. Arnhem was the strategic goal to capture. Without a bridgehead there and control of the crucial bridge over river Rhine the necessary conditions for the next step, capturing

Fig. 21-1 The road bridge over River Rhine (Nederrijn) at Arnhem was the primary objective for 1 British Airborne Division when landing on 17 September 1944. North is to the left in the picture (RAF photograph collection Robert Voskuil)

the area up to Ijsselmeer (Zuider Zee) and then advance into the Ruhr would not be available.

It was thought that it would be possible for the 1st Airborne Division to capture and hold the bridge and its surroundings for up to three days until XXX Corps could reach the area and link up with the 'Red Berets'. It is however important to note that only about half of the available resources could be landed the first day. The rest would come during the subsequent days when the battle was already raging and surprise would be lost.

The planned deployment areas at Arnhem for the three brigades of the 1st Airborne Division (1, 4 Parachute Brigades and 1 Airlanding Brigade) as well as the attached Polish Parachute Brigade are illustrated on **Map 21-2**, where the landing zones (broken lines) are also indicated.[364]

XXX Corps had to reach Arnhem within 72 hours at the latest, this after having advanced along one road only; with the Guards Division leading and the 43rd (Wessex) and the 50th Infantry Divisions following suit. No actions on the flanks were to be taken by the Corps. Protection of the flanks was to be entirely the roles of VIII Corps on the right and XII Corps on the left side.

In order to reinforce the protection of supply transport along *Club Route,* as the route of advance was called, three special battle groups were employed. The first one was to reinforce a regiment of the 101st U.S. Airborne Division (506 RCT [Regimental Combat Team]) which was to capture Eindhoven,. The group was to comprise a reinforced tank regiment from the British 11th Armoured Division, the 15/19th Hussars, supported by one battery from 86 Field Regiment RA equipped with SP guns.

The second battle group, which also came under American command, the 501 RCT, was given the task to reinforce the defence of Veghel. The group also comprised a reinforced British tank regiment, 44 Royal Tank Regiment, from 4 British Armoured Brigade. This group was supported by a battery from 4 Field Regiment RA which was normally supporting the brigade.

The third battle group was put under command of the 82nd U.S. Airborne Division to reinforce the protection of the large bridge at Grave. Here one of the tank regiments of 8 Armoured Brigade (which was under command of the 43rd (Wessex) Division), (the Nottinghamshire Yeomanry), was given the task. In its turn this regiment was supported by 513 Battery RA from 147 Field Regiment RHA.[365]

With these battle groups each American parachute battalion would thus be supported by at least one tank regiment and a British artillery battery in addition to the airborne divisions' own artillery units.

A smaller Dutch Brigade, the Princess Irene Brigade, was also engaged and was under command of the 43rd (Wessex) Division.[366] It was to be used for similar protecting tasks along 'Club Route'. Under command of VIII Corps, was a Belgian brigade employed in the same way.

It is worth noting that the two flank Corps had not yet crossed the heavily defended Meuse-Escaut Canal (the Dutch and Belgian called it Maas-Schelde Canal) whereas XXX Corps, by a daring advance, had managed to establish a small bridgehead north of the canal towards the Dutch border on 10 September.

The ground offensive from 'Joe's Bridge' at this bridgehead was 'Operation Garden' in the overall operation plan. But there was another formation available, although not much has been written about it. It was the 52nd (Lowland) Infantry Division, which had been attached to the British Airborne Corps. This division had been well trained for warfare in mountainous terrain – Norway being a potential area for engagement. But had, as we have seen in a previous chapter, commenced training in the summer 1944 for a role as an air-transported division for support of airborne divisions. Air transport meant neither parachute deployment nor transport to the battlefield with gliders, but conveyance by means of transport aircraft, primarily C47 Dakota (DC 3). Hence, it was necessary to have access to airfields, although these could be quite simple grass strips.

An opportunity for the employment of this division was Operation Market Garden. Although the main idea was to proceed towards Ruhr after Arnhem, the area between this city and Ijsselmeer (Zuider Zee) had first to be secured and all German forces in western Holland sealed off and prevented from interfering with the offensive towards the Ruhr.

The sealing off was to be undertaken by the Guards Division and the 43rd (Wessex) Division who were to be given half each of this front line from Arnhem up to Ijsselmeer (Zuider Zee). This meant that they both had to cover around 30km of this. The 50th (Northumberland) Division was also planned to capture an area north and east of Arnhem including the bridge at Doesburg. Reinforcement of the divisions mentioned was to be the role given to the 52nd (Lowland) Division just north of Arnhem.

The operation plan was based on the assumption that XXX Corps was able to reach Arnhem at D+2, in any case not later than D+3. A prerequisite for this timetable was that all major bridges, in particular the largest, could be captured intact. If this proved not to be possible the alternative plan required the Guards Division to spread out along the shore of the river where the bridge(s) had been blown up. The task assigned to the 43rd (Wessex) Division was then to attack across the river to capture a bridgehead. Protected by this a couple of temporary bridges should be built to make it possible for the tanks of the Guards Division to cross the river. The Wessex Division was trained for attacks across large defended rivers, as was demonstrated at river Seine in August 1944. To make it possible large stocks of bridge and ferry material had been provided and detailed plans drawn up as to how these resources would be used at the different rivers. In addition to this material, each brigade of the Wessex Division also brought 100 amphibious vehicles.

It is remarkable however that no plans seem to have been prepared for the relief of the 1st Airborne Division should one or several of the large bridges have been demolished, and the advance of XXX Corps thus been much delayed.

Operation *Market Garden* was finally approved by Eisenhower at a heated meeting with Montgomery in Brussels on 10 September. D-Day was fixed at 17 September and detailed planning commenced immediately as was the issuing of orders. Or more correctly, re-planning commenced, as much had already been done by the headquarters concerned. Operation Comet had just before the meeting been planned but been cancelled. This operation was a mini version of Operation Market Garden with only the 1st Airborne Division and the Polish brigade as participating actors. And a bit earlier in August, Operation Linnet had been planned with the same formations participating as those now to be employed in Operation Market Garden. The 1st Airborne Division had since Normandy prepared at least 15 operations that all had been cancelled in the last minute. So much planning material and data were available in the afternoon of 10 September.[367]

'A bridge too far' became a familiar expression which also became the title of Cornelius Ryan's well-known book about Operation Market Garden, which in its turn formed the basis for the grand Hollywood film also with the same title from the 1970s. It has been much debated who uttered the sentence in the first place. Often General Browning is said to be the 'father', but many others have stated that this is not true and nothing but a myth. Browning's Chief of Staff has, however, emphatically stated that his boss at a meeting with Montgomery when asked what he thought about the operation had said that it was feasible, but that he was afraid that it was 'a bridge too far'.[368] It may be as it was, but it later turned out to be correct, as realities have shown. Now, let us look at the artillery planning of the two separate sub-operations.

The artillery plan – Operation Market

It might be worthwhile first to recall that a British airborne division had one light artillery regiment with 24 mountain howitzers of American manufacture, or, if you like, air-landing howitzers. The British transported the guns in gliders, which also had the capacity to carry also the towing vehicles, one Jeep per gun, and ammunition trailers. The regiment had the normal organisation with three batteries, each with two troops, i.e. 24 guns in total. On the first day of this operation the regimental commander with staff and two batteries were to be landed, using 57 Horsa gliders for the transport to the battlefield. On the second day the remaining third battery and a few other regimental resources would come in 33 Horsas. In total thus 90 Horsas were needed for the artillery exclusive of anti-tank and anti-aircraft resources. The regiment was commanded by Lieutenant Colonel W.F.K. 'Sheriff' Thompson (**Fig. 21-2**).

On the first day 1 and 3 Battery should be landed. Both of them were under command of the divisional artillery commander (CRA), Lieutenant Colonel Robert Loder-Symonds, who had decided to keep the regiment under his command when all were in position.[369] But he ordered 1 Battery to support 1 Air-landing Brigade and 3 Battery to support 1 Parachute

Fig. 21-2 Lieutenant Colonel W.F.K. 'Sheriff' Thompson, Commanding Officer 1 Airlanding Light Regiment RA (RAHT)

which was given the task to protect parts of the landing zones until 4 Parachute Brigade had arrived on D+1.

Also under Loder-Symond's command there were two anti-tank batteries with 12 and 16 6-pounder guns respectively. Both batteries also had eight 17-pounder anti-tank guns to be kept as a reserve near divisional headquarters. Initially, command of the batteries was to be decentralised but gradually centralised later in order to establish a coherent and well-coordinated defence against tanks.

As it was expected that the airborne division would be relieved within 2–3 days it was not anticipated that very much artillery ammunition (75-mm) had to be brought to Arnhem particularly as daily re-supply from air (by means of parachutes) was planned. These considerations resulted in the decision that each gun would bring 137 rounds, most of which were high explosive (HE). Only 6 anti-tank and 6 smoke rounds per gun were included.[370]

The fire observation and control resources were limited due to the regimental organisation and only one divisional regiment being available. Normally troop commanders performed this role. While an ordinary infantry division had three regiments and thus 18 troop commanders to be engaged as FOOs for all the battalions, the airborne division here had only six. As we have seen (Chapter 7 and 20) it had been decided that airborne divisions should be allotted extra fire observation resources organised as Forward Observation Units (FOU) comprising several observation and liaison parties. The latter were employed at headquarters and artillery units expected to be available for support from the outside. The FOUs were allotted when airborne operations had to be launched. Observation parties for parachute battalions were accompanying them and thus dropped by parachute. Others were transported to the battlefield by gliders.

The FOU-resources were mainly needed for securing efficient radio communication between the air-landed units and the external artillery units when these came close enough to be in range for support.

In the plan for Operation Market Garden the 1st Airborne Division was allotted eleven FOOs from 1 FOU.[371] Another four and the commanding officer of 1 FOU were positioned for liaison with the artillery headquarters of

Brigade. When 2 Battery arrived later on D+2 it was ordered to support 4 Parachute Brigade.

When Loder-Symonds presented his artillery plan on 12 September it was based on the assumption that the airborne division had captured not only the road bridge at Arnhem but also a large part of the city area, as shown on **Map 21-2**. The only artillery regiment available had to be deployed at a fairly central position with its fire zone covering 360°, i.e. around the horizon. The site selected was just north of the shore of river Rhine where the railway from Nijmegen was turning eastwards towards the city centre (on the Brigade order the coordinates were given as 712777). During the initial phases of the battle a few more deployments would be needed, the first one just east of the landing zones, near Wolfheze.

Although Loder-Symonds wanted to keep all the regiment under his command it was necessary first to put 3 Battery under command of 1 Parachute Brigade during the brigade's advance to the road bridge at Arnhem. The guns, with a maximum range of around 9km, would otherwise be unable to reach targets near the bridge.

1 Battery should remain deployed near the landing zone and support 1 Air-landing Brigade,

XXX Corps and those artillery regiments which were expected to come within range of Arnhem first.

Loder-Symonds grouped his own and the allotted fire observation resources so that 1 Parachute Brigade would get six observation parties, i.e. each battalion would have two. 1 Airlanding Brigade was given six parties. 4 Parachute Brigade would also get extra observation parties after arrival so that each of its battalions would have at least one, preferably two observation parties.

He also decided that once the division had reached Arnhem and been deployed there as illustrated on **Map 21-2** all observation parties of 1 FOU should return under his command and some of them would be put under command of the Polish Brigade.

Of the eleven observation parties of 1 FOU, seven marched on foot and had the light wireless set No. 68R. Each FOO/OPO was assisted by two signallers. The other four parties were Jeep-borne and could therefore bring the more powerful, but heavier, No. 22 set. As was normal practice, the battery commanders also had this type of set, which also was the case as regards the regimental headquarters and Loder-Symond's staff. The latter also had a No. 19 set, which was normally installed in armoured vehicles, but was chosen because of its long range.

In his capacity as divisional artillery commander, Loder-Symonds, had his command net open for communication with subordinate units. The intention, furthermore, was that he, via this network, should be in contact also with XXX Corps and 5 AGRA. Once external artillery units later were close enough to support the airborne division he could attach these to his command net as well.

An ordinary regimental net was open between the regimental headquarters and the three batteries of the light regiment. Normally the latter would have their battery nets in operation. Here a special arrangement was made for 3 Battery. During the advance of 1 Parachute Brigade towards the Arnhem road bridge this battery was the only one that could support the brigade. As it was assumed that the two troops of the battery would have to engage different targets simultaneously, in particular against much feared 88-mm guns, a second battery frequency was allotted, by which two independent troop nets could be operated.

FOO/OPOs equipped only with the smaller No. 68R set would often be in a situation where they could not reach the batteries due to the short range of this set. Hence it was decided that relay signalling via brigade headquarters should be prepared. Initially the observation parties of 1 FOU should be attached to Loder-Symonds command net. But as soon as external batteries came in range, which was assumed to be the case once advance units had passed Grave, they should turn to their own net, the FOO Control Net, by which they would communicate with artillery units of XXX Corps. Another measure taken was that FOO/OPOs still at brigade headquarters should monitor the command nets of regiments advancing from the South. Hence their 'flick frequency' would be, as an example, the frequency of the 84 Medium Regiment RA command net. Once they heard traffic on this they could either switch their sets on to this frequency, or open up a reserve set for direct communication.

Fire preparation lists of all known enemy positions, in particular 88-mm deployments, had been prepared and distributed to the batteries, by which quick engagement of targets could be done. These lists were brought to the battle by all FOOs. Unfortunately, none of the lists seems to have been preserved, so we cannot know how extensive they were. No other pre-planned fire plans seem to have been prepared.

When planning Operation Market Garden, Loder-Symonds anticipated that three regiments from XXX Corps would be put under his command once the first units had reached Arnhem.[372] Naturally, he presumed that the two regiments of the Guards Division would be amongst them. The medium regiment under command of this division could be the third.

As regards the American divisions we will just record that they had three or four artillery battalions each. The 82nd Airborne Division had two parachute battalions, whose guns (dismantled) were dropped by parachute, and two glider-borne battalions.[373] The battalions had three 4-guns batteries; one battalion had four batteries. The 101st Airborne Division had one parachute battalion and two glider-borne.

Most of these battalions were equipped with the same 75-mm howitzer as the British airlanding regiment had. Twelve 105-mm guns were also landed by the Americans.[374] There are different statements in the literature as to which battalion(s) these guns had been provided. Most likely, as it seems to me, it was 319th Glider Field Artillery Battalion, which was part of the 82nd Airborne Division.

With the 105-mm howitzers included, the Americans would bring no less than 84 guns to the battlefield, albeit not all on the first day. According to the overall plan, the 82nd Airborne Division was to bring one of its artillery battalions the first day and 101st no artillery at all! The reason for the latter might be that the need for artillery was not considered to be large and it was assumed that artillery from XXX Corps could bring help very soon after the landings. This help would in particular come from the *Hunt Group,* which included 7, 64 and 84 Medium Regiment RA, a group designed for reinforcement and counter-battery bombardment during the advance towards Nijmegen and Arnhem.

The artillery plan – Operation Garden
A massive deployment of artillery south of Mass-Schelde Canal was planned to support the breakout of XXX Corps from its small bridgehead. Some 300 guns were to be deployed for this task within an area of 7 x 7km. Beside these all the artillery of the flank-protecting two Corps would also be deployed. As regards XXX Corps the following field regiments were engaged:

Guards Division
    55 Field Regiment RA
    153 Field Regiment RA
43rd (Wessex) Division
    94 Field Regiment RA
    112 Field Regiment RA
    179 Field Regiment RA
50th (Northumbrian) Division
    74 Field Regiment RA
    90 Field Regiment RA
    124 Field Regiment RA

Reinforcing these were the field regiments normally supporting the independent 8 Armoured Brigade, 147 Field Regiment RHA, which was now put under command of XXX Corps. The Army Field Regiment, 86 Army Field Regiment RA, was allotted as well.

Furthermore, in the initial phase, XXX Corps was given one of the many regiments of the flank-protecting Corps, 151 Field Regiment RA. This regiment normally belonged to the 11th Armoured Division. Also part of the same Corps, VIII Corps, was the independent 4 Armoured Brigade, under whose command 4 Field Regiment RHA fell. As we have seen, one of its batteries had been allotted to one of the special battle groups north of Eindhoven. We may also note the employment of the following units:

- A Belgian battery from the Belgian Brigade
- One troop of the Dutch Irene Brigade
- 165 Heavy Anti-Aircraft Regiment RA (for ground tasks)

Turning now to heavy artillery resources of the three Corps we can see that these were significant too. Each Corps was supported by one AGRA (Army Group Royal Artillery) comprising one Army Field Regiment, four medium regiments and one heavy. For Operation Garden, 7, 64 and 84 Medium Regiment RA from 5 AGRA were in support of XXX Corps. From the same AGRA's 52 Heavy Regiment RA, one battery, 419 Heavy Battery RA, was put under command of 64 Medium Regiment RA.

The two first mentioned medium regiments had a past from El Alamein, where one battery of each regiment was rearmed with 4.5-inch guns and the second with 5.5-inch guns. 84 Medium Regiment RA had been established later and had two batteries with 5.5-inch guns from the beginning.

The 4.5-inch gun had a maximum range of around 20,000 yards. The 5.5-inch gun had, as earlier mentioned, and could fire two types of shell. The first one provided was the 100lb shell, which could be launched up to around 16,000 yards. The 80lb shell developed in 1943, and delivered to the field units in mass from third quarter 1944, could increase the range to around 18,000 yards.

The gun with the largest range was provided by 419 Heavy Battery RA. This battery was equipped with the 155-mm 'Long Tom' gun of American manufacture, which could reach targets at ranges of up to about 23km.

Differences in range of the various guns of the Corps would later prove to be of great importance during the course of the battle.

The employment of resources dictated that

the two regiments of the Guards Division, 55 Field Regiment RA and 153 Field Regiment RA, should follow close behind the front units with the latter, equipped with SP guns, being the first. This regiment was in support of the leading battle group from 5 Guards Brigade, Irish Guards Group. A section of two guns from 84 Medium Regiment RA were attached to the leading battery of this regiment.

With the second brigade of the Guards Division, 32 Guards Brigade, 55 Field Regiment RA would follow with its towed 25-pounders and this regiment would also be accompanied by a section from 84 Medium Regiment RA.

The major part of 55 Field Regiment RA was to march close behind the divisional headquarters.

Behind the Guards Division with its 3,500 vehicles would march the three special battle groups allotted for support of the American 82nd and the 101st Airborne Division, including a battery in each one of them from 4 Field Regiment RHA, 86 Field Regiment RA and 147 Field Regiment RHA respectively. It was planned that the last vehicle of Guards Division would pass the starting point at 13.00 hours on D+1.

The next division would be the 43rd (Wessex) Division to which were attached 8 (Independent) Armoured Brigade and the Dutch brigade. Within its long column of some 5,000 vehicles, the three divisional field regiments would march as would 64 Medium Regiment RA, the latter under command of this division during the march. Attached to this regiment 419 Heavy Battery RA was to march. The plan called for all vehicles of the divisional column to have passed the starting point before dark on D+2, i.e. at around the same time as the first unit of the Guards Division was planned to reach Arnhem.

Finally, the third division of XXX Corps, the 50th (Northumbrian) Division, would march with its three divisional regiments. Under command of this division was 7 Medium Regiment RA. The vehicles of this divisional column were planned to pass the starting point at the Maas-Schelde Canal during the whole fourth day, D+3.

If the Guards Division could march without any interference all the way up to Arnhem, and no bridges on their way were demolished, the final vehicles would pass the starting point, 'Joe's Bridge', when the first vehicles arrived at Arnhem.[375] The first artillery units to be able to support the airborne division would be this division's two field regiments and 84 Medium Regiment RA, but they would have to move forward, passing numerous vehicles, crossing river Waal and deploying well into the 'Island', as the area between this river and river Rhine was called by the British. Otherwise their firing range would be insufficient for fire at targets north of Rhine. No detailed plans for such deployment seem to have been prepared.

Before the advance towards Arnhem by XXX Corps could be commenced on D-Day, a strong preparatory artillery fire had to be arranged north of the small bridgehead at the Belgian-Dutch border ('Joe's Bridge'). A couple of hours before the start all known enemy artillery deployments and fortifications were to

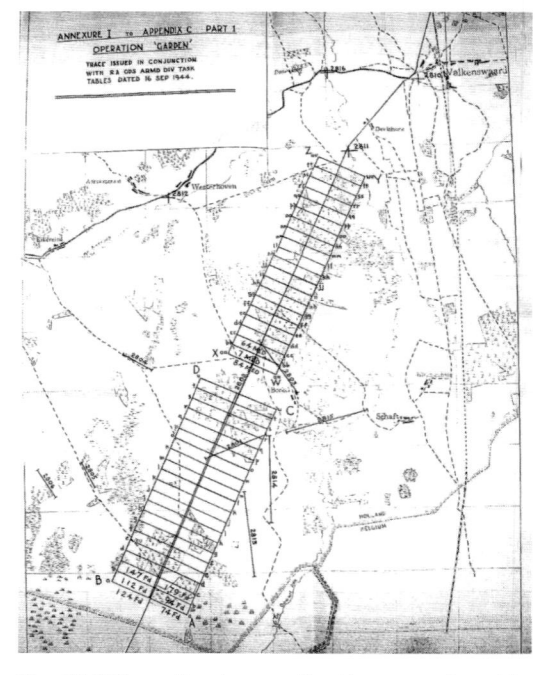

Fig. 21-3 The rolling barrage fired in connection with the break out by the Guards Division from its bridgehead at the Belgian-Dutch border on the 17th September. It was split into two parts, one in which six Field Regiments (144 guns) took part, B-A-C-D, and one further ahead in which three Medium Regiments (48 guns) were engaged, X-W-Y-Z. Other units fired against targets on the flanks and even further ahead along the 'Club Route'. The only heavy battery available fired against the village Valkensward [cf. upper right corner] (RAHT)

be bombarded, in particular by the medium and heavy guns. Then a rolling barrage would follow, coordinated with all the air-landings along 'Club Route'. In this fire plan six field regiments and the three allotted medium regiments would participate. The former would open with two regiments beside each other on the first line and the others two and two on the subsequent two lines of the barrage (**Fig. 21-3**).[376]

The distance between the different line targets was 200 yards, and a total of 21 lines were planned. This meant that the barrage would cover around 4km of the advance route northwards towards Valkenswaard. The width would be around 1,400–1,500 yards, i.e. around 700–800 yards per regiment. This required the regiments to place the fire of all three batteries beside each other.[377] The normal barrage design was, as we have seen, to place the fire of two of the batteries beside each other and to have that of the third battery superimposed across the fire of the others, which would imply a regimental barrage width of 500–550 yards.

The fire plan had been designed so that the attacking armoured units could follow close behind the artillery fire. The advance speed was thus set at 200 yards per minute, about twice the speed of the attacking infantry on foot. As a regiment needed about two minutes to shift from one line to another, the barrage must be a rolling one. This meant that although the barrage moved forward 200 yards per minute each regiment would stay on its line firing for two minutes, sometimes even three, before lifting to a new line further ahead as illustrated by the following scheme taken from the fire plan.

The barrage commenced three minutes before Z hour, which is '0' in the plan. The six regiments opened up on the following lines:

- Line a–a   74 and 124 Field Regiment RA
- Line b–b   94 and 112 Field Regiment RA
- Line c–c   147 and 179 Field Regiment RA

At '0' the first shift takes place when the a–a line is left free from fire and the two first mentioned regiments shift to the fourth line d–d, where they are firing for two minutes. One minute after their shift, line b–b is left free when 94 and 112 Field Regiment shift their fire to line e–e, where they are engaging for two minutes. And then the barrage and shifts are moving ahead like this, implying that all regiments is firing two or three minutes on each line engaged by them.[378]

In a similar way a barrage was planned for medium regiments. The difference is that the firing should commence ten minutes before Z hour and end at Z+10 minutes, i.e. when still ten minutes remained of the barrage fired by the field regiments, which undoubtedly looks a bit strange. On the other hand it is stated in the fire plan that it might prove necessary to repeat the barrage or a part of it a second time. The medium guns should therefore immediately be re-laid on the starting line once the first barrage had been completed.[379]

A unique feature thus is the separate barrage for medium regiments well beyond the one fired by field regiments. It was also a narrow concept as the three regiments were placed on different lines and not beside each other. The width was not more than around 900–1,000 yards, but the length was about the same as for the field regiments' barrage. Another 4km of the advance route and adjoining areas on both sides of it were thus to be covered with fire.

Fire density was ordered to be 'Normal' for both barrages, which meant that the 25-pounders should fire in average three rounds per minute and the medium guns one round per minute.

The fire plan did not make provision for a gap between the field regiments across the road to avoid craters on it as is sometimes stated in the literature. However, verbal orders may have been given late for this purpose.

In addition to the barrages, some timed concentrations were included in the plan. These were placed primarily on the flanks along roads and across potential advance routes of enemy armoured vehicles. The following units were allotted for such tasks:

- 86 Field Regiment RA
- 90 Field Regiment RA
- 151 Field Regiment RA
- 419 Heavy Battery RA
- Belgian battery
- Dutch troop
- 165 Heavy Anti-Aircraft Regiment RA

The plan for timed concentrations called for fire from '0' to '0+15'. Some targets were engaged as regimental concentrations, others as battery concentrations. The heavy battery was to fire at the village Valkenswaard with highest possible intensity. The HAA batteries were to fire airbursts over targets assigned to them, and they were good at that.

Apart from these fire plans at the start of the advance of the Guards Division no other were prepared but many would follow later, both written and verbal when Operation Garden was in full swing.

It is surprising that no protecting smoke belts along the flanks were prepared. The wind conditions do not seem to have prevented this type of artillery fire. The prevailing wind direction on 17 September was north and the wind speed was low.

Now let us leave the planning to see what actually happened.

From plans to action

Sunday 17 September 1944, D-Day, was a day with excellent weather for once. The 700 gliders to be taken to Arnhem with the British units the following days were loaded and ready for take-off.

The towing aircraft of equal number were also ready as were all the transport aircraft for transport of the British parachute formations. There was nothing to prevent the first phase of the operation, the bombing of located enemy anti-aircraft positions, airfields and other German positions that could interfere with the flying in of all the aircraft. 1,400 heavy bombers had been dispatched during the night and the morning for these tasks.[380] At 09.45 hours, the first aircraft of the huge armada that would transport half of the three airborne divisions to Holland in the first wave took off.

The British started from a large number of airfields in Southern England. First unit to leave was the glider-borne 1st Airlanding Brigade with the 1st Airlanding Light Regiment RA minus one battery. A few divisional units also left for Arnhem. As illustrated in **Appendix 5** the transport required 320 Horsa gliders and a few Hamilcar gliders. The latter were needed for transport of the heavy 17-pounder anti-tank guns with tractors being part of the two divisional anti-tank batteries. A number of gliders were required for transport of heavy equipment and ammunition to the parachute brigades.

A few American Waco gliders were attached to the British armada. They transported a detachment of liaison personnel from the American air force with jeeps and radio equipment who were to direct American aircraft

Fig. 21-4 A Stirling aircraft towing a Horsa glider on route to Arnhem on 17 September 1944. This glider was one of nearly 700 gliders to transport British airborne troops to Holland during the next few days (Wikimedia)

supporting the ground forces.

After 1 Air-landing Brigade, 1 Parachute Brigade followed with other units to be dropped by parachute the first day. The 150 Dakotas required were flying in two wide columns together with the gliders across the Channel. It has been estimated that the entire armada covered an area of about 10km wide and a length of some 150km (**Fig. 21-4**).

Along a southerly route the American divisions flew, also forming a large armada protected by strong fighter units, as were the British.

Blessed by the good weather and the minimum German interference from anti-aircraft guns and *Luftwaffe*, units could be landed at the planned landing and dropping zones. Losses were small and the number of gliders lost due to technical mishaps or incorrect navigation was limited (**Fig. 21-5**).

General Browning and his headquarters, around 150 people with jeeps and heavy equipment, were transported by 37 Horsa gliders and landed as planned at the Groesbeek Hill together with the 82nd US Airborne Division.

Having landed, all the units went towards their tactical objectives. Headquarters were established for leading the forces on the ground. But soon difficulties started and misfortunes followed, in particular for the British west of Arnhem.

Major Gough's reconnaissance squadron, which was intended to be a *coup-de-main* force, had lost all the jeeps of one of its four troops.

Fig. 21-5 On D-Day, 17 September 1944, 1 Parachute Brigade was dropped west of Arnhem. Heavy equipment was landed by means of gliders. The main parts of the Light Regiment RA and various divisional support units were landed at the same zone. A bit further north the 1 Air-landing Brigade was landed with gliders the same day (Shutterstock.com No. 249573877)

This was, however, not a major setback, his force was still big enough. Men and equipment had been dispersed widely during the landings, so it took time to assemble the squadron. The plans flawed quickly. The squadron had not driven far until it was stopped by a German ambush and became locked in heavy fighting without any possibility to get free and continue towards the Arnhem bridge.

The three battalions of 1 Parachute Brigade were dispatched along three pre-planned routes (**Map 21-3**). Two of the battalions, 1 and 3 Battalion, were stopped by the hastily deployed German training battalion, which was already in Arnhem when the British arrived. This battalion was commanded by the forceful *Obersturmbannführer* Krafft and ironically his battalion was just training to deal with an allied air-landed force. One of its companies was deployed near Wolfheze and could therefore immediately attack the British. Krafft's two other companies and support units were not far away and could soon seal off the area between the railway in the North and the road passing Oosterbeek, Utrechtsweg, in the South. In his war diary Krafft later regretted that he had not got time enough to bring all his companies with him from Western Holland.[381] If this had been the case he would have cut off all the area down to river Rhine, he stated.

Instead of this, the route was free for the 2nd Parachute Battalion, commanded by Lieutenant Colonel Frost, to follow the southernmost route along the river and they met hardly any resistance. After several hours of marching on foot they reached the bridge at Arnhem in the evening. Here they occupied the northern end of the bridge. The Germans managed, however, to blow up the railway bridge just before Frost's men could capture it. The pontoon bridge proved not to be in position.

In his war diary, which includes some interesting maps, Krafft says that the British passed his left flank, despite heavy counter-attacks to stop them, and encircled his battalion. This made him decide to make an attempt to break out in the dark and then to follow the railway towards the East. This is what happened when reinforcements began to arrive from the North during the late evening.

Krafft is making a thought-provoking reflection in his war diary: If the British had been satisfied with the encirclement and keeping his battalion tied down instead of trying with great efforts to annihilate it, they could easily have advanced without opposition to the Arnhem bridge also along the northern route and this before he had received reinforcements. Well placed in the city centre with the majority of their forces in place, the British would get help from what Krafft called 'terrorists', the Dutch resistance fighters. It would then have been extremely difficult to defeat them and retake the city before the British forces advancing from the South had reached Arnhem. As we know, the sequence of events turned out differently.

What could the gunners do the first days of the battle? The arrival and landing of 1 Airlanding Light Regiment RA was successful. Out of the regiment's 24 guns only two had been lost. It was one of the guns of F Troop which did not reach Arnhem on D-Day, and one of the guns of C Troop not arriving on the second day as had been planned. This was the first time a complete regiment had been transported by air to the battlefield with gliders and engaged directly in battle. It would later turn out to be the only operation in the war when as many as 22 guns were employed.[382] In this respect 1 Air-landing Light Regiment RA became unique.

After landing, the first two batteries assembled quickly and could be deployed near the landing and dropping zones close to Wolfheze. As regards 3 Battery this was only a temporary position as it was to accompany 1 Parachute Brigade towards the Arnhem bridge. Dark came before they could leave but during the afternoon the battery could provide efficient support for the parachute brigade, in particular 1 and 3 Parachute Battalion. Wireless communication failed with the 3rd Battalion advancing towards the bridge.[383] Maybe the first target engaged by 1 Battery (or was it 3 Battery?) was Wolfheze Hotel (still a hotel then) where Krafft established his headquarters during the afternoon.

The 1st Battalion of the Border Regiment, which had been landed by gliders the first day, had the task defending the landing and dropping zones to the South and dispatched a company down to Renkum at the river shore. The company was soon engaged in heavy fighting and during the night DF targets were engaged extensively to protect it from being overrun. Before the second wave of aircraft and gliders arrived on the second day, both batteries of the light regiment had to engage numerous targets at different places and later, all firing had to be concentrated southwards to make a retreat of the Border Company from Renkum possible.

The artillery starts the battle in the South – XXX Corps breakout

Excitement was peaking, expectations too. General Horrocks had, with his usual enthusiasm and determination in metaphorical terms, electrified his subordinate commanders the day before. This he did when he briefed them at the cinema in Leopoldbourg about the latest details of the plan for Operation Market Garden. The role of XXX Corps in the advance to Arnhem he summarised with the words 'we are the cavalry'.

Now, in the morning of 17 September, 300 guns were ready, crowded just south of the bridgehead at 'Joe's Bridge'. Certainly some of them were already engaged in firing northwards, but most of them just waited for the time when Operation Garden was to start, 'Z' hour. This would coincide with the first landings at Arnhem in Operation Market. They had to wait, but around 13.00 hours came the order, 'Z' is 14.35 hours!

During the Sunday afternoon, the Guardsmen would make their way up to Eindhoven, either to capture it as a first objective or to link up with the Americans if these had already done so. Preceded by the far-reaching but brief barrage, the tanks and other vehicles of the waiting divisions commenced their advance. Traffic control was a demanding task. The Guards Division had around 3,500 vehicles to move forward along the only route (the Corps had in total around 20,000 vehicles). At the head of the column the Irish Guards Group advanced. The Group was part of the informal organisation arranged during the summer.

A British Armoured Division comprised one armoured brigade and one infantry brigade. In the new informal organisation, four battle groups had been organised from these. Each group had one tank battalion, one infantry battalion and some command and support units. Another idea was that the two battalions should come from the same parent regiment, e.g. Irish Guards. The two brigade headquarters were to lead two battle groups each.[384]

Besides the leading battle group, the three others were the Welsh Guards Group, Grenadier Guards Group and Coldstream Guards Group.

Problems arose at the start. After only a couple of kilometres' march the first nine tanks were destroyed. The infantry had to leave their vehicles and get involved in fighting with the Germans at both sides of the road ahead. By and by they could continue the march but were stopped again, this time south of Eindhoven. A halt for the night at Valkenswaard became necessary. A fraction only of the distance to Arnhem had been covered (around 10 out of 100km).

The American divisions, neither of which could be flown in complete on D-Day, had been landed at the right places and thus had a successful start. Units from the 82nd Airborne Division quickly captured the large bridge at Grave intact, which was one of the most important results the first day of the battle. German counter-attacks against the Groesbeek Hill required the concentration of most of the division there, which made any surprise attack on the two large bridges at Nijmegen impossible.

The 101st Airborne Division also scored several initial successes, but the great setback was that the important bridge crossing Wilhelmina Canal at Son was blown up just as the Americans reached it. This proved to delay the advance of the Guards Division by about 24 hours.

The message to the gunners that 'Z' was 14.35 hours came from the artillery headquarters of XXX Corps and was quickly distributed to all regimental headquarters and then down to batteries and every gun.

The sound rangers and flash spotters (long bases) of 4 Survey Regiment RA had, during the days before D-Day, located all German artillery north of the bridgehead. The data were used as the basis for an extensive counter-battery programme, XXX Corps Counter Battery Neutralisation Programme No. 25.[385] This bombardment would mark the start of Operation Garden and began at 14.09 hours. One field regiment from the 50th (Northumbrian) Division, another from the 43rd (Wessex) Division, 7 Medium Regiment RA and 64 Medium Regiment RA as well began what General Horrocks called the 'Milk Round', the successive bombardment of all the enemy gun positions.

This time it was a fairly mild 'round'. Twelve or possibly thirteen targets were engaged for three minutes each. In the first series of the fire plan, at 14.09–14.12 hours, most of the targets were engaged by two troops of field artillery and two troops with medium guns, i.e. in total 16 guns. The second series was fired after a five-minute pause at 14.17–14.20 hours by 3–4 troops against each target.[386] In respect of the heavy enemy bombardment of the British bridgehead taking place the first days, the results of this first 'Milk Round' seemed quite limited. Some neutralisation effect was accomplished during the initial breakout.

After completing their firing, the medium regiments had five minutes to change laying and prepare for the rolling barrage, this being the signal for the tanks of the Guards Division to start their advance northwards. The field regiments had thirteen minutes to do likewise.

At 14.25 hours the medium regiments and 419 Heavy Battery RA opened fire, the barrage was on. This was the northernmost barrage that began, but at 14.32 hours the six field regiments started their barrage and when they made the first shift 200 yards forward at 14.35 hours, the tank engines roared into life and off they went.

During the preceding days 4 Survey Regiment RA had not only by means of its sound ranging and flash spotters located the targets for the initial 'Milk Round'. They had also surveyed all participating regiments into the same grid, which was a prerequisite for firing the barrages without extensive prior, revealing ranging.

The survey regiment had also by using short bases (two well-fixed observation posts) ranged the heavy anti-aircraft guns against the farthest ground targets. The observers made their measurements with theodolites against high airbursts (likely to be 40–50 yards above ground surface).

In the air some hundred fighter-bombers equipped with rockets and guns were ready (*Typhoons*). See **Fig. 21-6**.

Fig. 21-6 In connection with the break-out by the XXX Corps from the bridge-head at the Belgian-Dutch border on 17 September extensive air attacks with Typhoon fighter-bombers were launched against German positions. The aircraft was armed with automatic cannons and rockets. Observe the barrel-formed air-cooler under the engine that gave the aircraft a typical look (©Imperial War Museum CH 13344)

As we have seen, the battle group from 5 Guards Brigade, Irish Guards Group, was in the lead. Their first nine tanks destroyed were victims, according to the literature, of an anti-tank platoon, which had been dug in with their *Panzerfausts* close to the road. If so deployed, it seems not unlikely that they had survived the barrage, as this was not very tight nor intensive. At this part of the advance route only 25-pounders were engaged. Their shells were good for neutralisation but not for destruction of battle-experienced troops well dug in. Neither can it be ruled out that German anti-tank guns with their long range were employed as well (as is shown in the film *A bridge too far)*.

When the tanks were hit about ten minutes had passed. At the same time the barrage fired by the medium regiments ended. Another five minutes later all the concentrations at flank targets ended. But the rolling barrage fired by the six field regiments continued. According to the fire plan it would proceed another ten minutes along the road, with 200 yards lifts every minute. This was now to no use as the advancing column had been stopped.

While the infantry disembarked and attacked the enemy, fighter-bombers were also called in to fire their rockets against the German positions, a strong complement to the artillery.

The Typhoon fighter-bombers belonged to 83 Group RAF and were directed from the ground by a liaison detachment with radio travelling at the head of the Guards column. The aircraft came in groups of eight aircraft attacking every five minutes during the first 35 minutes and then eight aircraft every ten minutes. Later these aircraft were available for further attacks whenever needed. The fighter-bombers flew in at low height over the first vehicles and aimed their rocket attacks against targets around 50 yards on both sides and around 200 yards ahead of these vehicles.[387]

The battle went on for a couple of hours and at around 5 p.m. the medium regiments were ordered to repeat their barrage a second time, just as had been planned. The firing started at 17.35 hours and ended twenty minutes later. Behind it now followed the Guards battle group, which had been able to re-commence its advance. But this could not continue because of renewed enemy interference, which delayed it further. As already mentioned, they managed to reach Valkenswaard around 7 p.m. where they halted for the night. So they failed to reach Eindhoven 5km ahead as General Horrocks had hoped. The fact that his troops did not rush on in force during the night to capture the city has raised some criticism over the years. Further nightly halts would follow later, and this with even more serious consequences.

When the head of the column reached Valkenswaard no artillery unit had passed the start line. 153 Field Regiment RA that was to support the Guards group initially had some 600 vehicles ahead. If the ambush of the first tanks had not occurred, the regiment had been 20–25km behind the leading vehicles and would have passed the border during the evening of D-Day. The new situation with the leading unit at Valkenswaard 10km north of the border and more fighting meant that the ordered march had to be changed. The regiment was ordered to advance northwards at 15.00 hours and went into bivouac just north of the border at 22.00 hours.[388] With them followed, as we have seen, a section (2 guns) from 84 Medium Regiment RA.

The fighting north of the Rhine intensifies
On the second day, D+1, the enemy resistance at Arnhem increased when strong units from two SS Panzer divisions had reached the area. This definitely stopped all attempts to advance to the Arnhem bridge by the two battalions of 1 Parachute Brigade that Krafft's men had halted.

Progress by the 1st and 3rd Parachute Battalions failed when they reached halfway between Oosterbeek and the bridge. This forced the British to change from attack to defence. The pressure from the West now also increased when Kampfgruppe von Tettau comprised of several diverse units, began to assemble on the scene.

The same fate struck 4 Parachute Brigade, which, after having landed on the second day, was to proceed along Arnhem – Ede Road and the railway towards the northern part of Arnhem city. The brigade was soon stopped and had to withdraw down south of the railway. During the next days, the main parts of the British division were pressed more and more into a perimeter at Oosterbeek down to river Rhine. Frost's battalion at the bridge fought bravely during four nights and three days before it was forced to give in. By then, they had fought for twice as long as had been planned.

What had the gunners done?

On Monday 18 September (D+1), 3 Battery was ordered to re-deploy ahead and was ready for action near Oosterbeek Church at 10 a.m. It had not been possible to advance to the originally planned position at the eastern side of the Rhine near the railway crossing of the river, but the battery could now reach targets around the Arnhem road bridge, **Map 21-4**. The battery commander, Major Dennis Munford, had accompanied the parachute brigade headquarters and the 2nd Parachute Battalion to the bridge and could now observe and control fire at numerous targets on both sides of the river.

On Tuesday afternoon (D+2), the whole regiment was deployed with the three batteries together close to Oosterbeek Church. They were ready to fire at 18.30 hours and continued to support the 2nd Parachute Battalion for another day, but at around 7 p.m. on Wednesday 20th

Fig. 21-7 The air-landed light regiment was the only artillery available up to day D+4 for the hard-pressed red berets at Arnhem. During the final days the guns were deployed near Oosterbeek Churh as was illustrated in this former diorama at the Hartenstein Airborne Museum Oosterbeek. Note the fuze key used by the gunner in the centre (Author's collection)

Major Munford sent the message:

> We have been blown off the top Storey. We are quite O.K. We have killed 300 or 400 Germans for the loss of 30. The bridge is blocked with German half-tracks, armoured cars etc. We need small arms ammunition.[389]

This was the last contact with the bridge. The fighting there ceased during the night and the bridge was once again in German hands.

At the same time as the regiment engaged targets near the road bridge, fire was also requested in support of 4 Parachute Brigade and 1st Air-landing Brigade to the Northwest. These calls were answered as well as possible with regard to the limited availability of artillery ammunition. Both pre-planned fire and repeated fire against opportunity targets were executed in support of these units doing their best to press on towards the Arnhem bridge.

When the attacks from the western side increased during the following days the guns were mostly firing in that direction, in particular to help the Border Regiment battalion engaged there. The light regiment also had to fire a lot to protect its own positions. In addition this was needed to defend the positions where glider pilots were engaged. Much of manhandling of the guns was needed when firing around the horizon was necessary. An earlier diorama at the Airborne Museum, Ooosterbeek, **Fig. 21-7**, illustrated gunners in action near the Oosterbeek Church.

No external survey resources had been flown in, so the regiment had to take care of all survey actions themselves. With the tight deployment near Oosterbeek Church this was not a big problem, and the church must have been an excellent 'trig point' for quick fixing of the gun positions and bringing the guns parallel relative the zero line. The accuracy of fire has been much testified, which in this battle was extremely important as the points of impact were always very close to the positions of own troops. Good maps contributed to the good results. Topographical maps available in the scale 1:25,000 proved to be very accurate. Getting correct co-ordinates of targets was not a problem, at least not because of map quality.

Shortage of ammunition gradually increased when re-supply flights failed. Most of the

Fig. 21-8 Most of the re-supplies of artillery ammunition were, as other types of re-supply, dropped at wrong locations. Here men from the divisional headquarters at Hartenstein are trying to attract the attention of supply aircraft pilots (©Imperial War Museum BU 1119)

supplies were dropped on pre-planned dropping zones, which now were in German hands. All attempts to draw this to the attention of the Royal Air Force failed. The consequences became severe both for the aircraft and the batteries in much need of more ammunition, food, and spare parts etc. (**Fig. 21-8**).

In total large amounts of 75-mm shells, fuzes and cartridges were flown in. But large quantities of wrong type of 75-mm shells were also dropped. Due to flight restrictions and bad weather almost nothing could be dropped during the final four days. In total 1,220 shells of the correct type were taken to Arnhem during the first four days and on the sixth, out of which 120 were smoke shells and 90 anti-tank shells.[390] The quantities that could be collected during the various days were as follows:

18 September	80
19 September	250
20 September	330
21 September	400
22 September	—
23 September	160
24 September	—
25 September	—
Total	1,220

As we have seen before, each gun had brought 137 shells to Arnhem, so with the re-supplied shells, around 190 shells could be fired by each gun during the nine days of battle. For the final days only around 45 shells per gun were left.

At their positions near Oosterbeek Church the gunners were exposed to almost continuous shelling from enemy artillery and mortars day and night. Towards the end they were also under fire from tanks and tracked assault guns, not to mention infiltrating snipers. Despite this they managed to maintain their own activities at the guns and command posts. When not firing the guns they fought as infantry and also took part in the hunting of enemy armoured vehicles among houses and gardens. Besides their anti-tank guns, many carried anti-tank weapons of the 'PIAT' type.

Special actions had to be taken by the commander of the light regiment, Lieutenant Colonel W.F.K. 'Sheriff' Thompson. Surviving soldiers from the battalions that had tried to reach the road bridge but been stopped in the heavy fighting retreated back in groups, often demoralised and without any commanding officer or NCO. On approaching the church they were decisively halted by 'Sheriff' Thompson, sometimes at point-blank threat by his Sten Gun. He sorted them into units they belonged to and deployed them in defence positions facing East. He then arranged for them to get food and water from the light regiment's stock in the church. This improvised defence force was called Thompson Force and later, when he was wounded, Lonsdale Force after the officer then taking over as commanding officer.

What had happened further south?

The Guards Division head north

On the second day, Monday 18 September, the Guardsmen fought their way into Eindhoven where the American parachutists had now arrived. This made it possible to bring forward material for a field bridge at Son, where the construction immediately commenced. This was ready for tanks to pass at 06.00 hours 19 September. This in its turn made a quick advance possible via Veghel and Grave to the southern edge of Nijmegen. The Irish Guards reached it in the evening of this day. But the Germans had had time to bring forward reinforcements and very hard fighting followed. To advance into the city itself became impossible. The leading units of XXX Corps had now covered around 85km and 'only' 15 remained to Arnhem. A critical obstacle was the large road bridge at Nijmegen, which was in German hands. Also the second important bridge, the railway bridge, was controlled by the Germans.

After a night of preparations the Grenadier Guards Group launched an attack on the city defence well coordinated with the American 505th Parachute Regiment. In order to capture not only the city but also the two vital bridges, a spectacular crossing of river Waal was part of the plan. The 3rd Battalion of the 504th Parachute Regiment paddled across under murderous shelling by German artillery and mortars. Many casualties were the price. British tanks supported the American, as did the still small artillery resource available. In the evening both bridges were in the hands of the Americans and the British. And remarkably enough, they were intact!

This was the result of an attack executed decisively and with force, but it was blessed by great luck. The bridges were prepared for demolition and this was actually ordered. But when the Guardsmen's tanks began crossing the road bridge, nothing happened. For some unknown reason the ignition devices failed to work. The fact that the bridges had not been blown up days earlier is said to have depended on a strict order by Field Marshal Model, who wanted to use them for counter-attacks.

The strong resistance south of Eindhoven and the demolition of the Son Bridge had delayed the XXX Corps advance by 36 hours. And when the Americans were held back at Nijmegen and could not seize the two large bridges over river Waal by a *coup*, the consequence was a further delay of the Corps advance towards Arnhem by another two days.

A much debated issue over the years to this day is whether the Guards Division would have been able to reach Arnhem during the night between 20 and 21 September if they had pushed on immediately after the capture of the Nijmegen bridges, as the Americans wanted. They complained bitterly, 'the British had stopped for tea'. Others have declared emphatically that such an advance was not possible as the road to Arnhem had high banks over the surrounding terrain, which was soft or even marshy, so the tanks could not leave the road for protection. Hence they would be easy prey to German anti-tank guns already deployed and ready for them, it has been argued.

A counter-argument has been that the 10th SS Panzer Division was brought across Rhine by ferries and boats upstream of Arnhem, an operation taking much time, and that it thus had not been able that night to establish any strong defence with anti-tank guns along the road. And what action could British artillery been able to

Fig. 21-9 The defence of the perimeter at Oosterbeek required engagement of everybody, not only the fighting men of the parachute and infantry companies but all within the perimeter i.e. signallers, orderlies, drivers, mechanics etc. (AWM No. P02018.322)

do against unprotected enemy soldiers? The resources for this were available that night. This was a situation so critical for the success of the whole operation that one might wonder why the Corps commander, General Horrocks, was not in place to give support and clear directives to commanders and soldiers of the leading units, as he used to do.

When the British in the morning on 21 September renewed their advance it was too late to bring help to Frost's battalion at the bridge. The battle was over for them and the Germans had got time enough to deploy their anti-tank guns effectively, thus preventing any advance along the road up to Arnhem. After a few kilometres advance, the British forces were forced to stop. The objective now changed to saving what was left of the airborne division in the Oosterbeek perimeter by advancing instead in a more northwesterly direction. There the situation had begun to deteriorate quickly and was critical, exposed as the perimeter had been for several days and nights to strong enemy attacks from all sides and almost continuous shelling by artillery and mortars. All who could use small arms had to assist in the defence (**Fig. 21-9**). Losses in terms of killed and wounded increased rapidly.

More infantry than that left of the Guards Division was needed to make an evacuation possible. The 43rd (Wessex) Division was therefore called forward. It took them two days to reach the 'Island' and launch its attack there. This too has been criticised to have been too slow an advance. In particular the commanding officer, Major General Thomas, has been accused of having been too cautious and had not showed the aggressiveness that the situation demanded. Others, the Corps commander, General Horrocks amongst them have defended his actions. The traffic situation was such that no faster advance had been possible. The division had many subordinate units and thus had more than 5,000 vehicles as compared with the normal strength of around 3,500 vehicles. The Germans also made numerous attempts to cut 'Club Route' between Eindhoven and Nijmegen and were successful a couple of times.

Anyway, when arriving at the 'Island' on 22 September, 129 Infantry Brigade launched an attack on Elst along the Arnhem road and the railway from Nijmegen northwards. It was supported by a tank battalion: the 13/18 Hussars from 8 Armoured Brigade. The brigade was stopped as the Guardsmen had been before them. When 214 Infantry Brigade arrived supported by the 4/7 Dragoon Guards tank battalion it was immediately engaged in an attack towards Oousterhout northwest of the Nijmegen road bridge.

During the early morning two reconnaissance troops from the Household Cavalry had by a daring advance infiltrated through the German lines. Protected by morning fog and advancing on small roads along a long westerly turn and then northerly, they managed to reach the Poles at Driel. The arrival of the Polish brigade had been delayed by bad weather for several days landed at last on 21 September. On this day, around 1,000 men were dropped by parachute (out of a total of 1,500 men). The two reconnaissance troops making contact with them were around 20 men with eight light scout vehicles.[391]

On the same day, 22 September, the commander of 214 Brigade got the order to fight their way to the Poles on the southern shore of the Rhine at all costs, which they by some 'unorthodox' methods managed to accomplish.

During the evening that day the Poles attempted to get a force across the river to the northern side. Shortage of assault boats made it impossible to transfer more than 50 men that night out of the 1,000 that had landed at Driel. Of these, only a few got in contact with the British.

The next night another attempt was made. This time around 200 men got across the river Rhine and most of them managed to reach the besieged British soldiers as welcome reinforcement.

Late on Saturday evening the 23 September the third brigade of the 43rd (Wessex) Division, 130 Infantry Brigade, reached the southern shore of the Rhine and immediately began preparations for an attack across the river. The plan was that the 4th battalion of the Dorsetshire Regiment should lead the crossing and be followed by the other battalions. But this proved to be impossible. Assault boats and amphibious vehicles had been severely delayed by the repeated German attacks on 'Club Route' (now called *Hell's Highway* by all). The situation on the northern side of the river was now so serious that the brigade could not wait for these resources. The plan was changed and it was decided that only half of the Dorset Battalion should be shipped across that night, and now not any longer act as the leading unit of the brigade. The task was now to protect the western flank of the airborne perimeter down to the river to make an evacuation possible.

During the night 24/25 September half of the Dorset battalion was transported across the Rhine behind a protecting heavy artillery bombardment. Around 400 men embarked the boats but due to heavy fire from German positions only some 300 managed to get across, and they found themselves engaged in heavy fighting with the enemy west of Westerbouwing with further casualties as a consequence. Due to strong currents in the river the boats were dispersed over a longer distance than planned. The force was thus split up in small groups and these were unable to fight as a coherent unit. Only a handful managed to infiltrate through German positions into the airborne perimeter.

While the attempts to relieve the airborne division was going on, hard fighting was taking place at the Groesbeek Hill, southeast of Nijmegen, where the Americans were being attacked in force from the East and the Southeast. Around Veghel on 'Club Route' the battle also raged. As we have seen, several severe German counter-attacks closed the road to Nijmegen several times, which severely interfered with the advance of the two infantry divisions following the Guards Division. A severe shortage of artillery ammunition also occurred as the movement of the RASC vehicles was halted. Serious too was the fact that boats and amphibious vehicles, badly needed in the north, were delayed. 'Club Route' was completely closed to transport on 20 and 22–23 September. Once opened again, a renewed closure was enforced on 24–26 September.

On Sunday 24 September, the Corps commander, General Horrocks or possibly Montgomery himself, now promoted Field Marshal, decided that the attempts to relieve the airborne division by crossing the river should be cancelled. The remaining parts of the division were to be evacuated to the southern side of the river Rhine. General Urquhart had advised that his forces could not hold out any longer. The order went to the commander of the 43rd (Wessex) Division in the morning of Monday, 25 September, to organise the evacuation. The latter, in his turn, gave the order to 130 Infantry Brigade to execute the evacuation that night. A Canadian unit of Engineers with assault boats was put at their disposal. All available artillery units were to support the operation.

At 10.00 hours, Monday morning, the order reached General Urquhart: *Berlin tonight!* He immediately gave his orders to those of his subordinate commanders still available. We will come back to that, but first we will have a look at what happened to the infantry division, which was so anxious to assist, but never got the chance.

The air-transported reinforcement division

The 52nd (Lowland) Division had initially trained in a specialist mountain warfare role before carrying out further training to allow it to operate in an air-landing role.

The purpose of the division was now to reinforce other units when sealing off the area north of Arnhem towards Ijsselmeer. All were enthusiastic about this plan and being given opportunity to, at last, make a substantial contribution to the liberation of Europe.

The plan was to fly the division in to the Deelen airfield located on the northern outskirts of Arnhem towards Ijsselmeer. It was considered possible to do this on the fifth day of Operation Market Garden. It was thought that quite a lot of repair work first had to be undertaken at the airfield. For this purpose an American airfield Engineer battalion had been assigned, the 878th Aviation Engineer battalion, which in its turn likely would have to arrive by some 150 gliders.[392] The airfield had been an important centre for the direction of German fighter formations. It was also used as other command headquarters.

On 20 September it was obvious that the division could not be flown to Deelen. An alternative plan, of reduced scope, was hastily devised. It called for a battalion battle group with support units to be landed by gliders to reinforce the 1st Airborne Division. This operation too, was cancelled in the morning of 23 September.

Thoughts were raised about landing the whole of the division or parts of it at a suitable grass field south of river Waal. This field had been found during the initial days of the operation at Keent, which is located a few kilometres downstream of Grave where the river Maas makes a meandering turn. It had been overlooked when the original plans for Operation Market Garden were drafted, but when the opportunity to use it emerged it was quickly decided to change this by, in the first place, using it for supply flights, but also as a potential landing site for the 52nd (Lowland) Infantry Division.[393]

On 30 September, several days after the evacuation took place, it was finally decided that the division should not be employed. Disappointment was great. The division was eventually to be engaged in battle a month later when the northern shore of the river Schelde had to be cleared, this time as 'sea-borne', but this is another story.

How the gunners of this division had prepared themselves for action we will come back to later.

We will now see how the artillery units were used in Operation Garden after the initial days of the battle, and will take a step back in time.

The artillery dispersed but at last concentrated again

On 18 September, the second day, 153 Field Regiment RA supporting the Guards Division was able to advance and deploy just south of Valkenswaard. Here it could help in breaking the German barrier between Aalst and Eindhoven. The regiment reached the latter city during that afternoon and went on to the Wilhelmina Canal. The bridge there had been blown up as we have seen, so the regiment had to wait until the morning the next day, 19 September, before it could proceed over the new bridge. Then it became a speedy advance. Malden, a few miles south of Nijmegen, was reached in the afternoon and at 15.00 hours the regiment was ready to open fire. From this position they were able to support the heavy street fighting in the city. This culminated in the spectacular crossing of river Waal during the afternoon of 20 September.

During the evening that day, one of the batteries fired in support of the 82nd Airborne Division at Groesbeek Hill. Most likely one of the regiment's batteries, 129 Battery RA, crossed the river Waal at Nijmegen that evening and deployed half a mile southwest of the village of Lent. If so, this battery would have been the first from XXX Corps to cross the river and almost got Arnhem within range. The distance to the road bridge at Arnhem was not more than 13km, where the men of Frost's battalion were just facing the bitter end of their heroic struggle.

It is not known whether the two medium guns that were attached to the regiment during the march also had deployed north of the Waal. If so, the Arnhem Bridge had been within range.[394] Firing had, however, required radio communication with the gunners north of the Rhine. But the observation party of 1 FOU, that had tuned the flick frequency of its wireless set to the command net of 153 Field Regiment RA, had no contact with the regiment. The section with medium guns from 84 Medium Regiment RA was most likely connected on this net, which meant that neither of these could fire against targets north of the river Rhine.

The rest of 153 Field Regiment RA joined the battery near Lent around 12.00 hours the next day. Here they would remain in support of the Irish Guards Battle Group until the following day, 22 September until 18.00 hours when ordered to re-deploy back to its former position near Malden south of Nijmegen, so no help to their brothers north of the river Rhine could be provided by this regiment.

The second regiment of the Guards Division, 55 Field Regiment RA seems to have passed 'Joe's Bridge' on 18 September, D+1, and had to wait for the temporary Bailey bridge at Son to be ready the next morning. On 19 September the regiment reached the Maas-Waal Canal southwest of Nijmegen and deployed there. The bridges across the river Waal were within comfortable range about 6km to the North. So this regiment too could take part in the firing during the afternoon 20 September when the large bridges were captured.

After these two regiments, the three regiments of the 43rd (Wessex) Division would come closer (94, 112 and 179 Field Regiment RA). The first of these crossed the border in the afternoon 19 September, but the following day they had to wait for the road between Eindhoven and Son to be opened after the Germans had blocked it. The two other regiments crossed the border during the evening 20 September and the following night. All regiments were deployed late on 21 September near the place where 'Club Route' crossed the Maas-Waal Canal not far from Nijmegen. Here they remained deployed until 23 September when they could proceed and cross the road bridge over the river Waal for deployment at Slijk-Ewijk.

The reinforcing regiment that was to support the 130 Brigade of the 43rd (Wessex) Division with two batteries, 147 Field Regiment

RHA, began its advance northwards in the afternoon on 20 September. Its 413 Battery that was assigned the task to support one of the tank battalions of 8 Independent Armoured Brigade, the Sherwood Rangers, had crossed the border around 4 a.m. on this day. The battery had to stay in a 'hiding place' until the closed road north of Eindhoven had been cleared later the same day. During the evening the two batteries bivouacked close to the road between Veghel and Grave and proceeded the next morning at 7 a.m. They too then deployed close to the Maas-Waal Canal. A day later they redeployed a bit further north in order to support 214 Infantry Brigade in its attack north of the Waal. At 07.30 hours the batteries (431 and 511 Battery RA) crossed the Waal and deployed just north of the Nijmegen road bridge. The airborne perimeter north of river Rhine was still out of range.

The 50th (Northumbrian) Infantry Division was the last division of XXX Corps to commence the march towards Arnhem. Its three field regiments (74, 90 and 124 Field Regiment RA) would in accordance with normal practice support one brigade each. They were therefore allotted to respective brigade column for the march. Besides these regiments, 7 Medium Regiment RA was also to march in this divisional column. It was planned to have the leading unit of the division cross the border during the third day, i.e. on 19 September.

First to march was 69 Infantry Brigade with 90 Field Regiment RA attached. But due to the heavy fighting south of Eindhoven this regiment was already engaged on 17 September. During the night between 17 and 18 September the regiment was moved forward to positions just north of the border. The batteries were deployed very close to each other and were ready for action at 01.15 hours. A few series were fired there before the regiment was ordered at 05.30 hours to re-deploy forwards in order to support one of the battalions of the divisional brigades in its attack northwards. The new deployment was a couple of miles further to the North and here the regiment was ready for action at 07.15 hours.

They stayed in this new regimental position until 23 September and were heavily engaged in the fighting around 'Club Route' but could eventually move forward on this day. The next deployment was close to the road about halfway between Eindhoven and St. Oedenrode, where they took part in the hard fighting around Veghel.

During the period 24–26 September this regiment, 90 Field Regiment RA, redeployed to a few positions east of Uden where Operation Garden was over for them.

It would not be until 23 September that the sister regiment, 74 Field Regiment RA came away, so the operation had begun with much waiting. In their war diary for the period 19–22 September it was stated: 'Very quiet period. Nothing fired although regt partly in action.'[395]

But on 23 September the regiment redeployed, at last, around 2 p.m. to an area south of Eindhoven, but during the two following days no substantial firing was required. The war diary of 24–25 September notes: 'Quiet time and very few targets engaged. Weather had deteriorated and its quite wintry [!] now.' This regiment never came further north while Operation Garden was going on.

124 Field Regiment RA did not pass the Maas-Escaut Canal until the night 22/23 September after having been heavily engaged before that in support of the 3rd Infantry Division east of 'Club Route'. When advancing northwards it was stopped south of Eindhoven but could later move forward. And much firing was required during the fighting around Veghel the following days.

During the very final period, VIII Corps was made responsible for the southern area and the 50th (Northumbrian) Infantry Division was put under command of this Corps. Exempted from this was, however, 69 Infantry Brigade that was leading the column of the division and was heavily engaged in the fighting between Veghel and Uden. Hence it remained under command of XXX Corps and was now to be supported by 124 Field Regiment RA.

When the road once again had been opened on 23 September, the regiment again was 'on it wheels' northwards to support the brigade in an attack north of Nijmegen. In the early morning 24 September the regiment crossed the river Waal and deployed southwest of Elst with Oosterbeek within range.

Lieutenant Beck at 86 Field Regiment RA tells how his battery, 341 Battery RA, had been ordered to support the 15/19 Hussars (The King's Royal Hussars), which was part of the 11th Armoured Division. They were to reinforce the Americans in their defence of 'Club Route' between Eindhoven and Veghel. The battery was put under command of a tank squadron and was to cross the border with the squadron and move up to Son and meet the Americans of the 101st Airborne Division.[396]

Beck tells us that once his regiment had completed the initial Corps barrage they crossed 'Joe's Bridge':

> We went into action about 1000 yards or so from the bridge immediately in front of a Battery of Medium guns. Shells from our own guns on the other side of the canal were whistling overhead as the 'Milk-Round' went on and another barrage was fired. Our leading tanks were meeting stiff opposition. The first 9 were knocked out in the space of 200 yards! We dug in. At dusk the bridgehead area was subjected to heavy enemy shelling for nearly 45 minutes and although many shells fell close no one in the Battery was injured, although one man was evacuated with shell-shock.

The next day the regiment was still in this position and fired almost continuously. The battery was exposed to fire from snipers and others and when the night had fallen they were subjected to a violent air attack. Beck again:

> Several JU-88s dive-bombed the bridgehead area. Many H.E. bombs and A.P. bombs rained down bursting like crackers down the lines of guns, amongst the concentrated vehicle, down each side of the road, and around the bridge approaches. We spent a most uncomfortable half an hour shivering in our slit trenches, watching the scores of tracer shells weaving patterns in the sky. A troop had some remarkable escapes […] It was our first experience of deliberate air attack on our own position and it wasn't pleasant.

During Tuesday 19 September they could quickly move their SP guns forward and deploy just northwest of the new Bailey bridge at Son. Here they could see numerous gliders on the fields in front of them and soon they were visited by American glider pilots who were trying to find their way back to England. The battery was visited in the afternoon by the commander of the 101st Airborne Division, General Taylor, just as six Panther tanks attacked. An FOO was positioned in the tower of Son Church and began immediately to engage the attackers. A tank hit the tower, but the FOO, Lieutenant Craston, was able continue firing. Little by little the German tanks began to withdraw. But the next morning a renewed attempt was made. Beck noted:

> The enemy tanks returned to the attack in the morning [20th September]. 15/19 Hussars put in an attack supported by our gunfire. We got two and the 15/19 got four. Total bag for the morning six Panther tanks – and another dangerous threat to the supply lines was removed.

On 22 September the battery was ordered to re-deploy further ahead when the Germans cut off the road past Veghel and halted all traffic. This had enforced a quick reaction in the North. 32 Infantry Brigade of the Guards Division was ordered to turn around and move southwards from Nijmegen and with it followed one of the batteries of 153 Field Regiment RA. In the morning of 23 September the whole regiment was to link up with the brigade down at Uden.

We will follow Beck's account of this battle and his battery's experience for the whole operation which was so critical in the evening of 22 September:

> There was trouble further up the main axis where the enemy had cut the main road at Veghel. We were ordered forward and hurriedly packed up. The road was congested with traffic and there was a long stream of transport belonging to the British 1 Airborne Division [the Sea Echelon of the division comprised 2000 men and around 1000 vehicles]… Traffic was at a standstill in St. Odenrade but we found our way through and took up a position just east of the main road and south of Veghel. Our O.P.s found the Americans in Veghel hard pressed as the Germans were astride the road leading north from the town. A fire plan was quickly laid on and under cover of this the Americans succeeded in driving the enemy back some distance from the road.

On 23 September Beck wrote:

> A very exciting morning for our O.P.s and hard work for the gun end and command post staffs. The enemy, intent on preventing supplies reaching Arnhem, made repeated attempts to capture the road from Veghel. Supporting his attacks with 88-mm guns he kept the Americans and the 15/19 Hussars hard pressed all the morning. Our O.P.s, under constant shellfire, did

great work in bringing down fire from our guns on to enemy concentrations. Many attacks were broken up before they got moving. Others were stopped by our shell fire just when the Americans were in dangerous situation. The gun end were constantly on the alert answering many calls for fire. The Battery Command Post was now a miniature H.Q.R.A. A battery of 25-pdrs., a battery of mediums, and a battery of 3.7 H.A.A. guns had been surveyed on to our grid. Telephones were laid to them and all orders for fire were passed on so that the O.P.s had quite a useful concentration of artillery to call on. The H.A.A. guns put down airburst concentrations over the enemy, which proved particularly effective. By tea time the excitement died down and the enemy withdrew defeated, and the route was saved, for a time anyway.

The next day Beck and his fellow gunners could move forwards again and eventually passed Grave and from there through Nijmegen down to the Groesbeek Hill. There the task assigned was to support the Americans now pressed hard also here. For the moment we will leave them there.

The medium and heavy guns rush forward
For Operation Garden, a mini-AGRA was organised that comprised the three participating medium regiments, 7, 64, 84 Medium Regiment RA and the 419 Heavy Battery RA of 52 Heavy Regiment RA. They constituted the Hunt Group to which Beck's regiment, 86 Field Regiment RA, was later attached. As we have seen, all of them were under command of the various divisions for the march to Arnhem. They would of course thus be prepared to support these, but the type of support presumed to be most urgent when the plans were devised was support of the main positions of the 82nd Airborne Division at the Groesbeek Hill. Counter-battery engagement against enemy artillery and mortars in protection of the Americans was the focus. To advance as quickly and early as possible northwards to come within range of Arnhem with this forceful resource does not seem to have been in the mind of the planners, amazingly enough.

We have observed that the two batteries equipped with 4.5-inch guns (211 Battery of 64 Medium Regiment RA and 27/28 Battery of 7 Medium Regiment RA), i.e. the guns with the longest range, had been placed far back in the long marching column of the Corps. This was also the case regarding the battery with the most far-reaching guns, 419 Heavy Battery RA. The regiment marching furthest to the north was 84 Medium Regiment RA, which had 5.5-inch guns. These had a shorter range but the shells were more powerful, which could be an advantage in counter-battery bombardment.

It seems to have been realised by the Corps commander and his staff on 20 September, or possibly the day before, that the heavier guns must be moved forward as soon as possible. This coincided with the decision to speed up also the advance by the 43rd (Wessex) Division when it turned out to be impossible for the Guards Division alone to crack the enemy defence north of Nijmegen. So artillery support for the British soldiers north of the river Rhine now became the priority.

64 Medium Regiment RA crossed the Belgian-Dutch border around 6 p.m. on 20 September.[397] 'Club Route' was open again and the regiment began to overtake all vehicles that had been stopped during the morning when the Germans closed the road. But it was indeed not easy to rush forward!. The march continued all day and night until 4 a.m. 21 September when they halted for a short rest, but at 06.25 hours the order came to proceed.

At 08.45 hours the regiment was ordered to deploy close to the road between Grave and Nijmegen, approximately 5km from the Nijmegen bridges. This was the place where the first radio contact with the gunners in the perimeter at Oosterbeek was established at 09.35 hours. The range was almost 20,000 yards; so only 211 Battery with its 4.5-inch guns could engage targets there. The battery was deployed an hour later and after another hour fire orders from the perimeter could be executed. The FOO from 1 FOU at the headquarters of the 1st Airlanding Brigade then ordered fire against ten different targets, all located along the western boundary of the perimeter. But only five of them proved to be within range.

The second-in-command of the regiment, who normally was responsible for reconnaissance and deployment of the regiment, immediately went northwards to find new gun positions closer to river Waal. At 12.07 hours he ordered B Troop to re-deploy to a position close to the power station in western Nijmegen, almost at the river shore. They were ready for action at 14.10

hours. The A Troop was then ordered to leave its position and march as fast possible to the same area. Nothing has been found as to when they had deployed and were ready for action, but it seems likely that it was around 15.30 hours.

While the 211 Battery had been active, the sister battery, 212 Battery, reached the first position and deployed there around 13.00 hours. They fired a few rounds eastwards to 'control' the fixation of their position made by the surveyors. Arnhem was beyond the range of these guns, but soon they could execute harassing fire upon request from the Americans at the Groesbeek Hill and also fire against some DF targets to protect the infantry just north of the Nijmegen road bridge.

The regimental commander who had been at Corps headquarters returned to the regiment around 13.30 hours. He informed his staff that it had been decided that a special battle group would try to force its way up to Arnhem. The group would comprise a tank regiment, reconnaissance units and an infantry brigade. Support with artillery fire would be provided by a field battery (25-pounders) and a medium battery. The FOOs should be tuned to the command net of 64 Medium Regiment RA with their 'flick frequency' and thus be able to order fire from this regiment. But the whole operation was cancelled when it was found impossible to get the units involved forward before dark.

The first rounds from XXX Corps artillery in support of the hard pressed soldiers in the Oosterbeek perimeter had, as had been witnessed, a positive psychological effect. Spirit went up, and a feeling spread around the besieged 'Red Berets' that help across the river Rhine would come at last. When the gunners down at Nijmegen had fired numerous series during the night to 22 September the following message was received from the divisional artillery commander Loder-Symonds at 06.45 hours:

> Support excellent. Having magnificent results. Must have more regts at earliest opportunity, especially fld regts from relieving formation.[398]

The reason why Loder-Symonds wanted field regiments to support them was probably due to the fact that the fire must be very close to own positions within the perimeter. The shorter safety distance of the 25-pounder shells was therefore a distinct advantage.

Over the only radio connection working between the 1st Airborne Division and XXX Corps, being the one operated by the artillery via the headquarters of 64 Medium Regiment RA, a large volume of non-artillery messages had to be communicated. The net was now doubled and had been made more robust and safe thanks to a couple of relay sets at the foremost units north of the river Waal. Through Loder-Symonds' network, requests to the Corps headquarters for engagement of fighter-bombers and other army-cooperating aircraft were transmitted. Bad weather however limited this kind of assistance for some days.

During the night between 22 and 23 September, 212 Battery of 64 Medium Regiment RA was redeployed forward to the same area near the power station where 211 Battery was already in action. From around 7 a.m. the battery could start supporting the besieged in the perimeter. But the northernmost targets could only be reached with the 80-pound shells with their 2km additional range. There would soon be a shortage of this type of ammunition when the transport from the South was stopped for almost two days near Veghel.

On 23 September the artillery was reinforced when 275 Heavy Anti-Aircraft Battery RA was put under command of 64 Medium Regiment RA around 3.30 p.m. The battery was then ready to engage ground targets from its position north of river Waal opposite the power station. Within a couple of hours A Troop of 84 Medium Regiment RA could also be included in the regimental arsenal, although not formally under command. This unit was deployed in Nijmegen close to the power station; probably on 22 September.

The final unit to come under command of 64 Medium Regiment RA was 27/28 Battery RA from 7 Medium Regiment RA. It was equipped with 4.5-inch guns and came under command at 13.00 hours on 24 September. It is not known where it was deployed but as it was used for several different tasks around the perimeter it can be assumed that it was close to the southern shore of river Waal, or possibly just north of the river.[399]

So, in summary, 64 Medium Regiment RA became the core of the artillery group much engaged day and night from 21 September to the end of 26. The units fired almost continuously in support of the 1st Airborne Division north of river Rhine. They also provided much needed support to the 43rd (Wessex) Division. In the former case it was mostly a matter of defensive tasks. In the latter, it was offensive tasks including barrages and concentrations in support of several brigade attacks on the 'Island'. But numerous DF tasks were required as well. The group also had to support the remaining parts of the Guards Division north of Nijmegen and even eastwards on calls from the Americans.

One artillery unit remains to be mentioned in this context. It is 419 Heavy Battery RA with its 'Long Tom' guns with a range exceeding 20km. The battery commander, Major Palmer, had accompanied the armoured units rushing forward to link up with the Poles late in the evening 22 September. There he personally got an important role as relay station and provider of tactical information during the final days of the battle. Before arriving he had led the march of his battery from the South. His account of this is a good illustration of how the rushed advance of the medium and heavy guns was effectuated once the decision had been taken.

During the night 20 to 21 September he was still south of the Belgian-Dutch border and ready to march:

> There was no point in leaving the guns in action so we got them limbered up ready to move as soon as we got the word to go. At long last this came and, at 0830 hours on 21 Sep. I led the remainder of the Battery out on to the main road where we joined the advance part of the second Brigade of 43 Div. Soon afterwards I received a message over the wireless to report to the head of the Divisional column which was then in Eindhoven. This was easier said than done as I had to overtake all the vehicles ahead but eventually I made it and was told that 30 Corps HQ had ordered the Battery to be given top priority on the road and that as far as possible the route ahead was being cleared of other traffic to let us through. I was told that this was because, apart from the one 4.5" Battery of 64 Medium Regiment, our 'Long Toms' were the only guns, which could reach Arnhem from South of the Rhine at Nijmegen and so give support to 1st Airborne who were desperately in need of any support they could get from 30 Corps. I switched out of my rather slow half-track into my nimble jeep, although this reduced me to one wireless instead of my usual two, so that I could race ahead to tell Tod Slaughter [Gun Position Officer] to have everything ready for the guns arriving much earlier than planned and to warn the military police at all the Traffic Control Posts on the way forward that they must do all they could to ease the Battery's march.[400]

The battery was delayed by jubilant citizens in Eindhoven. The Dutch brigade was advancing just ahead of the battery and the enthusiasm had no limits when they arrived. But at 15.30 hours the battery finally reached Nijmegen and was ready to fire twenty minutes later, Palmer recalls. The gun positions were situated at the south-western outskirts of Nijmegen, about 2km south of the river Waal. There they remained in position for the rest of the battle. No problem with the range to Oosterbeek on their part, but soon enough problems with ammunition supply.

As we have seen, 84 Medium Regiment RA marched along with the Guards Division and deployed near Malden, south of Nijmegen.[401] From this position the regiment provided artillery support northwards and eastwards. A Troop was moved forward close to the river shore and was attached to 64 Medium Regiment RA as far as fire control was concerned. This was the only unit of 84 Medium Regiment RA that could reach Arnhem/Oosterbeek.[402]

In summary, we can note that the majority of the advancing artillery formations had reached the Nijmegen area by 21 September without interference of the repeated German attacks on 'Club Route' at Veghel, which became particularly serious 22–23 September. We can also note that 153 Field Regiment RA was the first formation deployed already on 19 September near Malden 5km south of the Nijmegen bridges after having passed the big bridge at Grave during the morning.

About 5km from the Nijmegen, five field regiments, two medium regiments and the heavy battery were deployed on 22 September, in total 156 guns. And to these we can add the American guns available in the area. Unfortunately all of these were out of range as far as the Oosterbeek perimeter was concerned. This was also the case for the only field regiment deployed on the 'Island', i.e. 153 Field Regiment RA. Towards 24–25 September several regiments were, however, deployed north of the river Waal and so close to Oosterbeek that they could engage targets around the perimeter.

Just before the final phase of the battle a few regiments were still south of Veghel, namely 74, 90 and 124 Field Regiment RA from the 50th (Northumbrian) Division and 7 Medium Regiment RA except its 27/28 Battery RA. The 86 Field Regiment RA was still in that area as well.

The most extensive artillery support for the 1st Airborne Division was delivered by the XXX Corps artillery. Without it the fighting at Arnhem/Oosterbeek would not have been possible for the division to undertake for such a long period as nine days. This is despite the fact that no artillery fire had been possible to deliver from the outside before 21 September.

The British airborne division had, right from the first day, been isolated from the outside world. Only occasionally had radio communication with the headquarters of the Airborne Corps at the Groesbeek Hill southeast of Nijmegen been possible to establish. Nor had morse communication with London worked. When such contacts had been opened they were immediately disturbed by German counter-communication transmitters and had to shut down.

Loder-Symonds headquarters had, as we have noted, two types of wireless set, No. 19 and No. 22, both to be used either for Morse traffic or orally (i.e. telephone communication). The range was dependent on weather and terrain conditions, interfering traffic, types of aerial, time of the day or night. As a rule of thumb a maximum range of 15–30km could be achieved, the longest range with telegraphy. With some luck it would have been possible technically to reach units approaching Nijmegen from Grave, but this had not taken place.

Maybe the reason was that Loder-Symonds staff did not have access to the correct frequencies, as some experts have argued. Whatever the reason, it was silent until the morning 21 September. A liaison officer of 1 FOU positioned at the headquarters of 1 Airlanding Brigade had, as normally was the case, his 'flick frequency' tuned to one of the approaching regiments command net, in this particular case 64 Medium Regiment RA. Around 9 a.m. he suddenly heard traffic on this 'flick frequency' and immediately opened up his reserve set on this frequency and made a call, which was received at the regimental headquarters. With much of fussy adaptations of the call, he managed to determine from where it came and direct contact was wanted.

Several versions have been published as to what really was said when from the regimental side attempts were made to get confirmation that the call was correct and not a German pirate radio trying to infiltrate, such as questions about mutual acquaintances, interests of wives and much more. When all felt satisfied Loder-Symonds opened a No. 19 set on the same frequency. From this moment there were two working connections open all the time. They were to be used over the following days intensively not only for artillery traffic but also as General Urquhart's only connection with the commander and headquarters of XXX Corps. Certainly he must have been very satisfied with this help from the gunners after all the mishaps with the divisional radio communication and failed attempts to contact the outside world.

The artillery had skilled and experienced signallers and officers used to getting contact under adverse conditions, which was now a great help. They were also used to arranging relay signalling when the range was too short, which normally was the case during the night with the technology available during the 1940s. This ability to arrange relay signalling was a special advantage in this particular situation, as we have learnt from Major Palmer's account.

Around 11 a.m. on Thursday, 21 September, the first rounds were shot by artillery from XXX Corps in support of the British at Arnhem. Or more correctly: in support of those inside the Oosterbeek perimeter. It was here that the remains of the airborne division were pressed together in their final bitter fight. Artillery support was called for more or less day and night during the subsequent phase, and this with good result. Often targets very close to own positions were engaged. Normal safety distances could not be respected. This required highest precision in the work by command posts and gun crews.

Many comments have been made on the incident when Loder-Symond himself ordered fire with the heavy battery against an infiltrating unit just south of Hartenstein. He began ranging and placed his first round around 400 yards south of the target to be on the safe side. After having observed the impact he gradually moved the fire towards the target before fire for effect was ordered, and this was fired with excellent result. It would certainly not have been appreciated if the shots, without ranging, had landed right upon the divisional headquarters!

On the last day of the battle, 25 September, the defenders on the eastern side of the perimeter had been pressed back to the light regiment's gun position close to Oosterbeek Church. Nothing could be done to prevent 1 and 2 Battery being overrun by enemy tanks and infantry that day. The surviving gunners retreated to the woods and continued to fight as infantry to the last. At 3 p.m. the German attempts to cut off the remaining part of the airborne division from the river shore suddenly ceased for unknown reasons. This caused an unexpected decline in the fighting for the dead tired, hungry and shabby 'Red Berets', which made the eventual evacuation possible the coming night.

During the days and nights that had passed since the first radio contact with XXX Corps artillery had been opened on 21 September, the artillery of XXX Corps had been engaged almost continuously against numerous targets. Forty regimental targets had been registered and engaged. And in addition to these, a further 120 different targets had been engaged to a varying extent. Particularly important had been the firing on targets west of the perimeter, where the 1st Airborne Division was exposed to numerous severe counter-attacks and infiltration. On the last day before the evacuation the British were, as we have seen, almost overrun from the eastern side. Had this been successful, the remains of the airborne division would have been cut off from the river and lost without any relief.

The XXX Corps artillery units had, besides providing support for the airborne division, also been very active in support of the various brigade attacks against Elst and other places on the 'Island'. The medium batteries also fired southwards and eastwards in support of the American 82nd Airborne Division in its exposed positions at the Groesbeek Hill and Nijmegen as some field regiments also had done. There were also 86 Field Regiment RA directly under command of this American division and 413 Battery RA from 147 Field Regiment RHA. Liaison and observation officers were frequently exchanged between the Americans and the

Fig. 21-10 A British Observation Officer assisting the Americans at the Groesbeek Height southeast of Nijmegen. Observe the white bursts over the wood edge from the on-going artillery fire. American Waco-gliders and parachutes are seen on the field close to the observation post (©Imperial War Museum, Robertson No. 03/55/1)

British units to facilitate cooperation (**Fig. 21-10**). All the extensive firing drew on the limited ammunition reserves.

How had the artillery intelligence resources been employed?

Amongst the artillery resources available when the operation commenced was 662 AOP Squadron RAF that was under command of XXX Corps. Besides its own three Flights (A, B and C), each with four aircraft, B Flight 658 AOP Squadron RAF had been allotted since Normandy. This was now called D Flight. 'A Flight' was under command of the 50th (Northumbrian) Division and 'B Flight' was now put under command of the Guards Division.

'C Flight' remained initially under command of the Squadron Leader but was later to be put under command of the 43rd (Wessex) Division.[403] 'D Flight' was attached to Corps Headquarters, to be used primarily for liaison/communication flights. One of its aircraft was shot down when undertaking such a task.

In the planning of Operation Garden it was assumed that these aircraft could not be used before the XXX Corps had established itself firmly north of Arnhem. Nor would there be any need for engaging them earlier. Therefore, the aircraft of B Flight were dismantled by removing the wings so that they could be transported on lorries that would accompany the Guards Division column northwards. The aircraft of the other Flights' were kept ready for flying sorties.

Now, when the planned fast advance along 'Club Route' failed, the 'B Flight' portee aircraft were unloaded near Nijmegen and the wings attached so as to make them ready for the air again. At the same time the CBO of XXX Corps had established himself and his staff with the Americans in the area. It then became a natural task to have the AOP resources engaged in locating enemy artillery and mortar positions, and also to observe and control fire against such targets.

It was therefore decided to bring forward also the two other Flights of 662 AOP Squadron RAF, i.e. 'A Flight' and 'B Flight'. They were somewhat delayed due to the repeated attacks on 'Club Route' by the Germans.

We may note from the war diary of the squadron that it was a dangerous undertaking to fly with these aircraft around Nijmegen with the enemy so close, both on the ground and in the air: In the war diary of 25 September one of the entries is as follows:[404]

> Captain Cracknell of C Flt today had a very narrow squeak, he had a seven minutes duel with a Focke-Wulf 190 and by really superb flying managed to escape. The F.W. had 3 separate attacks at him but twice fired over his head and one beneath his starboard wing.

During the final days of September, two Flights were redeployed forward to the 'Island' and used for counter-bombardment tasks against artillery and mortars.

The survey resources of 4 Survey Regiment RA were split up and allotted to the three divisions of XXX Corps by which the survey of divisional artillery formations into the same grid was quickly secured. Certain resources were kept centrally to make a Corps grid possible, if and when needed. This turned out to be the situation around 23 September when the number of units deployed southwest of Nijmegen became significant. A special requirement emerged also, namely survey of some American artillery units into the same Corps grid.

Another important task was to survey all the units that redeployed to positions on the 'Island' during the final days of the operation with all firing plans to be executed there, not least the extensive DF programme to be fired in protection of the evacuation from the Oosterbeek perimeter across river Rhine during the night 25 to 26 September. The success of that demonstrates clearly the precision of fire that had to be put down very close to own positions. No casualties due to 'friendly fire' have been registered.

We may recall that the 'Flash Spotting Troops' and 'Sound Ranging Troops' had been very active just before the breakout from the bridgehead at the Maas-Schelde Canal (Escaut) on 17 September.

During the first phase of the breakout, the main parts of the resources of the survey regiment were allotted to the two divisions towards the back of the Corps column, the 43rd (Wessex) and the 50th (Northumbrian) Division. To the former was attached 48 Composite Battery RA and to the latter 47 Composite Battery RA. Under the Commanding Officer and his small staff such batteries comprised, as we have seen, a 'Survey Troop', a 'Flash Spotting Troop' and a 'Sound Ranging Troop'. Attached to the regimental headquarters (4 Survey Regiment RA) was a central 'Survey Troop'.

These resources needed much time for deployment and could not be used during the march. It was not until 'Club Route' had been opened after it had been cut off 22–23 September that the intelligence resources were ordered forward. On the latter day, 48 Composite Battery established a 'Long Base' on the Groesbeek Hill measuring in an easterly direction. On the same day the 'Sound Ranging Troop' of this battery opened a 'Sound Ranging Base' with six microphones and two 'Advance Posts' mainly along the road from Nijmegen to the South, i.e. measuring towards the east as well.

The following day the latter base was extended with two additional microphones further to the South.

On 25 September the two troops of 48 Composite Battery RA were replaced by two troops of 47 Composite Battery, which had now been called forward. The former had been ordered to establish new observation bases on the 'Island'. The 'Sound Ranging Troop' of the relieving battery established two new bases with four and five microphones respectively. One of them was to measure in northeasterly direction from the Groesbeek Hill, the other in southeasterly direction from the Hill. With this arrangement good opportunities for location of enemy artillery and mortar positions threatening the American the 82nd Airborne Division were in place.

48 Composite Battery reconnoitred a sound ranging base on the 'Island' for measuring towards the Arnhem area. This could however not be deployed until the following day. It was to cover a distance from Valburg in northwesterly direction with six microphones. The 'Long Base' near river Waal established by the 'Flash Spotters' was complemented with an additional observation post near Slijk-Ewijk on the northern shore of the river.

A '4-pen recorder' sound ranging section had been attached to this battery, which could be deployed within a couple of hours only. When the Guards Division ran into trouble on 17 September the need for this new resource quickly emerged.

The section deployed along the Maas-Schelde Canal (Escaut) on both sides of 'Club Route' during the afternoon of 17 September and was ready to measure at 17.30 hours. The next day it was time for redeployment forward. On 20 September the section deployed at the Groesbeek Hill and was ready at 16.40 hours. It remained there for a couple of days during which it was heavily engaged in locating enemy mortars in particular. The next redeployment came on 23 September when the unit moved to the 'Island' and established its sound ranging base just north of the large Nijmegen bridges. On 25 September the section redeployed further north and established its sound ranging base northwest of the village Homoet, which meant that it was positioned about a mile and a half north of all the artillery now positioned around Valburg.

In summary, we can thus see that the artillery intelligence resources were quickly brought into action as soon as the tactical situation made this possible. During the final days of the operation they covered all front segments to the north and the east with 'Long Bases' and 'Sound Ranging Bases'. It was proved that these resources were the only ones that could provide good information from the depth of the enemy positions. The Army Cooperation resources of RAF, which would normally provide air photographs, were available on a limited scale only. The observation bases of the survey regiment became even more important when a more static situation followed after Operation Market Garden.

The role of airpower
The air forces were very busy before 17 September in order to secure air superiority. These operations were effective but it did not result in total superiority. The fighter-bombers' extensive rocket attacks carried out at the initial breakout of the Guards Division on the first day were, as we have seen, also very effective and successful. Close air support to all three divisions of XXX Corps had been carefully prepared by the provision of liaison staff from the Royal Air Force to the divisional headquarters, known as Tentacles. The Guards Division had a special liaison group with own vehicle and radio equipment for direct cooperation between the advancing ground forces and the aircraft. The British 1st Airborne Division had no possibility to call for help from the air before 21 September due to lack of radio communication.

Two circumstances limited air support before the last days. One was bad weather conditions both in England and in Holland for several days. The other was that the air space around 'Club Route' and the areas where the landings had taken place was reserved daily for the hundreds of aircraft flying in those airborne troops that had not been flown in the first day. Huge amounts of supplies would also be flown in daily to those already fighting on the ground. Together, these circumstances made it necessary to reject most requests for support from bombers and fighter-bombers. It was just a matter of lacking air space. For the British north of river Rhine, this was a severe disadvantage.

On 22 September, the 1st Airborne Division got some initial support when 24 Typhoons attacked targets near the perimeter, and this was repeated the following day. But on Sunday, 24 September an even more massive attack took place. For several hours numerous targets were attacked with rockets primarily mortars, '*Nebelwerfer*' units and artillery pieces.

Also during the critical following day, 25 September, it is recorded that 'a very large number of targets' were attacked by Typhoon formations. A large formation of bombers also dropped their bombs at 17.00 hours. One source tells that it comprised 74 bombers.[405]

No detailed reports have been found regarding the effects of these aerial attacks, but probably these were of significant importance. Loder-Symonds reported a couple of times how delighted he was over this help. It was reported too that, as soon as British fighter-bombers or bombers appeared over the battlefield, enemy artillery and mortar fire stopped around the perimeter. One may assume that the reason why the ground attacks weakened significantly during the critical afternoon of 25 September was due to the increased activities of the Royal Air Force.[406] Seen over the whole nine days period, the aerial support was however a disappointment.

Disappointed Scottish gunners

When the 52nd (Lowland) Infantry Division, in the summer 1944 was ordered to prepare itself for employment as an air-transported formation this naturally caused consequences for its artillery Regiments, 79, 80 and 186 Field Regiment RA and the attached 1 Mountain Regiment RA. We have seen that they had to prepare for two different alternatives. One was a scenario where the division and its artillery were to be transported by air to an area still partly under enemy control. The second was based on a tactical situation where the landings would take place behind the foremost lines of own forces. This meant that the gunners in the first alternative would be armed with 3.7-inch mountain howitzers instead of their normal 25-pounders. 186 Field Regiment RA would be flown in first, and if this was not sufficient in the first phase, 80 Field Regiment RA would follow suit. In the second alternative two regiments would be landed with 25-pounders. The remaining regiments would follow by sea, or be flown in later.[407]

As had been the case with the 1st Airborne Division many planned operations had been cancelled at the last minute with much disappointment following. Finally, Operation Market Garden materialised and transport to the Deelen Airfield north of Arnhem was to take place. This looked like an operation of the second type above, i.e. it was assumed that the Scottish division would fly in behind own forces. Hence the gunners would come armed with 25-pounders in the field regiments and 3.7-inch mountain howitzers in the Mountain Regiment RA.

It was a big setback when the employment of the division was cancelled on 20 September. The Deelen airfield had not been captured.

Preparations for alternative plans started immediately, one being a limited landing with gliders near Arnhem. This was a transport alternative never prepared, but it was not a reason for concern. The gunners were used adapting to new conditions!

A battle group from the division was to be landed, supported by a temporary artillery force comprising one troop of 25-pounders from 80 Field Regiment RA (B Troop), 452 Mountain Battery RA and an anti-tank battery. This force would use Horsa gliders but also quite a number of American Waco gliders.[408]

When bad weather and the changing tactical situation finally made this alternative employment impossible too, great disappointment was unavoidable. Major Ross wrote:[409]

> The weather had now definitely taken a turn for the worse, and further postponements rendered negligible our chance of going... when the gallant survivors of Arhem turned up in Lincoln, saying that with guns they would have held on, a wave of disappointment swept all ranks. It was the anticlimax after three months of particularly hard

work, and most people realized that there was now no hope of any similar air operation till the Spring. To The Serjeants' Mess goes the credit for the remark that we had now apparently four roles, the airborne, the seaborne, the ski-borne, and our present one – the still born. On this note of disillusionment, our association with the air-transportable role came to an end.

For the sea-transported brigade group employment was not cancelled. After being landed in Normandy they marched northwards. The attached field regiment, 79 Field Regiment RA, deployed on 16 September near Heusden, about 20km south of Joe's Bridge. It was later engaged in the fighting to the North after Operation Market Garden had been concluded.[410]

The end of the battle and evacuation

The final phase of the battle can be said to have begun during the evening of 22 September when the Poles made their first attempt to cross the river Rhine. This was followed by two more crossings the following two nights. On 23 and 24 September several brigade attacks on Elst (between Nijmegen and Arnhem) were also launched. Artillery was really busy on those days. The fact that the Operation Market Garden was on its way to a failure was as yet not on the minds of the gunners.

When parts of the 4 Dorset Battalion crossed the river during the night to 25 September two observation parties from 477 Battery RA of 112 (Wessex) Field Regiment RA accompanied them. One of them was under command of Captain Trotman and was never heard of again after they had left the southern shore.[411] The other party was under command of Captain 'Zeke' Rose who managed miraculously enough to reach Oosterbeek Church and link up with the light regiment. There 'Zeke's' portable radio was exchanged for a No.22 set by which excellent communication with his regiment was established. This became a good complement to the wireless line between the perimeter and 64 Medium Regiment RA, which was working well, but heavily loaded with traffic.

Peter Wilkinson has the story of 'Zeke's' destiny:[412]

> Captain 'Zeke' Rose of 112 Field Regiment took up a position in F Troop command post [3 Battery RA] in the porch of the church where he had a view across the open flats to the east. Through the morning, he directed fire from his Regiment's guns and the Division's artillery on to visible enemy targets and others that were called for by other observers. After midday, while standing in the church porch identifying targets with Lieutenant Moore [Troop Leader], it was unfortunate that, after such a brave effort to reach the bridgehead, he was hit and fatally wounded by machine gun fire.

During the final days the whole 1 Airlanding Light Regiment RA had as we have seen been deployed down at Oosterbeek Church (see **Map 21-4**) where they with efficient firing had stopped numerous attacks on different parts of the perimeter. Towards the end this became more and more difficult and eventually the regiment had to concentrate on defending its own positions. The gunners were all the time exposed to frequent attacks from infantry, tanks and assault guns, not to mention artillery and mortar shelling.

Before leaving the besieged, we must note that besides the light regiment the two anti-tank batteries made invaluable contributions with their shells during the hard close fighting along streets and in the gardens. Neither must the mortars of the airborne units be forgotten. Anti-tank guns and mortars had a most important role without which the perimeter could not have held out for so long. It is, however, beyond the scope of this book to discuss this in detail.

When a forceful crossing of river Rhine from the South could not be done in time, General Horrocks was forced to order the remnants of the 1st Airborne Division to evacuate to the southern side of the river. In the morning of 25 September, his order was passed on by the commander of the 43rd (Wessex) Division, Major General Thomas, to General Urquhart at his headquarters at Hartenstein: '*BERLIN TONIGHT!*' This was around 10 a.m. General Urquhart immediately called his subordinate commanders (those left in action), including his artillery commander Loder-Symonds, to his headquarters to give orders for the evacuation. Preparations then began. On the southern side of the river 130 Infantry Brigade now was in charge.

This brigade had been planning for an assault crossing and establishment of a second bridgehead at Renkum a short distance downstream from Oosterbeek. This was now cancelled.

According to General Urquhart's plan the evacuation was to commence at 10 p.m. and be concluded by first light the next morning (26 September). The soldiers should form up in groups of 14 men, equivalent to the capacity of assault boats to be used, and move silently down to the shore of the river and to wait there for their turn to cross. Their shoes should be wrapped with material to make their movement as soundless as possible. The whole evacuation was to start with groups from the northern part of the perimeter; and the final groups to withdraw were the gunners and the 'Lonsdale Force', already in positions close to the river.

Selected glider pilots were ordered to reconnoitre the footpaths to be followed so that enemy positions were avoided. These would be marked with white strips from parachutes in order to make it easier to follow in the dark. It would be seen that this was far from easy and some got lost or captured by the Germans.

Left behind were the wounded who could not walk. They were supported by medical doctors and orderlies who voluntarily stayed to look after them. There are numerous stories written and told as to how the evacuation was done. Many assault boats were shot to pieces with many men drowned as a consequence. Many tried to swim across the river in the cold water, which certainly not was easy due to the strong current. Many swimmers died unfortunately. Others were hit by enemy bullets from machine guns and other weapons.

The evacuation must, however, be regarded as a success. One must admire the exhausted and shabby soldiers, who managed to get down to the river without panic or lack of discipline and wait there patiently for their turn to cross to the southern shore in unsafe small boats, often exposed to enemy bullets. Reports and accounts over the years have quoted various numbers of those evacuated. The latest and most authoritative figures are given in Margry (2002).[413] He gives the following numbers of men evacuated:

Airborne Division	1,741
Glider Pilots	422
Polish Brigade	160
4 Dorset Battalion	75
In total	**2,398**

Some 300 men had to be left on the northern river shore. Many of them were taken care of by the Dutch Resistance and were hidden by them. In a spectacular secret evacuation on 20 October, which was coordinated with allied units on the 'Island', another 140 men would be saved across the river by means of assault boats assembled at the place.

How had the gunners contributed to making the evacuation possible?

After the breakout in the south, the artillery had been dispersed along almost the entire 'Club Route' but had later become more concentrated. 153 Field Regiment RA had crossed river Waal on 21 September and deployed just north of the Nijmegen road bridge. It has not been possible to get it confirmed, but it seems probable that its 129 Battery RA crossed over the night before. This regiment would anyway return back southwards in the evening of 22 September and did not take part in the final fighting on the 'Island'. But this is what all the regiments of the 43rd (Wessex) Division did. They deployed on the 'Island' beginning in the morning 23 September. The situation then was such that they first had to deploy just one or two kilometres northwest of the road bridge at Nijmegen. From these positions they could not reach the Oosterbeek perimeter, but played an important role supporting the attacks by 129 and 214 Infantry Brigade to capture Elst and establishing a stop for German infiltration further up the 'Island'. There they had to undertake extensive firing right from the beginning, but on the 24th these regiments could at last redeploy near Valburg, which meant that the range to the perimeter now was reduced to a comfortable 7–8km.

On 22 September, two batteries from 147 Field Regiment RHA moved in with their 'Sexton' SP guns. They first deployed near Lent and the following day further to the West, at Slijk-Ewijk. 431 Battery RA from this regiment deployed on 24 September just south of Valburg. 511 Battery RA was assigned to support 43 Reconnaissance Battalion (reinforced with the motor battalion of 8 Armoured Brigade) which was given the task to protect the western flank of the 43rd (Wessex) Division. It deployed near the village Andelst about 4km west of Valburg, where the division during 23–24 September had deployed its three field regiments.

More artillery crossed river Waal on 24 September. 55 Field Regiment RA from the Guards Division came in different batches during the afternoon and deployed a couple of kilometres northwest of the Nijmegen road bridge. From there they could possibly reach the northern shore of the Rhine, but hardly of any help to the besieged within the perimeter.

124 Field Regiment RA had a better position. I was one of the regiments from the 50th (Northumbrian) Division, which initially had been far back in the divisional columns and been stopped south of Veghel when 'Club Route' was cut off. But on 23rd September they could pass this village together with 69 Infantry Brigade and pass Nijmegen in the morning the following day. The regimental headquarters deployed southeast of Valburg. Probably the batteries were in positions a bit further to the north in order to get the whole Oosterbeek perimeter within range. Targets furthest away were at maximum range when Super Charge was used.

In the war diary of 64 Medium Regiment RA it is noted at 20.30 hours on 23 September that the second-in-command in the morning the following day should reconnoitre gun positions south of Valburg (coordinates 6669 and W1/2 6769 were given). No entry in the war diary confirms however if this was done or whether redeployment actually took place. But in the personal diary of the commanding officer, Lieutenant Colonel Hunt it is clearly stated that 212 Battery RA (5.5-inch guns), which had to come closer to Oosterbeek, really deployed on 25 September. The battery was ready for action at 15.00 hours.[414] The war diary of 47 Composite Battery RA confirms this. The surveyors fixed the location of the battery that day at 13.00 hours; the grid square was 6867.[415]

A redeployment of this battery with its 5.5-inch guns was indeed a necessity due to the ammunition situation. In the war diary it is noted at 10.50 hours on 24 September that 212 Battery RA had used all 80-lb shells, which is further confirmed at 17.15 hours that day. The battery on the other hand still had 175 100-lb shells, but this type of shell gave a shorter range by approximately 2km.

As regards the 211 Battery RA with 4.5-inch guns the situation was brighter. There were still about 120 shells per gun and another 105 shells per gun available at a rear ammunition depot.

When it comes to 155-mm ammunition for the guns of 419 Heavy Battery RA, the situation was critical. At the same time this battery had only 41 shells per gun left, and at the rear ammunition depot, Second Line, none! Major Palmer notes in his account for 25th September that they were down at only eight shells per gun.

Map 21-5 illustrates where the various artillery units were deployed in the evening of 25th September when Operation Market Garden was close to its end, as far as can be confirmed by original sources. For a couple of them, question marks prevail.

The evacuation was to be protected by a massive artillery fire during the final night. On one hand this was to conceal sounds and movements from the perimeter, on the other hand to give the Germans an impression that a large river crossing from the south was taking place. The fire plan was prepared by the divisional artillery commander Lieutenant Colonel Loder-Symonds, assisted by Major Taylor and Lieutenant de Burgh at his headquarters. The plan was transmitted on radio, slightly coded by means of Slidex, in two long messages. Unfortunately these messages have not been found. On the other hand two fire orders from the 43rd (Wessex) Division dated 25 September are available in archives. Most likely these have been prepared on the basis of the plan sent from the artillery headquarters of the airborne division.[416]

The smaller of these was called *'Swindon'* and was to be fired by 94 Field Regiment RA. This was part of a deception plan aimed at concealing the real intentions, evacuation at Oosterbeek. A deceptive attack was to be launched by 4 Battalion Wiltshire Regiment of 129 Infantry Brigade. The feint attack was to be executed a bit to the east of the village Heteren about 3km downstream of the Oosterbeek perimeter. Artillery fire was to be opened at 20.50 hours against 'targets' on the northern shore and later be moved step-wise further away from the river as if a landing of forces from the southern side took place. To add some confusion smoke belts were to be fired at 21.00–21.15 hours.

The fire plan was to be repeated a couple of times during the evening including addition of some new targets.[417]

The larger fire plan was called *'Java'* and is illustrated in **Map 21-6**. Targets were numbered and the time for their engagement is given by 'T1', 'T2' and 'OC' respectively. 'T1' means H-30 to H+120 minutes, and 'T2' means H+120 to H+270 minutes. 'OC' means 'On Command', i.e. the tactical situation would determine when these targets should be engaged. We can note here that units firing 'T' + 'T2' would fire continuously for five hours!

As shown on **Map 21-6** a line of defensive fire around the whole perimeter was to be fired. All units illustrated on **Map 21-5** would be engaged except the heavy battery and those units which had difficulties in reaching the perimeter, i.e. 55 Field Regiment RA and 511 Battery RA. The heavy anti-aircraft battery was also given an important role against ground targets. The 'H' hour was decided to be 21.00 hours, which implied continuous fire until 02.00 hours 26 September. The fire order had all details about targets and times for engagement, i.e. for a specific unit which targets to engage, when to start and when to finish firing. Ammunition expenditure and fire intensity were other details in the order. The limited availability of artillery ammunition implied a directive to the units to preferably fire short bursts rather than continuously. In particular the medium regiments had to be careful with their spending. As an example, for a task over two and a half hours, they were to fire only 20 rounds per gun, i.e. on average one round per 7–8 minutes.

The field regiments being better off could fire more, but for these still not more than one round on average per two minutes could be spent.

In addition to the pre-planned fire during the night, some targets could, as we have seen be engaged on order: those denominated 'OC' on **Map 21-6**. Exact time for firing was not given in the order. These targets were located just outside the western side of the perimeter with a certain concentration on the southern sector. It seems likely that the intention was to protect the evacuation of 4 Dorset Battalion with fire on these targets. This evacuation was assumed to begin at 02.00 hours at the earliest.

94 Field Regiment RA was to be employed by order only, and this particularly against targets further to the west, near those engaged in 'Swindon' as part of the deception plan.

In the literature the extensive defensive fire programme is often described in terms such as 'massive firing', 'violent artillery fire', etc. If the fire order 'Java' was followed, as much seems to confirm, this was hardly the case. The fact that the firing was still experienced as 'massive' and 'violent' might be a consequence of the large number of batteries with different types of gun employed (at least 142 guns) and that the fire from this came irregularly and unsynchronised. Hence, all the time shells whistled through the air on different targets and in numerous bursts within a fairly limited area. And against the same targets, fire continued for hours. The medium batteries fired, as mentioned, for five hours as did 431 Battery RA of 147 Field Regiment RHA and other field batteries.

Some field regiments also fired smoke shells during the morning hours to protect the crossing of late stragglers when light began to return. Responsible for this part of the overall artillery programme was the commander of 112 (Wessex) Field Regiment RA. Douglas Goddard noted that his battery fired smoke shells between 04.00 and 06.30 hours. For the 24 hours period 25–26 September his battery fired in total some 50 smoke shells, probably most of them were fired during these morning hours.[418]

Lieutenant Sidney Beck who on the 25 September was at the Groesbeek Hill with his SP Regiment in support of the Americans has in his personal diary described how they experienced the evacuation as 'spectators':[419]

> News was still vague and disturbing. Our thoughts were still with the boys at Arnhem. That night we stood outside our bivvies in the dark and watched the almost continuous flash of gunfire. To the north the skyline, as far as we could see, the brilliant yellow flashes of cordite were illuminated. The continuous dull roar of the guns throbbed in the air and at times the ground trembled with the intensity of the barrage. It went on for hours, seemingly without a pause, and we stood silent and fascinated wondering [. . .] We'd seen nothing like this before. There was something angry in the air, as though great dragons were at bay, roaring and spitting defiance. Was it the last assault crossing, the crown of the operation, or, and none dared to voice these thoughts, was it withdrawal, a desperate rearguard action? Sometimes after midnight there was a sudden hush and the horizon darkened and quietened. We turned in, puzzled but hopeful.

Operation Market Garden – still controversial

The operation ended with the evacuation from the Oosterbeek perimeter during the night 25–26 September 1944 although attempts were also made on the following days to save a few more stragglers from the northern shore of the river Rhine, but without any significant result.

The operation was a costly undertaking; Cornelius Ryan wrote that the losses were greater than those of D-Day in Normandy. On the allied side, he wrote, 17,000 men were lost in killed, wounded and missing/captured as compared with 10,000–12,000 in Normandy.[420]

The British at Arnhem lost 1 485 killed and almost 6,500 wounded and captured as prisoners of war (**Fig. 21-11**). A high human price.

A person who had to digest a number of difficult impressions was Major General Urquhart, who was amongst those evacuated and who would return to England within a couple of days.

The battle on the 'Island' and at Groesbeek Hill went on far into the month of October and became a tough fight. During this period the artillery played an important role, often decisive. The large bridges at Nijmegen, which remained intact during Operation Market Garden, were attacked on 29 September by German frogmen who, in a spectacular raid, blew up the railway bridge and badly damaged the road bridge. This, however, could be provisionally repaired with Bailey bridge material, by which traffic soon could be resumed.

Operation Market Garden was strategically a large failure according to many observers, a 90% success as seen by others, amongst them Montgomery. The strategic objective which was to secure a large bridgehead north of Arnhem, could not be accomplished. But, on the other hand, the Germans had been pushed back from a large area north of the Belgian-Dutch border. Risks must be taken in war, both strategic and tactical, but discussions will persist as to whether they here had been too large at the outset. To what extent had the allied side made them greater than they had had to be? The questions do not have a single definite answer. Without trying a deep analysis here, a set of issues and aspects that remain under debate to this day, will be commented briefly below.

Planning of landing zones
The zones determined for landings and droppings were perfect as such but were located too far away from the primary tactical objective, the Arnhem road bridge, which meant that all surprise was lost. Many say that this was a distinct failure on the part of the planners. Strong German anti-aircraft positions and unsuitable terrain near the bridge for gliders excluded alternatives, others have argued.

Insufficient air transport capacity
Shortage of air transport capacity made it impossible to land more than half the available airborne resources on the first day of the operation. Bad weather then resulted in several

Fig. 21-11 The two captured sappers Charles Gier and Dick Robb were among the some 6500 soldiers who became prisoners of war at Arnhem. This was equivalent to roughly 65 per cent of the landed force. The picture was taken on 20 September 1944 by the German photographer Kutzner and is said to be the first picture from Arnhem published by British newspapers. It has been assumed that it came to Britain via neutral Sweden or Switzerland at the beginning of October (©Imperial War Museum HU 2131)

delays of further transport, which had severe tactical consequences. The operation should not have been started when this shortage of capacity became obvious, some critics have stated.

Insufficient offensive capacity
The former transport factor in combination with unexpected bad weather had resulted in only one of the four British brigades (the Polish included) being used offensively on the first day. The Americans lacked resources for capturing the Nijmegen bridges that day before German reinforcements could arrive, which delayed the advance of the Guards Division towards Arnhem by two days. Were the risks reasonable?

Suppression of intelligence data
The intelligence situation was good as regards anti-aircraft positions around Arnhem and German formations that were active in this region. The late incoming information about the two SS Panzer Divisions' rehabilitation north of Arnhem was paid no attention to or was suppressed. This is one of the most debated examples of self-made risk taking. Whether this was reasonable or not there are many opinions.

Underestimated German battle worthiness
Affected by the quick breakdown of German resistance in France and Belgium the Allies underestimated the German resistance, which the planners presumed to be very weak. Losses and diminishing will to fight were wrongly thought to have reduced the battle worthiness of German formations.

Part of this problem area is the underestimate of the resources of the 15th German Army north of river Schelde that were not stopped immediately after the liberation of Antwerp. These resources could, without interference, reinforce the German defenders north of Maas-Schelde Canal. This threat, some argue, was underestimated by the planners. Others argue that by reinforcing the American airborne regimental combat groups between Eindhoven and Grave with British tank and artillery units from XXX Corps, this threat had been taken into account in a reasonable way by the planners.

Criticised also is that the well-known skill on the German side at all command levels to quickly improvise and take action in accordance with the local tactical situation was not better observed, i.e. what was called '*Auftragtaktik*' in the German language was overlooked in general.

Lack of offensive spirit
Here foremost three issues have been discussed. One is whether the Guards Division had been able to reach the planned objective of the first day, capture of Eindhoven, despite the darkness, had they demonstrated more aggressiveness. The second issue, and here the criticism is strongest, is whether the Division had been capable of fighting its way up to Arnhem in the evening of 20 September after having captured the large Nijmegen bridges. Some have stressed that this had been possible as German forces that evening had not yet arrived in force in the Elst area. Was it due to lack of offensive spirit and aggressiveness or a sound and realistic judgement of the terrain and the tactical situation?

Much debated too, is the third issue. Had the 43rd (Wessex) Division been able to reach the 'Island' much earlier than was the case, when it became obvious on 21 September that more infantry was badly needed there? Some have stated that the divisional commander, General Thomas, was too cautious and methodical in his approach, which delayed the appearance of his forces on the 'Island' by, say 24 hours. Others, including the Corps commander, General Horrocks, have defended him and argued that traffic jams and hindrances as well as German interferences made a faster advance impossible.

Catastrophic communications
Battle command in the 1st Airborne Division at Arnhem did not work as had been expected. The communication system required collapsed. Communication with the headquarters and units of XXX Corps neither worked as it should, nor was it the case with communication with the commander and staff of 1 Airborne Corps south of Nijmegen.

Many have wondered if it was due to neglected equipment maintenance and bad battery charging. Others have wanted to point to lack of training in using the equipment correctly under adverse conditions and over long distances. Relevant frequency tables had also been left behind in England, some have argued. Could all communication difficulties that 1st Airborne Division encountered been presumed in advance, and by that affected the planning, is another often discussed aspect of the battle.

Summary of the role of artillery in Operation Market Garden

This summary is limited to the role of British artillery only. The artillery battalions landed by the two American airborne divisions played important roles but it is beyond the scope of the above analysis to cover also their actions.

In this summary it has been practical to look at the two sub-operations separately, and I will begin with the air-landing operation.

Operation Market (one British and two American airborne divisions)
- As compared with an ordinary infantry division the British 1st Airborne Division went into action with only one third of the artillery of the former. This situation was planned to last for two days; it became four days. This risk accepted at the planning stage was significant and was not to be repeated in future operations. It was fortunate that 22 of the 24 guns of the light airlanding regiment could be brought to Arnhem, albeit it took two days.
- Thanks to the allocation of eleven observation parties from 1 FOU the division was not in a worse situation than the ordinary infantry division as regards fire observation and control resources.
- The divisional artillery commander (CRA) had at the planning stage decided that the light regiment should be used united under his command, although the three batteries were to be in support of one brigade each. Through this arrangement, direct support could be launched quickly to these brigades, but concentrated fire from the entire regiment was still always an option. As seen, it was not possible, however, to deploy the whole regiment at the same location (near Oosterbeek Church) until the third day. During the critical initial phase it was thus not possible to concentrate fire. Frost's battalion could be supported by one battery only (3rd Battery).
- From the selected deployment areas fire around the horizon was possible, and was also implemented. A restriction was however the shortage of ammunition. Most of the replacement supplies from aircraft were lost.
- The terrain made fire observation very difficult, in most cases impossible, by which ranging and control of fire was severely hampered. Radio communication was also difficult due to the terrain, but worked well with a few exceptions. The artillery nets were often the only ones working in the brigades. Despite being exposed to enemy shelling from artillery and mortars day and night the light regiment could most of the time meet requests for fire. The regiment did deliver what was expected from it, and did so in a most commendable way.
- One lesson learned was that the CRA headquarters lacked capacity to effectively manage and coordinate a large number of external regiments, when these came within range. Afterwards, this led to an upgrading for future operations, including upgrading of the CRA position to the rank of Brigadier.
- Close air support from medium bombers and fighter-bombers could have been a good complement to the artillery, but the number of sorties was fairly low. This was due to the fact that air space had to be reserved for several hours every day for the extensive supply transport. Bad weather during the week the battle was going on also reduced air activity. However, when it was possible to give the besieged forces at Arnhem (Oosterbeek) direct support from the air, the results were much appreciated.

Operation Garden (XXX Corps)
- The XXX Corps was initially supported by some 300 guns, which at the time was quite normal for a Corps attack. Due to allocation of these resources to individual divisions and brigades, which were spread out over the very long march route, 'Club Route', strong concentration of fire was possible only on the first day, when the Corps broke out northwards. During the final day, when the evacuation of the British survivors from the Oosterbeek perimeter took place, it was possible to concentrate about half of the initial artillery resources.
- The field regiments were given their ordinary role to support one brigade each within the divisional column. No other role seems to have been foreseen in the

planning. Fire concentration was not an option during the march forward.

- The medium regiments were allocated with one for each division and were to march at the rear of the divisional columns. An exception was the allocation of two sections (from 84 Medium Regiment), which marched under command of the leading batteries of 55 Field Regiment RA and 155 Field Regiment RA who were supporting the leading brigade groups of the Guards Division.
- The role planned for the medium regiments was reinforcement of the divisional regiments and to be prepared for counter-battery actions, in particular support of the 82nd American Airborne around Groesbeek Hill SE of Nijmegen. No role in support of the 1st British Airborne Division before arrival north of Rhine seems to have been planned.
- The formations equipped with guns having the longest range, 419 Heavy Battery RA and the two medium batteries with 4.5-inch guns from 7 Medium Regiment RA and 64 Medium Regiment RA, were to march at the rear of the Corps column, which implied start 2–3 days after the Guards Division had commenced its dash northwards.
- Corps artillery planning was thus not focused on bringing up much artillery within range of Arnhem as early as possible. Neither was there any plan to secure effective radio communication with the airborne division at the earliest possible time. Obviously there was not much of advance training in making radio contacts over long distances. The battle made these mistakes embarrassingly clear.
- The initial barrage in support of the breakout by the Guards Division had a unique design. Six out of ten available field regiments fired a rolling barrage, fairly narrow (1,400m), along the road northwards over a distance of 4km. It started three minutes before the tanks began moving and was completed 23 minutes later. No preparations were made for imposing pauses or to halt it in case of contingencies, which with hindsight is amazing. When the tanks were stopped after 2km, the barrage continued for another 2km for no purpose.
- At the flanks of the barrage four field regiments fired during the first 15 minutes, both concentrations and fire against line targets. It is not clear as to whether the intention was neutralisation or destruction of the targets, e.g. anti-tank guns. The overall fire plan also included harassing fire at targets many kilometres from the main road, which seems reasonable.
- Of particular interest is the fact that the fire of the medium regiments was not superimposed over the fire of the field regiments. Each regiment fired its own barrage simultaneously beyond the one fired by the latter. This was even narrower: about 900m. Contrary to normal practice it was fired long before any tanks nor infantry were up close to it. On the other hand it was planned for a repeat shoot, which took place three hours after the first one had been executed, this time with better effect. The whole arrangement with this division of fire resources cannot be seen as anything but a wrong use of artillery.
- The chosen fire intensity was moderate for both field regiments and medium regiments by which the barrage(s) can be said to have been fairly light. In view of the importance of the operation this is strange, particularly as the opponents were battle-experienced troops dug in and positioned in well-prepared fortified positions.
- The counter-battery programme preceding the barrages was quite moderate in terms of scope and intensity.
- Furthermore, it is strange that no need for smoke belts along the flanks to protect the tanks of the Guards Division from long range firing enemy tanks and anti-tank guns was foreseen.
- As the dash for Arnhem was not as quick as planned due to German interference, the distribution of artillery units along the long column (some 20,000 vehicles were on the road) had the advantage that some guns at least were almost everywhere available when and where the road was blocked.
- A decision at high level seems to have been made early morning of the 20 September that the guns with the longest range should

be brought forward as quickly as possible to support the airborne troops north of Rhine. On 21 September in the morning, one medium regiment was ready near Nijmegen with Arnhem within range, and towards the evening also the only heavy battery. We now know that it could have been two days earlier with better planning. Had this been the case, one can rest assured, that the 'Red Berets' had welcomed it very much.

- Cooperation between British and American headquarters and commanders worked very well, as was cooperation between their Forward Observation Officers. The key to this was, that the parties did not interfere on respective radio communication networks. Instead, the practice was to use liaison officers equipped with wireless sets netted on their own networks. By this arrangement it was easy to transmit fire orders etc. from an American unit to British units and vice versa. The liaison officer could be a regimental or battery commander, but many times subalterns were engaged.
- The field regiments brought much more ammunition with them than normal. Hence they did not suffer too much when the supply transports were interrupted by the Germans blocking the only available road – as they did many times. The medium regiments and the heavy battery had a worse situation, and a severe shortage of ammunition was unavoidable on their part during the last critical days of the battle.
- Appreciation was expressed from many supported units on the accuracy demonstrated by the British artillery again and again, despite long ranges and frequent re-laying of the guns in many directions. Often there was a need to fire very close to own troops. Normal safety distances could not always be respected, but to the credit of surveyors and gun layers no major mistakes with casualties from 'friendly fire' were reported.
- The intelligence resources of the artillery were effectively used despite the frequent needs for improvisation, and many times changed plans. In particular this was the case east and southeast of Nijmegen where the demand for target location was great. The dashing attitude on the part of the survey batteries with early and quick reconnaissance and deployment of sound ranging bases and flash spotters proved very valuable and was admirable.
- The plan for the long defensive firing around the perimeter to protect the 'Red Berets' withdrawal across the river Rhine the last night was prepared hastily, but was executed with normal effectiveness. Available artillery resources (some 140 guns) were well coordinated and used with great skill. Again, some of the artillery regiments played an important role when supporting the deceptive attack a few kilometres downstream of Oosterbeek.

Finally I conclude with a few words, which Major General Tony Richardson, subaltern at the 431 Battery, 147 Field Regiment RHA during the battle, said to me and some Dutch friends a few years ago in Arnhem: '*We came a long way and we did our best'!* To me this is a lasting impression of the role played by the gunners at the battle of Arnhem, albeit a few question marks regarding the planning of the operation must be raised.

22. The Final Onslaught – The Rhine Crossing

Since the failed operation at Arnhem in the autumn 1944, higher headquarters had been planning for a new massive attack across river Rhine. In respect of the need for replacement of all losses, and the necessity of boosting the supply lines for all armies with ammunition, fuel, livestock etc, they all needed several months of preparations. An important part of this was the clearing of the area north of river Schelde, which was a prerequisite for making the port of Antwerp available for the Allies. This was accomplished in November 1944. Based on this, it was thought possible to launch an offensive across Rhine in January 1945 provided the winter weather would not be too severe.

Everything did not go the Allies' way. The German offensive through the Ardennes changed the plans, but allied superiority finally gave the Allies the upper hand and the German attack was broken. They were pushed back roughly to the point where they had started. This made it possible for the headquarters of Montgomery and Bradley to return to the planning of the Rhine Crossing. But this must be preceded by a large operation to clear all the area between the rivers Maas and Rhine. The plan for this called for a British-Canadian attack southeastwards from the area between Nijmegen and Reichswald in parallel with the heavily fortified Siegfried Line down towards the city Geldern. This was the meeting point with the American 9th Army, which was to advance northwards from river Roer. This was the planned Operation Veritable in the North and Operation Grenade in the South.

Responsible for the British-Canadian operation was the 1st Canadian Army. The prime role was, however, assigned to the British XXX Corps under Lieutenant General Brian Horrocks. The Corps benefited from a temporary composition, which implied a grouping of a huge force, some 200,000 men. Four divisions would launch an initial attack with the objective of capturing the Reichswald woods. Behind them would several other infantry and armoured divisions follow suit. Planning for this huge operation without revealing place and time for it became a really demanding task, not least logistically. Staff work thus became an onerous undertaking of highest calibre.

The battle commenced on 8 February 1945 in the northern sector with a huge artillery programme. In the south, the Germans had opened dams in the Roer River, which had flooded the area where the Americans were to advance. Large areas were flooded in the British sector too (**Fig. 22-1**). The Americans had to wait until 23 February before their part of the overall operation could commence.

During the first two weeks, the Germans therefore got the advantage of concentrating most of their reserves against the British and the Canadians. The fighting became very hard and took a longer time than had been expected. Things were not made easier by the snow melting and rainy weather, which converted all roads to mud. In the vicinity of river Rhine where Canadian units were to attack, large areas were flooded.

On 10 March the struggle was over, however, when the last German units withdrew across river Rhine. The losses on both sides were very large.

Fig. 22-1 Before the Germans were forced to return across the River Rhine they had made the battle a real challenge for the Allies not least because of the extensive flooding they had arranged by breaking banks and dams. Amphibious vehicles were needed for many supply transports in the Nijmegen-Cleve area (AWM No. SUK 13839)

The initial attack in the north was supported by some 1,050 guns. The artillery programme commenced with a five hours long preparatory fire against German headquarters, fortified positions, and communication centres etc. A large counter-battery bombardment against enemy artillery was also launched. Not least, by means of the artillery intelligence resources and air reconnaissance some 45 enemy batteries with 150 guns had been located in advance. The counter-battery bombardment became a task for some 600 British guns.

Following the preparatory fire programmes, a large Covering Fire Programme had been prepared. This would include a tight fire plan for the four infantry divisions attacking close together. Superimposed on this, some 400 anti-aircraft and anti-tank guns would fire a special 'Pepperpot' Programme for several hours. Three of the divisions attacked behind a huge barrage. The fourth division, the Scottish Highlanders, preferred a fire plan based on timed concentrations against located enemy positions. Following the initial covering fire, direct support on opportunity targets was foreseen. Altogether, this was one of the largest pre-planned artillery programmes in the Second World War.

An indication of the implications of the initial artillery programmes as far as artillery was concerned is given by **Fig. 22-2**, which is illustrating the design of the barrage. The barrage covered the attack area southeast of Nijmegen over Groesbeek Hill down into Reichswald.

A creeping barrage was fired by 4–5 field regiments and 3 medium regiments in front of each division. These covered the front of the divisions up to a depth of some 500 yards from the start line. The fire during the first 70 minutes was aimed at the first lines of the barrage then a lift of 300 yards took place every twelve minutes. This exemption from normal practice and a few others were applied too. Routine was to be avoided. The barrage was planned to move forward about 5–8km from the start line of each division.

I will now conclude this background information by quoting Lieutenant Sidney Beck. He tells us how his battery with SP guns experienced a typical day in the middle of Operation Veritable. An attack by 160 Infantry Brigade on 24 February 1945 was to be supported by no less than 400 guns, amongst them Beck's guns:

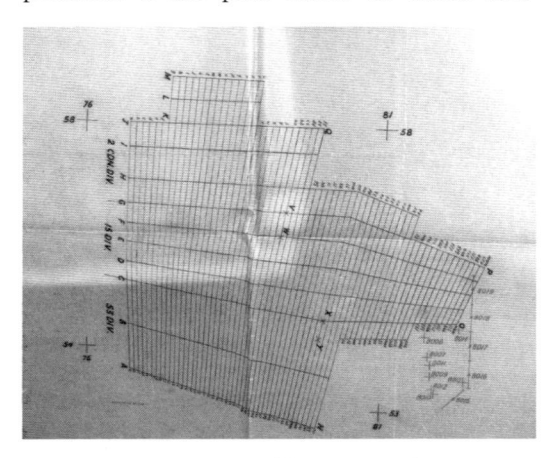

Fig. 22-2 Operation Veritable aiming at clearing the area between River Maas and River Rhine started on 8 February 1945 as a preparation for the final allied crossing of the River Rhine. The large attack was launched in south-easterly direction from Nijmegen down into Reichswald. The British-Canadian attack was made by four infantry divisions deployed beside each other. Three of them attacked behind barrages, the boundaries of which are shown. We can see pause lines included in the plan. The barrage moved 5–8km into the area held by the Germans. The fourth division, attacking south of the former three, had its covering fire planned as timed concentrations against German positions that had been well located in advance (RAHT)

> We were still unloading ammunition when the fire began at 01.30 hrs. It continued without pause until 05.15 hrs necessitating firing on a different target every 3 minutes. It says much for the high standard of training that, despite the weariness of the gunners after previous long days of firing, not a target was missed during the four hours bombardment. The attack by 53 Div progressed slowly and we were called upon for fire support during the day. Towards evening more ammunition arrived and another load around midnight. Tracks and fields were almost impassable to the ammunition lorries and we had to use our Sherman tanks to tow the trucks to the guns. This had its disadvantages as the tanks cut our telephone and tannoy wires. It was no joke for the signallers repairing torn wires in the mud and rain of a dark night. More enemy shells landed in the Regimental areas, both A and B Troops having shells on their positions, fortunately without casualties.[421]

And now to Operation Plunder, the final onslaught across river Rhine.

At the beginning of March 1945, Montgomery's 21st Army Group was deployed with the 1st Canadian Army south of Arnhem-Nijmegen and the 2nd British Army south of that along river Rhine down to the line Geldern-Wesel where the 9th US Army took over; this army under Montgomery's command too. Further south came two American armies. The 12th US Army Group in which two armies were attached, one of them Patton's 3rd Army, was closest to the British Army Group. The 6th US Army Group under Devers was deployed south of these. This consisted of one American and one French army (see **Map 22-1**).

The planning was based on extensive analyses of terrain, logistic requirements and the need for artillery and air support. The potential and possibilities of enemy counter-actions against the allied attackers were of course carefully considered also. In respect of the normal large width of the river, which had been further widened by the opened locks and dams, the attack would be of the same character as landings on a defended coast. A difference in comparison with the Normandy landings was, however, that no major concrete fortifications existed along the shore.

It was eventually decided that the main resource on the British side would be XII Corps reinforced with the 1st Commando Brigade. The Corps was to cross the river between Rees in the north and the city Wesel in the south. To the right of the British Corps, the 9th US Army would attack simultaneously with two divisions beside each other.

At a final stage of the planning process, it was decided that the attack across the river was to be done by two Corps in parallel. XXX Corps, who had carried the heaviest burden during Operation Veritable, got the task to cross to the left of XII Corps in the sector Rees – Emmerich in the north. Due to the flooding and lack of (likely) assault boats the final plan called for an advance towards Emmerich along the eastern shore of river Rhine from the Rees area once a bridgehead had been established there. The Corps attack in the north was to be launched a few hours before the main attack by XII Corps, this as a deception. But roughly at the same time, the 1st Commando Brigade in the South was to cross and attack Wesel. This would, it was thought; reinforce the impression that the prime attack would be at Rees.

Wesel was an important road and railway junction, and it was considered important to capture the city at an early stage. If so, the 9th US Army could establish a supply route with high capacity for support of the huge allied forces planned to proceed from the bridgehead into the heartland of Germany. These were to enclose the Ruhr industrial area from the north and attack towards river Elbe and the Baltic coast.

After all deliberations, Operation Plunder for the 2nd British Army had been broken down into three distinct sub-operations:

- Operation Torchlight, XII Corps
- Operation Turnscrew, *XXX Corps*
- Operation Widgeon, 1 Commando Brigade

As a protection for all these attacking formations and their preparations, the whole western shore area was to be defended by the 3rd Infantry Division in the north and the 52nd (Lowland) Infantry Division in the southern sector as soon as the whole area west of river Rhine had been cleared in Operation Veritable. The commander of the VIII Corps was to be in charge.

The tactical situation on the enemy side of the river was unclear during the planning period. The final judgement a few days before the attack was that the allies were to meet the German 1st Parachute Army. This consisted of II Parachute Corps, with three divisions, the 6th, 7th and 8th Parachute Divisions, and LXXXVI Corps, which in its turn comprised 84 and 180 Infantry Divisions. None of these formations were, however, up to nominal strength and lacked much of their heavy equipment.

The parachute formations could not any longer be regarded as airborne troops. They were more like ordinary infantry divisions, albeit with better training and battle experience. The overall battle worthiness of the German forces varied. In worst condition was the 84th Infantry Division, who had lost more than 6,000 men as prisoners of war. The parachute divisions had each lost 1,500–3,000 men.

As a reserve further back from the river on the German side, the XLVII Panzer Corps was deployed with its two divisions, the 116th Panzer Division and the 15th Panzer Grenadier Division.

Looking further to the north, the German

25th Army stood against the 1st Canadian Army.

We can briefly see the initial deployments just before Operation Plunder on **Map 22-2**.[422]

Large airborne resources had been allotted to Montgomery. The XVIII American Airborne Corps with the 13th and 17th Airborne Divisions and the British 6th Airborne Division were made available, at least on the paper. He gave directives to his staff as to how these were to be employed in principle:[423]

a) They should be used concentrated and in strength
b) The area in which they were to operate should be within artillery range of, at least, medium artillery
c) Following from (b), the timing should be such that the airborne drop was coordinated with the main assault across the river
d) There should be a quick link-up between the ground and airborne troops

We can here clearly see that Montgomery was affected by the experience from Arnhem. A lesson learned was that the weather could have a significant impact on air-landing operations. In this case, it was decided that the river crossing would be done even if the airborne part of the operation had to be cancelled due to bad weather. But a certain amount of flexibility was maintained by the decision that the whole operation could be postponed a couple of days while waiting for better weather. The postponement must never, however, be more than five days.

It was, furthermore, decided that the landings of all airborne troops would take place on one day only in order to minimise the risk of weather interference.

It was unknown as late as at the beginning of February when the airborne divisions would be landed, and how many of the tentative divisions that could be made available. This impacted on the timing of the operation. These issues were central on the agenda when a large planning conference with the concerned main actors took place on 9 February.[424]

One of the first decisions at the conference was that two airborne divisions would be employed with the task to capture the Diesfordt Woods and the closest area around it. The terrain here rises slightly above the area closer to the eastern shore of river Rhine. It was deemed serious a threat to the units attacking across the river. Furthermore, much artillery and numerous anti-aircraft guns were thought to be deployed by the Germans in the woods or its surroundings. Good observation conditions southwestwards towards the river and other lower areas were another critical factor. Besides Diesfordt Woods itself, the air-landed troops would capture a few nearby bridges across river Ijssel. Once the attacking units had linked up with the air-landed troops the latter would be either withdrawn or given special tasks in the area around Wesel.

The operation was assigned to the 6th British Airborne Division and the 17th US Airborne Division. If and how the third division, the 13th US Airborne Division, was to be employed was unclear. That was at the beginning of February an issue requiring further studies and deliberations. A possible alternative was to let it support the advance of the 9th US Army across the rivers Rhine and Lippe. There were, however, no transport resources available for bringing the division to the battlefield on the same day as the two others. Employing it later when all surprise was gone was deemed to imply unacceptable risks. As it was to be shown later, the division was never employed as an airborne formation.

As regards the timing of Operation Varsity, as the airborne operation was to be called, opinions differed.[425] The British 6th Airborne Division had in haste been transferred to Holland in December 1944 to reinforce XXX Corps when the German Ardennes offensive was to be stopped. The division had now been engaged as a fighting infantry division for more than a month. The British Command stated that the division could be employed at the Rhine 28 days after withdrawal from the fighting in Holland and returned to England. The division was well trained and an air-landing exercise with the whole division had been done just before it was taken to Holland. Furthermore, it had gained much battle experience in Normandy and later. Montgomery's wish to get the airborne units engaged at Rhine on 15 March was no problem as far as this division was concerned.

The situation was tenser as regards the American divisions. The 17th US Airborne Division was at the time of the conference also engaged in ground fighting but had never been trained as a complete formation in an air-landing operation. The Airborne Corps Commander stated as his opinion that this division could not be engaged before 1st April in respect of the need for further training. The division had also suffered from losses of 4,000 men who had to be replaced in total. This made the need for training even more acute.

After much of discussions, a compromise was agreed on. D-Day was set at 24 March. This meant that the German defenders got another two weeks for rehabilitation and preparations east of river Rhine. An officer who became worried about this was the commander of XXX Corps Lieutenant General Horrocks. On the other hand, the formations of the 2nd Army needed about a month of preparations too, before being ready to attack across river Rhine. It was now considered necessary to give the orders to the attacking divisions not later than two weeks before D-Day. If so, enough time would be given at lower levels for planning and distribution of orders. Time was also needed for further training and bringing forward the huge amounts of assault boats, ferries and bridge equipment required for this large-scale attack. Provision and stocking of artillery ammunition was another logistic challenge requiring at least one week.

XII Corps headquarters had plenty of time for their preparations. It was known by the staff at the beginning of February what the Corps role would be and a first set of planning instructions could be distributed to subordinate units already on 5 February. These had of course to be followed later by many other instructions when the staffs at higher levels continued their work and completed their planning and coordination. This was a good start. Final instructions were given to divisions and brigades at staff conferences on 8 and 10 March. The final Corps order was ready for distribution on 21 March.

The colleagues at XXX Corps had a much tougher situation. This Corps was, as we have seen, deeply engaged in Operation Veritable, the clearing of the whole area between rivers Meuse and Rhine. This battle implied an immense stress on the Corps commander and his staff week after week. The temporary Corps grouping was extremely unusual in terms of strength and the number of participating formations. At the beginning of March when the order was given to prepare for the attack across river Rhine on 24 March, all concerned were extremely exhausted.

In order to make it possible to fully concentrate on the new task, XXX Corps headquarters was relieved from the responsibility of controlling the still ongoing battle. This task was transferred to the II Canadian Corps and later to the VIII British Corps. Horrocks declared that he needed 21 days for planning and all preparations. His staff had to concentrate entirely on this task. They should be given a chance also to get some rest and time for recovery. But unfortunately this time was hardly available.

It was necessary with a quick start on 4 March when a first sketchy planning instruction was issued to all units of the Corps to take part in the operation. This was then followed by new instructions every day until 20 March when the final order to lower units must be given. The short time available made it necessary to work in parallel at Corps, Division and Brigade levels in order to meet the deadline. This called for leadership and efficient staff work of highest calibre. Horrocks was perhaps the only Corps commander in the British Army capable of bringing this process to a successful end in time.

In the XII Corps sector, the planning[426] resulted in the decision that the attack was to commence by the 1st Commando Brigade attacking on D-1 at 22.00 hours. The main attack would then follow on D-Day at H Hour, which was 02.00 hours when the 15 (Scottish) Division would attack. The division was to cross with two brigades beside each other and a third as reserve. The objective was to capture and secure an initial bridgehead on the eastern shore of river Rhine. Tanks equipped for swimming (*DD* tanks) from the 44th Tank Battalion would cross at an early stage to reinforce the infantry.[427] The Scots would of course attack headed by bagpipers in the first units. This can even today be heard in a recorded BBC-report from the attack.

Behind the Scots would follow a brigade from the 52nd (Lowland) Division and the independent 4 Armoured Brigade with the task to link up with and support the air-landed units in the Diesfordt Woods. Later (D+2 and D+3) another three divisions would cross the river as soon as the bridgehead had been enlarged and the necessary ferry lines and bridges had been arranged. This would include the 7th Armoured Division to the left and most of the 52nd (Lowland) Division to the right of this division.

Behind the former the 53rd (Welsh) Infantry Division would pass. Numerous artillery units would gradually cross the river.

In the XXX Corps sector in the north, the 51st (Highland) Division would attack, here too with two brigades beside each other, one on each side of Rees. After them, the third brigade and the attached 9 Canadian Infantry Brigade would be engaged east of the river too. The divisional attack would, as mentioned, be launched a bit earlier than the attack by XII Corps, this for the reason of deception. H Hour was here set at 21.00 hours on D-1.

The 51st (Highland) Division was to be followed as soon as possible by a Canadian Division the task of which was to attack along the left (northern) flank and capture Emmerich. This division would then return to II Canadian Corps after a couple of days.

The 43rd (Wessex) Division was planned to cross the river Rhine downstream of Rees, starting on 25 March. Later the 3rd Infantry Division, the 11th Armoured Division and 8 Independent Armoured Brigade would enlarge the bridgehead and prepare for a break-out. Much artillery would cross the river also in this sector.

Map 22-3 illustrates briefly the primary objectives on D-Day for the attacking divisions of the two Corps. There is shown also how the boundaries of the 18th US Airborne Corps were located. And the formations to follow after a couple of days are indicated as well.

The techniques of crossing the river were developed by XII Corps, together with the 79th Armoured Division (Major General Hobart). The 79th Armoured Division put numerous pieces of special equipment at the disposal. In the first wave of attack, the infantry would be transported by tracked amphibious vehicles – Buffalos, – which can be seen moving into the river in **Fig. 22-3**.

More infantry would then cross by means of small assault boats 'DD-tanks' would 'swim' across early, as mentioned.

When a first bridgehead had been secured, ferry routes could be established. These would first comprise of assault boats and 'Buffalos', but wheeled amphibious vehicles of the DUKW type as well. Larger ferries would then come, ferries that could carry light vehicles such as Jeeps and Universal Carriers. These were the Cl. 9 ferries/rafts. The figure gives the load capacity in tons. The plan was to have the first one in operation five hours after H hour.

Later the first day, ferries with capacity to carry tanks, artillery pieces and other heavier vehicles would come, 50/60 ferries/rafts. A rapid build-up of strength on the eastern side of river Rhine required much more capacity than that of the ferries although many of these were in action. More than 5,000 vehicles would be taken across in the XXX Corps sector during the first two days, this according to the plan. After six days no less than 35,000 vehicles would be over.

In order to accomplish the required capacity, bridges had to be built as soon as possible. The first type of bridge to be established was the FBE Bridge (Folded Boat Equipment), type CL 9. It was hoped in XII Corps that the first bridge of this kind would be in operation towards the evening of D-Day already.

Heavier Bailey-bridges were to be built on larger pontoons. Three classes were available, Cl 12, Cl 40 Tactical and Cl 40 High Level All Weather. The length of the bridges would be 300–600 yards. Most of the artillery was to cross the river for deployment east of it using such bridges, **Fig. 22-4**.

To make the traffic work, large resources from Royal Engineers were needed. Each division had around 20 Sapper Companies for establishing the ferries and bridges.[428] Special resources from the Royal Navy and others were also provided.

As to the wanted surprise, this could not be accomplished as regards the location of the

Fig. 22-3 The first wave of attackers across the River Rhine had to use amphibious vehicles, here 'Buffalos' leaving the Western bank of the river (AWM No. SUK 13979)

Fig. 22-4 Artillery units were redeployed east of River Rhine as soon as ferry lines had been organized and bridges built. The capacity of bridges was limited, causing long queues, with vehicles having to wait for hours before getting the opportunity to cross the river (AWM No. UK 2808)

crossings. The timing could on the other hand be kept secret to the last minute by carefully concealing the assembly of troops, stocking of ammunition and other commodities etcetera. The attacking units were deployed west of river Meuse till the very last days and nights. The artillery gun positions were prepared during the nights and the guns brought forward during the final night (cf. El Alamein).

A large programme for deception was initiated by 21 Army Group. The programme included a number of different measures. Faked radio traffic and other measures all aimed at giving an impression that the main attack would come within the area held by 1 Canadian Army near Nijmegen-Arnhem. In other words: an attack much further to the north than the selected section of river Rhine. Large-scale deceptive attacks, with complete artillery support with live ammunition, were executed by the divisions defending the western shore area as well.

In order to further reduce the risk that attack preparations were revealed in their details beforehand, smoke screens were operated along the river during the final week. These were established by units of Royal Engineers, equipped with smoke generators and covered up to some 80km along the river (**Fig. 22-5**).

Coordinated with Operation Plunder was a massive air campaign by the allied air forces. This aimed at acquisition of air superiority over the whole operational area. A large number of German airfields were bombed beginning D-3 and such attacks went on over D-Day. Each day some 1,400 bombers were engaged. It was important to make sure that enemy air resources would not interfere with the large airborne armada with its all slow-moving gliders.

Heavy bombers were, once again, to be employed in direct support of the ground forces. This time, the target was the city Wesel, which was to be completely bombed to pieces in connection with the attack by the 1st Commando Brigade during the evening and night D-1. 27 heavy bombers were to make an initial attack just before dark, later no less than 200 heavy bombers would follow suit attacking the city and fortified positions near the city. The bombers would arrive at 22.45 hours, i.e. 45 minutes after the time when the Commandos commenced their attack across river Rhine. The brigade was planned to have secured its bridgehead at this time and was prepared to attack the city.

Another important task on the part of fighter-bombers and medium bombers was to complement the counter-battery bombardment launched by the allied artillery. Enemy artillery and anti-aircraft gun positions just out of range of the artillery were the targets, basically east of the motorway (*Autobahn*) under construction. This runs in parallel with river Rhine (cf. **Map 22-3**).

When the attacks were well under way, the air resources were to be available for direct

Fig. 22-5 Smoke belts along River Rhine concealed during two weeks the preparations for the crossing. This did not stop the sound rangers from locating enemy artillery and anti-aircraft deployments, but for observation bases (Flash Spotters) it was much more difficult (©Imperial War Museum BU 1951)

support of the attacking units (Close Air Support). Extensive preparations with special liaison detachments, radio equipment etc., had been planned in order to facilitate quick and efficient support.[429]

We must note finally that a huge operation like Operation Plunder could not be executed unless much of training had been included in all the preparations. Training of the drivers of amphibious vehicles was important, as were exercises on loading and unloading of the vehicles. Construction of ferries and training of loading and unloading of vehicles on board these are other examples of what was needed.

The attacking units had also to rehearse in full strength including attached resources. Special weeklong brigade exercises were organised for all participating brigades. These took place as crossings of river Meuse, one exercise in daytime and one similar during the night.[430]

As regards the units of XII Corps, there was no problem finding time for exercises, but for those of XXX Corps, preparations were much more hectic. By taking advantage of the plans of the other Corps, it was possible, however, to get ready in time. And the fact that it was important with all the exercises and other training efforts is shown by a statement made by the commander of one of the units once it had crossed river Rhine: 'During the exercises everything went wrong, when the real crossing was made everything was perfectly done.'

All marching to the final deployment areas were made in the dark as was planned for the initial crossings. Artificial moonlight had to be arranged along the river and further backwards to make it easier for the attackers, 'movement light'. This was a task given to searchlight batteries of the Royal Artillery (**Fig. 22-6**).

Within the XII Corps section a line of searchlights was established around 3km west of the river and another one around 7km west from it. Searchlight batteries were used in a similar way in support of XXX Corps. Even further to the north, searchlights were used for purposes of deception.

Artillery planning initially concentrated at Corps headquarters

In the early planning stages, the need for artillery was analysed at the headquarters of the 21st Army Group and the 2nd Army, in particular in relation to the planned role of XII Corps and the XVIII US Airborne Corps. It was obvious, that a massive backing of both Corps was essential. A painful lesson from Operation Market Garden was that air-landing troops must have access to much more artillery than the limited own resources, which were an organisational part of such formations. In the 6th Airborne Division only one light regiment with twenty-four 75-mm air-landing howitzers was available, as we know (an American airborne division could at best bring four battalions each with twelve guns to the battlefield).

This might be compared with the armament of an ordinary infantry division, which was three regiments, i.e. in total 72 guns. This artillery force was often reinforced in battle by one or several field regiments as well as by medium and heavy regiments from army artillery groups (AGRAs).

Many changes of artillery grouping were made in February and March 1945. This was a consequence of Operation Veritable, which was not completed until 10 March. The uncertainty as to whether one or two British Corps were to be engaged simultaneously of course had an impact on the planning. To this must be added the uncertainty regarding the number of airborne divisions to be engaged; would it be one, two or three?

At the beginning of March, the artillery Order of Battle for XII Corps was eventually fixed,[431] soon also the one for XXX Corps.

At the disposal of the artillery commander

Fig. 22-6 Many searchlight detachments deployed in several lines parallel with the river were used to create artificial light over the battlefield. Rocket beams and tracer fire from anti-aircraft guns also gave guidance as regards correct direction of attacks (RAHT)

of XII Corps, Brigadier William Heath, a massive artillery force was allotted. This was about the double size of the normal artillery strength of a British Corps. The Order of Battle is presented in detail in **Appendix 6.** In this neither the anti-tank nor anti-aircraft resources not used for ground roles have been included, irrespective of the fact that these also were under his command. We can summarise the artillery strength as follows:

- 15 field regiments (25-pounders)
- 1 mountain regiment (3.7-inch mountain howitzers)
- 10 medium regiments (4.5-inch guns and 5-5-inch gun-howitzers)
- 2 heavy regiments (7.2-inch howitzers and 155-mm guns)
- 3 American artillery battalions (155-mm pieces)
- 1 Super Heavy Regiment (8-inch and 240-mm howitzers)
- 2 heavy anti-aircraft regiments in ground role (3.7-inch guns)

It should be noted that out of all medium regiments only one still had 4.5-inch guns. Standardisation to 5.5-inch guns (gun-howitzers) for medium regiments was now almost completed.

These formations, with a total of 640 guns, came from the regiments of participating divisions and from three army artillery groups, 3 AGRA, 8 AGRA and 9 AGRA. The latter groups had medium, heavy and super heavy formations but also a few army field regiments. From one of the independent armoured brigades, 4 Armoured Brigade, came 4 Field Regiment RHA which was armed with SP guns. This regiment was planned to be the first to be ferried across the river. It had been assigned the role to provide support for the 6th Airborne Division. The regiment was specially trained for this role and was given a forward deployment area close to the river.

In support of XXX Corps and the Canadian brigade attached to it, a large artillery force was also allotted. This force was planned to be large enough to support the enlargement of the initial bridgehead to accommodate one, later two divisions beside each other; eventually large enough for three divisions. From this enlarged bridgehead, the eventual breakout was to take place.

In this case, the artillery came from participating divisions and two army artillery groups, 4 AGRA and 5 AGRA. Significant resources from the II Canadian Corps in the north were also needed in addition to these. The Order of Battle for XXX Corps is presented in **Appendix 7.** From this we can summarise the resources made available for the Corps artillery commander, Brigadier S.B. Rawlins:[432]

- 16 field regiments, of which 3 were Canadian
- 1 mountain battery
- 11 medium regiments, of which 2 were Canadian
- 4 heavy regiments, of which 2 were Canadian
- 3 heavy anti-aircraft regiments (only a few batteries for a ground role)

In the background, a Super Heavy Regiment was deployed as an additional resource, if required.

This meant that this Corps was to be supported by 676 guns, hence somewhat more than those of XII Corps.

By these allotments, the 21st Army Group had assembled more than 1,300 guns to support the attacks by the two Corps across river Rhine, i.e. more artillery than the allotment for Operation Veritable. A huge artillery resource was furthermore available for reinforcement from other Corps further back should it be required.

The deployment areas adopted immediately before the attacks, and which had been prepared during the nights of the previous week, are schematically illustrated on **Map 22-4**. We can see that this large artillery force was squeezed into an area 6–10km deep and 30km wide. A large stock of ammunition was dumped at each gun position.

After deployment of the guns, their vehicles were taken to 'Wagon Lines' a few kilometres backwards, most of them south of Kevelaer.

For survey, establishment of sound range bases and observation bases, the resources of the survey regiment of XII Corps, 7 Survey Regiment RA, were reinforced by a battery from 10 Survey Regiment RA, which normally supported VIII Corps. The resources of XXX Corps, 4 Survey Regiment RA, were reinforced in the same way by a battery from the same regiment. The entire front of both Corps could thus be covered with resources for location of enemy artillery and mortars. I am indicating their deployment on **Map 22-5**.[433] We can see that two supporting sound ranging bases were established within each Corps sector and in addition to these, three 'light' sound ranging bases, 4-pen recorders, in the XII Corps sector and two in the XXX Corps sector. The 'heavy' bases had two advance posts each. These are not showed on the map.

In addition to the observation bases, i.e. 'long bases', numerous ordinary fire observation posts were deployed along the river as well. Those coming from the various army artillery groups (AGRAs) were netted to the counter-battery officer of each Corps (CBO) on the special radio net established for observations on enemy artillery and mortars, the Shell Rep Net. Those belonging to the divisional artillery were netted on the normal regimental net to their regimental headquarters from which their observations were passed on to CBOs and regiments.

Each Corps had for the first time been allotted three radar stations too. These were to be used for locating mortar positions.

As we have seen from Appendix 6 and Appendix 7, several AOP Squadrons were allotted as well. These were grouped to give all infantry and armoured divisions one Flight each (4 aircraft). Every AGRA got at least one Flight too. For reconnaissance and fire control deeper into the enemy area, Army Cooperation Squadrons of RAF were available (using Arty/R procedures). They were to be continuously flying in the area on D-Day. Certain medium regiments had been dedicated for cooperation with RAF. But firing should not be done only by a medium regiment acting as radio counter-part, but by all regiments of the Corps not engaged in other tasks. Hence, targets were to be engaged as Victor Targets.

The intelligence resources of the artillery were engaged one week before the attacks. They were the prime resource for collection of data on enemy artillery and mortar locations. They collected also general tactical information regarding enemy deployment of infantry, assault guns, vehicles etc., up to around 2km from the river.

In order to get a quick and efficient planning process regarding the employment of the large artillery resources, planning was initially concentrated to the Corps level. Planning was here particularly concentrated on the large preparatory fire programmes that were to precede the attacks. In this operation, extensive counter-battery programmes were to be prepared as well as were strong preparatory bombardment of enemy positions aiming at reducing the enemy's will to resist the attacks, i.e. Softening Bombardment. Not until a week or two before D-Day, the divisional headquarters took over detailed planning. The staffs had to prepare in detail fire support of the crossings as such and the fighting thereafter.

The headquarters of XII Corps and its divisions had another task to deal with. The landings of airborne forces were to be facilitated by a preparatory fire programme, which was to be ended by a short anti-aircraft bombardment near the dropping and landing zones. Another fire program to be prepared in detail was the artillery support for 1 Commando Brigade's initial attack on D-1.

The concerned regimental headquarters did not get more than a week for their preparations, sometimes only a few days. Information had to be distributed to subordinate commanders piece by piece. The gunners who were to undertake all firing missions were informed about the coming attack on D-2, in some cases as late as D-1.

Hard, exhausting staff work

So, numerous fire tasks had to be prepared down to the single gun within XII Corps area:

- Counter Bombardment (against enemy artillery and mortars)
- Preparatory bombardment of enemy positions east of river Rhine
- Support of the attack against Wesel by 1 Commando Brigade (Operation Widgeon)
- Support of the river crossing by 15 (Scottish) Division (Operation Torchlight)
- Preparatory bombardment of enemy positions preceding the arrival of airborne forces (Operation Varsity)
- Counter bombardment of enemy anti-aircraft positions just before the air-landings;
- Support of air-landed forces
- Direct support of formations that had crossed river Rhine

Governing the planning was the time schedule for the various attacks, which was:

- Operation Widgeon 23 March 1945 (D-1) 22.00 hours
- Operation Torchlight 24 March (D) 02.00 hours
- Operation Varsity 24 March (D) 10.00 hours

Much artillery ammunition was needed, although no exact figures on consumption could be given. During the nights D-7 to D-1, the following volumes were stockpiled at gun positions or more centrally:[434]

25-pounder HE Shells	600/gun
25-pounder Smoke Shells	5,000 – 6,000/divisional artillery group
25-pounder Flare Shells	100/colour (three available), supplied to divisional artillery of 7 Armoured Division
25-pound Flare Shells	900/colour (three available), supplied to divisional artillery of 15 (Scottish) Division
Super Charge (25-pounder)	250/gun
5.5-inch gun-howitzers	500/gun out of which 30–50% were 80-lb shells
4.5-inch guns	500/gun
Heavy guns/howitzers	300/gun
Super Heavy howitzers	100/gun
Heavy anti-aircraft guns	400/gun (ground roles)
Mountain Howitzers	350/gun

Sufficient stocks of rockets had to be arranged as well.

For all units that were engaged to complement the artillery by participating in *Pepperpot* programmes huge volumes of ammunition had also to be stocked beforehand. Such programmes included 17-pounder anti-tank guns, Bofors (40-mm) anti-aircraft guns, tanks, 4.2-inch mortars and heavy machine guns which all were to fire series of timed concentrations against carefully selected targets. With the exception of the machine guns, they were all to be engaged in indirect fire, indeed an unusual undertaking on their part.

Transporting all ammunition to the gun positions was a real logistic challenge. One hundred and twenty-four 3-ton lorries were required to bring forward in the dark the ammunition for one medium regiment only.[435]

Extensive firing without prior ranging required accurate survey of all firing units into the same grid. A Corps grid with fixed 'trig points' should be established at 16.00 hours on D-6, it was decided. Best possible and accurate weather data was another pre-requisite. Such data were to be distributed from the Corps headquarters to all regiments. Normally such distribution was to take place every four hours. The ambition was raised just before D-Day. It would take place every three hours, which required a tighter schedule for remote collection of wind, temperature and air pressure data.

Further measures taken in order to secure best possible accuracy were extensive gun calibration firing before the attacks. This was particularly a responsibility for medium and heavy regiments. The muzzle velocity of their guns had to be carefully calibrated after all the extensive firing they had been through during Operation Veritable. The units were in turn sent to the Lommel range in Belgium for such calibration.

As in Operation Veritable, an extensive counter-bombardment programme against artillery and mortars would, as mentioned, be fired in Operation Plunder too. A 'softening bombardment' over several hours was another fire programme similar to what had been executed in the former operation.

The major difference between the artillery programmes of the two operations was the design of the covering fire plans. In Operation Plunder the task was to protect the crossings of numerous amphibious vehicles and assault boats loaded with infantry, who were not to commence fighting until disembarking on the eastern shore had taken place. Hence, there was no need for large area-covering creeping or rolling barrages. Instead it was a matter of neutralising or destroying selected targets either by means of heavy concentrations or by 'Stonks', i.e. fire against line targets in the latter case. Several hundred targets were registered beforehand and detailed preparations were made for their bombardment.

Map 22-6, which is an extract of the fire plan, is illustrating the chosen concept. The targets were farms, road junctions, and sections of railways etc, where it was expected to find enemy positions or where he would bring reinforcements forward.

In order to conceal the exact timing of the crossings, the fire was shifted from targets close to the river some 400 yards inwards and after a short while, it was moved back to the shore. This was repeated several times, by which it was hoped that the enemy would be inclined to remain under cover when the ultimate shift had to take place in connection with the infantry's crossing.

We can now summarise the different fire plans within the XII Corps area with time, number of guns with different calibres etcetera. **Fig. 22-7:1** and **Fig. 22-7:2** give graphical illustrations for both Corps.

Ten hours of counter-bombardment

We will first look at the counter-bombardment programmes prepared by the commander of 9 AGRA and his staff, **Table 22-1**.

As we can see, this bombardment was a task assigned to medium and heavy units. These were also engaged in Operation Widgeon and Operation Torchlight for direct support of advancing formations. With only short breaks, the guns were firing continuously for about twelve hours. This required certainly well trained and determined gun crews (**Fig. 22-8**).

Bombardment of mortars seems to have been led by the 'Counter Mortar Officer' (CMO) of either 52 (Lowland) Division or 15 (Scottish) Division, but no documentation to confirm this has been found.

Strong support of the Commando Brigade – Operation Widgeon

Responsible for planning artillery support of 1

Fig. 22-7:1 The fire plans for Operations 'Plunder' and 'Varsity' were extensive and were to be fired over many hours in a way that was similar to the huge fire plans of the Great War 1914–1918. Here the different sub-plans for the support of XII Corps are summarised. The Rhine Crossing came to be the big final for the British artillery in World War II (Author)

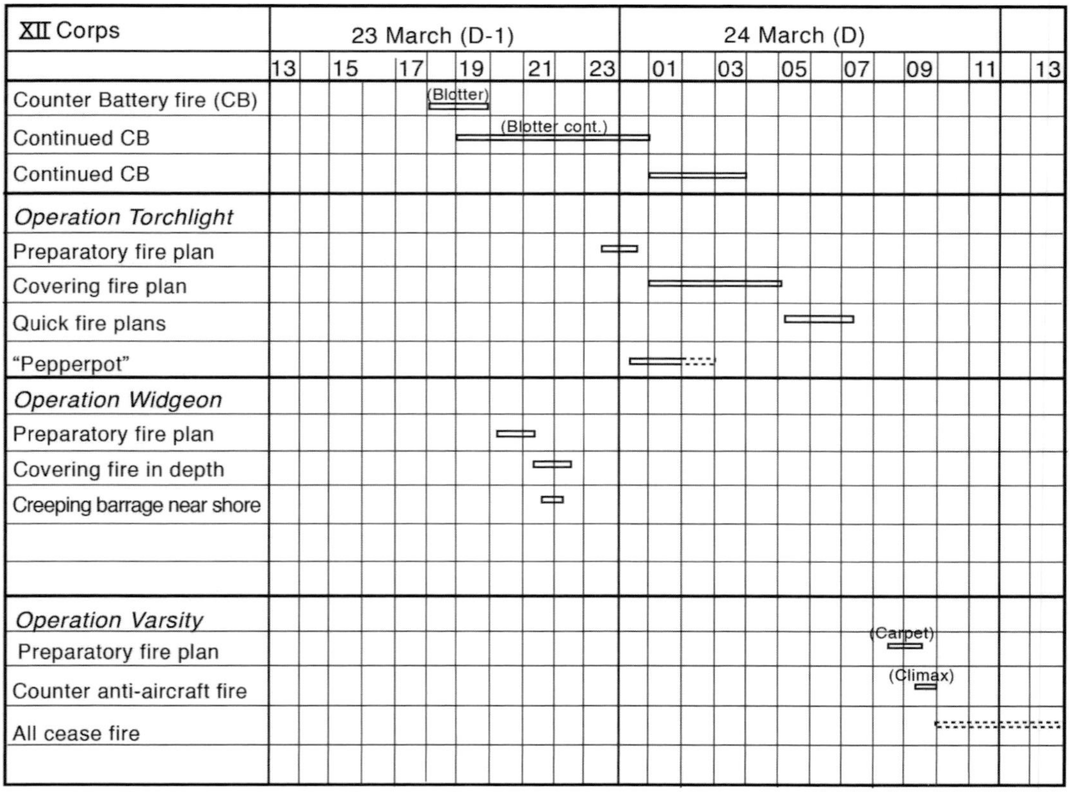

XII Corps	23 March (D-1)						24 March (D)						
	13	15	17	19	21	23	01	03	05	07	09	11	13
Counter Battery fire (CB)				(Blotter)									
Continued CB					(Blotter cont.)								
Continued CB													
Operation Torchlight													
Preparatory fire plan													
Covering fire plan													
Quick fire plans													
"Pepperpot"													
Operation Widgeon													
Preparatory fire plan													
Covering fire in depth													
Creeping barrage near shore													
Operation Varsity										(Carpet)			
Preparatory fire plan													
Counter anti-aircraft fire										(Climax)			
All cease fire													

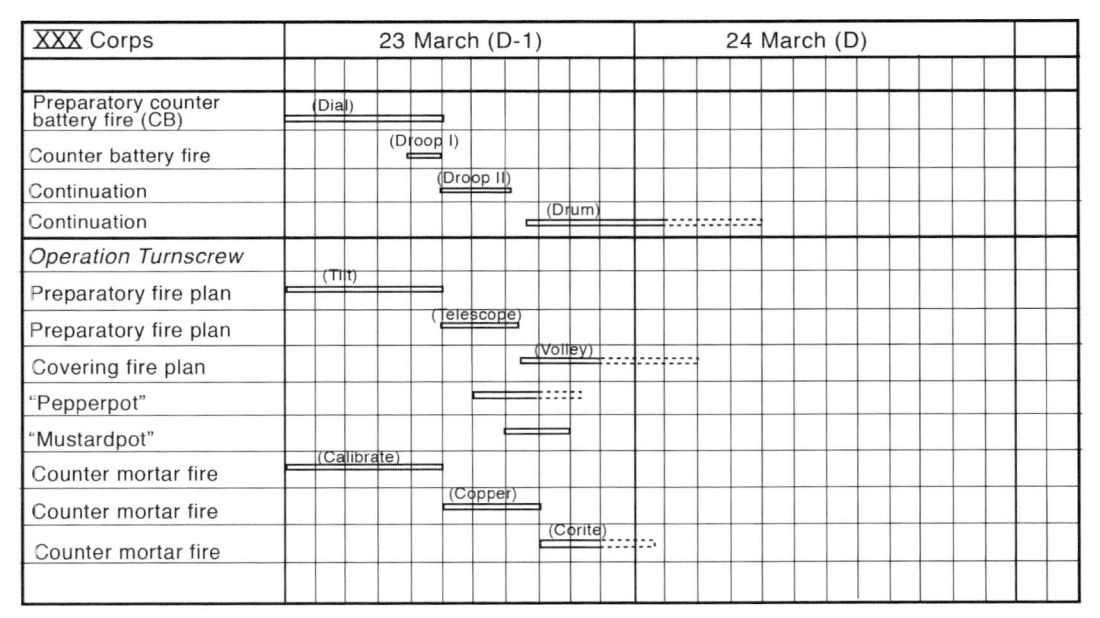

Fig. 22-7:2 Here the various fire plans that were devised for the support of XXX Corps at the Rhine Crossing are summarized (Author)

Commando Brigade was the artillery commander (CRA) of the 7th Armoured Division. His fire plan is attached to his order for Operation Widgeon and comprises several parts as shown in **Table 22-2**. 'H' hour was D-1 22.00 hours.[436]

The Mountain Regiment RA made available for the operation was put under command of the Commando Brigade. To compensate for the limited range of the mountain howitzer, the regiment was deployed as near Wesel as possible.

Forward Observation Officers from the regiment would accompany the brigade during its attack. One of the battery commanders, Major Ruston, was nominated 'Brigade Artillery Commander'. The reason for this arrangement had a communication background.

To make sure that fire observation data and fire orders would be possible to communicate, it was necessary to use the No. 22 wireless set with its longer range, but a problem was that no vehicles could be used during the attack for transport of the equipment. But the mountain

Table 22-1. XII Corps counter-bombardment programmes

Day, time	Fire Plan	Number of guns, types
D-1 18.00–20.00	BLOTTER	160 medium
		32 heavy (155-mm/7.2-inch)
		4 super heavy (240-mm)
		36 American heavy (155-mm)
		24 heavy anti-aircraft (3.7-inch)
D-1/D 20.00–01.00	Continued bombardment	16 medium
		32 heavy
		2 super heavy (8-inch)
		36 American heavy
		24 heavy anti-aircraft
D/D+1 10.00–04.00	Continued bombardment	Only heavy batteries

Table 22-2. Fire plans in support of 1 Commando Brigade

Day, time	Fire Plan	Number of guns, types
D-1, 20.30–21.28	Softening	160 medium
		16 heavy (7.2-inch)
		4 super heavy (240-mm)
D-1, 21.30–22.30	Covering fire, rear targets	168 25-pounders
		heavy guns as above
D-1, 21.50–22.10	Creeping barrage from the eastern shore	144 25-pounders
D-1, 22.15–22.50	Flank indication with green flare shells	4 25-pounders on each flank, firing every 30 seconds
D-1, 22.45–22.50	Moving fire along railway, high intensity	24 mountain howitzers (3.7-inch)

Fig. 22-8 Both Operation Veritable and Operation Plunder implied extensive night artillery firing. Here a Medium Regiment is seen in action (RAHT)

gunners had developed special means to overcome such problems. This included boards, strings and stretchers for carrying on foot the equipment including batteries. This was just what was needed here.

An exemption from the general concept of fire plans with concentrations and 'Stonks' was a barrage arranged as protection of the crossing by the Commando Brigade and the initial advance once ashore. It was planned as a creeping barrage where four field regiments opened fire against targets beside each other. Each one covered a front of 500 yards and together they thus covered around 2,000 yards. 200 yards ahead of these units, another two regiments were to fire, spread out over the same front line, i.e. 2,000 yards. When the former shifted 100 yards ahead, the latter made a similar shift forwards and so on.

The fire plan for 'Operation Widgeon' implied a remarkable concentration of firepower in support of one single brigade. The entire Corps artillery force was basically engaged just before and during the attack across river Rhine!

A quite strong resource was reserved for direct support of the Commando Brigade during another ten hours, namely:

- Two field regiments
- One mountain regiment
- Two medium regiments
- One heavy battery

This meant that around 108 guns were at the disposal of the brigade commander. This can be compared with the normal allotment of artillery for a brigade, which was just one field regiment, i.e. 24 guns (only 25-pounders).

And then: concentrated firepower in support of the main attack – Operation Torchlight

The main attack within the XII Corps section was carried out by the 15th (Scottish) Division, who also was to be supported by the majority of available artillery resources. Responsible for planning and execution was the divisional artillery commander (CRA) and his staff. This was a tough undertaking, which can be illustrated by the fact that they under strong pressure, due to the short available time, had to produce and distribute 269 copies of fire plans and coordinate lists for several hundred targets down to all organisational levels; not to mention the hundreds of traces (map overlays).

The fire programme had the overall structure with 'H' hour set at D-1 22.00 hours as is summarised in **Table 22-3**.

During the initial attack phase, the artillery resources were distributed roughly equal on the two attacking brigades, 227 Infantry Brigade to the left and 44 Infantry Brigade to the right.[437] When a shift of concentration southwards later took place (at 08.20 hours) in connection with softening bombardment before the air landings, the former could rely on support from four field regiments, one medium regiment and a heavy anti-aircraft regiment (ground roles), and the

Table 22-3. Fire plans in support of the 15th (Scottish) Division

Day, time	Fire Plan	Number of guns, types
D-1/D, 23.30–00.30	Softening	160 medium
		16 heavy (7.2-inch)
		4 super heavy (240-mm)
D, 01.00–05.30	Covering fire	288 25-pounders
		144 medium
		12 heavy guns (7.2-inch)
		4 super heavy (240-mm)
		24 heavy anti-aircraft guns (3.7-inch), in ground roles
		One rocket battery
D, 05.30–07.30	Continued direct support against pre-registered targets	Same employment

latter brigade one field regiment and one medium regiment. The Corps artillery commander could, however, allot further resources to a brigade, if needed. For all of the regiments, 'cease fire' was ordered for a few hours when the air landings were taking place. More about this later.

Three of the field regiments were reserved for firing smoke belts on order from the Corps headquarters. They constituted a special artillery group commanded by the commander of 25 Field Regiment RA. It was to be shown that they never had to be used for such tasks.

One medium regiment was retained at disposal of the commander of 9 AGRA (Army Group RA) to be used for counter-bombardment when special needs arose. This regiment was to be used also for fire in depth in cooperation with the Royal Air Force Army-cooperation Squadrons acting as observation posts. As mentioned, such engagements would be ordered as 'Victor Targets', which meant fire with all artillery within the Corps. It was about dealing with critical targets such as large enemy artillery deployments.[438]

Some ten salvos with the Canadian rocket battery were also planned. This only battery had 12 launching carriages for 32 rockets each (an earlier version was designed for 30 rockets).[439]

Finally, a few words about the *Pepperpot* programme, which was planned to begin one and a half hour before the main attack. This was the responsibility of the commander of 112 Light Anti-Aircraft Regiment RA. Three groups were organised, *HOOP, WHISTLE* and *TOP*, each one comprising quite a number of firing units of different kinds:

- 40-mm Bofors anti-aircraft guns
- 4.2-inch mortars
- 17-pounder SP anti-tank guns
- Machine guns

The groups were deployed to cover the entire Corps area.[440] During the period H-15 minutes to H+15 minutes, the Bofors guns would not be used, as they were to mark the flank boundaries of the attacking battalions with tracer fire bursts.

According to the plan for the Bofors guns of HOOP-group, they would engage nine different targets between H-90 to H-15 minutes. Each gun was to fire 180 rounds. In the second phase from H+20 to H+90 minutes, seven targets were to be engaged, and this with a total of 250 rounds per gun. This part of the 'Pepperpot' was in support of 44 Infantry Brigade.

Before turning to the air-landings, we will first have a summarising glance at the artillery planning in XXX Corps.

Massive XXX Corps Artillery support – Operation Turnscrew

In principle, more than 600 guns available to XXX Corps would be used in the same way as the artillery of XII Corps. Timings were, however, a bit different, and there was only one major attack across river Rhine to plan for. The 51st (Highland) Division was to cross with two brigades beside each other, one on each side of the city Rees. These were to be followed by the third divisional brigade and the temporarily attached 9 Canadian Infantry Brigade. The planning had to focus on the subsequent enlargement of the bridgehead and also the eventual breakout northwards and eastwards.

The violent, and in time stretched out, fire programme was to begin with a softening fire for four hours including counter-battery bombardment. This would then at H-30 minutes be followed by covering fire for the two attacking brigades. Available artillery was divided into two groups, 'A' and 'B'. The counter-battery programme was a 'milk round', much liked by the Corps commander, Lieutenant General Horrocks. A special counter-mortar programme was here included too. In this case, it is well documented. Responsible was the artillery commander of the 3rd Infantry Division. This programme was to go on for three hours.

Another important feature was the *Pepperpot* programme, which was planned also by the artillery commander of 3 Infantry Division. It was obviously given higher priority than that of the neighbouring southern Corps. The programme was here to begin two hours before 'H' hour and include engagement of ten different targets by the following resources:[441]

- 22 tanks with 75-mm guns
- 48 17-pounder anti-tank guns (towed and SP)
- 72 40-mm Bofors anti-aircraft guns
- 36 4.2-inch mortars
- Machine guns of seven machine gun companies

The tanks were allotted 200 rounds per tank, the anti-tank guns 90 per gun, the Bofors guns 750 per gun and the mortars 300 per each.

While the above programme included only targets outside Rees, a special program: *Mustardpot* was prepared for the city area itself. This programme, also intensive in its design, was prepared by the artillery commander of the attacking division.

We can now summarise the different fire plans prepared for XXX Corps. Due to lack of space, reference is made to the war diaries for details.[442] The counter-bombardment programme is summarised in **Table 22-4**, see also **Fig. 22-7:2**.

The first part, *DIAL*, was to be done by ranging and direct observation of the fire. The number of targets, and thus ammunition allotment, was limited. *DROOP I* and *DROOP II* were the main parts of the programme and ammunition allotment was thus good. The final part, *DRUM*, which was not limited in time, aimed at quick counter-bombardment against enemy batteries which were activated during the river crossing.

The counter-mortar programme comprised several separate fire plans as shown in **Table 22-5**.

The first fire plan, *CALIBRATE*, aimed at harassing enemy mortar units, but it was aimed at ranging/checking air burst heights with the support of the observation resources of the survey regiment. This was as a preparation for the main fire plan, *COPPER*, which was to be fired only as an air burst programme. The 25-pounders were to use the new VT fuzes for maximum height accuracy.

The final fire plan aimed to quickly answer fire from activated enemy mortars when the attack was under way, as had been planned for the artillery counter-bombardment programme.

The support of the 51st (Highland) Division when attacking across river Rhine, which was to commence at D-1 21.00 hours, was divided into several sub-programmes too. The first two fire plans were 'softening fire programmes' against enemy positions near the river aiming at reducing morale and will to resist. Then the main covering fire programme was launched in support of the crossing. The overall programme is summarised in **Table 22-6**.

The first part, *TILT*, can be seen as a 'ranging programme' with low ammunition consumption planned. The aim was to provide a foundation for good accuracy in the main pro-

Table 22-4. XXX Corps counter-bombardment programmes

Day, time	Fire Plan	Number of guns, types
D-1, 13.00–17.00	DIAL (preparatory bombardment)	16 medium 8 heavy (155-mm/7.2-inch) 2 super heavy (240-mm) 24 heavy anti-aircraft guns (3.7-inch
D-1, 17.00–18.00	DROOP I	216 25-pounders 160 medium 36 heavy guns (155-mm/7.2-inch) 4 super heavy (8-inch/240-mm) 72 heavy anti-aircraft guns (3.7-inch), in ground roles
D-1, 18.00–20.15	DROOP II	96 25-pounders 112 medium 20 heavy (155-mm /7.2-inch) 4 super heavy (8-inch/240-mm) 24 heavy anti-aircraft guns (3.7-inch), in ground roles
D-1, 20.30– on call	DRUM	32 medium 20 heavy (155-mm/7.2-inch) 2 super heavy 24 heavy anti-aircraft guns (3.7-inch) in ground roles

grammes, *TELESCOPE* and *VOLLEY*.

It might be added that certain units were to be engaged from D-1 21.00 hours in harassing fire against targets in depth from the front line, this to 'seal off' the area where the main attack was to take place.

Finally, it should be mentioned that the *Pepperpot* programme was to be executed between 19.00 hours and 20.55 hours on D-1 but could be extended thereafter by the engaged mortars. The *Mustardpot* programme against Rees was planned for D-1 20.00 hours to 22.00 hours.

The mistakes at Arnhem should not be repeated – Operation Varsity

There were several lessons learnt from Arnhem that affected the planning of the large Rhine crossing operation. First, complete airborne divisions should this time be landed the same day. Second, the landings should be done close to the objectives, partly on them.

Another important lesson was to make sure that the airborne units could count on support from artillery deployed west of the river directly after landing, at least from medium artillery with sufficient range. Particularly important in this

Table 22-5. XXX Corps mortar counter-bombardment

Day, time	Fire Plan	Number of guns, types
D-1, 12.00–18.00	CALIBRATE	12 heavy (7.2-inch)
		48 heavy anti-aircraft guns (3.7-inch), in ground roles
D-1, 18.00–21.00	COPPER	16 25-pounders
		20 heavy guns (7.2-inch)
		48 heavy anti-aircraft guns (3.7-inch), in ground roles
D-1, 21.00–on call	CORDITE	48 25-pounders
		4 heavy (7.2-inch)

context were the two batteries still equipped with 4.5-inch guns (range around 18.5km) and the 155-mm 'Long Tom' guns which had a range above 20km. It was of great importance to take advantage of these units.

From artillery point of view, it was also essential to make sure that early radio contacts between the air-landed troops and the ground forces west of river Rhine could be established.

The air-landings were, as we have seen, a Corps operation with one British and one American airborne division. The commander of the XVIII US Airborne Corps and his staff, including the artillery staff, were to take command of the landed units once they were on the ground. When this had taken place, the 1st Commando Brigade would leave XII Corps and also come under his command.

For each airborne division (the 6th British and 17th US Division) an artillery group from XII Corps was to be put at their disposal for support during the first 24 hours. As regards the British, the three field regiments of the 52nd (Lowland) Division, with two medium

Table 22-6. Fire plans in support of the 51st (Highland) Division

Day, time	Fire Plan	Number of guns, types
D-1, 13.00–18.00	TILT	16 25-pounders
		8 medium (5.5-inch)
		2 super heavy (240mm)
D-1, 18.00–20.20	TELESCOPE	360 25-pounders
		48 medium (5.5-inch)
D-1, 20.30–on call	VOLLEY covering fire	360 25-pounders
		128 medium (4.5-inch/5.5-inch)
		16 heavy (7.2-inch)
		One rocket battery

regiments under command, were allotted to the 6th Airborne Division. The divisional artillery of the 53rd (Welsh) Infantry Division and one medium regiment were put at the disposal of the American Airborne Division in a similar way.

As further assistance, 8 AGRA was reserved as a special supporting group as well. It consisted of one field regiment and the remaining medium regiments (after two had been allotted to the 52nd (Lowland) Division and one to the 53rd (Welsh) Division) and one heavy regiment. The three American 155-mm battalions in the area were attached as well (3x12 guns).

I will now concentrate the review and presentation on the planning for the 6th Airborne Division. This division was planned to land around the north-western part of Diesfordt Woods with 3 Parachute Brigade near the river, with 5 Parachute Brigade northernmost away from river Rhine and 6 Airlanding Brigade near Hammenkiln and Ijssel Canal.

The division would protect the northern and northwestern flanks of XVIII Corps and disturb the enemy defence east of river Rhine. By doing this, a large bridgehead would be secured much quicker. It was an important objective to capture three bridges across the Ijssel Canal just east of Hammenkiln.

We can see the incoming air routes on **Map 22-7**, the northern to be used by the British and the southern by the Americans. The map does not show the five supply dropping zones, to be used by the many transport aircraft during the first day. These were located close to the dropping zones.

The selected dropping zones implied that only 3 Parachute Brigade could be supported by field regiments west of river Rhine. The two other brigades were landed too far from the river. We may here recall that only some 30% of available shells could reach the maximum range due to the limited supply of 'Super Charges' for the 25-pounders. This would imply some consequences for the plans devised.

First, it was decided that the division's own regiment, 53 Airlanding Light Regiment RA, would be organised temporarily with two 12-guns batteries. Deployment and firing with this organisation was trained on Salisbury Plain before departure for Rhine. The regiment had in February started training on the use of 25-pounders and it was decided that the regiment would bring two of them to Rhine in addition to the normal armament of twenty-four 75-mm howitzers.

The two batteries were to be grouped for support of 5 Parachute Brigade and 6 Airlanding Brigade respectively. In order to strengthen the support to these brigades the two medium regiments of the 52nd (Lowland) Division's artillery group were allotted with one to each Brigade. Furthermore, when needed, 8 AGRA would reinforce them. With these well-conceived arrangements, the air-landed troops would be much better off than the 1st Airborne Division had been at Arnhem.

4 Field Regiment RHA belonging to 4 Independent Armoured Brigade would as mentioned with priority be ferried across river Rhine and as soon as possible link up with the air-landed formations. It was hoped that this could take place in the evening of D-Day already. The following day, it was planned to get a second field regiment across the river to reinforce the air-landed 'Red Berets'.

There were plenty of fire observation detachments as the 2 FOU was under command of 6 Airborne Division. Each brigade and battalion headquarters had such resources. Thanks to the allotment of 2 FOU, a special organisation for mortar counter-bombardment could also be established. An officer in charge, Counter Mortar Officer (CMO), was placed at the divisional headquarters with an assistant (ACMO) at each one of the three brigade headquarters.

The communication between the airborne division and the relieving forces had not been well prepared in Arnhem. Neither had it been trained for it properly. Hence, it did not work and required improvisations. The lesson was now learned. In order to make sure that the communication would work this time despite long distances and bad transmission conditions, skilled signallers well trained for this situation were used at all critical wireless stations. The airborne division was also to detach own signallers to all-important stations at the supporting units west of river Rhine. Signallers at both ends were to know each other and should have trained together.

It was decided that a liaison officer with signallers from the airborne division would be attached to the artillery headquarters of the 52nd (Lowland) Division and its three field regiments. At 8 AGRA and 4 Field Regiment RHA such detachments were organised as well. The value of relay stations had been obvious at Arnhem. They had there been improvised. Here, they were planned for in advance.

A problem at Arnhem was the limited range of the wireless sets used, in particular during the nights. In order to eliminate such problems, the gunners were now equipped with better equipment. FOOs were equipped with No. 62 sets instead of the usual No. 22. The range was thus 40–50 per cent longer when used for radiotelephony, i.e. around 22km (with Morse around 32km). This set had the advantage also that it could be carried by two men instead of the 3–4 men required for No. 22, this when sets were not transported with Universal Carriers or Jeeps. The set No. 68P had been introduced for communication with supported infantry commanders; it was a modernised version of the older No. 18.[443]

Based on learning's from Arnhem, No. 19HP sets were to be used for communication between the artillery headquarters and the supporting artillery west of river Rhine. The liaison groups from 2 FOU were also equipped with such sets, which had been developed for use in AFVs. Its long range, up to 40–80km in telephony mode, was here very attractive. At a later stage, it was replaced by the better Canadian set: No. 52, which had a range up to around 100km. In telegraphy/morse mode a range of as much as 800km was possible.[444]

Within the airborne division three divisional artillery nets were planned:[445]

- RA Command Net
- RA Support Net
- RA Counter Mortar Net

When needed the artillery commander could also open a special 'RA Information Net' for direct communication with his colleague at the 52nd (Lowland) Division. Special equipment was also reserved for communication with artillery headquarters of the XVIII US Airborne Corps.

At brigade level, a 'Brigade Support Net' was opened for communication with the liaison groups at the artillery headquarters of the 52nd (Lowland) Division and the two medium regiments under the division's command. 3 Parachute Brigade could order support from one or several of the divisional field regiments via this group. The two other brigades could get support

The Final Onslaught – The Rhine Crossing

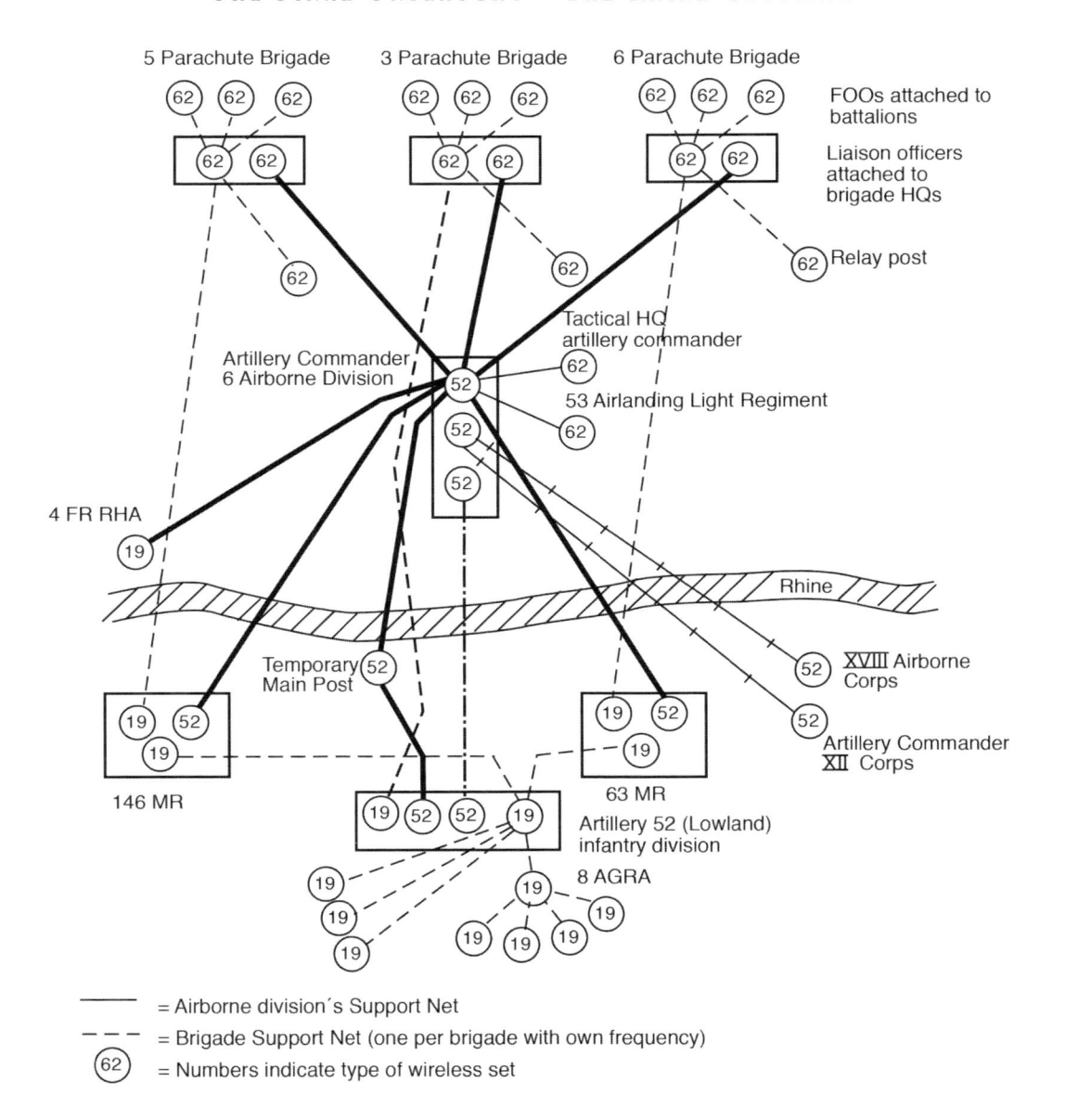

Fig. 22-9 The Order network of the 6 Airborne Division is here marked with full lines. With new more powerful wireless sets communication with artillery units west of River Rhine was not a problem; and artillery support from these units could immediately be established. When in range the battalions of the landed brigades could also get in contact with units west of River Rhine without having to communicate via headquarters (Author)

from the medium regiment assigned to support respective brigade.

Another important net was the normal regimental net for 53 Airlanding Light Regiment RA. By using this net all battery and troop commanders of the regiment, who normally acted as artillery commanders/FOOs at battalion and company levels, could fire with all regimental units. Via their regimental headquarters they could also engage all other artillery units within range. Within the regiment, there were in normal order the three battery nets too.

333

Interesting in this context is to note that the use of the divisional reconnaissance regiment's mortar troop, which was equipped with 4.2-inch mortars, in this operation was fully coordinated with the artillery regiment. By this, all regimental FOOs could use this additional resource when the range of the mortars so permitted.

The 'RA Support Net' was the most important net needed in order to make concentrated artillery fire possible from the airborne division's own resources and all those made available west of river Rhine. This and other nets here discussed are illustrated in **Fig. 22-9**.

The principal station in this net was initially a special Set-up Station located near the western shore of river Rhine. As soon as the divisional artillery commander and his staff had landed and established the headquarters they were to take over as the principal station in the network.

We may also note that the intended early support from 4 Field Regiment RHA had communication-wise been prepared.

As it was to be proved, all the well-conceived preparations regarding radio communication were a success. The large 'RA Support Net' could be opened already an hour after the first landings, around 11 a.m. and it seems likely that all stations were on the net around 12 a.m.

A short but intensive artillery fire preparation before the air-landings

The airborne armada was planned to arrive with first aircraft at 10.00 hours on 24 March 1945. This was 'P' hour in the plans. The fire plan had two parts. The first was a preparatory, softening fire against targets selected by the two airborne divisions. This was coordinated with further attacks by medium bombers and fighter-bombers. Responsible for this was the artillery commander of XII Corps. Basically all the Corps artillery was to be engaged, but for an hour only. After a ten minutes pause, the second part would follow which was aimed at combating enemy anti-aircraft units near the planned dropping and landing zones. The time for this part of the fire plan was 30 minutes and should be stopped when the first aircraft arrived on the scene.

In summary the fire plans in support of the airborne troops were as seen in **Table 22-7**.

During the second part, 'CARPET', the 25-pounders were planned to fire 60 rounds per gun and the medium and heavy guns 30 rounds per gun. In the final phase, the fire intensity was to increase to 100 rounds per gun for the 25-pounders, i.e. 6–7 rounds per gun and minute, and 60 for the medium guns whereas the heavies would continue firing 30 rounds per gun.[446]

An interesting detail was that VT fuzes ('radar' fuzes) would be used this time. Many targets were located close to, or on, the planned landing zones for gliders. In order to avoid craters there the fire against these targets would be airbursts by means of this type fuze. The decision was not obvious. This new type of fuze suffered still from 'teething' troubles and was thus not very reliable.

The initial task given to 53 Airlanding Light Regiment RA with its temporary two battery-organisation was preparation of defensive fire (DF) as protection for the landed troops. A second task was harassing fire in depth where the enemy could be expected to advance for counter-attacks. Targets would be bridges, road junctions, and concentration of buildings, etc.

It was important that the incoming aircraft would not be exposed to friendly artillery fire. Detailed safety instructions were prepared to reduce this risk. The responsibility was delegated down to the individual batteries and troops. But the prime responsibility was on the shoulders of two officers from the XII Corps artillery headquarters. One of them would be placed 10–12km west of river Rhine and via radio pass over a warning order that the armada was on its way. The second, positioned in a tower near the river, was the one to give the final order to all guns to stop firing when the first aircraft reached the river, undeniably a unique role!

When 'cease fire' was ordered, all the aircraft were without any protection. As we have seen the

Table 22-7. Fire plans in support of air-landings

Day, time	Fire Plan	Number of guns, types
D, 08.20–09.20	CLIMAX	216 25-pounders
		176 medium (4.5-inch/5.5-inch)
		24 heavy (155mm/7.2-inch)
		4 super heavy (240mm)
		36 American heavy (155mm)
		24 heavy anti-aircraft guns (3.7-inch)
D, 09.30–09.45	CARPET	264 25-pounders
		Other guns as above
D, 09.45–P	Continued bombardment	214 25-pounders
		Other guns as above

P = Arrival time of airborne armada

landings would last for 70 minutes for the British units to be dropped by parachute and landed with gliders, the Americans would need 210 minutes. It was necessary to take into account also the time needed for the 240 heavy bombers to drop supplies to the landed troops, beginning at P + 220 minutes, this concentrated to the British sector. The long postponement of artillery support to the troops on the eastern side of river Rhine would imply severe consequences, as we will see later.

A good start – the plans for Operation Plunder take effect

Preparations went on to the last minutes. But at 17.00 hours on D-1, 23 March, it was a huge roaring start along the whole XXX Corps front, and an hour later along the front of XII Corps. Minor counter-mortar bombardments and softening fire against enemy positions had commenced already at noon that day. Within the both Corps sectors the gunners from now on had to fire almost continuously for several days.

The 9th US Army began its Rhine crossing further south. One of the largest artillery concentrations in Northwest Europe was launched.

The presentations here are mainly based on operation orders and plans issued by the participating formations. But changes of these could come very late through new oral orders. Such orders are seldom well documented and are often completely missing. In this case, however, we can get a good picture of what happened. It is an account about the counter-bombardment programme. The CBO of XXX Corps, Major W.G. Edwards, who obviously was a meticulous person, wrote a detailed report after the operation about the Corps counter-bombardment actions.[447]

From this report, we can see that the first part of the initial plan, *DIAL*, was never fired. The main part, *DROOP I*, was executed exactly as planned between 17.00 and 18.00 hours, but the employed units had been reinforced. Instead of 216 25-pounders 160 were engaged, but this reduction was much compensated by engagement of 240 medium guns instead of planned 160. The following sub-programmes were basically fired as of the initial plan.

Edwards also informs that all targets were engaged four times and that in 'DROOP I' three up to forty guns were concentrated against each enemy gun. The hour-long programme implied that around 26,000 shells were fired by 512 guns. For all parts of the programme some 45,000 shells were consumed. The Corps Commander, General Horrocks, can be presumed to have been satisfied with his 'milk round'. He noted that the enemy artillery was very passive during the critical initial phase of the attack across river Rhine.

At 21.00 hours D-1, the first amphibious vehicles moved into the water opposite Rees. The BBC reporter Wynford Vaughan Thomas described vividly in a recorded report how he experienced the crossing of the Rhine when accompanying the commander of one of the attacking battalions. One can hear the sounds of bursting shells at the other side of the river. A bit further away, the weaker but demanding sounds of the Scots' pipers could be heard. The engines of all the *Buffalos* geared up with a mighty roar when all vehicles went towards the eastern shore. Halfway across excited comments about the crossing can be heard such as: 'We are racing across Rhine . . . ', 'We are waiting for the enemy to open fire', and …'Around us all Buffalos which seems an irresistible power.'[448]

The first British soldiers ran ashore at the city Rees after the crossing that took about seven minutes. Others followed suit and soon the first battalions of the 51st (Highland) Division were across on both sides of Rees. They were soon reinforced by 'swimming' Sherman tanks, some of which, however, failed to climb the shore.

Crossings then went on for several days, although short breaks had to be done when the riverbanks were shelled by German artillery and mortars. These breaks delayed the establishment of ferry connections for heavier vehicles and – not the least – construction of bridges. The ferries (rafts) had capacity only for a limited number of vehicles per hour, so the bridges were of critical importance for the planned build-up of resources in the bridgeheads.

In order to get tanks and artillery over the river, ferries and bridges of the 'CL 40' or 'CL40/50' classes were required (numbers give capacity in tons). During the first 24 hours the capacity was restricted as only 'CL 9' classes were then available. This capacity was sufficient for transfer of light supply transports, general carriers and much more, by which a first-hand need of ammunition, fuel, foodstuffs etc., could be met.

The fighting in the XXX Corps sector was hard. The British there had to meet battle-experienced parachute troops and armoured units, albeit far under nominal strength after the long battles west of river Rhine. The city Rees turned out to be a hard nut to crack. Despite the city was completely encircled; the resistance could not be completely broken until 26 March.

After about a week the objective of establishing a deep bridgehead for three divisions had been accomplished, the 43rd (Wessex) Division deployed in the north, the 51st (Highland) Division in the middle sector and the 3rd Infantry Division in the southern sector.

In the south, Horrock's Corps had linked up with XII Corps' bridgehead on 26 March, where the operation had begun as planned with the attack by the 1st Commando Brigade across river Rhine at 22.00 hours on D-1. The brigade quickly captured its first objectives outside the city Wesel, but the city itself proved to be as hard a nut as Rees. It would take a couple of days more until the city had been cleared from enemy soldiers.

The main attack by XII Corps, with two brigades in parallel, was launched by the 15th (Scottish) Division as planned on D-Day, 24 March 1945 at 02.00 hours. To the left, 227 Infantry Brigade crossed on 'Buffalos' and assault boats and further to the right, 44 Infantry Brigade crossed. The crossings went well, although some boats landed a few hundred yards away from the planned landing sites. The resistance met by these attackers was much lighter than those in the North had encountered. The objectives were taken during the night and early morning hours. The third brigade, 46 Infantry Brigade, could also cross as planned together with 'swimming' Sherman tanks. A few of the latter were lost but at 08.20 hours 57 tanks had managed to get ashore on the eastern side.

German counter-attacks came as had been expected, but they were fairly weak and easily broken up. Quick and very strong counter-attacks never emerged. This was very fortuitous, as the infantry had no available artillery support until later in the morning. This was a consequence of the large air-landings of Operation Varsity, which would commence at 10 a.m.

More ferry connections across the river could quickly be established and the first CL 9 FBE-bridge was ready for traffic in the evening of D-Day. After having been in use for a few hours, the bridge was damaged and had to be taken out of traffic until D+1 15.00 hours. Ferries of the heavier CL 50/60type, which were needed for taking SP-guns across, could be opened during the evening after a short delay due to enemy shelling. The first bridge of CL 40 Bailey bridge opened for traffic on D+1, 25 March, at 16.30 hours.

The transfer of 4 Field Regiment RHA could not be done as soon as it was hoped. According to a note in the war diary of the artillery headquarters of the 15th (Scottish) Division reconnaissance staff from 181 Field Regiment RA (one of the divisional field regiments) crossed river Rhine at 12.00 hours on D-Day already and a corresponding detachment from 4 Field Regiment RHA at 17.00 hours.[449] Furthermore, it is noted that a troop of the latter regiment was ferried across later in the evening. The regiment could avail itself of the first CL 9 bridge when this was ready at midnight. Before the whole regiment could cross, a section of the bridge collapsed. A few vehicles were stuck on the bridge, one went down and two men drowned. The next day, time is unclear; the whole regiment was, however, deployed and ready to fire on the eastern side of river Rhine. 181 Field Regiment RA was across on the second day too, i.e. D+1. The two regiments could deploy southwest of Hamminkeln and could then give support to the foremost formations.

Many artillery units gradually redeployed within the two Corps sectors on the eastern side of the river, but some were left behind during the first week. The reason was that there was a need for almost continuous firing. There was also a need to avoid overloading the ferries and bridges with too many ammunition transports. Re-supply of artillery ammunition required as we have seen numerous lorries.

Now back to D-Day when the large air-landings took place. Droppings were to take place at 10.00 hours as seen.

Operation Varsity – another catastrophe?
A short preparatory fire programme would precede the landings, as we have noted. This was started as planned at 08.20 hours by the artillery of XII Corps and went on for an hour. After a ten minutes pause, the bombardment of anti-aircraft positions began. This could, however, not go on during half an hour as planned. The first aircraft with parachute units arrived 8–9 minutes too early and brought the artillery fire to an end.

The officer given the task to stop the firing was the GSO2 of the XII Corps artillery headquarters, Major Gilbert Heathcote (later Brigadier Sir Gilbert Heathcote, Bart, CBE). He was now in an observation tower near river Rhine and after the warning notice from his colleague further west he ordered 'cease fire' at 09.52 hours when the head of the armada crossed river Rhine, **Fig 22-10**.

With this order not only the bombardment of the anti-aircraft positions stopped but also the direct support of the ground forces in the bridgehead (**Fig. 22-11**).

Sir Gilbert has in a letter to me told me about the unusual role he was assigned.[450] In an extract from his (unpublished) autobiography he tells about the agony felt by all concerned:

> The significance of the crossing of this great river was made plain by the presence of the Prime Minister accompanied by the Chief of the General Staff, Field Marshal Alanbrooke (Winston having with difficulty been dissuaded from taking part in the main assault) They were suitably ensconced on a small eminence overlooking the scene. So was I, for I had a lone yet significant role to play. This stemmed from the artillery fire plan that was then audible and visibly in full spate; the bark and thunder of field and medium guns came from below with, further to the rear, the rumble of heavy and super heavy artillery whilst ahead we could just see the dust and smoke of its effect on the shattered town of Wesel. How would this mass of metal in the air be integrated with the imminent arrival of the fleet of aircraft and gliders carrying two airborne divisions?
>
> This issue had been part of prolonged debate. The aircraft could be routed above the trajectories of the shells; they could risk flying through it or it could be stopped before leading aircraft entered it. The first was discounted by parachutists, who did not relish becoming slow-descending targets for too long. The risk involved in the second seemed low but unpredictable and unnerving. The airborne force chose the third alternative. This required the simple word 'Stop' to reach every gun but who would decide the moment and send the order? I never discovered whether I was given this task as prize or punishment. The certainty was cold feet on a warm March day as I checked and rechecked my wireless links to the guns whilst the crash and thunder seemed to intensify. It was the whisper from other spectators on our eminence that focussed my binoculars on the western sky; to see the approaching fleet looking like an ever-widening skein of geese.
>
> The airborne assault was to suffer heavily from enemy flak. I live today with the sense that I stopped the guns too soon, that the image of a flaming aircraft and its occupants tumbling from the sky above us distorted my judgement as it also affected the decision not to risk flying through the trajectories. Even the Almighty may find it difficult to decide whether the loss of life from enemy ground fire exceeded that which might have come from our own guns. Cold feet seem understandable.

Sir Gilbert is writing in his letter that his and his boss' (the Corps artillery commander, Brigadier W. Heath) opinion was that the decision to stop the firing was to cause larger losses than if they had taken the risk by not ordering cease fire that some aircraft had been hit by 'friendly' artillery fire. But they had been overruled by the commanders of the airborne formations.

Visibility was not the best when the airborne formations arrived. Morning mist in combination with dust and smoke after the bombings and artillery firing made it difficult for the pilots to find the right places for dropping the parachutists and landing the gliders. The armada was grouped in such a way that six battalions could be dropped within approximately ten minutes. 3 Parachute Brigade arrived first and then 5 Parachute Brigade. They were transported by 243 Dakota aircraft flying at the height of 200–300 yards.[451]

Fig. 22-10 Like huge swarms of birds the British and American airborne formations passed over an anti-aircraft battery on their way towards River Rhine on 24 March 1945. When they were around ten miles from the river a message was sent from an advance post to Major Gilbert Heathcote at Royal Artillery Headquarters attached to XII Corps. He was the one to order all artillery units west of River Rhine to cease fire, when the first transport aircraft approached the river (Drawing by J.T. Kenney, RAHT collection)

Glider-borne troops began to arrive around 10.20 hours in 440 Horsa and Hamilcar gliders. They were divided into six different groups transporting 6 Air landing Brigade and heavy equipment and ammunition etcetera. In the fifth group came the artillery headquarters, 2 FOU and 53 Air landing Light Regiment RA.

In the British sector, the northern route, all was over after about one and half hour. Along the southern route it would take a couple of hours more until the American division was in place. Well, not exactly. The major part of a parachute battalion landed far into the British sector. The latter thanked for the extra, unexpected help provided!

The first supply transport was delayed. The 240 bombers did not begin to arrive until 13.00 hours, and they flew too low causing many parachutes not to open. Destroyed and damaged canisters were a consequence. Another difficulty as regards supplies was that the RASC force allotted for collecting and distributing the supplies to the fighting units was much reduced in strength due to loss of several Hamilcar gliders. It has been estimated that only 30–35% of the supplies could be collected, a consequence of which was acute ammunition shortage during the afternoon at the parachute brigades.

The shortening of the artillery bombardment against flak positions, and the difficulties on the part of fighter-bombers to locate their targets due to bad visibility, resulted in a small number of anti-aircraft guns destroyed by direct hits. A limited neutralisation effect was all that could be accomplished. The commander of 7 Survey Regiment RA, Lieutenant Colonel Clegg, who could watch the course of the air-landing operation afterwards wrote that aircraft arriving first avoided flak fire, but then the German anti-aircraft units regained their power and went into full action again.[452] Of the estimated number of guns, 1,000, the majority, 70% were light anti-aircraft guns with calibres down to 20mm. These were very efficient against slow, low flying aircraft about to drop parachute formations and against gliders about to land. They caused immense destructions. In particular enemy guns deployed north and east of Diesfordt Woods had escaped the British bombardment and were excellently positioned in relation to the arriving airborne troops.[453]

The German infantry that was deployed near or even on the landing places caused terrific losses. The artillery headquarters, including the 'Brigade Major', landed with their Horsa almost on top of a German position. Those on board had no chance to take cover and were all killed. The position as 'Brigade Major' was transferred to the commander of 2 FOU, Major Harold Rice, who personally related these events to me.

The 6th Airborne Division lost almost 1,000 men the first day, out of which some 250 were killed in action. As regards heavy equipment, i.e. Jeeps, light tanks, carriers, anti-tank guns etc about 50% were lost.[454]

Was the light artillery regiment better off? What fire support could they provide? The first gliders of the 78 allotted for the transport of the airborne part of the regiment (a large part came on road, the sea tail) began their landing at 10.50 hours in landing zone 'P' where also the divisional headquarters and its artillery headquarters were to land. Harold Rice has described the landing as very rough as the farmland could not carry the weight of the Horsas. The wheels immediately sank and the glider body shuffling along the ground surface caused a huge cloud of dust.

The first gliders carried the reconnaissance staff of the two batteries of the light regiment. The gun positions had been selected from the

Fig. 22-11 At 10 a.m. 24 March 1945 one British and one American Airborne Division began crossing River Rhine over the bridgehead on the eastern side of the river. All artillery fire against enemy anti-aircraft units and other targets then had to stop. The landing of the British units was planned to take 70 minutes, whereas the Americans needed up to three hours to get all landed. During this period all artillery units west of the river were silent, no support could be provided! (©Imperial War Museum BU 2139)

map, but a detailed reconnaissance of them had to be done. A first task on the part of the glider pilots was to escort these detachments when carrying out this reconnaissance, which was done quickly and efficiently. The war diary reports that eleven guns were ready for action at 11.00 hours. Five of these were from 211 Battery RA, including one that had come from 210 Battery RA when the latter was split and its gun distributed to the two enlarged batteries. Six guns came from 212 Battery RA, out of which three had been allotted from 210 Battery RA.[455]

The time mentioned is seen in many sources. Provided the landing time, 10.50, is correct, ten minutes for reconnaissance, unloading the guns, transport to the site and deployment seems to be too short a time. Before being ready for action the guns should furthermore be surveyed in with parallel barrels and ammunition unloaded and prepared for firing.

The war diary anyway states that the regiment at 15.00 hours was well established and target rangings had taken place. Fire against enemy detachments had also been executed. It is however added that the latter primarily had been done with medium guns from positions west of river Rhine, this in order to be careful with ammunition spending. Bringing down the stock below 100 shells per gun required permission from the regimental headquarters. When only 60 rounds per gun were left, it meant 'cease fire' for that gun until replenishment could take place. It had been planned that 160 rounds per gun, complete with charges and fuzes, would be provided each day once supply arrangements were in full operation, but before that the guns had to rely on ammunition brought by themselves to the battlefield.[456] Besides this ammunition, four Hamilcar gliders would bring some extra ammunition and thus extend perseverance. But it did not go as planned in this respect. One glider disappeared and the three others landed too far from the planned landing zone.

Eleven guns were, as seen, ready for action early, without damages. What had happened with the thirteen other guns, and the two 25-pounders? Well, as was the case for other parts of the huge armada, losses for the artillery regiment were also large. Due to the bad visibility on the ground, many gliders landed far from the planned landing zones; in some cases some 3–5km away. Enemy fire reaped many victims too. The war diary summarises the landing results for the 78 gliders (inclusive 4 Hamilcars) employed:

- 35 gliders (45%) landed within 1,000 yards from the landing zone (LZ)
- 14 (18%) landed far from the LZ, but the gunners managed to find their way to the regiment with the glider loads intact later during D-Day or D+1
- 7 (9%) landed west of river Rhine, but could link up within four days
- 22 (28%) were destroyed:
  – 3 shot down by anti-aircraft guns
  – 3 destroyed when landing;
  – 15 landed far away and were destroyed by the enemy
  – 1 one was hit when landing and caught fire

From an interesting attachment that is available, we get detailed information about every single glider. We can read who were on board, what kind of load the glider carried, where the landing took place (coordinates given) and whether the load could be unloaded or was lost etc.

We can see from this list that most of the gliders were of the Horsa Mark II type, i.e. the latest version. Loading and unloading took place through a hinged nose section, which was opened after landing. In addition to the gliders transporting the twenty-four 75-mm howitzers three extra had been allotted for the transport of the two 25-pounders with ammunition and equipment. This seems to have been the only time such guns were transported like this.

Review of the list shows that six or possibly seven 75-mm howitzers were lost. Another six were landed away from the LZ, often about a kilometre, but in one case almost 5km wrongly. One of the two 25-pounders was lost. As mentioned none of the four Hamilcars fully loaded with extra artillery ammunition could make it, one of them landed 4km from the LZ. Maybe this was the Hamilcar load that was retrieved in a raid during the night to the 25 March and brought back to the regiment.

A patrol with glider pilots had left at 22.00 hours on D-Day and returned safely at 01.45 hours with the load. This is another example of the flexibility in action proved by British glider pilots. They certainly could do much more than flying and landing their gliders![457]

The two batteries had each eight guns in action at 4 p.m. Three of them had been provided from 210 Battery RA before the operation.

The regiment supported several of the brigade attacks launched by the 6th Airborne Division during the following days. This required redeployment once per 24 hours. It is, furthermore, noted in the war diary of 29 March 08.00 hours that the regiment returned to the normal three-battery organisation. The number of guns was still limited to 17 plus one 25-pounder. It was decided to act from then on with six guns per battery organised as one troop only.

The regimental headquarters was deployed and ready to lead the artillery from 12.45 hours on D-Day. It was then to act as a hub in the extensive communication network we have seen, which included all the reinforcing regiments west of river Rhine. Restrictions on firing had been cancelled in the British sector at 11.30 hours but had to be maintained in the southernmost section until 13.30 hours due to the American landings. A break also had to be done around 13.00 hours when the bombers were to drop supplies over the British sector.

War diaries give different points of time when the message '*Varsity all clear*' came over the radio networks, but it seems to have been around 13.45 hours. All firing restrictions were then lifted, and many FOOs were certainly now eager to get through with their fire orders!

Despite the great losses, the British airborne brigades captured their objectives already in the afternoon D-Day, 24th March. A first link-up with ground forces coming up from the Rhine was made around 2 p.m., amongst them 1 Commando Brigade. As was planned, the latter was put under command of XVIII US Airborne Corps when Wesel finally had been cleared.

Perhaps the success the first day was due to fairly weak resistance in the XII Corps area. They were spared from counter-attacks of armoured reserves as XXX Corps had been exposed to in the north. In retrospect, one may still wonder as to whether the air-landings with such large losses were worth its high price. Maybe it had been possible to break down the German resistance, with smaller losses, by the forces that crossed the river. In such a situation, these had been able to use more than 600 guns in support all the time instead of having to see them silent for several hours.

It should, however, be noted that for the coming breakout from the bridgehead the British in the 6th Airborne Division had a very strong, motivated and well trained formation with offensive capability. This capability was strengthened, not the least, by the artillery put at the division's disposal in addition to its own light regiment.

Breakout towards the Baltic coast

The scope and purpose of this book does not permit a detailed account of the battle during the final week of March when the bridgehead was enlarged. A large combined bridgehead was then established for both Corps with a depth of 10–15km in the north, where XXX Corps was, and 20–25km in the South where the XII Corps and the XVIII US Airborne Corps were deployed. The latter was to be relieved by the VIII British Corps after this initial period of fighting.

It had indeed been a tough week for all, the gunners included. The commander of 190 Field Regiment RA, Lieutenant Colonel R.J. Streatfield, wrote in the war diary of his regiment on 30 March 1945:

> The day was spent in cleaning and maintenance. Everything badly needed these after the operation, which had been one of the most intense ones we have ever performed. Rarely were the guns quiet for longer than an hour even during the nights and all command post staffs and gun detachments were worn out.[458]

As had been the case in Operation Veritable, 'Victor Targets' had again and again been engaged by all Corps artillery. Concentrated fire from all artillery of the various army artillery groups (AGRAs) had also been requested by FOOs and AOPs almost every day, i.e. 'Yoke Targets'.

No ammunition shortage arose despite all the firing. Pemberton (1950) shows that only about 50% of ammunition allotted to XII Corps was used, as regards smoke ammunition only 2.7%.[459]

While the British were to break out in north-easterly direction, the Americans would turn eastwards and take part in the encirclement of the Ruhr industrial area. For the British, a rush to the Baltic coast took place in April. This was not without any fighting and many artillery units were employed to the last day. The extension of the area controlled by the Russians had by this been constrained. The road to Denmark was closed to them, should the temptation to 'liberate' this country have been persisting in Moscow.

As regards the Royal Artillery, Operation Plunder and Operation Varsity had been the very last really big concentrations of firepower. They represented the big Finale! Montgomery's guests, Churchill and Alan Brooke, had been able to follow the first days of this battle. On 26 March 1945, a final 'picnic' took place on the western shore of river Rhine. We may here recall for a moment the initial pages of this book, where the picture so often published from this event is commented on (**Fig. 1-2**).

Summary of the artillery role in Operation Plunder – the Rhine Crossing

- Good planning at all levels secured an unusual concentration of firepower. Of particular importance here was that brigade attacks could be supported by larger numbers of guns than usual. Besides the large number of guns as such, the firepower was exceptional as roughly 50% of the guns were medium and heavy guns (El Alamein ca 5%, Normandy 20–40%).
- It was an impressive achievement by the various staffs to overcome all logistic challenges and hurdles. As was the case in the preceding Operation Veritable, all transports must take place in darkness and under strict traffic discipline to get the more than 1,300 guns deployed in time, with up to 600 shells per gun dumped in advance.
- As it this time was a matter of assault crossing over a wide river, it was not the role of the artillery to support the attacking formations with rolling or creeping barrages, this contrary to Operation Veritable. Extensive fire plans were instead devised with timed concentrations against numerous targets and fire, on demand, against recorded potential targets. Some targets were line targets (Stonks). Preparations for large smoke belts were also made, but these were fired only to a very limited extent. All the plans were based on a careful analysis of both the terrain and the possible and likely counter-actions by the Germans. Roughly speaking, preparations were made for covering an area of 5 x 30km with artillery fire in connection with the assault crossing (British sector).
- When the bridgehead was expanded, all now well-tested tools as regards artillery support were used; this included regimental and divisional concentrations (Mike & Uncle targets) as well as the use of the most powerful tool, concentrations against a single target from all available artillery of a Corps (Victor target). Concentrated fire from all artillery of an AGRA (Army Group Royal Artillery) was another option used (Yoke target). Certain attacks were supported by barrages. All types of quick defensive fire procedures to repulse counter-attacks were used.
- As was the case in Operation *Veritable*, the preparatory, softening fire plans were extreme and went on for many hours before the crossing commenced. The similarity with First World War huge barrages is here obvious. Question marks were raised as to whether the spending of artillery ammunition was indeed beyond the optimal level. There was, however, never any shortage of artillery ammunition.[460]
- The British adhered strictly to the doctrine of centralised tactical Command and decentralised Control. This made the large concentrations possible in a short time, but also direct support at opportunity targets down to Battery and even Troop level, when this was adequate. Centralised fire planning at Corps level was now much more common than it had been earlier in the war.
- A unique feature as regards the overall operational concept was the combination of the Rhine crossing with a huge air-landing operation, Operation Varsity. This caused a big problem seen from artillery perspective. Landing of the airborne troops after the initial phase of the river crossing, meant that a 'cease fire' had to be ordered to all the artillery west of the Rhine. During two to four hours this powerful resource of some 600 guns supporting XII Corps stood idle. Those brigade formations, which had already crossed the river and were engaged in battle, nor the air-landing formations, could get any substantial fire support during this period. The fact that the main objectives still were taken can be seen as the result of weaker resistance in this sector than further north, where the XXX Corps made its crossing.
- The air-landings as such were not a complete success. Too short a counter-anti-aircraft fire programme neutralised or destroyed only a few guns out of the total,

roughly 1,000, deployed by the Germans within or close to the dropping and landing zones. When the British artillery was ordered silent, most of the German anti-aircraft guns were back in action after only 15–20 minutes with devastating consequences for the air-landing troops. Bad visibility added to the problems. A large number of aircraft and gliders missed the dropping and landing zones. For the British, the losses the first day were over 1,000 men killed and wounded and half the heavy equipment was lost.

- A complete air-landing light regiment was, for the first time during war, flown in on one day, not only with its own 24 guns, but also with two extra 25-pounders attached. But the regiment suffered around 30% losses already during the landing phase. Due to the 'cease fire' imposed on all artillery west of the Rhine, this loss of initial fire support to the landed forces was a severe set-back, which was further worsened by the significant losses of ammunition that took place.
- A lesson learned at Arnhem, which in this operation was observed, was that airborne formations should not have to rely only on its own limited artillery resources. Artillery from relieving formations, in this case close to the Rhine, should be at hand for reinforcement soon after the landing. Strong resources could here be used in support only a few hours after the landings. It was furthermore possible to deploy some regiments east of the river already on D to D+1.
- Another problem which had been resolved, was the establishment of good and reliable radio communications between fire observers attached to the air-landed brigades and the artillery regiments west of Rhine, this right from the beginning. Selection of appropriate and controlled wireless equipment; good organisation; and well-trained signallers, made the communication this time, work very well.
- No airborne troops were landed in the sector allocated for the assault crossing by XXX Corps. Hence, no 'cease fire' order had to be imposed, except for a few units close to the XII Corps area. In respect of the much harder resistance encountered in the north, it would have been very difficult, not to say impossible, to establish a sufficiently large bridgehead there without the uninterrupted support from all the 700 guns available to the Corps. Backed by this huge resource, the Corps was successful.
- The survey and intelligence resources from the artillery, including many AOP Flights, were employed effectively, in particular for the collection of intelligence data needed for detailed planning, and this not only for the counter-battery planning.
- Close air support was applied effectively and the coordination with the artillery worked well.
- The implementation of the gigantic artillery resources made available for the Rhine crossing was effective. The use of artillery can be said to have represented the state-of-the-art of the time. Concentration of firepower from several hundreds of guns of a Corps within a few minutes was applied frequently (all Corps artillery on the target within 6–8 minutes was not an unusual feature). The prime characteristic of the arm to be an area-covering deadly weapon never failed when the numerous enemy counter-attacks were to be broken. The artillery was up to its reputation as a 'Battle Winner'.

In summary, the Royal Artillery contribution to the success of the Rhine Crossing and the subsequent swift increase of military strength made the British dash to river Elbe and the Baltic Coast possible, the latter reached one month after the Rhine Crossing.

This said, it does not mean that everybody was satisfied with the artillery procedures and how the 'tool box' had been used. The debate as to whether the use of artillery should be based more on surprise actions (through predicted fire), or if the artillery should strive for accuracy (through ranging), continued to the end of the war (e.g. by the Commander of 8 AGRA, Brigadier A.P. Campbell, who in a letter to the commander of VIII Corps in March 1945 expressed strong opinions on this issue).[461] Other topics for ongoing arguing was the emphasis on simplicity, which had been stressed many times by officers like Jack Parham and Sidney Kirkman, and the need for innovative, flexible use of artillery, thus avoiding plain routine.

23. From Defeat to Success – Burma

Ubique!
When we have now made some descents into British Second World War artillery history, we have got a pretty good view over the rearmament and the gradual build-up of new resources and how these were used. We have seen how battle techniques and technical methods were developed and adapted to different conditions, not the least the terrain and climate conditions. We will however not forget that the gunners had to fight in many more theatres than those discussed, and this under much varying terrain and climate conditions. They really had to meet the requirements of the first Latin word of the Royal Artillery motto, *Ubique Quo Fas et Gloria Ducunt*, which means 'Everywhere'.

In the north, gunners landed not only in Norway but also on Iceland, where a British force acted as a guard during the first years of the war until the Americans took over. They did not have to fight there, however, as the country was not invaded. In the Mediterranean area, gunners were engaged in Greece, Syria, Iraq, Persia and on the island Crete, albeit not on a big scale. The battle against the Italians took place not only in North Africa but also further to the South, in Abyssinia. An engagement took place in Madagascar in May 1942, with the first real amphibious landing of the Second World War. The aim was to prevent the island held by a French garrison, loyal to the Vichy Regime, being occupied by the Japanese.

Extensive fighting in North Africa went on after the battle of El Alamein in late 1942 and continued over the winter until the final defeat of the Axis powers took place in May 1943. The large invasion of Sicily, Operation Husky, then came in July. This was in its turn followed by the allied landings on the Italian mainland in September 1943. The artillery met new challenges and had to adapt again to new and more severe terrain conditions.

The final break-through of the 'Gustav Line' south of Rome in May 1944 (Fourth Battle of Cassino) was preceded by one of the largest artillery engagements of the Second World War. The capability of the artillery to meet and stop large-scale counter-attacks with huge concentrations of firepower was demonstrated many times, for instance, during the defence of the bridgehead at Anzio in the springtime 1944.

It can be noted that the trend shift as regards the use of artillery resources that took place at El Alamein was further firmly established during the subsequent battle in North Africa and later in Italy. Abundant artillery resources and efficient and concentrated use of these was the message of the day. The methods for close cooperation between air resources and ground forces were also refined during this period, as was the use of naval artillery against ground targets on land.

AOP Squadrons, belonging to the Royal Air Force, but manned by artillery officers as pilots and observation officers, had got their firm introduction. Airborne formations had become available at large scale towards end of 1942. One parachute brigade was landed on Sicily in July 1943 in connection with the allied invasion. But there were as yet no glider resources available for transport by air of the light artillery regiment of the 1st Airborne Division. The regiment stayed on in Tunisia until 9 September when the whole division was sea-transported to Taranto at the 'heel' of the Italian 'boot'. Once there, the regiment was much appreciated for its role as a sort of mountain regiment during the autumn 1943 before taken back home to England to prepare for engagement in Normandy together with the major part of the airborne division (except one parachute brigade).

The battles on Sicily and at the Italian mainland showed again the good ability on the part of the gunners to adapt to new conditions. Nowhere would the test, however, be as hard as in South East Asia, which the British included in the Far East.

The new enemy
Early in the morning of 7 December 1941 the Japanese surprise attack on Pearl Harbour took place, as is generally known. This made USA go to war against Japan immediately. The German

declaration of war against USA came soon afterwards. This meant that the enormous human and industrial resources of USA could directly benefit Britain in its war effort too.

At the same time, the Japanese launched also an attack against the British Empire. Capture of the Malayan peninsula and Singapore were the prime objectives. The attack began with the Japanese landing in the early morning of 8 December 1941 on both sides of the border to Siam (Thailand). Large air attacks took place, which the obsolete British fighters could not do much about. Japanese air superiority was soon secured. Hong Kong was attacked the same morning. The difference of dates, 7 and 8 December, is due to the fact that the Pearl Harbour and the Malayan peninsula are located on opposite sides of the International Date Line. See **Map 23-1** for a general view.

A humiliating blow on the Royal Navy came on 10 December 1941 when the battleship HMS *Prince of Wales* and the battle cruiser HMS *Repulse* were sunk in the South China Sea by Japanese aircraft. The ships that had arrived in Singapore on 3 December went to sea without any air protection and became thus easy prey to the Japanese Air Forces.

The British now met an enemy who was utterly motivated and well trained.[462]

As it would be shown, the Japanese was a different type of soldier compared with the German and Italian soldiers the British had met so far. Cultural, social and ideological differences meant that only victory or death mattered to the Japanese soldier. A Japanese unit never gave in and had to be killed to the last man. Becoming a Prisoner of War individually or collectively was unthinkable. The last hand grenade was reserved for the soldier's own ultimate death if no alternatives to being captured could be seen. With this attitude, they were also reluctant to take prisoners themselves, not even when the opponent was wounded or lacked possibilities to continue fighting. Better then to put the bayonet into him. Doctors, nurses, medical orderlies and wounded at aid posts or hospitals would meet the same destiny if there were no time to evacuate them. Many examples of collective massacres have been presented. The brutality and ruthlessness of the Japanese soldier made him a much-feared enemy, particularly as he at the same time was a very skilled opponent whatever his undertakings were.

First Phase – Malaya and Singapore

The British had prepared themselves for an attack from the north against Singapore, a plan that had been already prepared in 1937. According to this plan, the British were to quickly occupy the area just north of the Malayan border to Siam when an attack on the peninsula or Singapore was deemed imminent and unavoidable. A revised concrete plan was prepared in 1940–41, Operation Matador.[463] This was, however, politically sensitive and the relations not only with Siam, but also with USA complicated the issue. This had the consequence that necessary decisions were not taken in time, despite good intelligence information about the pending attack. Another complicating factor was the unclear command structure between the civilian side, primarily the Governor, and the military high command. A question mark must still be raised as to whether an early order to apply Operation Matador, had changed the outcome of the battle.

The few British formations were not well trained for jungle warfare. This was even more the case as regards the reinforcing formations coming directly from England and the Middle East. Nor were the forces trained to cooperate. All-arms-training had not been prioritised in the British Army during the first years of the war. Neither had any real preparations in terms of fortifications and mine fields to meet an attack from the North neither been made at Singapore.

Lieutenant General Arthur E. Percival was commander of the ground forces. He decided that the battle down through the Malaya Peninsula should initially be assigned to III Corps comprising of the 9th and 11th Indian Infantry Divisions. The 8th Australian Infantry Division was assigned the defence of the southern part of the peninsula, i.e. Johore and Malacca down to the island of Singapore where fortress troops were deployed. Amongst the latter were two Malayan local defence brigades who prepared to meet the invasion as well as they could. Lacking an operative plan for this, it was not easy. A number of permanent coast artillery guns built to defend the island with its naval base from seaborne attacks added to the fortress garrison. The Australians were the only formation that was to some extent trained for a jungle war (**Fig. 23-1**).

The 18th Infantry Division arrived in January 1942 as reinforcement directly from

Fig. 23-1 The Australians were better trained for jungle warfare than the English and Indian units. After the bitter defeats at Singapore and in Burma 1942, a systematic rearmament and training took place for the latter in India as preparation for the coming offensive against the Japanese. One part of this was to get all men used to the jungle and to take advantage of it, individually and when to fight in large formations. For those successful many opportunities for patrolling, for camouflage, surprise attacks and circumventing etcetera would emerge. Everyone had to become as skilled in this as the Japanese, if otherwise, one would stand small chances to survive (AWM No. 007179)

England. This division of course lacked training for jungle warfare. It could possibly have been kept as a strong reserve for counter-attack against the Japanese invasion of the Singapore Island, but was split up into minor units who got stuck in fighting far from the Island. And for that kind of campaign it was not trained.

On the Japanese side the 25th Army under command of General Yamashita Tomoyuki, (often just referred to as Yamashita.) His army comprised the 5th, 18th and 56th Infantry Divisions and the Imperial Guards Division. The initial landings were carried out by the 5th and 18th divisions. The 56th Infantry Division was kept in a stand-by position ready to move into Burma. The Guards Division had as a first task to subjugate Siam by quickly seizing Bangkok and then prepare for advance towards Singapore.

The Japanese attack towards Singapore was, as **Map 23-1** indicates, mainly carried out using the main roads southwards with a concentration of forces to the western part of the peninsula. The Japanese tactic was to attack by surprise and strength against British positions, which were then encircled through the jungle. Facing this risk the British quickly withdrew. This was repeatedly done all the way down to Singapore. Many outflanking movements at sea along the western coast of Malaya were performed by Japanese units as well.

The British divisions had 2–3 field regiments each. Armament was a mixture of guns: vintage 18-pounders and 4.5-inch howitzers and new 25-pounders. Some 3.7-inch mountain howitzers were also part of the arsenal. Neither medium nor heavy guns were available. Coast artillery positions on land had been constructed near Singapore. Some of these could be laid on targets in the north, but the necessary high explosive shells were missing. Armour piercing shells for maritime targets were abundant, but were of no use against advancing infantry.

The artillery could never stop the rapid Japanese advance. The terrain made close deployment of regiments impossible and, as we have seen, the necessary training of infantry and artillery together had never taken place.

At the beginning of February the Japanese entered the Singapore Island by launching a strong attack from the northwest, at the same time as a deception attack against the eastern part of the Island was arranged. The British forces were exhausted after having been exposed continuously to Japanese artillery fire and air attacks for ten days and nights. No reserves for strong counter-attacks had been organised, and local Japanese superiority claimed its right. The few artillery units were dispersed and, due to the short range of the old guns, had few opportunities to affect the final battle. Concentration of firepower was not possible, nor was any efficient counter-battery bombardment.

Lieutenant General Percival was on 15 February forced to surrender to the Japanese Commander-in-Chief, General Yamashita. Some 85,000 men went into harsh captivity. If depot personnel and civilian defence employees are included, the total number increases to some 130,000.[464] The defeat is the largest in British history. Churchill would never forgive Percival for not having stopped the Japanese. It is perhaps not surprising that discussions have been going on since this disaster about what could have otherwise been done. These discussions will probably continue in the future. General Farndale writes about this in his book about the regimental history:[465]

As is so often the case with the British Army, the regiments and units fought well. There was much individual heroism and men died in gallant defiance to the last or advanced in local counter-attack with great ferocity. Many times the Japanese reported the toughness of the fighting and many times they held back when they knew the consequences of attacking prepared positions. But it is above unit level that the problems arose. Units were cobbled together in brigades and commanders lacked experience at the operational level, co-ordination failed frequently, as will always be the case if training at this level is faulty. More than anything else the disaster in Malaya was caused by failure to keep the armed forces up to date and to make timely decisions once the die was cast.

Next Phase – Burma
The Japanese crossed the border to Burma in January 1942. The task to capture the country was assigned to the commander of the 15th Army. The attack was initiated by the 55th Infantry Division from Siam near the city of Moulmein. This division was followed in February by the 33rd Infantry Division. The division was assigned the task to seize Rangoon, the capital with its so important harbour for the build-up of the Japanese forces, **Map 23-2**.

Burma is a long country with high ridges and mountains stretching in north-south direction. The country is covered with dense jungle, except for plains with rice fields.

On the eastern side, Burma is bordering Siam and China, on the western side India (Assam) and the Bay of Bengal. The southernmost part of the country, a narrow coastal strip south of 16th Latitude, had no significance as regards military operations. The mountains in the country reach heights in the order of 3,000–4,000m.

Low farmland, with several large rivers, is located between the high land north of Rangoon. The largest river, the Irrawaddy, runs from the northernmost part of the country through the city Mandalay down to its large delta near Rangoon. East of this river, near the eastern highland, flows another river that was to prove important during the coming fighting, the river Sittang. The large river Chindwin also had great military significance. It runs from the high land in northwestern Burma and joins Irrawaddy near Mandalay.

The infrastructure of the country was in a poor state. The large rivers and the only railway running from Rangoon to Mandalay were the most important transport routes. The railway stretches beyond Mandalay up to the city of Myitkyina from which roads proceeded northwards and northeasterly towards China. The rest of the national road network was weak with only a few roads crossing the large mountainous parts. Numerous gorges, streams and marshy land added to the difficulties for road transport with motor vehicles.

The climate in Burma was hot and humid with heavy monsoon rains from May to October–November. The soldiers had to walk around all the time in damp clothes. The environment, so hard for Westerners, was made even worse by the abundant presence of snakes, mosquitoes and other insects. This made disease flourish among units, in particular malaria, dysentery, typhus and various kinds of jungle ulcers. Hardly any soldiers in the Second World War had such a demanding battle environment as the soldiers fighting in Burma; so completely different from North Africa and Northwest Europe. But for the gunners it was a matter of *Ubique*! They had to accept the situation and never give up their professionalism despite the appalling conditions. Anyone visiting the jungles of South East Asia today in monsoon rains may get a feeling what it was like, although being there under war conditions is something else and much worse.

The resistance that met the Japanese when the battle started was primarily put up by the 1st Burma Division and some local defence units. The 17th Indian Infantry Division should be added to these forces; the division had arrived in Burma in January 1942 and went to battle early but was soon struck by a major setback. The bridge over the violent river Sittang was blown too early due to fear for a strong Japanese attack to capture it. Half the division was left on the wrong side and all heavy equipment was lost; only a few soldiers managed to escape across the river.

The 5th and 6th Chinese Army was deployed in the border area towards China. These armies were parts of Chiang-Kai-Shek's Nationalist forces. They were actively supported by USA, who supplied them extensively by air from India. The two armies were under command of the American general Joseph

Stilwell, nick-named 'Vinegar Joe' due to his blunt manner, not least in his contacts with the British, whom he disliked very much.

The Japanese captured Rangoon on 8 March 1942 and a long delaying battle to the north then followed, basically along the large rivers in central Burma. See **Map 23-2**.

On the British side, the battle was from 19 March led by Lieutenant General William Slim. He assembled and grouped the scattered forces in one Corps, the Burma Corps. Slim's skill prevented all Japanese attempts to encircle and annihilate the Corps. After having fought a delaying battle over a long distance, some 600 miles, what was left of his Corps crossed river Chindwin and the border to India. This happened in the middle of May 1942, just before the arrival of the monsoon rains. Burma was now completely occupied by the Japanese. They stopped at the border: India could wait.

A small British success, but important to morale, was the rescue of ten 25-pounders and fourteen 3.7-inch mountain howitzers back into India.[466]

To the fury and frustration of Slim, his exhausted soldiers were not well-received and taken care of in India. This seems to have been caused by personal antipathies between senior commanders in India and by unwillingness to understand what the Burma Corps had been through, and what it had accomplished against appalling odds.

Slim, maybe the best British general in the war, was made commander of the new XV Corps, which he immediately began to train systematically for a coming offensive against the Japanese invaders. As the basis for his training programme, an analysis was made regarding what was needed to make it possible to match the Japanese in jungle warfare. Some of the points he stressed were the following (in summary):[467]

- All, officers and other ranks alike, should get accustomed to the jungle and learn to use it for their own benefit as a good environment for concealed movement, reconnaissance, ambushing, etc. The jungle should thus not be regarded as an hostile battle environment, but as a friend offering many opportunities
- At the unit level, patrolling in the jungle should be introduced and they should all be responsible for their own security. The Japanese should not be able to surprise any unit. And no 'non-combatants' were to be accepted
- At the operational level Japanese outflanking tactics and attacks on the rear of positions should be adopted. This also meant that frontal attacks should be avoided as much as possible. If encircled, the units should stay on and not retreat as had happened previously so many times. Counter-attacks should be well prepared and the terrain for these be well reconnoitred in advance. To make this operative policy work, units, even very large ones, should be re-supplied from the air
- The battle was to continue even during the monsoon period

Slim's experience and ideas were not well received initially; many conflicting wills within the Indian High Command delayed the necessary adaptation. Strong political pressure from London, Washington and Chiang-Kai-Shek made that the 14th Indian Infantry Division was employed in the Arakan towards the end of 1942 before it was well prepared for it.

The commander of Eastern Army, General Irwin, led the operation. Slim's proposal that his XIV Corps should be used instead, this in combination with an amphibious landing behind the Japanese lines, was rejected.

Several frontal attacks attempted by the 14th Division failed. Such operations had to be abandoned eventually and the division forced to retreat. The threat to be encircled by Japanese units through the jungle the usual way had become imminent. The Indian High Command had to give in and transfer regional command to Slim for stabilisation of the situation. He was given also the responsibility for the planning of a large-scale offensive into Burma.

The building of operative strength continued on both sides in 1943. The Allies prepared a massive ground offensive from Assam southwards. At the same time, Stilwell was to attack from Northeast with strong Chinese forces. Along the right (Western) flank several amphibious operations were to be prepared. The big offensive was to commence at the beginning of 1944.

The required forces were organised as the

14th Army with Slim as its commander.[468] The army was to comprise two British-Indian Corps to which two British infantry divisions from West Africa and East Africa were allotted. Strong air forces were to be made available for cooperation with the ground forces. The plans also called for air supply, not least of artillery ammunition, to large independent units.

The Japanese had in 1943 systematically increased their forces in Burma. These were not intended for an invasion of India, but to defend Burma when the expected allied offensive came. One part of their plan was, however, to attack northwards into Assam and capture Imphal, Kohima and end of the railway from central India, Daipur. Large British stores were there tempting objectives. If they were to succeed, the allied lines of supply would be much hampered, as would the supply lines to Chiang-Kai-Shek's armies. The Japanese offensive was planned to start in February 1944, which was the same time as the allied planned to launch their offensive. None of the parties knew about this coincidence, however.

A much discussed operational concept, being part of the allied strategy, was air-landings of large units behind the Japanese lines, this in accordance with ideas pursued by the eccentric Major General Orde Wingate who had gained the attention of Churchill when bypassing his superior commanders, Slim amongst them. Churchill was attracted by the ideas presented by the young general, whom he saw as a new 'Lawrence of Arabia'.

Wingate had in 1943 commanded a large force that moved on the ground behind the Japanese lines. His Chindits ambushed the Japanese and carried out other types of operation. After heavy losses, they returned the same way they had come. Now, in 1944, Wingate planned to land several special brigades by aircraft and gliders, organised as Columns. He planned to establish a number of strong points with these units, which were to be supplied from the air. From these positions, he planned to undertake major attacks on the Japanese positions and rear supply lines. Four artillery troops, each with four guns, were allotted for the protection of the strong points.

It is not possible within the scope of this book to make detailed presentations of the hard and large-scale battles, which both parties commenced in February 1944. The Allies obtained the upper hand gradually and would re-capture Burma a bit more than a year later. Slim's analysis of what was required and his masterly conducting of the operations are worth a separate study. It was Generalship of the highest class. Worthwhile studying are also the huge logistic challenges facing Slim's army and how the supply of it could be secured.

Nowhere in this war were the Engineers/Sappers exposed to such difficult tasks as here in Burma. It was a matter of road construction in the most difficult terrain and construction of numerous bridges. They had to arrange crossings of the large, wide rivers for the huge forces engaged as well. Lack of material from home did not make it easier and local solutions had to be devised. As an example, **Fig. 23-2** illustrates how a mass of rafts was arranged for transporting guns and vehicles across one of the large rivers.

How the Engineers/Sappers solved all their problems with technical skill, creativity and, not the least, ability to adapt to the adverse climate and terrain conditions prevailing in Burma cannot but be admired, and would of course deserve a closer study.

The offensive from the north towards Rangoon followed about the same routes as had been used in the retreat 1942. The capture of the

Fig. 23-2 Crossing the major rivers in Burma required large stocks of material and equipment, which if not supplied from outside, had to be manufactured close to the battlefield. The sappers of 14 Army became experts on improvisations. Besides building roads and bridges they also manufactured numerous rafts such as this one loaded with a 25-pounder and a Jeep, which is to cross River Chindwin (RAHT)

city Mandalay and the junction Meiktila, so important for the Japanese supply lines, were spectacular achievements of the operation. At the beginning of May 1945, Rangoon was recaptured by forces that were landed from the sea and reinforced by the airlanding of a Gurkha parachute battalion near the city. The forces advancing from the north were not far away.

We will now close this superficial visit to this special theatre of war by having a brief look at the special conditions facing the artillery in Burma and how the gunners met the challenges and how the resources were used.[469]

The many artillery problems in Burma
Divisional artillery
After completion of the overall rearmament in Britain, the availability of guns for divisional artillery was generally good. The firepower of the 25-pounder shell and the gun's fairly long range were much needed. A problem in Burma was the hilly terrain and the lack of roads. The 25-pounder with its towing 'Quad' was often too wide for the narrow pathways and the engine of the Quad too weak.

An innovative gun mechanic faced the problem and equipped the gun with a shorter wheel axle with attached Jeep wheels. The pivot plate was removed, and sometimes also the shield. By this arrangement the gun became lighter and easier to manhandle. Another advantage was that it could be towed by lighter vehicles, for instance one or two jeeps. The modified version was called '25-pounder Jury Axle'. Later the arrangement was further improved and officially approved (**Fig. 4-3**).[470]

A useful complement was the good old 3.7-inch mountain howitzer. There were plenty of them available in India. It had been modernised with pneumatic wheels and was easy to tow after a jeep and could in road-less terrain be carried by mules. The relatively high trajectory was an advantage in the hilly jungle terrain in Burma, where indirect fire with flat trajectory guns was not possible (**Fig. 23-3**).

The good accuracy of the gun was an advantage also when fire very close to own troops, say 10–50m, was required. The skill on the part of the Japanese to infiltrate and silently advance through the jungle to surprise their opponents made the need for this type of fire quite common.

The 3-inch mortar had similar characteristics. It was primarily an infantry support weapon, but in Burma it was used also as a weapon to complement the artillery. The very limited threat for tank attacks made it possible to use gunners of anti-tank regiments to man mortar units.

Reinforcing artillery
This was the great deficiency area. The 14th Army had never more than three medium regiments in Burma. They were armed with 5.5-inch guns. Just a few old 6-inch howitzers were also available. The latter had a good steep trajectory and proved more technically reliable than the new gun. The former got a bad reputation due to its technical deficiencies and poor ammunition. Maybe the gun was not adapted particularly well to the wet and hot climate of Burma.

Heavy regiments were completely missing. Only a few old 7.2-inch howitzers had been provided. But they were used more on a single basis and were manned by surplus gunners from anti-aircraft regiments.

Organisational adaptations
Just before the final great offensive in 1944, the artillery organisation was changed in order to get it better prepared for the tactical requirements and terrain conditions. This was a matter only for the divisional artillery. As a complement to the usual allotment of three field regiments per

Fig. 23-3 In the Burma campaign the old 3.7-inch mountain howitzer proved to be an efficient weapon in the hilly jungle terrain. Here the firing of a battery is watched by the American General Dan Sultan on visit to 36 British Infantry Division (RAHT)

division, each with 24 guns per regiment, some alternatives were introduced:[471]

1) To what was called Light Infantry Divisions were allotted one field regiment with 24 Jury Axle 25-pounders and two mountain regiments, each with two batteries. Each one of them had four mountain howitzers towed/carried by mules, and one battery with sixteen 3-inch mortars.
2) An ordinary Infantry Division was allotted one regiment with twenty-four 25-pounders of the ordinary type, one Jungle Field Regiment comprising two batteries, each with eight jeep-towed mountain howitzers and one battery with sixteen 3-inch mortars, and one mountain regiment comprising four batteries, each with four mountain howitzers.
3) An Armoured Division was to have two field regiments each comprising two battery with eight 25-pounders each and one battery with eight 'Priest' SP guns [a complete armoured division was however never provided for this theatre].
4) To 'Attack Divisions' for amphibious operations three 'Attack Regiments' were allotted each one comprising one battery with eight 25-pounders of the ordinary type, one battery with eight 'Priests' and a third battery with six mountain howitzers.

Deployment and local protection
The terrain seldom allowed for deployment of artillery in accordance with the 'book'. It became necessary to find tight positions, often wheel to wheel, or along roads with guns firing over each other. A special problem was crests in front of the guns. To get a free passage for the shells at the minimum elevation required by target positions gun deployment often included crest clearing. This was a task often given to Sappers who often used explosives, instead of saw and axe, to cut the trees.

Deployment was often difficult due to heavy rains making the bad roads muddy. Sometimes the guns had to be manhandled with ropes and tackles to high positions without any road or even a footpath. An example of manhandling a gun in muddy terrain is shown in **Fig. 23-4**, although it does not illustrate an extreme situation. The challenge could be much worse!

A pre-requisite for the necessary tight deployment was the air superiority gained by the

Fig. 23-4 For the gunners it was a matter of honour to follow the infantry wherever they had to fight. But it was often extremely hard work indeed to get the guns in place for support of them, in particular when the monsoon rains turned all roads to mud as here near Rangoon in May 1945 (RAHT)

Allies in 1944. There were hardly any major risks for Japanese counter-battery bombardment. The Japanese lacked artillery in Burma and gave counter-battery fire low priority, when employing their scarce resources. As mentioned, nightly infiltration into gun positions and headquarters followed by surprise attacks with bayonets and hand grenades was the preferred method.[472] They were extremely skilled in application of this tactics, which made local protection of gun positions in Burma a much more important task than it was in North Africa and Europe.

Local protection was normally arranged with barbed wire fences and alarm mines around the battery positions and the single gun. For gun crews it was important to get deep slit trenches and foxholes and other dugouts as soon as possible. Absolute sound and light discipline was necessary when no firing was ordered. Unplanned rifle fire against suspected movements or sounds outside the fences was forbidden. Otherwise gun and crew positions would immediately be disclosed.[473]

Fire observation
Acting as fire observer in the jungle was not an easy undertaking. Observation opportunities were very limited and the possibilities to fix own position by map reading, and those of the supported unit, were very small. Finding an observation post could in itself be cumbersome, **Fig. 23-5**, and always-required infantry escort.

Despite this, there was always a risk of being hit by a bullet through the head from a well-hidden sniper in a tree. Once in place it could prove difficult to establish radio communication with the guns. Line laying was often necessary, which in its turn exposed signallers to large risks.

It was normal practice in North Africa and Europe to have the two troop commanders of a battery acting as fire observers attached to forward battalions, but in Burma four or even more observers were needed due to the terrain.

Fire for effect must be placed very close to own positions, which required very good accuracy in battery and troop command post calculations and gun laying. Fire observers had often to put down the first rounds a bit behind the intended target in order to be on the safe side, and then gradually move the fire closer, say in hundred-yard shifts, until it was over the target. In order to make it easier to find out where the first round would hit ground, a usual practice was to have one gun firing smoke shells.

A special task for fire observers was to pinpoint targets for fighter-bombers and bombers. An efficient method for this was to cover the target area with coloured smoke shot by the artillery.

It must in this context be noticed that the 'Flash Spotters' of the survey regiment could not be of any use in the jungle, as this made it very difficult, not to say impossible, to observe muzzle flashes or muzzle smoke from firing Japanese artillery. Hence, there was no point in establishing short and long (observation) bases. Deployment of sound ranging bases with sufficient width was not easy, except where the terrain opened up: the Imphal plain being an example. Before the large offensive crossing of river Irrawaddy was launched in 1945, sound rangers managed to locate most of the enemy artillery.

Creeping or rolling barrages

When attacks through the jungle were prepared against fortified Japanese positions, which were often located high up on hills and ridges or on the back side of these, covering fire planned as barrages or timed concentrations was of little use. One reason was the difficulty to estimate the speed of infantry advance in the jungle. Another reason was that neutralising fire in accordance with normal British doctrine and practice did not work. The heavily fortified Japanese positions with strong bunkers and shelters, all with fortified connecting trenches, were almost immune against fire from light guns such as 25-pounders and mountain howitzers.

To help the attacking infantry, destruction of such positions by means of heavier artillery and – not the least – air attacks was necessary.

A special task preceding an attack was 'Bunker Busting'. The practice was to have light guns first to uncover the bunker from its protecting camouflage, which normally had been done with great skill by the Japanese. When this was done and the bunker could be clearly observed, a heavier piece – often a 5.5-inch gun – was used to destroy it including its crew. This could be accomplished with direct fire at a distance of 800–1,000 yards from the bunker, but indirect fire over a distance of 2,000–3,000 yards could also be applied. Around 10–15 rounds had to be fired in the latter case before a direct hit destroyed the bunker. And a direct hit it must be! Different fuze settings for direct bursts on ground impact and delayed bursts were tried depending on the type and location of bunkers.

Weaker concentrations as compared with Europe

The terrain and lack of gun positions enforcing dispersed deployment made it difficult to arrange large fire concentrations from numerous guns, as was the case in other theatres. Another factor was that the necessary surveying of gun positions into the same grid was very difficult. Availability of artillery was limited in Burma. When in Europe it was fairly easy to quickly concentrate fire from 500–600 guns, well, sometimes even more, the number in Burma was seldom above 100–200 guns. Direct support on opportunity targets with a troop (four guns) or a battery (eight guns) was dominating the artillery employment.

In this context, it must also be noted that the availability of artillery ammunition was much more restricted in Burma than in Europe, which of course affected how artillery resources could be used.

Air transport

No other theatre of war saw such a huge employment of air resources for sustained supply of encircled large forces as Burma, the battle of Imphal in 1944 being an excellent example. Extensive evacuations of tens of thousands wounded and non-combatants also took place, as were landings of large reinforcements.

Fig. 23-5 An Observation Party on its way to an observation post. This is Lieutenant D.A. Imlay with his signaller Kebby from 8 Field Regiment RA who are seen crossing one of the many rivers in Burma. Kebby is carrying a No. 18 type of wireless set. Dense jungle terrain made it extremely difficult to find suitable observation post where observations towards the enemy locations could be made. When supporting an infantry battalion in Burma often 6–8 Observation Parties were needed instead of the normal 2–3 (©Imperial War Museum SE 2531)

In no other theatre, redeployment of complete divisions and brigades by air transport took place as was done here, when the situation required this. Such a situation was when the large Japanese offensive against Imphal and Kohima was to be met in February 1944.[474] In connection with the lightning offensive by the 17th Indian Infantry Division towards Meiktila a year later, a complete infantry brigade was flown in as reinforcement to a just captured airfield; this at a critical initial phase of the battle.

As regards artillery units, these large-scale air transports offered no problems for the mountain regiments. Neither was it a problem to those units that had mule-carried guns, nor to those with jeep-towed guns. These units could be quickly loaded in the transport aircraft. Even the mules were tranquil and accepted patiently to be taken on board the aircraft. For batteries with 25-pounders it was more difficult. The normal gun version was too big for the doors of the aircraft. Hence such batteries had to come later by road. Guns equipped with the 'Jury Axle' and removable shield were on the other hand possible to take on board including their lighter vehicles.

The large availability of American transport aircraft in the region, which in its turn was a consequence of the American support to Chiang-Kai-Shek's armies, made the large-scale air transport operations possible. Occasionally he (and the Americans) had to accept that such resources were allotted for other purposes than transport of supplies to China.

The last artillery battle of the war

Guns became silent permanently in Europe on 8 May 1945 when Germany finally surrendered. Fighting continued for another three months in South East Asia and the Far East. In Burma, the liberation of Rangoon was followed by mopping-up operations, which were still going on when peace came on 15 August 1945. The cease-fire was a bit unexpected, but came true when the atomic bombs had been dropped over Hiroshima and Nagasaki and made the Japanese forces lay down their weapons and surrender.

The final operations in Burma had as their objective to annihilate the Japanese forces that had been in the Arakan region and the western part of the country. These forces tried to take refuge in Siam by crossing the British lines from Mandalay to Rangoon in the south. As regards the British artillery, the operations were hampered by the ongoing monsoon rains, which flooded large areas and made roads unusable. Gun positions had to be found at higher terrain sections near villages and farm buildings or on roads and railway embankments.

It was here east of Rangoon, close to river Sittang, that the Royal Artillery fired the last rounds in the Second World War. It has been stated that it was a troop of 384 Battery RA who made it, a few hours in fact after the point of time when hostilities should cease on 15 August 1945.[475]

When You Go Home,
Tell Them of Us and Say,
For Your Tomorrow,
We Gave Our Today

(From the 2nd Infantry Division obelisk in Kohima.)[476]

24. Gunners We Have Met

As mentioned earlier, units of Royal Regiment of Artillery constituted the largest arm of the British Army in the Second World War with more than 700,000 men serving. This includes all artillery units armed with artillery pieces of any kind, i.e. field artillery, anti-aircraft artillery, anti-tank artillery, coast artillery and units manning guns on merchant ships. Those serving in all these units proudly called themselves, and were called by others, Gunners, a sort of title even today earning high status. Their loyalty, readiness for sacrifices and – not the least – high standard as regards professional skills in what is called Gunnery made the arm such a forceful and effective resource to the benefit of the Allies' cause.

The contributions of many distinguished individuals would be worth highlighting and presentation, but that would not be possible in a book of this kind. Exceptions will, however, be made for some individuals whom we have met in previous chapters. Those selected will be briefly presented, as will their contributions and what is behind their names.

They forged the sword

Two officers who made special contributions to the development of the artillery and its methods during the war will be the first to be presented, namely the Generals Jack Parham and Sidney Kirkman. Who were they?

Major General Hetman Jack Parham, CB, CBE, DSO
He was born on 27 July 1895. His parents were farmers at a small farm in Wiltshire, in Southern England. He went to school in Sherborne before starting officer training at Royal Military Academy at Woolwich, South-East London. In November 1914, he was commissioned as 2nd Lieutenant of the Royal Artillery and was immediately sent to the British Expeditionary Force in France.

Jack Parham served in France for one year before being transferred to Salonika in Greece. Large British and French forces had landed there the year before. After the end of the war, in 1918, he returned to England and thereafter held many artillery positions in England and India up to 1939. He was promoted Major in 1934.

In the inter-war period, Parham got an interest in aircraft engineering and flying, which first came when he was a schoolboy already and which was to accompany him throughout his whole life. He saw, long before many others, the possibilities to improve observation of artillery fire by using an aircraft. He presented his ideas on this subject in an article in 1933 already; in this he proposed the autogiro as a suitable air vehicle for this purpose. He himself had learnt to fly autogiros and suggested that each battery would have one for fire observation. An artillery officer would be both pilot and observer. He did not spur any enthusiasm on the idea and soon began to think in terms of using a light winged aircraft instead. His interest thus turned in a new direction. He first bought a small single-engine aircraft at a very low cost and learned flying it. After the engine had broken down, he changed the aircraft to become a glider.

There were several other artillery officers interested in flying in the middle of the 30s. Together with some of them, Parham in 1934 established the Royal Artillery Flying Club, which was to play an important role when the Army a few years later was prepared to create special air units for fire observation and control. This process has already been described, but we may note here that without Jack Parham's enthusiasm on the matter nothing substantial had probably emerged.

In January 1940, Parham held the rank of Lieutenant Colonel and was the commanding officer of 10 Field Regiment RA, a regiment that was sent to join BEF in France. His regiment was there to take part in the intense fighting in May. Thanks to his cool and determined leadership, the regiment made a good contribution in the battle when BEF was pushed back to Dunkirk, from which the regiment was rescued back to England. During the first days of the battle, when BEF was deployed along river Dyle in Belgium, he one day concentrated the fire from all his 24 guns against the same target, an armoured enemy unit halted for refuelling and rest. He could do this by personally giving fire orders to the batteries on radio, which was a fairly untested procedure at that time. This artillery engagement has been described as the very first regimental concentration fired in the war.

Jack Parham was soon after his return in England promoted Brigadier and artillery commander of the 38th Infantry Division. He now had a platform for developing the methods for concentrating fire from a very large number of guns, for which he has been best known. His priorities were speed and simplicity based on the fact that artillery on technical grounds was an area-covering weapon. Targets were often scattered over a fairly large area. He turned a technical disadvantage into a tactical advantage. The earlier practice of prioritising accuracy by focusing on time-consuming ranging, was not a good doctrine, he used to argue. With the technology available absolute precision could still not be achieved. Long communication ways through the hierarchy for acquisition of permission to open fire should also be eliminated. That was another point that he stressed.

Parham proposed a simplified method for description of targets to be engaged, at the time used as an order for calling up guns for firing. If the FOO/OPO wanted a whole regiment (24 guns) to fire he just ordered *Mike Target* followed by its location and rounds to be fired. If he wanted all the divisional artillery (72 guns) to engage a certain target, he ordered *Uncle Target* over his radio set, and a real blow was *Victor Target*, where the entire Corps artillery was to fire (200–300 guns, or many more). Parham's message was, that large-scale concentrations were possible to effectuate by using modern survey and communication technology in the right way. A prerequisite was, however, that simplified fire ordering procedures including this set of target descriptions were applied. In late 1941 he invited a number of high officers to witness how the fire from no less than 144 guns could land at the same target within five minutes, the target to be pointed out by one of the spectators.

As we have seen, Parham's ideas were accepted, albeit not immediately. But eventually, they were officially approved of as methods for imposing quick and very strong blows against the enemy. Training manuals were soon revised accordingly. This contribution made by Parham was of utmost importance during the last three years of the war.

From autumn 1942, Parham served in turn as artillery commander of the 1st, 2nd and 14th Army. He had hardly assumed the latter position when the war was over in August 1945. He was known as the officer also responsible for planning the extensive preparatory fire programme preceding the Normandy invasion on 6 June 1944.

Parham was promoted Major General in 1946 and commander of the 3rd Anti-Aircraft Group in Scotland, a position he held until retirement in 1949. At the beginning of this period he acted as Aide-de-Camp to H.M. the King.

In retirement, Jack Parham got more time again to attend to his old interest in aviation and aircraft design. He studied the subjects both in theory and practice and wrote books and articles. He was fascinated by the shape of birds and their flying technique and tried to transfer some of his findings to the design of aircraft wings. Of his books, one in particular has been much observed and appreciated. Its title is *Bird Flights for Bird Lovers*. He made all the illustrations in the book himself. He was an eminent illustrator and artist, and many elegant panorama sketches from observation posts made by him have been preserved. He was always fond of combining various tactical reports with well-drawn sketches.

Another area of interest to Parham after retirement was sailing. In this field, he wanted to improve design of sails and masts with inspiration from the world of birds. He made several practical trials with his own-designed and built catamaran.

Major General Hetman Jack Parham died at the age of 79 on 29 December 1974 after having suffered a lot from bad health and diminishing sight during his final years.

General Sir Sidney Chevalier Kirkman, GCB, KBE, MC
Kirkman was born in 1895 in Bedford where he spent his school years before getting the opportunity to enlist at Royal Military Academy at Woolwich. He was commissioned 2nd Lieutenant in 1915 and served in the First World War to its end; this in France, Belgium, Italy and other places. He was appointed a Battery Commander before the war was over. He was

wounded three times and awarded the Military Cross (MC). During the inter-war period he served in Egypt, Palestine, Malta and India. He got further training at Staff College, Camberley, Surrey in 1931–1932. However, his career upwards was slow, despite all his qualifications.

When the war broke out, he was a Major and still a battery commander. But then his career gathered momentum. In 1940 he was promoted Lieutenant Colonel and the commander of 65 Medium Regiment RA, a Territorial regiment, and with this he took part in the battle of France. After having returned from Dunkirk, it took about a year until again promoted, this time to the rank of Brigadier and artillery commander of the 56th Infantry Division. Montgomery, who had seen Kirkman's qualities, made him artillery commander of XII Corps later the same year, 1941. It was now that Kirkman made his large contribution to the development of artillery doctrines and tactics. Thanks to him, the establishment of a new trend as to the use of artillery came about. His suggestions were presented in connection with the largest-ever peacetime exercise, Exercise *Bumper* in October 1941. Highest umpire in the exercise was Montgomery and Kirkman assisted him as chief umpire on the use of artillery.

Kirkman then showed convincingly that it would lead to serious consequences when command of artillery units was decentralised too much within Corps and divisions. When so done, he explained, concentration of firepower could not be arranged when much needed, and artillery units remained idle, or kept as a 'reserve', in critical situations. As a countermeasure he proposed a doctrine, which was to be very successful during the rest of the war. The doctrine said that Command, i.e. the tactical use of artillery units in the operative situation in question, should be kept as high as possible in the organisation, and Control, i.e. primarily fire observation and control, should be decentralised to lowest practicable level. By this, concentration of firepower across unit boundaries would be possible. A better co-ordination of the artillery plan with the overall operative plan would also be secured.

'Control' should, if the doctrine was followed, rest with the one having the best view of the tactical situation in detail. This was normally the Forward Observation Officer (FOO) acting together with the infantry, or armour, commander to be supported. Together with the latter he could best judge how the battle should be pursued. Based on this he could advise the infantry/armour commander as to whether fire from a troop of four guns or many more would be the best tactical alternative. If and when a strong and sudden enemy counter-attack threatened the infantry/armour, the FOO was in a position to immediately take action with all available artillery resources.

It can be said that Jack Parham in 1941 established the technical procedures for quickest and strongest possible concentration of firepower from all artillery within range. Sidney Kirkman established the necessary command and control structure for such an employment of artillery to become possible. Both of them broke by this an out-of-date doctrine on how artillery should be used. They were successful also thanks to personal qualities in convincing those hesitant or reluctant to accept new ideas. Furthermore, they had the capacity to get things done; they were real 'doers'.

Montgomery called for Kirkman when he needed a top-class artillery commander for the 8th Army in Egypt. He assumed his new role in mid-September 1942 and became immediately the principal advisor and co-ordinator of the huge artillery employment in the battle of El Alamein 23 October–4 November 1942. This made the application of the new doctrine possible. The 800–900 guns available to Montgomery were used very efficiently and made a decisive contribution to the success of the battle.

Before the fighting in North Africa came to an end in May 1943, Montgomery made Kirkman commander of the 50th Infantry Division with the rank of Major General. Just before this, he acted as artillery commander of 18 Army Group, which comprised the 1st and 8th Army. He led the 50th Infantry Division in the invasion of Sicily in July 1943 and the subsequent battle for the island. He also commanded this division when it later landed on the Italian mainland in September 1943. It was then time for the next step in Kirkman's career.

Kirkman was promoted Lieutenant General at the beginning of 1944 and appointed commander of XIII Corps, which on the British side was given the task to finally break through the German 'Gustav Line' south of Rome. This attack has been called the fourth battle of Cassino and commenced on 11 May 1944. It was well coordinated with simultaneous attacks by strong American, French and Polish units. The barrage fired along the 20km-long front line from Cassino to the sea was one of the largest artillery concentrations in the Second World War.

Sidney Kirkman stayed on in Italy until the beginning of 1945 when he was injured and had to leave his command and return to England. He had been a much-appreciated commander in Italy and he was much missed. After having recovered, he was appointed commander of all forces in Southern England. General Officer Commanding-in-Chief Southern Command. In this capacity, he received the German capitulation on the Channel Islands.

He was assigned several important positions after the war, amongst them commander of a Corps in the British Army of the Rhine and Deputy Chief of the Imperial General Staff. Another important task given to him was to assume command of all the administrative work of the British Army as Quarter Master General, now with the rank of a full General. Furthermore, he was member of the prestigious Army Council 1945–1950.

Kirkman retired from the Army in 1950, but other important responsibilities followed. He was nominated Special Financial Representative in Germany on behalf of the British Government 1951–1952. Finally, in 1954–1960 he was Director General Civil Defence. He never lost an interest in the Royal Artillery and his comrades-in-arm. In the period 1947–1957 he held the position of honour Colonel Commandant Royal Artillery. It must finally be mentioned that he was a popular lecturer and leader of seminars in military history at various universities as well.

General Sir Sidney Chevalier Kirkman died at the age of 87 years on 5 November 1982.

Distinguished Territorial officers
Lieutenant Colonel, Professor John T. Whetton, OBE, DSO, MC
Whetton was born on 27 October 1894 in New Fryston near Castleford as one of 13 brothers and sisters. He had to leave school already at the age of thirteen and start working in a coal mine, but he had an interest in, and the talent for, further study. In 1908–1914, he studied at Castleford Technical College. When the First World War broke out he finished his studies and got enlisted in the Army and served in France. He was seriously wounded in 1916 and sent home. His skill had been observed and he was promoted several times. In 1918, when he had recovered from his wounds, he was constituted Captain and became commander of a ski company (!), which was engaged in Russia against the Bolsheviks after the Russian revolution. He was awarded both a Russian Order and the British Military Cross (MC).

Back in England from Russia in 1920, he was demobilised and began studying mining techniques at the Leeds University and graduated as Bachelor of Science in 1923 and Master of Science in 1925. He continued along the academic route at Armstrong College in Newcastle, where he researched and lectured in mining techniques, applied geophysics and survey up to 1939 when the war broke out. His interest in the nation's defence and his experience from World War I soon made him an officer of the Territorial Army. In this capacity, he took part in the compulsory yearly training that the civilians of this army had to undertake. In parallel with his demanding academic career he also had embarked on a military career.

As a consequence of his first-class civil and military qualifications he was in 1937 requested to build a new survey regiment, which was given the name 4th (Durham) Survey Regiment TA. He now held the rank of Lieutenant Colonel. Before this, there were only three regular survey regiments in the Royal Artillery and it was now obvious that more were needed. Over the coming years, ten regiments would gradually come into operation in the British Army.

Whetton's regiment was set on war foot when the war broke out, and he arranged with strong hand systematic training of it including many exercises to make it ready for war service. As we have seen in a previous Chapter, the regiment was in 1940 sent to Egypt, where it was put under command of 8 Army as the only survey regiment! Here a horrible blow came upon it in June 1942 when one of the two batteries was caught at Tobruk, this when the locked-in British forces had to surrender to Rommel.

Whetton demonstrated his strong leadership in this severe situation and established quite soon a new battery with surveyors flown in from England. The regiment was again complete when the battle of El Alamein began on 23

October 1942. The rapid advance westwards by the 8th Army after this battle introduced many challenging survey problems to the regimental surveyors, but also to the 'Flash Spotters' and the 'Sound Rangers'. With his excellent background, Whetton quickly found good solutions to the problems emerging.

Whetton's regiment was later taken back to England to be attached to XXX Corps. The regiment was to support the artillery of the Corps when landing in Normandy on D-Day, 6 June 1944 and the subsequent battle of Normandy and North-West Europe. At the beginning of 1945, Whetton was once again wounded and had to leave the regiment. He was to experience the end of the war in England.

John Whetton's extraordinary successful and much appreciated contribution to the war effort was rewarded several times. He was made Officer of the Order of the British Empire (OBE) by H.M. the King in 1941 and awarded the Distinguished Service Order (DSO) in 1943. He continued as an energetic commander of 4th (Durham) Survey Regiment TA for three more years after the war.

Whetton returned to the academic world when being demobilised after the war. He was appointed Professor of Mining Sciences at Leeds University in 1945 and began immediately with well-known determination and enthusiasm to bring up research and academic education to high standard. In 1957–1959 he was Pro-Vice Chancellor of his university. He maintained a large international network with colleagues around the world up to high age. He was entrusted many posts also outside the academic world.

Professor John T. Whetton died at the age of 85 on 23 September 1979. He is a good example on how Britain's armed forces took advantage of the skill of talented civilians with preparedness to contribute in peace and war. Many were engaged as officers of 'Territorial Army' and some were promoted to high positions. Two of them I would like to just mention very briefly, but their achievements would be worth more complete presentations in another context.

Brigadier, Chief Dentist Alfred Francis Hely
Another good example of a distinguished territorial officer is Hely. Despite being a dentist, he served as artillery officer in the 'Territorial Army' and was commander of a regiment in North Africa during the first part of the war. Later he became divisional artillery commander (CRA) and deputy divisional commander in Burma, a most distinguished role indeed entrusted a territorial officer.

Brigadier, Sir Philip J. D. Toosey
Toosey is one of the most well known of senior territorial officers. In his civilian life, before and after the war, he was an investment bank executive. He too served as commander of a Royal Artillery regiment when the war broke out, and was a very skilled and by all appreciated officer. He served in Singapore commanding 135 Field Regiment RA when the British had to surrender to the Japanese on 15 February 1942. As prisoner of war he was to play a remarkable role as the head of several prison camps through the war, always making his utmost to assist his fellow prisoners, thus taking consistent large personal risks. He was the model for the character Colonel Nicholson in the cinema film *The Bridge on the River Kwai*, played by Sir Alec Guiness, who however plaid a much different role than the much-praised role Toosey played in real life. After the war, Toosey was promoted Honorary Brigadier and commander of an Army Group Royal Artillery (AGRA) for some years. He assumed this military responsibility in addition to an impressive post-war civilian career.

They used the sword – the subalterns

The large number of artillery formations during the war required numerous subalterns, i.e. officers with the rank 2nd Lieutenant and Lieutenant. They were needed to assist in deployment of batteries and their troops and, when this was done, to serve at the battery and troop command posts with fire planning, managing artillery boards, calculations of 'corrections of the moment', preparation of laying data for the guns and many more gunnery tasks related to 'the indirect fire system'. The workload was often extremely high. The subalterns had to be ready also to replace troop commanders in battle as FOOs/OPOs.

The subalterns were in most cases often young men, often of the age 20–22 years, who after school had been rapidly trained to be commissioned as officers (cf. Chapter 13). In that initial training they were given the basics of their profession, war service gave the necessary extra training, making them real gunnery specialists after some time.

Major General Hetman Jack Parham
CB, CBE, DSO

General Sir Sidney Chevalier Kirkman
GCB, KBE, MC

Lieutenant Colonel, Professor John T. Whetton
OBE, DSO, MC, TD

Lieutenant (later Captain) Sidney Beck

Lieutenant (later Major) Douglas Goddard
MBE FCIS

Lieutenant (later Major General) Tony A. Richardson
CB, MBE

Lieutenant (later Captain) Peter Wilkinson
MC

We have in this book met a few good representatives of this kind of professionals. One was Sidney Beck who landed on D-Day in Normandy with his SP regiment, 86 Field Regiment RA. I have with the kind permission of his son, Benjamin Beck, taken several quotations from his distinguished personal war diary. After the war, Sidney Beck left the Army and returned to his civilian life as a civil servant, first as a Customs Officer, later as Economist in various governmental authorities. His last position was as Parliamentary Commissioner for Administration (the Parliamentary Ombudsman). He died at the age of 82 years in 1998.

An ex-subaltern who has given me invaluable help was Douglas Goddard who served as Gun Position Officer with 112 Field Regiment RA during the campaign in North-West Europe. His regiment played as we have seen an important role in the battle of Normandy and when the remnants of 1 Airborne Division were rescued back over river Rhine in September 1944. He continued as a regular officer after the war until 1957 when he left the Army with the rank of Major. He held thereafter many distinguished positions in the industry and was also entrusted with important community posts. H.M. the Queen demonstrated her appreciation of Goddard's distinguished services by appointing him Member of the Order of the British

Empire (MBE). Douglas Goddard died at the age of 91 on 11 December 2011.

Another distinguished and skilled representative of the ex-subalterns is Tony Richardson who served with 147 Field Regiment RHA, a SP regiment. He too assisted in the evacuation of the 'Red Berets', the 1st Airborne Division, at Arnhem. He stayed on in the Army after the war, eventually reaching the rank of Major General as commander of 'British Army Air Corps'. With his kind permission, I have availed myself of several of his articles on military subjects. General Richardson died at the age of 92 on 26 March 2015.

A young officer who experienced the fierce battle of Arnhem on site was Peter Wilkinson. He served there as 'Battery Command Post Officer' of 3 Battery of 1 Airlanding Light Regiment RA. After having taking part in the battles both in North Africa and Italy he was an experienced 'airborne officer' long before being landed at Arnhem. He was awarded the Military Cross in recognition of his service in Italy. Having returned from Arnhem with the remnants of the 1st Airborne Division, he was promoted Captain and made Troop Commander. In this capacity he took part in the disarming and repatriation of German forces in Norway in 1945. His final assignment was as an AOP pilot in Germany before being demobilised in 1946. He then served as economist and chartered accountant over the years before assuming the position as Managing Director of Anglia Building Society. I had the privilege of translating and publishing his excellent book, *The Gunners at Arnhem*, in Sweden in 2004.[*]

Two ex-subalterns who have published detailed accounts of the roles played by their regiments during the war are G.W. Robertson and Robert Woolacott. The former served with 136 Field Regiment RA and took part in the Burma campaign. His book, *The Rose & The Arrow: A life Story of 136th Field Regiment Royal Artillery 1939–1945*, has been an important source for this book. I am with gratitude pleased to acknowledge that Woolacott's book, *The Winged Gunners*, also has been an excellent source in my research. The book covers the history of 1 Airlanding Light Regiment RA from its creation in 1942, through the war to its short post-war role (see also Truesdale et. al. in the literature list).

The presented ex-subalterns are good representatives of all those who 'used the sword' that Parham and Kirkman had 'forged'.

[*] Peter Wilkinson died at the age of 94 on 20th January 2017.

Epilogue

Interview with Major General (retd) Jonathan B.A. Bailey CB, MBE, PhD

Major General Jonathan B. A. Bailey CB, MBE, PhD

This book deals with British artillery history from World War II, after a brief look at the historical background. It does not include the postwar history and the Cold War. In order to get a perspective on the British Army in general, and specific strategic issues during that period and the near future, I have turned to a distinguished authority, Major General (ret.) Jonathan B.A. Bailey CB, MBE, PhD. He was Director of the Royal Artillery (and Inspector of Artillery) in 2000–2002. During the period 2002–2005 he was Director General Development and Doctrine British Army. After his retirement he has worked in the industry, but also as Visiting Research Fellow of the Oxford Leverhulme Programme on the Changing Character of War. General Bailey has published several books and articles on national and international defence strategies and the historical development of British artillery. The future development of the national defence strategy has also been one of his subjects for articles and lectures.

We met in September 2011 when I had the opportunity to raise a set of questions, which are presented in bold below. The answers and comments kindly given by General Bailey are with his permission summarized here.

Has observation of traditions and history always been important to The Royal Regiment of Artillery? What has it meant as regards morale and fighting spirit?

– I must answer this question in the context of British Army overall. Yes, it has over time been demonstrably important in terms of performance and morale. I have for instance a survey about battalion commanders in the first Iraqi war of 1991, which clearly confirmed the importance of history. One Commander stated that he felt very pressed to perform in line with the proud history of his formation. So, knowledge about the history strengthens the identity of the formation, and this leads to a sense of pride of serving there.

In The Royal Regiment of Artillery the battery seems to be the bearer of traditions?

– The Royal Regiment of Artillery, as an umbrella organization for all artillery units, is of course the bearer of all artillery traditions, but batteries are in daily life the real bearers of traditions. This is marked by the fact that almost all regular batteries have a title of honour attached to it, such as 'J Battery (Sidi Rezegh) Royal Horse Artillery'. Another example that may be of interest to Swedish readers is the 'O Battery (The Rocket Troop) Royal Horse Artillery' commemorating the battle at Leipzig 1813 when the '2nd Rocket Troop Royal Horse Artillery' was attached to the Swedish Army. You can also find a 'Room of History' at the barracks of most of the batteries. This is not the case with regiments, which in most cases are much younger than the batteries.

Why so?
– The reason for this role on the part of batteries is Britain's long history. Batteries were often deployed to support the infantry when 'policing' the various corners of the Empire. They were equipped for this role to act as independent formations capable of supporting themselves. From time to time they were 'brigaded' into temporary regiments. Infantry companies on the other hand were seldom used independently as batteries were. Their battalions were their natural homes.

Is it in your mind important to learn from history?
– War is always a matter of human endeavour. Clausewitz said that the purpose of study [of history] was to establish an educated judgment. With knowledge and understanding of history you prepare your power of intuition for decision-making in new situations. Technology and tactics change, but man's nature does not. Therefore you can learn much from history. Trying to judge the future without knowing the history is a grave misguidance and can prove to be dangerous. This is not to say that history will be copied, but understanding the mechanisms behind it may prove important in new situations. However, when judging the future it is not necessarily the recent history that is most important, it might well be the much earlier history. Looking for instance on the situation in the mid-90s, when the future role of the armed forces was to be judged for the next twenty years, the Cold War history with its linear deployment and logistics had become irrelevant. The types of conflict prevailing after this period have called for manoeuvre capability, including concentration of power at the right place at the right point in time. There is much to be learned about this in the history of the fluid battles of the 18th Century. So, what seems irrelevant in history now, might well become very relevant in a new situation in the future.

What were the key issues for the development of the British Army after World War II?
– One should be clear about the fact that both world wars were significant aberrations from the traditional role of the British Army. Britain had never had a huge standing army. The Royal Navy was to protect Britain from getting involved in a large continental war. But in both the major wars Britain had to mobilize a huge army of civilians. The inevitable question afterwards therefore was, will this be the future? Or, can we go back to real 'soldiering' in the Empire only? After World War II the British Empire was bankrupt, but we had residual interests to protect militarily during the process of colonial disbandment. At the same time we had to retain a military capability to meet the Soviet threat in Europe. For this task we had, as a member of NATO, the British Army of the Rhine (BAOR), or as would have been more correct to call it, the British Army of the Elbe. So, the key issue was to find a balance of capabilities for both tasks. We had to retain the conscript system until 1963, when it was finally abolished. Britain had always disliked the conscript concept and wanted to get rid of it as soon as possible.

And tactically?
– That was to further develop the capability of mass concentration of artillery fire at shortest possible time. A continuation of the successful doctrine of close cooperation of ground forces and the air forces was also to be pursued.

Does it mean that all-arms-cooperation, which often failed during World War II, was improved in the post-war period?
– The forces of the various member states of NATO were to be used only within their own allotted sector of the front, they had their 'slot in the wall', so to speak. Hence there was not much room for manoeuvre. The role of artillery was defensive, not to support infantry and armour in attack. There was an endeavour to further develop cooperation between armoured formations and the infantry; but not with an emphasis on just three-arms cooperation, i.e. armour-infantry-artillery, but also on cooperation between land and air forces. By the late 1980's NATO had adopted plans that required greater manoeuvre and ideas of air-land cooperation reached their height with US-led thinking on 'Air Land Battle'.

– This change of NATO strategy in the mid-80s took place upon British initiative (Field Marshal Nigel Bagnall). The restrictions of national sectors on NATO's Inner German borders were reduced to permit huge NATO counterattacks. Instead of linear defence and linear logistics, manoeuvre was to be the new operational strategy. There was an emphasis on land-air cooperation, but artillery again developed an offensive role, supporting armoured manoeuvre from the line of march, and with increased ranges and precision It also called for development of improved target acquisition and communication technologies.

Turning to the question as to whether what the Germans call '*Auftragtaktik*' has been in line also with British traditions and mentality?

Background to the question: Some historians have stated that the British during the big wars emphasized rigid plans and control based on hierarchy with less room for initiatives by individuals at lower levels. On the other hand, it has been stated, the Germans were much more flexible and stimulated personal initiatives, when it came to how best a given task should be executed, i.e. '*Auftragtaktik*' was the doctrine. Would you say this is correct?

– First, I am against too superficial generalisations like this. Britain could not have run an empire successfully for about 200 years in the days before electronic communications without a very high degree and expectation of devolved responsibility and decision-making in its all-volunteer forces. Britain never had conscription until 1917.

Looking at the Royal Navy for example, they have always emphasized personal initiatives. Nelson called his ship commanders to his cabin and told them the outline of his plan and what he wanted to accomplish. From this he expected his subordinates to plan and execute their part of the battle. And he himself quite often disobeyed orders when the situation changed, and he believed a revised plan would be better in respect of the overall objectives. This was a kind of '*Auftragtaktik*' and was after him for decades called 'the Nelson touch'.

As regards the Army, the mentality was similar. An officer's wish was always to independently command a battalion or whatever at the North-Western Frontier or any other place in the Empire a long way from London. So, the British mentality certainly has been in favour of '*Auftragtaktik*' long before the Germans started to use the word. But we must realize that the situation was quite abnormal during the big world wars. Britain had to throw large armies of civilians into battle with relative little training. In such a situation you have to go to basics as regards training and leadership in battle, i.e. there was no room for '*Auftragtaktik*', '*Befehlstaktik*' was more likely to succeed.

We must furthermore realise that the '*Wehrmacht*' went to war with well-trained formations. Most of the conscripts and their commanders at lower levels had got a basic training in '*Hitlerjugend*', which was a good basis for '*Auftragtaktik*'. A German '*Feldwebel*' in World War II [corresponding British rank was Sergeant] had more military training than a new British or American Lieutenant.

But historically, '*Auftragtaktik*' has always been the heart of the British Army, even though this might be harder to identify if one looks only at the two World Wars.

But what happened to '*Auftragtaktik*' after the war as far as the British are concerned?

– Much did not change as long as we had a big conscript army, but when we returned to a regular army of professionals after 1963, more emphasis on '*Auftragtaktik*' could again be implemented. It would also become the basis for training. Another important basis for this was the change of NATO strategy towards strong counterattacks and manoeuvre, which became the accepted strategy in the mid-1980s, This required a general implementation of '*Auftragtaktik*' and this then became the official doctrine. But today the debate is also going in the opposite direction, implying that local personal initiatives are not enough. Circumstances, in particular when huge combined operations of land and air forces will be the case, may again call for more strict control from higher levels of command.

Finally, about '*Auftragtaktik*', what is officially the corresponding word in English?

– In the official doctrine from mid-1980s it is 'Mission Command'. In British military doctrine, 'Mission' means a task plus the purpose of it. So, if the task given proves impossible or unsuitable for any reason to undertake, the commander, e.g. a company commander, is expected to change or revise it in order to accomplish the purpose.

What role do you foresee for artillery in the future?

– Linear types of conflict between national forces

seem to be a thing of the past, if only because we have the ability to strike deep throughout a theatre of operations. Simple combat between military forces without the friction and ambiguities created by civilian populations seem unlikely. Will it ever happen again? Now we have to face asymmetrical conflicts like Afghanistan and just now Libya. As mentioned, there will be a need for capability in manoeuvre warfare in the future. A consequence will be much more focus on long range and precision, and improved means for long-range target acquisition and communication. Besides cruise missiles, Unmanned Armed Vehicles (UAVs), attack helicopters and advanced aircraft resources, the artillery will have its share. Although new precision ammunition will be a priority, the artillery will definitely retain its capability to launch fire against area targets. Sometimes precision can be too good!

We have seen that the existence of a large number of Terriorial regiments in 1939 made a fairly quick rearmament possible. What has the Territorial Army meant in the post-war period?
– It is true that the Territorial Army could mobilise a strong force in both world wars, although the Territorials were not prepared for the type of war they were called upon to fight. It should be noted that this force was, however, nothing like the reserve forces of Germany and France whose systems of conscription allowed them to support much larger reserve forces; and ones with a high level of training based on the training of individual members, who had already served their periods of conscription.

After the Second World War the Territorial Army has gradually been reduced and is today small as compared with its strength in 1939. Another change that has taken place, is that the Territorial formations are not intended for use as formed combat units. Their role has been reduced to provide qualified individual replacements for the regular formations, replacement of specialists in for instance logistics, communication and headquarters functions in particular. They are still collectively trained in regional units as before, but there is not anything like Territorial battalions to be deployed for attacking the enemy.

For the moment this is the situation. The future of the Territorial Army and Reserves is now being reviewed, although I do not know anything about the deliberations that might introduce a change back to formed combat units. We will learn more about this towards the end of this year [2011], when the report will be issued.

Author's comment December 2015:
From the document *Transforming the British Army An Update – July 2013* (British Army) it is seen that the Army of 2020 will comprise 82,000 Regular personnel and 30,000 trained Reservists. The Army will retain five regular artillery regiments being part of a new Artillery Brigade. In addition to these a parachute artillery regiment will also be retained. Reserve artillery will be organised in three regiments attached to the artillery brigade. They are to be trained to act as complete formations for combat as the regular formations. Hence, the previous more limited role to provide replacements for regular formations will be relinquished. Furthermore Royal Artillery will provide four regiments for an Intelligence and Survey Brigade to which The Honourable Artillery Company will be attached as well. It is not known as to whether 29 Commando Regiment Royal Artillery will be retained by Royal Marines.

Finally, if for any unforeseeable reason a significant rearmament will prove necessary in the future, what will be the major problems to overcome?
– First, we have to identify clearly the type of threat that is emerging and what kind of resources that will be required to meet it. For the time being it is difficult to see a threat requiring such a significant increase of artillery resources in UK. We are again discussing the future in the terms of the 10-year rule, as we did in the 1930s. This would imply that we can for the time neglect some elements of capability, as we will have at least ten years to prepare for a major threat requiring any significant rearmament.

If rearmament is found necessary, however, we have to decide whether we are to develop a large number of regiments with 155-mm howitzers and, if so, what types of target acquisition system and ammunition these will require. Or shall we develop regiments with MLRS [Multiple Launch Rocket System] or UAVs, or would the money best be spent on cruise missiles and other types of missile? There are several important questions of this kind to clarify before launching any artillery programme.

Should a large number of 155-mm howitzers prove to become the preferred option, where shall we get them? Are they stored from the Cold War, or must they be manufactured? The latter case implies certain problems. Most likely there will exist only a few factories in the western world that can manufacture 155-mm barrels. And should we decide to acquire a large number due to the threat we see internationally, many other countries will most likely do the same. This would certainly imply that 'buying from the shelf' will prove very difficult, not to say impossible. Hence, we have to be prepared to re-create our own arms industries. This will be possible but before it can commence, much time will be needed for arriving at decisions on necessary funding priorities. I am not sure that short range artillery and a great number of barrels will be the preferred priority, more likely it will be fewer guns with long range capability firing smart precision ammunition. I am with this not arguing against artillery capability to fire against area targets. This capability must be retained too.

Before such a situation as discussed above will emerge the general trend will thus be to further develop weapons for extended ranges and improved precision. The 'stand-off capability' will be the future, as it looks just now. And, quite frankly, hitting valuable targets far beyond our manoeuvring forces is what artillery always has done since it was first introduced.

With these interesting reflections about the future our discussion ended.

Selection of Symbols, Terms and Acronyms

Types of unit

⊠ Infantry

▭ Armour

● Artillery

⌒ Airborne

Unit size

XXXX   Army (>500 000 men)

XXX   Corps (50 000 – 100 000 men)

XX   Division (15 000 – 20 000 men)

X   Brigade (3 000 – 5 000 men)

III   Infantry Regiment (1 500 – 2 000 men)

II   Battalion / Artillery Regiment (600 – 1 000 men)

I   Company, Battery (100 – 150 man)

•••   Platoon, troop

••   Group, Section

Examples

Infantry Division (15 000 – 20 000 men)

Artillery Regiment (600 – 1 000 men)

Unit number to the right of symbols

Guns

╫ Light gun (calibre < 11 cm)

╫ Medium gun (calibre 11 – 15 cm)

╫ Heavy gun (calibre > 15 cm, < 20.3 cm)

╫ Super Heavy gun (calibre > 20.3 cm)

⊤ Light anti-aircraft gun (calibre < 45 mm)

⊤ Heavy anti-aircraft gun (calibre > 45 mm)

Selection of Symbols, Terms and Acronyms

Terms and Acronyms

The artillery arm and its institutions

'Firepower'	Royal Artillery Museum, Woolwich Arsenal, London. James Clavell Library is the library and archives of the museum (closing in 2016 prior to a move to Larkhill where a new museum will open some years later)
HAC	Honourable Artillery Company, oldest army unit
RA	Royal Regiment of Artillery
RAA	Royal Australian Artillery
RCA	Royal Canadian Artillery
RFA	Royal Field Artillery, older part of RA
RGA	Royal Garrison Artillery, older part of RA
RHA	Royal Horse Artillery, part of RA
RAA	Royal Artillery Association (established 1920)
RAHT	Royal Artillery Historical Trust (principal of Royal Artillery Museum and the owner of its collections)
RAI	Royal Artillery Institution (established 1838)
SAA	South African Artillery

Armies, other arms and corps

BAOR	British Army of the Rhine, in Germany from 1945
BEF	British Expeditionary Force, in France 1939–1940
NWEF	North-Western Expeditionary Force, Norway 1940
TA	Territorial Army
ACC	Army Catering Corps
RAMC	Royal Army Medical Corps
RAOC	Royal Army Ordnance Corps
RASC	Royal Army Supply Corps
RE	Corps of Royal Engineers
REME	Royal Electrical & Mechanical Engineers

Artillery formations and commanders

AGRA	Army Group Royal Artillery
AOP	Air Observation Post
FR	Field Regiment (<11cm calibre), normally given as Fd Regt.
MR	Medium Regiment (<15cm), normally given as Med Regt.
HR	Heavy Regiment (<20.3cm), normally given as Hvy Regt.
SHR	Super Heavy Regiment (>20.3cm), normally given as SH Regt.
SuR	Survey Regiment
HQRA	Headquarters of artillery commanders at corps and higher levels. could also be found at divisional level
MGRA	Major General Royal Artillery
CAGRA	Commander Army Group Royal Artillery
CCMA	Corps Commander Medium Artillery (from 1943 CAGRA)
CCRA	Commander Corps Royal Artillery
CRA	Commander Royal Artillery, commander of all divisional artillery
COR	Commanding Officer Regiment, normally only given as CO
RHQ	Regimental Headquarters
Tactical Headquarters	Commander with detachment of key staff officers

366

Selection of Symbols, Terms and Acronyms

BC	Battery Commander
BK	Battery Captain, Battery Commander's deputy

Deployment and fire management

CBO	Counter Bombardment Officer, Counter Battery Officer
CMO	Counter Mortar Officer
BGP	Battery Gun Position
DA	Deployment Area
TGP	Troop Gun Position
Wagon Lines	The location to which vehicles were assembled after gun deployment, normally under command of the BK
Bearing Picket (BP)	A steel pole with a card giving accurate bearings and coordinates to be used for battery fixation
Trig Point	Trigonometry Point, which was accurately surveyed by topographic surveyors and from which artillery surveyors could start surveying in their units
Battery Command Post	Acting as battery fire calculation and control centre
Troop Command Post	Acting as troop fire calculation and control centre
CPO	Battery Command Post Officer
GPO	Gun Position Officer, same role as CPO but at the troop level

Fire observation and control

AOP	Air Observation Post. The pilot was a gunner, the plane a Taylorcraft Auster managed by RAF
FOO	Forward Observation Officer. He was attached to the unit to be supported
FOP	(Forward) Observation Post
OPO	Observation Post Officer. He acted independently, not attached to any unit, with his own battery
OPP	Observation Post Party, which included signaller(s) and assistant(s)
Zero Line	Centre line of arc to be covered by fire. Guns of a battery were normally oriented with parallel barrels along this line before engaging targets
CoM	Correction of the Moment. Applied to sight data and registered target data to take into account factors affecting the ballistics of the flight of shells such as wind direction and strength, air pressure, weight of shell etc.
CP Fire	Counter-Preparation Fire (until 1941). A concentration of fire against an enemy formation assembling and preparing for an attack, see also DF
Covering Fire	Fire in support of own attacking formations. Planned as barrages or time concentrations for all artillery available. See also Neutralization
Barrage	Standing or moving belt of fire behind which own infantry or armour attack. When several belts make up a pattern, often with 100–200 yards distance between them, the barrage could be either 'creeping' or 'rolling' depending on how participating units are planned to lift their fire from one belt to another. Other types existed as well, one being the 'box barrage'
Destruction	Fire delivered for destroying enemy infantry, armour, installations etc.

Selection of Symbols, Terms and Acronyms

DF	Defensive Fire. Pre-planned fire to be launched for the protection of own positions when the enemy is attacking
DF(SOS)	Defensive Fire ordered in case of emergency. If no other fire mission was ordered guns should rest aimed, and loaded, at such a target for quickest possible engagement when needed. A 'gun sentry' was often left when the detachment was at rest, thus the first round could be fired without any delay
Gunfire	A fire order where each gun fired as rapidly as possible, without concern for the other guns in the Battery, or if an interval (a specified number of seconds) had been ordered by the originator, it was fired at that required time interval after its previous round.
Met/met	Meteorological
Met Telegram	Gave air pressure, wind speed and direction at certain projectile flight times as one input to calculation of CoM
Neutralization	Fire which was delivered in order to hamper or interrupt movement and/or firing of weapons by the enemy. It used much less ammunition than fire for destruction. See also Covering Fire and Destruction
Predicted Fire	Target engagement prepared with necessary gun data including Corrections of the Moment but before ranging or fire for effect
Preparatory Fire	Fired prior to an attack to disrupt enemy communications, headquarters, artillery positions etc. See also Covering Fire
Ranging	The observer's procedure for directing the fire to the target before ordering fire for effect onto the target. Normally this was done by 'bracketing' over the target, successively halving the brackets
Registration	Targets recorded for future engagement, either after ranging or as 'silent registration', i.e. all gun data prepared only. See also Predicted fire

Some British awards
CBE Commander of the Order of the British Empire
KBE Knight Commander of the Order of the British Empire
MBE Member of the Order of the British Empire
OBE Officer of the Order of the British Empire
CB Companion of the Order of the Bath
GCB Knight Grand Cross of the Order of the Bath
KCB Knight Commander of the Order of the Bath
TD Territorial Decoration
DSO Distinguished Service Order
MC Military Cross
MM Military Medal
VC Victoria Cross

Measurement units
1 mile = 1,609m
1 yard = 0.91m
1 foot = 30.48cm
1 inch = 2.54cm
1 cwt (long hundredweight)
 = 112 pounds (lb) = 50.8kg
1 pound (lb) = 0.45kg
1 ounce = 28.35g

Maps

Map 16-1 The British Expeditionary Force (BEF) was deployed around the cities Lille and Arras in Northern France between 1 and 7 French Army when the German attack commenced on 10 May 1940. A large number of French armies were deployed to the right of them along the whole border down to Switzerland in the Southeast.

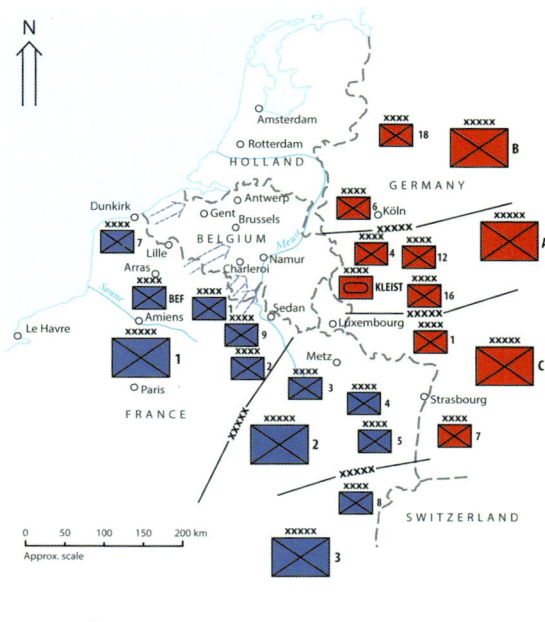

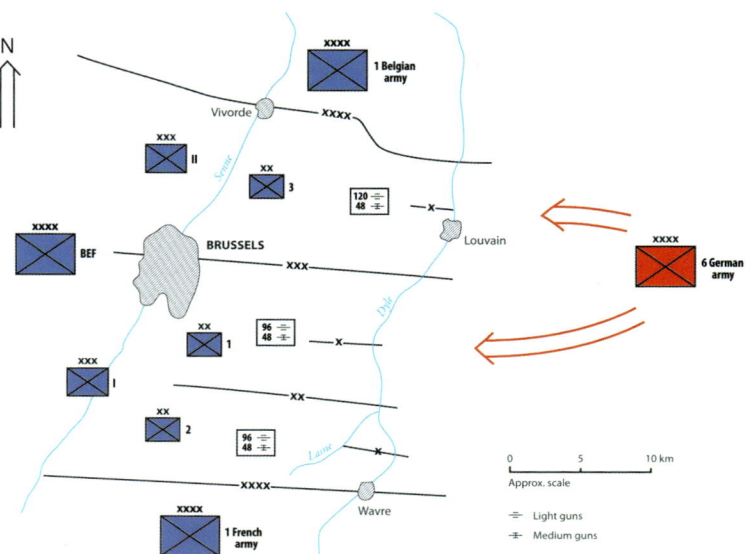

Map 16-2 When BEF had been deployed along the River Dyle in Belgium, each infantry division could be supported by at least four Field Regiments and three Medium Regiments. The map illustrates the number of field and medium guns within the deployment area of the three foremost divisions (The map is a revised and simplified version of a map from Farndale: The Years of Defeat).

MAPS

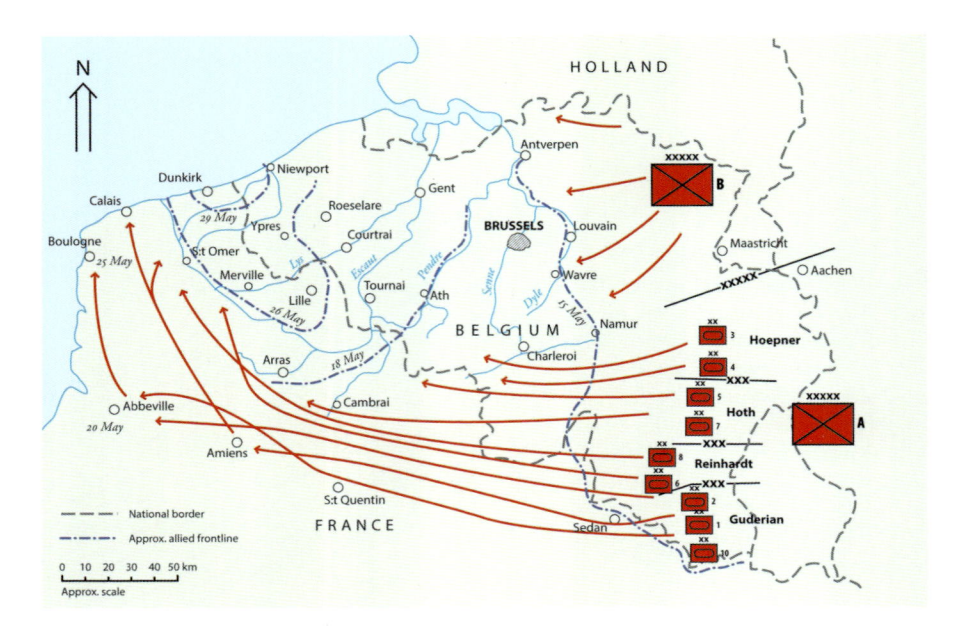

Map 16-3 On 13 May 1940 the German Army Group A commenced its 'Blitz' offensive with four armoured Corps south of the allied positions in Belgium and on 20th May the first units reached the Channel. Thereby were the supply lines of BEF cut and an evacuation at Dunkirk was made unavoidable, in particular so as the German Army Group B pressed very hard from north and northeast. The map shows the approximate front lines at different dates during the gradual retreat into the final bridgehead at Dunkirk in late May.

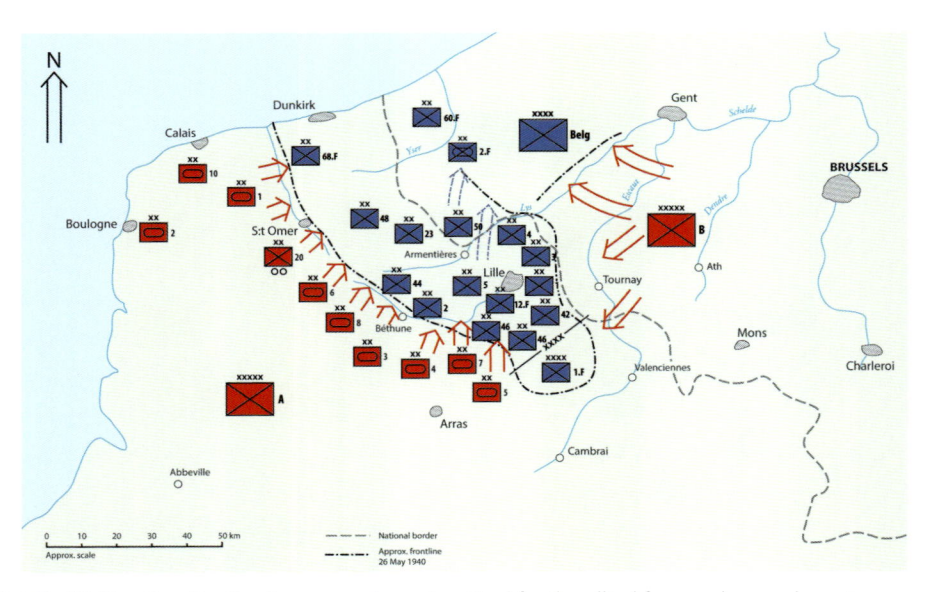

Map 16-4 On 26 May the situation became extremely critical for the allied forces when under extreme pressure from Army Groups A and B. Further north a Belgian collapse was imminent which would imply a completely opened right flank of BEF as a consequence. The British 5th and 50th Division therefore were hastily redeployed up towards Ypres to fill the gap. They were followed a day later by Montgomery's 3rd Division, which made an exceptional redeployment during the night behind the former divisions. In the Southeast, French 1 Army was enclosed and had to capitulate.

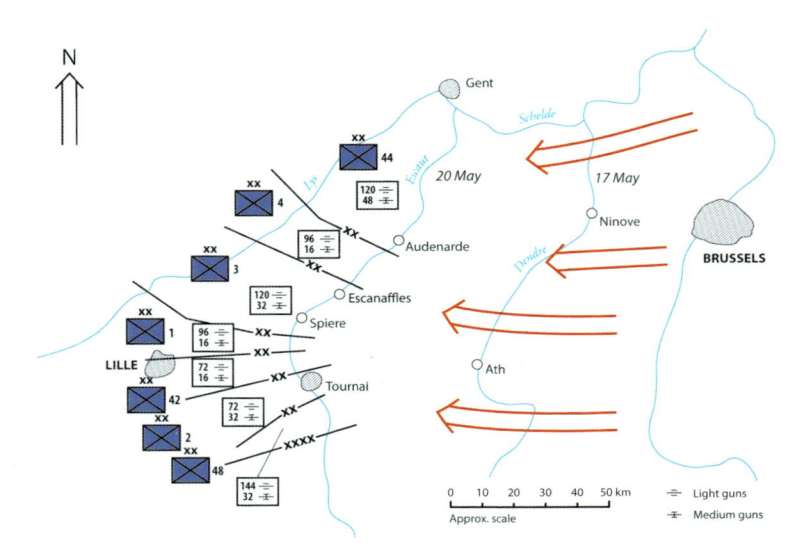

Map 16-5 At a defence line along River Escaut the retreating divisions, with support from BEF's strategic reserve, were to make a final stand. However, when they risked to be circumvented around both flanks they had to give up and continue the retreat towards Dunkirk. As we can see from the map all divisions had plenty of field guns as well as medium guns (The map is a revised and simplified version of a map from Farndale: The Years of Defeat).

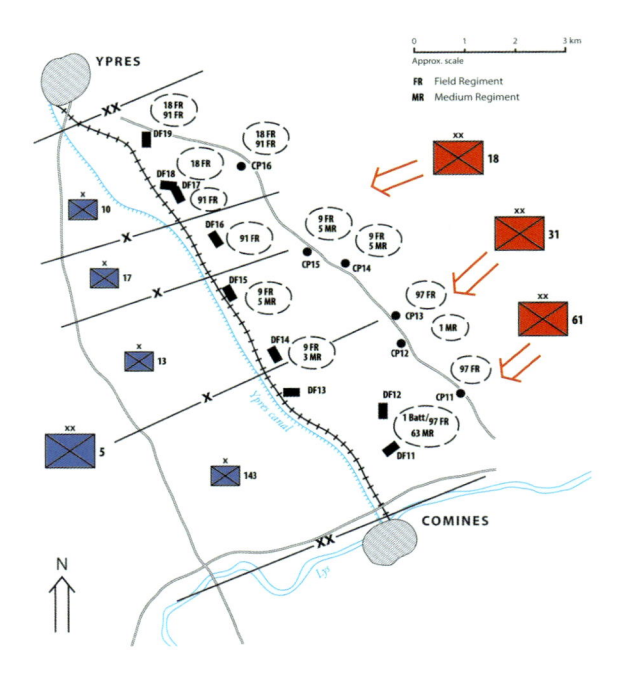

Map 16-6 The artillery commander of the 5th Infantry Division and his staff managed to prepare a fire plan after the hasty redeployment of the division on 26 May 1940 to the Ypres region, just before the decisive battle on 27–28 May commenced. The Gunners did what they could do with the limited resources still available. This saved the situation. 'CP' means Counter Preparation Fire and 'DF' Defensive Fire where the Germans were to be stopped finally. The regiments that planned fire against the respective targets are indicated by their numbers within the broken circles. 'FR' means Field Regiment and 'MR' Medium Regiment.

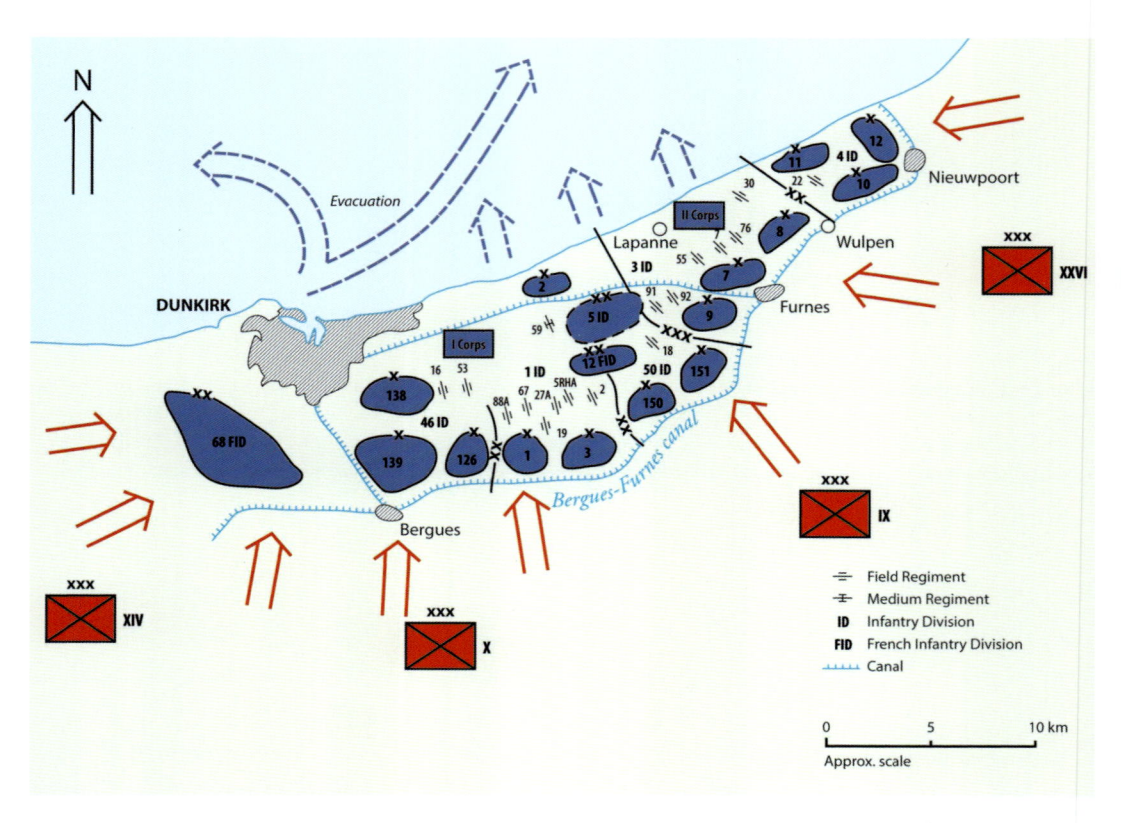

Map 16-7 In the evening of 30 May 1940 the reminiscences of BEF were in the bridgehead together with remaining parts of six French divisions. Four of the latter were in the eastern part of the bridgehead and are not marked on the map. As to British artillery, parts of sixteen Field Regiments were left, less than one third of the artillery force available when the fighting commenced on 10 May. All Medium Regiments, except a tiny portion of one regiment, were already lost (The map is a revised and extended version of Map 19 in Farndale: The Years of Defeat).

MAPS

Map 17-1 The only British artillery formation sent to Norway was 203 Battery RA, which came to Harstad with 12 guns in three Troops with four guns each, six of the guns only were engaged in battle. These were abandoned when the evacuation took place, the remaining six could be brought back to Britain though. The evacuation dates given here are uncertain as different dates are given in various source documents. However, the error is expected not to be more than 1–2 days.

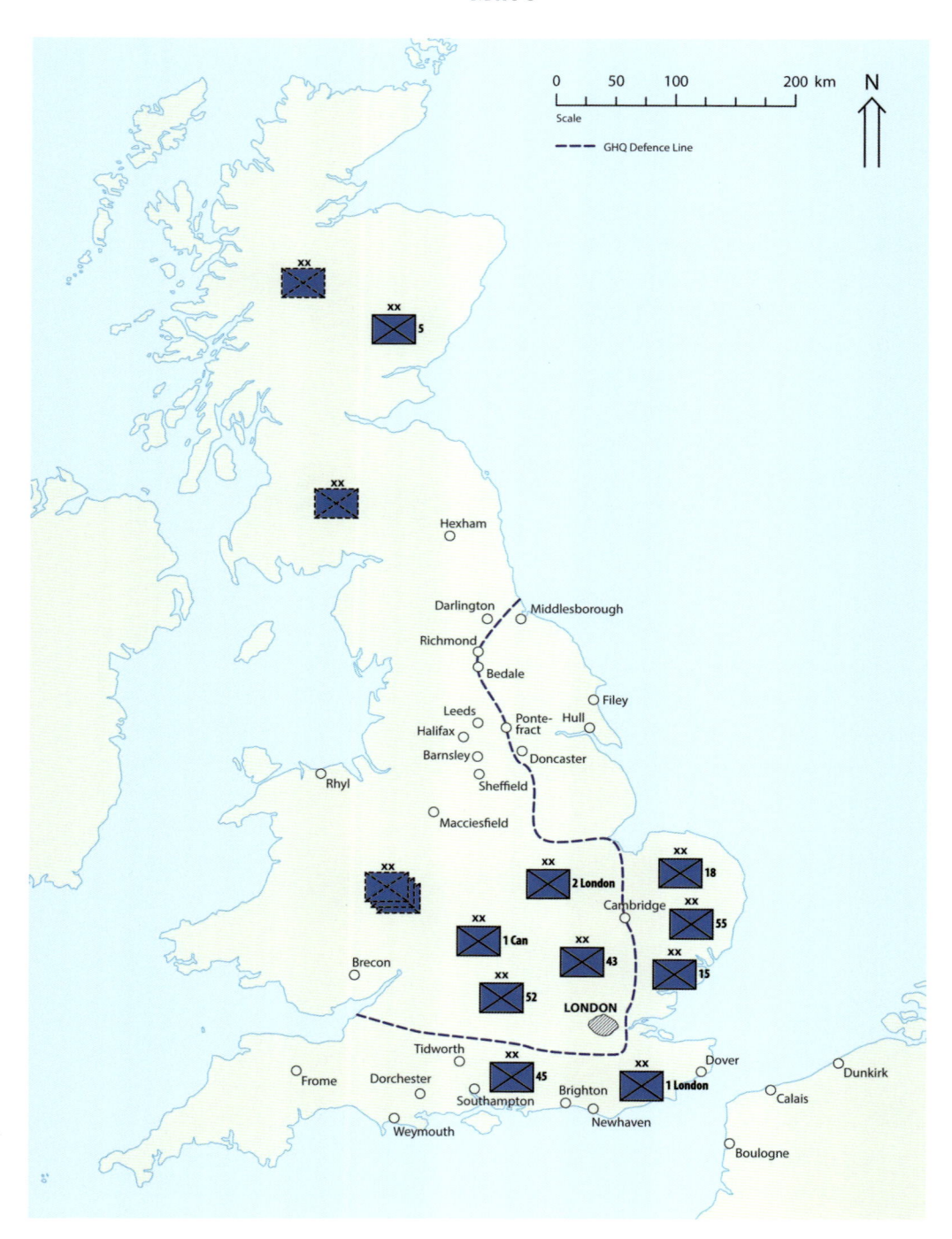

Map 18-1 The divisions available in Britain in 1940 for defence lacked, in most cases, much personnel and equipment. Many formations also lacked appropriate training. Until mid-July the strategy yet applied was to offer a firm stand against an expected German invasion and to finally stop it along the fortified defence line 'GHQ Defence Line', illustrated on the map. When Field Marshal Alan Brooke took over as Commander-in-Chief, he changed to a more offensive strategy: The enemy should be attacked and beaten already on the beaches!

MAPS

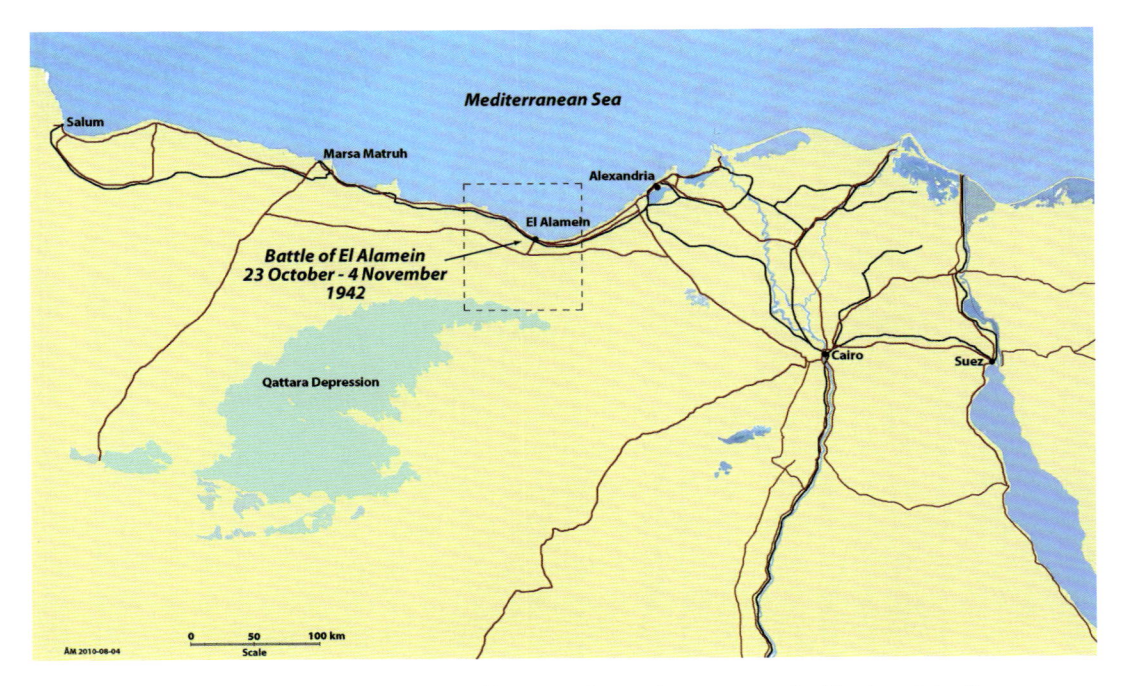

Map 19-1 The battle at El Alamein was inserted between the Mediterranean in the North and the Qattara Depression in the South. Here, some 200,000 men on each side were to fight the decisive battle of Egypt.

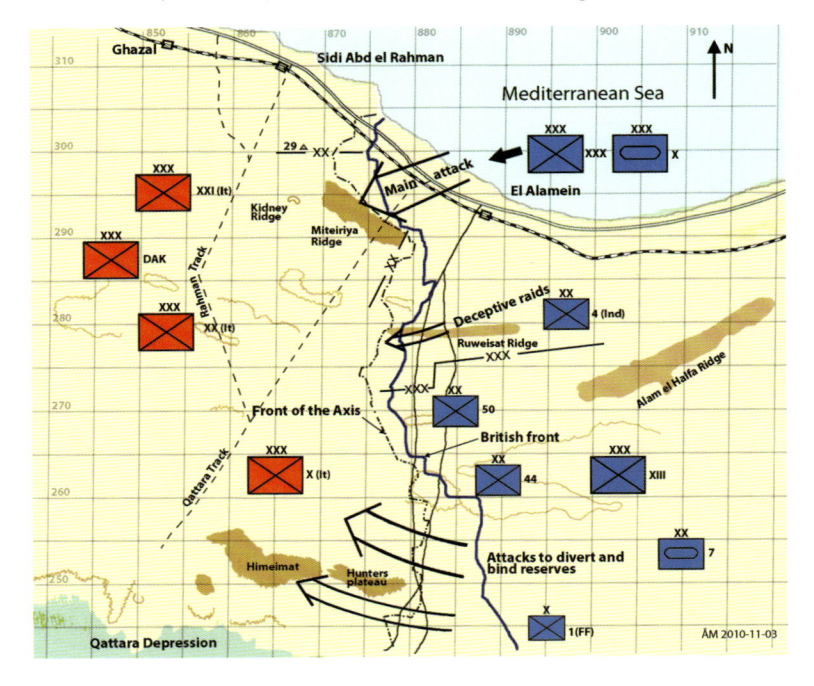

Map 19-2 The main attack in Operation Lightfoot commenced at 21.40 hrs on 23 Oktober 1942 with a concentration to the Northern sector. Deceptive attacks took place in the Southern sector aiming at concealing the direction of the concentrated main attack and also to tie down the armoured reserves of the Axis Powers in the South (the grid square is 5x5 kilometres).

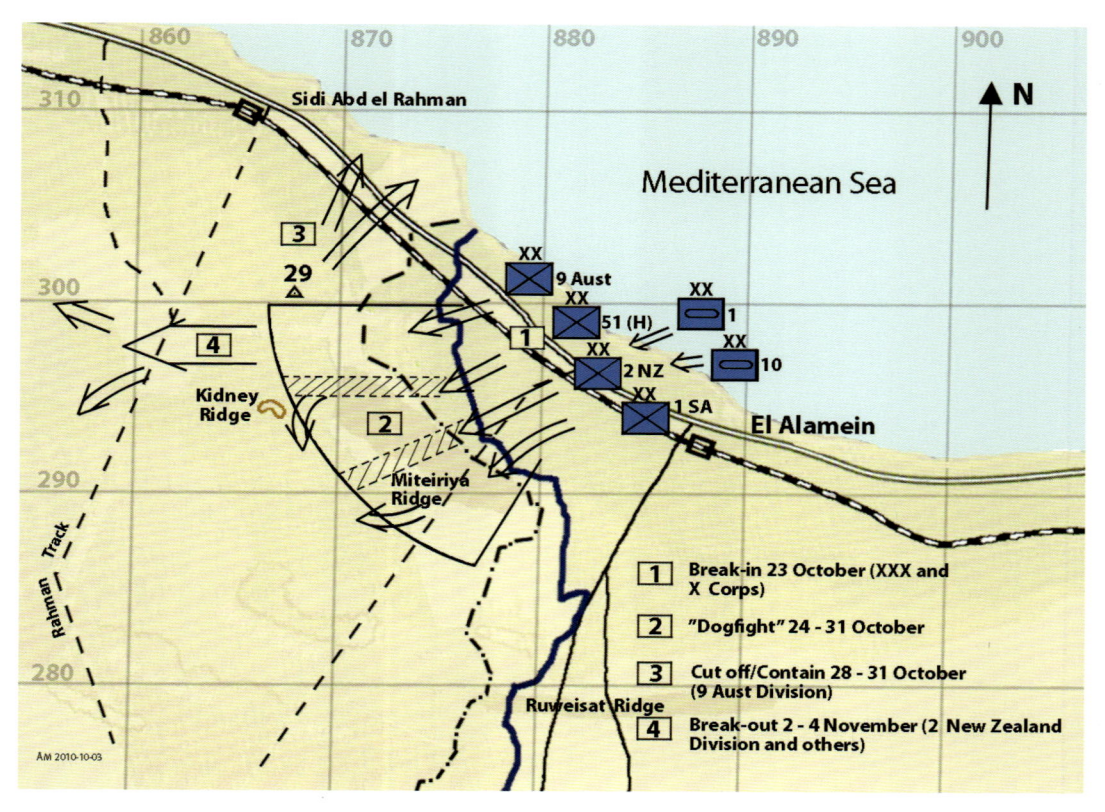

Map 19-3 After the initial main attack, which commenced at 21.40 hrs on 23 October 1942, the fighting continued within the captured area for about a week. Montgomery called it 'the dog fight', which was aimed to clear that area and wear down his opponent during the many counter-attacks that followed. The Australian division also attacked northwards to cut off and circumvent German units closer to the beach. The final break-out, called Operation Supercharge, took place on 2-3 November (the grid square is 10x10 kilometres).

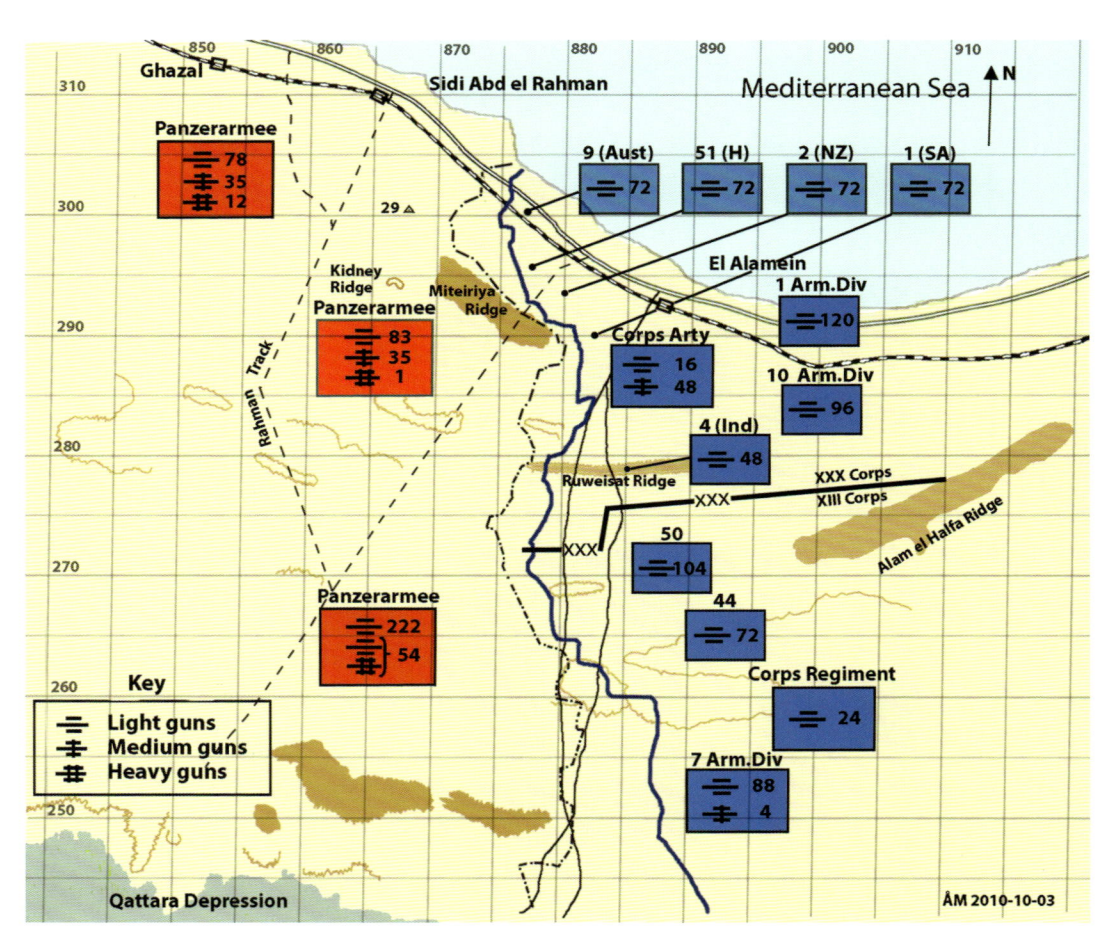

Map 19-4 Available artillery just before Operation Lightfoot on 23 October 1942. Besides the own artillery of the four attacking divisions, which are indicated on the map in blue colour, another 18 Troops (72 guns) from the two armoured divisions were at their disposal. The latter were split with 3-6 Troops per attacking division and within these attached to the divisions' own regiments. Those reinforced in this way thus could muster three Troops per Battery, i.e. 12 guns. The Axle Powers also had significant artillery resources. Regarding medium and heavy guns, they were superior to the British in terms of number of guns (the grid square is 5x5 kilometres).

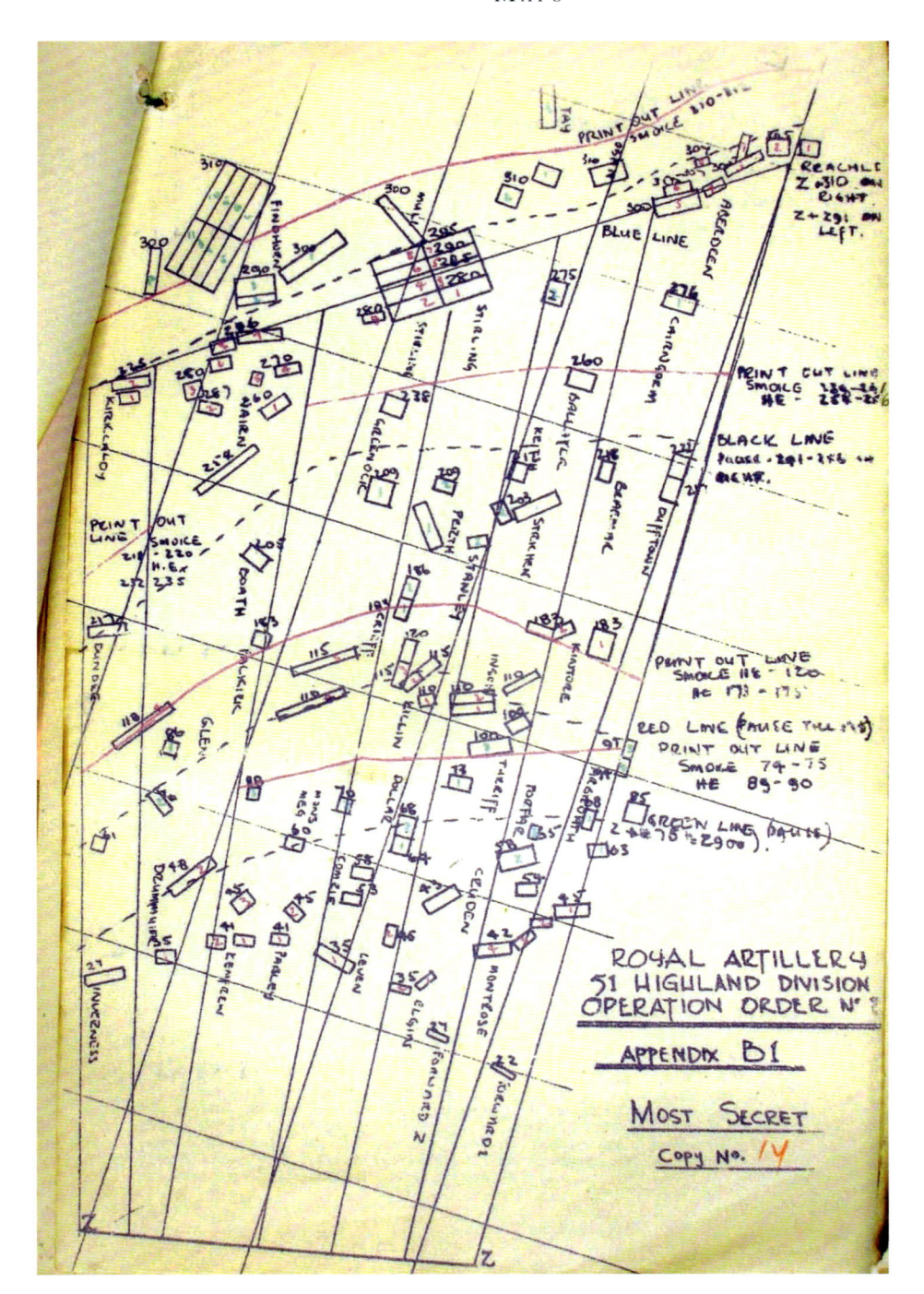

Map. 19-5 The covering fire in support of the Scottish Division was designed as a number of timed concentrations against known enemy positions. The fire was systematically moved forward. As can be seen here, pause lines were included (Green, Red and Black line). The location of these was marked with artillery fire slightly beyond respective line (called 'Print Out lines'). Closer to the final attack objectives a few smaller barrages were part of the plan. These were applied when the location of the enemy positions was not certain enough (RAHT).

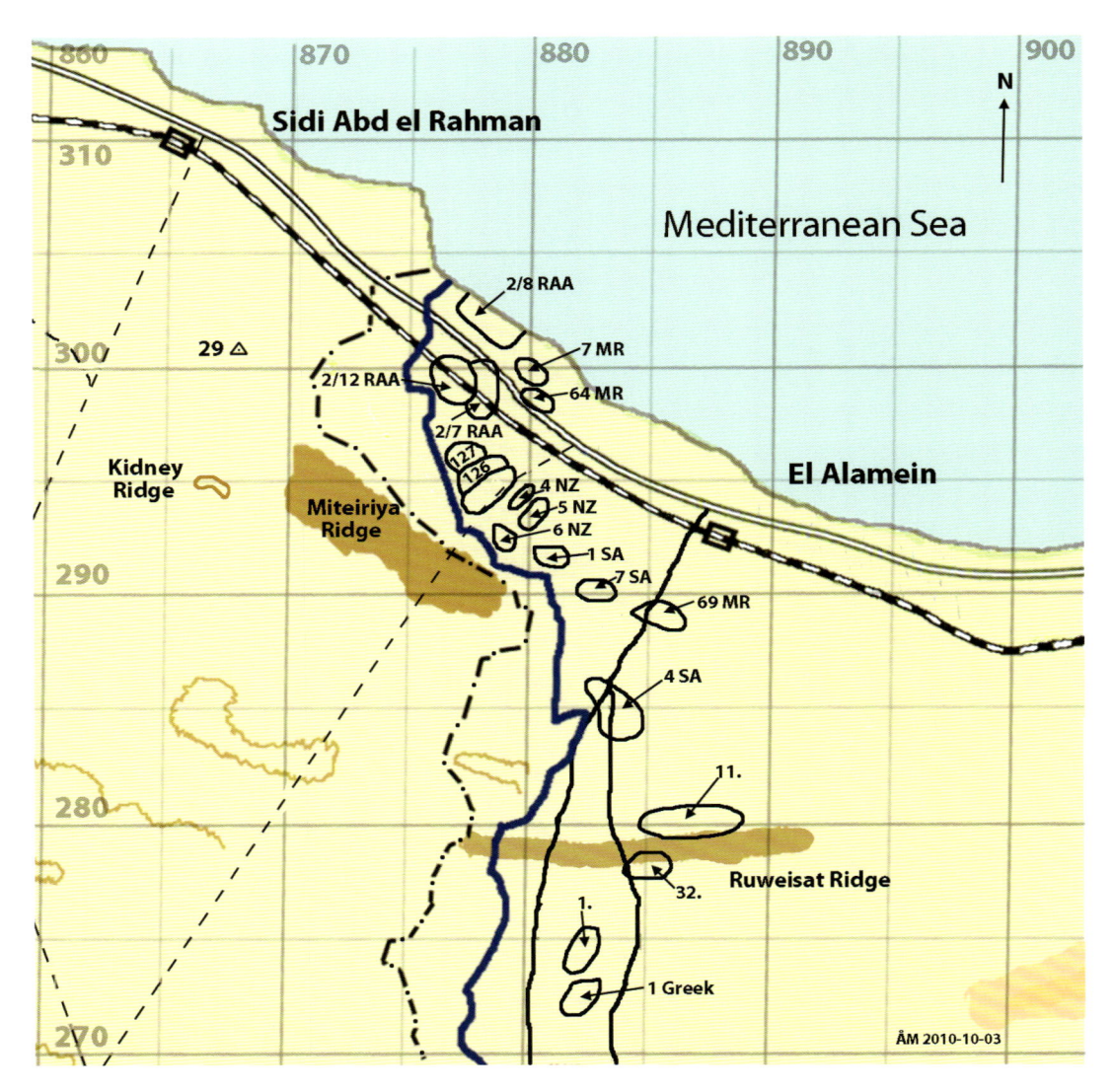

Map 19-6 Approximate deployment of the British artillery within the XXX Corps area before the main attack in Operation Lightfoot, which took place on 23 October 1942. Necessary ranges to cover were initially 5–8 kilometres, but then quickly approached maximum ranges for the 25-pounders, which necessitated early redeployment. The medium and heavy batteries of the Axis could only be countered by the rare British Medium Batteries. Numbers without additional letter are British Field Regiments. Those with NZ added are New Zealand Field Regiments and those with RAA Australian. SAA in addition to the numbers are South African regiments. British Medium Regiments are denominated MR after the number (the grid square is 5x5 kilometres).

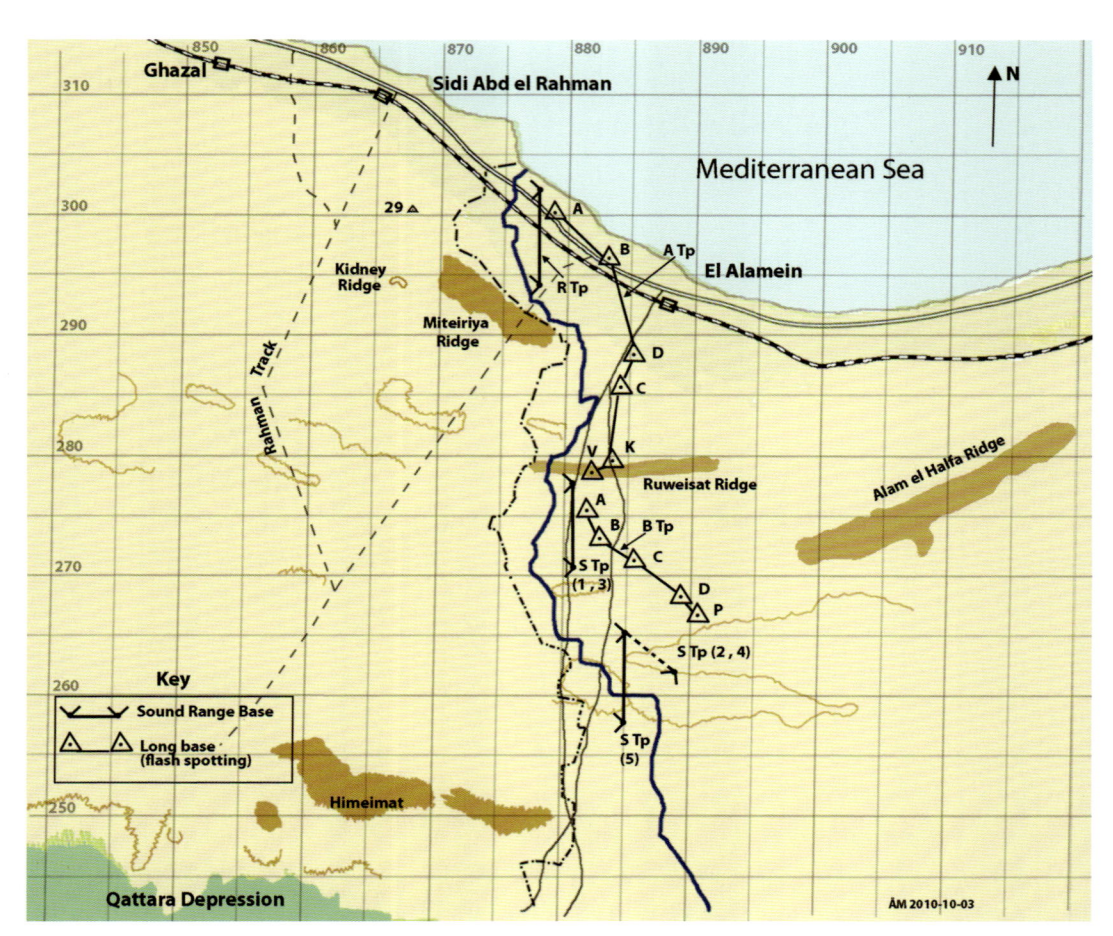

Map 19-7 The British sound ranging and observation bases on 23 October 1942. On the Northern towers 'B' and 'D' lanterns were applied which could be used when laying guns during nightly attacks. When these had commenced the intensive battle noise made sound ranging impossible. The staff instead had to assist the observation bases with repair and extension of telephone lines to their evaluation centres. After two days' fighting the long-bases were redeployed and reinforced forward both in the North and in the South (the grid square is 5x5 kilometres).

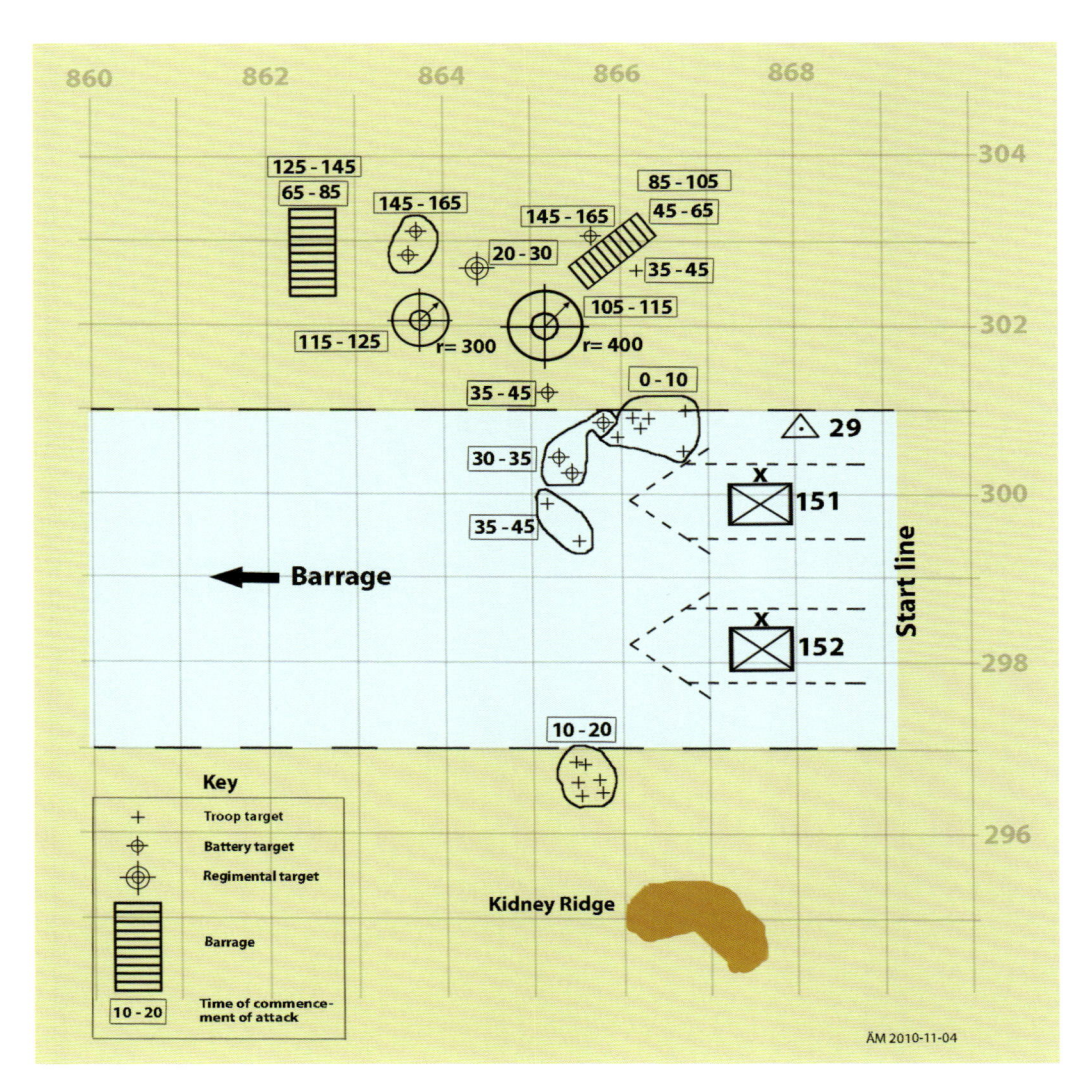

Map 19-8 During the main attack in Operation Supercharge eight Field Regiments (192 guns) fired a creeping barrage along the whole front, four kilometres. It was located between the broken lines on the map. It was here that the two attacking infantry brigades advanced beside each other. In addition, five Field Regiments (120 guns) fired timed concentrations against targets all over the attack area and at the flanks. The fire plans were complicated and comprised fire against Troop- and Battery-targets as well as Regimental targets, as here is illustrated for 2/7 Australian Field Regiment. We can see that they also fired some minor rolling barrages and fire over some large circular target areas. Some guns also fired smoke shells. The firing went on for 165 minutes (the grid square is 1x1 kilometres) (Data from Concentration Table attached to the War Diary of 127 Field Regiment RA which also took part with a similar fire plan of its own).

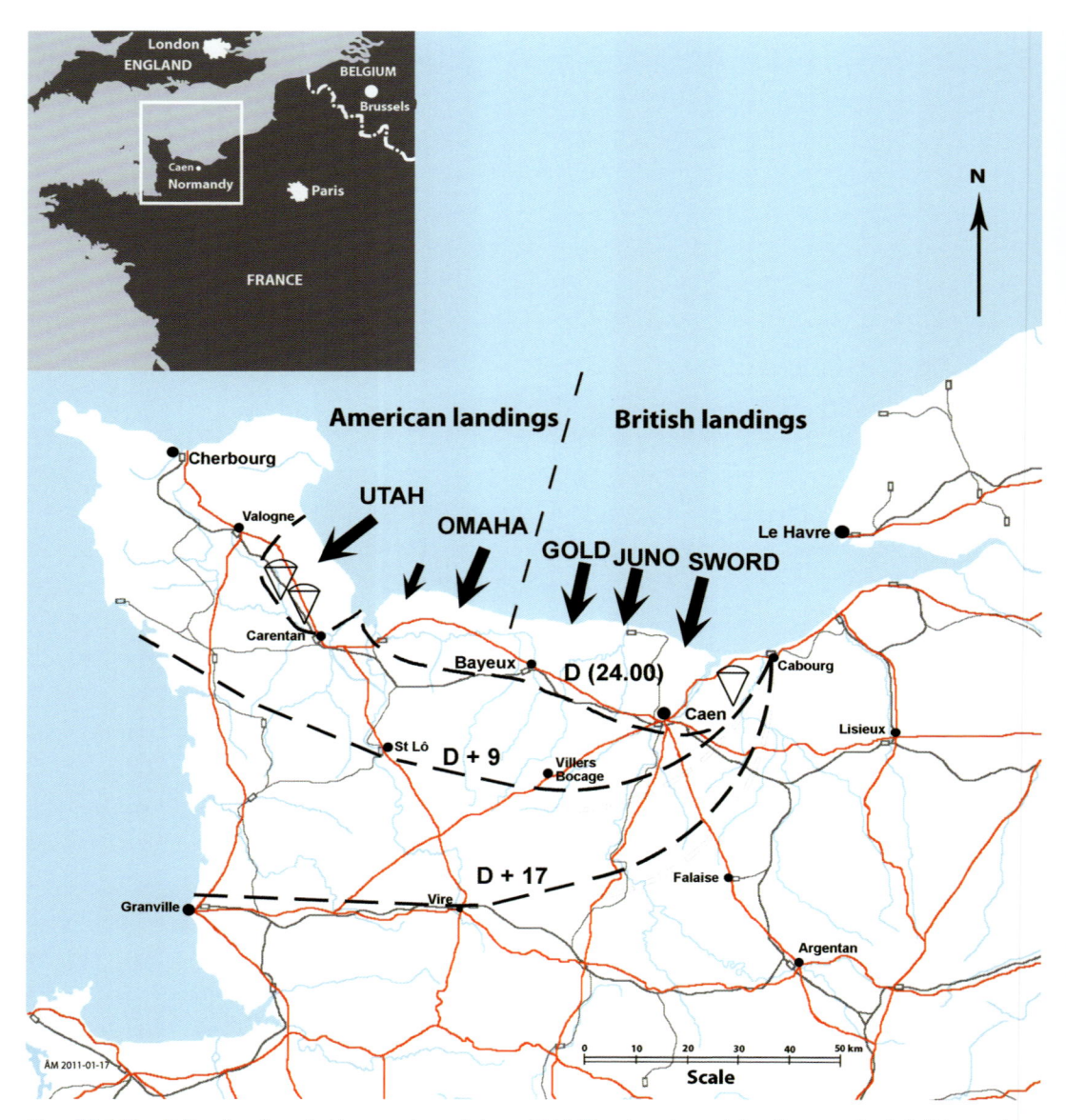

Map 20-1 The D-Day landings in Normandy on 6 June 1944. The American air-landings on the left (Western) flank were made by the 82nd and 101st Airborne Division. At the Eastern flank 6 British Airborne Division landed. Within the American beach sector 1 and 4 Infantry Division were landed as well as a unit of Rangers. The British landed the 3rd and 50th Infantry Divisions, as well as the 3rd Canadian Infantry Division, all reinforced by Armoured and Commando units. The planned extension of the bridgehead at 24.00 hrs on D-Day and during the subsequent weeks are illustrated by broken lines. Reality was to show that this advance planning had been too optimistic.

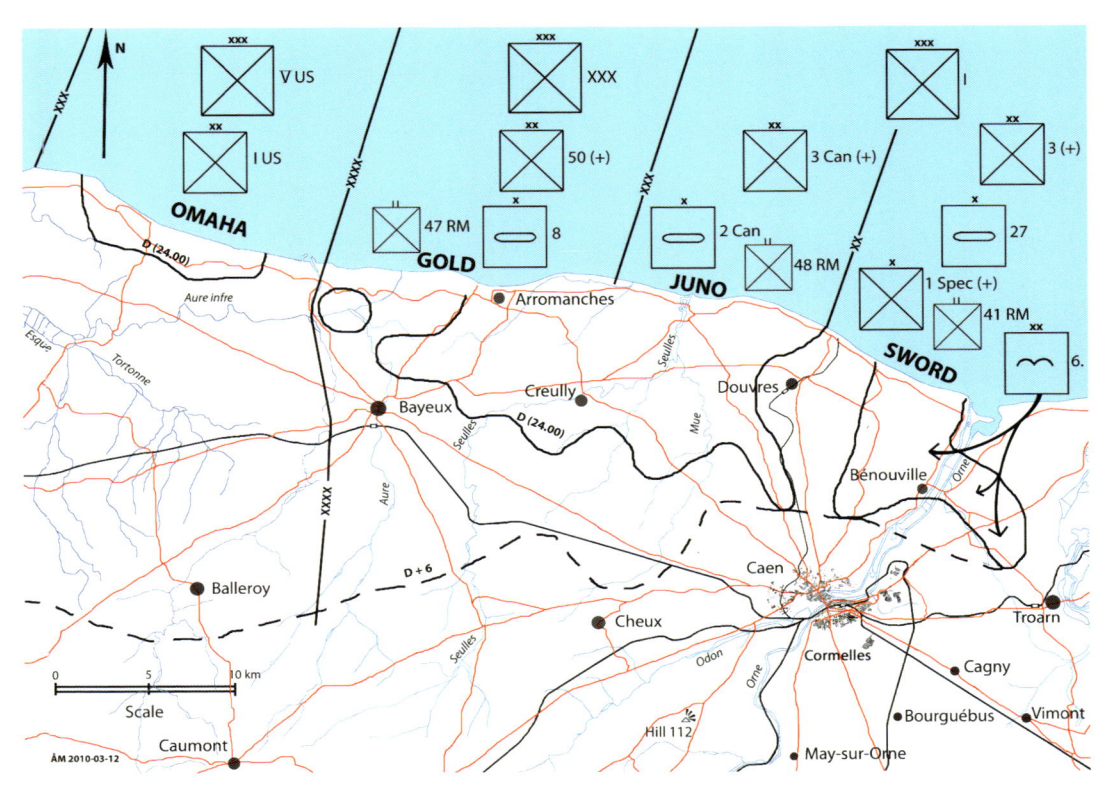

Map 20.2 The British landed on three beach sectors, Gold, Juno and Sword. Immediately to the right they had one of the American sectors, Omaha. At the Eastern flank the 6th British Airborne Division landed. The approximate extension of the bridgehead at the end of D-Day is indicated and as it was after six days of fighting. Montgomery's plan was to capture Caen the first day, but as we can see this had not been achieved, not even after a week.

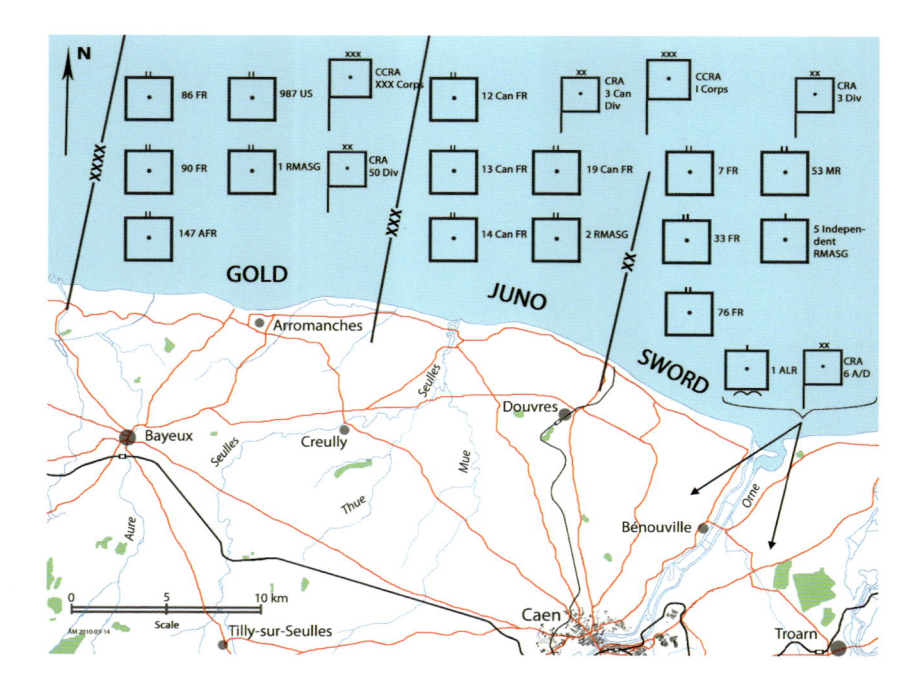

Map 20-3 During D-Day, 352 self-propelled guns were landed within the British sectors. They were distributed amongst the formations as indicated on the map, where also artillery commanders at Corps and divisional levels are indicated. One light Air-landing Battery with eight guns arrived on D-Day with gliders as a first support unit for the 6th Airborne Division East of River Orne.

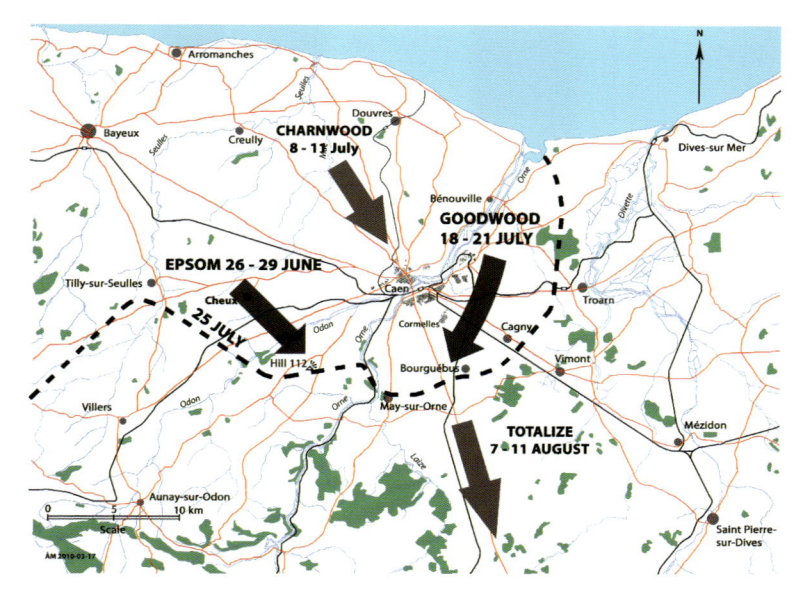

Map 20-4 The approximate extension of the bridgehead around Caen on 25 July 1944. The American break-out now took place further to the West. In the British sector the bridgehead had been extended through 'Operation Epsom' and its successor Operation Jupiter as well as Operation Bluecoat west of the city and Operation Goodwood on the Eastern side. Still some weeks of heavy fighting remained until the battle of Normandy was over. The British break-out was initiated through Operation Totalize on 7–11 Augsust.

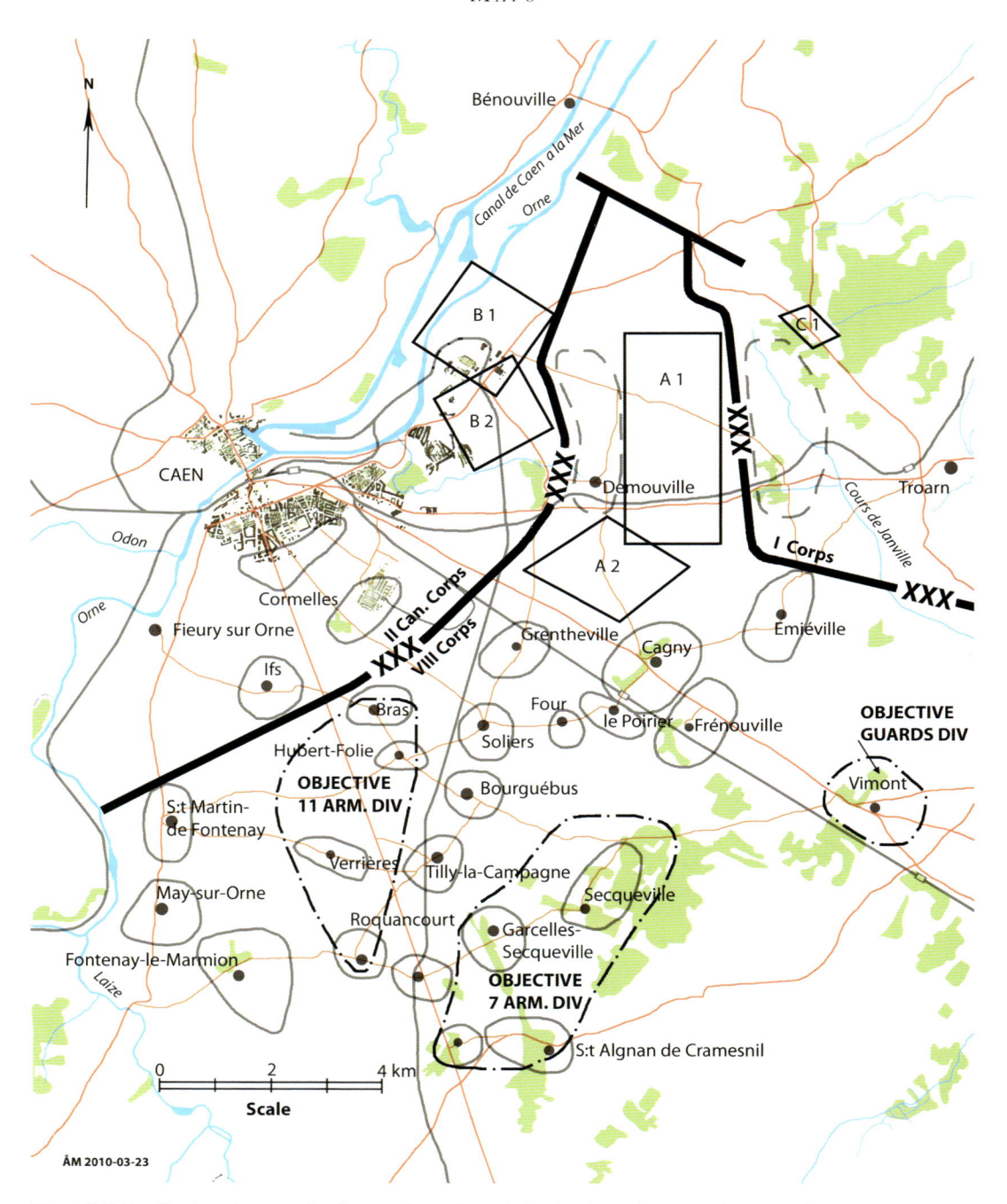

Map 20-5 The first-hand targets for the attack southwards by the three divisions of VIII British Corps in Operation Goodwood, which commenced on 18 July 1944. The aim was to establish the right conditions for a definite break out from the Normandy bridgehead. Areas marked A1 and A2 indicate the location of rolling barrages behind which the 11th Armoured Division was to proceed. Similarly B1, B2 and C1 indicate barrages fired for the two Corps attacking on the flanks. Encircled areas indicate where artillery was planned in support of attacking units. Fire at these could in most cases, however, not be accomplished from the first deployment locations of artillery to the North and Northeast of Caen. Redeployment forwards was first necessary.

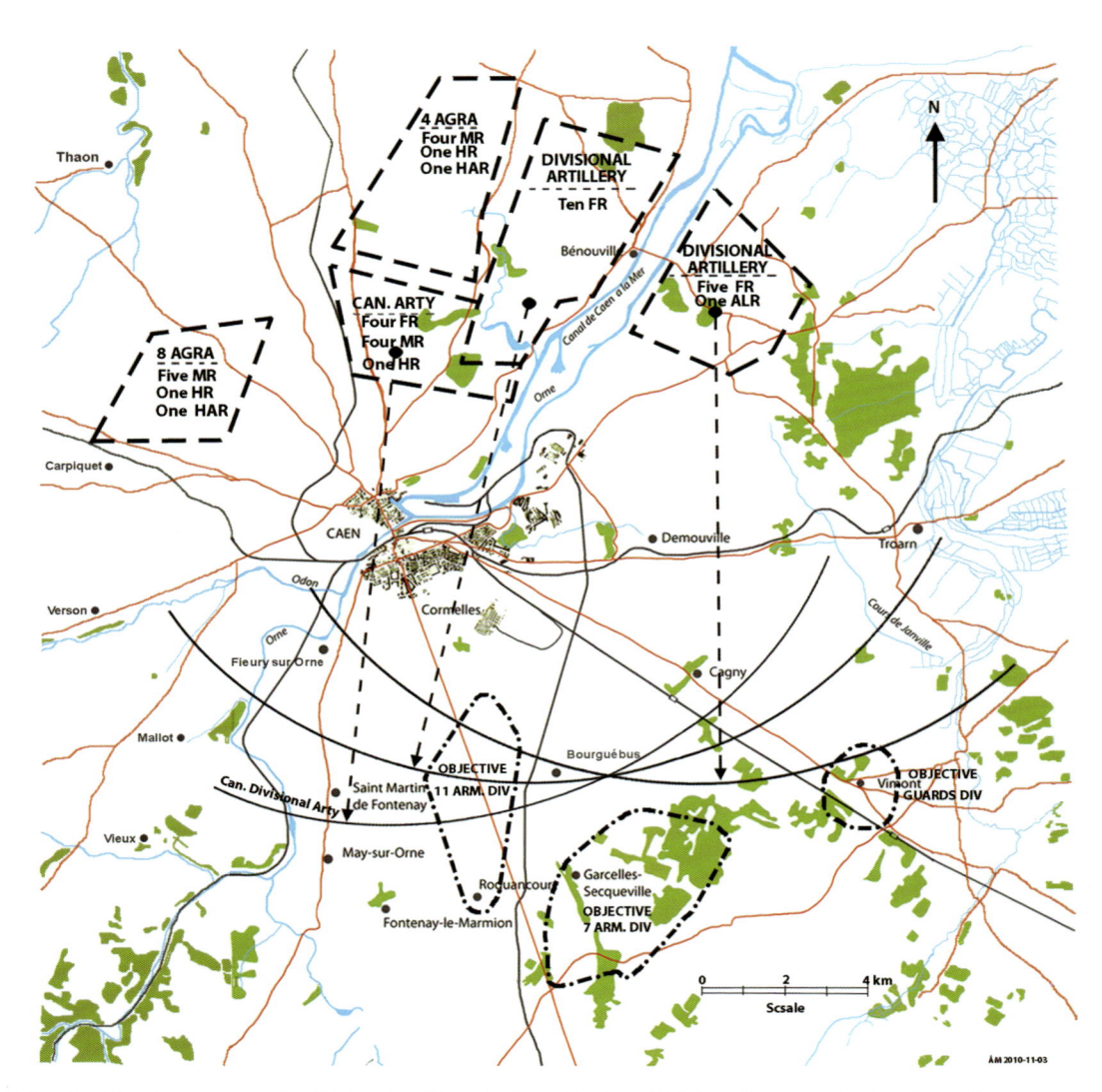

Map 20-6 Maximum range for divisional artillery deployed in the initial three key areas before Operation Goodwood. Indicated range could only be accomplished with guns firing with Super Charge, which normally comprised 20–30 % of the battery ammunition stock. This implied no restriction during the initial phase when the barrage was to be fired, but quite soon redeployment became necessary. Also the heavier regiments were forced to fire at very long ranges initially.

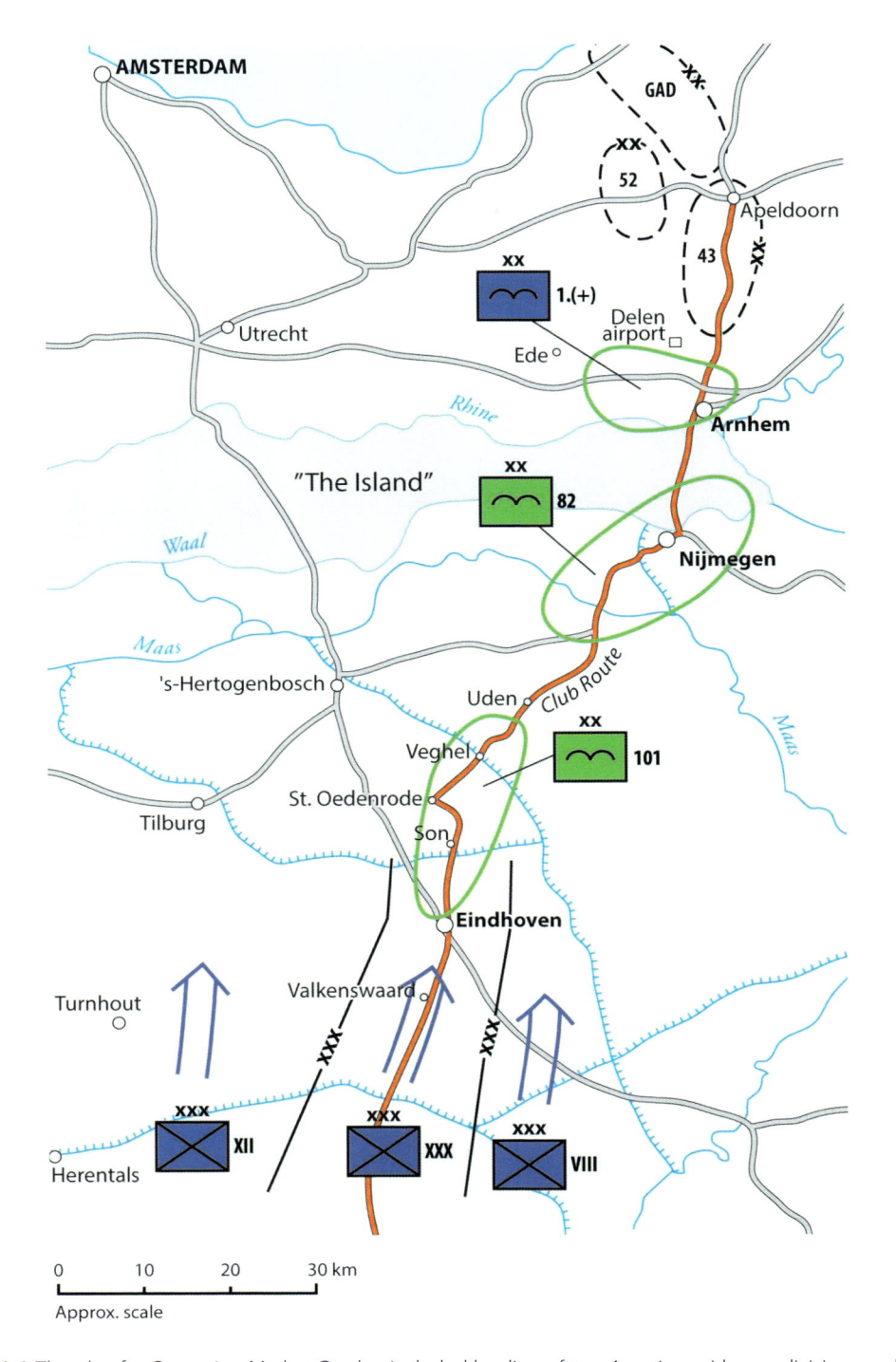

Map 21-1 The plan for Operation Market Garden included landing of two American airborne divisions and one British to secure Club Route, along which XXX Corps was to proceed as fast as possible, at first to Arnhem and then to Ijsselmeer (Zuider Zee). The two American divisions are here marked with green colour and the British with blue. XII British Corps was to protect the Western flank and VII Corps the Eastern flank.

MAPS

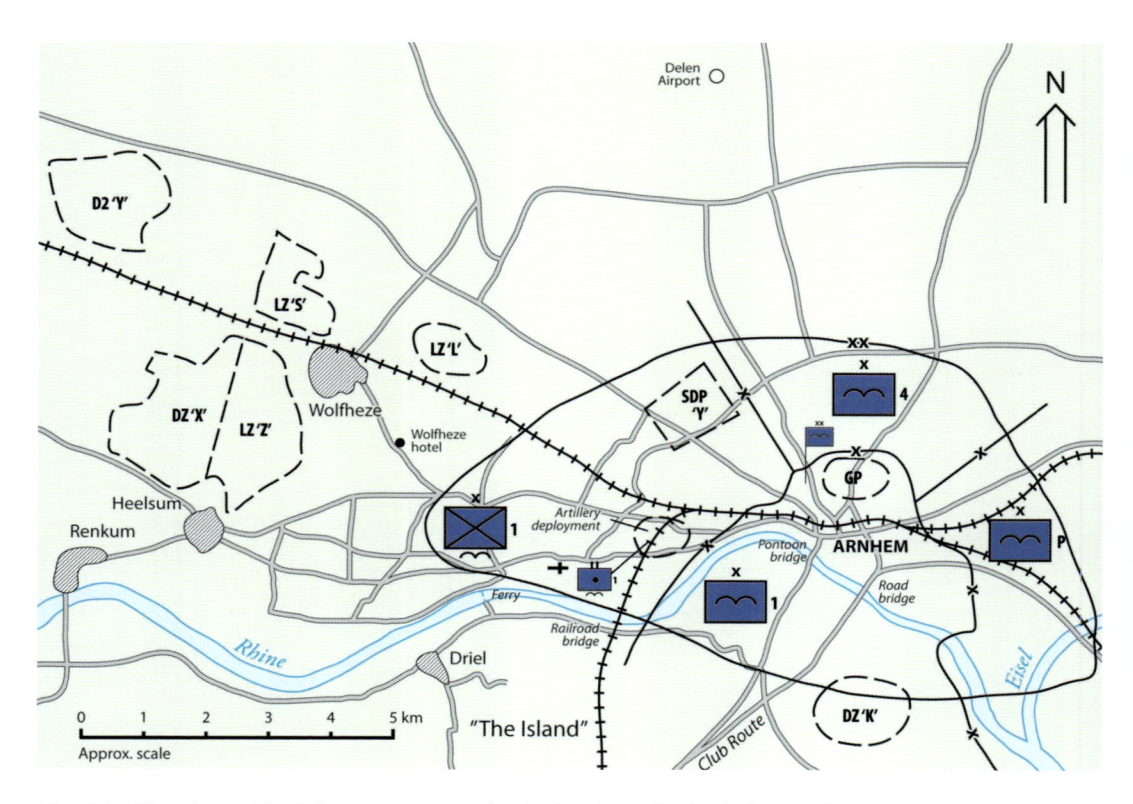

Map 21-2 The planned final deployment areas for the four brigades landed west of Arnhem. Observe the intended area for deployment of the Light Air-landing Regiment RA close to the railway coming from the South. There, it had had to fire in all directions around the horizon, which had been possible. DZ mark dropping zones for parachute brigades and LZ glider landing zones. SDP marks the planned area for dropping of supplies. GP is where glider pilots would be deployed for fighting after landing.

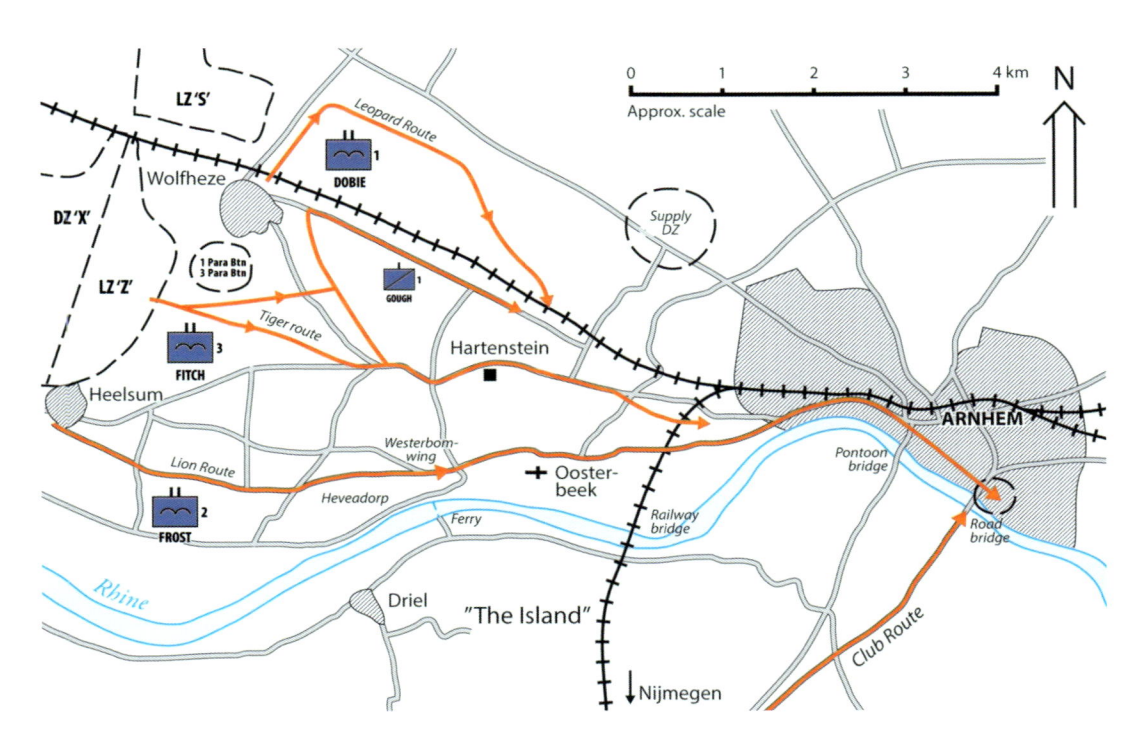

Map 21-3 After landing on 17 September 1944 the three parachute battalions of 1 Parachute Brigade were to march towards the road bridge at Arnhem as quickly as possible, only the 2nd Battalion under command of Lieutenant Colonel Frost succeeded. The reconnaissance squadron of the division, which was intended to act as a 'coup-de-main' force, was as two of the battalions stopped by quickly improvised fierce resistance from the Germans. This first day of the battle two batteries from the Light Air-landing Regiment RA were in action close to the dropping and landing zones. None of them could with fire reach targets close to the principal attack objective, the road bridge at Arnhem.

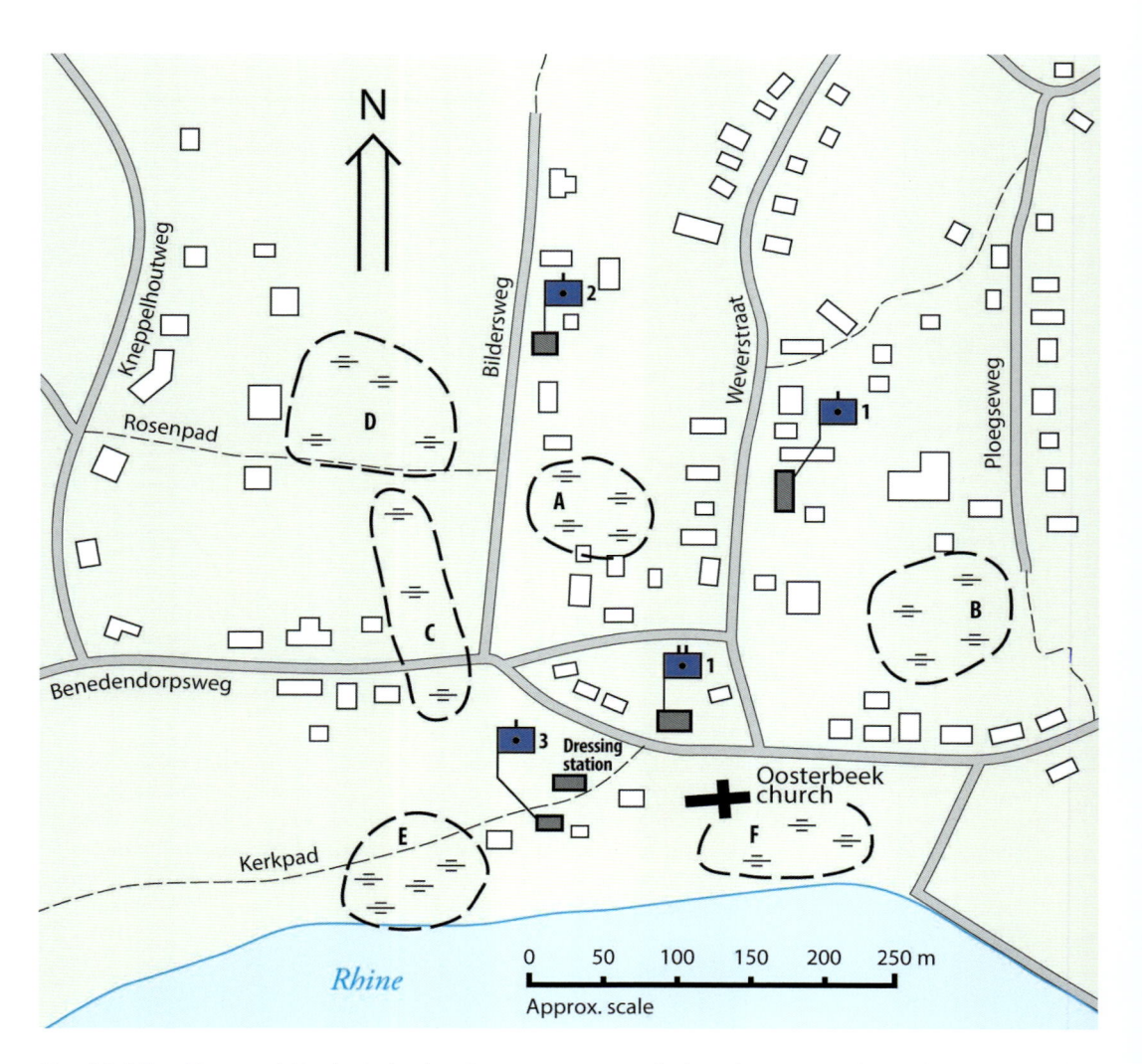

Map 21-4 The 22 guns of 1 Light Air-landing Regiment RA were deployed near Oosterbeek Church on 19–25 September and managed to efficiently provide support to the last days, although subject to extensive artillery and mortar fire. During the last afternoon several of the gun positions were overrun north of Benedendorpsweg and the risk emerged that the whole divisional perimeter might be cut off from the shore of River Rhine. 'Flags' with a stripe on top of them mark the command posts of the batteries, the one with two stripes marks the regimental headquarters. The latter had during the first days been located in a house near A Troop.

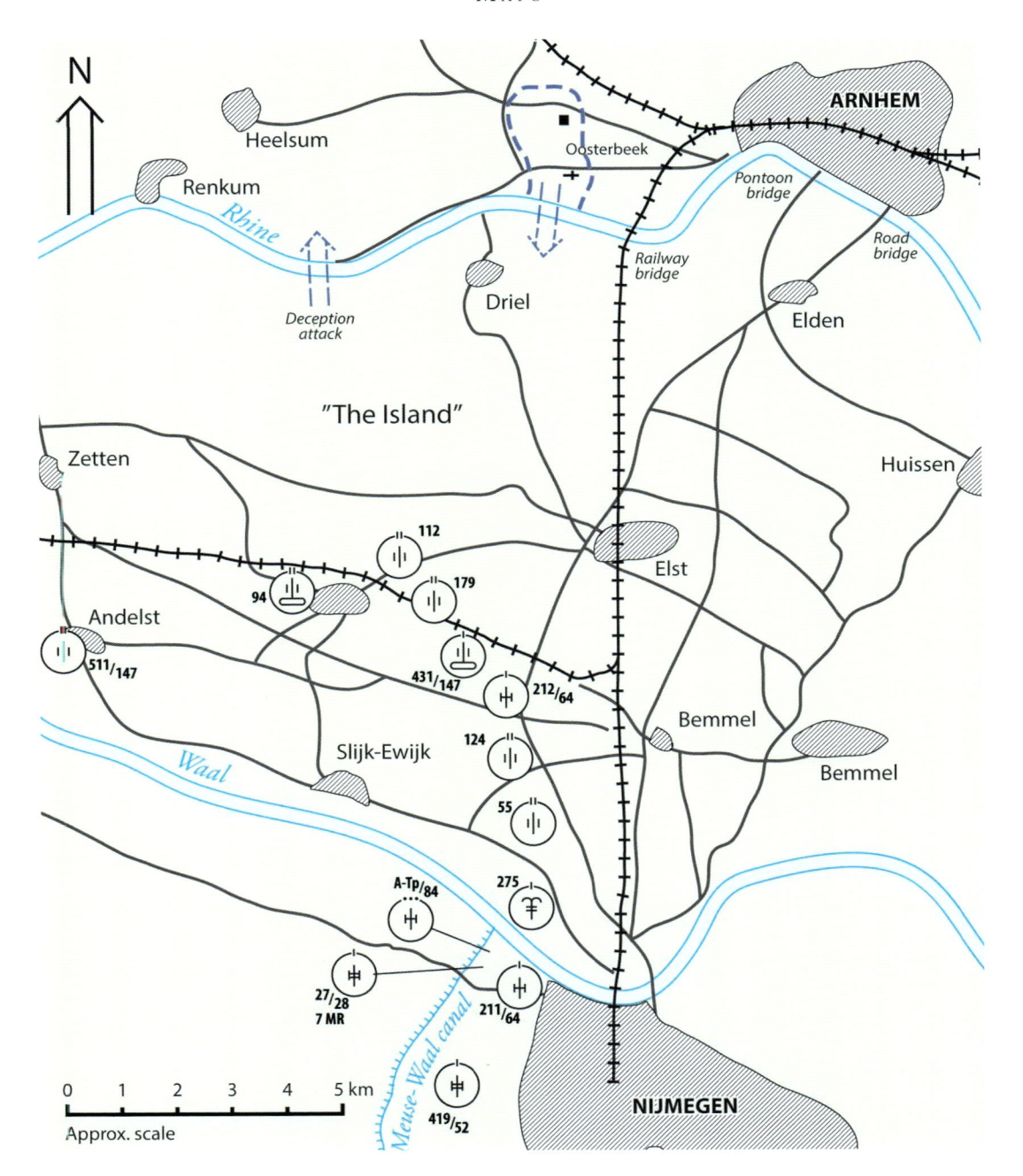

Map 21-5 Available artillery was ready from the afternoon 25th September to take part in the extensive defensive fire plan, which was to protect the evacuation of the remaining part of the 1st Airborne Division the following night. The exact deployment location of the 27/28 Battery, 7 Medium Regiment RA, has not been able to confirm. The same applies to A Troop, 85 Medium Regiment RA. 55 Field Regiment RA was deployed north of River Waal as indicated on the map, but could not participate in the fire plan due to the range. Furthermore, the regiment was probably much needed for fire towards East and Southeast. A major problem for all was the ammunition shortage. The deceptive attack launched by a battalion west of (downstream) the perimeter inc uded 'a barrage' fired during the evening by 94 Field Regiment RA.

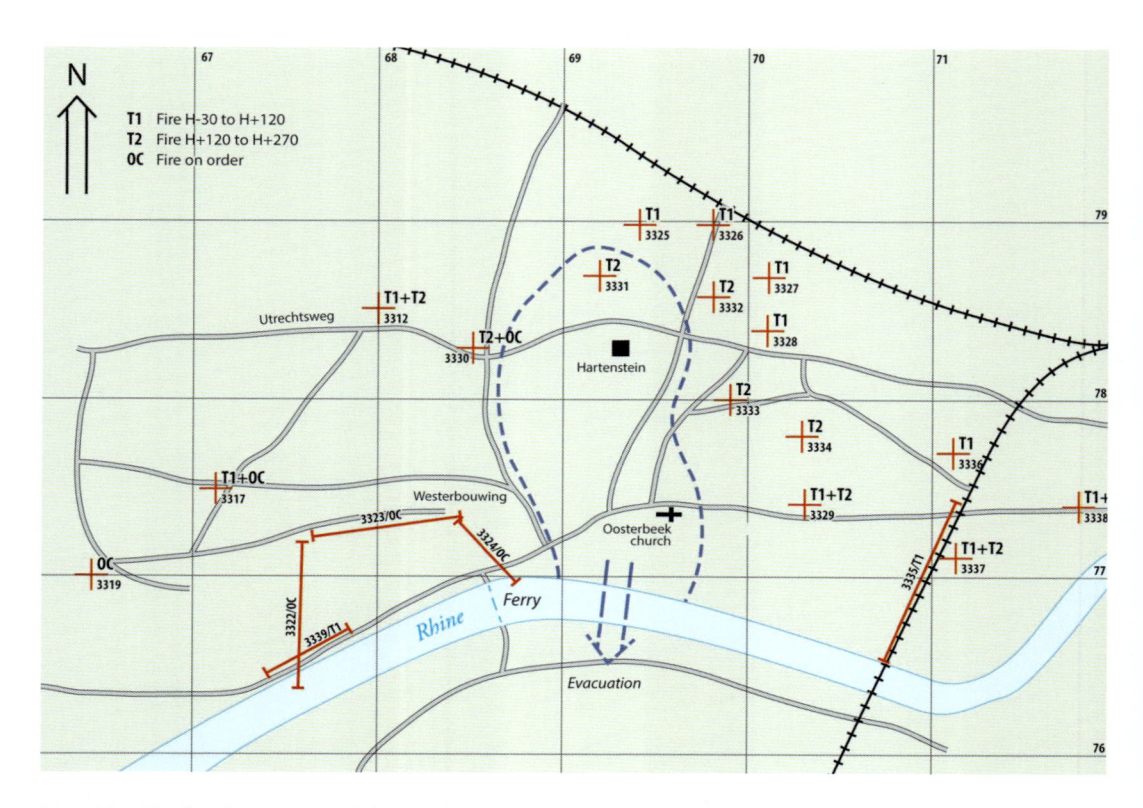

Map 21-6 The fireplan 'Java', with here indicated target numbers, was hastily prepared during the afternoon 25 September and was fired beginning at 20.30 hrs for the protection of the evacuation of the remaining part of the 1st Airborne Division. Around 140 guns took part, most of them fired continuously for five hours, albeit with fairly low intensity due to the acute ammunition shortage. Targets to be fired on command, here indicated with 'OC', were most likely to be fired when the companies of 4 Dorset Battalion, which had crossed River Rhine west of the ferry line, were to start evacuation at 02.00 hrs on 26 September. The formation was then dispersed into many small groups and many soldiers had already been killed or taken prisoner and there was no radio contact with them. Therefore, it is not clear as to whether this part of the plan was ever executed. Well known is, however, that smoke was fired during the morning for protection of the last evacuees.

MAPS

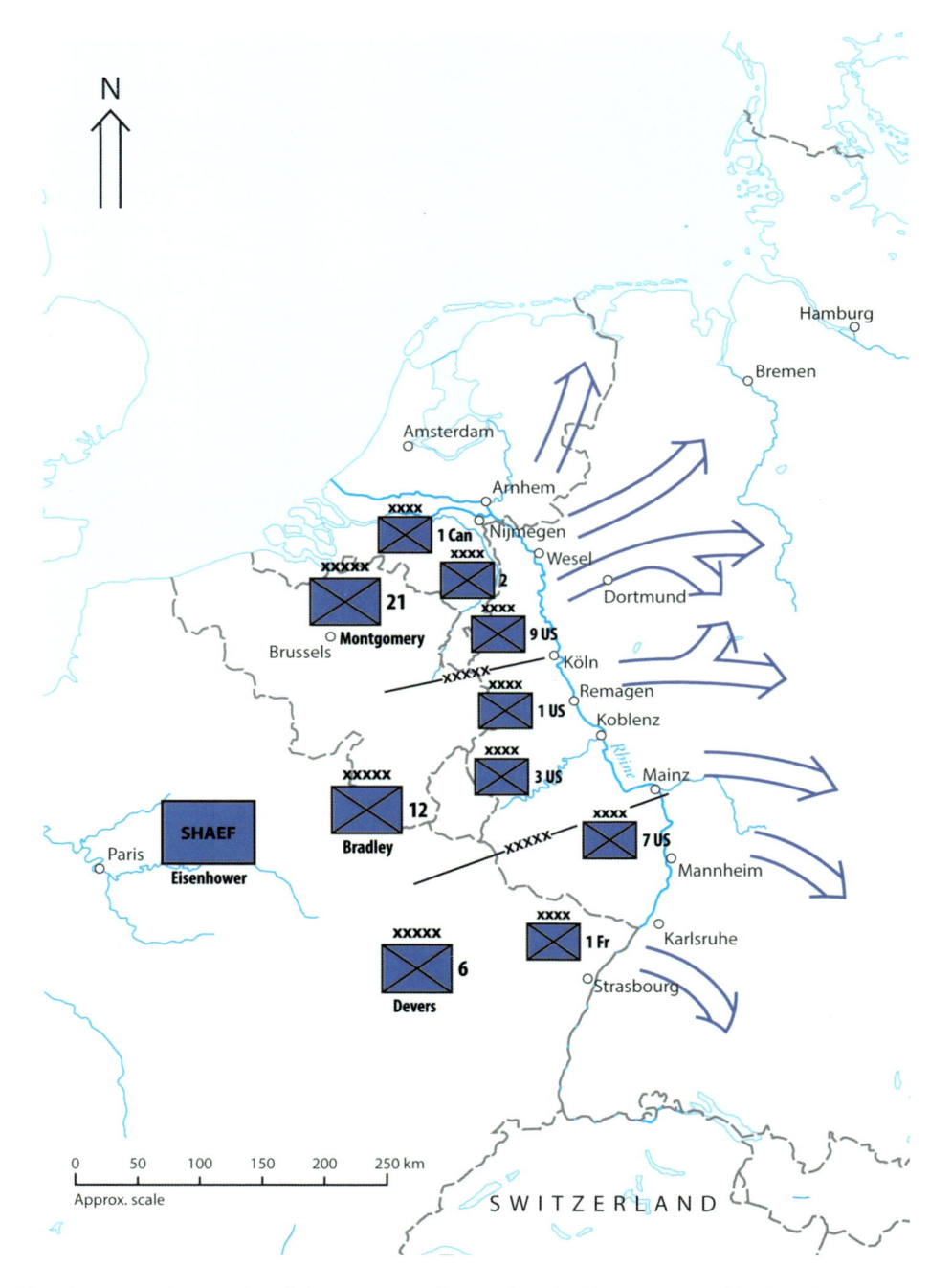

Map 22-1 On 10 March 1945 the whole area west of River Rhine had been captured by the Allies and preparations could commence in detail for the large Rhine Crossing. Seven armies, being part of the British 21st Army Group under Field Marshal Montgomery, 12th US Army Group under General Bradley and the 6th US Army Group under General Devers, would in well coordinated operations cross the river on 24 March and the following days. Artillery preparations were to begin late on 23 March. The armies would after the crossing proceed in various directions into Germany. During the first day two airborne divisions would land east of River Rhine just north of the city Wesel in support of the British attack.

MAPS

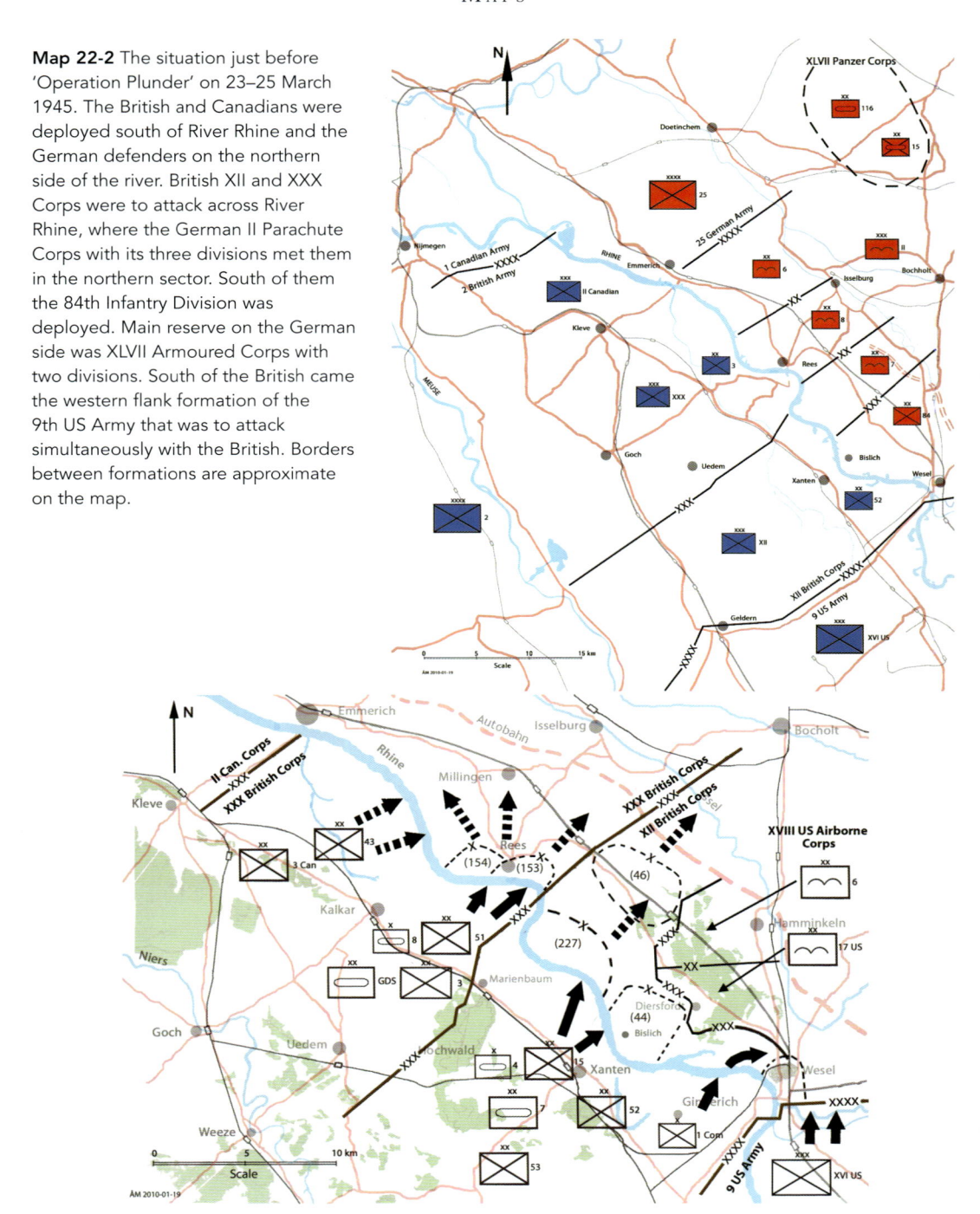

Map 22-2 The situation just before 'Operation Plunder' on 23–25 March 1945. The British and Canadians were deployed south of River Rhine and the German defenders on the northern side of the river. British XII and XXX Corps were to attack across River Rhine, where the German II Parachute Corps with its three divisions met them in the northern sector. South of them the 84th Infantry Division was deployed. Main reserve on the German side was XLVII Armoured Corps with two divisions. South of the British came the western flank formation of the 9th US Army that was to attack simultaneously with the British. Borders between formations are approximate on the map.

Map 22-3 Attack objectives of the British divisions at the Rhine crossing on 23–25 March 1945 (Operation Torchlight and Operation Turnscrew). The attack by the separately detached 1 Commando Brigade to initially take the city Wesel is also illustrated (Operation Widgeon) as are the air-landings north of the river during D-Day by two airborne divisions (Operation Varsity). Together the various sub-operations constituted Operation Plunder. To the right of the British the attack by XVI American Corps southeast of Wesel can be seen.

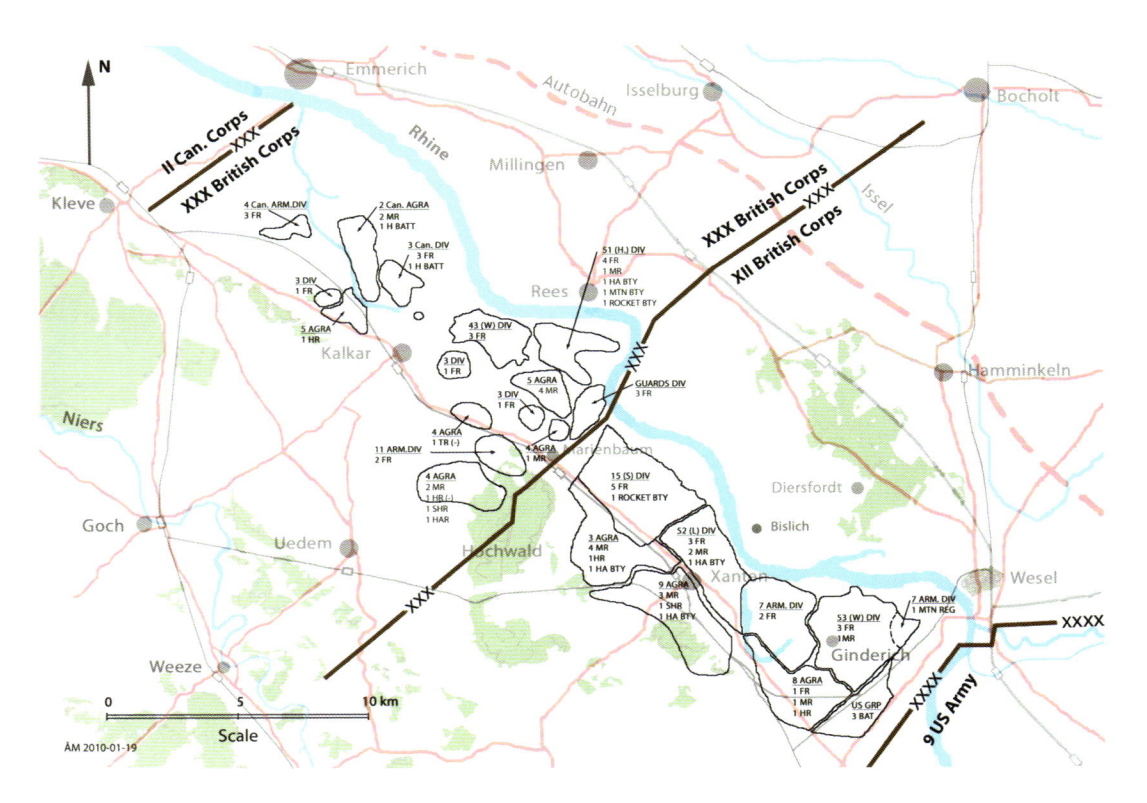

Map 22-4 More than 1,300 guns were deployed near River Rhine to support the British attack across the river. Here are seen the areas where the various divisional artillery and the reinforcing Army Artillery Groups (AGRA) were deployed, including rocket artillery and heavy anti-aircraft units engaged in a ground role. The number of regiments by type is indicated (FR=Field Regiment, MR= Medium Regiment, HR= Heavy Regiment, HAR= Heavy Anti-Aircraft Regiment).

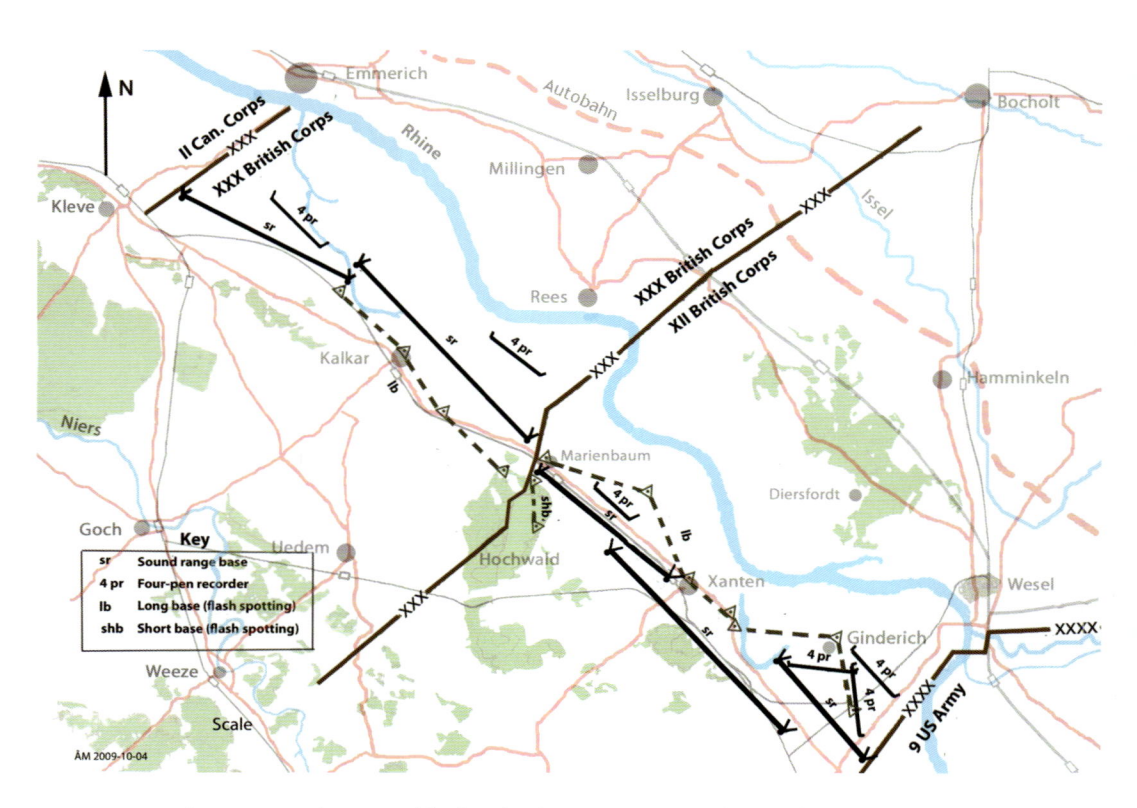

Map 22-5 In order to acquire best possible data for the coming counter-battery fire, the entire front of the two Corps were covered by sound-ranging and observation bases for more than a week before the attack across River Rhine. Besides locating artillery these also located anti-aircraft batteries and – not the least – mortars. The latter task was in particular performed by the light sound-ranging bases (4-pen Recorders). Observation Officers flying Austers added to the intelligence resources, as did the reconnaissance squadrons of RAF.

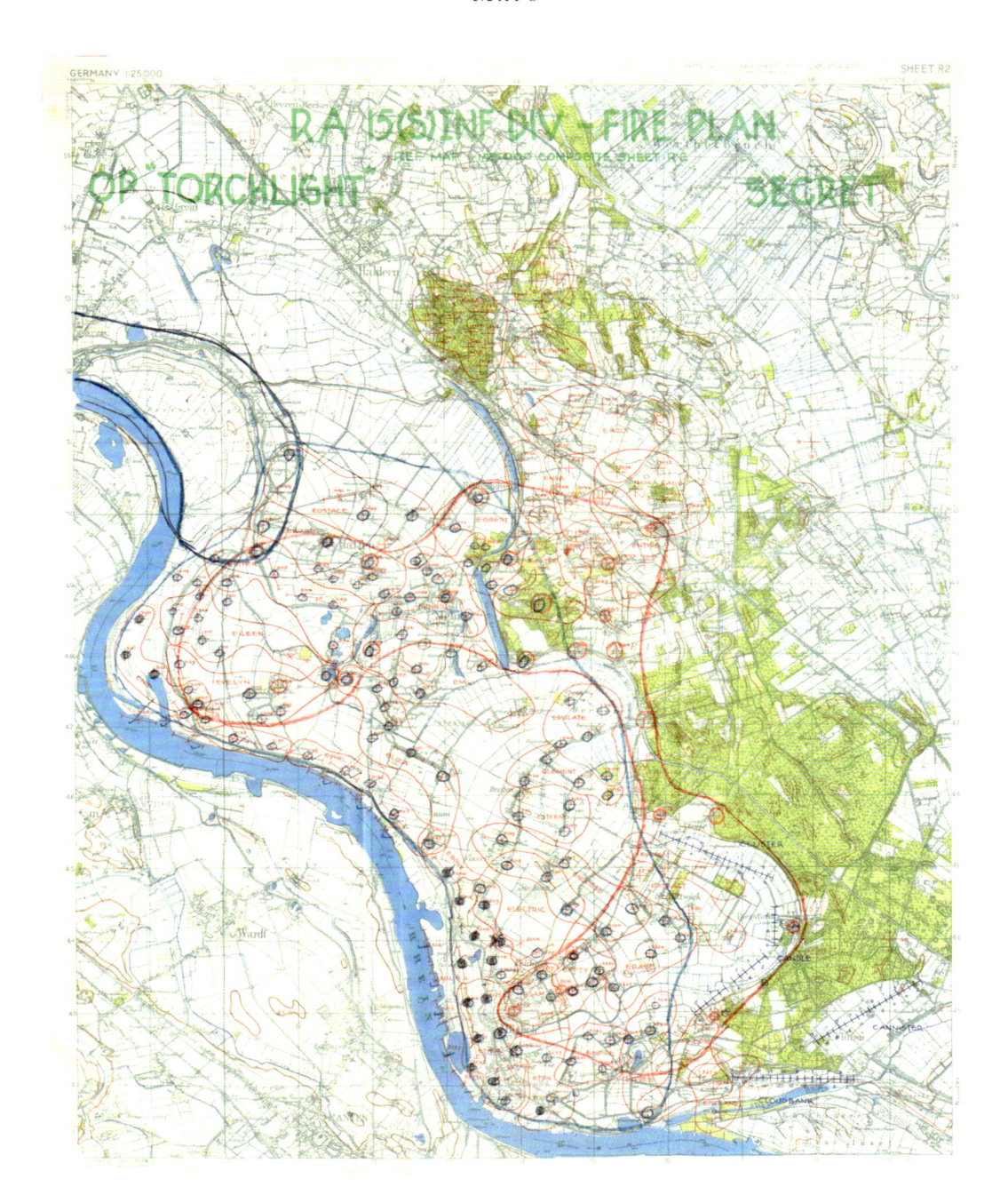

Map 22-6 The fireplan for the support of the attack across River Rhine by the 15th (Scottish) Infantry Division comprised a large number of concentrations within the attack areas planned for the different brigades. In addition smoke belts around Diesfordt Woods were planned, here indicated in blue to the right on the map (The National Archives, WO 205/925).

MAPS

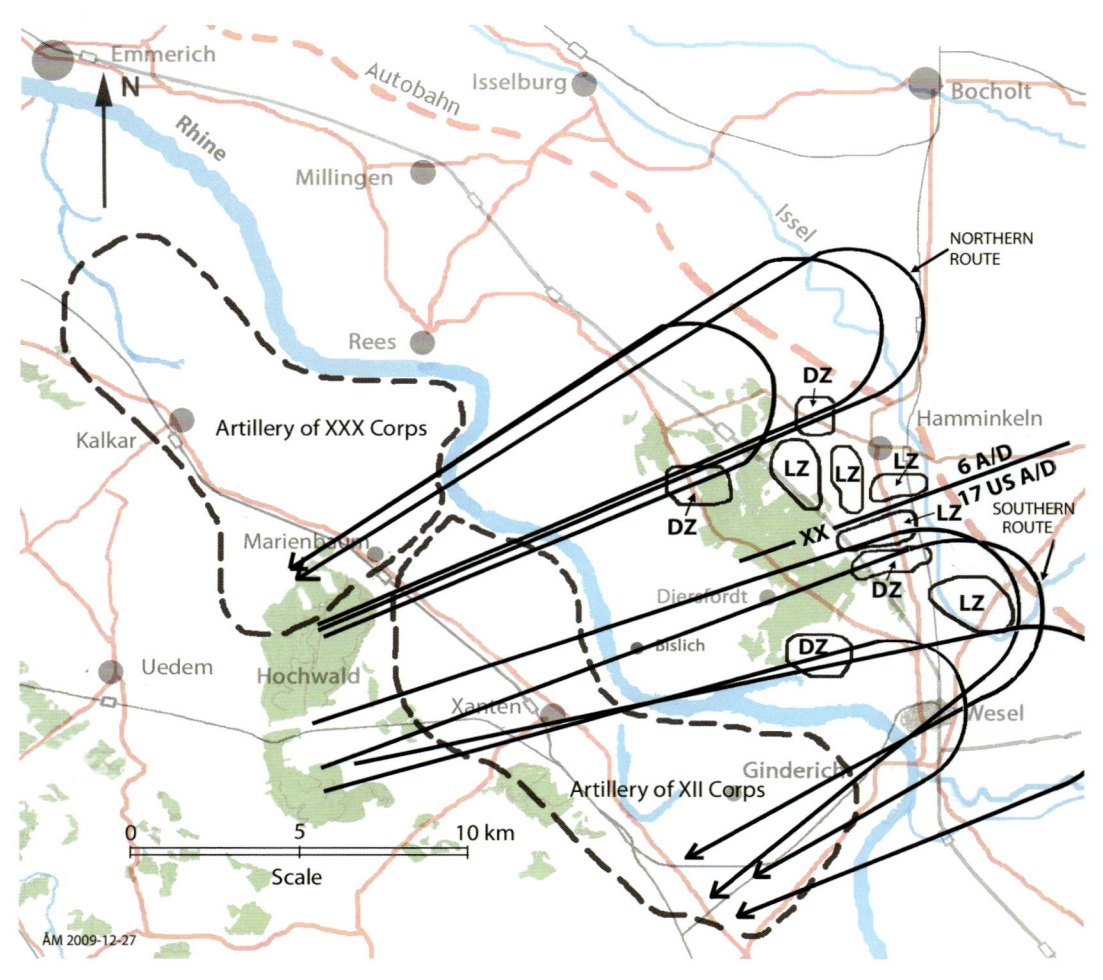

Map 22-7 The landings of the 6th British Airborne Division along the northern route was planned to take 70 minutes, whereas the landings of the 17th American Airborne Division along the southern route would take 210 minutes according to the plan. After these landings 240 heavy bombers would fly in and drop a first stock of supplies to the landed forces. During all aircraft movements 'cease fire' was ordered to all the guns of XII Corps. As seen also the southernmost artillery of XXX Corps had to stop firing.

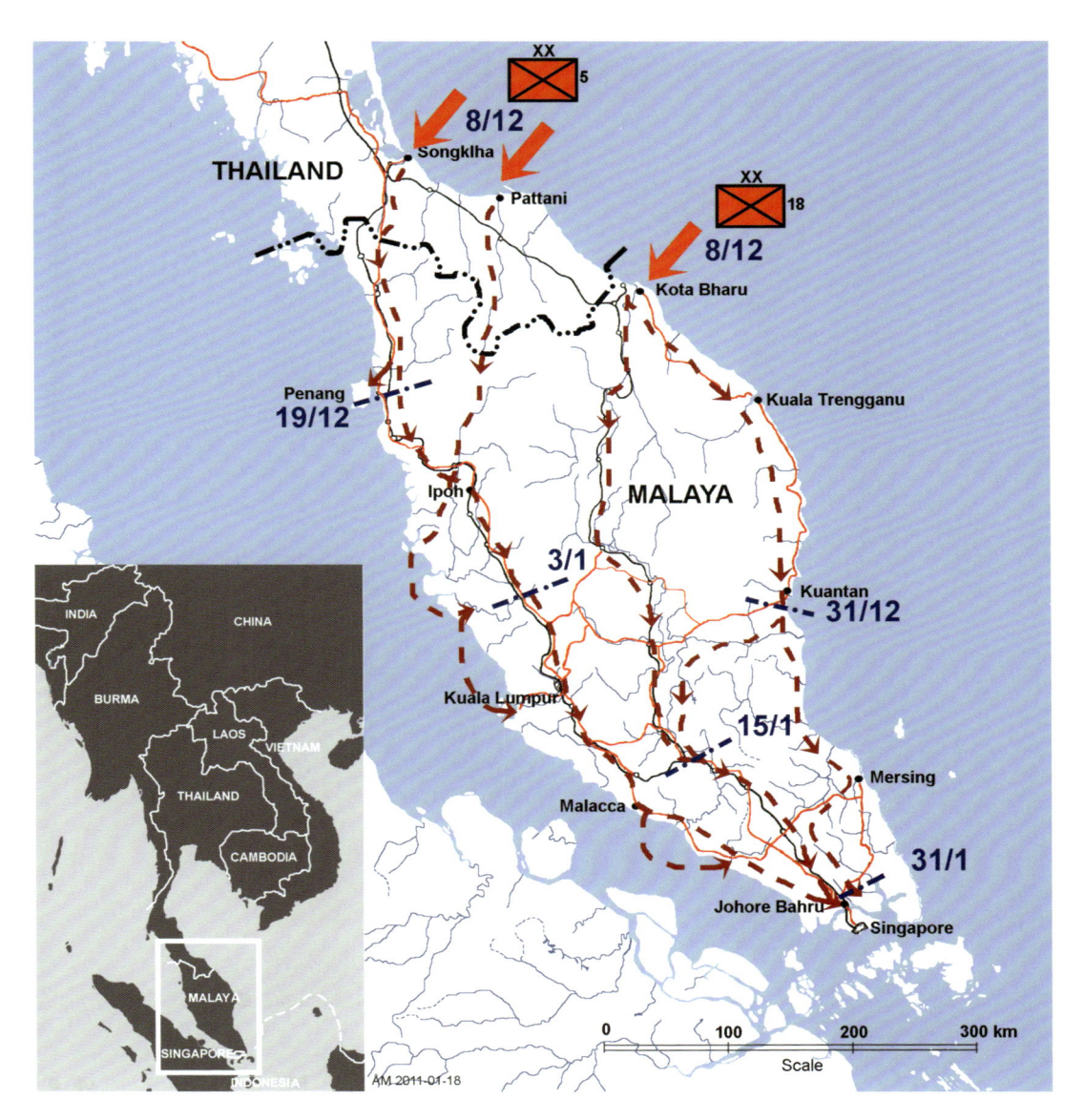

Map 23-1 The Japanese landings at the Malayan peninsula on 8 December 1941 took place in the border area between today's Thailand and Malaysia. Later the Japanese Guards Division arrived in the peninsula from Bangkok. The Japanese advance mainly took place along roads and railways, but also a number of bypasses at sea took place. The last day of January 1942 they reached the straits towards Singapore.

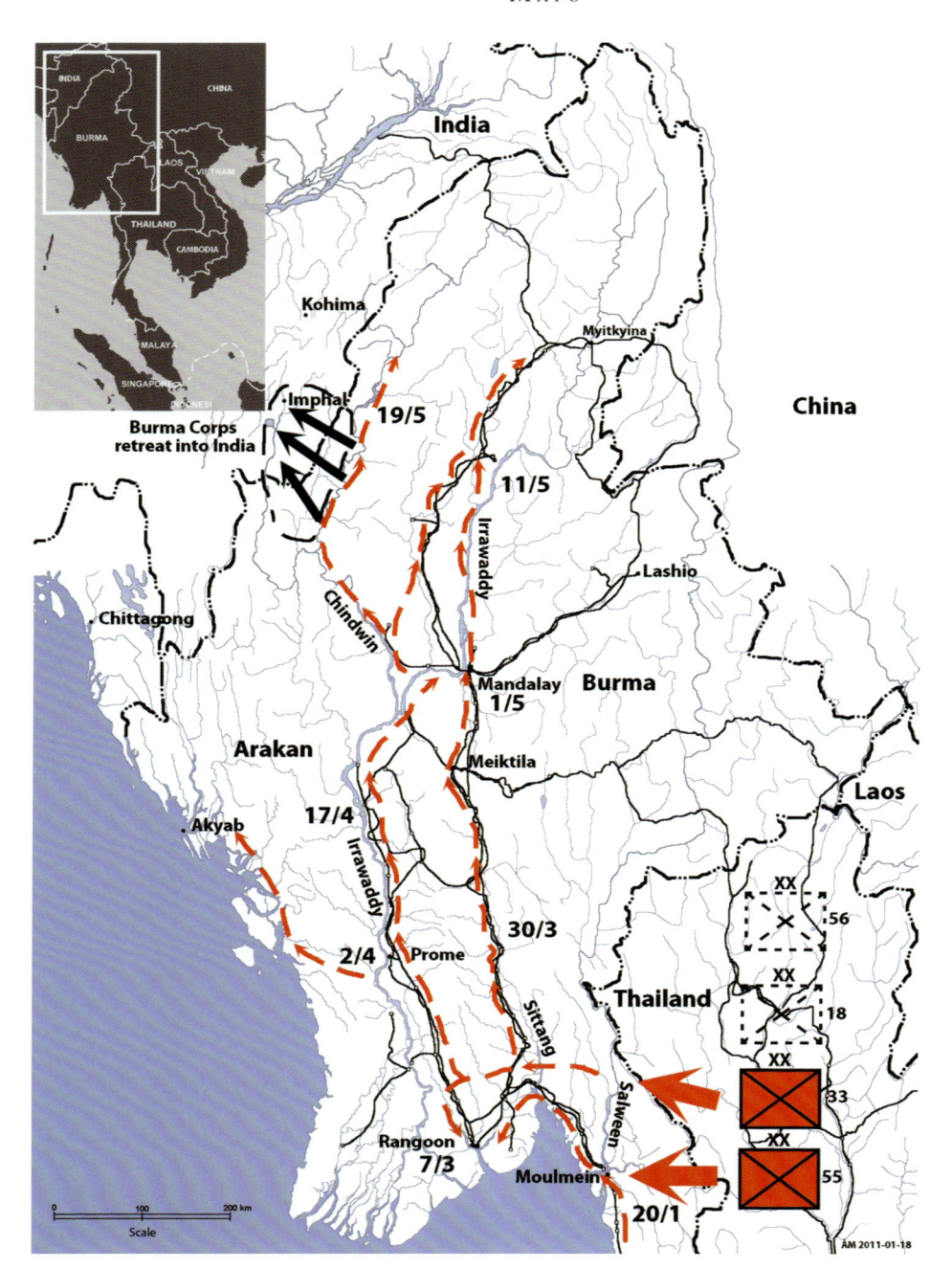

Map 23-2 After having secured some airfields in the southernmost part of Burma the main Japanese invasion of Burma was launched from around the city Moulmein beginning on 20 January 1942. The 55th Division was in the lead and pressed the British northwards along River Sittang. The 33rd Division first conquered Rangoon and then headed northwards along the big river Irrawaddy. In mid-May all was over, when the British crossed the border to India. It meant a great defeat, but the retreat fighting had been skillfully performed and enclosures and destruction been avoided. In the eastern part of Burma, large Chinese formations were forced out of the country by the Japanese 18th and 56th Infantry Division. However, one Chinese Division followed the British into India.

Appendix 1

Order of Battle BEF 1940 (except anti-tank and anti-aircraft regiments)
(Based on Farndale, The Years of Defeat 1939–1940, Annex A)

BEF GHQ:
Major General Royal Artillery (MGRA) — Major General S.R. Wason

Field Regiments
1st Regiment RHA (A/E & B/O Battery)	Lt.Col. W.T.H. Peppé
2nd Regiment RHA (H/I & L&N Battery)	Lt.Col. D.F. Aitkinhead
32nd Army Field Regiment (107/121 & 115/120 Battery)	Lt.Col. W.B. Mackie
98th Army Field Regiment (TA) (391 & 392 Battery)	Lt.Col. G.A. Ledingham
115th Army Field Regiment (TA) (238 & 240 Battery)	Lt.Col. M.R. Simpson
139th Army Field Regiment (TA) (362 & 364 Battery)	Lt.Col. G. Ames

Medium Regiments
1st Medium Regiment (1/3 & 5/22 Battery)	Lt.Col. A.A. Middleton
2nd Medium Regiment (4/7 & 8/12 Battery)	Lt.Col. C.H. Brittan
4th Medium Regiment (9/13 & 14/16 Battery)	Lt.Col. F.H. Sterling
51st Medium Regiment (TA) (215 & 240 Battery)	Lt.Col. E.A. Lea
56th Medium Regiment (TA) (174 & 221 Battery)	Lt.Col. C.L.O. Tayleur
58th Medium Regiment (TA) (229 & 230 Battery)	Lt.Col. M. MacEwan
61st Medium Regiment (TA) (243 & 244 Battery)	Lt.Col. G.E. Fitzhugh
63rd Medium Regiment (TA) (214 & 216 Battery)	Lt.Col. E.R. Culverwell
65th Medium Regiment (TA) (222 & 223 Battery)	Lt.Col. S.C. Kirkman
69th Medium Regiment (TA) (241 & 242 Battery)	Lt.Col. J.C. D'Arcy

Heavy Regiments
1st Heavy Regiment (16 & 28 Battery)	Lt.Col. R. Hilton
51st Heavy Regiment (A, B, C, & D Battery)	Lt.Col. D. McDowell
52nd Heavy Regiment (417, 418, 419 & 420 Battery)	Lt.Col. A.A. Comerford

Super Heavy Batteries
1st Super Heavy Battery
2nd Super Heavy Battery
3rd Super Heavy Battery

I Corps:
Commander Corps Royal Artillery (CCRA)	Brigadier F.H.N. Davidson
Commander Corps Medium Artillery (CCMA)	Brigadier F.W.H. Pratt

Corps Artillery
27th Army Field Regiment (21/24 & 37/47 Battery)	Lt.Col. L.C. Griffiths-Williams
140th Army Field Regiment (TA) (366 & 367 Battery)	Lt.Col. T.F.K. Howard
3rd Medium Regiment (2/11 & 6/10 Battery)	Lt.Col. R.H. Stacpoole
5th Medium Regiment (15/17 & 20/21 Batttery)	Lt.Col. Heaton-Ellis
1st Survey Regiment (1st Survey, 1st Flash Spotting & 1st Sound Ranging Battery)	Lt.Col. C.I. Beckett

1 Infantry Division
Commander Royal Artillery (CRA) — Brigadier C.W.P. Perceval

Divisional Artillery
2nd Field Regiment (35/87 & 42/53 Battery) — Lt.Col. G.S. Leventhorpe
19th Field Regiment (29/97 & 39/96 Battery) — Lt.Col. H.B. Latham
67th Field Regiment (TA) (265 & 266 Battery) — Lt.Col. A.C.W. Hobson

2 Infantry Division
Commander Royal Artillery (CRA) — Brigadier C.B. Findlay

Divisional Artillery
10th Field Regiment (30/46 & 51/54 Battery) — Lt.Col. H.J. Parham
16th Field Regiment (22/72 & 34/86 Battery) — Lt.Col. H.A. Tyler
99th Filed Regiment (TA) (393 & 394 Battery) — Lt.Col. J.P. Whiteley

48 (South Midland) Infantry Division
Commander Royal Artillery (CRA) — Brigadier E.F. Lawson

Divisional Artillery
18th Field Regiment (59/93 & 94/95 Battery) — Lt.Col. G.N.C. Martin
24th Field Regiment (50/70 & 22/56 Battery) — Lt.Col. W.H.F. Crowe
68th Field Regiment (TA) (269 & 271 Battery) — Lt.Col. M.S. Clutterbuck

II Corps:
Commander Corps Royal Artillery (CCRA) — Brigadier E.C.A. Schreiber
Commander Corps Medium Artillery (CCMA) — Brigadier R. Staveley

Corps Artillery
60th Army Field Regiment (TA) (237 & 239 Battery) — Lt.Col. F.P. Hallifax
88th Army Field Regiment (TA) (351 & 352 Battery) — Lt.Col. H.M. Stamford
53rd Medium Regiment (TA) (209 & 210 Battery) — Lt.Col. W.R. Brazier
59th Medium Regiment (TA) (235 & 236 Battery) — Lt.Col. H.C. Servaes
2nd Survey Regiment (2 Survey, 2 Flash Spotting & 2 Sound Ranging Battery) — Lt.Col. J.A. Leigh

3 Infantry Division
Commander Royal Artillery (CRA) — Brigadier R.H. Towell

Divisional Artillery
7th Field Regiment (9/17 & 16/43 Battery) — Lt.Col. J. Wedderburn-Maxwell
33rd Field Regiment (101/113 & 114/109 Battery) — Lt.Col. R.H.A. Kellis
76th Field Regiment (TA) (302 & 304 Battery) — Lt.Col. W.E. Vaudry

4 Infantry Division
Commander Royal Artillery (CRA) — Brigadier G.E.W. Franklyn

Divisional Artillery
22nd Field Regiment (32/33 & 36/55 Battery) — Lt.Col. H.A. Young
30th Field Regiment (104/111 & 112/117 Battery) — Lt.Col. H.C.R. Roquette
77th Field Regiment (TA) (302 & 303 Battery) — Lt.Col. W.H. Denholm

5 Infantry Division
Commander Royal Artillery (CRA) — Brigadier J.R. Barry

Divisional Artillery
9th Field Regiment (19/28 & 20/76 Batteriey)	Lt.Col. L.C. Tyson
91st Field Regiment (TA) (361 & 363 Battery)	Lt.Col. W. Buffey
92nd Field Regiment (TA) (365 & 368 Battery)	Lt.Col. C.B. Wood

50 (Northumberland) Infantry Division
Commander Royal Artillery (CRA) — Big.gen C.W. Massy

Divisional Artillery
72nd Field Regiment (TA) (285 & 286 Battery)	Lt.Col. R.M. Graham
74th Field Regiment (TA) (296 & 298 Battery)	Lt.Col. R.T. Edwards

III Corps:
Commander Corps Royal Artillery (CCRA) — Brigadier W.E. Duncan
Commander Corps Medium Artillery (CCMA) — Brigadier K.W. Hervey

Corps Artillery
5th Regiment RHA (G & K Batteries)	Lt.Col. A.A.M. Durand
97th Army Field Regiment (TA) (385 & 387 Battery)	Lt.Col. F. Lushington
51st Medium Regiment (TA) (215 & 240 Battery)	Lt.Col. E.A. Lea
56th Medium Regiment (TA) (174 & 221 Battery)	Lt.Col. C.L.O. Tayleur
3rd Survey Regiment (3 Survey, 3 Flash Spotting & 3 Sound Ranging Battery)	Lt.Col. E.R.S. Ames

42 (East Lancashire) Infantry Division
Commander Royal Artillery (CRA) — Brigadier A.S. Archdale

Divisional Artillery
52nd Field Regiment (TA) (205 & 206 Battery)	Lt.Col. F.C.F. Cleeve
53rd Field Regiment (TA) (209 & 210 Battery)	Lt.Col. G. Bennet

44 (Home Counties) Infantry Division
Commander Royal Artillery (CRA) — Brigadier E.A. Osbourne

Divisional Artillery
57th Field Regiment (TA) (225 & 226 Battery)	Lt.Col. T. Syon-Smith
58th Field Regiment (TA) (60/100 & 89/90 Battery)	Lt.Col. G.W.E. Heath
65th Field Regiment (TA) (257 & 258 Battery)	Lt.Col. C.C. West

Saar-front:
51 (Highland) Infantry Division
Commander Royal Artillery (CRA) — Brigadier J.O. Shepherd

Divisional Artillery
17th Field Regiment (10/26 & 13/92 Battery)	Lt.Col. K.F.W. Dunn
23rd Field Regiments (60/100 & 89/90 Battery)	Lt.Col. L.F. Garrett
75th Field Regiment (TA) (299 & 300 Battery)	Lt.Col. G.T. Nugee

Other divisions:
12 (Eastern) Infantry Division
23 (Northumbrian) Infantry Division
46 (North Midland & West Riding) Infantry Division
None of these had any artillery of their own

BEF II:
1 Armoured Division
Its divisional artillery was attached to BEF I

52 (Lowland) Infantry Division
Commander Royal Artillery (CRA)   Brigadier G.C. Kemp

Divisional Artillery
70th Field Regiment (TA) (277 & 279 Battery)   Lt.Col. G.E. Suddards
71st Field Regiment (TA) (281 & 281 Battery)   Lt.Col. C. Wardlow
78th Field Regiment (TA) (309 & 310 Battery)   Major G.A. Usher

Appendix 2

Third Battle of El Alamein – Artillery Order of Battle 23 October 1942

X Corps:
1 Armoured Division
    2 FR RHA   24 25-pounder
    4 FR RHA   24 25-pounder
    11 FR RHA (HAC)   24 'Priest' (105-mm howitzer)
    78 FR RA   24 25-pounder
    146 FR RA (Hammer force)   24 25-pounder

10 Armoured Division
    1 FR RHA   24 25-pounder
    5 FR RHA   24 25-pounder
    98 FR RA   24 25-pounder
    104 FR RHA   24 25-pounder

Number of guns X Corps:
    25-pounder   192 (out of which 18x4=72 were attached to XXX Corps)
    Priest (105-mm)   24
    4.5-inch guns   0
    5.5-inch gun-howitzers   0

XIII Corps:
Corps formations
    4 Survey Regiment RA
    53 AFR RA   24 25-pounder

7 Armoured Division
    1 French FR (1 French Brig)   16 25-pounder + 4 5.5-inch gun-howitzers
    3 FR RA (1 French Brig)   16 25-pounder + 4 5.5-inch gun-howitzers
    3 FR RHA   16 25-pounder + 4 5.5-inch gun-howitzers
    4 FR RA (22 Armoured Brig)   16 25-pounder + 4 5.5-inch gun-howitzers
    97 FR RA (22 Armoured Brig) 24 25-pounder + 4 5.5-inch gun-howitzers

44 Infantry Division
    57 FR RA (131 Brig)   24 25-pounder
    58 FR RA   24 25-pounder
    65 FR RA   24 25-pounder

50 Infantry Division
    74 FR RA   16 25-pounder
    111 FR RA   24 25-pounder
    124 FR RA   16 25-pounder
    154 AFR RA   24 25-pounder
    1 (Greek) FR (1 Greek Brig)   24 25-pounder

Number of guns XIII Corps:
    25-pounder   288

4.5-inch Guns	0
5.5-inch Gunhowitzers	4

XXX Corps:
Corps formations

7 MR RA	8	4.5-inch guns
	8	5.5-inch gun-howitzers
64 MR RA	8	4.5-inch guns
	8	5.5-inch gun-howitzers
69 MR RA	16	4.5-inch guns
121 FR RA (23 Armoured Brig)	16	25-pounder

1 South African Infantry Division

1.FR SAA	24	25-pounder
4 FR SAA	24	25-pounder
7 FR SAA	24	25-pounder

2 New Zeeland Infantry Division

4. FR NZA	24	25-pounder
5. FR NZA	24	25-pounder
6. FR NZA	24	25-pounder

9 Australian Infantry Division

2/7 FR RAA	24	25-pounder
2/8 FR RAA	24	25-pounder
2/12 FR RAA	24	25-pounder

51 (Highland) Infantry Division

126 FR RA	24	25-pounder
127 FR RA	24	25-pounder
128 FR RA	24	25-pounder

4 Indian Infantry Division

1 FR RA	16	25-pounder
11 FR RA	16	25-pounder
32 FR RA	16	25-pounder

Note. A test formation was 66 Mortar Company RE, which had 18 4.2-inch mortars. 12 of these were attached to the Australian Division, the remaining were kept as a Corps formation

Number of guns XXX Corps:

25-pounder	352
4.5-inch guns	32
5.5-inch gun-howitzers	16

Number of guns 8 Army:

25-pounder	832
Priest (105-mm)	24
4.5-inch guns	32
5.5-inch gun-howitzers	20

Note. In addition to the number given, 908 , another 31 guns were in workshops for repair or kept as a reserve

Sources: For X and XXX Corps the source is *Battle of El Alamein Order of Battle Eighth Army 2200 hrs 23 October 1942 Forward Area Only* Cabinet Office, Historical Section, 13th March 1956 (©RAHT Collection MD 272)

For XIII Corps the Order of Battle and the number of guns per regiment have been taken from *Form at a Glance – 13 Corps Arty Number Twenty-Seven As per 23 Oct 42* (to be found in The National Archives, WO 169/4010)

Appendix 3

Consumption of Ammunition by the Field Regiments (25-pounders) during the Third Battle at El Alamein 1942 (rounds per gun)

Day	X Corps	XIII Corps	XXX Corps
October			
24	28	190	577
25	9	71	64
26	33	71	84
27	80	30	103
28	106	10	88
29	49	24	159
30	95	25	48
31	137	18	209
November			
1	34	47	90
2	309	28	314
3	35	37	80
4	85	27	123

Source: RA Notes on the Offensive by Eighth Army from 23 Oct–4 Nov on the Alamein Position, Appendix 1 (authored by Commander Royal Artillery 8th Army Brigadier Sidney Kirkman, 24 November 1942) (The National Archives, WO 201/431)

Note. Ammunition consumption was normally reported daily from 15.00 hrs till 15.00 hrs the next day. When Kirkman writes '24' it is assumed to be consumption 23/24 October etc.

Appendix 4

Operation Goodwood Meeting – Artillery Order of Battle 18 July 194

I Corps:

3 Infantry Division
7 FR RA	24 'Priest' (with 105-mm howitzer)
33 FR RA	24 'Priest' (with 105-mm howitzer)
76 FR RA	24 'Priest' (with 105-mm howitzer)

51 (Highland) Infantry Division
126 FR RA	24 25-pounders
127 FR RA	24 25-pounders
128 FRA RA	24 25-pounders

4 Artillery Group RA (AGRA)
150 FR RA	25 25-pounders
191 FR RA	24 25-pounders
53 MR RA	16 5.5-inch gun-howitzers
65 MR RA	16 5.5-inch gun-howitzers
68 MR RA	16 5.5-inch gun-howitzers
79 MR RA	16 5.5-inch gun-howitzers
51 HR RA	8 155-mm guns 'Long Tom'
	8 7.2-inch howitzers
107 HAR RA	24 3.7-inch anti-aircraft guns (in ground roles)

VIII Corps:
Guards Division
153 FR RA	24 'Sexton' (with 25-pounders)
53 FR RA	24 25-pounders

7 Armoured Division
3 FR RHA	24 25-pounders
5 FR RHA	24 'Sexton' (with 25-pounders)

11 Armoured Division
13 (HAC) FR RHA	24 'Sexton' (with 25-pounders)
151 FR RA	24 25-pounders

8 Artillery Group RA (AGRA)
25 AFR RA	24 25-pounders
61 MR RA	16 5.5-inch gun-howitzers
63 MR RA	16 5.5-inch gun-howitzers
77 MR RA	16 5.5-inch gun-howitzers
107 MR RA	16 5.5-inch gun-howitzers (från 9 AGRA)
146 MR RA	16 5.5-inch gun-howitzers (från 9 AGRA)
53 HR RA	8 155-mm guns 'Long Tom'
	8 7.2-inch howitzers
165 HAR RA	24 3.7-inch anti-aircraft guns (in ground roles)

II Canadian Corps:
3 Canadian Infantry Division
12 FR RCA	24	'Priest' (with 105-mm howitzer)
13 FR RCA	24	'Priest' (with 105-mm howitzer)
14 FR RCA	24	'Priest' (with 105-mm howitzer)
19 FR RCA	24	'Priest' (with 105-mm howitzer)

2 Canadian Artillery Group RCA (AGRA)
3 MR RCA	16	5.5-inch gun-howitzers
4 MR RCA	16	5.5-inch gun-howitzers
7 MR RCA	16	5.5-inch gun-howitzers
15 MR RA	16	5.5-inch gun-howitzers
1 HR RA	8	155-mm guns 'Long Tom'
	8	7.2-inch howitzers

Total number of guns:
- 72 'Sexton'
- 168 'Priest'
- 216 25-pounders
- 208 5.5-inch gun-howitzers
- 24 155-mm guns 'Long Tom'
- 24 7.2-inch howitzers
- 48 3.7-inch anti-aircraft guns (in ground roles)

Total 760 guns

FR = Field Regiment
MR = Medium Regiment
HR = Heavy Regiment
HAR = Heavy Anti-aircraft Regiment

RA = Royal Artillery
RCA = Royal Canadian Artillery
RHA = Royal Horse Artillery

Source: *RA 8 Corps Operation Order No 2, Appendix 'A'* (WO)

Appendix 5

Distribution of Gliders within 1 Airborne Division for Operation Market Garden

Formation	1. tranche	2. tranche	3. tranche
Division HQS	10	19	—
Reconnaissance Squadron	22	—	—
Light Regiment RA	57	33	—
1 Anti-tank Battery	21	—	—
2 Anti-tank Battery	—	27	—
17-pounder Anti-tank guns	11 (incl. 8 Hamilcar)	11 (incl. 8 Hamilcar)	—
9 Company RE	16	6	
1 Parachute Brigade	23 (incl. 3 Hamilcar)	20	—
4 Parachute Brigade	—	43 (incl. 3 Hamilcar)	—
1 Air-landing Brigade:			
-HQS	10	—	—
-Air-landing Battalion	57 (incl. 1 Hamilcar)	6	
- Air-landing Battalion	57 (incl. 1 Hamilcar)	6	
- Air-landing Battalion	22 (incl. 1 Hamilcar)	41	
181 Field Ambulance	7	5	—
21 Independent Parachute Company	—	1	—
Supply	7	36 (incl. 3 Hamilcar)	—
Polish Parachute Brigade	—	45	35
Corps HQS	38	—	—
Miscellaneous	—	2	—
Total	**358**	**301**	**35**

i.e. 694 gliders in total, out of which 665 Horsa and 29 Hamilcar

Source: 1 Airborne Division Operation Instruction No. 9

Appendix 6

Allocation of Artillery for XII Corps – Operation Plunder

The Order of Battle below excludes light anti-aircraft and antitank formations and is based on war diaries and Appendix A2 of 'BAOR Battlefield Tour Operation Plunder 12 British Corps crossing the River Rhine 23–25 March 1945' (see references)

Attached to Commander Corps Royal Artillery (CCRA)
Counter-Battery Section (CBO)
7 Survey Regiment RA with one Battery from 10 Survey Regiment RA attached
Two light Sound Ranging Sections (*4-pen recorder*). These were attached to 7 Survey Regiment RA
653 AOP Squadron RAF (except three Flights)
A Troop 100 Radar Battery

15 (Scottish) Infantry Division Artillery Group
131 FR
181 FR
190 FR
6 FR (from 3 AGRA)
4 FR RHA (from 4 Armoured Brigade)
C Flight from 653 AOP Squadron RAF
Rocket Battery

52 (Lowland) Infantry Division Artillery Group
79 FR
80 FR
186 FR
63 MR (from 8 AGRA)
146 MR (from 8 AGRA)
One Battery from 108 HAR attached to 146 MR

53 (Welsh) Infantry Division Artillery Group
81 FR
83 FR
133 FR
77 MR (from 8 AGRA)
One Battery from 108 HAR attached to 77 MR
A Flight from 653 AOP Squadron RAF

7 Armoured Division Artillery Group
3 FR RHA
5 FR RHA
1 Mountain Regiment RA
B Flight from 653 AOP Squadron RAF

3 Artillery Group RA (AGRA)
13 MR
59 MR
One Battery from 108 HAR attached to 59 MR
67 MR
72 MR
59 HR
A Flight from 658 AOP Squadron RAF

8 Artillery Group RA (AGRA)
25 FR
C Flight from 658 AOP Squadron RAF attached to 25 FR
61 MR
53 HR
40 American Artillery Group (3 battalions 155-mm guns)
C Flight from 658 AOP Squadron RAF

9 Artillery Group RA (AGRA)
9 MR
11 MR
107 MR
3 SHR
90 HAR, in ground roles
C Flight from 659 AOP Squadron RAF

Abbreviations
FR = Field Regiment
MR = Medium Regiment
HR = Heavy Regiment
SHR = Super Heavy Regiment
HAR = Heavy Anti-aircraft Regiment

BAOR = British Army Of the Rhine
CBO = Counter Battery Office
CCRA = Commander Corps Royal Artillery

Appendix 7

Allocation of Artillery for XXX Corps – Operation Plunder

Attached to Commander Corps Royal Artillery (CCRA):
Counter Battery Section (*CBO*)
4 Survey Regiment RA with one section from 10 Survey Regiment RA
Two light Sound Ranging Sections (*4-pen Recorder*). These were attached to 4 Survey Regiment RA
662 AOP Squadron RAF (except three Flights)

Guards Division
55 FR
153 FR
86 AFR (to 43 (Wessex) Infantry Division at H+24 hrs)
B Flight from 662 AOP Squadron RAF (from 3 Infantry Division H+24 hrs)

3 British Infantry Division
7 FR
33 FR
76 FR
B Flight from 662 AOP Squadron RAF
One Troop from 100 Radar Battery (except one Section)

3 Canadian Infantry Division
12 Canadian FR
13 Canadian FR
14 Canadian FR
One Battery from 1 HR
C Flight from 660 AOP Squadron RAF

43 (Wessex) Infantry Division
94 FR
112 FR
179 FR
C Flight from 662 AOP Squadron RAF

51 (Highland) Infantry Division
126 FR
127 FR
128 FR
147 FR
454 Mountain Battery
79 MR
One Survey Section from 4 Survey Regiment RA
A Flight from 662 AOP Squadron RAF
1 Canadian Rocket Battery
One Section from 100 Radar Battery

2 Canadian Artillery Group RCA (AGRA)
3 Canadian MR
7 Canadian MR
One British 7.2-inch Battery

4 British Artillery Group RA (AGRA)
53 MR
65 MR
68 MR
79 MR
51 HR
61 SHR (two Batteries)
B Flight from 652 AOP Squadron RAF

5 British Artillery Group RA (AGRA)
7 MR
64 MR
84 MR
121 MR
52 HR
B Flight from 658 AOP Squadron RAF

Abbreviations
AFR = Army Field Regiment
FR = Field Regiment
MR = Medium Regiment
HR = Heavy Regiment
SHR = Super Heavy Regiment
HAR = Heavy Anti-aircraft Regiment

CBO = Counter Battery Office
CCRA = Commander Corps Royal Artillery

Notes

CHAPTER 1 – THE PERIOD BEFORE THE FIRST WORLD WAR

1. The situation is mentioned by Montgomery in his Memoirs, p. 329. The battle went on 16–19 October 1813 and resulted in a decisive defeat of Napoleon.
2. See Bailey 2004: *Field Artillery and Firepower*, p. 177.
3. The role played by the Rocket Troop in the Swedish Army is presented in *Engelskt ridande raketbatteri under svenskt överbefäl i kriget 1813–1814*. This account was prepared by the Historical Section of Swedish Army General Staff and an original copy in Swedish as well as a translated copy in English have been found by the author in the archive of the Royal Artillery History Trust at the Royal Artillery Museum at Woolwich Arsenal, James Clavell Library.
4. From letter to the author 26 October 2005 in which Major McCleery mentions that by tradition a toast is proposed in honour of the King of Sweden and that telegrams are exchanged with the Swedish Court.
5. Hedberg (1994), p. 32.
6. Bonnet (1994), p. 4.
7. Ibid. p. 4.
8. www.landrovercentre.com/guntroop/HAC.htm
9. One might wonder what influence on this development the foremost lady at the Queen's court had. Her name was Helena Snakenborg from an estate in Sweden. She arrived in England together with a Swedish Princess at the age of 16 and remained there for the rest of her life. She became a very close and trusted friend of the Queen. Her remarkable life story is presented in the book *Helena Snakenborg. En svenska vid Elizabeth I:s hov* authored by Gunnar Sjögren, Askild & Kärnekull 1973.
10. *The Royal Artillery Journal*. Vol. LXXV, No. 4, p. 257.
11. Ibid. p. 258.
12. Bonnet (2004), p. 4–5.
13. Bailey (2004), p. 169.
14. Ibid. p. 175.
15. Ibid. p. 176 where it is mentioned that from 1804 19% of ammunition supply to guns was of this type, and around 50% to the howitzers.
16. Bonnet (2004), p. 9.
17. Ibid. p. 8.
18. Bailey (2004), p. 174.
19. Ibid. p.179 and p. 183.
20. Ibid. p. 179.
21. At an academic lecture in Sweden a Swedish officer discussed this problem with rocket fire as compared with traditional artillery, but he presumed that 'one day rockets might come in general use as a complement to conventional artillery, as it might be possible to implement bigger calibres and as it also will be easier to deploy rocket launchers in terrain not suitable for ordinary pieces'. Isander (1827). Vol. III–IV, p. 3–4.
22. Bailey (2004), p. 187.
23. Counter-Battery fire doctrines existed in most armies stating the importance of this task.
24. One account of the struggle is Hibbert: *The Great Mutiny India 1857*. Harmondsworth, Middlesex Reading 1978.
25. The 'Sea-Brigade' comprised some 530 men including fifty Marines and they had a number of ship guns of various calibres and was attached to a larger formation under Brigadier Adrian Hope. In his account Lind af Hageby wrote: 'At last the day which I had so long looked forward to arrived, when I was to close in on the enemy and demonstrate that I was worth the task of honour to fight for and under Albion's proud Banner, the on so many blood-stained battlefields planted Banner of Victory' [from Swedish]. The account from his service in the Royal Navy has the title *Minnen från ett tre-årigt vistande i engelsk örlogstjänst 1857–1859* and was published in1860.
26. Bonnet (1994), p. 13.

CHAPTER 2 – THE PERIOD UP TO THE SECOND WORLD WAR

27. Bailey (2004), 212, Note 30.
28. Ibid. p. 211.
29. Ibid. p. 220.
30. Barnett (2000), p. 366.
31. Bailey (2004), p. 252, Note 131.
32. Ibid. p. 233, Note 140.
33. Hughes (1992), p. 162.
34. A photograph of this tractor is to be seen in Hughes (1992), p. 101.
35. At Woolwich Arsenal some 80,000 persons manufactured guns and ammunition during the war. Most of them were women. Indeed a remarkable war effort.
36. Hughes (1992), p. 160.
37. During the large battle at Cambrai in November 1917 e.g. seventy 60-pounders fired 16,000 tear gas shells. Bailey (2004), p. 257.
38. Ibid. p. 257, Note 53.
39. Ibid. p. 241.
40. Bonnet (1994), p. 27.
41. Barnett (2004), p. 404.
42. Bailey (2004), p. 274. The formation was sometimes also called *Experimental Armoured Force*.
43. Ibid. p. 284.
44. Artillery Commemoration Book (1950) has a complete list of all the converted Yeomanries, p. 680–684.
45. Bonnet (1994), p. 52.

CHAPTER 3 – TWILIGHT – WAR AND MOBILISATION

46. An exciting report on this was made by the Swedish journalist G. Persson who was present. This can be found in his book *Tjekoslovakiens Ödestimma*. Stockholm 1938 [in Swedish].
47. Goddard et al. (2004), p. 20.
48. Falvey (2002), p. 10–11.
49. Ibid. p. 15–16.
50. The numbers have been estimated from the last issue before the war of the *Royal Artillery Blue List*.
51. RA Commemoration Book (1950), p. 677.
52. Here presented data are slightly adapted data from Ian Hogg (see References) and data from Farndale (2002). *The Far East Theatre 1941–46*, Annex F.
53. The exact number of guns delivered from USA is uncertain. Other sources claim 800 guns. May it be so, but any way it was a significant interim solution for the Royal Artillery.
54. Walker in discussion with the author on 7 December 2004. Later in the war, Johnny Walker became officer of the airborne artillery.
55. Robertson (1986), p. 47–48.
56. Evans, Nigel: *British Artillery in World War 2*, Chapter *Artillery Communications* (http://nigelef.tripod.com).
57. *What Did You Do in the War, Daddy – Part 1*. BBC WW2 People's War Article A4045943, 10 May 2005.
58. This recorded at the Royal Artillery Museum, Woolwich Arsenal.
59. Barnett (2000), p. 427.
60. *Royal Artillery Blue List*, May 1938.
61. Lewendon/Robertson: *The Royal Artillery Journal*. Vol CXXI, No. 2, p. 43.

CHAPTER 4 – A DECISIVE REARMAMENT

62. Op cit, Note 61, p. 43–44.
63. Bonnet (1994), p. 33.
64. The graph is based on data from Farndale: *The Years of Defeat*, Annex M. Some other sources have also been used, amongst them *General Return of the Strength of the British Army*. As mentioned the various sources are not fully consistent and coherent. The results of the author's analysis are however deemed to give correct order of magnitude.
65. Hughes (1992), p. 178 informs that around 1,400 carriages of the types Mark IV and V were at disposal in 1936 for conversion of 18-pounder guns to 18/25-pounders. Pemberton (1950) writes on p. 12 that around 1,000 guns had been converted by 1939.
66. Henry (2002), p. 23.
67. Hughes (1992), p. 200–202.
68. This presentation is based on data from *The Production History of the 25 pdr. Field Equipment*. Ministry of Supply. February 1947. The Directorate of Weapons Production. (RAHT MD/1599).
69. Robertson (1986), p. 90.
70. Data have been retrieved from many sources, most of them from Evans. Op cit. Note 56, 25-pdr Chapter *The Guns, 25-pdr*. Another source has been *Range Tables* for 25-pdr Mark II. It should be

71. Quoted in Woollacott (1994), p. 5.
72. Pemberton (1950), p. 15 and Hughes (1992), pp. 183 and 185.
73. Falvey (2002), p. 59.
74. Evans, op cit Note 56, Chapter *The Guns, Data Sheets.*
75. Based on data from *The Production History of the 4.5"/5.5" Field Equipment.* Ministry of Supply. The Directorate of Weapons Production. July 1946 (RAHT MD/1599.
76. Evans op cit Note 56, Chapter *The Guns.*
77. Ibid., Chapter *The Guns, 25-pdr*, p. 2. Manufacture continued after the war and Hogg, p. 256, informs that in total 2150 pieces were manufactured.
78. The presentation here is based on Pemberton (1950), pp. 249–250 and Napier: *Royal Artillery Journal.* Vol. LXIII, No. 1, p. 11–20.
79. See e.g. Farndale (1996), *The Years of Defeat,* Annex A, p. 241.
80. Fransson (1996), p. 127.
81. Farndale (1996), *The Years of Defeat,* **Fig. 13**, illustrates the gun without its original shield. It is said that a number of guns with this shield were captured in Sudan in 1941.
82. Hogg (2002), p. 141.
83. Ibid. p. 147.
84. Steckzén (1946), p. 527. Regarding the enormous American manufacture of more than 100 000 pieces, partly in conflict with the license agreement, see Fransson (1996), pp. 160–162.
85. Farndale (2002), *The Far East Theatre 1941–46.* Annex F, pp. 342–343.

CHAPTER 5 – ARTILLERY GROUPING, ORGANISATION AND EQUIPMENT

86. The organization of formations at higher levels, Corps and Divisions, changed during the war, in particular this was the case as regards armoured divisions. The presentation here reflects the organization applied during the last years of the war. More about this in Forty (2002).
87. The presentation is based on data from Evans, op. cit. Note 56, Chapter *Organization for Manoeuvre.*
88. Henry (2002), p. 20.
89. Data from Table 5-2 have been retrieved and summarized from Evans, op. cit. Note 56, *Organisation for Manouevre* as representing 1944.
90. Goddard (2002), p. 61.
91. Woollacott (1994), p. 65.
92. Robertson (1986), p. 165.
93. Evans, op. cit. Note 56, Chapter *Artillery Communications.*
94. Forty (2002), Appendix 5, pp. 350–351 and other sources.
95. The Gunner 1944, p. 43.
96. Woollacott, p. 34.
97. The Slidex system is described and illustrated in Forty (2002), pp. 91–93.

CHAPTER 6 – LOOKING FAR INTO THE BATTLEFIELD

98. War Diary March 1945 HQRA 17 Ind. Div; C.B. Intelligence Summary (WO 172/6988).
99. Parham presented his proposal in an article in RUSI Journal, August 1933, see Farndale: *The Years of Defeat,* p. 11. In the latter book all the complicated arguing rounds which eventually resulted in the establishment of the Air Observation Squadrons with artillery officers as pilots are recorded, pp. 11–12.
100. Farndale (1996): *The Years of Defeat,* p. 32.
101. Ibid. p. 33.
102. See 'Unpublished Sources – Miscellaneous', Gibson, p. 10.
103. Ibid. p. 14.
104. Forty (2002) gives slightly different data for the first squadrons, see p. 78.
105. One statement of this kind is given in Gibson, op cit Note 102, p. 11.
106. Farndale (2002), *The Far East Theatre 1941–1946,* Annex N and Robertson (1986), pp. 271–273.
107. Farndale (2002), op. cit. Note 106, p. 378.
108. RA Notes 1944, Para 836.
109. *5 Survey Regiment RA. Its formation, training and operational roles in the United Kingdom,* p. 6. (RAHT MD/ 3376)
110. Lewis, T.W., *'Long Traverse from Juno'. Recollection of the Campaign in North West Europe by members of 7 Survey Regiment RA June 1944 to May 1945.* (RAHT MD/2664).
111. A hyperbola is a plane curve, such that the difference of the distances from any

point on it to two fixed points, the foci, is constant. In sound ranging a pair of microphones represents the foci and the time difference between arrivals of the sound wave to the pair gives the hyperbola. At long distances from the foci the hyperbola can be approximated by its asymptote. In practical sound ranging this was the case, hence, the asymptote gave the direction to the gun from which the sound wave originated. An alternative plotting method was the 'Circle Method', which however was not normally used by the British during the war.
112 Lewis, op. cit. Note 110.
113 Evans, op. cit. Note 56, Chapter *Target Acquisition and Counter Battery*, p. 9–10.
114 It is not clear as to whether this number is correct. Some sources are giving the number to be twelve, but this might include an Indian Survey Regiment. Here the number is taken from data in Farndale (1996), *The years of Defeat*, Annex M.

CHAPTER 7 – AIRBORNE ARTILLERY
115 Captain Peter Wilkinson MC in letter to the author on 4 April 2004.
116 The presentation of the Regiment and its equipment is based on an article in *Royal Artillery Journal*, Vol. LXXIV, p. 36–54 authored by Lt Col W.F.K. Thompson, who commanded the Regiment from July 1943 to September 1944.
117 Pemberton (1950), p. 207.
118 Ross, Walter J.M., Major: *The Airtransportable Role – A Diversion.* Chapter VIII in his unpublished war account on 80 (Lowland) Field Regiment RA. (RAHT).

CHAPTER 8 – HOW TO HIT THE TARGET – TECHNICAL GUN CHARACTERISTICS
119 Evans, op cit Note 56, Chapter *Fire Control Meteor*, pp. 11–12.
120 Letter to the author from Douglas Goddard on 6 March 2007.
121 *War Diary 69 Medium Regiment RA, October 1942* (WO 169/4654).
122 Kirkman: *RA Notes on the Offensive by Eighth Army from 23 Oct–4 Nov on the El Alamein Position*, 24 November 1942. Para 8 (iv), p. 9. (WO 201/431).
123 See *Range Tables (Part 1) QF 25-pr, Mark I and II, 1944*, pp. 100–101.

124 Evans, op. cit. Note 56, Chapter *Errors and Mistakes*, p. 3.
125 Op. cit. Note 123, p. 48 and 50.
126 Evans, op. cit. Note 56. Chapter *Methods.* p. 29.
127 Pemberton (1950), p. 101.
128 This is comprehensively discussed by Evans, op. cit. note 56. See his Chapter *Ammunition..*
129 Ibid. p. 16.

CHAPTER 9 – HOW TO HIT THE TARGET – GEODETIC REQUIREMENTS
130 *AT Volume III, Pamphlet No. 14 A, Regimental Survey. August 1944*.
131 Conversation with Captain Johnny Walker on 6 December 2004.

CHAPTER 10 – HOW TO HIT THE TARGET – GUN LAYING
132 Firing with increasing elevation in the Upper Register implies reduced range.

CHAPTER 11 – PREPARATIONS FOR OPENING OF GUNFIRE
133 Robertson (1986), p. 216.
134 Goddard el al (1997–2002), pp. 188–189.
135 Robertson (1986), p. 253.
136 From *Gunner, 1944, August*, p. 88.
137 Also quoted in Mead (1982), p. 35.
138 See e.g. *AT, Volume III, Pamphlet No. 13*, p. 9 and further.
139 *Artillery Notes 1944, Para 1331*, p. 17.
140 Ibid, *No. 19, Appendix 'A'*.

CHAPTER 12 – ARTILLERY BATTLE TECHNIQUES AND TACTICS
141 *Royal Artillery Journal*, Vol. LXXV, No.3, p. 216.
142 More details about ranging are to be found in *AT Volume III, Pamphlet. No. 3, Part I*.
143 *AT Volume III, Pamphlet No. 3* gives details on the communication between the OPO and the gun positions for various ranging alternatives.
144 Op. cit. Note 142, p. 41.
145 Ibid. p. 8
146 See e.g. Pemberton (1950), pp. 229–230.
147 Evans, op. cit. Note 56, Chapter *Effects and Weight of Fire*, p. 5–6.
148 Ibid. p. 5.
149 Robertson (1986), p. 216 (in a newsletter

by the regimental commanding officer Armstrong).
150 Carver (2001), p. 50.
151 At Balaklava during the Crimean War 1854–1856 the British Light Cavalry Brigade attacked in October 1954 straight towards Russian artillery and cavalry positions. The losses were catastrophic.
151 R.G.S. Bidwell, Brigadier: *The Development of British Field Artillery Tactics*. Royal Artillery Journal, Vol. XCIV, No. 2, p. 10.
153 Ibid. p. 11.
154 In RA Notes 1944 No. 13, Appendix 'F' is a summary of experiences from the engagement of more than 600 targets from artillery ships in the Mediterranean after the fall of Tunisia. See also Bailey (2004), p.99. Experiences from cooperation with bombers and fighter-bombers in Italy are also presented in the same RA Notes, para 891.
155 Robertson (1986), p. 218.
156 Goddard et al. (2002), p.106.
157 Crews well trained could reach even higher rates, The record is said to be held by a Canadian gun crew which claimed 17 rounds in one minute.
158 The term is defined in AT, Volume III, Pamphlet No.6, p.1.
159 Carver (2001), p. 196.
160 Ibid. p. 46.
161 Foreword in a book about 4 Survey Regiment RA, *'Z Location'*.
162 Keene: *The value of Predicted Harassing Fire*. Royal Artillery Journal, Vol. LXXIII, No. 4, p.355
163 Goddard (2002), p.76.
164 In RA Notes 1944, No. 21, Appendix 'E' is a summary of experiments regarding artificial light in various tactical situations made by 21 Army Group.
165 *Operational Research in NW Europe – the work of No. 2 Operational Research Section of 21 Army Group, June 1944–July 1945*. Report No. 21, *Accuracy of Predicted Fire – Operation Veritable*, Appendix D (RAHT MD/1479) .
166 The graph is drawn by the author based on data from Ibid, Appendix D, Figure 5.
167 The rationale behind these changes is well described in *RA Notes 1944, Para 891*, pp.14–15.

168 Pemberton (1950), pp.198–199.
139 Powell, Robin, Major: *The Battle for Able*. Unpublished personal account of his war experiences. (RAHT Blue Box 2).
170 *Artillery Lessons Campaign in Italy 1943–45*. A report to a conference at the Royal Artillery School in August 1945 (RAHT MD/486)

CHAPTER 13 – TRAIN, TRAIN, EXERCISE, EXERCISE…!
171 Robertson (1986), p. 13.
172 Ibid. p. 69 gives a good example.
173 Farndale (1996): *The years of Defeat*, p. 289. It has not been possible for the author to get the numbers confirmed. They seem to be uncertain.
174 See e.g. Robertson (1986), p. 65. He gives many other good examples of basic training of a TA unit during the first years after mobilisation.
175 *RA Notes 1943, No. 11, Appendix 'D'*.
176 Woollacott (1994), p. 1.
177 Op. cit. Note 175.
178 How this type of training was started without proper preparations is described for the different units in *Royal Artillery Commemoration Book*, p. 71.
179 Major Douglas Goddard in letter to the author on 26 May 2005.
180 Op. cit. Note 175.
181 *Royal Artillery Journal, Vol. LXVIII, No.4*. p. 411.
182 See e.g. how 136 Field Regiment RA used to train their gunners in India, Robertson (1986), p. 235.

CHAPTER 14 – SUCCESS REQUIRES EFFICIENT STAFF WORK
183 'Grade 1' was a Lieutenant Colonel position, 'Grade 2' was a Major and 'Grade 3' a Captain. See Forty (2002), p. 55.
184 *Handbook of the British Army 1942*. British War Office and U.S. War Department, TM 30–410, 1942, p. 23.
185 For more details see Forty (2002), pp. 52–62.
186 Detailed presentations can be found in Evans. Op. cit. Note 56, Chapter *Headquarters Royal Artillery*.
187 Material for a speech to young officers (RAHT MD/1689).
188 The presentation is based on Field

Marshal Slim's account in *Defeat into Victory (1999)*, pp. 209 ff.

CHAPTER 16 – ARTILLERY TO THE FIELD – ACROSS THE CHANNEL

189 Barnett (2000), p. 429, has a slightly smaller number of divisions, but the same order of magnitude as Farndale (1996): *The Years of Defeat*, p. 25. The numbers given in this book are the same as those of the latter book.
190 The graph has been prepared by using data from Farndale (1996): *The Years of Defeat*, pp. 6–23.
191 Data from Ibid., Annex A.
192 Permberton (1950), p. 27.
193 Both the Order and the Instruction are attached to the *War Diary HQRA 3 Div* (WO 167/220).
194 See e.g. Pemberton (1950), p. 27, about the situation within BEF.
195 The instruction is attached to the regimental war diary (9 Field Regiment RA, WO 167/469).
196 *7 Field Regiment RA War Diary*, 8 April 1940 (WO 167/468).
197 *War Diary HQRA 3 Div*, 9th April 1940 (WO 167/220).
198 This is attached to the war diary of 1 Survey Regiment RA and is dated 22 April 1940 (WO 167/571).
199 This is attached to the war diary of 1 Survey Regiment RA and is dated 13th April 1940 (WO 167/571).
200 See *War Diary HQRA 3 Division May 1940* (WO 167/220). The War Diary is probably written after the end of the battle
201 The presentation onwards is based on *War Diary HQRA 3 Div* (WO 167/220)
202 *War Diary 7 Field Regiment RA*, 13 May 1940 (WO 167/468).
203 Montgomery (1958), p. 61.
204 About the air battle see Tamelander (2002): *Slaget om Västeuropa*.
205 Parham, Jack, Lieutenant Colonel: *Personal Account 10th Field Regiment, May–June 1940*, p. 7 (WO 197/128).
206 From *War Diary HQRA 3 Division, May 1940* (WO 167/220). The subsequent presentation is mainly based on this source.
207 *War Diary HQRA 3 Div, 14 May* (WO 167/220).
208 *War Diary 7 Field Regiment RA, 14 May 1940* (WO 167/468).
209 *War Diary 99 Field Regiment RA, 15 May 1940* (WO 167/504)
210 Parham, op cit Note 205, p. 13.
211 Ibid. p. 14–15.
212 In Farndale (1996): *The years of Defeat* it is stated that the firing took place at the Escaut-line on 20th May and included 18 Field Regiment RA, p. 54. Farndale is also making reference to Bidwell, Shelford (1970): *Gunnners at war*. My presentation is, however, based on Parham's own account.
213 Gordon-Finlayson, R., Major: *Personal Diary 10th Field Regiment, May–June 1940* (WO 197/91).
214 Parham, op cit Note 205, p. 27.
215 Parham, *Royal Artillery Journal*, Vol LXVII, No. 3, p.254.
216 Onderwater (1992), p. 60.
217 Parham, op cit Note 205, p.18.
218 Ibid. p. 45.
219 Ibid. pp. 26–27.
220 *War Diary 92 Field Regiment RA, 21 May 1940* (WO 167/501).
221 Farndale (1996), *The years of Defeat*, p. 52.
222 Ibid. p. 53.
223 The presentation of the redeployment of 5 Infantry Division to the area around Ypres and its engagement there, in particular during the period 26–29 May 1940, is based on the War Diary with attachments of the divisional artillery commander (WO 167/246).
224 *RA 5 Division Operation Order No. 13*. This is dated on 26 May 1940 and was distributed by means of dispatch riders to the various regiments at 22.30 hours.
225 *War Diary 91 Field Regiment RA, 27th May* (WO 167/500).
226 Ibid., May 1940.
227 *War Diaries 1939–1945. Field Marshal Lord Alanbrooke*. Second Impression London 2003, p. 72.
228 Ibid. P. 73
229 Farndale (1996), *The Years of Defeat*, p. 60.
230 Parham, op cit Note 205, p. 39.
231 See the war diary of *1 Sound ranging Battery* which is attached to *War Diary 1 Survey Regiment RA* (WO 167/571).
232 The map is from *War Diary 1 Survey Regiment RA* (WO 167/571) but it is probably made after the return to England

on data brought home from France.
233 Parham, op cit Note 205, p. 49.
234 The account is attached to Parham's account, op cit Note 205, p. 51.
235 Palmer, *Royal Artillery Journal, Vol. CXVII, No.2*, p.20.
236 Ibid. p.20.
237 Pemberton (1950), p. 42.
238 How the surrender was seen from a German point of view can be studied in von Luck (2005), p. 54.
239 Pemberton (1950), p. 37.
240 Mentioned in Spears (1954), Volume I, p. 302.

CHAPTER 17 – FAILED INTERVENTION IN NORWAY

241 *War Diary HQRA 5 Division, April–May1940* (WO 167/246).
242 Churchill, Winston (1948): *The Second World War*, Vol. I, p. 443.
243 Ibid. p. 457.
244 Ibid. p. 422.
245 The Orders of Battle for allied and German forces in Norway are presented by Dildy (Osprey), pp. 28–29.
246 This is presented in several books about the campaign in Norway including Tamelander & Zetterling (in Swedish).
247 A few old 95-mm howitzers only were landed for direct support of the marine infantry.
248 *War Diary 51 Field Regiment RA, April–May 1940* (WO 166/1483).
249 *War Diary 203 Battery RA, April–June 1940* (WO 168/49).
250 *Movement Control Summary Norway 1940* (WO 198/4).
251 A few observations suggesting that the battery did not have the 25-pounder Mark II, the 'real 25-pounder', but the Mark I version, i.e. the18/25-pounder are the following:
 – We have seen that only a very limited number of gun carriages had been delivered to the Royal Artillery in March 1940;
 – The war diary of the actual unit, 51 Field Regiment RA, says nothing of rearmament to the new gun. The regiment prepared for transport from its quarters in the last week of March and embarked troop carriers at the beginning of April, obviously with the intentions to get it engaged in Norway early in April had not the Germans forestalled British plans by invading the country on 9 April. It seems unlikely that the regiment would have had time for rearmament, undertake necessary training etc. under these circumstances;
 – The war diary of 203 Battery RA has no indication that new guns had been transported to Norway. In a document about equipment transported to Norway it is said that it was 25-pounders and 25-pound ammunition, but as we know the 18/25-pounder often was called just the '25-pounder';
 – In General Auchinleck's report from the campaign it is specified that guns taken back to England were 18/25-pounders and, furthermore, that the British left 4000 shells for 18/25-pounders, when the forces were evacuated.
252 General Auchinleck's Report, Appendix C. See Note 254.
253 Keegan (1991), pp. 145–147.
254 Auchinleck, C.J.E., Lieutenant General: *Report on Operations in Norway from 13 May 1940 to 8 June 1940.* (WO 168/9).
255 The quotation is taken from Auchinleck's Report, op. cit. Note 254, p. 1.
256 The Independent Companies sent to Norway were predecessors to the later *Commandos*.
257 Op. cit. Note 254, pp. 8–9.
258 Ibid. p. 9.
259 Ibid. p. 21.
260 Tamelander & Zetterling, op. cit. Note 246, p. 250.
261 *Movement Control Summary Norway 1940* (WO 198/4).
262 *War Diary 203 Battery RA, 9May 1940, 09.45 hours* (WO 168/49).
263 *NWEF Operation Instruction No. 1, 13 May 1940.* This instruction is attached to the war diary of 24 Guards Brigade (WO 168/24).
264 *HQ NWEF Conference No. 4, 22 May 1940, para 8* (WO 198/16).
265 *HQ NWEF Conference No. 8, 26 May 1940, para 2* (WO 198/16).
266 Farndale (1996): *The Years of Defeat*, p. 28 and Map 5.
267 Auchinleck writes about the postponement in his report (op. cit. Not 254, p. 26): 'The

original programme of evacuation was timed to begin on the night 2nd/3rd June, but was postponed for 24 hours at the urgent request of Sir Cecil Dormer [British Ambassador to Norway] in order to enable the Norwegian Government to try to implement the so called "Mowinckel Plan" through the Swedish Government and so secure that Narvik should become a neutral area under Swedish protection. In view of the probability of heavy enemy air attacks on Harstad I agreed to this postponement with great reluctance.'
268 In the plan all allied units had been divided into detachments of 150 men each. By this everyone could see from the plan which night they were to leave.
269 The war diary of 203 Battery RA (WO 168/49) gives many details and time schedules about the evacuation of the battery.
270 Op. cit. Note 254, p. 31.
271 Ibid. p. 36

CHAPTER 18 – FROM IMMINENT INVASION THREAT TO OFFENSIVE TRAINING
272 *War Diary 16 Field Regiment RA, June 1940* (WO 167/472).
273 *War Diary 92 Field Regiment RA, June 1940* (WO 167/501).
274 Fleming (2003), p.199.
275 *War Diary 2 Regiment RHA, June 1940* (WO 167/463).
276 *War Diary 76 Field Regiment RA, June 1940* (WO 167/496).
277 *War Diary* 99 Field Regiment RA, June 1940 (WO 167/504).
278 *War Diary 74 Field Regiment RA, June 1940* (WO 167/494).
279 *War Diary HQRA 5 Division, June 1940* (WO 167/246).
280 Robertson (1986), p. 39
281 *War diary 72 Field Regiment RA, June 1940* (WO 167/483).
282 More details about the programme can be seen in Farndale (1996): *The Years of Defeat, Annex B.*
283 *War Diary 69 Medium Regiment RA, June 1940* (WO 167/550).
284 Fleming (2003), p. 199.
285 Farndale (1996): *The Years of Defeat.* p. 95.
286 Fleming (2003), p. 65.
287 Goddard et al. (2002), p. 26.
288 Farndale (1996), p. 99.
289 *Exercise Bumper. Notes by R.A. Adviser for Chief Umpire* (Kirkman Papers RAHT MD/3138).
290 Ibid. p. 3.
291 Ibid. p. 5.
292 Ibid. p. 6.
293 *The Employment of Artillery in Mass. Paper by General Parham in the Summer 1942, issued by C-in-C Home Forces at a conference at Larkhill on 8 June 1942, and used as the basis of Artillery tactics in the First Army Campaign in Tunisia* (Parham Papers RAHT MD/188).
294 Goddard et al. (2002), p. 26.
295 Ibid. p. 27.

CHAPTER 19 – 'IT WILL BE A KILLING MATCH' – EL ALAMEIN
296 *'Lightfoot'. General Plan of Eight Army,* para 38–39. The memo is dated 14 September 1942 and is part of a set of documents compiled by HQRA XXX Corps about the third battle at El Alamein (WO 201/646. See also WO 201/648).
297 In discussions after the war with Sir Basil Liddell Hart General von Thoma stressed that a pincer operation against the Middle East never existed on the German side. Liddell Hart (1948): *The Other Side of the Hill.*
298 Bidwell, R.G.B., Brigadier: *The Development of British Field Artillery Tactics 1940–1942. The Desert War.* Royal Artillery Journal, Vol. XCIV, pp. 83.
299 The name came from one of the first officers commanding such a battle group, Major General Jock Campbell, originally a Gunner. He was one of only three Gunners awarded the Victoria Cross in World War II. He was killed in a car accident a few weeks after having received this award of honour. Campbell is said to have explained that the wrong employment of artillery was just due to severe shortage of artillery.
300 Bidwell, op. cit. Note 298, p. 84.
301 Kirkman was later to command 50 (Northumbrian) Division at the invasion of Sicily in July 1943, and early 1944 he was promoted to command XIII Corps and assigned the task to plan for the break-through of the 'Gustav Line' in Italy, which became the fourth battle at

Cassino which began on 11 May 1944.
302 The regimental catastrophe was completed when the ship transporting the captured surveyors across the Mediterranean fell victim to torpedoes from the Royal Navy and went down with the POWs.
303 *'Lightfoot'*, op. cit. Note 296, pt. 14.
304 Ibid. pt. 18.
305 Ibid. pt. 22.
306 Ibid. pt. 11.
307 Ibid. pt. 23
308 Ibid. pt. 24 and pt. 29.
309 Ibid. pt. 32.
310 Ibid. pt. 41.
311 The letter with its attachment is included amongst the documents that the HQRA XXX Corps compiled after the battle at El Alamein (WO 201/646).
312 *War Diary BRA Eighth Army, September 1942* (WO 169/2340).
313 Detailed Orders of Battle for both sides are presented in Latimer (2004): *El Alamein, Appendix*.
314 *War Diary HQRA XIII Corps* (WO 169/4010).
315 The data for this Attachment have been compiled basically from Latimer (2004), *Appendix* and war diaries.
316 A good illustration is *El Alamein C.B. Chart Night 23/24 October*. This map was drawn in January 1943 by 524 Pal. C Field Survey Company RE and is slightly revised reprinted in Pemberton (1950), Map 4. Reference is also made to British Library.
317 *War Diary 1 Composite Battery, 4th Survey Regiment RA* (WO 169/4685) and *War Diary 'R' Troop 1 Composite Battery* (Wo 169/4685).
318 *War Diary 2 Composite Battery RA* (WO 169/4690).
319 *War Diary 'S' Troop 2 Composite Battery* (WO 169/4692).
320 Kirkman, Sidney: *RA Notes on the Offensive by Eighth Army from 23 October–4 November on the El Alamein Position*. 24 November 1942, Pt. 5, p. 6 (WO 201/431).
321 Pemberton (1950), p. 146.
322 Ibid.
323 *30 Corps Artillery Operation Order No. 18, Appendix F* (WO 201/646)
324 *2 NZ Div Operation Order No. 17, pt. 23* (see WO 201/646 where this order is kept).
325 Bidwell, R.G.S., Brigadier: *El Alamein and Memories of E Battery H.A.C. – 25 Years Ago* (RAHT MD/761).
326 *War Diary 30th Corps CBO* (WO 169/4039).
327 Kirkman, op. cit. Note 320, pt. 5, p. 6 (WO 201/431).
328 *Minutes of Conference held at Tac HQ, Eighth Army, at 02.30 hrs 25 Oct. 1942.* The minutes can be found in WO 201/648.
329 *Decisions given by Army Commander at Conference held at H.Q. 2 N.Z. Div at 12.00 hrs 25 Oct 1942.* The document is signed by Montgomery himself and is to be found in WO 201/648.
330 Kirkman, op. cit. Note 320, pt. 8 (iv) (WO 201/431).
331 Ramsay, A., Brigadier: *Summary of Artillery Operations in 9 Aust Div in Sidi Abd El Rahman from 23 Oct to 4 Nov 42*, p. 11 (WO 201/597)
332 Kirkman, op. cit. Note 320, pt. 3 (ii).
333 Ramsay, op. cit. Note 331, p. 6.
334 Pemberton (1950), p. 143.
335 Kirkman, op. cit. Note 320, pt. 10 (WO 201/431).
336 Mangilli-Climpson (2007), p. 128.
337 Ramsay, op. cit. Note 331, p. 3.
338 Ibid. p. 8.
339 Rowe, Tim: *Steve Weir New Zealand's Master Gunner*. Article No. 4, 2004. New Zealand Army Military Studies Institute, p. 2829 (RAHT MD/3520).
340 Kirkman, op. cit. Note 320, pt 1 (v) (WO 201/431).
341 Latimer (2004) refers to this statement, p. 229.
342 The plan was attached to the artillery order of the New Zealand Division for 'Operation Supercharge'. It can be found in the voluminous War Diary of 127 Field Regiment RA, which regiment had similar tasks (WO 169/4607).
343 Kirkman, op. cit. Note 320, pt. 14 (WO 201/431)
344 Ibid., pt. 14 and Appendix 1 (WO 201/431).

CHAPTER 20 – A NEW FRONT IS OPENED – NORMANDY

345 Stjernfelt (2004), Appendix.
346 In the 2 Army artillery plan it is stated that this battalion was equipped with SP guns.

347 A map with these 'trig points' is included in the Kirkman Papers at James Clavell Library, Royal Artillery Museum (RAHT MD/3138).
348 In Whetton/Ogden: *Z Location*, pp. 83–84 a detailed presentation is given as to how the units of 4 Survey Regiment RA were landed and the tasks assigned to them.
349 Ibid. pp. 87–88.
350 Good presentations of the employment of SP guns can be found in several articles of *The Gunner*. See for instance the article by Major General Jack Parham in the March 1969 edition and a follow-up article by Brigadier G.G. Mears in the June 1969 edition. Here a later article (1994?) by Major General T.A. Richardson has been the source used. Meirs and Richardson both were subalterns and engaged in the 'run-in-shoot' on D-Day, on 6 June 1944.
351 Beck, Sidney, Lieutenant: *341 Battery 86th Field Regiment RA (Herts Yeomanry) War Diary 3 June 1944 to 9 April 1946*, entry 6th June 1944.
352 These plans are summarised as *Landing Tables* and are included in the Parham Papers at James Clavell Library, Royal Artillery Museum (RAHT MD/188).
353 Tamelander & Zetterling (2003), *Avgörandets ögonblick*, p. 240.
354 Goddard et al. (2002), p.49.
355 O'Conner, Lieutenant General: *Corps Comd's Notes on 'Goodwood Meeting', 9 Sep 1944*. The report is attached to *2nd Army 'G' Operation Goodwood* (WO 205/1121).
356 *8 Corps Operation Instruction No. 4. Operation Goodwood. 16 Jul 44*. The order is part of a report prepared by HQS 2nd Army (WO 205/1121).
357 *Notes by Comd 8 Corps on the Employment of Armour in Battle*. This document was an attachment to his report from the battle, see op. cit. Note 355.
358 *RA Artillery Notes 1944, No. 20*, para. 1146 and its Appendix B.
359 Extract from the un-published article *The attack on Rauray by the 12th Battalion The King's Royal Rifle Corps on 26 June 1944*, which I have received from its author, Major General T.A. Richardson, on 13 October 2008.
360 Goddard (2009), *Master of None*, p.p. 63–64.
361 Whetton/Ogden, *Z Location*, p. 91.
362 Goddard (2009), op. cit. Note 360, p. 69.

CHAPTER 21 – 'BERLIN TONIGHT' – ARNHEM

363 Margry (2002), Volume 1, p. 73.
364 The map is a revised and extended version, made by the author, of a map attached to *1 Airborne Division Operation Instruction No. 9*.
365 *30 Corps Operation Instruction No.24. 'Operation Garden' 15 September 1944* and *Amendment to 30 Corps Operation Instruction No. 24 16 September 1944*. (Attached to War Diary HQ 'G' XXX Corps [WO 171/341]).
366 The brigade was fairly small, around 1,500 soldiers. A troop of four guns was attached.
367 A complete list of the cancelled operations is presented in Margry (2002), Volume 1, p. 18.
368 Brigadier A.G. Walch Papers, IWM (No. 01/11/2).
369 This account is primarily built on the report prepared by Loder-Symonds after the war. See e.g. RAHT MD/1437. In a slightly shortened edition the report is also reproduced in RA Notes 1944, para 1312.
370 In 'Sheriff' Thompson's article in Royal Artillery Journal, Vol. LXXIV, No. 1, he shows in detail how the regiment was to be loaded on board 87 Horsas, when available. One Horsa could carry three tons, so detailed loading tables had to be prepared. In order to bring 137 shells per gun these had to be dispersed to all gliders. Those carrying a gun with its Jeep could only bring nine shells to avoid overloading. The number 137 per gun is often mentioned in the literature, but in reality it was less as four gliders and two guns were lost.
371 Wilkinson (2002) gives the names of 16 observation officers with the Captain's rank and another five including the CO, Major R.D. Wight-Boycott, who were positioned at the Corps HQS, p.158.
372 *Operation Market. Notes on CRA's Order given at 12 Sep* [1944] (IWM 92/4/1).
373 Margry (2002), Volume i, p. 97 (101 A/B Division) and p. 133 (82 A/B Division).
374 The piece was called M3 105mm Pack

Howitzer and had been developed for use by glider-borne formations. The design of several existing guns were used. The barrel was for instance a shorter version of the barrel of the standard 105mm field howitzer and the buffer/recuperator from the 75mm pack howitzer. The intention was to get a gun with a stronger shell than the HE shell of the latter. As the weight must be kept down to just over a ton, the price became a short barrel and thus shorter range. The maximum range was around 7.6km as compared with 8.9km of the 75mm gun. The number of guns in the operation is found in the report *Allied Airborne Operations in Holland. September–October 1944*, which probably was prepared by the divisional headquarters of 1 British Airborne Division. The report is included in Walch archive (IWM 01/11/2).

375 In the Corps' plan for the march it was prescribed that the vehicle density should be 35 vehicles per mile, i.e. 50 yards between the vehicles (WO 171/341). The divisional column would then be spread over a distance of some 160km. In the order for Guards Division it was, however, stated that the density should be 60 vehicles to the mile, i.e. only 30 yards between vehicles. If so, the divisional column would cover 98km (WO 171/380).

376 Many sources show the design of the barrage, e.g. war diaries of the participating field regiments. It is also presented in the report *Operation Market Garden 17–26 September 1944* prepared by XXX Corps headquarters (IWM Walch Papers 01/11/1–2).

377 The layout is confirmed by a pencil note on the issue of the fire plan attached to the war diary of 94 Field Regiment RA (WO 171/983).

378 The fire plan shows in detail how the shifts are to take place all the way to the final line target u-u, where all regiments remain firing during the last minute. The plan is attached to the war diary of most of the participating field regiments.

379 The fire plan was prepared by the artillery headquarters of Guards Division and is attached to war diaries of several of the participating regiments, e.g. 7 Medium Regiment RA (WO 171/1047). It can be assumed that 'Z' hours was the same for both barrages, but it is amazing that this is not mentioned in the plan.

380 Margry (2002), Volume 1, pp. 90–92 have the details of these attacks and their results.

381 Krafft, Sepp: *SS Panzer Grenadier Ausbildungs- och Ersatzbat. 16 in den Kämpfen bei Arnhem 17.9.44 – 7.10.44*. An English translation is kept by National Archives, Kew (WO 205/1124).

382 The second time a complete regiment was transported to the battlefield was Operation Varsity being part of the large Rhine Crossing in March 1945. Of the 24 guns only 11 could be employed directly. The remaining 13 guns had either been lost or landed far away from the planned landing zone. The regiment (53 Air-landing Light Regiment RA) could later recover more guns bringing the total number up to 18 guns, which were organised temporarily in three 6-guns batteries.

383 The presentation here is primarily based on the report prepared by the artillery headquarters of 1 Airborne Division after the battle, which is attached to RAHT MD/1437 and also in a summarised version in RA Notes 1944, Para 1312.

384 Margry (2002), Volume 1, p. 208.

385 The fire plan is attached to the war diary of 7 Medium Regiment RA (WO171/1047).

386 In the literature it is often stated that the counter-battery programme commenced at 14.00 hours, see e.g. General Horrock, but the war diaries of both 124 Field Regiment RA and 64 Medium Regiment RA confirm 14.09 hours as the time when the first rounds were fired. A note by pencil at the fire order attached to the war diary of 7 Medium Regiment RA also confirms the time.

387 *Air Notes No. 134, 18 September 44*. The report is attached to War Diary HQ 'G' XXX Corps (WO 171/4077).

388 *War Diary 153 Field Regiment RA, September 1944* (WO 171/998).

389 *War Diary 1 Air-landing Regiment RA, September 1944* (WO 171/1016).

390 Details are presented in a report included in Brigadier P.N.R. Steward-Richardson's Paper (IWM 92/43/1).

391 Margry (2002), Volume 2, p. 592. There

392 Margry (2002), Volume 1, p. 22, gives this number for the cancelled Operation Comet.
393 Margry (2002), Volume 2, pp. 702–703, describes how the field was 'detected' and came into use from D+9 when 209 C-47 landed with equipment and supplies of different kind.
394 In a regimental history for 52 Heavy Regiment RA this is said to have been the case. An extract of this history document was made available to the author by Douglas Goddard.
395 *War Diary 74 Field Regiment RA, September 1944* (WO 171/975).
396 A personal diary introduced on Internet by his son Benjamin Beck, who in communication with the author has given additional information about his father's war service and also granted permission to quote from the diary http://web.ukonline.co.uk/benjamin-beck/batterydiary.htm. See also op. cit. Note 351.
397 *War Diary 64 Medium Regiment RA, September 1944* (WO 171/1059).
398 Ibid.
399 In his article *Market Garden September 1944* in Royal Artillery Journal, Vol. CXXV, No.2 Major General Tony Richardson has on a sketch map marked the position of 7 Medium Regiment RA close to the southern shore but a few kilometres east of the Nijmegen road bridge. The main parts of the regiment were then deployed and engaged south of Veghel and had been ordered to redeploy forward to the marked position. It is possible that 27/28 Battery RA moved to this site already in the night between 24th and 25th September, but more likely is that it deployed close to 64 Medium Regiment RA, to which it had been put under command.
400 Personal report prepared by the battery commander, Major E.R.D. Palmer, p. 30 (Douglas Goddard's archive).
401 *War Diary 84 Medium Regiment, September 1944* (WO 171/1066).
402 The war diary of this regiment obviously has several errors as regards dates and actions, e.g. that A Troop already at 15.40 hrs on 21st September should have been redeployed to the southern shore of Waal.
403 *RA Notes 1944, Para. 1589, Appendix A.*
404 *War Diary 662 AOP Squadron RAF* (WO 171/1029).
405 Margry (2002), Volume 2, p. 713.
406 The discussion here has been based primarily on *Air Notes No. 134-No. 140* which are attached to the war diary of XXX Corps headquarters (WO 171/341).
407 This presentation is based on an unpublished report by Major Walter J. M. Ross serving with 80 Field Regiment RA (RAHT MD Series).
408 *War Diary HQRA 52 (Lowland) Division, September 1944* (WO 171/543).
409 Ross report, op. cit. Note 407 (RAHT MD Series).
410 *War Diary 79 Field Regiment RA, September 1944.* Reference is also made to the war diary of 4 Survey Regiment RA (WO 171/1072).
411 Captain Trotman had been posted to the regiment in August as replacement for a troop commander. He was therefore not very well known by others when he was ordered to accompany the 4 Dorset Battalion across River Rhine. He was immediately taken prisoner of war, unharmed, and taken to Germany. He survived the capture. Nothing was heard from him after the war, and he himself did not approach any of his former comrades in arms until 60 years had passed. He then came 'out of the shadows' and got in touch with Douglas Goddard, who learnt that Trotman after the war became a Priest in Northern Ireland. In a long letter to Goddard he told his story from the night when he accompanied the Dorset infantry across River Rhine. The author has got an extract from this letter from Douglas Goddard.
412 Wilkinson (2002), p. 138.
413 Magry (2002), Volume 2, p. 683.
414 Hunt's diary is available at Imperial War Museum (IWM 06/4/1).
415 *War diary 47 Survey Battery RA, September 1944* (WO 171/1078). This is also stated in *Situation Report No. 12, War diary 4th Survey Regiment RA, September 1944* (WO 171/1072). In the 'Situation Report' from the evening 26th September

by the artillery headquarters of the 43rd (Wessex) Division it is stated that both troops of 212 Battery RA were deployed near the road to Elst about 2km south of this village (C Troop at 689680 and D Troop at 687684). There was hardly any reason to have the units deployed to these positions on 26 September as the evacuation of the remaining part of 1 Airborne Division then had been completed. Hence this is another indication that the battery's re-deployment took place on 25 September.

416 These orders are attached to the war diaries of 64 Medium Regiment RA and 94 Field Regiment RA. The commanding officer of the former (Hunt) has in his personal diary noted that it was the artillery commander of 43 (Wessex) Division who had issued the fire plan for the night, which strengthens the assumption that the fire order 'Java' was the one to be fired in protection of the evacuation.

417 The fire order is attached to the war diary of 94 Field Regiment RA.

418 Douglas Goddard's archive.

419 Beck, op. cit. Note 351, diary entry on 25 September 1944.

420 Ryan (1974), p. 599.

CHAPTER 22 – THE FINAL ONSLAUGHT – THE RHINE CROSSING

421 Beck, op cit Note 351, *24 February 1945*.

422 The map is based on *Operation Plunder. 12 British Corps crossing the Rhine 23–25 March 1945, Map 1*. British Army of the Rhine Battlefield Tour. December 1947.

423 *Minutes of Conference held at Main Headquarters 21 Army Group on 9 February 1945 to consider Operation Varsity* (are attached to WO 205/11).

424 Ibid.

425 Ibid.

426 *RA 12 Corps Op Instruction No. 41, 22 March 45.* An attachment to the war diary (WO 171/4059).

427 DD means *Duplex Drive*.

428 Op. cit. Note 422.

429 Ibid. pp. 28–31.

430 Ibid. Appendix H.

431 Op. cit. Note 426.

432 *30 Corps Operation Instruction No. 49 dated 20 March 45, Appendix A* has all the details. The document is attached to the war diary of 'G' Staff HQ XXX Corps March 1945, section 'Op Instructions' (WO 171/4077).

433 As regards sound ranging bases and observations bases within the XII Corps section the deployment has been taken from a map presented by Lieutenant Colonel Clegg, commander of 7 Survey Regiment RA, dated 17 June 1945. It is found in several sources, amongst them RAHT MD/2664. The corresponding deployment within XXX Corps section is based on reports attached to the war diary of 4 Survey Regiment RA (WO 171/5112).

434 *RA 12 Corps Planning Instruction. Second Army Op 'Plunder' 11 March 45* (WO 171/4059).

435 *9 AGRA Admin Instr No. 6 14 March 45.* Instruction is attached to the war diary of 9 AGRA March 1945 (WO 171/4746).

436 In the literature various data have been presented regarding the artillery employment for 'Operation Widgeon'. I have based my presentation on attachments to *RA 7 Armd Div Operation Order No. 46 dated 22 March 1945*, which in its turn is attached to the war diary (WO 171/4173) and *Operation Plunder: Royal Artillery target maps* (WO 205/925). This Operation Order seems to be the most authoritative source.

437 *RA 15 (S) Inf Div Op O No. 1 dated 14 March 45*, which is attached to the war diary of 52 (L) Infantry Division (WO 171/4264).

438 More about this is in *RA 12 Corps Planning Instruction Second Army Op 'Plunder' 11 March 45* (WO 171/4059).

439 Op. cit. Note 422, Table 1.

440 Op. cit. Note 434.

441 *Notes for CRA's 2nd Conference on Pepperpot. 18 March 45.* Attachment to the war dairy of HQRA 3 Division (WO 171/4134).

442 Unfortunately the RAHQ XXX Corps war diary is missing, but the *Planning Notes* and *Operation Instructions* issued by the Corps Headquarters provide some information about the thoughts about artillery employment (WO 171/4077). The artillery order for 'Operation Plunder', *RA 30 Corps Operation Instruction No. 35 Operation Plunder, 20*

March 45 can however be found attached to war diaries of some subordinate units, e.g. 73 Anti-tank Regiment RA (WO 171/4776). The HQRA 51(H) Division war diary, in particular the attached *RA 51 Highland Div OO No. 13, 22 March 45* with all attachments provide valuable information about the details of the divisional fire plans (WO 171/4249).
443 Forty (2002), Appendix 5.
444 Ibid.
445 The presentation here is a summary of *RA 6 Airborne Div OO No.7, 16 March 45* and in particular its *Appendix 'F'*. See the war diary of HQRA 6 A/B Division (WO 171/4160).
446 Ibid. Appendix 'A'.
447 *Operation Plunder – Concentrations fired during neutralization programmes on hostile batteries.* Undated attachment to the war diary of March 45 for *Counter Battery Officer XXX Corps* (WO 171/4087).
448 Part of the report is included as No. 22 track of the CD disc *Churchill and Friends*. The Green Label Music Company. Leatherhead KT 24 6WQ.
449 *War Diary HQRA 15 (S) Division* (WO 171/4197).
450 Letter to the author from Brigadier (ret.) Sir Gilbert Heathcote Bart CBE, dated 4 February 2006.
451 Several references to the height can be found in the literature. Saunders (2001) writes 800–1,000 feet, i.e. 270–330m, others have the height to be around 200m.
452 Clegg's report is dated 17 June 1945 and was written for all the members of his regiment and includes a map over all regimental deployments in connection with Operation Plunder. The report and map is kept at British Library.
453 Saunders (2001), p. 303.
454 *Operation Varsity. Operation of XVIII US Corps in support of the Rhine Crossing 24–25 March 1945, Appendix E.* British Army of the Rhine. Battlefield Tour. December 1947.
455 *War Diary 53 (Airlanding) Light Regiment RA March 1945* (WO 171/4762).
456 Ibid. The figures are found in *53(WY) Airldg Lt Reg RA OO No. 1 19 March 1945*, which is attached to the war diary.
457 See the regimental war diary.
458 *War Diary 190 Field Regiment RA, 30 March 1945* (WO 171/4857).
459 Pemberton (1950), p. 273.
460 See e.g. Pemberton (1950), p. 273, and Bailey (2004), pp. 326–327.
461 In his letter (exact date of it unknown) Campbell argues in favour of restrictions in the application of large fire concentrations on just map references and not prior ranging. Too extensive lists with numerous target coordinates that might be used were wearing down command post staffs and increased the risk that their work is losing in precision and accuracy, a consequence of which is artillery fire at the wrong place and waste of ammunition. With his own words: 'It has lead everyone to believe that if a gun is aimed at a point that it will hit that point. This of course is far from the case as no gun, except by chance, will hit a point aimed at without ranging and a considerable expenditure of ammunition.' A consequence of the practice was to make the observation parties more like liaison detachments than fire controllers. So, he wanted much more of ranging and that FOOs/OPOs should act in their real capacity. He concluded: 'The un-ranged fire for all concentrations in front of our own troops is the method of fire which should be avoided.'

Campbell touches another problem, namely the importance of having the infantry to advance close behind the artillery fire in attack in order to be able to cut in on the enemy directly when the fire is lifted forwards, this irrespective of the nature of the covering fire, a creeping or rolling barrage, or timed concentrations. Often the infantry was far behind, often due to bad accuracy of large concentrations without prior ranging. We can see that this was a repeated 'system problem' through the war, and Campbell's letter was one of many expressions of opinions on central issues. His letter is attached to the war diary of 8 AGRA, March 1945 (WO 171/4745).

CHAPTER 23 – FROM DEFEAT TO SUCCESS – BURMA

462 Tsuji (1988) describes how the jungle battle technique was developed, e.g. on Formosa. pp. 1–13.

463 Aldrich (1993), pp. 189–194, 290–294, 319, 337–339, 345–347.
464 It might here be added that the famous cinema film *The Bridge on River Kwai* with Sir Alec Guiness as the main star character, Colonel Nicholson, has a certain true background from the campaign. It was the commanding officer of 135 Field Regiment RA, Lieutenant Colonel Tosey, and his captured gunners who built the bridge, or more correctly two bridges, one temporary and one permanent, the latter still existing. After the construction of the bridges Colonel Tosey became a much appreciated leader of the POWs in various prison camps, where he restlessly did what he could to improve the severe situation the prisoners encountered, often taking large personal risks. Thus assuming quite different a role than the one Colonel Nicholson had been given in the film. More about this in Davies (1991).
465 Farndale (2002): *The Far East Theatre 1941–1946, p. 50.*
466 Ibid. p. 105.
467 A more elaborated list is given by Lyman (2004), p. 77.
468 Slim had at this time gained great popularity amongst all units, and the soldiers affectionately called him 'Uncle Bill'.
469 Primary sources for this section has been Pemberton (1950), Bailey (2004) and – not the least – articles and books by Brigadier Bidwell. *RA Notes 1944* also have many interesting testimonies from the field. An attempt to summarise is e.g. *Employment of Artillery in Jungle Warfare*, RA Notes 1944, Para. 1260.
470 At Royal Artillery Museum in London a gun of this type is on display.
471 Farndale (2002): *The Far East Theatre 1941–46*, p. 341.
472 A summary of British experience of Japanese battle techniques and how local defence must be arranged is found in M.G.R.A. *Training Instruction No. 3 1944. Japanese methods of Counter Battery. 30.3 44* (RAHT MD/2791).
473 An often told example of what the Japanese could accomplish as regards infiltration was a case where a battery one morning found that a whole Japanese platoon during the night had dug in between the two troops of the battery without anybody noticing it. A company of Sikhs was needed to get the platoon wiped out to the last man.
474 Young (Osprey) tells that during the period 18th April to 22nd June 1944, when the encircled IV Corps comprised four infantry divisions and two armoured brigades, in total some 150,000 men, 1,043 tons of ammunition, 5,960 tons of other supplies and replacements were flown in. Around 15,000 wounded and 45,000 'non-combatants' were taken out with returning aircraft. At its peak around 200 aircraft/day arrived.
475 A gunner playing a distinguished role during the final months of the battle was Brigadier A.H. Hely, who was a much appreciated divisional artillery commander (CRA) of the 7th Indian Infantry Division. He is a good example of a skilled territorial officer whose capacity was observed early and taken advantage of. He was a dentist in his civilian life but in parallel with this served in the Territorial Army back home in England. When the war broke out his regiment was transferred to Egypt and there took part in the fighting 1940 and later. In 1942 he was regimental commander with the rank of Lieutenant Colonel until August that year when he was promoted Brigadier and positioned as artillery commander of the mentioned division. He established good relations and efficient cooperation with subordinate regimental commanders and superior commanders. In 1944 and 1945 he was the natural second-in-command of the division and was for periods during the final fighting acting divisional commander, maybe the only non-regular officer to reach this position. After the war he returned to civilian life and served as Chief Dentist.
476 Farndale (2002): *The Far East Theatre 1941–46*, p. 325.

Sources and Literature

Unpublished sources
Sources are listed below for the various operations presented in the book. It should be observed that also published sources listed below have been used for these presentations. Notes indicate which have been used. The list below is ended with 'Miscellaneous', which comprises some general sources such as handbooks, regulations, range tables and also important people contacted by the author. These have all been sources for the initial chapters as well.

CHAPTER 16 – BEF IN FRANCE 1939/1940
Excerpts from *War Diaries* (National Archives, Kew) with plans, orders, reports, battle logs etc. September 1939–June 1940:
-HQ 46 Infantry Division (WO 167/286)
-HQRA 3 Corps (WO 167/173)
-CCMA 1 Corps (WO 167/128)
-CCMA 2 Corps (WO 167/152)
-CCMA 3 Corps (WO 167/174)
-HQ 44 Division Signals Section (WO 167/279)
-HQRA 1 Division (WO 167/193)
-HQRA 2 Division (WO 164/206)
-HQRA 3 Division (WO 167/220)
-HQRA 4 Division (WO 167/232)
-HQRA 5 Division (WO 167/246)
-HQRA 42 Division (WO 167/268)

-2nd Regiment RHA (WO 167/463)
-7th Field Regiment RA (WO 167/468)
-9th Field Regiment RA (WO 167/469)
-10th Field Regiment RA (WO 167/471)
-16th Field Regiment RA (WO 167/472)
-18th Field Regiment RA (WO 167/474)
-19th Field Regiment RA (WO 167/475)
-57th Field Regiment RA (WO 167/485)
-70th Field Regiment RA (WO 167/491)
-72nd Field Regiment RA (WO 167/483)
-74th Field Regiment RA (WO 167/494)
-76th Field Regiment RA (WO 167/496)
-91st Field Regiment RA (WO 167/500)
-92nd Field Regiment RA (WO 167/501)
-99th Field Regiment RA (WO 167/504)

-1st Medium Regiment RA (WO 167/534):
-3rd Medium Regiment RA (WO 167/536)
-5th Medium Regiment RA (WO 167/538)
-51st Medium Regiment RA (WO 167/539)
-53rd Medium Regiment RA (WO 167/540)
-59th Medium Regiment RA (WO 167/545)
-69th Medium Regiment RA (WO 167/550)

-1st Survey Regiment RA (WO 167/571)
-2nd Survey Regiment RA (WO 167/572)
-3rd Survey Regiment RA (WO 167/573)

-*Personal Account Lieutenant Colonel Jack Parham, CO 10th Field Regiment, May-June 1940* (WO 197/128)
-*Personal Diary Major R. Gordon-Finlayson, 10th Field Regiment, May-June 1940* (WO 197/91)
-*1 Corps Operation Instruction No. 24, 22 April 1940. [Plan D]* (attached to War Diary of 1 Survey Regiment WO 167/571)
-*RA 1 Corps Operation Instruction No. 17, 13 April 1940. [Plan D]* (attached to War Diary of 1 Survey Regiment WO 167/571)
-Barry, J.R. Brigadier: *Extract from The Story of 5th Division RA in May 1940 as seen from HQRA.* (RAHT MD/2136)

CHAPTER 17 – NORWAY 1940
Excerpts from *War Diaries* (National Archives, Kew) with plans, orders, reports, battle logs etc. April–June 1940:
-HQ 24 (Guards) Brigade (WO 168/24)
-51st Field Regiment RA (WO 166/1483)
-203 Battery RA (WO 168/49)
-HQ NWEF Norway 1940 (WO 198/16)
-DAQMS (WO 168/10)

-*Movement Reports* (WO 198/10)
-*The Administrative History of the Operations in Scandinavia 1940* (WO 198/17)
-Auchinleck, C.J.E., Lieutenant General: *Report on Operations in Northern Norway from 13 May 1940 to 8 June 1940* (WO 168/9)
-*O.B. NWEF. Extracted from General Auchinleck's Report Box 1/6 13.5.40* (WO 169/9)

429

-*Movement Control Summary Norway 1940* (WO 198/4)
-Kolin, M.L.: *Polish Troops in Norway. A Photographic record of the campaign.* London 1943

Chapter 18 – Home Front
Excerpts from *War Diaries* (National Archives, Kew) with plans, orders, reports logs etc. June–September 1940, September–October 1941:
-HQRA 5 Corps (WO 166/253)
-HQRA 5 Division (WO 167/246)
-HQRA 50 Division (WO 167/302)
-HQRA 52 Division (WO 167/328)

-2nd Field Regiment RHA (WO 167/463)
-7th Field Regiment RA (WO 167/494)
-10th Field Regiment RA (WO 167/471)
-16th Field Regiment RA (WO 167/472)
-72nd Field Regiment RA (WO 167/483)
-74th Field Regiment RA (WO 167/494)
-76th Field Regiment RA (WO 167/496)
-92nd Field Regiment RA (WO 167/501)
-99th Field Regiment RA (WO 167/504)

-59th Medium Regiment RA (WO 167/545)
-69th Medium Regiment RA (WO 167/550)

-*Minimum Army Requirements for the first two years of the war.* Report from Ministry of Supply March, August and October 1940 (WO 185/95)
-*Exercise Bumper. Notes by RA Adviser for Chief Umpire.* Kirkman Papers, (RAHT MD/3138)
-*Comments on first exercise in which a modern divisional concentration was fired in England.* RA 38 Div. Instruction of Dec 1941. Parham Papers, (RAHT MD/188)
-*The Employment of Artillery in Mass.* Paper by General Parham in the Summer 1942, issued by C-in-C Home Forces at a conference at Larkhill on 8 June 1942, and used as the basis of Artillery tactics in the First Army Campaign in Tunisia. Parham Papers (RAHT MD/188)
-*Order of Battle of the Field Forces in the United Kingdom. Part 3. Royal Artillery* (amended up to December 26th 1940). (WO 212/4)
-*Order of Battle of the Field Forces in the United Kingdom. Part III. Infantry Divisions.* 4th July 1940 (WO 212/10)
-*Munitions situation at beginning of June 1940. Notes on Sir Walter Layton's Statement.* (WO 196/33).

Chapter 19 – El Alamein
Excerpts from *War Diaries* (National Archives, Kew) with plans, orders, fire plans, reports, battle logs etc. August–November 1942:
-BRA Eight Army (WO 169/2340)
-HQ 'G' XXX Corps (WO 169/4035)
-HQ 13th Corps (WO 169/4007)
-HQRA 10th Corps (WO 169/3983)
-HQRA XIII Corps (WO 169/4010)
-HQRA XXX Corps (WO 201/468)
-30th Corps CBO (WO 169/4039)
-HQ 'G' 7 Armd Division (WO 169/4087A)
-HQRA 1 Armd Division (WO 169/4056)
-HQRA 10 Armd Division (WO 169/4118)
-HQRA 44 Division (WO 169/4135)
-HQRA 50 Division (WO 169/4147)
-HQRA 51 (Highland) Division (WO 169/3938)

-1st Field Regiment RA (WO 169/4573)
-3rd Field Regiment RA (WO 169/4573)
-4th Field Regiment RA (WO 169/4575)
-11th Field Regiment RA (WO 169/4577)
-32nd Field Regiment RA (WO 169/4583)
-53th Field Regiment RA (WO 169/4586)
-57th Field Regiment RA (WO 169/4587)
-74th Field Regiment RA (WO 169/4593)
-98th Field Regiment RA (WO 169/4601)
-104th Field Regiment RA (WO 169/4562)
-111th Field Regiment RA (WO 169/4602)
-121st Field Regiment RA (WO 169/4604)
-124th Field Regiment RA (WO 169/4605)
-146th Field Regiment RA (WO 169/4610)
-154th Field Regiment RA (WO 169/4612)

-1st Field Regiment RHA (WO 169/4555)
-3rd Field Regiment RHA (WO 169/4557)
-4th Field Regiment RHA (WO 169/4558)
-5th Field Regiment RHA (WO 169/4559)
-11th Field Regiment (HAC) RHA (WO 169/4560)

-7th Medium Regiment RA (WO 169/4649)
-64th Medium Regiment RA (WO 169/4651)
-69th Medium Regiment RA (WO 169/4654)

-1st Survey Regiment RA (WO 169/4681)
-4th Survey Regiment RA (WO 169/4684)
-No. 1 Composite Battery, 4th Survey Regiment RA (WO 169/4685)
-No. 2 Composite Battery, 4th Survey Regiment RA (WO 169/4690)
-'A' Tp 4th Survey Regiment RA (WO

169/4686)
-'B' Tp 4th Survey Regiment RA (WO 169/4691)
-'R' Tp 4th Survey Regiment RA (WO 169/4687)
-'S' Tp 4th Survey Regiment RA (WO 169/4692)

-*RA Notes on El Alamein* [Kirkman] (WO 201/431)
-*Planning Defensive Operations* (WO 201/423)
-*Eight Army 'Lightfoot'. Planning* (WO 201/646)
-*HQRA 13th Corps 'Lightfoot'* (WO 201/648)
-*30 Corps Artillery Operation Order No. 18, 13 Oct 42* (RAHT MD/301)
-*2 NZ Division Operation Order No. 17,* (see WO 171/646)
-*Minutes of Conference held at Tac HQ, Eight Army, at 02.30 hrs 25 Oct 1942* (see WO 601/248)
-*Decisions given by Army Commander at Conference held at HQ 2 NZ Div at 12.00 hrs 25 Oct 1942* (see WO 171/648)
-*9 Aust Division Summary of Artillery Operations 23 Oct–4 Nov 42* (WO 201/597)
-*Lessons from Operations* (WO 204/7000)
-Bidwell, R.G.S., Brigadier: *El Alamein and Memories of E Battery HAC – 25 years ago* (RAHT MD/761)
-Bingham, C.W., Captain, 60. FR RA: Brev till Brigadier Hallifax 12-1-42 (RAHT MD/1689)
-Brown, W.J., Captain: *Battle of Alamein. Account of 126th (Highland) Field Regt. RA* (RAHT MD/4312)
-Horrocks, Brian, Lieutenant General: *Battle of El Halfa* (CAB 201/423)
-Rowe, Tim, Sergeant: *Steve Weir – New Zealand's Master Gunner*. New Zealand Army Military Studies Institute, No.4 – May 2004 (RAHT MD/3520).

CHAPTER 20 – NORMANDY
Excerpts from *War Diaries* (National Archives, Kew) with plans, orders, fire plans, reports logs etc. June–August 1944:
-HQRA 2nd Army (WO 171/234)
-HQRA I Corps (WO 171/263). Many attachments, e.g. regarding counter-mortar plans, intelligence reports about German air activities etc.
-HQRA VIII Corps (WO 171/294). Several Operation Orders, *Battle Log* etc.
-HQ 4 AGRA (WO 171/907)
-HQ 8 AGRA (WO 171/909)

-HQRA 3 Division (WO 171/414)
-HQRA Guards Armd Division (WO 171/380)
-HQRA 11 Armd Division (WO 171/458)
-HQRA 43 (Wessex) Division (WO 171/486)

-7th Field Regiment RA (WO 171/969)
-14th Field Regiment RA (WO 171/987)
-25th Field Regiment RA (WO 171/970)
-33rd Field Regiment RA (WO 171/971)
-55th Field Regiment RA (WO 171/972)
-76th Field Regiment RA (WO 171/976), attached is divisional order for *Operation Overlord*
-94th Field Regiment RA (WO 171/983)
-112th (Wessex) Field Regiment RA (WO 171/985)
-126th Field Regiment RA (WO 171/988)
-147th Field Regiment RA (WO 171/995)
-150th Field Regiment RA (WO 171/996)
-151st Field Regiment RA (WO 171/997)
-153rd Field Regiment RA (WO 171/998)
-179th Field Regiment RA (WO 171/999)
-191st Field Regiment RA (WO 171/1004)

-3rd Field Regiment RHA (WO 171/1009)
-13th Field Regiment (HAC) RHA (WO 171/1015)

-61st Medium Regiment RA (WO 171/1057)
-63rd Medium Regiment RA (WO 171/1058)
-77th Medium Regiment RA (WO 171/1064)
-10th Survey Regiment RA (WO 171/1076)

-Three articles which the author has received from Major General Tony Richardson, who served as a subaltern with 147th Field Regiment RA and landed in Normandy:
  -*The Assault of the Normandy beaches by 231 Brigade of 50 Northumbrian Division, supported by 147 Essex Yeomanry Field Regiment (SP) RA 6–8 June 1944*
  -*The Battle of the Bridge-head*
  -*The attack on Rauray by the 12th Battalion The King's Royal Rifle Corp on 26 June 1944.*
-*Landing Tables Overlord 1 Corps & 30 Corps.* Parham Papers RAHT MD/188
-Fanshawe, G.D., Major General: Personal account on the preparations before the landing in Normandy and how this was done, as he experienced it as commander of 86th Field Regiment RA. The regiment landed with 'Sexton' SP guns (RAHT MD/1661)
-Neilson, I.G., Lieutenant Colonel: *The Story of B Flight 652 AOP Squadron RAF 11th June–15th August 1944.* The account is part of a

longer presentation by Neilson, which is available in RAHT MD/3301/5
-*2nd Army 'G' Ops Operation Goodwood* (WO 205/1121). Includes:
  -*The 'Goodwood Meeting' 18–21 July 1944.* D.T.I. War Office 30 Oct 1944
  -*Operation by Bomber Command in Close Support of the Army – Caen, 18th July, 1944.* Tactical Bulletin No. 38. Prepared by Air Ministry, July 23rd 1944
  -*Corps Comd's Notes on 'Goodwood Meeting'.* Lieutenant General R.N. O'Connor, Commander 8 Corps, 9 Sep 1944
  -*Notes by Comd 8 Corps on the deployment of armour in battle.* Lieutenant General R.N. O'Connnor, Commander 8 Corps, 26 Jul 44
  -*RA 8 Corps Op Order No. 2.*
-*Artillery Re-organisation Programme.* 21 Army Group July 1944 (WO 205/22)
-Beck, Sidney: *341 Battery 86th Field Regiment RA (Herts Yeomanry) War Diary.* Personal diary, letters etcetera covering his service as *Gun Position Officer* in the regiment from June 1944 to the end of the war in 1945 (, a more complete version is IWM 03/28/01)
-RA Notes No. 20, 1944:
  -*French Comments on Allied Artillery in Normandy.* Appendix 'B'
-RA Notes 1944, Para 1204:
  -*Operations in France since 6 June 44.*

CHAPTER 21 – OPERATION MARKET GARDEN
Excerpts from *War Diaries* (National Archives, Kew) with plans, orders, fire plans, reports logs etc. August–September 1944:
-HQRA 2nd Army War Diary (WO 171/3970)
-HQ 'G', XXX Corps War Diary (WO 171/ 341)
-HQ 69 Infantry Brigade War Diary (WO 171/651
-HQ 130 Infantry Brigade War Diary (WO 171/660)
-HQ 214 Infantry Brigade War Diary (WO 171/708)
-HQRA Guards Armoured Division War Diary (WO 171/380)
-HQRA 43 (Wessex) Division War Diary (WO 171/486)
-HQRA 50 (Northumbrian) Division War Diary (WO 171/517)
-HQRA 52 (Lowland) Division War Diary (WO 171/543)
-'B' Counter Battery Officers Staff, 30 Corps War Diary (WO 171/350)
-1 Air Landing Light Regiment RA War Diary (WO 171/1016)
-1 FOU War Diary (WO 171/964)

-55th Field Regiment RA War Diary (WO 171/972)
-74th Field Regiment RA War Diary (WO 171/975)
-79th Field Regiment RA War Diary (WO 171/977):
-90th Field Regiment RA War Diary (WO 171/982)
-94th Field Regiment RA War Diary (WO 171/983)
-112th Field Regiment RA War Diary (WO 171/985)
-124th Field Regiment RA War Diary (WO 171/987)
-147th Field Regiment RA War Diary (WO 171/995)
-151st Field Regiment RA War Diary (WO 171/997)
-153rd Field Regiment RA War Diary (WO 171/998)
-179th Field Regiment RA War Diary (WO 171/999)
-477 Bty/112th Field Regiment RA War Diary (WO 171)

-7th Medium Regiment RA War Diary (WO 171/1047)
-64th Medium Regiment RA War Diary (WO 171/1059)
-84th Medium Regiment RA War Diary (WO 171/1066)

-4th Survey Regiment RA War Diary (WO 171/1072)
-7th Survey Regiment War Diary (WO 171/1073)
-47th Battery/4th Survey Regiment War Diary (WO 171/1078)
-48th Battery/4th Survey Regiment War Diary (WO 171/1079)

-73th Anti-Tank Regiment RA War Diary (WO 171/924)
-662 AOP Squadron RAF War Diary (WO 171/1029)
-*Air Notes No. 134–140, 18–26 September 44.* The reports are attached to War Diary HQ 'G' XXX Corps (WO 171/341)

-*Operation Market Garden 17–26 September.* Report prepared by headquarters XXX Corps (IWM Walch Papers 01/11/1–2
-*30 Corps Operation Instruction No. 24 Operation 'Garden'. 15 Sep 44 with Amendments 16 Sep 44.* Appendix B of this summarizes the Operation Order for '*Market*'. Is included in WO 171/341, which also comprises Intelligence Log and various Orders of Battle. A detailed Order of Battle for 52 (Lowland) Infantry Division is also attached
-*30 Corps Movement Instruction for Operation 'Garden', 15 Sep 44.* Also comprising an instruction for traffic control. To be found in WO 171/341
-*30 Corps Operation Instruction No. 25. 23 Sep 44,* see WO 171/241
-*'1st Airborne Division September 1944'*, Album (WO 205/1250)
-*Artillery at Arnhem.* RA Notes 1944, para 1312
-Personal account from battle of Arnhem by Lieutenant Colonel 'Sheriff' Thompson, 1 Airlanding Light Regiment RA (WO 171/1016)
-Extract from History of 420 & 419 Batteries, 52nd (Bedfordshire Yeomanry) Heavy Regiment, September/October 1944, (Douglas Godddard's Archive)
-*On the Banks of Rhine.* Chapter Seven, Personal Account by Major E.R.D. Palmer, OC 419 Battery 52nd (Bedfordshire Yeomanry) Heavy Regiment (Douglas Goddard's Archive)
-Personal War Diary by Lieutenant Douglas Goddard, 220 Battery/112th Field Regiment RA (Douglas Goddard's archive)
-*112 Fd Regt. RA Operation Order No.2 17 Sep 44* (Douglas Goddard's Archive)
-*Operation 'Market'. Instruction No 1 to Major General R.E. Urquhart DSO, Commander 1 British Airborne Division, with 1 Polish Parachute Brigade under Command, 13 September 44* (Douglas Goddard's Archive)
-*1 Airborne Division Operation Instruction No. 9 12 September 44* (Douglas Goddard's Archive)
-*Operation Market Garden 1944 as recorded by* T.W. Kent [BSM] *in the personal scrapbook of his 30 years service in the Royal Artillery. April 4th 1932 to April 3rd 1962* (RAHT MD/1390)
-*RA Gds Armd Div Op Order dated 16 Sep 44. Operation 'GARDEN'* (WO 171/380)
-*Operation MARKET. Notes on CRA's Orders given at 12 Sep.* (IWM 92/4/1)
-*Operation Market Garden.* Report in HQRA 1 Airborne Division Report on the Arnhem Operation 17–26 September 1944 (RAHT MD/1437)
-*Lessons Learned September 1944* (WO 205/623)
-RA Notes 1944, Para 1312: *Artillery at Arnhem*
-de Burgh, P.R.R., Colonel: *Research Notes on 1 Air Landing Light Regiment RA and other units of 6th Airborne Divisional Artillery in North West Europe 1944–1945 especially at Arnhem.* (RAHT MD/2213)
-Baines, David, Brigadier: *25/26 Medium Battery North West European Campaign 1944–45. The Battle Axe Company Maude's Battery. Personal War Diary*
-*Battery Diary 341 Battery 86th Field Regiment RA (Herts Yeomanry) 3 June 1944 to 9 April 1946. Compiled by Lieutenant Beck (B Troop GPO) from the Battery Cmd Post Log and Extracts from Letters to his Wife*
-Berry, John, BSc: *Communications at the battle of Arnhem: A modern day technical analysis.* ATDI Ltd, Crawley, White Paper, 2004
-Briggs, Jack, Bombardier: *Arnhem A Personal View.* Briggs was NCO Signals at E Troop of 1 Airlanding Light Regiment RA. His report is included in the archival material of Colonel Paddy de Burgh at James Clavell Library (RAHT MD/2213)
- J.T. Whetton & R.H. Ogden: *Z Location or Survey in War. The story of the 4th Durham Survey Regiment Royal Artillery.* (www.94locating.net)
-Harrison, C.A., Captain: Unpublished memoirs from his service as troop commander of 1 Airlanding Light Regiment during the battle of Arnhem (IWM 82/33/1)
-Robertson, J.P., Major: *Sixty Glorious Days.* Unpublished memoirs covering the period August–September 1944 when he served as troop commander in 55 Field Regiment RA (IWM 03/55/1)
-Ross, Walter J.M., Major: Personal report regarding the preparations made by 80th (Lowland) Field Regiment RA for employment in Holland.. The regiment belonged to 52 (Lowland) Infantry Division. See – inter alia – Chapter VIII with the headline *The Airtransportable Role – A Diversion* (RAHT archive at James Clavell Library)
-Stewart-Richardson, P.N., Brigadier: Personal archive with many documents about British airborne operations 1942–1960 (IWM 92/43/1). Here the report that 1 Airborne Division presented on 10 January 1945 signed

by General Urquhart: *1 Airborne Division Report on Operation Market Garden, Part I–V* is included. In the archive all divisional and brigade orders for this operation are available
-Walch, A.G., Brigadier: Personal archive (IWM 01/11/1–2) with his memoir for the years 1926–1945. Walch was General Browning's Chief of Staff in 1 British Airborne Corps at the time of Operation Market Garden. Much material about all British airborne operations in 1942–1945 are available including a detailed report about the landings of 82nd and 101st American Airborne Division and their battle engagement. Other important documents are the report on Operation Market Garden prepared by XXX Corps and the report prepared by Walch himself with the title *Allied Airborne Operations in Holland September–October 1944*
-Hunt, H.S., Lieutenant Colonel: Personal archive (IWM 06/4/1) with his diary from the whole period when serving as commander of 64 Medium Regiment
-Krafft, Sepp: *SS Panzer Grenadier Ausbildungs- und Ersatzbat. 16 in den Kämpfen bei Arnhem 17.9.44 –7.10.44* (English translation of the German original is available in WO 205/1124)
-About American airborne artillery see http://www.ww2-airborne.us/units
-*Lessons Learned Operation 'Market Garden'* (WO205/623).

CHAPTER 22 – THE RHINE CROSSING – OPERATION VERITABLE AND OPERATION PLUNDER.
Excerpts from *War Diaries* (National Archives, Kew) with plans, orders, fire plans, reports logs etc. January–March 1945:
-HQ 21 Army Group (WO 205/11)
-Operation Plunder. Targets March 1945 (WO 205/925)
-HQRA 12 Corps. War Diary February–March 1945 (WO 171/4059)
-HQ 30 Corps 'G' Staff. War Diary. March 1945 (WO 171/4077)
-HQ 30 Corps 'G' Staff. Planning Notes. March 1945 (WO 171/4077)
-HQ 30 Corps 'G' Staff. Operation Instructions. March 1945 (WO 171/4077)
-HQ 30 Corps 'G' Staff. Operation Log. March 1945 (WO 171/4077)
-CBO 30 Corps. War Diary February–March 1945 (WO 171/4087)
-HQRA 3 AGRA. War Diary February–March 1945 (WO 171/4742)
-HQRA 4 AGRA. War Diary February–March 1945 (WO 171/4743)
-HQRA 5 AGRA. War Diary February–March 1945 (WO 171/4744)
-HQRA 8 AGRA. War Diary February–March 1945 (WO 171/4745)
-HQRA 9 AGRA. War Diary February–March 1945 (WO 171/4746)
-HQRA 3 Division. War Diary January–March 1945 (WO 171/4134)
-HQRA 4 Armoured Division. War Diary March 1945 (WO 171/4173)
-HQRA 6 Airborne Division. War Diary January–April 1945 (WO 171/4160)
-HQRA 7 Armoured Division. War Diary February–March 1945 (WO 171/4179)
-HQRA 15 (S) Division. War Diary February–March 1945 (WO 171/4197)
-HQRA 51 (H) Division. War Diary. February–March 1945 (WO 171/4249)
-HQRA 52 (L) Division. War Diary March 1945 (WO 171/4264)
-HQRA 53 (W) Division. War Diary February 1945 (WO 171/5472)
-HQRA 53 (W) Division. War Diary March 1945 (WO 171/5473)

-53rd (Airlanding) Light Regiment. War Diary January–May 1945 (WO 171/4762)
-4th Field Regiment RHA. War Diary WO 171/5081)
-25th Field Regiment RA. War Diary (WO/171/4814)
-131st Field Regiment RA. War Diary (WO 171/4843)
-181st Field Regiment RA. War Diary (WO 171/4854)
-190th Field Regiment RA. War Diary (WO 171/4857)

-4th Survey Regiment RA. War Diary February–March 1945 (WO 171/5112).
-73rd Anti-Tank Regiment RA. War Diary February–March 1945 (WO 171/4776)
-658 AOP Squadron RAF. War Diary February–March 1945 (WO 171/4751)
-*RA 12 Corps Planning Instruction Second Army Op 'Plunder' 11 March 45* (WO 171/4059)
-*RA 30 Corps Operation Instruction No. 35 Operation Plunder 20 March 45* (available in

War Diary of 73 Anti-tank Regiment RA WO 171/4776)
-30 Corps Operation Instruction No. 49 dated 20 March 45 (available amongst Op Instructions in WO 171/4077)
-RA 15 (S) Inf Division Op O No. 1 14 March 45 (available as attachment to the War Diary of 52 (Lowland) Infantry Division WO 171/4264)
-RA 6 Airborne Div OO No. 7 16 March 45. Important attachment is *Appendix F* (WO 171/4160)
-Notes for CRA's 2nd Conference on Pepperpot 18 March 45 (available as Attachment to the War Diary of 3 Infantry Division WO 171/4134)
-9 AGRA Adm Instr No. 6 14 March 45 (available as Attachment to the War Diary WO 171/4746)
-*Operation Plunder – Concentrations fired during neutralization programmes on hostile batteries* (is undated Attachment to the War Diary of Counter Battery Officer XXX. Corps WO 171/4087)
-*Z Location*. Chapter Twenty Two. Operation Plunder 24 March to 2 May 1945
-*CB Air Support (WO 205/545)*
-*Air Support in Counter Bty Role*. Main HQ First Cdn Army, 4 Mar 45 (WO 205/545)
-Norman Marshall, William, Lieutenant Colonel CO 90 HAA Regiment: *The Crossing of Rhine March 1945*. (RAHT MD/3189/1)
-*Report on the Operation to clear the area between the River Maas and the River Rhine 8 February to 10 March 1945*. Besides XXX Corps Operation Order a detailed map on the artillery deployment south-east of Nijmegen for Operation Veritable is available (RAHT MD 1385)
-RA Notes 1945, Para 1698–1701: *Artillery Support in Operation Veritable*. Based on a Canadian report
-Norman, William, Lieutenant Colonel (CO 90 Heavy Anti-Aircraft Regt. RA): *The Crossing of the Rhine March 1945* (RAHT MD/3189/1)
-Ruston, E.W., Major (Commanding Officer 451 Battery/1. Mountain Regt RA): *The Rhine Crossing at Wesel, March 23 1945* (RAHT MD/4018)
-*A Short History of 12 Corps in France, Belgium, Holland & Germany. May 1944–May 1945* (WO 205/1163)
-*12 Corps Lessons From The Campaign in N.W. Europe. June 1944 – May 1945* (WO 205/1163).

CHAPTER 23 – BURMA
Excerpts from *War Diaries* (National Archives, Kew) with plans, orders, fire plans, reports logs etc. 1944–1945:
-HQRA 4th Corps War Diary March–Aug 44 (WO 172/4193)
-HQRA 4th Corps War Diary Jan–July 45 (WO 172/6898)
-HQRA 2 Division War Diary Feb–July 44 (WO 172/4250)
-HQRA 2 Division War Diary Jan–July 45 (WO 172/6954)
-HQRA 5 (Ind) Division War Diary Jan–July 44 (WO 172/4203)
-HQRA 7 (Ind) Division War Diary 1944 (WO 172/4292)
-HQRA 7 (Ind) Division War Diary Jan–Aug 45 (WO 172/6978)
-HQRA 17 (Ind) Division War Diary Jan–June 45 (WO 172/6988)
-HQRA 20 (Ind) Division War Diary 1945 (WO 172/7011)
-HQRA 23 (Ind) Division War Diary Jan–Feb 45 (WO 171/7023)

-4th Field Regiment RA War Diary Jan–July 44 (WO 172/4638)
-9th Field Regiment RA War Diary Jan–July 44 (WO 172/4640)
-158th Field Regiment RA War Diary Jan–June 44 (WO 172/4657)

-*2 Div Arty Operation Order No. 3, 23 Feb 45* (RA MD/ 2791)
-*MGRA's Training Instruction No. 3, Japanese Methods of Counter Battery, 30.3.1944* (RAHT MD/2791)
-Bailey, R.D.W., 'C' Flight, 656 Air Op Squadron RAF: *Personal Experiences in the 7th Div 'Admin Box' 4th–24th February 1944*. (RAHT MD/ Blue Box 2)
-Brown, J.F., Captain: *Guns over Burma* (RAHT MD/1463)
-Ferguson, I.M, Captain: *Field Artillery in Jungle Warfare* (RAHT MD/1844)
-Leigh, R.F.D, Colonel: *33 Ind Corps Artillery supporting the crossing of Irrawaddy by 2 and 20 Divs*. (RAHT MD/2135)
-Leach, L.H., Lieutenant Colonel *Personal Story of his Service in India 1942–1945* (RAHT MD/Blue Box 2)
-Leigh, R.F.D, *Action of 33 Ind Corps Artillery in mopping up Operations*. (RAHT MD/2135)

-Nicholson, R.A.G., Brigadier: *The Road to Mandalay. The March of 115 Field Regiment RA, 19 Indian (Dagger) Division* (RAHT MD/ 3372)
-Sewell, E.R.A, Colonel: *Diary of 155 Field Regiment (Lancashire Yeomanry) RA in Malaya 8 December 1941 to 15 February 1942.* (RAHT MD/2386)
-Tucker, K.W: *Artillery in the Campaign in Burma.* [large transcript] (RAHT MD/ 2635)
-Uniacke, R.J., Lieutenant Colonel: *Diary 16th Field Regiment RA* (RAHT MD/Blue Box 2)
-*18 Divisional Artillery – War Diary relating to Singapore and Chiangi February 1942.* (RAHT MD/2673)
-*135 Field Regiment RA (TA) diary of the Campaign in Malaya and Singapore 13 January 1942 to 11 February 1942.* (RAHT MD/ 2756)
-*Jungle Jottings 1945* [presentation of experiences, around 100 pages] (RAHT, likely MD/1156)
-Royal Artillery Notes contain a large number of reports and summaries of experiences from Burma, including the following (only paragraphs given):
    -1943, paragraph 281 with attachment
    -1944, paragraphs 823, 824, 934, 1070–1075, 1160, 1201–1203, 1260 with attachments
    -1945, paragraphs 1594, 1941 with attachments.
-Messervy Papers, The Liddell Hart Military Archives, King's College:
    7 Div Commander's Operational Notes Crossing of Irrawaddy by 7 Indian Division 14 Febr 1945
    History of Twelfth Army
    Japanese Account of their Operations Dec 1941–Aug 1945
    Operations 4 Corps Oct 44–6 May 45
    Operations 4 Corps 6 May 45–15 Aug 45

CHAPTER 24 – GUNNERS WE HAVE MET
About General Parham:
—Evans, Nigel: *British Artillery in World War 2.* The Chapter *Distinguished Gunners*, pp. 8–9
-Farndale (1996): *Some Prominent Gunners of the Second World War*, p. 306
-Mead, Peter, Brigadier: *Gunners at War 1939–1945*, pp. 16–17, 53
-Who Was Who 1971–1980, Vol. VII, London 1981
-Mead, P.W.: *Major General Hetman Jack Parham, CBE, DSO.* Manuscript for obituary (RAHT MD/188/6)
About General Kirkman:
-Evans, Nigel: *British Artillery in World War 2.* Chapter *Distinguished Gunners*, p. 4
-Hughes, B.P., Major General: *General Sir Sidney Chevalier Kirkman, GCB, KBE, MC, 29 July 1895–5 November 1982.* Royal Artillery Journal, Vol. CX, pp. 3–5
-Parker, K.A.L., Assistant Under Secretary of State: *A Personal View.* Royal Artillery Journal, Vol. CX, pp. 5–6
-Farndale (1996): *Some Prominent Gunners of the Second World War*, pp. 301–302
-Who Was Who 1981–1990, Vol. VIII, London 1991

About Lieutenant Colonel, Professor John Whetton:
Sources used are obituaries and documents provided by his nephew Jim Whetton. The latter is writing a biography about his uncle.

About the subalterns:
Sources used are in the first place discussions and correspondence with the ex-subalterns as well as articles and books published by them. As regards Sidney Beck all correspondence has been with his son Benjamin Beck.

UNPUBLISHED SOURCES – MISCELLANEOUS
-*Royal Artillery 'Blue List' May 1938*
-*General Return of the Regimental Strength of the British Army* (selected points of time 1939–1943)
-*Engelskt ridande raketbatteri under svenskt överbefäl i kriget 1813–1814.* Försvarsstaben Krigshistoriska Avdelningen (In Swedish, available at James Clavell Library)
-*Sound Ranging and Observation (Flash Spotting). A Survey of the Operational Methods and the Accuracies Achieved in B.L.A. and Italy (June 1944 – May 1945).* Operational Research Group (Weapons & Equipment) Report No. 338
-*The Production History of the 25 pdr Field Equipment.* Ministry of Supply. The Directorate of Weapons Production. Feb 1947 (RAHT MD 1599)
-*The Production History of the 4.5"/5.5" Field Equipment.* Ministry of Supply. The Directorate of Weapons Production. July 1946 (RAHT MD 1599)
-*Extract from the Company History concerning the production of 25, 17 and 6 pr Guns during the Second World War.* G.J. Weir Limited (RAHT

MD/3059)
-*Artillery Lessons Campaign in Italy 1943–45. Report for a conference at Artillery School, Larkhill August 1945* (RAHT MD/486)
-Gibson, John D.: *'The Eye in the Sky' The Evolution of Artillery Air Observation Part II 1918 to the Present*. April 1997 (RAHT MD 2794)
-*Royal Artillery Notes 1943*
-*Royal Artillery Notes 1944*
-*Royal Artillery Notes 1945*
-Lewis, T.W.: *'Long Traverse from Juno'. Recollections of the Campaign in North West Europe by members of 7 Survey Regiment RA June 1944 to May 1945* (RAHT MD/2664)
-Powell, Robin, Major: *The Battle of Able* (RAHT Blue Box 2)
-Artillery Training Volume I:
    -Pamphlet No. 5, *Information, Reconnaissance, Local protection and Ammunition supply* 1942
-Artillery Training Volume III, Field Gunnery (RAHT):
    -Pamphlet No. 2 *Preparation For Opening Fire* 1943
    -Pamphlet No. 3, Part I *Fire Discipline and Observation of Fire* 1942
    -Pamphlet No. 3, Part III *Concentrations of Observed Fire* 1943
    -Pamphlet No. 4, *Engagement of Targets by Observed Fire* 1947
    -Pamphlet No. 6 & 6A, *Programme Shoots (Barrages and Concentrations)* 1942
    -Pamphlet No. 12A, *Concentrations of Observed Fire* 1944
    -Pamphlet No. 13A, *Engagement of Targets by Observed Fire* 1944
    -Pamphlet No. 14A, *Regimental Survey*, August 1944
-Flash spotting training (RAHT):
-Pamphlet No. 1 *Air Burst Ranging* (for use by Survey Regiments RA) 1944
Pamphlet No. 2 *Short Base Observation* (for use by Survey Regiments RA) 1942
-Directions for the use of Artillery Instruments, Pamphlet No. 2, *Artillery Boards* 1936 with Amendments 1944
-*Handbook for the Q.F. 18.pr, Marks IV, IVA abd IVB Guns, Addendum (No. 2) Ordnance, Q.F. 25-pr, Mark I, 1938*
-*Handbook for the Ordnance Q.F. 25-pr, Marks II and III, 1944*
-*Identifivation List for Ordnance Q.F. 25-pr Mark I Gun on 25/18-pr Mark IVP Carriage, 1942*
-*Identifivation List for Ordnance Q.F. 25-pr Marks 2, 2/1, 3, 3/1 & 4, 1950*
-*Range Table (Part 1) QF 25-pr Guns Mark I and II, 1944*
-*Range Tables B.L. 5.5-inch Gun Mark III, 1943 (100 lb shell)*
-*Protractors* (RAHT MD/4583)
-*Gun Drill for B.L. 5.5-inch Mark 3 Gun, 1945*
-*Operational Research in NW Europe – the work of No. 2 Operational Research Sections with 21 Army Group, June 1944–July 1945*, Report No. 21: *Accuracy of Predicted Fire – Operation Veritable*
-Army Operational Research Group Report No. 217: *Study of Accuracy of Artillery Fire. Preliminary Trials*, 28 September 1944 (WO 291/200)
-Army Operational Research Group Report No. 249: *Study of Accuracy of Artillery Fire. Trials 2, 3 and 4*, 5th April 1945 (WO 291/231)
-Wilkinson, Peter, Captain MC: *Early Times with the Royal Artillery. Some notes for the information of Stig Moberg, Sweden*. April 2004
-Correspondence with a large number of distinguished persons in Great Britain (Author's archive). I would like to mention the following in particular:
    -Bailey, Jonathan B.A., Major General, CB, MBE, Ph D
    -Coghlan, John, Lieutenant Colonel, MBE, TD
    -Goddard, Douglas, Major, MBE, FCIS
    -Heathcote, Sir Gilbert, Brigadier, Bart, CBE
    -Richardson, Tony, Major General, CB, MBE
    -Townend, William, Lieutenant Colonel
    -Wilkinson, Peter, Captain, MC.

The correspondence with L van Aardt has been interesting. He is living in South Africa, but was brought up in a farmer's family in Kenya, maybe due to this he was an officer of King's African Rifles during the war. He served in Burma as a platoon commander in 11 (East African) Division.

With military historians in the Netherlands I have had over the years an extensive correspondence, in particular with persons with special interest in British organisation, equipments and operations in World War II such as:
-Bob Gerritsen (specialist on Operation Market Garden. Co-author of *Arnhem Bridge – Target Mike One*)
-Meulstee, Louis (specialist on British wireless equipments)

-Hans Onderwater (although a Dutch citizen official historian of No. II Army Cooperation Squadron RAF)
-Voskuil, Robert, Drs (specialist on Operation Market Garden).

Published sources and a selection of literature

Ailsby, Christopher: *Hitler's Sky Warriors, German Paratroopers in Action 1939–1945.* Dulles Virginia, Brassey's 2000
Alanbrooke, Field Marshal Lord: *War Diaries 1939–1945.* London, Phoenix Press 2003
Aldrich, Richard J.: *The Key to the South. Britain, the United States, and Thailand during the Approach of the Pacific War 1929–1942.* Kuala Lumpur, Malaysia, Oxford University Press 1993
Bailey, J.B.A., Major General: *Field Artillery and Firepower.* Annapolis, Maryland, Naval Institute Press 2004
Bailey, J.B.A., Major General: *Great Power Strategy in Asia. Empire, culture and trade 1905–2005.* New York, Routledge 2007
Barnett, Correlli: *Britain and her Army. A Military, Political and Social History of the British Army 1509–1970.* London, Cassell & Co 2000 (1970)
Barnett, Correlli: *Hitlers Generaler* (in Swedish). Stockholm 2004 (English original, London 1989)
Bayly, Christopher and Harper, Tim: *Forgotten Armies. The Fall of British Asia 1941–1945.* London, Allen Lane 2004
Bazeley, H.C., Lieutenant Colonel: *The History and Development of Counter-Battery Operations by Air O.P.* Royal Artillery Journal, Vol. LXXV, No. 1, pp. 31–44
Bevis, Mark: *British and Commonwealth Armies 1939–43.* Solihull Westmidlands, Helion and Company 2004
Bidwell, R.G.S., Brigadier: *The Development of British Field Artillery Tactics. Old Principles – New Methods 1940–1943.* Royal Artillery Journal, Vol. XCV, No. 1 1968
Bidwell, R.G.S., Brigadier: *The Development of British Field Artillery Tactics 1940–1942. The Desert War.* Royal Artillery Journal, Vol. XCIV, pp. 83–93
Bidwell, Shelford: *Gunners at War.* London, Arrow Books 1972
Bidwell, Shelford & Graham, Dominick: *Fire-Power. British Army Weapons and Theories of War 1939–1945.* London 1982
Bonnet, P.R.F., Major General: *A Short History of the Royal Regiment of Artillery.* London, Royal Artillery Historical Trust 1994
British Army of the Rhine: *Operation Plunder. 12 British Corps crossing the Rhine 23–25 March 1945. Battlefield Tour.* December 1947
British Army of the Rhine: *Operation Varsity. Operation of XVIII US Corps in support of the Rhine Crossing 24–25 March 1945. Battlefield Tour.* December 1947
Bungay, Stephen: *Alamein.* London, Aurum Press 2003
Burlison, C.J., Lieutenant Colonel: *Dunkirk to D-Day – At Home.* Royal Artillery Commemoration Book, pp.46–59
Carver, Field Marshal Lord: *El Alamein.* Ware, Herfordshire, Wordsworth Editions 2000
Carver, Field Marshal Lord: *The Imperial War Museum Book of the War in Italy 1943–1945.* London, Pan Books 2002
Chant, Christopher: *Artillery of World War II.* Near Rochester, Kent, Grange Books 2001
Chant, Christopher: *Warfare and the Third Reich. The Rise and the Fall of Hitler's Armed Forces.* New York 1996
Churchill, Winston S.: *The Second World War* Volume I–VI. London, Cassell & Co. 1948–1954
Clark, Lloyd: *Anzio The Fricition of War.* London, Headline Review 2007
Daglish, Ian: *Operation Goodwood.* Barnsley, South Yorkshire, Pen & Sword Military 2004
Davies, Peter N, Professor: *The Man behind the Bridge. Colonel Toosey and the River Kwai.* London, Athlone Press Ltd. 1991
Deighton, Len: *Blitzkrieg. From the rise of Hitler to the fall of Dunkirk.* London, Jonathan Cape Ltd. 1979
Delaforce, Patrick: *Monty's Iron Sides.* Stroud, Glousterhire, Sutton Publishing 2002
Dildy, Douglas C: *See Osprey*
Dimmock, H-L-F, Lieutenant Colonel: *Artillery Recruit Training.* Royal Artillery Journal, Vol. 69, No. 3, pp.163–171
Doyle, Paul A.: *Where the Lysanders were.* North Weald Essex, Forward Airfield Research Publishing 1995
Dunn, R.H.W., Major: *Reminiscences of a Regimental Officer, Horse Artillery at Knightsbridge.* Royal Artillery Journal, Vol. LXXV, No. 1, pp. 1–8
Falvey, Denis: *A Well-known Excellence. British Artillery & An Artilleryman in World War Two.* London, Brassey's 2002

Farndale, Sir Martin, General: *History of the Royal Regiment of Artillery. The Years of Defeat – Europe and North Africa 1939–1941*. London, Brassey's 1996

Farndale, Sir Martin, General: *History of the Royal Regiment of Artillery. The Far East Theatre 1939–1946*. London, Brassey's 2002

Fleming, Peter: *Operation Sea Lion*. London, Pan Books 2003 (1975)

Ford, Ken: *See Osprey*

Forty, George: *British Army Handbook 1939–1945*. Thrupp, Stroud, Gloucestershire, Sutton Publishing 2002

Fransson, Stig A.: *Bofors 350 år* (in Swedish). Stockholm 1996

'G.E.S.' (pseudonym): *Survey in Burma*. Royal Artillery Journal, Vol. 73, No. 1, pp.33–36

Goddard, Douglas, Major Rankin, Eric, Captain & Vigers, James, Captain: *112th (Wessex) Field Regiment RA, TA 1938 – 1946*. Wargrave-on-Thames 2002

Goddard, Douglas, Major: *Master of None. The Life Enriched Reminiscences of a 20th Century Survivor*. Kibworth Beauchamp Leicester, Troubador 2009

Gorle, Richmond: *The Quiet Gunner at War. El Alamein to the Rhine with the Scottish Divisions*. Barnsley, South Yorkshire, Pen & Sword Military 2011

Gudmundsson, Bruce I.: *On Artillery*. Westport CT 06881, Praeger Publishers 1993

de Guingand, Sir Francis, Major General: *Operation Victory*. London, Hodder & Stoughton 1947

de Guingand, Sir Francis, Major General: *Generals at War*. London, Hodder & Stoughton 1964

Hackett, Sir John, General: *I Was a Stranger*. London, Sphere Books Ltd. 1979

Hammond, B.A.T., Lieutenant Colonel: *The Guns at Kohima – Part 1*. The Gunner, April 1994, pp. 8–9. *Part 2*, The Gunner, May 1994, pp. 22–23

Hart, Peter: *To the Last Round. South Notts Hussars 1939–42*. Barnsley, South Yorkshire, Leo Cooper 1996

Hastings, Max: *Nemesis. The Battle for Japan 1944–45*. Kondon Hammersmith Perennial 2008

Hastings, Max: *Overlord. D-Day and the Battle for Normandy 1944*. London, Pan Books 1985

Hedberg, Jonas, major, redaktör: *Kungl. Artilleriet. Medeltid och äldre vasatid*. Stockholm 1994 (in Swedish)

Hendrie, William F and Smith, Jack: *The Scots Guards*. Stroud, Gloucestershire, Tempus Publishing 2002

Hepper, J.M., Lieutenant Colonel: *A light Mountain Regiment in the Imphal Campaign*. Royal Artillery Journal, Vol. 74, No.1, pp.74–80

Hibbert, Christopher: *The Great Mutiny India 1857*. Reading, Penguin Books 1978

Hogg, Ian: *Twentieth-Century Artillery*. Nr Rochester, Kent, Grange Books 2002

Hogg, Ian V.: *The Illustrated Encyclopedia of Artillery*. London, Quantum Publishing 2003

Horrocks, Sir Brian with Eversley Belfield and H. Essame: *Corps Commander*. London, Sidgwick & Jackson 1977

Hughes, B.P. Major General: *History of the Royal Regiment of Artillery. Between the Wars 1919–1939*. London, Brassey's 1992

Jackson, Robert: *Dunkirk. The British Evacuation, 1940*. London, Cassell Military 2002

James, N.D.G., Major: *France – An Extract from the Diary of Major J.H. Brooke Dean 21st – 25th May 1940*. Royal Artillery Journal Vol. XCV, pp. 168–184

Jobson, Philip: *Royal Artillery Glossary of Terms and Abbreviations Historical and Modern*. Port Stroud, Gloucestershire, The History Press Ltd. 2008

'Kaitch' (pseudonym): *The Okydoke Pass*. Royal Artillery Journal, Vol. LXXV, No. 1, pp. 64–72

Keegan, John, Editor: *Churchill's Generals*. New York, Grove Weidenfeld 1991

Latimer, Jon: *Alamein*. First Harvard University Press, USA 2002

Lewendon, R.J., Brigadier, and Robertson, G.W., Major: *RA Manpower in World War II*. Royal Artillery Journal, Vol. CXXI, No. 2, pp. 43–45

Lewin, Ronald: *SLIM The Standardbearer*. Ware, Hertfordshire, Wordsworth Editions 1999

Liddell Hart, Sir Basil: *Vi var där! Tyska generaler berättar om andra världskriget*. Stockholm 2010 (in Swedish). The original in English is *Other Side of the Hill*, 1948 and 1951

Lind af Hageby, Axel, Premierlöjtnant: *Minnen från ett tre-årigt vistande i engelsk örlogstjänst 1857–1859* (in Swedish). Stockholm 1860

Lindsell, Sir Wilfred, Lieutenant General: *The Fourth Front. India and S.E.A.C. 1943–1945*. Royal Artillery Journal, Vol. 74, No. 4, pp. 297–313

Lowry, See Osprey

Luto, James: *Fighting with the Fourteenth Army*

in Burma. Barnslkey, South Yorkshire, Pen & Sword Military 2013
Lyman, Robert: *Slim, Master of War. Burma and the Birth of Modern Warfare*. London, Constable & Robinson 2004
Lyman, Robert: *The Generals. From Defeat to Victory, Leadership in Asia 1941–45*. London, Constable & Robinson 2008
MacArthur, Brian: *Surviving the Sword. Prisoners of the Japanese 1942–45*. London, Abacus 2005
Macksey, Kenneth: *Military Errors of World War Two*. Edison NJ 08837 USA, Castle Books 2003
Majdalany, Fred: *The Battle of El Alamein*. London 1965
Majumdar, R.C., General Editor: *Struggle for Freedom*. Bombay, Bharatiya Vidya Bhavan 1978
Mangilli-Climpson, Massimo: *Larkhill's Wartime Locators. Royal Artillery Survey in the Second World War*. Barnsley, South Yorkshire, Pen & Sword Military 2007
Margry, Karel: *Operation Market Garden. Then and Now, Volume 1–2*. London, Battle of Britain International Ltd. 2002
McCaig, R., Lieutenant Colonel: *The Second World War – The Far East. Part 3 – Gunners in India Half a Century Ago*. Royal Artillery Journal, Vol. CXXII, No. 2, pp. 14–23
Mead, Peter, Brigadier: *Gunners at War 1939–1945*. Shepperton, Surrey, Ian Allan Ltd. 1982
Mears, G.G., Brigadier: *A Divisional Artillery in the Normandy Landings*. The Gunner, June 1969
Mears, G.G., Brigadier: *Reminiscences of D-Day 6th June 1944*. Royal Artillery Journal Vol. CXXI No. 1, pp. 33–41
Military Library Research Services Ltd. (MLRS), Reprints:
-*Operation Goodwood. 8 Corps east of Caen 18–21 July 1944*. British Army of the Rhine 1947
-*Operation Plunder. 12 British Corps crossing the River Rhine 23–25 March 1945*. British Army of the Rhine 1947
-*Operation Varsity. Operations of XVIII US Corps in support of the Rhine Crossing 24–25 March 1945*. British Army of the Rhine 1947
-*A Short History of 30 Corps in the European Campaign 1944–1945*. 1945
-Mitchell, Alister J.: *Technology for Artillery Location 1914–1970*. Glasgow 2012
Montgomery, Bernard Law, Field Marshal Viscount: *Memoirs*. London, Collins 1958
Münnich, Ralph: *Panzer in Nord-Afrika 1941*. Friedberg 1977

Napier, A.F.S., Brigadier: *British Rockets in the World War*. Royal Artillery Journal Vol. LXXIII No. 1. p. 11
Nicholson, R.A.G, Brigadier: *With the Gunners on the Road to Mandalay – and Rangoon*. Royal Artillery Journal, Vol. 76. No. 3, pp. 174–179
Onderwater, Hans: *Second to None. The History of No II (AC) Squadron Royal Air Force 1912–1992*. Shrewsbury, Airlife Publishing Ltd. 1992
Osprey Publishers series of presentations of various operations in World War II:
-Chappell, Mike: *Scottish Divisions in the World Wars*. Oxford 2004
-Dildy, D.C.: *Dunkirk 1940. Operation Dynamo*. Oxford 2010
-Dildy, D.C.: *Denmark and Norway 1940. Hitler's boldest operation*. Oxford 2007
-Ford, Ken: *El Alamein 1942. The Turning of the Tide*. Oxford 2001
-Ford, Ken: *D-Day 1944 (3)*. Oxford 2002
-Ford, Ken: *D-Day (4)*. Oxford 2002
-Ford, Ken: *Caen 1944*. Oxford 2004
-Henry, Chris: *The 25-pounder Field Gun 1939–72*. London 2002
-Lowry, Bernard: *British Home Defences 1940–45*. Oxford 2004
-Shepperd, Alan: *France 1940. Blitzkrieg in the West*. Oxford 2005
-Young, E.M.: *Meiktila 1945. The Battle to Liberate Burma*. Oxford 2004
Owen, Frank: *The Fall of Singapore*. London, Classic Penguin 2001 (1960)
Page, Malcolm: *KAR A History of the King's African Rifles*. Barnsley, South Yorkshire, Leo Cooper 1998
Palmer, E.R.D., Colonel: *Last Days at Dunkirk*. Royal Artillery Journal Vol. CXVII, No. 2, pp. 19–24
Parham, Jack, Lieutenant Colonel (pseudo. D/101): *Some experiences of a Field Regiment R.A. in May 1940*. Royal Artillery Journal Vol 58, No. 3, pp. 245–263
Parham, Jack, Major General: *The Royal Artillery in the Normandy Landings*. The Gunner March 1969
Parker, Matthew: *Monte Cassino The story of the hardest-fought battle of World War II*. London, Headline Book Publishing 2004
Pemberton, A.L., Brigadier: *The Development of Artillery Tactics and Equipment*. London 1950. (Military Library Research Service Ltd (MLRS) have published a new edition in 2003)
Persson, Gösta: *Tjeckoslovakiens Ödestimma* (in Swedish). Stockholm 1938

Powell, R. D., Major: *The Battle for Able*. Royal Artillery Journal, Vol. CXII, No. 2, pp. 23–26

Pugh, L.H.O, Lieutenant Colonel: '*Jock Columns and the like*'. Royal Artillery Journal, Vol. LXXV, No. 2, pp. 148–156

Pugh, L.H.O, Lieutenant Colonel: *Ukhrul*. Royal Artillery Journal, Vol. LXXIII, No. 4, pp. 345–354

Richardson, T.A., Major General: *Normandy 1944. The Actions of a Battery of Self-propelled Close Support Artillery from D-Day to D+7*. A published article which the author has received from Richardson, unknown in which magazine it was published

Richardson, T.A., Major General: *Market Garden September 1944*. Royal Artillery Journal, Vol. CXXV/2 p. 46

Roberts, Owen N: *31st Field Regiment RA A Record*. Bristol, Old Comrades Association 1994

Robertson, G.W.: *The Rose and the Arrow. A Life Story of 136th (1st Lancashire) Field Regiment 1939–1946*. Reigate 1986

Royal Artillery Journal, Vol. LXXV No. 4. *The War Services of Lieutenant General Albert Borgard*

Rowe, Tim, Staff Sergeant: *Weir, Steve, New Zealand's Master Gunner*. Military Studies Institute, Occasional Paper Series No.4 May 2004

Rowse, A.L.: *The Story of Britain*. London, Artus Publishing Co. 1979

Royal Artillery Commemoration Book. London 1950

Ryan, Cornelius: *A Bridge Too Far*. Popular Library Edition, USA 1974

Sainsbury, J.D.: *The Hertfordshire Yeomanry Regiments, Royal Artillery, Part 1: The Field Regiments 1920–1946*. Welwyn, Hertfordshire, Hart Books 1999

'Sankie' (pseudonym): *A Gunner's Night Out*. Royal Artillery Journal, Vol. LXIX, No.1, pp. 45–49

Saunders, Tim: *Nijmegen*. Barnsley 2001

Sixsmith, E.K.G.: *British Generalship in the Twentieth Century*. London, Arms and Armour Press, Lionel Leventhal Limited 1970

Slim, William, Field Marshal Viscount: *Defeat into Victory*. London, Pan Books 1999

Smyth, John: *Percival and the tragedy of Singapore*. London, MacDonald & Co. (Publishers) Ltd. 1971

Spears, Sir Edward, Major General: *Assignment to Catastrophe Vol. I–II*. London, William Heinemann Ltd. 1954

Steckzén, Birger: *Bofors. En kanonindustris historia*. Stockholm 1946 (in Swedish)

Stjernfelt, Bertil: *Alarm i Atlantvallen*. 4:e utgåvan (in Swedish), Stockholm 2004

'Sterno' (pseudonym): *A Field Regiment in the Battle of Egypt. October–November 1942*. Royal Artillery Journal, Vol. LXX, No. 3, pp. 189–199

Stewart, Adrian: *Six of Monty's Men*. Barnsley, South Yorkshire, Pen & Sword Military 2011

Summers, Julie: *The Colonel of Tamarkan. Philip Toosey & The Bridge on the River Kwai*. London, Pocket Books 2005

Swaab, Jack: *Field of Fire. Diary of a Gunner Officer*. Thrupp, Stroud, Gloustershire, Sutton Publishing 2005

Tamayama, Kazuo and Nunneley, John: *Tales by Japanese Soldiers*. London, Cassell & Co 1992 and 2001

Thompson, Julian: *The Imperial War Museum Book of the War in Burma 1942–1945*. London, Pan Books 2003

Thompson, W.F.K., Lieutenant Colonel: *Some Airborne and Mountain Artillery Techniques and Tactics Developed by 1 Airlanding Light Regiment RA*. Royal Artillery Journal, Vol. LXXIV, No. 1, p. 36 ff

-Tilgner, Daniel: *Jede Stunde dem Schicksal abgestohlen. Das Brieftagebuch der Magdalene Krippner vom Kriegsende in Bremen 1945*. Bremen 2005

Truesdale David, Cornelissen Martijn, Gerritsen Bob: *Arnhem Bridge Target Mike One*, Renkum (NL), R.N. Sigmond 2015

Tsuji, Masanoubu, Colonel: *Singapore 1941–1942. The Japanese Version of the Malayan Campaign of World War II*. Singapore, Oxford University Press 1988

Tower, Philip: *Second Army Artillery in the Battle of Arnhem*. The Gunner, November 1945

War Department, *Handbook on the British Army 1942*. Military Library Service Ltd. (MLRS) have published a new edition in 2003

Warner, Philip: *Horrocks The General who led from the front*. London, Hamish Hamilton Ltd. 1984

Wilkinson, Peter, Captain: *The Gunners at Arnhem*. East Haddon, Northampton, Spurwing Publishing 2002

Woollacott, Robert: *Winged Gunners*. Harare, Zimbabwe 1994

'X' (pseudonym): *There and Back*. Royal Artillery Journal, Vol. 69, No. 4, pp. 235–253

Young, Edward M: See Osprey

Index

A
Aa Canal 190
Aalst 294
Abyssinia (see Ethiopia)
Afghanistan 363
Aire Canal 178
Alam el Halfa 230, 235, 236, 431
Albert Canal 175, 177, 275
Alberville 170
Aldbourne 205
Alde 216
Aldrich, R.J. 428
Alexander, Harold, Field Marshal 230
Alexandria 231
Alfriston 228
Algeria 241
Allen, J.E., Major 21
Alost 183
Alresford 208
Altmark 200
Alton 152
Amesbury 97
Andelst 307, 391
Ankarcrona, G., Colonel 1.Cl. 21
Ankenes 207, 210–213
Antwerp 175, 275, 311, 315, 369
Anzio 79, 343, 438
Arakan 347, 352
Archangelsk 37
Ardennes 174, 177, 315, 318
Arendal 200
Armentières 188, 192
Armstrong College 356
Armstrong, Gun designer 31
Armstrong, G., Lieutenant Colonel 117, 418
Arnhem 10, 19, 93, 96, 97, 118, 119, 162, 164, 275–314, 315, 317, 318, 321, 330, 332, 342, 359, 387–389, 391, 393, 423, 424, 433, 434, 437, 448
Arras 8, 178, 187, 188, 369, 370
Arromanches 273
Assam 346–348
Atlantic Ocean 201
Atlantic Wall 258
Auchinleck, Claude, Field Marshal 8, 208–213, 229, 230, 420, 429
Australia 77, 220, 226
Austria 40
Avry, W&T 53

B
Bagnall, Nigel, Field Marshal 361
Bailey, J.B.A., Major General 11, 16, 17, 19, 33, 34, 36, 37, 360, 414, 415, 418, 428, 437
Bailey, R.D.W. 435
Baines, D., Brigadier 18, 433
Baker Perkinson 53
Balaklava 134, 418
Ballangen 207
Baltic Coast 317, 340, 342
Baltic Sea 199
Bangkok 345
Bare Ridge 235
Barnett, Correlli 37, 415, 419
Barry, J.R., Brigadier 403, 429
Bayeux 26
Bazely, Charles, Captain 83
Beardmore 52
Beck, Benjamin 18, 358, 425, 436
Beck, Sidney, Lieutenant 18, 263, 264, 296–298, 309, 316, 358, 423, 426, 432, 433, 436
Bedford 354
Beisfjord 211, 212
Belgium 34, 50, 93, 134, 164–169, 171, 174, 175, 177, 179, 183, 193, 311, 325, 353, 354, 435
Bengal Bay 346
Bergen 200
Bergues 194, 195
Berlin 10, 46, 275, 276, 294, 306, 423
Berkshire 93
Berry, J. Brigadier 429, 439
Béthouart, Antoine, Brigadier 202, 207, 209
Bidwell, R.G.S., Brigadier 134, 135, 231, 232, 252, 418, 419, 421, 422, 428, 431
Billotte, General 165, 175
Bingham, C.W., Cpl 431
Bjerkvik 211, 213
Black Prince 27
Bock, Feder von, General 175
Bodö 208–213
Bofors 61–63, 209, 212, 244, 246, 325, 329, 330
Bogen 207, 210
Bogue, Captain 26
Bohusz-Szysko, Major General 211
Bonnet, B.R.F., Major General 414, 415
Borgard (Borgaard), Albert, Lieutenant General 28
Borkenes 211, 212
Boulogne 165, 275
Boyle, P., Lieutenant 133
Boyle, William, Earl of Cork and Orey, Admiral (see Cork)

Bradley, Omar, Lieutenant General 258, 315
Breda 175
Briggs, J., Bombardier 433
Brighton 222
Brocks, Major 170
Brooke, Alan (Alanbrooke), Field Marshal 25, 38, 84, 134, 135, 165, 175, 188–190, 196, 197, 219, 221, 223, 229, 337, 341, 419
Brown, J.F., Captain 435
Brown, W.J., Captain 431
Browning, Frederick, Lieutenant General 276, 278, 284, 434
Brussels 169, 172, 181, 182, 184, 192, 275, 278
Buck, M. 20
Bulford 93
Burma 18, 19, 50–52, 54, 57, 59, 63, 66, 69, 79, 85, 95, 102, 104, 105, 109, 112, 116, 149, 157, 164, 343, 345–352, 357, 359, 427, 435, 436, 437
Burnes, R 12
Buthidaung 149
Båtberget 207

C
Caen 265–271, 432
Cairo 231, 233, 235
Calais 165, 186, 275
Camberley 355
Cambrai 415
Campbell, A.P., Brigadier 342, 427
Campbell, Jock, Major General 421
Canada 53, 72, 77, 226
Candlin, R.E., 2nd Lieutenant 170
Cape of Good Hope 205, 221
Cardiff 52
Carver, Field Marshal, Lord 418
Cass, E.E.F., Lieutenant Colonel 204
Cassino 82, 145, 156, 343, 355, 356, 422
Castleford 356
Catterick 152
Caumont 270
Chamberlain, Neville, Prime Minister 40, 46
Channel Island 356
Charleroi 175, 182, 192
Cherbourg 50, 165, 166, 174, 196, 197, 265
Cheux 272

Index

Chiang-Kai-Shek, Generalissimo 346–348, 352
Chiangi 436
China 40, 346, 352
Chindits 348
Chindwin 346–348
Churchill, Sir Winston, Prime Minister 25, 26, 40, 93, 198–200, 203, 214, 218, 219, 227, 229, 230, 232, 233, 341, 345, 348, 420, 427
Clapham, 2nd Lieutenant 211
Clausewitz 361
Clegg, Lieutenant Colonel 338, 426
Cleve (Kleve) 315
Clyde 206
Coghlan, J., Lieutenant Colonel 18, 437, 448
Comines 179, 188, 192, 199
Congreve, Sir William 26, 30, 60
Contentin 265, 269
Copenhagen 30
Corbet 133
Cork, Lord (Earl of Cork and Orey) 202, 203, 207, 208, 212
Cotterill, Bob, Sergeant 120
Cox, Air Force Officer 170
Cracknell, Captain 303
Crawley 433
Crawley, Ph. 19
Craston, Lieutenant 297
Crécy 27, 177
Crete 229, 343
Crossley Bros. 53
Czechoslovakia 40, 41, 415

D
Dagenham 152
Daglish, J. 19
Daipur 348
Daladier, Prime Minister 40, 46
Dalmuir 52, 55
Danzig 46
Davies 427
de Burgh, Paddy, Lieutenant 308, 433
de Fonblanque 193
de Gaulle, Charles, Colonel 177
de Guingand, Sir Francis, Major General 158, 233, 247, 248, 258
Deelen 294, 305
Dehli 30
Dempsey, Sir Miles, General 258
Dendre 177, 182, 183, 184
Denmark 28, 93, 171, 340
Dieppe 60
Diesfordt Woods 318, 319, 331, 338
Dietl, Eduard, General, 209
Dill, Sir John, General 165
Dinant 177
Doesburg 278
Dormer, Sir Cecil, Ambassador 421
Dottiginies 184
Douai 188
Dover 43

Driel 118, 293
Dungeness 228
Dunkirk (Dunkerque) 43, 50, 69, 81, 134, 164, 177–180, 182, 186, 192–197, 199, 212, 214–216, 219, 220, 222, 224, 233, 275, 353, 355
Dyle 169–177, 179–187, 190–193, 197, 353

E
Ede 289
Eden, Anthony, Minister of Foreign Affairs 218
Edward III, King 27
Edwards, R.T., Colonel 403
Edwards, W.G., Major 335
Egersund 200
Egypt 61, 108, 145, 205, 214, 221, 222, 226, 229, 232, 233, 355, 356, 428
Eindhoven 276, 277, 281, 286–288, 291–296, 300, 311
Eisenhower, Dwight D., General 158, 258, 275, 278
El Aghelia 229
El Alamein 9, 15, 54, 55, 57, 59, 62, 63, 66, 101, 102, 107, 108, 113, 129, 164, 229–231, 233–237, 240–242, 244, 245, 247, 250, 252, 254–257, 267, 268, 281, 321, 341, 343, 355, 356, 407, 408, 417, 421, 422, 430, 431
Elbe 317, 342, 361
Elizabeth I, Queen 27, 414
Elles, Sir Hugh, General 60
Elst 118, 293, 296, 302, 306, 307, 311, 426
Emmerich 317
England (see Great Britain)
English Channel 169, 174, 177, 192, 218, 284
Enveruie 216
Ere 184
Ervik 206, 207, 210, 211
Escaut 169, 171, 175, 177, 178, 182–187, 191–193, 197, 275, 277, 296, 303, 304, 310, 315, 419
Essex 218
Ethiopia 40, 229, 343
Evans, Nigel 19, 54, 56, 107, 133, 415–418, 436
Evans, Paul, Librarian 20
Evelegh, W., Major General 159
Everberg 176
Evill, J., Brigadier 118

F
Falaise 267, 270, 272
Falvey, Dennis 41, 56, 415, 416
Fanshawe, G.D., Major General 431
Farndale, Sir Martin, General 16, 22, 159, 187, 190, 204, 206, 211, 345, 401, 415–421, 428, 436

Ferguson, I.M., Captain 435
Festing, F.W., Major General 157
Finland 199, 204, 205, 208
Flanders 169, 196
Fleming, P. 421
Folkestone 222
Fontaney-le-Pesnel 271
Forth of Firth 205, 216, 218, 220, 222, 229, 265
Fort 416, 418
France 15, 27, 29, 34, 40, 43, 46, 48, 50, 69, 81–83, 108, 134, 144, 164, 166, 169, 174, 175, 177, 179, 180, 182, 185, 186, 190, 191, 193, 195–197, 199, 200, 203, 204, 205, 208, 209, 212, 214–216, 218, 220, 222, 229, 265, 270, 311, 353–356, 363, 366, 420, 429, 432, 435, 439, 440, 446
Fransson, S. 416
Fraser, William, Brigadier 207, 208
Frederick the Great, King of Prussia 29
Freyberg, Sir Bernard, Lieutenant General 238, 242, 243, 249, 251, 252
Frost, J., Lieutenant Colonel 285, 289, 293, 295, 312
Frundsberg 272
Furnes 194, 195

G
Gandhi, M. 40
Gatehouse, Alec, Major General 248
Gazala 234
Geldern 315, 317
Gennap(e) 28
Georges, Alphonse Joseph, General 165
Germany 26, 33, 34, 37, 40, 41, 46, 60, 72, 93, 171, 197, 199, 200–202, 208, 209, 213, 219, 220, 226, 227, 239, 250, 265, 317, 352, 356, 359, 363, 366, 425, 434
Gerritsen, B. 18, 437
Gibraltar 28
Gibson, John D. 416, 437
Gier, C. 309
Gitting, Len 55
Givenchy 186, 190
Glasgow 205, 206
Glücksburg 26
Goddard, Douglas, Major 18, 19, 74, 102, 136, 140, 144, 152, 222, 227, 228, 266, 271, 272, 309, 358, 359, 415–418, 421–426, 433, 437
Goddard, N. 19
Godwinsson, Harold, King 26
Gold Beach 258, 260
Gordon-Finlayson, R., Major 184, 185, 419, 429
Gort, Lord, General 46, 165, 167,

443

Index

168, 178, 188, 190, 193
Gott, General 230
Gough, F., Major 284
Gratangen 207
Grave 277, 280, 287, 291, 294, 296, 298, 300, 301, 311
Great Britain (see also Scotland) 12, 14, 26, 27, 29, 33–35, 37, 40, 43, 46, 48, 50, 62, 63, 72, 83, 84, 86, 93, 95, 104, 108, 132, 151, 164–166, 169, 175, 180, 185, 186, 195–200, 203–205, 208, 212, 214, 215, 217–221, 227, 229, 230, 233, 234, 257, 261, 264, 275, 284, 297, 304, 310, 311, 318, 343–345, 349, 353, 354, 356, 357, 361–363, 414, 419, 420, 428, 430, 437
Great Yarmouth 218
Greenock 205
Greece 229, 343
Greig, Captain 263
Groesbeek 284, 287, 294, 295, 298, 299, 301–304, 309–313, 316
Gudbrand Valley (Gudbrandsdalen) 204
Guderian, Heinrich, Colonel General 175, 177, 178
Gudmundsson B.I. 439
Guiness, Sir Alec, Actor 357
Guiness, C.D., Captain 33
Gustavus Adolphus, King of Sweden 27
Gustav Line 343, 355, 421
Gällivare 199, 208
Göring, H. Air Marshal 219

H

Haldane, Richard Burton, Minister of Defence 34
Halifax 214, 402, 431
Halldin, A. 21
Hallifax, Brigadier 158, 431
Hamminkeln 331, 336
Hardy, B. 19
Harmonworth 414
Harrison, C.A., Captain 433
Harstad 203, 206–212, 421
Hartenstein 289, 290, 301, 306
Hastings 26, 222
Hawick 213
Hayes 52
Heath, William, Brigadier 118, 323, 337
Heathcote, Sir Gilbert, Brigadier 18, 118, 337, 427, 437
Hely, A.F., Brigadier 357, 428
Henderson, Sir Neville, Ambassador 46
Henry 415, 416
Henry VII, King 27
Henry VIII, King 27
Hestefjell 211
Heteren 308

Heusden 305
Hibbert 414
Himiemat 230, 237
Hiroshima 352
Hitler, Adolf, Chancellor of Germany 40, 46, 48, 174, 179, 200, 201, 219–221
Hobart, P.R.C., Major General 38, 320
Hogg, I. 415, 416
Holbaek 28
Holland (see Netherlands)
Homoet 304
Hope, Adrian, Brigadier 414
Horrocks, Sir Brian, Lieutenant General 12, 14, 141, 162, 233, 239, 275, 286–288, 294, 306, 311, 315, 319, 335, 336, 431
Hoth, Hermann, General 175
Hughes, B.P., Major General 415, 416, 436
Hulse, Brian 45
Hunt, H.S., Lieutenant Colonel 307, 425, 434
Hunters Plateau 237
Hutton, T. 19
Håkvik 207

I

Iberian Peninsula 27, 29
Iceland 343, 345
Ijssel 331
Ijsselmeer (Zuider Zee) 277, 294
Ilkley 152
Imlay, D.A., Lieutenant 352
Imphal 348, 352
India 14, 26, 27, 29–31, 33, 40, 42, 46, 93, 95, 208, 213, 226, 229, 345–349, 353, 355, 414, 418, 435
Iran (see Persia)
Iraq 19, 229, 343
Ireland 29, 425
Ironside, E., Field Marshal 169, 208, 218, 219
Irrawaddy 346, 351, 435, 436
Irwin, General 347
Isander, J., Captain 414
Italy 18, 26, 40, 50, 59, 60, 79, 82, 86, 91, 93, 94, 96, 104, 108, 116, 125, 126, 135, 144, 149, 156, 214, 229, 343, 354, 356, 359, 418, 421, 436, 437

J

Japan 15, 16, 33, 40, 48, 343
Jedburgh 205, 212
Jobbit, Jack 88
Jobson, Ph. 20
Joe's Bridge 277, 282, 286, 295, 297, 306
Johore 344
Juno Beach 260, 437

K

Kahn, M. 21

Kalapanzin Valley 135
Karl Johan, Crown Prince of Sweden 26
Keegan, J. 420
Keene, T.P., Lieuteant Colonel 143, 418
Keent 294
Kemp, Sam 88
Kenney, J.T. 63, 124, 125, 337
Kent 151, 294, 438, 439
Kent, T.W., Battery Sergeant Major 433
Kenya 437
Kevelaer 323
Kidney Ridge 230
King, S., Major 19
Kipling, R. 33
Kirkman, Sir Sidney, General 12, 110, 134, 222–224, 227, 232, 233, 238, 250, 251, 254, 256, 257, 342, 353, 354–359, 401, 408, 417, 421–423, 430, 431, 436
Kiruna 199, 208
Kolin, M.L. 430
Kohima 348, 352
Kola Peninsula 37
Krafft, Sepp, Sturmbannführer 285, 286, 288, 424, 434
Kristiansand 200
Kristianstad 21, 28
Kuala Lumpur 438

L

La Bassée 186, 190
La Glaneri 184
Labergdal 207
Laize 266
Lake District 153
Lamont, S., Captain 187
Larkhill 31, 150–154, 223, 226, 227, 366, 421, 430, 437
Latimer, J. 236, 422
Lawrence of Arabia 348
Layton, Sir W. 430
Le Havre 165, 174, 196, 197, 199, 204, 215
Leach, L.H., Lieutenant Colonel 435
Leeb, Wilhelm Ritter von, Colonel General 175
Leeds 52, 356, 357
Leese, Sir Oliver, Lieutenant General 238, 239, 247, 248
Lent 295, 307
Leigh, J.A., Lieutenant Colonel 402
Leigh, R.F.D., Colonel 435
Leipzig 21, 24, 26, 39, 360
Leith 205
Lent 295, 307
Leopoldburg 286
Lewendon, R.J. Brigadier, 415, 439
Lewes 222
Lewis, T.W. 416, 417, 437, 439
Libya 363

444

Liddell Hart, Sir Basil 421, 436
Liland 210
Lille 167, 174, 178, 193
Lincoln 305
Lind af Hageby, Axel, Premier Lieutenant 30, 414
Lippe 318
Llandrindod 152
Loder-Symonds, R.G., Brigadier 278–280, 299–301, 305, 306, 308, 423
Lommel 325
London 20, 25, 27, 28, 40, 41, 85, 152, 180, 203, 206–209, 211, 212, 220, 230, 233, 301, 347, 353, 362, 366, 419, 428, 430, 436
Lonsdale 291, 307
Louvain 176, 181
Loyd, Major General 185
Luck, von 420
Lucknow 30
Luleå 199, 200, 208, 209
Lumsden, Herbert, Lieutenant General 233, 247–249, 254
Lund 28
Lund, Otto M., Major General 135, 223
Lunn-Rochliffe, W.P., Major 126
Luxembourg 169
Lydd 151, 222, 228
Lyman 428
Lyme Regis 216
Lys 192, 193

M

Maas 87, 143, 276, 277, 282, 294–296, 303, 304, 311, 315, 316, 435
Mace, M. 21
MacGregor 190
Mackesy, P.J., Major General 202, 203, 207, 208, 213
MacRae 185
Madagascar 343
Maginot Line 165, 175, 191, 198
Malaya Peninsula 46, 74, 344–346, 436
Malacca 344
Malden 295, 300
Malta 355
Mandalay 346, 349, 352, 436
Mangilli-Climpson, M 422
Mannerheim, C.G., Field Marshal 199
Manstein, Erich von, Field Marshal 174
Margry, K. 307, 423–425
Marlborough, Duke of 28
Mason, Air Force Officer 170
Massy, H.R.S., Brigadier 83
Mattingley 149
Maxwell, J., Brigadier 159
Mayu 136
McCaig, Dick 149
McCleery, W., Major 21, 24, 26, 414
McKillop, Lieutenant 236
Mead, Peter 417, 436
Mead, Tom 187
Mears, G.G., Brigadier 423
Mediterranean 40, 214, 229–231, 234, 245, 343, 418, 422
Meieri 210
Meiktila 349, 352
Messervy, Frank, Lieutenant General 436
Metro-Vickers 52
Meulstee, L. 19, 78, 437
Meuse 177, 196, 277, 319, 321, 322
Metz 165, 191
Minassieb 237
Miteiriya 230, 237, 238, 248, 249
Mo 208, 209, 211–213
Moberg, J. 21
Moberg, Å. 21
Model, Walther, Field Marshal 291
Moerbeke 184
Moesjöen 210, 211
Molotov 199
Mont Fleury 263
Mont Pincon 270, 272
Mont St. Aubert 193
Montgomery, Bernard L., Field Marshal 9, 12, 14, 25, 26, 135, 156, 158, 159, 167, 168, 171, 174–176, 178, 179, 222, 223, 226, 227, 229, 230, 232, 238, 245–251, 254, 257, 258, 265, 267, 275, 278, 294, 310, 315, 317, 318, 341, 355, 414, 419, 422
Montrose 97
Moore, Lieutenant 306
Morris Brown, S. 233
Moscow 37, 340
Moulmein 346
Moulton, J. 182, 194
Mowat, Fairley, Subaltern 141
Munford, Dennis, Major 289, 290
Munich 40
Murmansk 37
Mussolini, B. 40, 229
Myitkyina 346
Mårtensson, L. Colonel 21

N

Nagasaki 352
Namsos 203, 204, 206
Namur 171
Napoléon 21, 24, 26, 29, 30, 414
Narvik 8, 9, 199–214, 421
Neilson, I.G., Lieutenant Colonel 431, 432
Nelson, H., Admiral 362
Netherlands 27, 93, 165, 168
New Fryston 356
Newbury 93
Newcastle-on-Tyne 215, 356
New Zealand 220, 226, 422

Nicholson, R.A.G., Brigadier 436
Nieuwpoort 186, 193
Nijmegen 276, 279, 281, 287, 291–304, 306–308, 310–317, 321, 425, 435
Nile Delta 233–235
Normandy 19, 59, 60, 89, 93, 95, 96, 102, 110, 135, 141, 142, 164, 228, 258–261, 263–266, 269, 270, 272–275, 278, 303, 306, 310, 317, 318, 341, 343, 354, 357, 358, 422, 431, 432
Norman, W. M. 435
Northern Ireland 425
Northumberland 150
Norway 8, 9, 15, 69, 93, 164, 171, 199–208, 210, 212–214, 220, 221, 230, 277, 343, 359, 366, 420, 421, 429, 430
Nottingham 56

O

O'Connor, Sir Richard, General 229, 267–269, 432
Odon 266
Oedenrode 296
Ofot Fiord 207, 210
Ogden 272, 423, 433
Okehampton 31, 150, 151
Omaha Beach 258
Onderwater, Hans 19, 82, 419, 437
Onega 37
Oosterbeek 118, 285, 289, 290, 292, 293, 296, 298–303, 306–308, 310, 312, 314
Oosterhout 293
Orne 266–268
Orneset 211
Oslo 200
Ostvleteren 195
Otterburn 150

P

Palestine 229, 365
Palmer, E.R.D., Colonel 81, 195, 299–301, 308, 420, 425, 433
Parham, Jack, Major General 12, 83, 84, 124, 134, 181, 182, 185, 186, 190, 193, 194, 217, 222, 224–227, 241, 254, 257, 259, 264, 342, 353–355, 358, 359, 402, 416, 419–423, 429–431, 436
Parker, K.A.L., Assistant Under Secretary 436
Parkhead 52
Patton, George S., Lieutenant General 317
Paunsdorf 26
Pearl Harbour 343, 344
Pemberton, A.L., Brigadier 16, 196, 198, 340, 415–420, 422, 427, 428
Percival, Arthur E., Lieutenant General 344, 345

INDEX

Perry, Captain 263
Persia 229, 243
Persson, Gösta, Journalist 415
Perth 216
Ploegsteert 188, 193
Plymouth 203
Poland 37, 46
Pope, W.H., Lieutenant 141
Portobello 205
Powell, Robin, Major 149, 418, 437
Preussia 46

Q
Qattara Depression 9, 230, 235, 245

R
Rahman Track 230, 251, 422
Ramcke, Bernard Hermann, Major General 238
Ramsay, A., Brigadier 251, 253, 422
Ramsbury 205
Ramsgate 218
Ranks, C., Bombardier 79
Rangoon 346–350, 352
Rauray 271, 423, 431
Rawlins, S.B., Brigadier 323
Redesdale 150
Rees 317, 320, 329, 330, 335, 336
Reichswald 315, 316
Reinhardt, Hans, General 175
Renaix 184
Renescure 190
Renkum 286, 306
Rhine 10, 15, 25, 37, 40, 61, 95, 109, 145, 147, 162, 164, 275, 276, 279, 282, 285, 288, 289, 292–295, 298–300, 303–308, 310, 313–342, 356, 358, 361, 366, 412, 424–427, 433–435
Ribbentrop, Foreign Minister 199
Rice, Harold, Major 338
Richardson, Tony, Major General 18, 314, 358, 359, 423–425, 431, 437
Rob, R. 309
Robertson, G.W., Major 18, 76, 135, 136, 216, 359, 415–418, 421, 439
Robertson, J.P., Major 433
Robson, R. Colonel 20
Roer 315
Roermond 143
Romania 40
Rombaksfjorden 209, 211
Rome 343, 355
Rommel, Erwin, Field Marshal 107, 129, 175, 177, 178, 187, 229–232, 234, 235, 239, 250, 256, 257, 356
Rose, T. 'Zeke', Captain 305, 306
Ross, Walter J.M., Major 97, 305, 417, 425, 433
Rowe. T., Sergeant 422, 431

Rowland, D. 262
Ruge, Otto, Major General 203
Ruhr 276, 277, 317, 340
Rundstedt, Gert von, Colonel General, 174
Ruston, Major 327, 435
Ruweisat 230, 239
Ryan, C.E., Colonel 153
Ryan, Cornelius, Author 278, 310, 426
Rye 227

S
Saar 83, 165, 166, 191, 193, 196, 403
Sabrum, Captain 210
Salerno 272
Salisbury Plain 31, 331
Saloniki 353
Sambre 175
Saunders, T. 427
Scandinavia 199, 200, 429
Scapa Flow 205
Scotland 151, 205, 216, 219, 222, 354
Sedan 177
Seine 102, 144, 275, 278
Sennybridge 150
Sewell, E.R.A., Colonel 436
Schelde (see Escaut)
Sheil, Major 194
Shelford 419
Sherborne 353
Shoeburyness 31
Shoreham 222
Shrapnel 4, 29
Shrivvenham 152
Siam (Thailand) 344, 346, 352
Sicily 59, 117, 141, 272, 343, 355, 421
Siegfried Line 315
Sierra Leone 19
Sing, Captain 31
Singapore 40, 74, 146, 226, 229, 344, 345, 357, 436
Sittang 346
Skjomnes 210
Skuvtua 211
Skåne 28
Skånland 207
Slaughter, Tod 300
Slijk-Ewijk 295, 304, 307
Slim, William, Viscount, Field Marshal 158, 159, 161, 347, 348, 418, 427
Small, Captain 88
Smith, Sergeant 194
Smith, A&W 52
Smith, Mark, Curator 20, 113
Snakenborg, Helena 414
Somme 166, 174, 196
Son 287, 292, 295, 297
South Africa 437
South Cina Sea 344
South Downs 151, 221, 222, 228
Southampton 206, 218

Southend 218
Soviet Union (Russia) 16, 33, 37, 40, 60, 93, 199, 201, 208, 226, 227, 229, 356
Spain 27
St. Just 144
St. Leger 261
St. Nazaire 197
St. Omer 190, 193
St. Oodenrode 297
St. Valery 197
Stalin 46
Stavanger 200
Steele, M., Major General 20
Stewart-Richardson, P.N.R., Brigadier 424, 433
Stilwell, Joseph, General 346, 347
Stjernfelt, B. 422
Stockholm 415
Stoney, Tom Butler, Captain 245
Storey, B.B., Captain 170
Strangways, Lieutenant 26
Streatfield, R.J., Lieutenant Colonel 340
Stubbs, Jock 86
Stumme, Georg, General 239
Sudetenland 40
Sudbourne Hall 216
Suez Canal 229
Suffolk 218
Sultan, D., General 349
Surrey 355
Sweden 21, 28, 199–203, 208, 309, 359
Switzerland 165, 175, 309
Sword Beach 258, 260, 261
Syria 234, 343

T
Taranto 343
Tarnapol 272
Taylor, Major 308
Taylor, M.D., General 297
Taylor, R.B., Captain 194
Tell el Aqqaqir 230
Tetta, von, Major General 289
Thamelander 419, 420, 422
Thames 218
Thoma, Wilhelm Ritter von, Major General 239, 250, 252, 421
Thomas, G.I., Lieuteannt General 293, 306, 311
Thompson Glover, Peter, Captain 245
Thompson, Teddy 80
Thompson, W.F.K., Lieutenant Colonel 278, 279, 291, 417, 423, 433
Tilshead 150
Timbers, K., Brigadier 5, 13, 21
Tobruk 229, 231, 234, 241, 356
Toosey, J. D., Brigadier 357, 437
Tournai 184, 191, 193
Townend, W., Lieutenant Colonel 19

446

Index

Trawsfynydd 150
Tripoli 231
Tromsö 202, 209, 212
Trondheim 200, 201, 203–205
Trotman, A., Captain 306, 425
Tsuji, M., Colonel 427
Tucker, K. W. 436
Tunisia 84, 126, 159, 343, 417, 421, 430
Tvedalsryggen 211
Tyler, Tubby, H.A., Lieutenant Colonel 185

U
Uden 296, 297
Uniacke, R.J., Lieutenant Colonel 436
Urquhart, R.E., Major General 294, 301, 306, 307, 310, 433, 434
USA (United States of America) 43, 48, 50, 57, 77, 227, 343, 344, 346, 415
Utah Beach 258
Utrechtsweg 285

V
Valburg 303, 304, 307
Valkenswaard 282, 283, 287, 288, 295
Van Aardt, L. 18, 437
Vaughan Thomas, Wynford, BBC Reporter 335
Veghel 277, 291, 294, 296, 297, 299, 301, 308, 425
Venlo 143
Vickers Armstrong 52, 53, 56, 215
Violaines 186
Vologda 37
Voskuil, Robert, Drs. 19, 276, 438

W
Waal 276, 282, 291, 292, 294–296, 298–300, 304, 307, 308, 425
Walch, A.G., Brigadier 423, 424, 433, 434
Wales (see Great Britain)
Walker, Johnny, Captain 18, 43, 112, 152, 415, 417
Wancourt 178
Washington 347
Waterloo 26, 29, 30, 60
Watson Leindlaw & Co. 52
Watts, Air Force Officer 170
Wavre 172
Weir Ltd. 53, 62, 437
Weir, Steve, Brigadier 238, 253, 422, 431
Wellington, Arthur Wellesley, Duke of 26, 29
Westdown 151
Westerbouwing 293
Weygand, Maxime, General 177
Weymouth 216
Wezel (Wesel) 317, 318, 321, 324, 327, 336, 337, 340, 435
Whetton, Jim 18, 436
Whetton, John T., Lieutenant Colonel, Professor 18, 234, 257, 272, 356–358, 423, 433, 436
Whitworth-Jones, Captain 236
Widdicombe, J.W., Lieutenant 79
Wight-Boycott, R.D., Major 423
Wilhelmina Canal 287, 295
Wilkinson, Peter, Captain 18, 75, 80, 93, 94, 227, 306, 358, 359, 417, 423, 425, 437
William the Conqueror 26
William IV, King 32
Wiltshire 353

Wilson, Captain 236
Wimberley, D.N., Major General 246
Wingate, O., Major General 348
Wm. Beardmore (Parkhead) 52
Wm. Beardmore (Dalmin) 52
Wolfheze 279, 285, 286
Woollacott, Robert, Captain 18, 391, 416, 418
Woolwich Arsenal 28, 29, 52, 93, 152, 353, 354
Wright, Lieutenant 26

XYZ
Yamashita (Tomoyuki), General 345
Young, D., Lieutenant 236
Young, Edward M. 428, 431, 440
Ypres 178, 179, 188, 197, 199, 419
Yser 178, 179, 189
Zenne 177, 182
Zetterling 420, 423

ÅÄÖ
Åndalsnes 203, 205
Öyjord 211

Note. The reader is advised also to check Appendix 1, Order of Battle, BEF artillery in France 1940, where names of a large number of officers are presented. Only those mentioned in the main text have been included here.

Author (Stig H. Moberg) with three veterans at lunch in August 2005. From right to left:

Douglas Goddard MBE, FICS (1920–2011). Landed in Normany in June 1944 as Lieutenant and Gun Position Officer in 112 (Wessex) Field Regiment RA TA. His regiment was engaged during the battle of Arnhem in September 1944 together with several other regiments, the fire of which made possible the evacuation across Neder Rijn of 2,300 men of the 1st Airborne Division (out of 10,000) during the night 25/26 September 1944. The regiment took part in several battles in North West Europe until the end of the war in May 1945. Douglas Goddard remained in the Army after war as a regular officer until 1957 when he, then a Major, retired for a civilian career which saw him in high positions in Chartered Institute of Building and society.

Peter Wilkinson MC (1922–2017) was Battery Command Post Officer in the 1st Airlanding Light Regiment RA during the battle of Arnhem, then as a Lieutenant. Before that he served with distinction with his regiment in North Africa and Italy. After the evacuation from Arnhem he was promoted Captain and took part in the restoration of the 1st Airlanding Division. In May 1945 his regiment was sent to Norway, landing at Stavanger, to take part in the disarmament of German forces in Norway. In 1946 Peter Wilkinson returned to civilian life and became a Chartered Accountant. Towards the end of his career he was Chief Executive of Anglia Building Society.

John Coghlan MBE, TD (1923–2016) served in 1944 as Lieutenant in the Black Watch and took part in the decisive fourth battle at Cassino, Italy. His division was then transferred to Greece to help subdue the communist insurgency going on in that country. After the war John Coghlan served has headmaster at several schools before being engaged by the British Sports Council where he held senior positions before retiring. In parallel with his civilian career he served with the Territorial Army, eventually promoted to Lieutenant Colonel.

Stig H. Moberg (1937–). Graduated in 1963 from Royal Institute of Technology in Stockholm, Sweden as Master of Science in Electrical Engineering. He has held several managerial and executive positions in Swedish and international power supply industries as well as in engineering and investment companies. After retirement in 1997 he acted as consultant and advisor to development organizations and energy ministries in many countries. Served as an Officer of the Royal Swedish Artillery Reserve 1960–2000.